A *Glossary of*
Contemporary
Literary Theory

This new edition is for Richard and Joanna,
Nancy and Simon, Dinah and Joe
and new arrival Sylvie

A Glossary of
Contemporary
Literary Theory

Fourth Edition

JEREMY HAWTHORN
Professor of Modern British Literature,
Norwegian University of Science and Technology,
Trondheim, Norway

A member of the Hodder Headline Group
LONDON

Co-published in the United States of America by
Oxford University Press Inc., New York

First published in Great Britain in 2000 by
Arnold, a member of the Hodder Headline Group,
338 Euston Road, London NW1 3BH

http://www.arnoldpublishers.com

Co-published in the United States of America by
Oxford University Press Inc.,
198 Madison Avenue, New York, NY 10016

© 2000 Jeremy Hawthorn

British Library Cataloguing in Publication Data
A catalogue record for this book is available from the British Library

Library of Congress Cataloging-in-Publication Data
A catalog record for this book is available from the Library of Congress

ISBN 0 340 76066 4

1 2 3 4 5 6 7 8 9 10

Production Editor: Julie Delf
Production Controller: Priya Gohil
Cover Design: T. Griffiths

Printed and bound in Great Britain by
MPG Books Ltd, Bodmin, Cornwall

Introduction to the Fourth Edition

In preparing this fourth edition I have had access to a range of very useful suggestions for amendments and additions that have been made by various readers. Many of these suggestions have allowed me to fill in gaps and to correct inadequacies in the third edition, and I thank those who have given me their advice.

Readers will doubtless be relieved to know that I have resisted the temptation to call this new edition *Literary Theory: The Millennial Edition*, although as I used the search-and-replace function in my computer to substitute 'the twentieth century' for 'the present century', I was, against my will, drawn to feel that this is perhaps a more than usually propitious time to survey the field of Literary Studies and literary theory. At any rate, working on my revisions I found myself meditating on the nature of the 'field' covered by the glossary. It is undeniable that the theory with which students of literature are expected to be conversant today comes from a far wider range of sources and disciplines than would have been the case twenty or thirty years ago. Not only is it associated with a range of different cultures and national literatures, but in many cases it is theory that is by no means primarily or exclusively concerned with literature or with literary criticism. As I point out in my section on using the glossary, there is an element of overlap between this work and companion volumes published by Arnold which have to do with feminist theory and cultural theory – and the same can be said for other reference works concerned with postcolonialist theory, linguistic theory, media theory, and so on. Some of the terms that I decided, rightly or wrongly, *not* to include in the present volume are: chaos theory; end of history; uncertainty/complementarity (as in Heisenberg and Bohr); the prisoner's dilemma game; and synergy. In each case I felt either that their bearing on Literary Studies was too indirect to justify inclusion, or that they fell outside my criteria for inclusion (see page viii below). Maybe I was wrong to exclude them – in which case they may be in the fifth edition if there is one. My point, however, is that deciding what *is* appropriate for inclusion in a glossary of contemporary literary theory is by no means as straightforward as it once was.

Academic disciplines have their periods of infancy, adolescence, maturity – and perhaps also senility and death. New or young disciplines are characteristically very conscious of the need to establish and preserve a distinct identity; like newly independent nations they patrol their own borders vigilantly, eager to ensure that powerful neighbours do not violate their territorial integrity. I can remember being told by lecturers in Film Studies twenty-five years ago that as they were working hard to gain acceptance for the view that Film Studies was not a sub-division of Literary Studies, they were not sure that the time was ripe for collaborative work with colleagues in this field.

Work on this glossary has convinced me that Literary Studies today is in a very different situation: perhaps it is entering old age – it certainly suffers from none of the fears manifested by my erstwhile colleagues in Film Studies. The shift from syllabuses which included courses on criticism (literary, of course, and Anglo-American, if the department was a department of English), to syllabuses offering courses on theory, is indicative of an opening up of Literary Studies to a far wider range of intellectual influences. Teaching a new course on literary theory in my own (English) department earlier this year I was struck by the realization that a hefty majority of the essays and extracts on the syllabus I had chosen were originally written in languages other than English, while many had no direct connection with literature. And yet it had seemed to me impossible to offer a course in literary theory that did not include coverage of such topics as structuralism and post-structuralism, psychoanalysis, Marxism, feminism, and so on. Even topics such as narratology which have a very direct and immediate connection with the study of prose fiction are by no means exclusively concerned with literature.

Although the change that I am reporting brings with it problems – more theory leaves less time for the reading of literary works; a student who moves between different disciplines may find him- or herself being introduced to, say, structuralism three or four times in different departments – I feel that the opening up of Literary Studies has made the discipline more intellectually exciting and more academically challenging. I have therefore absolutely no wish to turn the clock back.

At the same time, this is perhaps an appropriate moment to stress that the reading and studying of literature is – among other things – a *craft*. By this, I mean that something has gone wrong when bright research students feel that their biggest problem is to 'choose a theory' for their project, a belief that seems to carry with it the assumption that once this choice has been made, the encounter between a corpus of literary works and a theory will itself generate the required thesis. Literary study is a craft to the extent that there is no theory that can replace or compensate for that set of skills and sensitivities that the careful reading, analysis, and interpretation of literary works brings with it.

This is an argument that sets off warning bells for many, and for two separate reasons. First, because it may suggest that such things as careful reading, analysis, and interpretation are theory-independent, and second because it is an argument that has been used as part of a case against the study of theory *in toto*. I would associate myself with neither of these views. So far as the first is concerned, I believe that the study of theory and criticism makes us better readers of literature, and that it should complement and inform the reading, analysis, and interpretation of literary works. Having been educated during the period of the (fading) hegemony of the New Critics, one of the things that I was acutely conscious of during my time as an undergraduate was that a study of literature based upon close reading, analysis and interpretation naturally threw up theoretical issues and problems that were then ruled out of court by those who believed that the nature of literary criticism was such that its philosophical premises could not be stated. (See for example F. R. Leavis's 'Criticism and Philosophy', in his *The Common Pursuit* [1952], an essay much cited by those intent on keeping theory out of Literary Studies.)

But if it is wrong to assume that skills of close reading, analysis and interpretation are theory-independent, there are many today who are guilty of a comparable error in assuming that literary theory does not need to be informed and enriched by these same skills. Too many research students today are skilled theorists but indifferent close readers.

If the reading and studying of literature is a craft that is informed by theory, it is also one possessed of a certain autonomy or specificity. Some issues of critical method or philosophical underpinning may be shared with other disciplines, but some are not, and the student of literature needs to remember that an exclusive diet of theory that is not literature-specific will leave a gap. In making my revisions for the present new edition I have included more references to film, and there is no doubt that literary works and films throw up a number of common problems for the reader or viewer, problems that are susceptible to analysis by means of conceptual tools drawn from overarching bodies of theory. But there is a tendency for students of literature – and especially at higher levels – to believe that it is enough to read literary texts and literary theory. It is not. The study of literature must also include extensive acquaintance with literary criticism. Theory alone will show no one how to be a critic, nor will theory alone bring with it an understanding of scholarship. To make a division between theory and criticism is of course arbitrary and potentially misleading: the best literary criticism is overtly informed by theory, just as the best theory feeds upon traditions of critical debate.

As I have said, there have been times when such arguments have been presented in the form of either/or. Either theory or criticism. Either theory or scholarship. Either theory or skills of reading, analysis and interpretation. But the truth is that all are needed. The trick – the very difficult trick – is to achieve a creative tension between these different elements and activities, so that an engagement with literary works is informed by scholarship, critical acuity, and theoretical understanding. And also, of course, so that one's critical practice and one's involvement in theoretical issues are informed and enriched by the challenge that literary works have always presented to our ideas and to our lives. 'Lives' is a term that has become less fashionable since the 'death of the author'. But the historical perspective that even such an arbitrary and artificial watershed as a new millennium imposes upon us can force us to recognize that of all the different elements that encourage us to bring new perspectives to literary works, the changes in the ways we live constitute the most powerful.

The occasion of this new edition is an appropriate time to thank my publisher, Arnold, for their continued support, and for their willingness to allow me regularly to update the work. I must also thank my employer, the Norwegian University of Science and Technology, and in particular the English Department and the Faculty of Humanities, for providing me with regular research leave, travel support, and up-to-date computer equipment. And thanks to many friends – among them Maroula Joannou, Paul Goring, Ruth Sherry, Mike Pickering and Domhnall Mitchell – who have helped with suggestions.

Jeremy Hawthorn
Trondheim, December 1999

Using the Glossary

1 Conventions of presentation

I have attempted to group related terms in common entries so as to avoid repetition and so as to permit entries that have a certain completeness. Thus rather than having separate entries for *plot*, *story*, *fabula* and *sjužet*, I have a single entry for STORY AND PLOT. The negative result of such a policy, inevitably, is that those searching for the meaning of terms must frequently tolerate having to find their way to the substantive entry via cross-entries. In this fourth edition I have attempted to make cross-referencing more comprehensive.

The use of small capitals (e.g. DECONSTRUCTION) indicates the existence of an entry on the term so presented. Sometimes the actual entry may be under a cognate term; thus DECONSTRUCT refers the reader to the entry for the term DECONSTRUCTION. I have normally limited this use of small capitals to the *first* mention only of the term in question within each entry. To avoid confusion the use of small capitals generally directs the reader to substantive (rather than cross-reference) entries, although I have made exceptions to this rule in the case of particularly important terms or connections.

Parenthetical references with page numbers refer the reader to the bibliography at the end of the book, which provides full publication details of all works from which quotations have been taken.

Many of the terms with which I deal are of foreign origin, and often it has had to be a matter of personal judgement as to whether they are sufficiently assimilated to be written without the use of the italics that indicate a loan word. I have based my decision here upon the extent to which the words in question can be said to be in frequent use amongst theorists: thus I give *épistémè* and *méconnaissance* italics, but not écriture or flâneur. In transliterating Russian names and terms I have adopted the more traditional versions (e.g. Eichenbaum rather than Èjxenbaum), unless I am referring to a published source. Thus both of these variants appear in the bibliography and in textual references.

American readers should note that British spelling is used throughout except where I quote from a source in American English. Thus there is no entry for center, but there is one for CENTRE.

2 Criteria for selection of terms

My aim in the pages that follow has been to provide the reader with sufficient information to enable him or her to make sense of those of the more common specialist terms used by recent literary critics or theorists that cannot be found in more general dictionaries or glossaries of literary terms. By 'recent' I mean, generally, from about 1970, although I have allowed myself to be inconsistent on this point and I have included some entries on older terms such as the New Criticism where I have judged that this will be helpful to the readers I have in mind. Terms that have entered Anglo-American theoretical discussion via recent English translations of older works (by Bakhtin and Ingarden, for example) are also included.

It is not, however, enough for my purposes for a well-established term to have become very fashionable of late: to merit inclusion it needs to have been granted a significantly changed or extended meaning. Thus, for example, AUTHOR is included but *trope* is not.

3 Schools and approaches

As an additional aid to those using this glossary I append here a list of most of the terms included in it grouped according to their intellectual associations or origins. It will be seen that the groups belong to very different categories: academic disciplines such as Linguistics, critical schools such as the 'Bakhtin group' and the Prague Linguistic Circle, ideological and political groupings such as Marxism and feminism, groups categorized according to a methodology or a focus of concern such as reader-response criticism, and so on.

My groupings are crude, and should be treated only as a convenient indication of which glossed terms have something of interest for, for example, those interested in deconstruction, or feminism. Some terms do not fit in to any of these groupings, and some find a home in more than one. Where terms are asterisked this is to suggest either that they represent concepts central to the grouping in question, or that the entry thus indicated contains information about the school or approach. Those wanting a fuller account of such groupings should consult Ann Jefferson and David Robey (eds), *Modern Literary Theory* (2nd edn, Batsford, 1986), or Raman Selden, Peter Widdowson and Peter Brooker, *A Reader's Guide to Contemporary Literary Theory* (rev. 4th edn, Harvester Wheatsheaf, 1997).

Anthropology and Cultural Studies
*binary/binarism; *bricoleur; *culture; *Cultural Studies; fiction; formulaic literature; *myth; New Historicism and cultural materialism; Sapir-Whorf hypothesis; script; *structures of feeling; *thick description/thin description

Bakhtin group
assimilation; *carnival; *centrifugal/centripetal; character zone; *chronotope; contiguity; *crowning/decrowning; *dialogic; discourse; dominant; enthymeme; exotopy; hetero-biography; *heteroglossia; horizon; hybrid/hybridization; orchestration; *polyphonic; refraction; register; reification; semantic position; *skaz*; transgredient; utterance

Deconstruction
agon; aporia; *arche-writing; author; *centre; coherence; Copernican revolution; *deconstruction; desire; *différance; *dissemination; echolalia; *écriture; ephebe; erasure; *grammatology; heterobiography; hinge; hymen; *logocentrism; *logos; *ludism; *mise-en-abyme*; *Nachträglichkeit*; New Readers; phallogocentrism; *post-structuralism; *presence;

Using the Glossary

*radical alterity; reference; revisionism; *s'entendre parler*; site; subject and subjectivity; *supplement; *tain; textualist; *transcendental pretence/signified/subject

Discourse analysis
*archaeology of knowledge; closure; *différend*; *discourse; *dispositif*; *épistémè*; exteriority; genotext and phenotext; multivalent; New Historicism and cultural materialism; *signifying practice; slippage; speech; suture; text and work; topic; *utterance

Electronic media/Science fiction
browsing; *cyber/netics/punk/space; *cyborg; *fantastic; hyperspace; hypertext; IF; morphing; mundanes; precession; *Shannon and Weaver model of communication; virtual reality

Feminism
androcentric; *androgyny; biocriticism; biologism/biological determinism; *body; *consciousness-raising; cross-dressing; cyborg; *desire; *difference; dubbing; *écriture féminine; erotics; *female affiliation complex; femaling; *feminism; *gaze; *gender; genre; gothic; *gynocratic; *gynocritics; *immasculation; logic of the same; magic realism; *male-as-norm; *marginality; *masquerade; *matriarchy; minoritizing/universalizing; *muted; nominalism; *object-relations theory/criticism; other; *patriarchy; pejoration; *phallocentrism; pleasure; pornoglossia; *queer theory; quest narrative; reading position; realism; *recruitist; romance; script; second wave feminism; *sexism; *standpoint theory; *stereotype; subject and subjectivity; wild zone

Linguistics
actualization; *arbitrary; aspect; *competence and performance; cratylism; *diachronic and synchronic; diacritical; difference; *discourse; *displacement; *functions of language; idiolect; *langue and parole; *linguistic paradigm; markedness; metalanguage; punctuation; *register; *Sapir-Whorf hypothesis; shifter; *sign; sociolect; speech; *speech act theory; *syntagmatic and paradigmatic; text and work

Marxism
absence; against the grain; *alienation; *alienation effect; always-already; *aura; *base and superstructure; *class; coherence; co-optation; Copernican revolution; *critical theory; *dialectics; economism; English; *epistemological break; *fetishism; flâneur; formation; *Frankfurt School; gest; *hegemony; homology; ideologeme; *ideology; *incorporation; instance; *intellectuals; *interpellation; legitimation; *literary mode of production; *Marxist literary theory and criticism; *materialism; moment; montage; myth; popular; praxis; problematic; *realism; *reification; slippage; structure in dominance; *structure of feeling; subject and subjectivity

Media Studies
*agenda-setting; digital and analogic communication; *gatekeeping; hot and cool media; mediascape; *Media Studies; *technological determinism; *uses and gratifications

Modernism and Postmodernism
*abject; *alienation; archetypal criticism; aura; *bricoleur; cancelled character; character; *closure; *erasure; *flâneur; frame; *heterobiography; *hyperspace; hypertext; *ludism; marginality; metafiction; *modernism and postmodernism; montage; nomad; polyphonic; popular; *precession; realism; repetition; *short-circuit; syntagmatic and paradigmatic; *True-Real

Narratology
achronicity/achrony; act/actor; actualization; anachrony; analepsis; architext; aspect; attribute/function; author function; cancelled character; *connotation and denotation; crisis; *defamiliarization; deferred/postponed significance; deixis; deviation; *diegesis and mimesis; digital and analogic communication; *discourse; disnarrated; *distance; *double focalization; *double-voiced; *duration; ellipsis; energetics/geometrics; *enunciation; euphoric text; event; fiction; figuralization/reflectorization; figure; figure and ground; flicker; flip-flop; force; *frame; *Free Indirect Discourse; *frequency; *function; geometrics/energetics; grammar; heteroplasty; hinge; homology; homonymy; hypotaxis; inside/outside view; *interior dialogue; interpolation; *intertextuality; intertitle; intrusive narrator; isochrony; *linguistic paradigm; magic realism; master narrative; metalanguage; metalepsis; *mise-en-abyme*; mode; montage; mood; move; *Nachträglichkeit*; *narratee; narration; *narrative; *narrative situation; *narratology; obstination; order; palimpsest text; Pamissa; paralepsis; paralipsis; parataxis, paratext; pentad; *perspective and voice; positioning; power; prehistory; privilege; prolepsis; quest narrative; reflector (character); repetition; script; semantic axis; *skaz*; short-circuit; slow-down; *story and plot; suspense; suture; syllepsis; synonymous characters; *text and work; theme and thematics; topos; Uncle Charles Principle; *Verschrift-ung/Verschriftlichung*

New Criticism
*ambiguity; autotelic; coherence; essentialism; *functionalist criticism; icon; *image; *intrinsic criticism; *New Criticism; *organicism

New Historicism and Cultural Materialism
circulation; *emplotment; energy; exchange; *New Historicism and cultural materialism; resonance; structure

Phenomenology and Geneva School
eidetic; *epoché*; *phenomenology; polyphonic

Postcolonialism
affiliation; Africanist/nationalist; alterity; authenticity; bolekaja critics; comprador; contamination; *creolization; diaspora literature; disidentification; double colonization; double consciousness; double-voiced; dubbing; ethnoscope; *Eurocentric; fictograph; *hybrid/hybridization; imagined community; *liminal; marvellous realism; master narrative; mediascape; *mimicry; nation/nationalism; nativism; *négritude*; neo-Tarzanism; *nomad; orature; *orientalism; other; passing; *postcolonialism; relativism; relexification; subaltern; syncretism; transculturation; *west

Pragmatics
*discourse; double-bind; *politeness; *pragmatics; *speech act theory

Prague School/Prague Linguistic Circle
actualization; aesthetic; *concretization; *defamiliarization; *deformation; *dominant; *literariness; norm; *Prague School

Psychology and Psychoanalysis
abject; alterity; archetypal criticism; arche-writing; body; *censorship; chora; *condensation and displacement; contiguity; crosstalk; desire; disavowal; double-bind; *fetishism; figure and ground; *fort/da; *gaze; Gestalt; hommelette; imaginary/symbolic/real; intersubjectivity; *jouissance; *linguistic paradigm; *méconnaissance*; *mirror stage; *Nachträglichkeit*; name-of-the-Father; *object-relations theory/criticism; *objet a/objet A;* other; overdetermination; *panoptism/panopticism; phallocentrism; pleasure; *point de capiton*; primary process; projection characters; *psychoanalytic criticism; repression; revisionism; schizoanalysis; scopophilia/scopophobia; scotomization; sinthom; slippage; solution from above/below; subject and subjectivity; symptom; syntagmatic and paradigmatic; *topographical model of the mind; *transference; True-Real; *unconscious

Reader-response criticism
appreciation; code; coduction; crosstalk; ecological validity; exegesis; genre; *hermeneutics; ideation; *interpretation; *interpret[at]ive communities; interrogate; intersubjectivity; jouissance; *meaning and significance; ontological status; *open and closed texts; oppositional reading; parabolic text; performance; *politeness; prepublication/postpublication reading; punctuation; readerly and writerly texts; *readers and reading; *reading community; *reading position; *reception theory; *self-consuming artifact; *sense and reference; sub-text; suspense; theme and thematics; topic; *transactional theory of the literary work

Russian Formalism
*defamiliarization; *deformation; deviation; *dominant; fantastic; figure and ground; *function; *functions of language; *literariness; *Russian Formalism

Semiotics and Information Theory
autopoiesis; *binary/binarism; *code; *digital and analogic communication; echolalia; *epoché*; icon; index; myth; *redundancy; sememe; *semiology/semiotics; *Shannon and Weaver model of communication; *sign; signifying practice

Sexual politics/Queer theory
*camp; *closet criticism; code-switching; cross-dressing; cruising-zone; decipherment/deciphering; drag; faghag/fagstag character; ghettoization/deghettoization; lavender culture/language/sex; *masquerade; minoritizing/universalizing; outing; passing; punk; queen/butch; *queer theory; *ravissement*; stonewall; straight; *transgender; vanilla sex

Sociology of literature
affiliation; *apparatus; capital; field; *habitus; script; symbolic power

Structuralism and Post-structuralism
allography; *arbitrariness; *author; *bricoleur; convention; deviation; *diachronic and synchronic; diacritical; *difference; digital and analogic communication; *écriture; *formulaic literature; *function; *functions of language; *heterobiography; homology; hymen; *langue and parole; *linguistic paradigm; nominalism; *post-structuralism; reference; *sign; speech; structure in dominance; *syntagmatic and paradigmatic; *structuralism; textualist; transgressive strategy

Style and Stylistics
affective; chiasmus; closure; commutation test; *connotation and denotation; deviation; kernel word or sentence; punctuation; *style and stylistics; terrorism; text and work

4 Other useful glossaries and dictionaries

I have generally restricted my recommendations in this section to dedicated glossaries or dictionaries, although many other books and articles now include brief glossaries of specialist terms. I have included one web site, and reference material is increasingly being made available via the Internet. Internet searches can often throw up valuable results.

This glossary now has two companion volumes both published by Arnold. *A Glossary of Feminist Theory*, by Sonya Andermahr, Terry Lovell and Carol Wolkowitz (1997), and *Cultural Theory: A Glossary*, by Peter Brooker (1999). Each is available in a longer, hardback version and a concise, paperback edition, and both are highly recommended. Inevitably there is some overlap with my own glossary, and I have on occasions referred the reader to longer entries in both works where these deal with terms more marginal to Literary Studies.

Of the general glossaries of literary terms, the one I would recommend most remains M. H. Abrams's *A Glossary of Literary Terms* (Harcourt Brace Jovanovich). This appears regularly in revised editions and has intelligent entries that are both accessible and critically sophisticated. J. A. Cuddon's *A Dictionary of Literary Terms* has now appeared in a fourth edition (revised by C. E. Preston), published in hardback by Blackwell (1998) and in paperback by Penguin (1999). It contains a much larger number of entries than the Abrams glossary, but these are, inevitably, rather less detailed than those in Abrams. *The Concise Oxford Dictionary of Literary Terms* by Chris Baldick (Oxford University Press, 1990) places its emphasis on the succinct explanation of 'those thousand terms that are most likely to cause the student ... some doubt or bafflement'. *The Bedford Glossary of Critical and Literary Terms*, edited by Ross Murfin and Supryia M. Ray (Bedford Books, 1997, 469 pages), as its title suggests includes both literary and critical/theoretical terms. It is usefully comprehensive and accessibly written, and terms are related to specific examples. There are again more terms than in Abrams, but these are generally shorter.

Wendell V. Harris's *Dictionary of Concepts in Literary Criticism and Theory* (Greenwood Press, 1992) contains short, essay-length entries on 71 topics ranging from

'Allegory' to 'Unity', and taking in more recent terms such as 'discourse', 'postmodernism' and 'semiotics'. Each entry closes with a useful bibliography. Leonard Orr's *A Dictionary of Critical Theory* (Greenwood Press, 1991) has a mixture of longer and shorter entries, and is rather less Eurocentric than many similar works.

The *Johns Hopkins Guide to Literary Theory and Criticism* (Johns Hopkins University Press, 1994) is a massive (775 double-column pages) work edited by Michael Groden and Martin Kreiswirth. Entries are individually authored and cover theorists and critics, terms, and movements. Bibliographical information is provided in each entry. Slightly less massive (656 pages) is the *Encyclopedia of Contemporary Literary Theory: Approaches, Scholars, Terms* edited by Irena R. Makaryk (University of Toronto Press, 1993). This work again contains individually authored entries, and is usefully divided up into the three sections indicated in its title, with over 200 pages for approaches, a little under 300 for scholars, and 150 for terms. *Critical Terms for Literary Study*, edited by Frank Lentricchia and Thomas McLaughlin (University of Chicago Press, 2nd edn, 1995) contains essay-length entries on 22 central terms in use in Literary Studies, including 'interpretation', 'figurative language', 'author', 'canon' and 'discourse'. The standard of the essays (all by different contributors) is high.

The *Columbia Dictionary of Modern Literary and Cultural Criticism*, edited by Joseph Childers and Gary Hentzi (Columbia University Press, 1995) is 374 pages long with a format not dissimilar to my own glossary, except that the focus is more 'modern' than 'contemporary'. My impression is also that the emphasis is rather more literary than cultural. Another work that spans literary critical and cultural theory is *A Dictionary of Cultural and Critical Theory*, edited by Michael Payne (Blackwell, 1996; paperback 1997). This is 656 pages long, and includes entries on individual theorists, movements, and terms. It appears to cover fewer terms than my own glossary, but more theorists and movements.

Two useful reference books that concentrate on theorists are *The A–Z Guide to Modern Literary and Cultural Theorists*, edited by Stuart Sim (Prentice Hall/Harvester Wheatsheaf, 1995), and *Dictionary of Cultural Theorists*, edited by Ellis Cashmore and Chris Rojek (Arnold, 1999).

Bernard Dupriez's *A Dictionary of Literary Devices* (Harvester Wheatsheaf, 1991) has been translated from the French and adapted by Albert W. Halsall. It offers perceptive and often amusing definitions of a range of terms taken from Linguistics, Prosody, Rhetoric, and Philology. Richard A. Lanham's *A Handlist of Rhetorical Terms* has now appeared in a second edition (University of California Press, 1991). The terms are very often quite technical, but the explanations are very clear and well illustrated.

Also to be recommended are *The Longman Dictionary of Poetic Terms* by Jack Myers and Michael Simms (Longman, 1989), and *The New Princeton Handbook of Poetic Terms*, edited by T. V. F. Brogan (Princeton University Press, 1994).

Two reference works by Gordon Williams are both strongly recommended. *A Dictionary of Sexual Language and Imagery in Shakespeare and Stuart Literature* (Athlone, 1994) is a massive (three-volume) work that is both extremely scholarly but also accessible and well presented. *A Glossary of Shakespeare's Sexual Language* (Athlone, 1997) is available in paperback. Given the renewed interest in sexual terminology attendant upon the rise of such movements as Queer Theory and Masculinity Studies, these works allow students of literature to explore such terminology historically.

It will be seen that with all of these works one chooses between breadth and depth: the more entries, the shorter and less detailed they tend to be; the more fields covered, the less concentration there will be upon – for example – literary theory, and so on.

Of the more specialist sources, the following are worth noting.

Bakhtin group

M. M. Bakhtin, *The Dialogic Imagination*, Michael Holquist (ed.) (University of Texas Press, 1981) contains a useful 11-page glossary of some of the many coinages for which Bakhtin is responsible. Tzvetan Todorov's *Mikhail Bakhtin: The Dialogical Principle* (University of Minnesota Press, 1984) contains many illuminating discussions of Bakhtin's more idiosyncratic terms.

Cultural Studies

Raymond Williams's *Keywords* (Fontana, 1976) describes itself in its subtitle as 'a Vocabulary of Culture and Society', and makes fascinating reading. The concentration upon the origins and historical changes in meaning of key terms is especially illuminating. The 1988 edition was revised by Williams not long before his death. See also the glossaries mentioned at the start of this section.

Feminism

See above for my recommendation of *A Glossary of Feminist Theory*, by Sonya Andermahr, Terry Lovell and Carol Wolkowitz (Arnold, 1997). Maggie Humm's *The Dictionary of Feminist Theory* (Harvester Wheatsheaf) appeared in a second edition in 1995. *Feminism and Psychoanalysis: A Critical Dictionary* (Blackwell, 1992) is highly recommended; it is edited by Elizabeth Wright, and contains a large number of well-informed and clearly written entries from a range of contributors.

Gay Studies

A very brief *Glossary of Historic Gay Terms* can be found on the Internet at: http://www.psn.net/~martyn/slang.html#GlossR

Linguistics and Stylistics

Katie Wales, *A Dictionary of Stylistics* (Longman, 1989) contains useful explanations of many of the specialist terms from Linguistics and Stylistics which are likely to be of interest to students of literature and literary theory. R. L. Trask, *A Dictionary of Grammatical Terms in Linguistics* (Routledge, 1993) is recommended, as is *Key Concepts in Language and Linguistics* (Routledge, 1999), by the same author. The latter is an ideal reference text, accessible, well referenced and cross-referenced.

Media Studies

James Watson and Anne Hill, *A Dictionary of Communication and Media Studies* (4th edn, Arnold, 1997), gives concise definitions of most of the specialist terms from this area which are likely to be of interest to students of literature and literary theory. Frank Beaver's *Dictionary of Film Terms: The Aesthetic Companion to Film Analysis* (revised and expanded edition, Twayne, 1994) focuses more on technical than on theoretical terms, but is well worth consulting.

Using the Glossary

Narratology
A Dictionary of Narratology by Gerald Prince (Scolar Press, 1988) is highly recommended. Most of the entries are relatively short, but they are clear and detailed, and the dictionary is very comprehensive. *COGNAC: A Concise Glossary of Narratology from Cologne* by Manfred Jahn, Inge Molitor and Ansgar Nünning is an admirably compressed and informative 32-page duplicated pamphlet published by the Englisches Seminar at the University of Cologne (1993).

Postcolonialism
Key Concepts in Post-Colonial Studies, by Bill Ashcroft, Gareth Griffiths and Helen Tiffin (Routledge, 1998) covers this field comprehensively and engagingly.

Russian Formalism and the Prague School
A very useful source here is L. M. O'Toole and Ann Shukman, 'A Contextual Glossary of Formalist Terminology', which is to be found in the journal *Russian Poetics in Translation*, vol. 4, 1977, pp. 13–48. The entries consist of brief quotations from the key texts, grouped under central terms and concepts.

Semiotics
Vincent M. Colapietro, *Glossary of Semiotics* (Paragon House, 1993) is a handy guide, although the entries are generally short and contain little bibliographic detail.

Structuralism and Post-structuralism
Although not a dictionary or a glossary, Richard Harland's *Superstructuralism: The Philosophy of Structuralism and Post-structuralism* (Methuen, 1987) contains useful and intelligent discussions of many of the relevant central terms.

A

Aberrant decoding See CODE

Abject A concept taken from the work of Julia Kristeva, one which she discusses and defines in great detail in her book *Powers of Horror: An Essay on Abjection* (1982) – especially in the first essay in the book, 'Approaching Abjection'. For Kristeva the abject is a 'twisted braid of affects and thoughts' which 'does not have, properly speaking, a definable *object*'.

> The abject is not an ob-ject facing me, which I name or imagine. Nor is it an ob-jest, an otherness ceaselessly fleeing in a systematic quest of desire. What is abject is not my correlative, which, providing me with someone or something else as support, would allow me to be more or less detached and autonomous. The abject has only one quality of the object – that of being opposed to *I*. (1982, 1)

Kristeva suggests that 'food loathing' is 'perhaps the most elementary and most archaic form of abjection' (1982, 2), and she relates it to boundaries and ambiguous entities such as food, filth, waste or dung – items typically found on ambiguous borderlines between self and not-self. The abject is 'a wellspring of sign for a non-object, on the edges of primal repression', it is thus *'the "object" of primal repression'* (1982, 11, 12).

Judith Butler has related the concept to the way in which conventionality defines itself by creating what we can term an excluded OTHER: 'oppression works not merely through acts of overt prohibition, but covertly, through the constitution of viable subjects and through the corollary constitution of a domain of unviable (un)subjects – *abjects*, we might call them – who are neither named nor prohibited within the economy of the law' (1991, 20).

The abject has, moreover, a close relationship to (especially MODERNIST) literature. 'Approaching abjection' opens with a quotation from Victor Hugo's *La Légende des siècles*, and closes with sections linking the concept to Dostoevsky, Proust, Joyce, Borges and Artaud. Thus Kristeva argues that the 'abject is, for Dostoevsky, the "object" of *The Possessed*: it is the aim and motive of an existence whose meaning is lost in absolute degradation because it absolutely rejected the moral limit (a social, religious, familial, and individual one) as absolute – God' (1982, 18). Molly Bloom's monologue (in Joyce's *Ulysses*), Kristeva continues, spreads out the abject not because in it there is a woman speaking, but 'because, *from afar*, the writer approaches the hysterical body so that it might speak, using it as springboard, of what eludes speech and turns out to be the hand to hand struggle of one woman with another, her mother of course, the absolute because primeval seat of the impossible – of the excluded, the outside-of-meaning, the abject' (1982, 22).

See also DESIRE.

Abrogation See INCORPORATION

Absence An interest on the part of READERS and critics in what is not to be found in a literary WORK as against what is, did not suddenly emerge in the twentieth century: a concern to note what is lacking in one or more of an AUTHOR's works seems to be a natural component of literary-critical discussion. But recent theorists have drawn more particular attention to this issue, and since the publication of Pierre Macherey's *Pour une théorie de la production littéraire* (1966; translated as *A Theory of Literary Production*, 1978) such absences have been accorded more overt theoretical attention. According to Macherey the book is not self-sufficient but is necessarily accompanied by a certain absence without which it would not exist, and he draws our attention to the fact that Freud relegated the absence of certain words to the UNCONSCIOUS. Perhaps not surprisingly, the more a critic or theorist sees the author as in less than complete conscious control over his or her creation, the more likely it is that absences from the work will be seen to be significant. At the time of writing this work Macherey was a disciple of the French MARXIST philosopher Louis Althusser, and Althusser had argued that novels could allow us to see (but not know) the IDEOLOGY from which they were born and in which they bathed, from the inside (1971, 204). In like manner Macherey, and others following him, gave the concept of absence a specifically ideological importance. As it is seen by such theorists to be typical of ideologies that they are unable to confront their own conditions of existence, any ideology imposes blank spots and absences upon those in its grip. Thus by a process of logical retracing of steps it should be possible to read off the ideological underpinnings of a work by isolating its significant absences. From this perspective a work's absences are as significant as was the dog that did not bark to Sherlock Holmes.

An absence can, according to such theorists, be *determinate*. In other words, it can be so central that it structures the work around itself, determining the final form of the work. Thus using both Althusser and Macherey, Graham Holderness (1982, 12) has argued that the determinate absence of D. H. Lawrence's novel *Sons and Lovers* is the bourgeois CLASS; this is the missing element which forms and controls the novel, and which has to be perceived in order fully to understand it. There is no direct engagement with the bourgeoisie in the novel, but the importance of that class to Lawrence and in his society ensures that even its exclusion from the novel is determining. This is an absence on the level of content, but absences may also occur with regard to formal and technical matters: in the final section of James Joyce's *Ulysses* or in the poetry of e e cummings we notice the absence of many conventionally expected PUNCTUATION marks.

The Freudian concept of *lack*, associated most with the castration complex and the female's definition in terms of her lack of a penis and her attendant penis envy, has not surprisingly attracted a fair amount of FEMINIST criticism. Some feminist writers have suggested that for the female author there are writerly parallels to the Oedipus complex: see the entry for FEMALE AFFILIATION COMPLEX.

The centrality of the concept of PRESENCE in the work of Jacques Derrida leads perhaps inevitably to a comparable stress on absence, to an absence which is the complete antithesis of presence and of any LOGOCENTRIC restriction on play: 'Only *pure absence* – not the absence of this or that, but the absence of everything in which all presence is announced – can *inspire*, in other words, can *work*, and then make one work' (1978a, 8).

See also OPPOSITIONAL READING ('hermeneutics of suspicion').

Achronicity/achrony Achronicity is a state in which temporal relationships cannot be established; applied to a NARRATIVE it implies the impossibility of establishing an accurate chronology of events. An achrony is an EVENT in a narrative which cannot be located on a precise time scale, cannot be temporally related to other events in the narrative.

Thus the sentence 'Both John and Albert were to have unhappy love affairs with the same woman' informs us that two unhappy love affairs will take place, but nothing about which comes first (or whether both were simultaneous). Many narratives include achronicity. Thus in Henry James's *The Turn of the Screw* many temporal relationships are established, but it is not possible to establish whether Miss Jessel died before or after Peter Quint, which adds a productive AMBIGUITY of a minor sort to the tale.

Not to be confused with ANACHRONY.

See also ISOCHRONY.

Act/actor An actor is an agent in a NARRATIVE that performs actions, while for an agent in a narrative to act is for that agent to cause or experience an EVENT (Bal: 1985, 5). An actor does not have to be an individual, or even human. Steven Cohan and Linda M. Shires (1988) suggest a main division of actors into SUBJECT and object roles, depending upon whether they act or are acted upon. They further suggest four additional categories of actor with an indirect relation to events: *sender, receiver, opponent* and *helper* (1988, 69).

These categories clearly owe something to the influence of the SHANNON AND WEAVER MODEL OF COMMUNICATION. The French terms *destinateur* and *destinataire* are, following the narrative theorist A. J. Greimas, often used instead of *sender* and *receiver*.

A number of theorists use the term *actant* rather than actor, although Prince defines an actant as a role rather than as an agent (1988a, 1). Thus as Genette (following Spitzer) points out, any narrative in autobiographical form divides the subject of the auto-biography into two actants: the narrating I and the narrated I (1980, 252).

Bernard Dupriez provides a neat diagram of the ways in which Etienne Souriau, Vladimir Propp and A. J. Greimas – three important narrative theorists – see the varied 'actantial paradigms': see the diagram on page 4.

Actant See ACT/ACTOR

SOURIAU	PROPP	GREIMAS	EXAMPLES
directed power	hero	subject	philosopher
object of desire	princess	(desired) object	the world
desired obtainer	dispatcher	dispatcher/donor	God
antagonist		receiver/ beneficiary	humanity
arbiter/referee	aggressor/false hero	opposer	matter
helper			the Mind

(After Dupriez 1991, 16)

Actualization Many contemporary linguistic and literary theories distinguish between underlying abstract SYSTEMS and the particular implementations, manifestations, or *actualizations* which these enable or from which they are generated. Thus *parole* can be seen as an actualization of LANGUE; PERFORMANCE of COMPETENCE; the particular literary READING of a general literary competence; a given folk tale of a set of possibilities contained in the set of FUNCTIONS, and so on. In a broad sense PRAGMATICS can be defined as the study of actualizations.

What generally characterizes systems and their actualizations in such subjects as Linguistics and Literary Criticism is that the implementations are much richer than the formalized system: in other words, that the real, actual system which researchers assume lies behind the actualizations is more complex and extended and has greater generative force than the formalized systems which researchers have been able to construct. No grammarian has been able to construct a GRAMMAR that can unfailingly distinguish between grammatical and non-grammatical utterances with the degree of accuracy of a native speaker of the language in question. Thus study of actualizations normally feeds back to system-construction: we refine our systems partly through abstract work, but also by adapting them to the evidence acquired from pragmatic investigations.

In some usages *actualization* is interchangeable with CONCRETIZATION: see this entry for a more detailed account of what is meant by a reader's concretization of a literary work. Some writers have also used *actualization* as a synonym for FORE-GROUNDING because of its similarity to the original Czech form of the latter term, but this usage is not common. Nevertheless, the larger concept of actualization is central to a number of PRAGUE SCHOOL positions. These include, for example, the belief that those means of expression at various levels of a linguistic system that become automatic in ordinary communication are actualized in poetic language, or to put it another way, that poetic language makes visible the full potency of the SIGN. (This should explain why foregrounding is an example of actualization for the Prague School theorists: once the full potency of the sign is made visible, or actualized, one's attention is necessarily drawn to it.)

In the model constructed by Claude Bremond (1966), a NARRATIVE consists of functions each of which allows for two alternatives: actualization and non-actualization. Thus each function introduces two possible directions for the STORY to take.

Addressee/addresser See FUNCTIONS OF LANGUAGE

Aesthetic The concept of the aesthetic plays a central role in the writing of the PRAGUE SCHOOL theorists, who relate it to the process of FOREGROUNDING in their work. Jan Mukařovský, for example, suggests that a given component in a literary WORK can achieve aesthetic effect 'only by its difference from other components, the so-called *foregrounding*' (1964, 65). He further argues:

> Being a structure, that is, an indivisible whole, the work of poetry constitutes an *esthetic value*, a complex phenomenon which is at the same time unique and regular. Its uniqueness is given by the indivisibility of its composition, its regularity by the mutual equilibration of the relations between the components; being unique the work of poetry is nonrepeatable and accidental; being regular, however, it lays claim to general and permanent recognition. (1964, 65)

It will be noted that Mukařovský's definition of an aesthetic value does not of itself suggest a limitation to works of art or literature, and in this his approach is representative of much more recent theory. Literary theorists of the past two decades in particular have (to use a distinction which emerged in recent debates among historians) been 'lumpers' rather than 'splitters', more interested in seeing what works of art and literature have in common with that which is non-artistic than in isolating that which is unique about them. Or, as Frank Kermode puts it in his *An Appetite for Poetry*, 'Despite their common devotion to the complexities of language, the newer criticism differs from the old New Criticism in that it challenges "the specificity of the aesthetic"' (1989, 10). For this reason the term *aesthetic* has tended to crop up in theoretical discussion mainly as a corrective to REDUCTIONIST views of literature than as a prelude to detailed discussion of the specificity of art or literature. Indeed, Terry Eagleton's *The Ideology of the Aesthetic* (1990) is, as its title suggests, representative in its attempt to DECONSTRUCT the concept of the aesthetic and to explore its historical and ideological roots and variations.

One explanation for this is that typically the concept of the aesthetic has been applied to what are claimed to be universal and/or irreducible rather than context-dependent characteristics, and much recent theory has been unsympathetic to views of literature or art which are founded upon such universal or irreducible elements. Those recent writers on literature for whom the concept has played a central and key role have tended to be those with some connection to the study of aesthetics within the academic discipline of Philosophy, a study which typically appeals to traditions of thought which go back to the Classical study of art.

The following statement from the first page of the Preface to Stein Haugom Olsen's *The Structure of Literary Understanding* (1978) is thus also representative: 'It has always been acknowledged by those who have cared for literature that at least a part of the reader's judgements on a work, provided he reads it as a literary work, will be concerned with its aesthetic qualities' (1978, ix).

Aesthetic norm See NORM

Affective Of the seven definitions of this word provided by the Oxford English Dictionary (*OED*) only the last, 'Of or pertaining to the affections or emotions; emotional', is not described as obsolete. In the twentieth century, however, the fifth meaning provided by the *OED* is nearest to that commonly associated with literary-critical usage: 'Having the quality of affecting; tending to affect or influence; influential, operative.' This usage owes much to two sources: I. A. Richards's *Principles of Literary Criticism* (1924) and the essay 'The Affective Fallacy' by W. K. Wimsatt and Monroe Beardsley (1949). Richards's highly psychologizing approach led him to talk about 'affects' when discussing the READER's experience of literary WORKS, while the NEW CRITICAL commitments of Wimsatt and Beardsley led them to warn against paying attention to the *results* of a poem instead of the poem itself (Wimsatt: 1970, 21). By *results* they had in mind, in their own words, 'vivid images, intense feelings, or heightened consciousness' (Wimsatt: 1970, 32). While Richards felt that the *affects* of a literary work were the legitimate concern of the critic and Wimsatt and Beardsley thought that they were not, they seem generally to have agreed about what they meant by this and cognate terms.

More recently, a reaction against what has been seen as an overstressing of the rational MEANING of a literary work at the expense of its emotive affects (part of a more general reaction against the New Critics), has led to a partial reinstatement of the term *affective* in accepted critical vocabulary, although normally without a return to the sort of psychologizing associated with Richards. Thus for example Stanley Fish's *affective stylistics* stresses the regularity of affects within a particular INTERPRET[AT]IVE COMMUNITY. According to him the term (which replaces his earlier term *new stylistics*), describes a STYLISTICS 'in which the focus of attention is shifted from the spatial context of a page and its observable regularities to the temporal context of a mind and its experiences' (1980, 91).

In many usages *affective meaning* is closely related to CONNOTATION.

Affiliation According to Edward Said,

> [i]t is the case with cultural or aesthetic activity that the possibilities and circumstances of its production get their authority by virtue of what I have called affiliation, that implicit network of peculiarly cultural associations between forms, statements, and other aesthetic elaborations on the one hand, and, on the other, institutions, agencies, classes, and amorphous social forces. (1984, 174)

Said associates this usage with a passage from Antonio Gramsci's *Prison Notebooks* in which Gramsci refers to the need for individuals to order and systematize 'one's own intuitions of life and the world' and to do this in the context of the history of philosophy (Gramsci: 1971, 327). Said distinguishes affiliation from 'the facile theories of homology and filiation' (1984, 174), and for him affiliation is 'what enables a text to maintain itself as a text, and this is covered by a range of circumstances: status of the author, historical moment, conditions of publication, diffusion and reception, values drawn upon, values and ideas assumed, a framework of consensually held tacit assumptions, presumed background, and so on and on' (1984, 174–5). Affiliation stands thus in contrast to over-simple views of literary *filiation*, according to which literary works have to be understood in terms of and relation to other literary works. Certain critics antagonistic to F. R. Leavis's 'Great Tradition' have seen this as a classic example of a filiative view of literary influence and identity. Said's view clearly relates to a conception of modernity in which the affiliations established by an individual were of greater moment than lines of descent or family connections.

Robert D. Newman builds upon Said's term to construct a model of *disaffiliation*, in which 'structure is situated as a perpetually sliding signifier, generated by the revisionary mix of desires and repressions at work in the interaction between the narrative memories of text and reader (or events and interpreter)'. He thus aims to recreate the exile as his paradigm for narrative engagement and the interpretive experience (1993, 294).

Compare Bourdieu's concepts of the FIELD and of cultural and symbolic CAPITAL, and Brecht's more material APPARATUS. See also FEMALE AFFILIATION COMPLEX.

Africanist/nationalist Biodun Jeyifo uses this opposition polemically in order to be able to distinguish between two schools of scholars and critics concerned with African literature, an 'Africanist' rubric which 'implies professional specialism rendered as a sort of Weberian ideal type', and the 'Nationalist' rubric which 'connotes a heuristic-polemical rendering of critical positions which span a spectrum involving, among others, cultural-nationalist, Marxist or "Fanonist", feminist or even "nativist" views on African literature' (1996, 170 n15). 'Fanonist' denotes an individual or position indebted to the work of Frantz Fanon. Jeyifo's further comments suggest that whereas the term 'Africanist' is given an ESSENTIALIST sense by those studying African literature and CULTURE (especially by non-Africans), 'nationalist' is used in a more flexible manner such that it can encompass cultural and historical specificities and processes.

See also AUTHENTICITY; FEMINISM; MARXIST LITERARY THEORY AND CRITICISM; NATIVISM.

Against the grain In the seventh of his *Theses on the Philosophy of History*, which he completed in the spring of 1940, Walter Benjamin writes that

> [t]here is no document of civilization which is not at the same time a document of barbarism. And just as such a document is not free of barbarism, barbarism taints also the manner in which it was transmitted. A historical materialist therefore dissociates himself from it as far as possible. He regards it as his task to brush history against the grain. (In Benjamin: 1973, 258–9)

A READING which is 'against the grain' thus brings to light such concealed social guilts and responsibilities, by resisting the WORK's NATURALIZATION and DEFAMILIARIZING it. The expression comes from carpentry: if one planes a piece of wood against the grain one disrupts its smooth surface and reveals its hidden STRUCTURES.

Edward Said's *contrapuntal reading* has a comparable force to Benjamin's formulation; Said takes the term from musicology: a contrapuntal reading provides us with a counterpart to or critique of the text. Said's term has tended to involve an exposure of the hidden colonialist or imperialist presence in canonical literature: he suggests that cultural identities need to be analysed not as god-given essences, 'but as contrapuntal ensembles, for it is the case that no identity can ever exist by itself and without an array of opposites, negatives, oppositions: Greeks always require barbarians, and Europeans Africans, Orientals, etcetera' (1993, 60).

Compare OTHER.

Agenda-setting From committee procedure: if you control what goes on the agenda of a meeting then you can make sure that certain things are considered first while others are not considered at all. The term originally arose from debates within MEDIA STUDIES and has been especially applied to the way in which television is allegedly able to manipulate the thought of viewers not just by telling them *what* to think, but by telling them *about what* they are to think. Some critics have found it useful to extend the term to the manner in which a literary WORK can cause a READER to consider certain problems on the basis of the writer's consciously or unconsciously adopted premises, or the manner whereby a reader's allotting of a work to a particular GENRE limits the range of the expected in his or her reading experiences. See also GATEKEEPING; IDEOLOGY.

Agon From the Greek meaning a contest: the part of a classical Greek drama in which the CHORUS splits in two to support two protagonists engaged in verbal debate. The term is invoked by Harold Bloom in his collection of essays of the same name (1982), especially in the chapter 'Agon: Revisionism and Critical Personality' in which he develops his ideas of misreading and misprision.

For Bloom, REVISIONISM unfolds itself only in fighting, it is a spirit which portrays itself as agonistic, and he relates this to 'the American religion of competitiveness, which is at once our glory and (doubtless) our inevitable sorrow' (1982, viii). Revisionism, then, for Bloom, carries on a tradition of struggle that goes back to the beginning of our CULTURE and our literature.

Aleatory technique Aleatory means 'depending upon the throw of a die', or on chance: any work of art produced by an aleatory technique has reached its final form at least in part because of chance, unplanned events. The term is more common in film criticism, where it is used to describe films that have incorporated unplanned elements 'caught' during filming. William Burroughs's 'cut-out' and 'fold-in' techniques involve an aleatory element, as does the *objet trouvé* of experimental art. The term needs to be distinguished from *improvisation*, although there is an area of overlap between the two. In both cases the final decision to include or exclude the results of accident in an artwork involves judgement.

See also ROOT/RADICLE/RHIZOME.

Alienation In its more specifically MARXIST sense alienation refers to an experience believed by Marx to be the result of the development of the capitalist mode of production, wherein the worker was related to the product of his or her labour 'as to an alien object', and that 'the more the worker spends himself, the more powerful becomes the alien world of objects which he creates over and against himself, the poorer he himself – his inner world – becomes, the less belongs to him as his own. ... Whatever the product of his labour, he is not' (Marx: 1970b, 108).

In discussion of MODERNIST literature the term has come to be used in a rather more general sense to characterize the feeling of 'non-belonging', exclusion and loneliness seen to be typical of the modernist vision.

Some translations of the work of Mikhail Bakhtin use *alien* and cognate terms to represent Bakhtin's view of language as stamped with and soiled by the ownership marks of other people. See the entry for DIALOGIC.

Not to be confused with ALIENATION EFFECT.

Alienation effect From the German *Verfremdungseffekt* as defined and used by the German dramatist Bertolt Brecht. Given Brecht's commitment to MARXISM the proposed English translation is somewhat unfortunate as it may suggest (misleadingly) some connection with the Marxist concept of ALIENATION.

In developing his theory Brecht used a variety of different terms including *befremden, Fremdheit* and *entfremden*, which are to be found with earlier formulations in the useful index listing of 'Alienation' in Willett (1964). The concept matured in Brecht's thought as new terms were selected, and eventually reached the form in which it achieved fame as *V-Effekt* (*Verfremdungseffekt*). Terms such as *dislocation* and *estrangement effect* probably offer better translations of the final German form of the concept, and attempts have been made to establish them as the standard English terms, but *alienation effect* is probably too well established now to be displaced.

The notion shares common elements with the RUSSIAN FORMALIST concept of DEFAMILIARIZATION, but Brecht was concerned more specifically with the stage and a particular dramatic technique than were the Russian formalists. Alienation effects were aimed at dispelling the audience's empathy with what they witnessed on stage and at preventing their sinking into the 'world of the play' as well as preventing, too, the illusion that what they were witnessing was 'real life'. Instead the production and PERFORMANCE were constantly to remind the audience that they were watching a play, a depiction of events not as they necessarily were but as they might conceivably be.

The concept accompanies Brecht's development of a theory of *epic theatre* designed to replace that of *dramatic theatre*. In 'Theatre for Pleasure or Theatre for Instruction', which according to sources quoted by Willett was written in about 1936 or earlier, Brecht makes the distinction between these two clear:

> The dramatic theatre's spectator says: Yes, I have felt like that too – Just like me – It's only natural – It'll never change – The sufferings of this man appal me, because they are inescapable – That's great art; it all seems the most obvious thing in the world – I weep when they weep, I laugh when they laugh.
>
> The epic theatre's spectator says: I'd never have thought it – That's not the way – That's extraordinary, hardly believable – It's got to stop – The sufferings of this

9

man appal me, because they are unnecessary – That's great art: nothing obvious in it – I laugh when they weep, I weep when they laugh. (Willett: 1964, 71)

To achieve such results, Brecht's epic theatre used an episodic presentation of events very often involving NARRATIVE of an extra-MIMETIC nature broken up by songs, back-projected pictures or texts, commentaries, and so on. There is a striking parallel here with Mikhail Bakhtin's distinction between the epic and the novel in his essay 'Epic and Novel', in which he argues that whereas the reader can enter the world of the novel he or she cannot enter the world of the epic (Bakhtin: 1981, 32).

In narrative theory the term *words of estrangement* refers to elements in a narrative which clearly distinguish and distance the NARRATOR's consciousness from that of one or more CHARACTERS.

Allography According to the *OED* an allograph is a 'writing or signature made by one person on behalf of another'. POST-STRUCTURALIST critics convinced by or desirous of the death of the AUTHOR have adapted the term in order to suggest that the author no longer writes for him- or herself, but have stopped short of suggested that he or she writes for anyone else. Nicholas Royle considers using the term 'allography – a writing on behalf of another', 'only if this "other" is acknowledged as being non-human, unpresentable and irremediably cryptic' (1991, 33).

Alterity Otherness (see the longer entry for OTHER). The concept of the other or of otherness is important in a number of different theories, and all may make use of the term *alterity*. However, its use is especially associated with PSYCHOANALYSIS and POST-COLONIALISM.

See also EXOTOPY; RADICAL ALTERITY.

Always-already A phrase that is still used often enough for it to merit a gloss. It became popular in the 1970s and was associated with the work of Louis Althusser. A problem faced by Althusser and other STRUCTURALIST MARXISTS was that of ranking determining forces in order of strength and importance in an essentially synchronic model which did not allow for temporal alternation as a measure for judging cause-and-effect. Thus the word 'already' invokes that temporal and historical element which has already been neutralized or revoked by the word 'always'.

In explaining the concept of INTERPELLATION, Althusser provides an illustration (a man being hailed in the street), and then insists that 'in reality these things happen without any succession'(1971, 163), and that as 'ideology is eternal, I must now suppress the temporal form in which I have presented the functioning of ideology, and say: ideology has always-already interpellated individuals as subjects' (1971, 164). He is then able to deliver 'one last proposition': '*individuals are always-already subjects*' (1971, 164).

Always-already, then, is a phrase used to denote relations of subordination or influence while attempting to exclude that sense of temporality that use of a cause-and-effect model would bring with it.

See also CHORA; STRUCTURE IN DOMINANCE.

Ambiguity This is a less fashionable term today than it was for the NEW CRITICS, whose work owed a lot to William Empson's extension of the literary-critical importance of this concept in his *Seven Types of Ambiguity* (first published 1930). Empson defined *ambiguity* loosely, and this looseness remained in spite of a number of attempts to tighten the definition in successive editions of his work. By the third edition he was content to call an ambiguity 'any verbal nuance, however slight, which gives room for alternative reactions to the same piece of language' (1961, 1).

What has rendered Empson's usage less fashionable, perhaps, is its location of multiple MEANING in the WORK itself rather than in the READER or reading, or in the rules which define LITERARINESS itself. Thus alternative terms such as *polysemy* and *plurisignification* have emerged because they locate the lack of semantic CLOSURE elsewhere: in the reader, in language itself, or in the constituting rules of literariness. Empson's ambiguities were, after all, limited and finite even if they were multiple, whereas the polysemies of DECONSTRUCTION are never-ending. (Technically, *polysemy* locates the multiple meanings in the word itself, whereas ambiguity normally refers to the level of expression.)

Moreover, in spite of the fact that Empson is often unproblematically described as a New Critic, he never accepted the embargo on authorial control over meaning proclaimed by 'The Intentional Fallacy', before or after its formulation by W. K. Wimsatt and Monroe Beardsley in 1946, and the strongly biographical element in his use of the concept of ambiguity has also met with less sympathy among those convinced of the death of the AUTHOR. Finally, in spite of his concern with ambiguity Empson frequently stressed both the way in which ambiguities produced *meanings* in a work, and also how these often contradictory meanings could, nevertheless, merge into an AESTHETIC or artistic unity – and again these positions are likely to find less universal support than they once enjoyed.

See also FLICKER.

Anachrony Also, following Bal (1985), *chronological deviation*. Any lack of fit between the ORDER in which EVENTS are presented in the PLOT or *sjužet*, and that in which they are reported in the STORY or FABULA, is termed an anachrony. Both ANALEPSIS and PROLEPSIS are examples of anachrony.

Bal isolates two sorts of anachrony: *punctual anachrony*, when only one instant from the past or future is evoked, and *durative anachrony*, when a longer span of time or a more general situation is evoked.

Film theory has provided some useful related terms around the basic concept of the *cut*: a cut occurs when what the audience sees is not the result of continuous filming by one camera. A *matched cut* occurs when chronological sequentiality is maintained even though a cut has taken place, whereas a *jump cut* involves a break in sequentiality, either forwards or back in time. *Crosscutting* involves the movement between two different lines of action, whether or not these are occurring at the same or different times, while *intercutting* involves movement between different lines of action that are taking place at the same time.

See also DURATION; MONTAGE.

Analepsis Also, following Prince (1988a), *flashback, retrospection, retroversion, cutback* or *switchback*. An analepsis involves 'any evocation after the fact of an event that took place earlier than the point in the story where we are at any given moment' (Genette: 1980, 40).

As with PROLEPSIS the inclusion of evoked as well as NARRATED events extends the reach of analepsis rather beyond that traditionally accorded to a term such as flashback in pre-STRUCTURALIST days. With this extension, for example, the whole 'second generation' section of Emily Brontë's *Wuthering Heights* can be categorized as an example of analepsis as it continually evokes – to us and to CHARACTERS such as Heathcliff – EVENTS that took place earlier in the novel. Again, as with the extended meaning proposed by Genette for prolepsis, it may be argued that this runs the risk of giving the term too broad and vague a scope.

An *internal analepsis* does not reach back prior to the chronological point at which the STORY started, while an *external analepsis* does. A *completing analepsis*, according to Genette, fills in a gap or ELLIPSIS left earlier on in the NARRATIVE, while a *repeating analepsis* or *recall* repeats that which has already been narrated. Analepses can be measured according to their *extent* (how long a period of time they cover), and *reach* (how far back in time they go) (Genette: 1980, 48; Prince: 1988a, 5).

Alfred Hitchcock has a revealing commentary on one of the conventions governing the use of flashbacks in film – a convention which, typically, he broke. He is in conversation with the French film director François Truffaut.

A. H.   I did one thing in that picture [*Stage Fright*] that I never should have done; I put in a flashback that was a lie.

F. T.   Yes, and the French critics were particularly critical of that.

A. H.   Strangely enough, in movies, people never object if a man is shown telling a lie. And it's also acceptable, when a character tells a story about the past, for the flashback to show it as if it were taking place in the present. So why is it that we can't tell a lie through a flashback? (Truffaut: 1986, 275)

See also DIEGESIS AND MIMESIS (heterodiegesis and homodiegesis).

Analgon/analogic communication See DIGITAL AND ANALOGIC COMMUNICATION

Analysis According to T. S. Eliot, comparison and analysis are the chief tools of the critic. Analysis is conventionally distinguished from INTERPRETATION on the ground that it involves a separation of that which is to be studied into its component parts. Thus just as the chemical analysis of a substance would require that it be divided into the different chemical elements of which, in combination, it consists, so literary analysis would involve the dividing of a literary WORK (or in some cases a literary response) into the separate elements by which it is constituted.

The parallel indicates, however, that discussion of analysis leads naturally into treatment of the literary work as if it were an object. Not surprisingly, then, critics such as the NEW CRITICS, who frequently discussed the literary work in just this way, were perhaps more at ease with this concept than critics less happy to view the literary work as object have been. Literary analysis – the concept and the activity – is thus a good deal less fashionable so far as literary *works* are concerned than it once was, especially during the 1940s and 1950s when the influence of the New Critics was at its peak.

However, if analysing literary *works* has become somewhat less of a fashionable activity, the analysis of such things as IDEOLOGIES, MYTHS and even CULTURES has become something of a growth industry during the past couple of decades. The title of Perry Anderson's influential 1969 essay 'Components of the National Culture' is representative in its implication that a total culture may itself be objectified or even REIFIED, and then analysed by means of a separation into its constitutive elements. Analysis can be historical, but the analysis most favoured in recent years by literary and cultural theorists has been SYNCHRONIC rather than DIACHRONIC, and has frequently based itself on the model of synchronic syntactical or grammatical analysis. The popularity of the LINGUISTIC PARADIGM has had an important influence in recommending forms of analysis of linguistic origin – in the study of NARRATIVE, for instance.

Another influential factor is that of PSYCHOANALYSIS: Freud's analyses in particular have had a traceable effect on techniques of analysis within literary criticism, especially with regard to the utilization of concepts such as CENSORSHIP and CONDENSATION AND DISPLACEMENT. The emphasis in such cases has frequently been more on AUTHOR or READER than on literary work.

Anchoring A common METAPHOR in a number of contexts, used to indicate that a particular link in a chain of MEDIATIONS is at least relatively fixed. In his essay 'Rhetoric of the Image', Roland Barthes refers to what he terms 'the denominative's function', which 'corresponds nicely to an *anchoring* of every possible (denoted) meaning of the object, by recourse to a nomenclature' (1991, 28).

Androcentric Literally: centred on the male. The term has been coined by FEMINIST theorists wishing to describe a habit of mind and set of attitudes which are based upon a male perspective and which ignore female experience and interests. The opposite of androcentric is *gynocentric*: centred on the female. Gynocentricity is advocated by some feminists as a counter-balance to androcentricity, and in the field of literature requires writers and READERS to attempt to ground themselves on female experience and to view the world from a female perspective.

Compare FEMALING.

Androcratic See GYNOCRATIC/GYNECOCRATIC

Androgyny Technically, the union of both sexes in one individual. The *OED* gives this as a biological term and equates it with hermaphrodism, but in recent FEMINIST writing the term is used to refer to CULTURALLY acquired characteristics rather than to biologically determined ones. The writer who probably contributed most to this shift of emphasis was Virginia Woolf. Towards the end of her long essay, 'A Room of One's Own' (1929), she reports the train of thought inspired in her by looking out of her window on what she claimed was a particular day (26 October 1928) and seeing a taxi-cab stopping for a girl and a young man (her terms), picking them both up, and driving off.

> [T]he sight of the two people getting into the taxi and the satisfaction it gave me made me also ask whether there are two sexes in the mind corresponding to the two sexes in the body, and whether they also require to be united in order to get complete satisfaction and happiness? ... The normal and comfortable state of being is that when the two live in harmony together, spiritually co-operating. If one is a man, still the woman part of the brain must have effect; and a woman also must have intercourse with the man in her. Coleridge perhaps meant this when he said that a great mind is androgynous. (Woolf: 1929, 147–8)

Those who have sought to use and develop Woolf's suggestion have generally paid less attention to the GENDER of writers and more to the gender of, as it were, their productions – that is to say, to the attitudes, IDEOLOGIES and assumptions encoded in their writing. Donald Spoto provides an interesting insight into Alfred Hitchcock's views on gender and acting in his biography of the film director.

> 'Some people might be surprised by this,' said an actress who knew him well, 'but Hitchcock was always comfortable with homosexual or bisexual people. He always told his actors that they really had to be part masculine and part feminine in order to get inside any other character. Subjectivity, he felt, and feeling, transcended gender.' (Spoto: 1983, 86)

However, given the now-common assumption that there are two sexes but many genders, for many the BINARY implications of the term *androgyny* are now seen to be somewhat limiting. A number of recent FEMINIST writers have recognized that extension of the term beyond the realm of the biological was historically important, but that its use today is ideologically problematic. Radical feminists in particular have expressed opposition to feminist use of the term. Mary Daly, for example, comments as follows:

> Experience proved that this word [androgyny], which we now recognize as expressing pseudowholeness in its combination of distorted gender descriptions, failed and betrayed our thought. ... When we heard the word echoed back by those who misinterpreted our thought we realized that combining the 'halves' offered to consciousness by patriarchal language usually results in portraying something more like a hole than a whole. (Daly: 1979, 387)

And K. K. Ruthven has quoted Adrienne Rich's not unrelated objection, that 'the very structure of the word replicates the sexual dichotomy and the priority of *andros* (male) over *gyne* (female)' (Ruthven: 1984, 106, quoting from Rich: 1976, 30). In response to such criticisms, Sandra Gilbert and Susan Gubar have suggested the alternative term *gyandry*, but this coinage has not gained general acceptance. It seems that a more fluid and nuanced definition of the term *gender* may be rendering these other terms obsolete.

Compare CROSS-DRESSING; TRANSGENDER.

Anisochrony See ISOCHRONY

Anthumous/posthumous A distinction taken by Gérard Genette (1997) from Alphonse Allais. In his discussion of the PARATEXT Genette defines an anthumous paratext as one produced during the lifetime of the AUTHOR of the TEXT, while a posthumous one is produced after his or her death.

Anticipation See PROLEPSIS

Anti-novel See METALANGUAGE

Anxiety of influence/authorship See REVISIONISM

Apophrades See REVISIONISM

Aporia From the Greek for an apparently irresolvable logical difficulty, this term was traditionally used to describe statements by CHARACTERS in just that state – normally in soliloquy. (Hamlet's 'To be or not to be' soliloquy, for instance.)

More recently Jacques Derrida has adopted and developed the term, and Alan Bass, the English translator of *Writing and Difference*, glosses Derrida's usage of it as follows: 'once a system has been "shaken" by following its totalizing logic to its final consequence, one finds an excess which cannot be construed within the rules of logic, for the excess can only be conceived as *neither* this *nor* that, or both at the same time – a departure from all rules of logic' (Derrida: 1978a, xvi). For Derrida, according to Bass, this excess is often posed as an aporia.

In the wake of Derrida the term has become more popular as a way of referring to those insoluble doubts and hesitations which are thrown up by the READING of a TEXT. The term is not normally used (by those who normally use it) in a pejorative sense or to indicate disapproval, but rather to point to SITES within a reader's experience of a text in which he or she is given the freedom to play with the text by the irresolvability revealed at its stress points or FAULTLINES.

Apparatus A term with a number of meanings in contemporary theory. The dominant one, so far as I can ascertain, stems from the German dramatist Bertolt Brecht's term *Apparat*, meaning an ensemble of CONVENTIONS, conditions, modes of production, which lies partly hidden from the GAZE of the participant. Brecht names opera, the stage and the press as varied examples of an apparatus in his notes to the opera *Aufstieg und Fall der Stadt Mahagonny*. He suggests that such apparatuses 'impose their views as it were incognito'. The concept is related to Brecht's belief in the need for the artist not just to create new WORKS, but to create new possibilities for the creation, dissemination, and reception of art. Thus he attacks 'a general habit of judging works of art by their suitability for the apparatus without ever judging the apparatus by its suitability for the work' (Willett: 1964, 34). John Frow has suggested that the literary SYSTEM can be seen as such an apparatus, and that, accordingly, social functions need to be understood as a component of TEXTUALITY (1986, 84). Not to be confused with *scholarly apparatus*, which refers to those PARATEXTUAL elements specific to academic writing such as footnotes, references, and the conventions which govern their use.

Appreciation

Martin Jay has pointed out that the term was 'very much in the air in the post 1968 era', and he provides examples of a range of different usages.

'[A]pparatus' was employed by Bachelard to examine 'phenomeno-technologies' rather than unmediated phenomenological perception, by Althusser to designate 'ideological state apparatuses (*appareils*),' and by Foucault to talk of *dispositifs* of power and sexuality. But it was a renewed interest in Freud's usage that most inspired its adoption by film theorists. In a widely discussed passage from *The Interpretation of Dreams*, he had suggested that rather than conceptualizing the psyche as monolithic and undifferentiated, 'we should picture the instrument which carries out our mental functions as resembling a compound microscope, or a photographic apparatus, or something of the kind. On that basis, psychical locality will correspond to a place inside the apparatus at which one of the preliminary stages of an image comes into being.' (1993, 471; the quotation from Freud comes from the 5th volume of the standard edition, 536)

For the Foucauldian use of this term see *DISPOSITIF*; for ideological state apparatuses see IDEOLOGY.

Appreciation The critic Stein Haugom Olsen has given this term a rather more central and carefully defined function than it perhaps enjoyed before. According to him, 'appreciation involves an experience of value, positive or negative, that does not come into understanding. . . . Appreciation *is* the apprehension of a type of value, and the experience *consists in* and *is defined in* the apprehension' (Olsen: 1987, 152). He suggests that an analysis of appreciation 'is a way of identifying that core in criticism which is constitutive of our concept of literature' (1987, 137). Thus a person who reads a literary WORK may understand it without appreciating it, following Olsen; that is to say he or she will comprehend what the words mean but will not recognize or respond to the AESTHETIC features of the work.

Appropriateness conditions See SPEECH ACT THEORY

Appropriation See INCORPORATION

Arbitrary In Linguistics a SIGN is arbitrary if the relationship between it and whatever it stands for or represents is fixed by CONVENTION rather than by any intrinsic or inherent resemblance beyond the scope of the particular sign SYSTEM to which it belongs. Thus human word language typically rests primarily upon arbitrary signs. The French word *chien*, the German *Hund*, and the English *dog* are all used in their respective languages to represent the same animal; none of these words in spoken or written form resembles a dog independently of the conventions governing the use of the three languages in question. A Chinese person speaking no European language would have no way of knowing what these words mean, or that they are all used to represent the same animal. In contrast, speaking onomatopoeic words such as *pop* and *hiss* may be said to produce a noise not dissimilar to the sounds the words are used to represent. As signs, therefore, it can be said that these words are not totally arbitrary. Different writing systems can be more or less arbitrary: *pictographs*, for instance, are less arbitrary than words written in *phonetic script*. This is why labels that are to be read by people of many nationalities make frequent use of pictures rather than of script representing a single language. Faced with the words *a smiling face* in print a monoglot Chinese person would understand nothing, but even someone who had never encountered forms of representation such as photography and painting could make some sense of a photograph of a smiling face or of the sign ☺, however much the INTERPRETATION of such forms of representation is conditioned by a range of CULTURALLY learned CODES and conventions.

The linked terms *motivated* and *unmotivated*, or *natural* and *conventional* are sometimes used to convey a similar point: a motivated or natural sign is one which is linked to that which it represents by a resemblance or connection existing independently of the conventions of the sign system to which the sign belongs. These terms also have application outside of formal sign systems. A motivated or natural symbol, for example, is a symbol which has some natural, extra-systemic resemblance to or connection with that for which it stands. For *night* to symbolize danger is more natural than for *biscuit* to do so: night is generally a more dangerous time than day because of the concealment it grants to predators and malefactors. As a symbol of evil, then, *night* is a more motivated example than is *biscuit*; a writer can rely on a pre-existing association between the former and danger, but must construct such an association in the case of the latter example. For Roland Barthes's argument that the photograph is a message without a code, see the discussion of *analgon* in the entry for DIGITAL AND ANALOGIC COMMUNICATION.

That human language is essentially a system which makes use of arbitrary relationships is fundamental to its power and flexibility; non-arbitrary systems may sometimes be recommended because they are easier for users to understand and adapt to, but their potentialities are generally very restricted.

Ferdinand de Saussure's insistence upon the arbitrary relationship between SIGNIFIER and SIGNIFIED has been very influential in the twentieth century, partly – it is arguable – as a result of misunderstandings of Saussure's point. Certainly some followers of Saussure have used the arbitrary nature of this relationship (between, on the one hand, a sound image or its written equivalent and, on the other, the concept to which it refers) as a basis for seeing language as a self-enclosed system with no necessary connection with extra-linguistic reality. But this is to misunderstand Saussure's point. As Thomas G. Pavel has observed, the principle of arbitrariness maintains only that there is no motivated link between the conceptual and the phonetic sides of a linguistic sign, 'it does not deny the stability of linguistic meaning, once the semiotic system has been established' (1986, 8). In other words, although it is certainly true that it is possible to imagine a different course of history to that which actually occurred having led to the word *car* in English being replaced by another (*auto*, for example), once *car* has achieved an established meaning the relationship between this word and what it stands for in the English language community is relatively fixed.

For the RUSSIAN FORMALIST use of the term *motivation* see FUNCTION.

Archaeology of knowledge The title of an influential book by Michel Foucault in which the author attempts to describe DISCOURSES (as he defines this term), their internal rules and STRUCTURES, interrelationships, continuities and discontinuities, rules of transformation, and the conditions of their emergence, development and decline. He stresses that he does not want to suggest, by his use of the word archaeology, that he is concerned with something frozen and out of time. As a back-cover note to a paperback edition of his book expresses it, 'The domain of things said is what is called the *archive*; the role of archaeology is to analyse that archive'.

For Foucault the *archive* is a particular level that comes between the LANGUE that defines the system of constructing possible sentences, and the *corpus* that passively collects the words that are spoken. The archive is 'a practice that causes a multiplicity of statements to emerge as regular events', it is *'the general system of the formation and transformation of statements'* (1972, 130). The job of uncovering the archive 'forms the general horizon to which the description of discursive formations, the analysis of positivities, the mapping of the enunciative field belongs'. And the term archaeology is given to the totality of all these searches (1972, 131).

Archetypal criticism A type of criticism that attracted renewed attention in the 1970s and 1980s, largely as a result of a FEMINIST interest in the implications a new form of archetypal criticism might hold for an understanding of women's experience of PATRIARCHY.

Archetypal criticism has, however, something of a patriarchal history: its two founding fathers are generally taken to be Sir James Frazer and Carl Gustav Jung. Frazer's *The Golden Bough* appeared in 12 volumes from 1890 to 1915, and represents an exhaustive study of the interconnections of art, religion and MYTH through long processes of historical transmission and transformation. In addition to having a significant influence upon the study of ancient art and CULTURE, the work left its mark on *contemporary* literature: in his prefatory comments to the notes to *The Waste Land* (1922), T. S. Eliot acknowledges his deep indebtedness to Jessie Weston's *From Ritual to Romance* (1920) and adds the following comment:

> To another work of anthropology I am indebted in general, one which has influenced our generation profoundly; I mean *The Golden Bough*; I have used especially the two volumes *Adonis, Attis, Osiris*. Anyone who is acquainted with these works will immediately recognise in the poem certain references to vegetation ceremonies.

The widespread influence of Eliot's poem in the twentieth century is certainly one important factor in the spread of interest in archetypes (from the Greek words *archi*, a beginning or first instance, and *typos*, a stamp or impression), that is, in particular SYMBOLIC patterns and MOTIF-complexes which span cultural and historical boundaries. (Archetypal critics tend to divide into two camps when it comes to explaining this spanning process: we can call these, crudely, the 'spontaneous generationists' and the 'complex processes of transmissionists'.) But other MODERNIST writers of the same period exhibited great interest in the archetypal content of myths: we can cite Yeats, Joyce and Lawrence as obvious examples.

Outside of the work of creative artists we come near to archetypes in the work of Sigmund Freud, and certain Freudian uses of, for example, the Oedipus complex come close enough to universalized cross-cultural patterns of MEANING to invite the term 'archetypal'. But the theory of archetypes is given more direct theoretical justification in Jung's theory of the collective UNCONSCIOUS, the survival of primitive forms of thought in the psyches of the members of developed cultures.

The primary accessible source for these archetypes is myth, and in its first flowering archetypal criticism is very closely related to the study of ancient myth: so much so that it is sometimes known as mythic or mythopoeic criticism.

It is with Maud Bodkin's *Archetypal Patterns in Poetry* (1934) that archetypal literary criticism comes of age, and this study initiated a flood of myth-seeking analyses of literature, especially in the United States.

By the 1950s, however, archetypal criticism was under pressure. It was treated as a variant of extrinsic criticism by the NEW CRITICS, while simultaneously incurring the disfavour of MARXIST and sociological critics for its alleged failure to confront the socially or culturally specific nature of myth – although the critical theories of Northrop Frye helped to keep an archetypal light burning during the decades after the Second World War, and Leslie Fiedler's *Love and Death in the American Novel* (1960, revised edition 1966) demonstrated that it was possible for a literary criticism to trace archetypal patterns in modern literature in a manner that was both creative and culture-specific.

With the resurgence of feminist criticism, however, a new approach to the study of archetypes emerged. If the oppression of women was universal, then this would explain why myths reflecting this repression appeared at all times and all places – without the need for any mystical or even biological explanation. Annis Pratt's *Archetypal Patterns in Women's Fiction* (1982) is representative of the feminist appropriation of archetypal criticism. Pratt argues that Jung defined archetypes as primordial forms springing from the preverbal realm of the unconscious, and that he did not intend his archetypal categories to be taken as fixed absolutes but more as 'images, symbols, and narrative patterns that differ from stereotypes in being complex variables, subject to variations in perception' (1982, 4). Her book focuses upon such examples as the 'rape-trauma archetype' which can be traced from the Apollo-Daphne myth to much women's FICTION, the 'green-world archetype' which, in many female *Bildungsromane*, represents a special world of nature in which the pain and suffering experienced by the heroine will be unknown, and the 'growing-up grotesque archetype'. She concludes that it is possible to trace a relationship between the rise of women's fiction and three interrelated repositories of archetypal materials: 'the *Demeter/Kore* and *Ishtar/Tammuz* rebirth narratives, the *grail legends* of the later Middle Ages, and the cluster of archetypal and ritual materials constituting the *Craft of the Wise*, or *witchcraft*' (1982, 167). She concludes that the archetypal patterns to be found in women's fiction constitute signals from a buried feminine tradition that conflict with cultural NORMS, and this view of archetypes as potentially *oppositional* sums up much of the attraction that investigation into archetypes holds for feminist literary critics today.

Arche-writing Also *archi-trace, archi-writing, proto-writing*. A term invented by the French philosopher Jacques Derrida and derived in particular from Sigmund Freud's essay 'Note on the Mystic Writing Pad'. The writing pad in question was a toy sold for children on which messages could be written with a hard stylus, but apparently removed by detaching its double covering sheet from the wax slab on which this rested. What interested Freud was that although this operation rendered the writing in question invisible, it did not remove it utterly. The written message was still there, imprinted on the wax, hidden but not completely erased. Thus the wax base could be compared with the UNCONSCIOUS, from which (as Freud repeated on several occasions) nothing was ever completely erased, while the outer layer of celluloid and translucent waxed paper would accordingly be taken to represent the conscious mind which sends information on to the Unconscious without retaining it.

Moreover, the writing that becomes visible on the pad as a result of the use of the stylus was already there, in the sense that the use of the stylus only makes visible part of the wax block that pre-existed the act of writing. This development of Freud's analogy thus involves a conceptualizing of the unconscious mind as constituted by *writing* (see ÉCRITURE) in the form of an arche-writing or ur-writing in the brain which precedes all physical writing and, even, all speech – both phylogenetically and ontogenetically. As Derrida puts it,

> [w]riting supplements perception before perception even appears to itself [is conscious of itself]. 'Memory' or writing is the opening of that process of appearance itself. The 'perceived' may be read only in the past, beneath perception and after it. (1978a, 224)

From this perspective no perception is virginal or direct, but is given MEANING by a pre-existing arche-writing. The theory has points of contact (but only points) with Noam Chomsky's theory of a Language Acquisition Device (LAD) which, because it must predate the actual learning of any language, has the effect of situating language (again in the form of an ur-language or set of language universals) in the biological brain rather than on a social or CULTURAL terrain.

Derrida takes his use of the word *trace* from the same source in Freud. When the words written on the writing pad are removed, a slight scratch or trace of them remains on the surface. Freud sees this to be representative of the manner in which a trace 'is left in our psychical apparatus of the perceptions which impinge upon it' (quoted by Derrida: 1978a, 216). But the perceptions themselves are more than this trace: they are constituted by the relation between this trace and that which makes them visible (in the writing pad, the pressure of the wax slab behind; in the human mind, the coming together of trace and the Unconscious – the two linked by Freud in a passage quoted by Derrida: 1978a, 225).

Derrida then moves to apply this to writing (or, perhaps more properly, écriture). Freud 'performs for us the scene of writing', according to Derrida, but Freud's concept of the trace must nevertheless be 'radicalized and extracted from the metaphysics of presence' (1978a, 229). For Derrida, the trace would thus be

> the erasure of selfhood, of one's own presence, and is constituted by the threat or anguish of its irremediable disappearance, of the disappearance of its disappearance. An unerasable trace is not a trace, it is a full presence ... (1978a, 229)

This carries us back to some familiar Derridanean themes: the need to escape from the metaphysics of presence (see the entry for PRESENCE) involves the rejection of all fixed or hierarchical determinants. The trace must be really a trace, something that is left behind with no connection to that which caused it, and no guarantee of its own survival.

Only then will it represent a view of writing purged of the metaphysics of presence, a writing that can never catch up with that which will underwrite its own meaning. As Richard Harland puts it, 'perception is forever divided from the presence of "the things themselves"' (1987, 144), whereas for Freud the trace is safely linked to the presence of the wax tablet, the Unconscious which confirms the trace's meaning.

We must ask whether the first stage of Derrida's extension of Freud here is so very different from the argument that if the statue pre-exists the sculptor's labour, waiting, hidden in the block of stone, to be 'discovered', then statues therefore predate sculpture. Certainly the psychological evidence would appear to be that perception is partly constituted by biologically inherited elements common to all cultures, but that these elements are outweighed and can be modified by culturally specific learning. Moreover, one would want to ask what it was that caused human beings to be possessed of a particular biological inheritance.

See also CENSORSHIP; REPRESSION.

Architext Following Gérard Genette's book *L'Introduction à l'architexte* (1979), that ideal TEXT implied by the generic tradition to which a particular text belongs.

Archive See ARCHAEOLOGY OF KNOWLEDGE

Articulation See MEDIATION

Askesis See REVISIONISM

Aspect According to Mieke Bal the aspects of a given STORY are those traits which are specific to it and which distinguish it from other stories (1985, 7). Gerald Prince, in contrast, defines aspect as the *vision*, or point of view in terms of which a story is presented (1988a, 7), while Gérard Genette's definition of the same term is 'the way in which the story is perceived by the narrator' (1980, 29). As with many recent terms within NARRATIVE theory, *aspect* is borrowed from Linguistics, and its use rests upon an argued HOMOLOGY between the STRUCTURE of narratives and the structure of sentences.

What grammarians categorize as aspect is, in Genette's terminology, known as FREQUENCY (1980, 113).

See also PERSPECTIVE AND VOICE.

Assimilation In Mikhail Bakhtin's theories of DIALOGUE: the process whereby an individual temporarily adopts the viewpoint or IDEOLOGY of another person, or *assimilates* these to his or her own consciousness. Such assimilation will be more or less complete, more or less whole-hearted, to the extent that the individual's viewpoint or ideology are, or are not, at odds with those of the interlocutor. The concept can be seen as comparable in certain ways to Samuel Coleridge's 'willing suspension of disbelief', although Bakhtin seems to move more in the direction of 'adoption of belief'.

Compare CROSS-DRESSING; MASQUERADE; MIMICRY; and see also the entry for NOMAD.

Attribute/function A distinction used in determining the role of a CHARACTER in a NARRATIVE. A character may be possessed of attributes which have thematic significance, but which are not necessarily connected to that character's function in the development of the narrative.

See also FUNCTION.

Aura The German MARXIST Walter Benjamin used the term aura (adj. auratic) to describe the mystical sense that surrounds artistic or ritual objects like a halo, an aura that, according to him, is ultimately destroyed by techniques of mechanical reproduction such as photography. In his essay 'The Work of Art in the Age of Mechanical Reproduction' (first published 1936; included in *Illuminations*, 1973), he writes that

> that which withers in the age of mechanical reproduction is the aura of the work of art. This is a symptomatic process whose significance points beyond the realm of art. One might generalize by saying: the technique of reproduction detaches the reproduced object from the domain of tradition. (1973, 221)

In another essay included in *Illuminations*, 'On Some Motifs in Baudelaire', he further designates aura as 'the associations which, at home in the *mémoire involontaire*, tend to cluster around the object of a perception' (1973, 188). The *mémoire involontaire*, for Benjamin, is taken from the novelist Marcel Proust's distinction between involuntary and voluntary recollection, and rests on the belief (attributed by Benjamin to Freud) that memory fragments are often most powerful and most enduring when the incident on which they are based never entered consciousness (1973, 162). For Benjamin, mechanical reproduction interrupts the process whereby such auratic components enter the involuntary memory and enrich the art-work.

John Urry has extended the loss of aura from art(istic) objects to CULTURAL spheres:

> To say that a cultural phenomenon had aura was to say that it was radically separated from the social, it proclaimed its own originality, uniqueness and singularity, and that it was based in a discourse of formal organic unity and artistic creativity. Postmodernist culture is anti-auratic. Such forms do not proclaim their uniqueness but are mechanically and electronically reproduced. There is a denial of the separation of the aesthetic from the social and of the contention that art is of a different order from life. The value placed on the unity of the artistic work is challenged through an emphasis on pastiche, collage, allegory, and so on. Postmodern cultural forms are not consumed in a state of contemplation (as in the classical concert) but of distraction. Postmodern culture affects the audience via its immediate impact, through what it does for one, through regimes of pleasure, and not through the formal properties of the aesthetic material. And this serves to undermine any strong distinction between a high culture, enjoyed by an elite knowledgeable about the aesthetics of a given sphere (painting, music, literature), and the popular or low culture of the masses. (1990, 84–5)

See also AESTHETIC; MODERNISM AND POSTMODERNISM; ORGANICISM; PLEASURE; POPULAR.

Authenticity A term which in recent POSTCOLONIALIST usage has gathered to itself a number of negative CONNOTATIONS. The demand for 'authenticity' on the part of European or North American critics of Third or Fourth World literature has been attacked as an ESSENTIALIZING desire to fix 'native' peoples and their CULTURES in a timeless and static ethnic quaintness or DIFFERENCE. The demand for authenticity is thus a demand that 'native' peoples should stay safely STEREOTYPED as the OTHER of the western observer, not challenging paternalistic or semi-racist assumptions by revealing that there is no reason why they should not have as close a relationship to technological advance or cultural modernity as Europeans or North Americans. As Margery Fee puts it:

> The demand for 'authenticity' denies Fourth World writers a living, changing culture. Their culture is deemed to be Other and must avoid crossing those fictional but ideologically essential boundaries between Them and Us, the Exotic and the Familiar, the Past and the Future, the 'Dying' and the Living. Especially, 'authentic' writing from the Fourth World must steer clear of that quintessentially 'new' and ever renewing genre, the novel.
>
> . . .
>
> Given the destruction inflicted by Whites on indigenous cultures one sympathizes with this view, but indigenous peoples may well feel it is suicidal to devote the time of their best-educated to cultural preservation at the cost of political renewal. (1995, 243)

Author The concept of authorship was a relatively unproblematized one until comparatively recently. But subsequent to the publication of two essays in particular – Roland Barthes's 'The Death of the Author' (1977) and Michel Foucault's 'What is an Author?' (1980b) – the term *author* has, from being one of the least problematic of terms, become the SITE of much complex discussion. Clearly, on a simple level an author is a person who writes a WORK: Emily Brontë is the author of *Wuthering Heights*. But as Foucault reminds us, one cannot be an author by writing just anything: a private letter may be signed by the person who wrote it, but it does not have an author, nor do we normally speak of the author of a scientific theory: such writing is seen to have a relationship to the person who wrote it which is different from an author's relationship to a literary work.

In other words, the term *author* does more than attach a piece of writing to its individual human origin: it has to be a special sort of writing, and the relation thus posited is more than a certificate of origin. As Foucault puts it, 'The author-function is therefore characteristic of the mode of existence, circulation, and functioning of certain discourses within a society' (1980b, 148). To talk of an author is to appeal to a shared knowledge of these DISCOURSES and of the CONVENTIONS governing their transmission and circulation.

Foucault states that the concept of authorship comes in the train of 'penal appropriation': it is when writers become subject to punishment for what they have written that works acquire authors, and he dates the emergence of authorship at the point at which writers entered the 'system of property that characterizes our society' (1980b, 149). Barthes makes a similar point, claiming that the author is a modern figure, 'a product of our society insofar as, emerging from the Middle Ages with English empiricism, French rationalism and the personal faith of the Reformation, it discovered the prestige of the individual, of, as it is more nobly put, the "human person"' (1977, 142–3).

Perhaps the most challenging of Foucault's arguments is that *author* and *living person who wrote the work* are not to be equated, as the author function can give rise to several selves, several SUBJECTS, 'positions that can be occupied by different classes of individuals' (1980b, 153). When we talk of an author, in other words, we have in mind a range of characteristic actions and relationships which we do not attribute to every writing individual. What these are is, of course, a complex matter – especially as (according to both Barthes and Foucault), the author function (those conventions and attributes which attach to authorship) is not a historically stable one. It should be added that in certain usages 'author function' has a slightly different meaning: thus the Jane Austen of *Emma* would be one of Austen's author functions, so that when in the context of a discussion of *Emma* we refer to 'Austen' we have in mind certain characteristics which are possessed of the real-life author but are also text-specific (see the discussion of the term *career author* below).

Barthes in particular is keen (as the title of his essay suggests) to *challenge* the power of the author, a power to which he attributes a range of specifically IDEOLOGICAL functions. For him, to seek to explain a work by reference to the person who wrote it is (by implication) to be in thrall to a pernicious sort of individualism, and to imprison the work in the imagined self of its individual producer. The alternative view involves moving from work to TEXT, seen not as personal statement from author-God but as 'a tissue of quotations drawn from the innumerable centres of culture' (1977, 146). Clearly here the author is seen in representative POST-STRUCTURALIST manner as site rather than originating PRESENCE.

Barthes's view here is intimately tied up with theories of ÉCRITURE, translated rather less than satisfactorily in the English version of his essay as 'writing'. For him, writing

> is the destruction of every voice, of every point of origin. Writing is that neutral, composite, oblique space where our subject slips away, the negative where all identity is lost, starting with the very identity of the body writing. (1977, 142)

A similar theoretical basis underlies Barthes's claim that, for Mallarmé, it is language which speaks, not the author. 'The death of the author' is, then, an aspect of the POSTMODERNIST and post-structuralist attack on *origins*, on the belief that we can explain (or even help to understand) anything by referring it to where we think that it comes from or to any process of cause and effect. And (as both proponents and opponents of such recent critical positions have argued) to reject such a belief involves an acceptance of the impossibility of arriving at a final MEANING or INTERPRETATION of a text. Barthes closes his essay by claiming that the birth of the READER must be at the expense of the death of the author: in other words, to allow the reader unlimited interpretative play, the text must be removed from the author's control.

Recent critics untouched by postmodernism and post-structuralism have argued against individualizing views of the literary work in ways which subject the concept of the author to a related set of criticisms. A textual critic such as Jerome J. McGann (1983) has drawn attention to the gap between the author seen as sole creator of the work, and the real process of literary composition involving negotiation between historically located individual author and a range of other individuals and institutions – publishers, editors, censors, collaborating friends, critics, and so on.

Perhaps one note of caution is appropriate here. Although it is true as I have claimed that the concept of the author was relatively unproblematic prior to the recent work that I have discussed, earlier readers and critics (not to mention writers) perhaps held less simplistic views than some modern critics have attributed to them. Take the following two comments: 'if authors are as good after they are dead as when they were living, while living they might as well be dead'; 'If the real author is made of so little account by the modern critic, he is scarcely more an object of regard to the modern reader'. Both come from essays by the early nineteenth-century essayist William Hazlitt, from, respectively, 'On Thought and Action', and 'On Criticism' (Hazlitt: n.d., 107, 214).

The term *implied author*, along with the matching term *implied reader*, comes from Wayne C. Booth's *Rhetoric of Fiction* (1961). The term has entered into current critical vocabulary and is used to refer to that picture of a creating author behind a literary work that the reader builds up on the basis of elements in (or reading experiences of) the work. (Note the singular – each literary work has its own implied author, although some critics have used the term to refer to that composite sense of an author that we construct on the basis of more than one literary work.) The implied author may be very different from the real-life individual responsible for writing the work in question, and indeed Seymour Chatman argues that what we get from the concept of the implied author 'is a way of naming and analyzing the textual intent of narrative fictions under a single term but without recourse to biographism' (1990, 75). Thus when a critic writing on the novels of Jane Austen refers to 'Jane Austen', he or she may be referring to the historical figure, but is often referring to the author implied by one or more of her novels. To all intents and purposes the matched terms 'textual author' and 'textual reader'/'mock reader' are synonyms for 'implied author' and 'implied reader'. As Susana Onega and José Ángel García Landa comment:

> The textual author is a virtual image of the author's attitudes, as presented by the text. The textual reader is a virtual receiver created by the author in full view of the actual audience he or she presumes for his or her work. The textual reader need not coincide with the author's conception of the audience: this reader-figure may be a rhetorical strategy, a role which the author wishes the audience to assume (or even to reject). (1996, 9)

The term *career author*, in contrast, is used by the narratologist Seymour Chatman to denote 'the subset of features shared by all the implied authors (that is, all the individual intents) of the narrative texts bearing the name of the same real author' (1990, 88). In other words: that sense of a personality or human presence which readers construct from the historical author's (= the author as 'real person') works (note the plural). We would, for example, have a sense of a person and personality to which we could give the name 'Jane Austen' even if we had no information about this person beyond that provided by her works of fiction. It is this 'sense of a person' that Chatman calls the career author.

Authorial See NARRATOR

Authoritative discourse See DISCOURSE

Autodiegetic See DIEGESIS AND MIMESIS

Autoethnography/autoethnographic expression See TRANSCULTURATION

Autographic/allographic Richard Macksey states that Gérard Genette took this distinction from Nelson Goodman's *The Languages of Art* (1968), and used it in his *L'Œuvre de l'art* (1994). Macksey explains that the terms allow one to make a distinction between

> the status of those art works where the authenticity of the immanent object is crucial (e.g. painting or sculpture) and those where it is not (e.g., a literary text or a musical composition). The former are styled 'autographic,' the latter 'allographic'. (1997, xvi–xvii)

Unfortunately, as Macksey points out, in his earlier work *Paratexts: Thresholds of Interpretation* (1997; first published in French as *Seuils* in 1987), Genette had defined '"allography" in its various forms' as 'a text (preface, review, etc.) that one person writes for another person's work' (1997, 5 n8).

Automization See DEFAMILIARIZATION

Autopoiesis Taken by Jerome J. McGann from *Autopoiesis and Cognition: The Realization of the Living*, by Humberto Maturana and Francisco Varela (1980). McGann suggests that the term can be applied to literary texts, as these are paradigms of the interactive and feedback mechanisms studied by Maturana and Varela. Such mechanisms are distinguished from 'vehicular textual models' whose textual paradigm is one that does not interfere with or 'distort' a message. With vehicular textual models one can easily distinguish vehicle of transmission from message, whereas this is not the case with *autopoiesis* (McGann: 1991, 11).
    Compare the discussion in the entries for CODE and SHANNON AND WEAVER MODEL OF COMMUNICATION.

Autotelic A term popular with the NEW CRITICS which appears to be creeping back into theoretical use. From the Greek meaning self-completing, the term was used to suggest those qualities of autonomy and self-sufficiency beloved of the New Critics, and well glossed in the closing two lines of Archibald MacLeish's poem 'Ars Poetica' (1926): 'A poem should not mean I But be'.

Avant-garde See MODERNISM AND POSTMODERNISM

B

Backgrounding See DEFAMILIARIZATION

Base and superstructure Also *basis and superstructure*. Central to the traditional MARXIST analysis of society and history is the analytical distinction between base and superstructure. The most famous statement of this distinction is to be found in Karl Marx's *A Contribution to the Critique of Political Economy*, in which he states that

> In the social production of their existence, men inevitably enter into definite relations, which are independent of their will, namely relations of production appropriate to a given stage in the development of their material forces of production. The totality of these relations of production constitutes the economic structure of society, the real foundation, on which arises a legal and political superstructure and to which correspond definite forms of social consciousness. The mode of production of material life conditions the general process of social, political and intellectual life. It is not the consciousness of men that determines their existence, but their social existence that determines their consciousness. (1971, 20–21)

Working from the position outlined here, traditional Marxists have distinguished between elements in society which, with regard to their emergence and their historical effect, are either primary or secondary. On the one hand the *economic structure of society, the real foundation* (seen as primary), and on the other the *superstructure* (seen as secondary). Along with law and politics (mentioned by Marx), the superstructure has generally been taken to include other CULTURAL and intellectual phenomena such as (in some accounts) literature.

Such an analytical position leads inexorably to the view that to understand literature one must understand the primary phenomenon of which it is the secondary product, reflection or extension: the economic base of society.

Terry Eagleton, for example, has suggested that 'Marxist criticism is part of a larger body of theoretical analysis which aims to understand *ideologies*', and he locates IDEOLOGIES firmly within the superstructure (1976b, viii, 4).

There have been attempts within Marxism to modify and soften Marx's position as expressed above, and after Marx's death Marx's colleague and collaborator Friedrich Engels himself accepted that in order to stress the theoretical primacy of the economic base he and Marx had both understressed the extent to which the superstructure reacts back upon the base.

In his essay 'Literature and Sociology: In memory of Lucien Goldmann', Raymond Williams argued that in the 1930s Marxist literary criticism was 'weak in just the decisive area where practical criticism was strong: in its capacity to give precise and detailed and reasonably adequate accounts of actual consciousness: not just a scheme or a generalization but actual works, full of rich and significant and specific experience', and he attributed this weakness to 'the received formula of base and superstructure, which in ordinary hands converted very quickly to an interpretation of superstructure as simple reflection, representation, ideological expression – simplicities which just will not survive any prolonged experience of actual works' (1980, 18–19). For Williams, the base–superstructure model was inescapably REDUCTIONIST, and possessed of a 'rigid, abstract and static character' (1980, 20). For Terry Eagleton, in contrast, the usefulness of the distinction between base and superstructure becomes apparent only when an engaged historical perspective is added to its structural-analytic force. In an essay entitled 'Ideology and Scholarship' he writes that the

> distinction between more specific and more general senses of social interest, then, is among other things a distinction between the short term and the long term, historically speaking. This is also, one might claim, what is involved in the much criticized classical Marxist metaphor of base and superstructure. We can best distinguish between these two 'levels' not 'vertically,' as the model itself misleadingly suggests, but 'horizontally' – a matter, so to speak, of time scale. To say that the changes you have effected in a particular form of social life are only 'superstructural' is less a philosophical doctrine that [= than?, *J.H.*] a political warning and reminder: it is to argue that you have not yet run up against that outer limit or horizon which will prove most resistant to transformation – for Marxism, the property system – and that therefore not only is there more to be done, but until your political practice bumps up hard against that limit, what changes you have managed to bring about are not as radical as they might look. (McGann: 1985a, 120–21)

Seen from this perspective, the base–superstructure distinction has its utility not in so far as it exposes every aspect of social or cultural reality, but in as much as it enables the analyst to distinguish between determining and non-determining elements in social and historical change, and between temporary and accidental changes and those which are likely to be more long-lasting.

It is also worth remembering that the 'material forces of production' do not just consist of machines and factories, but also of human skills. To take a relevant example: a wholly or largely illiterate society is less able to produce wealth in the modern world than one possessed of a literate workforce. Clearly, then, literacy is an element in the forces of production. Following Marx's comment in the first volume of *Capital* that the difference between the worst architect and the best of bees is that 'the architect raises his structure in imagination before he erects it in reality' (1970a, 178), it can be inferred that human imagination is implicated in the productive forces. Thus if literature contributes to the development of literacy and imagination it is hard to relegate it lock, stock and barrel to Marx's superstructure.

Richard Harland has coined the term *superstructuralism* to refer to a range of recent theories which 'invert our ordinary base-and-superstructure models until what we used to think of as superstructural actually takes precedence over what we used to think of as basic' (1987, 1–2). Harland has in mind not just STRUCTURALISTS and POST-STRUCTURALISTS but also SEMIOTICIANS, Foucauldians and Althusserian Marxists.

See also STRUCTURE OF FEELING.

Belatedness See REVISIONISM

Bibliology Defined by Gérard Genette as 'the study of "technical givens" involving the "outermost peritext" such as the cover, title page and the book's material construction' (1997, 16). For *peritext* see the entry for PARATEXT.

Binary/binarism Binary oppositions form the basis of DIGITAL systems of communication which involve the transformation of *continuous variations* to *discrete either/or distinctions*. This process is fundamental to human language: the classic example involves the colour spectrum which, although continuous in nature, is broken up into discrete segments which are given separate colour terms in various human languages. We become aware of this when our attention is drawn to the fact that not all human languages digitalize the colour spectrum in exactly the same way or by means of the same series of DIFFERENCES.

Binary distinctions are fundamental to much of modern Linguistics, and Jonathan Culler quotes the linguist Charles Hockett's remark that 'If we find continuous-scale contrasts in the vicinity of what we are sure is language, we exclude them from language' (Culler: 1975, 14).

STRUCTURALISM has adopted this principle of modern Linguistics and has given it a – perhaps *the* – central position in structuralist theory. Structuralist ANALYSIS typically searches for hierarchical strings of binary oppositions in the material or TEXT under investigation: a classic example is indicated in the title of Claude Lévi-Strauss's *The Raw and the Cooked*. Jacques Derrida's coinage DIFFÉRANCE is a direct descendant of the structuralist emphasis upon binary oppositions.

While the making of binary distinctions was indulged in without too much heart-searching when structuralism enjoyed most prestige, more recently it has become a much more controversial process. One general point of contention relating to binary oppositions concerns their status: are they useful *analytical tools*, or are they *fundamental linguistic (or other) units*? Many CULTURAL phenomena are based upon binary oppositions: 'If you are not with us you are against us' involves the forced cultural imposition of a binary opposition upon what is often a range of essentially ANALOGUE variations. Moreover, as this example demonstrates, binary distinctions often play an indispensable role in the formation and preservation of STEREOTYPES, and for this reason much recent cultural theory has set itself in opposition to the making of binary distinctions. This is especially true of POSTCOLONIAL theory, in which a rejection of simple binary distinctions between 'the west and the rest', European and 'native', observer and observed, Self and OTHER, is fundamental to much recent work.

The suspicion felt by many FEMINISTS with regard to binary distinctions is summed up in the following comment by Mary Eagleton: 'According to binary thinking the male and the masculine constitutes the norm, the positive and the superior; the female and the feminine is the aberration, the negative, the inferior' (1996, 287).

See also ANDROGYNY; DIGITAL AND ANALOGIC COMMUNICATION; ENERGETICS/GEO-METRICS; LIMINAL; LINGUISTIC PARADIGM; QUEER THEORY; ROOT/RADICLE/RHIZOME; STRAIGHT; TRANSGENDER.

Biocriticism Criticism (normally but not necessarily) FEMINIST which considers biological elements to be pre-eminent among those factors which cause or condition the production or reception of literary WORKS. Feminist biocriticism typically places a very high premium upon DIFFERENCE of sex.

See also ÉCRITURE FÉMININE.

Biologism/biological determinism The view that biological characteristics and DIF-FERENCES play a significant or (in the case of biological determinism) a determining role in social or CULTURAL matters, thus attributing to biological forces what opponents argue should rightly be set at the door of IDEOLOGIES and socially constructed roles. Thus differences between men and women would be seen as the result of innate biological factors rather than as the product of particular social pressures and influences, or of cultural conditioning. A related example is the view that wars are the product of innate biological urges and drives in human beings. Such views have sometimes been referred to as *Naked ape-ism*, after an influential popularizing book by Desmond Morris which attempts to understand human beings as 'naked apes'.

The term has currency particularly in FEMINIST and feminist-influenced circles in connection with arguments concerning the role of biological elements in GENDER formation and construction. Thus Stevi Jackson and Sue Scott have pointed out that 'Challenging biological determinism is . . . an important political strategy for feminists and not just an academic matter', and they refer to Christine Delphy's persuasive argument that

> [p]eople do not revolt against what is natural, therefore inevitable; or inevitable, therefore natural. Since what is resistible is not inevitable; what is not inevitable could be otherwise – it is arbitrary therefore social. The logical and necessary implication of women's revolt, like all revolts, is that the situation can be changed. Belief in the possibility of change implies belief in the social origins of the situation. (Jackson and Scott: 1996, 6, quoting Delphy: 1984, 211)

Block characterization An explicit, introductory characterization of a literary character by overt description rather than 'showing' through action or dialogue. The first sentence of Jane Austen's *Emma* provides us with an example: 'Emma Woodhouse, handsome, clever, and rich, with a comfortable home and happy disposition, seemed to unite some of the best blessings of existence; and had lived nearly twenty-one years in the world with very little to distress or vex her.'

Body For many recent theorists the body is no longer merely a purely physical system the study of which can safely be left to the medical profession. Instead, the body is also a concept or set of ideas which are seen to be implicated in, and already in part constructed by, the non-physical: IDEOLOGY and history, for example.

Jacques Lacan sees the infant's changing attitude to his or her body as crucial to progress through the MIRROR STAGE. Michel Foucault has suggested that instead of power writing its version of truth directly on the body through torture, in the modern world this function has been taken over by schools and prisons which attempt to reform (see his *Discipline and Punish: The Birth of the Prison* [1979]).

Moving in a rather different direction, many recent FEMINISTS have stressed the importance for women of reinscribing the body in their writing. This is a different direction, because (at least in some accounts of écriture féminine) this treats the body more as source than as SITE. Stevi Jackson and Sue Scott have suggested that the challenge – one to which feminists are now responding – 'is to develop a theory of the body as itself socially constructed while being experienced as a material, physical presence' (1996, 11). (See the entry for ÉCRITURE FÉMININE for more consideration of these issues.)

What perhaps all of these accounts have in common is an attempt to historicize the body, to come to terms with the fact that the body is conceptualized differently in a range of CULTURES and historical periods – not just because such things as disease and nourishment vary culturally and historically, but also because individuals and cultures have different understandings of the relationship between the self and the body, different views of the contribution made by the body to the way a picture of personal or social identity is constructed.

Bolekaja critics In their preface to the first volume of their *Toward the Decolonization of African Literature* (1983), Chinweizu, Onwuchekwa Jemie and Ihechukwu Madubuike descibe themselves as '*bolekaja* critics', and explain that the italicized word, which means 'Come down let's fight!' is 'a term applied in Western Nigeria to passenger lorries ("mammy wagons") from the outrageous behavior of their touts'. Thus they see themselves as 'outraged touts for the passenger lorries of African literature' who are 'administering a timely and healthy dose of much needed public ridicule to the reams of pompous nonsense which has been floating out of the stale, sterile, stifling covens of academia and smothering the sprouting vitality of Africa's literary landscape' (1983, xii).

Their book declares its anti-EUROCENTRISM on page 1, and argues polemically for the need to root out 'imperialist rot' and to plant 'fresh African seeds'. At the same time, African writers and critics are urged to attend to African traditions and to build on African realities (there is, for example, a stress laid upon the importance of oral as against written traditions). The authors are suspicious of Africans writing in non-African languages, and non-Africans writing in African languages (1983, 12), and they counsel the African writer to shun what they term 'euromodernism' (1983, 165). *Toward the Decolonization of African Literature* is written in an assertive and polemical tone which does not avoid *ad hominem* comments:

Then Wole Soyinka, with his brand-new reputation, is parachuted in (1960) from Leeds and the Royal Court Theatre, and lands amidst much fanfare blown by such colonialist propaganda organs as *Encounter* magazine, and goes into action to flush out and swat the remnants of the native resistance to Anglo-Saxon pseudo-universalism. (1983, 203–4)

31

Bricoleur

In his critical account, Uzoma Esonwanne has claimed that bolekaja criticism has many unacknowledged debts, including some to 'imagined communities' such as those of the nation and the continent, and others to 'European history, epistemologies, and theories of art'.

> Bolekaja criticism is, like afrocentrism in North America, a form of nativism. Caught in the logic of eurocentrism, it cannot formulate a hermeneutic by which the generic, linguistic, and expressive eclecticism of African cultural practices can be most productively explicated. (1996, 72)

See also IMAGINED COMMUNITY; NATIVISM; NEO-TARZANISM.

Bottom up (perspective) See SOLUTION FROM ABOVE/BELOW

Bracketing See *EPOCHÉ*

Bricoleur In his *The Savage Mind* Claude Lévi-Strauss distinguishes between the SIGN systems of modern human beings and those of primitive CULTURES. Modern man (Lévi-Strauss's gendered term), like an engineer, makes use of specialized and custom-made tools and materials, whereas primitive man resembles an odd-job man or *bricoleur*, who makes use of those odds and ends of material which he has to hand to construct pieces of *bricolage*.

> The characteristic feature of mythical thought is that it expresses itself by means of a heterogeneous repertoire which, even if extensive, is nevertheless limited. It has to use this repertoire, however, whatever the task in hand because it has nothing else at its disposal. Mythical thought is therefore a kind of intellectual 'bricolage'... (1972, 17)

As a literary example of a *bricoleur* Lévi-Strauss points to the CHARACTER Wemmick, from Charles Dickens's *Great Expectations*, because Wemmick creates a sort of MYTH from the raw materials at hand: the parts of his suburban villa are mythically transformed into a castle (1972, 17 and 150n).

Lévi-Strauss argues, accordingly, that the sign SYSTEMS of primitive man tend to be less ARBITRARY or unmotivated, more MOTIVATED than those of modern man. This, he continues, reflects back upon systems and habits of thought, as whereas modern man is able to separate the abstract sign systems he uses from the CONCRETE realities to which they refer, for primitive man the motivated nature of his sign systems means that reality and sign systems are perceived as more interdependent and involved in each other. For Lévi-Strauss this leads, paradoxically, to the position that the thought of primitive man is at the same time concrete and abstract, and that separating the concrete from the abstract is much easier for modern man than it is for primitive man.

In the course of the same discussion of *bricolage* Lévi-Strauss suggests that it 'is common knowledge that the artist is both something of a scientist and of a "bricoleur",' and that art 'lies half-way between scientific and magical or mythical thought' (1972, 22). He further suggests that art is to be distinguished from myth in as much as whereas the artist starts with objects and events, and attempts to reveal a common STRUCTURE in them by means of AESTHETIC creation, myths 'use a structure to produce what is itself an object consisting of a set of events (for all myths tell a story)' (1972, 26). The distinction is worth comparing with attempts made by various writers to distinguish between the epic or other pre-novelistic NARRATIVES and the 'novel proper'. Such attempts have typically pointed to the fact that what is revolutionary about the novel is that it uses as its starting-point concrete (and 'novel') particulars, not traditional stories or characters. With the novel the aesthetic structure, as Lévi-Strauss calls it, is found or created, whereas with the epic it is the initial given.

Jacques Derrida has attempted to DECONSTRUCT the opposition between *bricoleur* and engineer by claiming that if by *bricolage* one refers to the necessity of borrowing one's concepts from 'the text of a heritage which is more or less coherent or ruined, [then] it must be said that every discourse is *bricoleur*' (1978a, 285). This clearly attracts Derrida because it is easier to argue against the unity or absolute source of a *bricolage* than of some other TEXTS – unless, of course, *all* texts are *bricolages* in which case no text can be possessed of such a unity or absolute source – or PRESENCE, CENTRE, or any other hierarchically organizing discipline.

Those writing about the phenomena of MODERNISM and POSTMODERNISM have also considered the notion of *bricolage* to be useful, for it seems to have a relevance to the typically (post)modernist incorporation of 'found' objects together in new structures which celebrate their diversity and heterogeneity.

Brisure See HINGE

Browsing Now enjoying an extended usage in the realms of IF (interactive FICTION), where the act of browsing involves the exploration of links and *cul de sacs* along different electronic pathways. Also known as *errance*.

See also HYPERTEXT.

C

Camera-eye narrative See PERSPECTIVE AND VOICE

Camp Nigel Wheale has usefully defined this term as follows:

> Theorists of camp behaviour define it as the culture and taste of marginal groups who celebrate the fact of their marginality through parody and self-mockery. Although it is most often associated with homosexuality, camp in this broader definition can be practised by other kinds of outsider group, for example by the dandy, the declassed intellectual, or ethnic minorities. . . . Camp style therefore originates as a private language, shared by a group as part of a common identity and a protection from outsiders; it is a perverse elitism, taking pleasure in tastes and

values which are conventionally scorned. Camp in this sense can also be applied to the valuation of normally despised objects, where a taste is developed and shared among a cult following. (1995b, 49)

I would, further, suggest that camp can also be seen as the (semi-) tolerated public face of the unaccepted: in the past it has, for example, been the way in which homosexuals have been able to display their sexual orientation without admitting to it.

By extrapolation, then, a camp reading of a literary work is one that digs beneath the publicly acceptable face of camp to uncover the more serious issues of sexual politics that it both signals and conceals. Fabio Cleto's edited collection *Camp: Queer Aesthetics and the Performing Subject: a Reader* (1999) gathers together a number of valuable pieces, including Susan Sontag's very influential 'Notes on "Camp"' (1964).

Compare the discussion in the entry for QUEER THEORY.

Cancelled character A term coined by Brian McHale to describe a technique whereby a literary CHARACTER is exposed as TEXTUAL function and no longer seen as 'integral creature' possessed of self-identity. McHale gives as example Tyrone Slothrop, from Thomas Pynchon's *Gravity's Rainbow*, who

> demonstrates this textualized concept of character: beginning as at best a marginal self, he literally becomes *literal* – a congeries of *letters*, mere words. The zone in which he is lost and scattered is not only a heterotopian projected space but, literally, a space of writing, and his disassembly 'lays bare' the absorption of character by text. (1987, 105)

According to McHale, this example lays bare what is more or less implicit in a range of other POSTMODERNIST characters: 'the ineluctable writtenness of character' (1987, 105). The technique can be seen to be implicit in MODERNIST portrayals of character, such for example as that of Klamm in Kafka's *The Castle*.

See also BLOCK CHARACTERIZATION; CHARACTER; CHARACTER ZONE.

Canon The term originates in debate within the Christian Church about the authenticity of the Hebrew Bible and books of the New Testament. That which was termed canonical was accepted as having divine authority within the Church, while writing of no, or doubtful, authority was termed apocryphal. Thus the Protestant canon and apocrypha differ slightly from those of the Catholic Church.

In ecclesiastical use, then, *canon* refers both to *origin* and *value*. By extension the term in literary-critical usage came to be applied (i) to WORKS which could indisputably be ascribed to a particular AUTHOR, and (ii) to a list of works set apart from other literature by virtue of their literary quality and importance. By the middle of the twentieth century such a decision was to a large extent decided institutionally: just as the church (or different churches) decided upon the Biblical canon, so the universities decided of which literary works the literary canon consisted. This is not to say that there were no disagreements concerning the canon: many of the disputes in which F. R. Leavis was involved during the 1930s and 1940s were essentially concerned with the canon. Leavis's view of the canon was highly restrictive: his novelistic Great Tradition consisted essentially of a part of the work of just four novelists.

Debates about the composition of the canon do not of course challenge the institution as such – rather the reverse. When the pressure for membership of or exclusion from a particular club is strong then the club as such occupies a secure position. What is likely to challenge this position is the opening of a rival club which appeals to those who have either been excluded from the first one, or who do not even want to seek membership in it. Thus when certain literary critics began to speak of canon*s* (cf. Robert von Hallberg: 1985) the move had important theoretical implications. After all, although the Protestant and Catholic Churches may disagree about canon and apocrypha, they all agree that only one of them can be correct. But were a church suddenly to state that no one canon had absolute authority, as canons only represented the needs and viewpoints of particular churches, then the idea of the canon as somehow linked to divine origin and authority would inevitably be open to question.

This at any rate is what appears to have happened in literary-critical circles. For when FEMINIST critics started to construct a rival canon or canons, not always as a *replacement* for the 'official' canon but also as an *alternative* to it, then this struck at the *claim to universality* that lay behind the idea of a single canon. For if there were several canons then, in the traditional sense, there was no canon. And increasingly the arguments of feminist critics, or of those interested in POPULAR literature, or the literature of ethnic minorities, were directed towards the establishment of alternative, non-universal *canons* rather than towards modifications of *the* canon.

For Mikhail Bakhtin, *canonization* is a process towards which all literary GENRES have a tendency, in which temporary NORMS and CONVENTIONS become hardened into universal ones so that evaluations too are considered to reflect universal rather than CULTURE- or time-bound values. Thus Bakhtin suggests that in its own time the HETEROGLOSSIA in a novel will be readily recognized, but as the work recedes in time this heteroglossia is more and more obscured by the process of canonization, which standardizes and reduces the ways in which the work can be read (1981, 417–18).

In recent years we have witnessed a growing interest in the investigation of *the* (historical) canon, along with attempts to explain it by reference to those groups whose interests it has been seen to reflect or to further. But these views have not gone unchallenged. There are still many critics who, while accepting that the concept of a single canon is more problematic (particularly at the edges) than was previously assumed, nonetheless insist that certain works are distinguished by a quality and importance that is not culture or time-specific, and that such works still merit a central place in the field of literary education and critical discussion.

John Guillory has argued, interestingly, that the establishment and modification of the canon are intimately connected with the pedagogy of language teaching, and that those works that have been canonized have been so chosen – at least in part – because they have been found suitable for the more or less sophisticated needs of language teaching at different educational levels and at different periods of history (Lentricchia and McLaughlin: 1990, 240–43).

Debates about the canon – or canons – are not unconnected with important recent debates concerning INTERPRETATION. Do different generations find *King Lear* of major importance because of something fixed 'in' the play which can be discovered and rediscovered again and again? Or is it that *King Lear* allows each generation to write part of itself and its problems into the play, thus making Shakespeare (as the title of Jan Kott's study had it), 'our contemporary'? Or does the fact that so much critical attention has been paid for so long to *King Lear* mean that the TEXT we peruse or the PERFORMANCE we witness is necessarily plumped out with the interpretations of former generations? Is it possible to envisage a future British or American culture in which *King Lear* would not be an important work of art, worthy of membership of the canon? Is it possible to envisage a society in which literature was of great cultural and educational significance but which did not have a single (or any) canon? Is our own society perhaps moving towards such a situation?

A few critics have attempted – covertly or overtly – to restrict the term *literature* to works within the canon, thus necessitating the use of other terms to describe non-canonical poetry, FICTION and drama. The term *paraliterature* has been coined to describe such work which is seen to be 'literary' in a broad sense but non-canonical, such as crime fiction, romantic fiction, the sort of poetry published in mass-circulation magazines, and so on. The emergence of such new terms is associated with a historical development which alters the scope of 'literature' from that of being a broad descriptive term to the far narrower, honorific term favoured by critics such as F. R. Leavis. In recent years, however, a counter-movement to expand the scope of this term and to reject what have come to be seen as élitist attempts to narrow its scope has become apparent.

Canons are to be found, of course, in many different fields. Thus if one used the term in the context of a discussion of orthodox Marxism it would be understood that one was referring to works by 'founding fathers' such as Marx, Engels, and Lenin. A more complex situation can occur when works deemed to be non-literary enter the literary canon: Boswell's *Life of Samuel Johnson* is a good example.

Debates about the canon have, inevitably, led to the coining of a range of sub-terms. Thus a 'canon war' is what happens when members of an academic department engage in battle for and against proposals to change the syllabus in line with what is perceived to be a need to change (or to recognize that a change has taken place in) the canon. A 'canon buster' is a person or a proposal dedicated to overturning the accepted canon.

Capital Now frequently used in an extended and metaphorical sense as with CULTURAL or SYMBOLIC capital – a usage associated with Pierre Bourdieu. According to Randall Johnson's Introduction to Bourdieu's *The Field of Cultural Production*, 'Bourdieu thus developed, as an integral part of his theory of practice, the concept of *symbolic power* based on diverse forms of capital which are not reducible to economic capital', so that academic capital, for example, 'derives from formal education and can be measured by degrees or diplomas held' (1993, 7). The 'banking system' within which *symbolic capital* circulates accepts a currency of knowledge-and-recognition, whereas *'cultural capital* concerns forms of cultural knowledge, competences or dispositions' (1993, 7).

Other writers have followed Bourdieu's lead, and I have to confess to having myself used the term 'ideological capital'.

See also AFFILIATION and FIELD, and contrast APPARATUS.

Career author See AUTHOR

Carnival In the writings of Mikhail Bakhtin the significance of the carnival in the Renaissance and Middle Ages assumes a representative importance, indicative of a particular form of POPULAR counter-culture. During this period, according to Bakhtin, 'A boundless world of humorous forms and manifestations opposed the official and serious tone of medieval ecclesiastical and feudal culture' (1968, 4). No matter how variegated and diverse these forms and manifestations they nonetheless, claimed Bakhtin, belonged to a single CULTURE of folk carnival humour (1968, 4). Bakhtin sees this culture as existing on the borderline between art and life, 'life itself, but shaped according to a certain pattern of play' (1968, 5). There is no firm distinction between actors and spectators, and during the period of the carnival it embraces all the people and there is no life outside of it.

By extrapolation Bakhtin dubs as *carnivalesque* all manifestations of a comparable counter-culture which is popular and democratic, and in opposition to a formal and hierarchical official culture. Important here is the idea of unity-in-diversity, of the hetero-geneous unison or POLYPHONY of the many VOICES that make up the carnival. In more recent usage, then, *carnival* and *carnivalesque* refer to traditional, often spontaneous, cultural phenomena which, although assuming many different surface forms, are nonetheless deemed to express a common oppositional or counter-culture. For Bakhtin, a sure distinguishing feature of the carnivalesque is laughter, which is never allowed in official celebration – something that Bakhtin, writing in the Soviet Union under Stalin, knew all about.

In his study of Dostoevsky Bakhtin suggests that the influence of carnival is responsible for a set of 'genres of the serio-comical', and that these have three main defining features. First, that 'their starting point for understanding, evaluating, and shaping reality, is the living *present*'; second, that they do not rely on *legend* but, *consciously*, on *experience* and *free invention*; and third, that they are deliberately 'multi-styled and hetero-voiced' (1984, 108).

To what extent such manifestations offer genuine opposition to the official culture has been the topic of some debate. Is the carnival like the licensed fool, the permitted safety-valve which reinforces the culture it mocks and PARODIES? Or is it the unassailable SITE to which a genuine oppositional force retreats when more overt challenges to official culture (and the political power that lies behind it) are not possible? (See the entry for INCORPORATION.)

Bakhtin argues that the carnival is the place for working out, 'in a concretely sensuous, half-real and half-play-acted form, a *new mode of interrelationship between individuals*, counterposed to the all-powerful socio-hierarchical relationships of non-carnival life'. He further suggests that the *eccentricity* legitimized by carnival permits 'the latent sides of human nature to reveal and express themselves' (1984, 123), a suggestion that obviously has a bearing upon his interest in Dostoevsky's use of eccentrics in his FICTION.

Such debates have a clear relevance to current discussions of popular culture and popular literature, and to debates about the distinction between 'of the people' and 'for the people', or folk and commercial culture.

Catachresis See INCORPORATION

Catalyses See EVENT

Censorship The idea that one psychical agency in the mind might exercise censorship over another is first found in Sigmund Freud's work in the volume *Studies on Hysteria* which Freud wrote with Joseph Breuer, and which was first published in German in 1895. The idea became central to Freud's theories and is closely related to the CONDENSATION AND DISPLACEMENT which Freud sees in the transformation and REPRESSION to be found in the process of dream composition.

In *The Interpretation of Dreams*, Freud refers overtly to the analogy of the political writer with disagreeable truths to tell those in authority. Direct expression of such truths will lead to suppression, but disguised or allusive references may get past the censor and have an effect upon the targeted authorities. Moreover, 'The stricter the censorship, the more far-reaching will be the disguise and the more ingenious too may be the means employed for putting the reader on the scent of the true meaning' (1976, 224).

This is one of the most important theoretical justifications behind Freud's INTERPRETATIONS not just of dreams, but of all other material in which psychic truths are deemed to be present in disguised form. Interestingly, this leads Freud to develop methods of interpretation which not only have much in common with previous and subsequent methods of decoding censored material or material composed in the shadow of censorship, but which resemble and influence literary-critical interpretative methods. Thus many of Freud's psychoanalytic interpretations are extremely reminiscent of literary-critical interpretations of complex or 'difficult' TEXTS.

Compare MARXIST and other theories of determining ABSENCES in literary WORKS.

Centre In the work of Jacques Derrida the term *centre* is used to represent 'a point of presence, a fixed origin' (1978a, 278) which imposes a limit on the play of the STRUCTURE in which it is found or placed. Following Derrida, then, much of the energy of DECONSTRUCTIVE criticism is directed towards freeing structures from the tyranny of whatever centre or centres to which they are seen to be subject. Derrida also uses a range of other terms, including *origin, end, archē,* and *telos* as roughly equivalent to centre.

Building on such usages, Vincent Crapanzano explains that his own use of the term posits

> an image, an event, or even a theoretical construct functioning as a nucleus or point of concentration that holds together a particular verbal sequence. The center gives coherence, a semblance of order at least, to what would otherwise appear to be a random, meaningless sequence of expressions. (1992, 28)

Crapanzano argues that centring can operate both precursively and recursively – that is, that a centre can condition or determine the meaning of that which precedes and also that which follows the centre. He illustrates his point with a passage from an early Henry James novel, *Confidence* (first published 1880), in which a conversation between a man and a woman shows the man trying to 'centre' their relationship, to find some firm point which will throw all of their encounters into meaningful relief.

Louis Althusser's essay 'Freud and Lacan', which is reprinted in his *Lenin and Philosophy* (1971) was influential in suggesting that the SUBJECT could (and should) be decentred. (See also the entries for DESIRE and COPERNICAN REVOLUTION.) Such views accord with a dominant trend in contemporary theory which is in opposition to hierarchical lines of control – whether in a society or in a human subject. The human subject is thereby denied a unity that is underwritten and orchestrated by a controlling centre which, like an all-powerful micro-chip in a super-computer, brings the whole system into synchrony with and through its all-pervasive PRESENCE and discipline. In the light of such an approach the human subject becomes SITE rather than point of origin, and a site, moreover, on which unrelated campers come and go (and sometimes fight) rather than one united by an all-powerful scoutmaster. A representative example of the POSTMODERNIST claim that the subject has been decentred can be found in Michel Foucault's Introduction to *The Archaeology of Knowledge*:

> Lastly, more recently, when the researches of psychoanalysis, linguistics, and ethnology have decentred the subject in relation to the laws of his desire, the forms of his language, the rules of his action, or the games of his mythical or fabulous discourse, when it became clear that man himself, questioned as to what he was, could not account for his sexuality and his unconscious, the systematic forms of his language, of the regularities of his fictions, the theme of a continuity of history has been reactivated once again ... (1972, 13)

A related term is 'the god trick', which refers to the way in which God (or any divinity) can be used as a centre to fix the meaning of all in the experience of the believer. Normally the divinity referred to is a metaphoric rather than a literal one: the term tends to be used in a sarcastic or dismissive manner.

An unrelated use of *centre* can be found in NARRATIVE theory, in the work of Seymour Chatman.

> 'Point of view' ('vision,' 'perspective,' 'focalization') has named still a third narrative function: that is, the presentation of a story in such a way that a certain character is of paramount importance. But this is quite different from filtration, since we may or may not be given access to that central character's consciousness. This function, I think, should be called *center*. (1990, 147–8)

See also LOGOCENTRISM; REFERENCE (for *head referent*); TRANSCENDENTAL SIGNIFIED.

Centrifugal/centripetal Mikhail Bakhtin uses these terms which describe the impulse either outwards or inwards, from or towards the centre, to refer to social and IDEOLOGICAL rather than physical forces. (Bakhtin's use of the word CENTRE is different from that of Jacques Derrida: see the separate entry for this term.)

Both of these forces, for Bakhtin, are to be found in language: there is the impulse and pressure towards a standardization imposed and maintained by a central authority, and at the same time the urge towards diversity and POLYPHONY. Every language, he claims in his essay 'Discourse in the Novel', 'participates in the "unitary language" (in its centripetal forces and tendencies) and at the same time partakes of social and historical heteroglossia (the centrifugal, stratifying forces)' (1981, 272).

Changing same

For Bakhtin, certain literary GENRES have a centripetal force, driving READERS towards a centre of conformity and uniformity, whereas others have the opposite effect, urging people away from conformity and towards diversity and heterogeneity. He accords poetry an essentially centripetal tendency, while the novel is granted the opposite, a centrifugal force. Not surprisingly, he argues that the novel flourishes during times of diversity and the slackening of central control.

Centripetal See CENTRIFUGAL/CENTRIPETAL

Changing same A theory of generational continuity in Afro-American culture. In her article '"The Changing Same": Generational Connections and Black Women Novelists' (1987), Deborah E. McDowell attributes the term to an article by Leroi Jones/Amiri Baraka: 'The Changing Same: R and B and New Black Music' (1971). In her note on this article, McDowell explains that Jones 'traces the continuities in the black musical tradition, which he argues has its roots in African religion and spirit worship', and that he 'submits that even as it has changed, in both vocal and instrumental forms, black music has remained the same, continuing patterns and impulses that originated in Africa and were transplanted and "Christianized" in America' (1987, 298 n1).

McDowell's own article compares Frances E. W. Harper's 1892 novel *Leroy* with Alice Walker's 1982 novel *The Color Purple*. She argues that these two novels 'represent the two most salient paradigms in the black female literary tradition in the novel', two traditions which 'derive from a common center in black women's novels' (1987, 282).

Character The concept of literary character has had a generally hard time in Anglo-American and European critical theory of the twentieth century. The NEW CRITICS and F. R. Leavis were united in their disapproval of A. C. Bradley's alleged treatment of Shakespearian (and other) characters as if they were real people, and Alan Sinfield has reminded us that G. Wilson Knight set aside 'the character' as a category of analysis because of his belief that each play was a visionary whole, and was 'close-knit in personification, atmospheric suggestion, and direct poetic-symbolism' (Sinfield: 1992, 56–7, quoting from Knight's *The Wheel of Fire*).

Subsequent critical approaches have generally shown little more enthusiasm for the concept or category. This has much to do with the anti-HUMANISM of much recent theory: humanism has been accused of privileging a human essence and of situating this within the bourgeois SUBJECT. As Francis Mulhern has expressed it, ' "Anti-humanism" is confident in rejecting the notion of a human essence (its principal definition) and the putatively bourgeois conception of the subject as self-transparent originator of meaning (its longest-running theme)' (1992, 33, n32).

If the human individual or subject is more SITE than source, more puppet or response than puppet-master or cause, then the category of *literary* character has rather less chance of being considered worthy of serious attention. The attack on literary character can thus be seen as an aspect of the anti-individualistic bias of much recent theory. To quote a representative example: in his *The Postmodern Condition: A Report on Knowledge* Jean-François Lyotard comments that

A *self* does not amount to much, but no self is an island; each exists in a fabric of relations that is now more complex and mobile than ever before. Young or old, man or woman, rich or poor, a person is always located at 'nodal points' of specific communication circuits, however tiny these may be. Or better: one is always located at a post through which various kinds of message pass. (1984, 15)

One could hardly find a better exemplification of that view of the individual as site rather than source than this.

To a large extent theorists who have questioned the concept of character are following in the wake of those MODERNIST and POSTMODERNIST writers whose works abandoned traditional forms of characterization. A comment taken from a letter written by D. H. Lawrence to Edward Garnett in 1914, and much-quoted since, warns:

You mustn't look in my novel for the old stable *ego* of the character. There is another *ego*, according to whose action the individual is unrecognisable, and passes through, as it were, allotropic states which it needs a deeper sense than any we've been used to exercise, to discover are states of the same single radically unchanged element. (1961, 18)

'Allotropy' is the variation of physical properties without change of substance: Lawrence maintains a belief in human singleness at base, a singleness which is, however badly expressed by the visible, stable *ego*. Later novelists abandoned even this belief: the unity of the human individual – real or literary – is an illusion; human beings are sites of struggle and division, and the conscious self has nothing like a full inventory of the components of the self.

Even within the study of NARRATIVE, no doubt as a result of the STRUCTURALIST foundations of NARRATOLOGY, the individual character – whether traditional or modernist – is rigorously DECONSTRUCTED. Gerald Prince's definitions of the term 'character' – 'An existent endowed with anthropomorphic traits and engaged in anthropomorphic actions; an actor with anthropomorphic attitudes' (1988a, 12) – almost leads one to feel that considering a literary character as in some way equivalent to a real human being is akin to talking to one's cat. But just as people have gone on talking to their cats so too critics and READERS have gone on treating literary characters as in certain ways equivalent to human individuals.

Thus in his essay 'When is a Character Not a Character? Desdemona, Olivia, Lady Macbeth and Subjectivity', which is to be found in his book *Faultlines*, Alan Sinfield clearly finds the category less than fully played out. Indeed, by arguing that Desdemona 'is a disjointed sequence of positions that women are conventionally supposed to occupy', and that she 'has no character of her own; she is a convenience in the story of Othello, Iago, and Venice' (1992, 53, 54), he forces the reader to compare her with those others in the play who, he suggests, *are* so possessed of a character.

See also ATTRIBUTE/FUNCTION; BLOCK CHARACTERIZATION; CANCELLED CHARACTER; CHARACTER ZONE; CHORUS CHARACTER.

Character zone Coined by Mikhail Bakhtin. According to his account, character zones are formed from the characters' semi-discourses, from various forms of hidden transmission for the discourse of the other, by the words and expressions scattered in this discourse, and from the irruption of alien expressive elements into authorial discourse (ellipsis, questions, exclamation). Such a zone is the range of action of the character's voice, intermingling in one way or another with the author's voice. (Quoted in Todorov: 1984, 73)

In other words, the READER of a novel builds up a picture of the CHARACTER's identity not just from direct descriptions of his or her actions or from 'transcriptions' of his or her speech, but from a wider zone of verbal implication.

See also CANCELLED CHARACTER; CHARACTER; ERASURE (discussion of erased character).

Chiasmus Originally a rhetorical figure in which the pattern AB BA is set up in more or less complicated versions. The last sentence of James Joyce's short story 'The Dead', for example, starts: 'His soul swooned slowly as he heard the snow falling faintly through the universe, and faintly falling . . .', and the REPETITION-with-inversion of the words *falling* and *faintly* gives us an example of chiasmus.

The Finnish critic Ralf Norrman has extended the use of this term in books on Henry James (1982) and Samuel Butler (1985), suggesting that both writers are obsessed with patterns of symmetry and that their writing is characterized by chiasmic patterns at the macro-level.

Brook Thomas has argued that chiasmus is the 'favourite figure' of the NEW HISTORICISTS, and that 'the historicity of texts and the textuality of history' (he is quoting from Montrose: 1989, 20) is both one of the most famous (or infamous) of New Historical catch-phrases and also a perfect example of chiasmus. According to Thomas, 'Chiasmus is the perfect figure to express Greenblatt's notion of a mimetic economy, since its balanced structure mimes the very circulation that he writes about' (1991, 184). See also the discussion in the entry for CIRCULATION.

Chinese box narrative See FRAME

Chora A term introduced by Julia Kristeva in her *Revolution in Poetic Language* (first published in French in 1974 as Kristeva's thesis for the French *Doctorat d'Etat*). The term is complex and difficult to gloss; Kristeva herself takes several pages to introduce it. She situates the term within a specifically Freudian context:

Discrete qualities of energy move through the body of the subject who is not yet constituted as such and, in the course of his development, they are arranged according to the various constraints imposed on this body – always already involved in a semiotic process – by family and social structures. In this way the drives, which are 'energy' charges as well as 'psychical' marks, articulate what we call a *chora*: a non-expressive totality formed by the drives and their stases in a motility that is as full of movement as it is regulated. (Moi: 1986a, 93)

(Motility: 'capability or power of moving', *OED.*) Kristeva notes that she borrows the term 'chora' from Plato's *Timaeus* to denote 'an essentially mobile and extremely provisional articulation constituted by movements and their ephemeral stases' (Moi: 1986a, 93). Thus all DISCOURSE 'moves with and against the *chora* in the sense that it simultaneously depends upon and refuses it' (Moi: 1986a, 94). Further definition is by negation: the *chora* is not a SIGN, it is not a SIGNIFIER, it is neither model nor copy, 'the *chora* precedes and underlies figuration and thus specularization, and is analogous only to vocal and kinetic rhythm' (Moi: 1986a, 94). According to Andrew Gibson, 'The *chora* is the endless flow of pulsions that precedes and underlies the symbolic order and its structures' (1996, 159). Kristeva uses the phrase ALWAYS ALREADY, which is glossed in the entry for this term.

Chorus character A character who plays a role comparable to that played by the chorus in drama, who provides necessary information and comments on CHARACTERS, situation, or action. Very often applied to minor characters in novels or short stories who themselves play little part in the events of the NARRATIVE.

Chronological deviation See ANACHRONY

Chronotope Coined by Mikhail Bakhtin to designate 'the distinctive features of time and space within each literary genre' (Todorov: 1984, 83). According to Bakhtin he took the term from mathematical biology, but introduced it into literary studies in a metaphorical sense (Bakhtin: 1981, 234). In his essay on the *Bildungsroman*, for example, Bakhtin suggests that the 'local cults' associated with particular literary works and linked to specific geographical locations in the mid-eighteenth century 'attest above all to a completely *new sense of space and time* in the artistic work' (1986, 47).

In the course of a discussion of Toni Morrison's novel *Beloved*, Lynne Pearce has proposed an extension of Bakhtin's term: *polychronotopic*, to describe the coexistence of multiple chronotopes within the same text (Pearce: 1994, 71). She suggests that within a single polychronotopic text,

> individual chronotopes, like individual voices, are distinguished by their autonomy and independence: they are both, as it were, 'independent centres of consciousness'. Without ever merging, however, the chronotopes enter into a complex dialogue with one another which is, at all times, a dialogue inscribed by power. .... (1994, 175)

Circulation A term favoured by the NEW HISTORICIST writer Stephen J. Greenblatt to describe the manner in which CULTURAL artifacts or IDEOLOGICAL meanings (for example) are transmitted from place to place by means of 'practical strategies of negotiation and exchange' (1990, 154). Greenblatt acknowledges the influence of Jacques Derrida in his use of the term, and what seems to be important is the way in which it presupposes a sequence of *transformations* of the artifact or MEANING as it is passed on by means of the aforesaid strategies. (Thus an object in a museum has been transformed from what it was when it was, for example, an item in daily use.)

See also RESONANCE and TRAVELLING THEORY, along with the other cross-references given in the entry for NEW HISTORICISM AND CULTURAL MATERIALISM.

Class Discussion of social class entered into literary-critical discourse most obviously with the emergence of a MARXIST literary criticism in the 1930s. Marxist views of class are not completely homogeneous (even in Marx's own writings), and they have become more sophisticated in recent years. What is common to them all, however, is an insistence upon defining class by relation to the economic STRUCTURE of society. This is in contrast to more recent sociological views of class which emphasize such matters as status, individual wealth, CULTURAL and IDEOLOGICAL commitments, and so on. Thus the traditional Marxist definition of a member of the working class is that he or she is one who lives by selling their labour power (rather than, for example, living off CAPITAL, off subsistence farming, or as a self-employed worker). Accordingly, as Alan Hunt has pointed out, two men who clean windows for a living, earn identical amounts of money, and share a common culture and lifestyle must from a traditional Marxist perspective be assigned to different classes if one is self-employed and the other is the employee of a large window-cleaning concern (1977, 89). In general, of course, Marxists have believed that membership of different classes (so defined) does result in differences in economic level, culture, and beliefs, and it is this belief which has made this concept of class appear relevant to literary criticism, for if accurate it would seem to offer the possibility of relating the content of a writer's work to his or her class origins or associations.

It is perhaps obvious that it is difficult to keep a concern with social class out of discussion of the work of a writer such as D. H. Lawrence, but it is arguable that light can also be thrown on the work of very different writers by an examination of their class origins and associations, along with a similar examination of READERS and critics of their work. A complicating factor which has to be confronted is that both writers and critics can occupy rather indefinite class positions (like window cleaners, their relation to the economic structure of society is not fixed by the job).

FEMINIST critics have directed a certain amount of criticism towards the tendency of more traditional Marxist discussions of class to limit themselves to the (male) 'heads of family' and assign women to the class to which their husbands or fathers belong. Many Marxist feminists have insisted upon the need to pay attention both to production and reproduction in defining class.

More recently, the development of academic interest in POPULAR culture has brought the issue of class under renewed scrutiny, with reference to both the producers and the consumers of this material.

Cleavage See HINGE

Clinamen See REVISIONISM

Closed texts See OPEN AND CLOSED TEXTS

Closet criticism According to Eve Kosofsky Sedgwick, 'the phrase "the closet" as a publicly intelligible signifier for gay-related epistemological issues is made available, obviously, only by the difference made by the post-Stonewall gay politics oriented around coming *out* of the closet' (1991, 14). In Gay (and subsequently general) parlance 'staying in the closet' meant keeping one's homosexuality secret, and as Sedgwick points out, before the events following the STONEWALL demonstrations of June 1969, even the phrase 'the closet' was itself in the closet. Coming out of the closet (frequently now abbreviated to just 'coming out') thus involved making an open and public declaration of one's homosexuality, and as Gay people came out of the closet, so too did the term 'the closet'. (Publication of Sedgwick's own 1991 book *Epistemology of the Closet* itself did much to give the term wider currency.)

From these usages have sprung a number of associated terms. The separate entry for OUTING can be consulted for this term; *closet criticism* is generally understood to refer to criticism written by Gays and depending upon a familiarity with Gay culture that does not openly admit its affiliations.

Care should be taken to avoid confusion with the much older term *closet drama*, which has nothing to do with sexual orientation but is a term used to denote dramatic works intended to be read ('in the privacy of one's closet') rather than PERFORMED.

See also PASSING.

Closure All literary WORKS come to some sort of close or conclusion, but such conclusions do not always provide the same sense of satisfaction or inevitability. According to Barbara Herrnstein Smith, closure 'may be regarded as a modification of structure that makes *stasis*, or the absence of further continuation, the most probable event'. She further adds that closure allows the READER to be satisfied by the failure of continuation or, to put it another way, it creates 'the expectation of nothing' in the reader (1968, 34).

Closure, in other words, is more than just the ending of a literary work: it requires that the ending or discontinuation have a certain AESTHETIC force. It need not imply that the reader is so satisfied at the end of the work that he or she stops thinking or that the work leaves no problems to be resolved, only that the reader recognizes that the ending of the work at this point and in this way is of aesthetic significance.

An absence of closure is frequently associated with MODERNIST or experimental art, including literature. Modernist writing often seems to challenge those literary CONVENTIONS which arouse certain expectations in the reader regarding what is acceptable as an ending for a literary work. Such works are often described as *open-ended* or lacking closure. This can refer not just to matters of STORY or PLOT, but also to aesthetic and IDEOLOGICAL issues.

Consonant and *dissonant* closure occur when the ending of a literary work either confirms and underwrites, or challenges and destabilizes, what has gone before. Of course, 'what has gone before' is always INTERPRETED in the light of GENERIC expectations, so that a final scene may involve events that are astounding to a CHARACTER or even NARRATOR, but not so much to the well-read reader.

Code The influence of Linguistics and SEMIOTICS has led to an increased recourse to the term *code* on the part of literary critics and theorists during the past two decades. This may be at least in part because the term implies that writer and READER are linked by their common possession of a set of CONVENTIONS governing systematic transformations, an implication which appeals to many contemporary theorists interested in issues raised by the sociology of literature and by the concept of LITERARINESS. The term also, of course, suggests that the literary work contains that which is hidden to those not possessed of the right code-book. (In this context, see also INTERPRET[AT]IVE COMMUNITY.)

Code

In one of the more influential examples of the development of a theory of literary codes, Roland Barthes has suggested five codes of reading which allow readers to recognize and identify elements in the literary WORK and to relate them to specific FUNCTIONS. The five codes are as follows.

The *proairetic code* controls the manner in which the reader constructs the PLOT of a literary work.

The *hermeneutic code* involves problems of INTERPRETATION, particularly those questions and answers that are raised at the level of plot.

The *semic code* is related to those TEXTUAL elements that develop the reader's perception of literary CHARACTERS.

The *symbolic code* governs the reader's construction of symbolic MEANINGS.

The *referential code* is made up by textual references to CULTURAL phenomena. (Based on Barthes: 1990, 19–20; the codes are also discussed in Barthes: 1975.)

Few critics apart from Barthes himself have put these terms to extended literary critical use, although one who has is Robert Scholes in his book *Semiotics and Interpretation*. The book contains a chapter dealing with James Joyce's short story 'Eveline', in which Barthes's various codes of reading are pressed into explanatory service (1982, 99–104).

Elsewhere in his work Barthes uses references to a variety of other codes. Thus in the course of two pages of his 'Textual Analysis of Poe's "Valdemar"' (1981a) there are references to the metalinguistic code, the socio-ethnic code, the social code, the narrative code, the cultural code, the scientific code, the scientific deontological code and the symbolic code. Barthes's usage suggests that different DISCOURSES in a culture or interpretative community are coded in such a way as to direct the reader's attention towards the right interpretative technique at the appropriate point in the reading of a literary work.

The use of the word 'code' by literary critics has an important relevance with regard to debates about interpretation. To decode a SIGN or sequence of signs is to return to a meaning or MESSAGE that pre-existed sign or signs, whereas to engage in interpretation (at least according to certain theorists) is to generate something new (see the discussion in the entry for SHANNON AND WEAVER MODEL OF COMMUNICATION).

Given that a key dispute between rival theories of interpretation centres on whether or not the interpreter is in part creator of something original, use of terms such as *code* or *decoding* tends to ally one with those who do not see interpretation as a creative activity. Jonathan Culler thus raised an important and early objection to the use of these terms when he remarked that 'listeners interpret sentences rather than decode them' (1975, 19). Although his objection concerns the study of natural languages, it would appear to have even greater force in the field of literary criticism.

It is perhaps noteworthy that although, as has been stated, use of the term *code* suggests that both writer and reader are in possession of a common set of rules for systematic transformations, much more has been written about the reader's decodings than about the writer's encodings – perhaps because at least one of the theorists concerned (Roland Barthes) has also been involved in arguing for recognition of the AUTHOR's death.

Umberto Eco has coined the term *overcoding* to refer to a process of meta-communication about an expression. According to him, overcoded rules tell the reader whether a given expression is used rhetorically: thus the opening statement 'Once upon a time' is deemed by him to convey the facts (i) that the events take place in an indefinite non-historical epoch, (ii) that the reported events are not 'real', and (iii) that the speaker wants to tell a FICTIONAL story (1981, 19). The term *aberrant decoding* is also credited to Eco, and draws attention to the fact that different 'consumers' of the same art-work may read or respond to it in varied and even eccentric ways. Eco refers to the artist of the palace of Knossos in Crete, whose work was aimed at a well-defined community of receivers, but which was looked at in a completely different way by the Achaeon conquerors, who used different attributes to – for example – express royalty (1972, 104–5).

The term *delayed decoding* was coined by Ian Watt in his *Conrad in the Nineteenth Century* (1980) to describe a particular impressionist technique of Joseph Conrad's whereby the experiences of a character who understands what is happening to him or her only while these experiences are taking place (or afterwards), is recreated in the reader. Thus in Conrad's *Heart of Darkness* we share Marlow's belief that lots of little sticks are dropping on the ship, up to the point when Marlow realizes that the 'sticks' are in fact arrows, and that the ship is being attacked.

For Roland Barthes's claim that the photograph is a message without a code, see the discussion of *analogn* in the entry for DIGITAL AND ANALOGIC COMMUNICATION. See also CODE SWITCHING; HERMENEUTICS; INTERPRETATION; FUNCTIONS OF LANGUAGE.

Codes of reading See CODE

Code switching Originally used by sociolinguists to denote the alternation between two varieties of the same language by the same user, but more recently applied within GENDER studies to denote a comparable movement between language varieties associated with different gender identities or sexual preferences; with this meaning sometimes referred to as *sexual* or *gender code switching*.

Compare DOUBLE CONSCIOUSNESS and MASQUERADE, and see also REGISTER.

Coduction A term coined by Wayne C. Booth to describe a process of evaluation which is not purely personal but a communal enterprise which places a due reliance upon 'the past experiences of many judges who do not have even a roughly codified set of precedents to guide them' (1988, 72). He explains 'Coduction will be what we do whenever we say to the world . . . "Of the works of this general kind that I have experienced, *comparing my experience with other more or less qualified observers*, this one seems to me among the better (or weaker) ones, or the best (or worst)"' (1988, 72).

Coherence Coherence involves the imposition of some form of unity upon disparate elements, and many commentators have attributed a belief in the essential coherence of the significant work of art to the NEW CRITICS. It is claimed that much New Critical ANALYSIS was dedicated to laying bare this coherence through the study of the controlled tensions, AMBIGUITIES, paradoxes and so on which imposed some form of coherence on the different elements of the individual WORK.

The idea of STRUCTURE carries with it a suggestion of necessary internal coherence, suggesting that just as the rules of GRAMMAR and syntax impose coherence on disparate parts of speech, so the LINGUISTIC PARADIGM implies that a comparable coherence can be found in non-linguistic structures.

A slightly different application of the concept of coherence is found in Lucien Goldmann's view that '[w]orld-views are social facts. Great philosophical and artistic works represent the *coherent* and adequate expression of these world-views' (1969, 129). This implies rather strongly that literary and other works fulfil the IDEOLOGICAL function of presenting that which lacks coherence with at least the appearance that its component parts cohere.

A number of recent theorists have certainly argued that attempts to find coherence in literary texts or in other structures involve the ideological imposition of a dissembling order onto struggle, contradiction, inconclusiveness. Robert Young, for example, refers to Pierre Macherey's objection to that part of the STRUCTURALIST project which searches for 'the secret coherence of an object' (1981, 4), while Michel Foucault has suggested that one of the roles performed by the AUTHOR has been that of giving the 'disturbing language of fiction . . . its nodes of coherence' (1981, 58).

Critics committed to or influenced by versions of DECONSTRUCTION have a complex relationship with the issue of coherence, one which is summarized to perfection in Robert Young's introductory remarks to Paul de Man's essay 'Action and Identity in Nietzsche'. Young quotes the following comment from de Man's foreword to Carol Jacob's *The Dissimulating Harmony*, published in 1978: '[Deconstruction] has the sequential coherence we associate with a demonstration or a particularly compelling narrative. But what is being argued (or compellingly told) is precisely the loss of an illusory coherence' (Young: 1981, 266). Deconstructive writing often seems to possess that paradoxical combination indicated by de Man: the use of arguments which seem ordered according to strict rules of logical progression (or which, at any rate, at least MIMIC such ordering), but which lead to various forms of dissolution, chaos, logical collapse, *MISE-EN-ABYME*.

Coloured narrative See FREE INDIRECT DISCOURSE

Commissive See SPEECH ACT THEORY

Commodity fetishism See FETISHISM; REIFICATION

Commutation test Commutation involves the substitution of one thing for another; the commutation test involves investigating the FUNCTION or significance of one thing by substituting it with another.

In literary ANALYSIS one might, accordingly, substitute a first-person NARRATOR for an omniscient one, or substitute Direct Speech for FREE INDIRECT DISCOURSE, in order to assess what the substituted element contributed to the passage or WORK in question.

Competence and performance A distinction introduced into Linguistics by Noam Chomsky, by means of which those language rules internalized by a native speaker which enable him or her to generate and understand grammatically correct sentences (competence), can be distinguished from the actual generation of particular correct sentences by such a speaker (performance). Competence also enables a native speaker to recognize whether or not a particular sentence is or is not grammatically well formed.

The distinction has been extended to literary criticism by a number of theorists who have sought to draw an analogy between the internalized rules of a language and the internalized rules or CONVENTIONS which enable competent READERS to read and understand literary WORKS. The analogy has the virtue of reminding us that there is a difference between literacy and the ability satisfactorily to read and respond to literary works, but it has some shortcomings too. First, that whereas Chomsky's competence is mainly concerned with the *generation* of correct sentences, the posited literary competence has often been concerned mainly or exclusively with the *reading or reception* of literary works. Second, that literary competence seems to be based upon capacities which are transmitted by means of CULTURE rather than nature (there is no literary equivalent to Chomsky's genetically transmitted 'Language Acquisition Device'). And third, literary competence is not universally present in adult human beings. We do not have to undergo formal education to learn how to speak.

Umberto Eco suggests a formulation which may go some way to resolving these problems, when he argues that the well-organized TEXT both presupposes a model of competence coming from outside of itself, but that it also attempts to build up such a competence by merely textual means (1981, 8).

Compare attempts to apply the distinction between LANGUE AND PAROLE to literature (see the separate entry for these terms). See also the separate entry for PERFORMANCE.

Completion In his *The Formal Method in Literary Scholarship* P. N. Medvedev makes use of this concept in the course of distinguishing poetic from other utterances. His argument is complex and, as Lynne Pearce has commented, not fully convincing (1994, 36). For Medvedev, social evaluation organizes scientific utterance at all stages of scientific work, but not for the sake of the utterance: the organization of the work of cognition and of the word, forms 'only... a necessary but dependent aspect of this work', so that in scientific utterance, 'evaluation is not complete in the word' (Medvedev/Bakhtin: 1978, 126). But for Medvedev, the poetic work presents quite a different case.

> Here the utterance is detached both from its object and from action. Here social evaluation is complete within the utterance itself. One might say its song is sung to the end. The reality of the utterance serves no other reality. Social evaluation pours out and concludes in pure expression. Therefore, all aspects of the material, meaning, and concrete act of realization without exception become equally important and necessary. (Medvedev/Bakhtin: 1978, 127)

It is arguable both that Medvedev (unusually) concedes too much to FORMALIST views of the art-work here, and also that he fails to appreciate that the semi-autonomy of the art-work does not necessarily involve the obliteration of hierarchies of SIGNIFICATION within the WORK.

Comprador Originally, according to the *OED*, a Portuguese word adopted in the East to denote a 'native' servant employed by Europeans 'to purchase necessaries and keep the household accounts'. The term subsequently became established in China to describe the chief Chinese agent of a European 'house'. It became a (somewhat clichéd) term in MARXIST discussions of neo-colonialism, where it was used to refer to local rulers who obeyed the dictates of colonial powers. If, as an old Marxist characterization had it, African neo-colonialism was like a white octopus with black tentacles, then those black tentacles were constituted by a comprador class.

After falling into disuse the term has recently enjoyed a new lease of life in POST-COLONIALIST writing, and is used rather more widely than before to describe any local authority – CULTURAL and IDEOLOGICAL as well as political – which owes allegiance to a foreign ruling or dominating power.

Conative See FUNCTIONS OF LANGUAGE

Concretization *Concrete* was a favourite word of the NEW CRITICS and of F. R. Leavis, used honorifically to distinguish literature (mostly poetry) which called particulars to mind, often by means of the direct evocation of the recalled testimony of the senses. Take for example Leavis's discussion of four lines from John Keats's 'Ode to Melancholy':

> Then glut thy sorrow on a morning rose,
> Or on the rainbow of the salt sand-wave,
>   Or on the wealth of globed peonies;
> Or if thy mistress some rich anger shows , . .

Leavis comments: 'That "glut", which we can hardly find Rossetti or Tennyson using in a poetical place, finds itself taken up in "globed", the sensuous concreteness of which it reinforces; the hand is round the peony, luxuriously cupping it' (1964, 214).

In Roman Ingarden's *Das Literarische Kunstwerk* (published in German in 1931 and in English translation as *The Literary Work of Art* in 1973) we find a use of *concretize* as a verb which has exerted considerable influence subsequent to the appearance of this work in English. According to Ingarden there are two types of concretization if one speaks purely ontically (i.e. 'of or having real being or existence'): on the one hand, 'the purely intentional concretization, ontically heteronomous in form and relative to the subjective operation' and on the other hand, 'the objectively existing concretization, characteristic, in form, of the respective ontic sphere and thus, in a state of affairs that exists in the real world, in the form of an ontically autonomous realization of the corresponding essences or ideas' (1973, 162). The distinction is, it will be seen, a complex one, but it allows Ingarden to talk about the way in which the literary WORK is concretized by being read. Central to his argument is that because literary works typically contain 'spots of indeterminacy', 'the reader usually *goes beyond* what is simply presented by the text (or projected by it) and in various respects *completes* the represented objectivities, so that at least some of the spots of indeterminacy are removed and are frequently replaced by determinacies that not only are not determined by the text but, what is more, are not in agreement with the positively determined objective moments' (1973, 252). READING is a creative process in this view of things, one in which the reader not only concretizes that which is in some sense 'there' in the TEXT but also adds to and goes beyond what the AUTHOR has provided or even intended.

In Brian McHale's account, the 'complexity of the literary artwork, [Ingarden] tells us, lies first of all in its being *heteronomous*, existing both autonomously, in its own right, and at the same time depending upon the constitutive acts of consciousness of a reader' (1987, 30).

The PRAGUE SCHOOL theorist Felix Vodička adopts and develops Ingarden's category in his essay 'The History of the Echo of Literary Works'. For Vodička the study of the concretization of past and present literary works involves 'the study of the work in the particular form in which we find it in the conception of the period (particularly its concretization in criticism)' (1964, 73). Vodička stresses the key point that 'since there is . . . no single correct esthetic norm, there is also no single valuation, and a work may be subject to multiple valuation, during which its shape in the awareness of the perceiver (its concretization) is in constant change' (1964, 79). Ingarden's 'spots of indeterminacy' lead directly to some of Wolfgang Iser's theories about the creative role of the reader; see the entry for PHENOMENOLOGY.

See also ACTUALIZATION; NORM.

Condensation and displacement According to Freud, a comparison of the dream-content with the dream-thoughts reveals that 'a work of *condensation* on a large scale has been carried out. Dreams are brief, meagre and laconic in comparison with the range and wealth of the dream-thoughts' (1976, 383). In other words, a large amount of MEANING is *condensed* into a relatively small size by making individual SIGNS or IMAGES signify more than one thing: the dream-thoughts are thus OVERDETERMINED. Freud's INTERPRETATIONS accordingly involve a work of unpacking; out of a single scene or figure in a dream a number of different meanings can be salvaged. As Freud also points out, the interpretation of a dream may occupy six or twelve times as much space when written out as does the written account of the dream itself (1976, 383). Dreams involve extreme *concentration* of meaning. Freud suggests a number of ways in which the process of condensation can be carried out – by means of collective figures (one known person in a dream standing for a number of different people, for example), of composite structures (a dream person who combines the appearance and characteristics of a number of different people, for example), or by verbal means (puns, for instance, which unite a number of different words). All of these argued techniques have been of interest to literary critics, and particularly critics of poetry, who have found points of comparison with the concentrated nature of the poetic image or symbol, and indeed many aspects of Freud's dream ANALYSES are remarkably similar to, for example, aspects of NEW CRITICAL analyses of lyric poems.

The film critic and theorist Laura Mulvey has noted that 'because [condensation] acts as a point of intersection, a nodal point, it can spark apparently random lines of association or thought, that then generate new movements or developments in a story-line' (1989, 131).

For Freud, condensation is typically associated with *displacement*, and he argues that '*Dream-displacement* and *dream-condensation* are the two governing factors to whose activity we may in essence ascribe the form assumed by dreams' (1976, 417). Freud sees displacement as a means whereby CENSORSHIP is outmanoeuvred; for example, if a person cannot consciously admit his or her hatred of another as a result of the operation of the censor, this hatred may be transferred to something associated with the person in question, *displaced* from one object protected by the censor to another one about which the censor is unconcerned. This again has been of interest to literary critics who have used the concept (often in association with that of condensation) to explore the way symbolism functions in literary WORKS.

Linguisticians use the term DISPLACEMENT in a rather different way: see the separate entry. See also the discussion of *metaphor* and *metonymy* in the entry for SYNTAGMATIC AND PARADIGMATIC: following Lacan, a number of commentators have observed that the condensation/displacement distinction has much in common with Roman Jakobson's distinction between metaphor and metonymy (see the discussion in Scholes: 1982, 75–6).

In NARRATOLOGY, *condensation* is sometimes used to indicate that a passage of Indirect or FREE INDIRECT DISCOURSE condenses the (implied) utterances of many different people, perhaps made at many different times, into one represented utterance. Compare *pseudo-iterative*, in the entry for FREQUENCY.

Conjuncture See MOMENT

Connotation and denotation The two terms distinguish between two forms of REFERENCE: the word 'military' as defined in the dictionary involves that which is connected to armies or soldiers (denotation), but it carries with it a range of associations which spring to the minds of those who share a common CULTURE – uniforms, marching, discipline, force, masculinity, rigid collectivity – and these are the *connotations* of the word. Denotations are almost invariably more fixed than connotations, changing only over much longer periods of time than it takes for a word's connotations to alter.

Roland Barthes points out in the introductory comments to his *S/Z* that the precise relationship between connotation and denotation is a matter of dispute. There are thus those for whom denotation is primary and connotation either secondary or non-existent. Some ('the philologists, let us say'), declaring every text to be univocal and possessed of a true, canonical meaning,

> banish the simultaneous, secondary meanings to the void of critical lucubrations. On the other hand, others (the semiologists, let us say) contest the hierarchy of denotated and connotated; language, they say, the raw material of denotation, with its dictionary and its syntax, is a system like any other; there is no reason to make this system the privileged one, to make it the locus and the norm of a primary, original meaning . . . (1990, 7)

Such objections have not generally undermined a widespread belief in the utility of the distinction.

In his essay 'Rhetoric of the Image', Barthes further attempts to link connotation to IDEOLOGY via rhetoric:

> [The] common realm of the signifieds of connotation is that of *ideology*, which cannot help being one and the same for a given history and society, whatever the signifiers of connotation to which it resorts.
>
> To the general ideology, then, correspond signifiers of connotation which are specified according to the substance chosen. We shall call these signifiers

connotators and the totality of the connotators a *rhetoric*: thus, rhetoric appears as the signifying aspect of ideology. (1991, 38)

A number of recent theorists have suggested that there are similarities between the connotation/denotation distinction and the METONYMY/METAPHOR distinction. This is because both connotation and metonymy involve relations of CONTIGUITY, whereas denotation and metaphor involve relations mediated by CONVENTION. The difference is, however, that whereas denotation involves unmotivated relations, metaphor normally relies upon motivated relations, or upon some aspect of similarity which is external to the system of MEANING involved. Warmongers and peacemakers bear some resemblances to hawks and doves which are external to any single language, whereas the denotation of 'war' as 'armed conflict' is specific to the English language and is therefore unmotivated. (For 'motivated', see the entry for ARBITRARY.)

Connotation and denotation are not exclusively linguistic phenomena: the sign of the cross, uniforms, expressive bodily actions, representations of the physical landscape – all these can have both connotations and denotations.

Whether or not the terms themselves have been used, literary critics and READERS have almost inevitably had to be concerned with the processes of connotation and denotation; Gérard Genette suggests that literature is the 'domain *par excellence*' of connotation (1982, 31). It was, however, probably the NEW CRITICS and those associated with them who drew most overt attention to the distinction. An insistence upon the importance of connotation to the way in which a poem worked necessarily underwrote the dangers of what was termed 'the heresy of paraphrase': other words might have the same denotations, but they would have different – and probably inappropriate – connotations. Another aspect of this issue was, however, rather neglected by the New Critics: if connotations are volatile and culture- or person-specific, then the 'meaning' of a poem is likely to be less fixed than the New Critics generally intimated it was.

It is this aspect of the connotation/denotation distinction that has interested more recent theorists. The distinction directs attention outwards from individual writer or reader, and from the literary WORK, to the wider culture and its historical movements. It has been of some polemical use to those concerned to argue for the volatility, instability, and even non-existence of TEXTUAL meaning.

See also SYNTAGMATIC AND PARADIGMATIC, and compare 'MASCON' WORDS.

Conscious and unconscious narrative versions See NARRATIVE

Consciousness-raising A term coined within the Women's Liberation Movement during the late 1960s which describes processes of IDEOLOGICAL renewal and morale-building based on interaction and discussion within groups of women concerned to bring collective support to such processes. Consciousness-raising was typically (but not exclusively) looked upon as a temporary strategy to be resorted to in the early stages of building up a strong women's movement not dominated or infiltrated by PATRIARCHAL ideas or influences.

Consciousness-raising groups borrowed techniques from PSYCHOANALYSIS and encounter group processes, but generally speaking they sought (successfully) to establish STRUCTURES and processes that were new and reflective of FEMINIST and anti-patriarchal ideologies, procedures and assumptions. It was commonly agreed, for example, that these should be non-hierarchical in nature. Very often they involved the examination or reconstruction of individuals' personal histories from a new and feminist perspective.

The concept has been influential in discussions of the role to be accorded to literature in combatting patriarchal ideas, and it has had a more diffuse influence on techniques of discussion and debate – in seminars and lectures and at academic conferences, for example.

Consonant closure See CLOSURE

Consonant psycho-narration See FREE INDIRECT DISCOURSE

Constatives See SPEECH ACT THEORY

Construction See DECONSTRUCTION

Contact See FUNCTIONS OF LANGUAGE

Contact language/literatures See CONTACT ZONE

Contact zone A coinage of Mary Louise Pratt's. According to her, she uses the term to refer to the space of colonial encounters, the space

> in which peoples geographically and historically separated come into contact with each other and establish ongoing relations, usually involving conditions of coercion, radical inequality, and intractable conflict. I borrow the term 'contact' here from its use in linguistics, where the term contact language refers to improvised languages that develop among speakers of different native languages who need to communicate with each other consistently, usually in context of trade. ...'Contact zone' in my discussion is often synonymous with 'colonial frontier'. (1992, 6)

Pratt notes that Ronald Carter has suggested the term 'contact literatures' to refer to literatures written in European languages from outside Europe (1992, 6).

See also TRANSCULTURATION (*contamination*).

Containment See INCORPORATION

Contamination See TRANSCULTURATION

Context See FUNCTIONS OF LANGUAGE

Contiguity Literally, the relation of touching or adjoining. METONYMY is defined as that relation based on contiguity, and has led to important theoretical work in both SEMIOTICS and literary criticism. The Freudian concept of DISPLACEMENT also relies to some extent on relations of contiguity: thus my fears about my boss may be displaced in a dream on to a fear of the colour blue if that is the colour of the suits he wears. The process of displacement follows a path based on the contiguous relation: boss → blue.

Mikhail Bakhtin distinguishes between relations of contiguity and those of mutual REFLECTION; merely contiguous lives, he writes,

> are self-enclosed and deaf; they do not hear and do not answer one another. There are not and cannot be any dialogic relationships among them. They neither argue nor agree. (1984, 70)

See also CONNOTATION AND DENOTATION.

Contrapuntal reading See AGAINST THE GRAIN

Convention In traditional usage, either the allowances which are made by READERS and audiences and required by certain GENRES, or the framework of formal requirements imposed by the same genres or sub-genres. Thus it is a theatrical convention that the actors normally face towards the audience, while other conventions place a certain pressure on both poet and reader with regard to a poem's formal STRUCTURE.

Recent literary and other theory has been much occupied with the larger extent to which systems of rules or conventions underlie the production or recognition of SIGNS and MEANING. A key role in the more general concern with this issue has been played by STRUCTURALIST theorists and critics. As Jonathan Culler has put it, structuralism 'is thus based . . . on the realization that if human actions or productions have a meaning there must be an underlying system of distinctions and conventions which makes this meaning possible' (1975, 4). Culler's position is somewhat vulnerable to the charge that it simplifies a complex and volatile situation: there does not have to be '*an* underlying system . . .', there may be many interacting and changing systems which are continually modified as a result of the uses to which they are put in the social and historical world.

Generally speaking, a sign that derives its force from a system of conventions is said to be *unmotivated* (see the entry for ARBITRARY), whereas one which has a force independent of any such agreed or accepted conventions is said to be *motivated*. 'Agreed or accepted' is important: conventions may be technically *artificial*, that is to say they may be drawn up, agreed upon, and abided by on the basis of conscious human planning and acceptance. Alternatively, they may be more *natural*, growing in a more unplanned manner, as particular tasks require a set of rules to enable and standardize communication. The conventions governing the presentation of academic papers are more artificial: they have been collated and regularized by a group of people, whereas those governing the behaviour of INTERPRET[AT]IVE COMMUNITIES are (to a much greater extent) natural: they have grown up through tacit consent without necessarily ever having been considered or written down.

It is typical of natural conventions that very often they are not even recognized as such, but are NATURALIZED by those who are familiar with and accept them. Thus *changing* such conventions may require shock techniques: a good example is that of the ALIENATION EFFECT pioneered by Brecht to make his audiences aware of, and reject, the theatrical conventions within the grip of which they were imprisoned. The pejorative use of the term *conventional* stems from the recognition that when conventions are applied mechanically and unfeelingly in literature and art then they have a deadening effect: if we describe a play as 'merely conventional', we mean that its conventions have become clichés, and far from being invisible are more like bare bones gaping through the flesh of the work.

See also CONVENTIONALISM; REGISTER.

Conventionalism Terry Lovell suggests that the main thrust of the conventionalist attack on empiricism is that the 'neutral observation language' posited by empiricism cannot be found, and that 'the concepts in terms of which experience is ordered and recorded are not and cannot be theory-neutral' (1980, 14–15). She cites Thomas Kuhn (see the entry for PARADIGM SHIFT) as an exponent of 'flamboyant conventionalism'; according to her he

> declared that all languages of observation and experience are theory-impregnated. He contended that sense perception itself depends upon theory, so that the way in which we perceive the world, the sensations and experiences we have, depend on the theoretical presuppositions we bring to it. (1980, 15)

As she points out, this means that knowledge cannot be validated by experience because the very terms of our experience presuppose certain knowledge. As a result, people with different knowledge are cut off from communication with one another, and indeed Kuhn's position has been criticized for positing a set of *paradigms* which are self-enclosed and cut off from one another. As Lovell puts it, 'Because the terms of rival paradigms are incommensurable, reality becomes a function of the paradigm, rather than something independent of all paradigms against which rival interpretations can be measured' (1980, 15). Kuhn's paradigm thus has more than a passing resemblance to Stanley Fish's INTERPRET[AT]IVE COMMUNITY, and both concepts have been subjected to similar criticisms.

Both are, arguably, examples of conventionalism – although the term itself has a pejorative ring and is not usually welcomed by those to whom it is applied. Lovell suggests that there is a strongly conventionalist element in the work of both Ferdinand de Saussure and Louis Althusser, although they have little else in common. But they were influential during much the same period (the decades of the 1970s and the 1980s), and conventionalist positions can be detected in the work of many theorists of this time.

Howard Felperin has argued that there is a conventionalist element in the work of the NEW HISTORICISTS, and he criticizes Stephen Greenblatt in particular for this alleged failing. According to Felperin, Greenblatt's 'theoretical retrenchments of the 1970s and early 1980s' allow him to modify an essentially realist model of history, culture, and literature by the addition of a 'sleeker "textualist" and inevitably "conventionalist" model' (1992, 151; for textualism see the entry for TEXTUALIST).

In other words, just as (according to Lovell) the conventionalist gives up the idea of a reality existing independently of our perceptions of it, and thus makes it impossible to adjudicate between different views of the world in terms of their 'correctness' or conformity to this independently existing reality, the New Historicist loosens his or her grip on the idea of a historical reality independent of 'narratives' of it and thus drifts in the direction of history as a set of TEXTS which all reflect the beliefs of their creators and between which no adjudication is possible.

See also CONVENTION.

Conversational implicature/maxims See SPEECH ACT THEORY

Cool media See HOT AND COOL MEDIA

Co-operative principle See SPEECH ACT THEORY

Co-optation See INCORPORATION

Copernican revolution A favoured metaphor of much recent theory, used to suggest a range of decentring processes allegedly comparable to the way in which the theories of Copernicus rendered untenable a belief in the earth as the CENTRE of the universe. In his essay 'Freud and Lacan' Louis Althusser refers to Sigmund Freud's comparison (on more than one occasion) of 'the critical reception of his discovery with the upheavals of the Copernican Revolution'. Since Copernicus, Althusser continues,

> we have known that the earth is not the 'centre' of the universe. Since Marx, we have known that the human subject, the economic, political or philosophical ego is not the 'centre' of history – and even, in opposition to the Philosophers of the Enlightenment and to Hegel, that history has no 'centre' but possesses a structure which has no necessary 'centre' except its ideological misrecognition. (1971, 201)

He adds that, in like manner, since Freud we know that the real SUBJECT, 'the individual in his unique essence', has not the form of ego which is centred on consciousness or existence, but rather that 'the human subject is decentred' (1971, 201). Jacques Lacan has an interesting extended discussion of the metaphor of Copernican revolution in his essay 'The Subversion of the Subject and the Dialectic of Desire in the Freudian Unconscious' (1977, 295–6). To this list of 'decentrers' Catherine Belsey has added the name of Ferdinand de Saussure, who, according to her, decentred language and thus put into question the metaphysics of PRESENCE which had dominated western philosophy (1980, 136).

The relevance of all this for students of literature is that Belsey reaches the conclusion that the epoch of the metaphysics of presence is doomed, 'and with it all the methods of analysis, explanation and interpretation which rest on a single, unquestioned, pre-Copernican *centre*' (1980, 137). In particular, the TEXT (literary or otherwise) is no longer seen as source and centre of its own MEANING; instead, the meaning of the text is detached from a fixed centre and thus deprived of that fixity that comes from self-identity. Such a position ties in with a number of other arguments which have a direct relevance to INTERPRETATION: the death of the AUTHOR and the movement from WORK to text, for example.

It is worth asking to what extent such arguments set up a parodic view of the position they wish to attack. It is possible to find those who defend 'the text itself' or 'the author's INTENTION' as exclusive meaning-determining 'centre', but to argue that such positions are representative of all modern (or even of twentieth-century) literary criticism or theory is to go beyond the evidence. To take just one example: William Empson's highly influential *Seven Types of Ambiguity* (first published in 1930) contains very many ANALYSES and interpretations of poems and parts of poems, but none that posits what could meaningfully be termed a Copernican view of the poem or of the interpretative process.

See also *ÉPISTÉMÈ*; EPISTEMOLOGICAL BREAK; PARADIGM SHIFT; PROBLEMATIC.

Counterhistory Sometimes hyphenated or written as two words. An account of the past which consciously rearranges known and/or hitherto unknown events in an explanatory pattern which counters a previously accepted pattern or patterns. Counterhistories are IDEOLOGICALLY or politically motivated: they attempt to usurp 'standard' views of the past in order to replace them with an INTERPRETATIVE rearrangement of processes and EVENTS which illustrates or justifies a (normally oppositional) set of principles or theories.

Counter-memory: Foucauldian term for a memory which counters the sense of a continuous, self-aware and homogeneous identity, whether of a person or a CULTURE, with a history of oppositions, discontinuities and exclusions.

Covert narrator See NARRATOR

Covert plot See STORY AND PLOT

Cratylism From Plato's dialogue *Cratylus*, in which the participants discuss whether names are motivated or not: the theory that the relationship between words and what words refer to is existential rather than CONVENTIONAL.

See also *motivated* and *unmotivated* in the entry for ARBITRARY.

Creolization See RELEXIFICATION

Crisis In traditional usage, the point at which the fortunes of the hero change. More recently, Mieke Bal (1985) distinguishes between *crisis* and *development*: the former a short span of time into which many events are compressed, the latter a longer span of time in which, as the name suggests, a development takes place.

Critical theory This is a term that has both a general and a (different) specific meaning. In the 1970s the term was often used alongside *literary theory* to refer to that body of theory associated with the study of literature or literary criticism. This usage is much less common now, partly because *literary theory* has become the preferred term and partly because of confusion with the more specific sense.

In Sociology and Cultural Studies the term is generally applied to that body of work associated with the 'FRANKFURT SCHOOL' – the Institute for Social Research established at the University of Frankfurt in 1923. The most influential member of the school was Theodor Adorno, and his condemnations of mass CULTURE and opposition to the standard Soviet and Lukácsian condemnation of MODERNISM are probably the most important aspects of his work so far as students of literature are concerned.

See the extended discussion in Brooker (1999).

Critics of consciousness See PHENOMENOLOGY

Critifiction Novels and short stories, often written by academics, which use academic settings and/or explore, sometimes humorously, issues from current literary-critical theory. See Siegfried Mews (1989). Mews borrows the term from Leo Truchlar, who uses it about the writing of Raymond Federmann.

Critique Used both as noun and verb, sometimes in the form of 'X's critiquing of Y's position'. At times more or less synonymous with more traditional terms such as INTERPRET[ATION] and ANALYSIS, but normally with the implication that a more aggressive, polemical and committed attitude towards the studied TEXT is being adopted. The term thus typically signals opposition to a more traditional view of the need for openness and the 'suspension of disbelief' in our engagement with literary works. (See the entry for *EPOCHÉ*.)

Cross-censorship See MASQUERADE

Cross-dressing Originally a term used to describe forms of transvestism (otherwise TV), but now often extended metaphorically to include not just the wearing of opposite-sex clothes but the adoption of other gender-associated tokens or forms of behaviour.

In criticism, the adoption of the viewpoint of a GENDER which is not one's own, whether from sympathy, envy, dislike of exclusion, or an attempt to colonize. See Elaine Showalter (1987).

See also DRAG; MIMICRY; PHALLOCENTRISM; TRANSGENDER.

Crosstalk 1. A concept developed by psychologists investigating perception, who confirmed that the human brain deals with *consecutive* messages far more efficiently than it deals with simultaneous ones. (Compare: 'God hands save the up Queen' with 'God save the Queen'; 'Hands up'.) When we want to listen carefully to something we normally ask our companion(s) to remain silent: crosstalk overloads our ability to process speech. Compare our inability to see Wittgenstein's duck-rabbit as both duck and rabbit at the same time. Experimental material concerned to explore this fact, and to discover the different strategies developed to overcome the problems it causes, have been of particular interest to students of the mass media, but also to those studying NARRATIVE and the READING process.

Although all written language presents the reader with an essentially linear sequence of SIGNS, when read these signs may be capable of generating different (and, potentially, simultaneously available) MEANINGS. The obvious example of this is a pun, but a sequence of words in a literary TEXT will also work on a number of different levels, not all of which can be followed at the same time. It is likely that one of the reasons why the APPRECIATION of literary WORKS demands moments of pause and recapitulation is to allow us to go back over what has been responded to in one way, so as to explore the possibility of alternative responses. We like to pause every now and then when reading a novel; PERFORMANCES of plays normally provide intervals.

2. The term is used in a rather different sense by the linguist John Gumperz, for whom it betokens that sort of misunderstanding which is occasioned by having to negotiate complex interactions with, for example, bureaucracies of one sort or another. Thus an Asian living in Britain may have difficulty during a job interview – may get caught in crosstalk – because he or she is abiding by a different set of regulatory CONVENTIONS. (See Gumperz: 1982a and 1982b.)

See also PUNCTUATION.

Crowning/decrowning Also throning/dethroning. According to Mikhail Bakhtin, 'the primary carnivalistic act is the *mock crowning and subsequent decrowning of the carnival king*'. This he refers to as a 'dualistic ambivalent ritual, expressing the inevitability and at the same time the creative power of the shift-and-renewal, the *joyful relativity* of all structure and order, of all authority and all (hierarchical) position' (1984, 124). Crowning and decrowning are forms of DEFAMILIARIZATION, and it is likely that this concept influenced Bakhtin's account. Literary WORKS which encourage the READER either to treat that which is normally despised or disregarded with interest and respect, or to treat that which is normally admired and respected with contempt or familiarity, are engaging in processes of crowning or decrowning.

Cruising zone In Gay slang *cruising* involves the search in a public or semi-public space for a new sexual partner. Its heterosexual near-equivalent is 'kerb-crawling', although this is associated with a motorised search for a prostitute. David Oswell (1998) attributes the term 'cruising zone' to Joseph Bristow, and cites his suggestion that the TEXT is a cruising zone, a 'site where desire charts its spaces for others to share the pleasures of contact: contact between those who are able to identify each other but who have not – as with most cruisers – ever met before' (Bristow: 1989, 79).

It is interesting that Oswell himself, writing about Hanif Kureishi's *The Buddha of Suburbia* (1990), compares the leading character of this work to a FLÂNEUR, and there is a sense in which the cruiser is the modern equivalent of a flâneur.

Cultural code See CODE

Cultural materialism/cultural poetics See NEW HISTORICISM AND CULTURAL MATERIALISM

Cultural Studies CULTURE, it should be clear from the separate entry for this term, is itself an extremely complex concept – one which has involved related but nonetheless separate traditions of research and theory in a range of different academic disciplines (Anthropology, Social History, Linguistics, Sociology, and Literary Studies, among others). Cultural Studies has emerged as a separate field of interdisciplinary study during the past three decades, initially in Britain, but more recently in the United States and in other countries.

In a long review-article subtitled 'Is Culture too important to be left to Cultural Studies?', Stefan Collini has claimed that in explaining what Cultural Studies is, more illumination is gained 'by reflecting on the shifting relations among disciplines and on the trajectories of those who have been led to claim the label of Cultural Studies for their very various activities' than from looking for a definition of its subject matter (1994, 3). He gives an ironic summary of three such possible trajectories, from the dissatisfied scholar of English Literature who seeks to study a wider range of contemporary and 'relevant' TEXTS, and sets up a unit to study the tabloid press or soap operas or DISCOURSE analysis, to the dissatisfied social scientist who rejects misguided SCIENTISM and pursues a more PHENOMENOLOGICAL study of the relations between public MEANINGS and private experience and sets up a unit to study football crowds or house-music parties or Tupperware mornings, to the person who starts with his or her own major grievance, theorizes opposition to making this a recognized academic study as an aspect of the repressive operation of power in society, and sets up a unit to study the (mis)representation of Gays in the media or the imbrication of literary criticism in colonial discourse. All three imagined individuals end up by situating their work within Cultural Studies (1994, 3).

This is both parodic and hostile, but it does have the virtue of showing how very different academic routes have led to the formation of Cultural Studies. Collini names three books and a university institute as the constitutive parts of the founding myth of Cultural Studies. The books are Richard Hoggart's *The Uses of Literacy* (1957), Raymond Williams's *Culture and Society* (1958), and E. P. Thompson's *The Making of the English Working Class* (1963), while the university institute was the Centre for Contemporary Cultural Studies, which was founded at Birmingham University in 1964. The Centre was initially a graduate research group within the ENGLISH Department, although it now has the status of an autonomous department. The association with the English Department was not fortuitous: the key figure in the setting up of the Centre was Richard Hoggart, whose main academic/institutional affiliation had been with English Literary Studies even though his own work (*The Uses of Literacy,* for example) had moved beyond a concern with CANONICAL literature by the mid-1950s. Hoggart, Williams, and Thompson, as Collini states, were undoubtedly the most influential figures in the formation of Cultural Studies in the 1960s. Although very different, they had much in common. Hoggart and Williams had a background in English Literary Studies, but both were drawn outside the then accepted limits of this academic area, to larger historical, cultural, and political issues of both a pragmatic and a theoretical nature. All three had more or less explicit and committed links to the political left.

A North American commentator has argued that 'the early Birmingham [Centre] scholars were influenced, directly or indirectly, by two very British institutions: the Fabian Society, whose socialist theories they espoused, and the Leavis/Arnold conservative literary tradition, against which they rebelled' (Gaunt: 1996, 92).

Right from its inception, Cultural Studies was academically expansionist if not downright colonialist, basing itself upon some of the methods and principles developed within Literary Studies but applying them in new ways to different objects of study. Thus by 1970 Richard Hoggart was able to write an essay entitled 'Contemporary Cultural Studies: An Approach to the Study of Literature and Society' – which had echoes from the debates between F. R. Leavis and the MARXIST critics of the 1930s – while referring to the fourth Occasional Paper published by the Centre, 'Lévi-Strauss and the Cultural Sciences', by Tim Moore. Hoggart's article is prefaced by a bibliographical note, the composition of which is interesting. It starts with references relevant to what Hoggart calls the English 'culture and society' debate, including of course Raymond Williams's *Culture and Society* (1958), but also L. C. Knights's *Drama and Society in the Age of Jonson* (1937), Lionel Trilling's *Beyond Culture* (1966), Georg Lukács's *The Historical Novel* (English translation, 1962), and other work on 'the sociology of literature'. This is one important branch in Cultural Studies' family tree: literary criticism that is anti-formalist and that seeks to establish connections with History and with theories of society. In the opening part of his essay Hoggart argues that what Raymond Williams has termed 'the culture and society debate' 'runs from Blake to T. S. Eliot through Coleridge, Arnold, Carlyle, Ruskin, Morris and many others' (1970, 155–6).

The bibliography then moves to list material concerned with the analysis of POPULAR literature, starting with Q. D. Leavis's *Fiction and the Reading Public* (1932) and ending with *The Popular Arts* by Stuart Hall and Paddy Whannel (1964). There are then works on mass communication, and works related to the social sciences, including psychology. Works on STRUCTURALISM and SEMIOTICS follow, along with texts concerned with 'mass culture' and with the sociology of knowledge. And finally, at the bottom of this complex family tree, are the Centre's own publications.

Referring to 'the culture and society debate' mentioned above, Hoggart argues that ' "[c]ulture" there means the whole way of life of a society, its beliefs, attitudes and temper as expressed in all kinds of structures, rituals and gestures, as well as in the traditionally defined forms of art' (1970, 156). This urge towards a totalizing and inclusive perspective, towards the tracing of connections, relationships and influences, along with a concomitant rejection of academic compartmentalization, has continued to characterize Cultural Studies, and makes it hard to pigeon-hole the area by means of traditional academic category distinctions such as that between the social sciences and the Humanities. Thus in an article published in 1976 entitled 'Cultural Studies at Birmingham University', Michael Green is able to list six main areas in which research at the Centre is clustered: *the mass media*; *cultural history*; *women's studies*; *art and politics* (particularly Marxist and semiological); *subcultures*; and *work*. As Green admits, by this time the activities of the Centre have broadened out considerably beyond the early concentration on the popular arts and the recovery and assessment of forms of working-class culture (1976, 140). (Another important influence which should be mentioned is the *Mass Observation* movement of the 1930s.) In the 1970s and 1980s courses in Cultural Studies developed outside Birmingham, with full or part degree courses (both undergraduate and postgraduate) on offer in a number of British polytechnics (now known as 'new universities'). In general such courses have been characterized by similar commitments to those of the Birmingham Centre, along with a strong interest in theory and a generally radical flavour.

For Collini, developments in the last three decades 'have transformed the enterprise almost out of recognition' (1994, 3), as a result of the assimilation of successive waves of European theory – Marxism (Gramscian, Althusserian, Frankfurt), structuralism, PSYCHOANALYSIS and POST-STRUCTURALISM, and FEMINISM. And as he notes, the last ten year or fifteen years

> have seen an extraordinary boom in the popularity of the term in the United States, where it has come to seem the most enabling disciplinary label under which to

pursue theoretical and practical inquiries into gender and sexuality, race and ethnicity, colonialism and post-colonialism, mass media and popular culture, and much else besides. (1994, 3)

He argues, however, that 'Cultural Studies in Britain still tends to be more historical, more empirical, and more nostalgic', whereas in the United States Cultural Studies 'has been shaped above all by the marriage between literary theory and what has been called "the politics of identity"'. And in a telling point he explains the replacement of 'society' by 'culture' as 'the preferred object of study in a range of academic fields' by the fact that in the 'frequently incanted quartet of race, class, gender and sexual orientation, there is no doubt that class has been the least fashionable in recent years' (1994, 3).

Collini's account is hostile, but it is not without its shrewd insights. What it fails to do is to concede the importance of individual projects within the field, and also of the effect – liberating, challenging – that Cultural Studies has had on its ancestors and cognate fields of study. Thus, for example, Cultural Studies has drawn much from Literary Studies, but it has also repaid much. Work within Cultural Studies has often fed back into Literary Studies, particularly with regard to the study of popular, non-canonical writing, the drawing of relationships between literature and the wider culture, and the development of specialized bodies of theory.

Culture According to Raymond Williams's *Keywords*, *culture* is 'one of the two or three most complicated words in the English language' (1976, 76). Williams attributes this complexity partly to the word's intricate historical development in several European languages, but mainly to the fact that it is now used for important concepts in several different intellectual disciplines. His discussion of the word should be consulted in its entirety, but his isolation of three interrelated modern usages is worth summarizing here. These are, first: 'a general process of intellectual, spiritual and aesthetic development'; second: 'a particular way of life', of either a people, a period or a group; third: 'the works and practices of intellectual and especially artistic activity' (1976, 80).

Williams is also responsible for an influential proposal concerning certain sub-categories into which 'culture' can be divided. In his essay 'Base and Superstructure in Marxist Cultural Theory' he distinguishes first of all between dominant, alternative and oppositional cultures – thus making it clear that for him 'culture' is not to be understood as a monolithic concept. Distinguishing between alternative and oppositional forms is relatively straightforward: it is the difference 'between someone who simply finds a different way to live and wishes to be left alone with it, and someone who finds a different way to live and wants to change the society in its light' (1980, 41–2). 'Alternative' and 'oppositional' cultures include, for Williams, both *residual* and *emergent* forms (1980, 40). This aspect of Williams's work has been especially influential so far as the later development of CULTURAL MATERIALISM is concerned.

In recent literary-critical discussion the term 'culture' has undoubtedly been used by those who wish to set literature in a socio-historical context without the use of terms which might invoke a specifically MARXIST methodology or ANALYTICAL framework, although to this one should add the point that Marxists have offered their own definition of the term. In an article published first in 1937, Edgell Rickword claimed that for the Marxist, 'culture is not a mass of works of art, of philosophical ideas, of political concepts accumulated at the top of the social pyramid by specially-gifted individuals, but the inherited solution of problems of vital importance to society' (1978, 103). This certainly distinguishes culture from, for example, the related terms BASE and SUPERSTRUCTURE, but it also restricts culture to *solutions*. More recent usages, many associated with the newly emergent academic area of CULTURAL STUDIES, have seen culture in terms of inheritance, not just of solutions, but of elements from all three of Raymond Williams's alternative definitions. For FEMINISTS it has been important to be able to attribute some or all GENDER characteristics and roles to cultural rather than to biological influences.

The term *popular culture* refers to the culture of a subordinate group or CLASS which is distinct from the dominant culture of a particular society, dominant in the sense either of more widely disseminated or valued, or in the sense of belonging to and reflecting the interests of a dominant group or class. The term POPULAR is itself problematic, invoking either that which is *for*, or that which is *of*, the people (for which the term *folk culture* has sometimes been reserved). Thus novels by Agatha Christie and Robert Tressell could either or both be included in or excluded from the categories of popular culture or popular FICTION depending upon one's definition of these terms.

For *cultural materialism* see NEW HISTORICISM AND CULTURAL MATERIALISM; for cultural capital see CAPITAL.

See also STRUCTURE OF FEELING; TRANSCULTURATION.

Cut(ting) See ANACHRONY

Cutback See ANALEPSIS

Cyber/netics/punk/space From the Greek word meaning steersman, the term *cybernetics* was coined by Norbert Wiener, whose book *Cybernetics: Or Control and Communication in the Animal and the Machine* (1949) introduced the term. Wiener was primarily interested in what became known as feedback systems, and in more scholarly circles *cybernetics* is still used to refer to complex feedback systems in (as Wiener's title has it) animals and machines – nowadays normally electronic 'machines'.

In less scholarly and more general usage *cyberspace* is used broadly to refer to the whole universe of electronic communication and (simulated) experience: missing e-mails are referred to as 'lost in cyberspace', electronic chat-lines allow for meetings in cyberspace, and so on. In such general usage the associations are exclusively electronic and never with animals. The term was coined by the American science FICTION writer William Gibson in his 1984 novel *Neuromancer*. Gibson is one of a number of Canadian and American writers whose work has become known collectively as *cyberpunk*. This work extends science fiction through the incorporation of detail from existing and predicted electronic technologies, presented in a format that owes much to the 'action' film. Ridley Scott's film *Blade Runner* (based on Philip K. Dick's 1968 novel *Do Androids Dream of Electric Sheep?*) is perhaps the best known cyberpunk film. According to Fredric Jameson, cyberpunk needs to be understood in terms of the social and historical contexts in which it emerged; for him, cyberpunk 'is fully as much an expression of transnational corporate realities as it is of global paranoia itself' (1991, 38).

Compare PUNK.

Cyborg According to Nigel Wheale,

> [t]he term 'cyborg' was coined in 1960 as a definition of a 'self-regulating man-machine system' (Tomas 1989: 127) but every period has imagined such 'human-Things', entities which test or define the contemporary sense of intrinsic human value over against its simulacrum: the incubus or succuba in Christian tradition, the Golem in Jewish folklore, Prospero's Ariel and Caliban (and perhaps even Miranda too?), E. T. A. Hoffmann's Sandman, and of course Mary Shelley's Frankenstein . . . . The robot also has a long and influential life in film history, beginning with Fritz Lang's eerie adaptation of the Golem legend in *Metropolis* (1926). (Wheale: 1995c, 102)

In her 1985 article 'A Manifesto for Cyborgs: Science, Technology, and Socialist Feminism in the 1980s', Donna Haraway explains further that the cyborg 'is a creature in a post-gender world; it has no truck with bisexuality, pre-Oedipal symbiosis, unalienated labor, or other seductions to organic wholeness through a final appropriation of all the powers of the parts into a higher unity' (in Mary Eagleton: 1996, 399). Haraway's explanation clearly bears witness to a FEMINIST extension and appropriation of the term; she has since refined and developed her ideas about the cyborg in her 1991 book *Simians, Cyborgs, and Women: The Reinvention of Nature*. In this work the cyborg is treated as an entity able to display in utopian form what human beings are not – but what they might just perhaps become.

Andermahr, Lovell and Wolkowitz comment that if 'feminism hesitates before the figure of the cyborg, it is less because of the fears imagined by Mary Wings of a plot to bypass and control women's bodies (1988) than of cyborg manifestations in the form of cosmetic surgery and other body modifications in the direction of an idealized FEMININITY' (1997, 52).

D

Daemonization See REVISIONISM

Data driven See SOLUTION FROM ABOVE/BELOW

Death of the author See AUTHOR

Decentring of the subject See CENTRE

Decipherment/deciphering Occasionally also *decoding*. Used with a specifically GENDER-politics sense to refer to INTERPRETATIVE processes whereby concealed clues relating to gender identity or sexual preference are read and their meaning brought to the surface. Such READING processes typically involve the detection of clues associated with homosexuality in a CULTURE or a CHARACTER. Such clues had to replace more overt reference in societies and times that outlawed homosexuality.

See also CODE; INTERPRETATION.

Declarations See SPEECH ACT THEORY

Decoding See CODE

Deconstruction The term originates in the writings of the French philosopher Jacques Derrida, and rests upon the implication, as Jonathan Culler puts it, that the hierarchical oppositions of Western metaphysics are themselves constructions or IDEOLOGICAL impositions (1988, 20). Deconstruction thus aims to undermine Western metaphysics by undoing or deconstructing these hierarchical oppositions and by showing their LOGOCENTRIC reliance upon a CENTRE or PRESENCE, which reflects the idealist desire to control the play of signifiers by making them subject to some extra-systemic TRANSCENDENTAL SIGNIFIED. As will be seen, Derrida is a great coiner of neologisms, and to avoid the necessity for repetition the reader is advised to look up these separate terms – along with DIFFÉRANCE, DISSEMINATION, and PHONOCENTRISM. Deconstruction is generally taken to represent an important – even dominant – element in POST-STRUCTURALISM.

In spite of the fact that Derrida in particular and deconstructionists in general are hostile to or dismissive about accounts of intellectual heritage and lines of descent, Derrida has not been without his formative influences. According to Martin Jay it is difficult to ignore hearing in Derrida's work the echo of other arguments, some of which he lists:

> Bergson's protest against the spatialization of time, Nietzsche's critique of Apollonian art, Bataille's strictures against heliocentric notions of form, Starobinski's exposure of the dialectic of transparency and obstacle in Rousseau, Heidegger's attack on enframing in the age of the worldview, Merleau-Ponty's interest in the chiasm of the visible and invisible, and Barthes's rejection of the traditional French fetish of linguistic clarity all provided threads for the intertextual web that can be called deconstruction. So too did Emmanuel Levinas's elevation of Hebraic iconoclastic notions of ethics over idolatrous Hellenic ontology and Edmond Jabès's stress on the word over the image. ... Here the effects of Derrida's own Jewish background must be acknowledged. And finally, the impact of the twentieth-century revolution in communications media, which was so important for thinkers from Heidegger to Baudrillard, may also be detected in Derrida's work. (1993, 498–9)

There is no absolute agreement concerning the implications that Derrida's more general positions hold for literary criticism and theory. At one extreme their implications can appear modest: Jonathan Culler quotes Barbara Johnson to the effect that deconstruction is 'a careful teasing out of warring forces of signification within the text' (Culler: 1981, ix) – a statement with which the NEW CRITICS would surely have been in full accord. In an interview with Imre Salusinszky, Johnson has further commented that if it is indeed the case that people approach literature with the desire to learn something about the world, and if it is indeed the case that the literary medium is not transparent, then a study of its non-transparency is crucial in order to deal with the desire one has to know something about the world by reading literature. (Salusinszky: 1987, 166)

This, one may be forgiven for noting, is so buttressed with qualifications that it would be hard to disagree with – although it does hedge its bets on whether it really is possible to learn something about the world through literature or whether this is a delusion experienced by 'people' who can be relieved of their inappropriate 'desire' through a study of the literary medium's non-transparency.

Johnson does, however, go on to distance herself and deconstruction from the 'self-involved textual practice of "close reading" ' of the New Critics mentioned by her interviewer, suggesting that deconstruction necessarily involves a political attitude, one which examines authority in language, and she notes that Karl Marx was as close to deconstruction as are a lot of deconstructors – particularly by virtue of his bringing to the surface the hidden inscriptions of the economic system, uncovering hidden presuppositions, and showing contradictions (Salusinszky: 1987, 167).

It would certainly seem that deconstruction involves one inescapable implication for the process of INTERPRETATION – literary or otherwise. This is that the interpretation of a TEXT can never arrive at a final and complete 'meaning' for a text. As Derrida himself remarks about a READING of the Marxist 'classics':

These texts are not to be read according to a hermeneutical or exegetical method which would seek out a finished signified beneath a textual surface. Reading is transformational. (1981b, 63)

Not just reading in general, but (clearly implied) each act of reading. Thus for Derrida the MEANING of a text is always unfolding just ahead of the interpreter, unrolling in front of him or her like a never-ending carpet whose final edge never reveals itself. Introducing a volume of essays entitled *Post-structuralist Readings of English Poetry*, the volume's editors, Richard Machin and Christopher Norris note that post-structuralist readings tend to 'feature the text as active object' (1987, 3): the AUTHOR is no longer seen as the source of meaning, and deconstruction is guilty of being an accessory after the fact with regard to the death of the author. Later on in their Introduction they seek to establish that whereas each reading in the collection 'develops an insistent coherence of its own that drives towards conclusive and irrefutable conclusions', the possibility is nonetheless held open of 'a multitude of competing meanings, each of which denies the primacy of the others' (1987, 7). The possibility of such a paradoxical blending of linear rigour and pluralistic co-existence has not always convinced the sceptical, however, and one of the most recurrent criticisms of the readings or interpretations generated by deconstruction is that they are not subject to falsification. Another objection is that these readings and interpretations have a tendency to end up all looking the same, all demonstrating the ceaseless play of the signifier and nothing much else, just as crude psychoanalytic readings of the 1930s and 1940s tended all to end up demonstrating certain recurrent items of Freudian faith. And indeed the more a criticism holds that interpretations are not subject to the control of textual meaning (however defined), the more it has to cope with the problem that the choice of text necessarily becomes a matter of less and less moment. How can one talk about rigorously grappling with a text if there is said to be nothing fixed 'in' the text?

See also COHERENCE; HERMENEUTICS.

Decrowning See CROWNING/DECROWNING

Deep structure See STRUCTURE

Defamiliarization Also *singularization*. From the Russian meaning 'to make strange', the term originates with the RUSSIAN FORMALISTS and, in particular, the theories of Viktor Shklovsky. In his essay 'Art as Technique', Shklovsky argues that perception becomes automatic once it has become habitual, and that the function of art is to challenge automization and habitualization, and return a direct grasp on things to the individual perception.

> Habitualization devours works, clothes, furniture, one's wife, and the fear of war. 'If the whole complex lives of many people go on unconsciously, then such lives are as if they had never been.' And art exists that one may recover the sensation of life; it exists to make one feel things, to make the stone *stony*. (1965, 12; the quotation is from Leo Tolstoy's *Diary*)

The PRAGUE SCHOOL theorist Bohuslav Havránek provides useful definitions of both *automization* and *foregrounding* in his essay 'The Functional Differentiation of the Standard Language'.

> By *automization* we ... mean ... a use of the devices of the language, in isolation or in combination with each other, as is usual for a certain expressive purpose, that is, such a use that the expression itself does not attract any attention ...
>
> By *foregrounding* ... we mean the use of the devices of the language in such a way that this use itself attracts attention and is perceived as uncommon, as deprived of automization, as deautomized, such as a live poetic metaphor (as opposed to a lexicalized one, which is automized). (1964, 9, 10)

For Shklovsky the purpose of art is to impart the sensation of things as they are perceived and not as they are known, and the technique used to achieve this end is that of making objects *unfamiliar*. One variant of this technique which Shklovsky attributes to Tolstoy is that of not naming an object but of describing it as if one were seeing it for the first time (1965, 13). This technique actually predates Tolstoy by many years: think for example of the Lilliputian descriptions of the contents of Gulliver's pockets in Jonathan Swift's *Gulliver's Travels*. Boris Tomashevsky, one of Shklovsky's fellow Russian Formalists, refers to Swift's defamiliarizing techniques in *Gulliver's Travels* in his essay 'Thematics' (1965, 86).

It is important to note that members of the Prague School believed that automization could occur at various levels: a CANON, for instance, could become automized, and subsequently defamiliarized by a WORK which forced readers to recognize this fact.

Theories of defamiliarization base themselves upon the assumption that outside the realm of art perceptual evidence is often overridden by what we know, such that we end up with familiar STEREOTYPES instead of knowledge constructed from the concrete information given to us by our senses. Mikhail Bakhtin, arguing along similar lines, suggests that by creating an extraordinary situation it is possible to 'cleanse the word of all of life's automatism and object-ness', thus forcing a person to reveal the deepest layers of both his personality and his thought (1984, 111).

In as much as defamiliarization involves challenging existing habits and assumptions, the view of art associated with the concept grants art – to a greater or lesser extent – a revolutionary rather than a reflectionist role, although for the Russian Formalists in general defamiliarization relates more to the challenging of linguistic than of political or IDEOLOGICAL habitualization (although there is no reason why the latter could not to some extent at least be seen to be involved in the former). There are interesting points of similarity here with Brecht's ALIENATION EFFECT, although for Brecht the defamiliarization process is certainly accorded a much more overtly political and ideological function.

The term *foregrounding* represents a development of the concept of defamiliarization which builds on FIGURE-GROUND theories developed by researchers into perception. Nowadays, *foregrounding* and *defamiliarization* are often used interchangeably. Both concepts are related to the view that 'poetic language' is to be sharply distinguished from other forms of language; according to Jan Mukařovský, the 'function of poetic language consists in the maximum of foregrounding of the utterance', while the 'foregrounding of any one of the components is necessarily accompanied by the automatization of one or more of the other components' (1964, 19–20). *Foregrounding* has led to the coining of a complementary term: *backgrounding* – meaning the process whereby certain elements in a literary work are presented in such a way as *not* to stand out or be noticed. The clearest example of backgrounding is probably to be found in detective novels, in which part of the AUTHOR's skill lies in blending in crucial clues with the unperceived background of the work so that the reader only fully understands the full significance of the clue later on. (See also the entry for ELLIPSIS for Gérard Genette's comments on *hypothetical ellipses*; and also the entry for DEFERRED/POSTPONED SIGNIFICANCE.)

The verb *to naturalize*, which also gives us the process of *naturalization*, is often used as an alternative term in English for automization. The term seems to have entered the lexicon of literary criticism in English via a long section in Jonathan Culler's *Structuralist Poetics* (1975) entitled 'Convention and Naturalization'. For Culler, the READER of a literary work wishes 'to reduce its strangeness' so that 'the strange, the formal, the fictional, must be recuperated or naturalized, brought within our ken, if we do not want to remain gaping before monumental inscriptions' (1975, 134).

According to Gérard Genette, for Roland Barthes the 'major sin of petty-bourgeois ideology' is the naturalization of culture and history (1982, 36). By this is meant that CULTURE and history are made so familiar that their historico-cultural specificity, and thus the possibility of changing them, is obscured. Anne Cranny-Francis has argued that

69

part of the formation of subjectivity of men and women involves the naturalization of SEXIST DISCOURSE 'as the obvious mode of representation and self-representation of women and men' (1990, 2). The term *doxa* is sometimes used to stand for that which is conventional, unquestioned, or naturalized.

See also DEFORMATION; LITERARINESS.

Default interpretation According to Geoffrey Leech, the 'initial and most likely interpretation' that will be accepted '*in default* of any evidence to the contrary' (1983, 42). The term comes from Leech's book *Principles of Pragmatics* and is proposed in the context of a discussion about the PRAGMATICS of ordinary interpersonal speech communication. So far as literature is concerned it will be clear that what one's initial and most likely INTERPRETATION of a TEXT or a part of a text is will be dependent upon a range of contextual factors, including those relating to GENRE. Now although contextual factors also influence and condition interpersonal speech communication, the fact that an UTTERANCE is delivered in person to its recipient means that the extreme variation of contextual factors with which one can meet when interpreting a literary text is unlikely to be encountered. For this reason, the concept of default interpretation is likely to be of limited value in literary studies.

Deferred/postponed significance Also referred to as *enigma* by Roland Barthes. Any element in a NARRATIVE the full significance of which is only appreciated at a stage later in the telling than that at which it appears.

Compare *delayed decoding* in the entry for CODE, also *backgrounding* in the entry for DEFAMILIARIZATION.

Deformation In Roman Jakobson's essay 'On Realism in Art' the term *deformation* is given a meaning very similar to that given to the term *defamiliarization* by the RUSSIAN FORMALISTS. According to Jakobson, as artistic traditions develop, 'the painted image becomes an ideogram, a formula, to which the object portrayed is linked by contiguity' (1971a, 39). (Compare what is said about *automization* in the entry for DEFAMILIARIZATION.) To break into this STEREOTYPED encoding of reality in art, according to Jakobson, the ideogram 'needs to be deformed' (1971a, 40), and he outlines a number of different ways in which this can be done. He thus makes REALISM a RELATIVE term, dependent upon the operation of processes of disruption which prevent artistic CONVENTIONS from hardening into what he calls ideograms, or stereotypes.

For the PRAGUE SCHOOL theorists deformation is, in like manner, linked to the concept of *foregrounding* (again see the entry for DEFAMILIARIZATION). According to them, deformation can be used either to make an element stand out so that it is foregrounded, or (as Yuri Tynyanov in particular argues), in the opposite manner: so as to reduce non-foregrounded elements to the status of neutral props.

See also DEVIATION; DOMINANT.

Degree zero (writing) See ÉCRITURE

Deixis Those features of language which fasten UTTERANCES temporally or spatially: 'here', 'now', for example. *Deictics*, or *deictic elements* (*deictic* can perform as either noun or adjective) play an important role in NARRATIVE; they constitute an important token of FREE INDIRECT DISCOURSE, for example.

See also SHIFTER.

Delayed decoding See CODE

Denaturalize See NATURALIZE

Denotation See CONNOTATION AND DENOTATION

Desire Both as noun and as verb *desire* indicates a central but diffuse and by no means unified concept or set of concepts in a cluster of different contemporary theories, very often in connection with attempts to DECONSTRUCT or theorize the SUBJECT or subjectivity. According to Michel Foucault, the more recent researches of psychoanalysis, linguistics and ethnology have 'decentred the subject in relation to', among other things, 'the laws of his desire' (1972, 13), and the concept of desire has assumed an important but varied function within theories concerned to see the subject as more SITE than determining origin or PRESENCE. For Jacques Lacan, because the subject is split between a conscious mind the contents of which are unproblematically retrievable, and an unconscious set of drives and forces (*Trieb*), and because the subject knows that what it knows is not all that it is, desire for the OTHER is a constituting part of the subject. This is my own précis of a notoriously difficult author's position; those wishing to check it against the original should consult, among other sources, Lacan (1977, 292–325). The following quotation should illustrate the difficulty involved:

> For it is clear that the state of nescience in which man remains in relation to his desire is not so much a nescience of what he demands, which may after all be circumscribed, as a nescience as to where he desires.
> This is what I mean by my formula that the unconscious is *discours de l'Autre* (discourse of the Other), in which the *de* is to be understood in the sense of the Latin *de* (objective determination): *de Alio in oratione* (completed by: *tua res agitur*).
> But we must also add that man's desire is the *désir de l'Autre* (the desire of the Other) in which the *de* provides what grammarians call the 'subjective determination', namely that it is *qua* Other that he desires (which is what provides the true compass of human passion). (1977, 312)

For Lacan, moreover, desire is necessarily linked to PHALLOCENTRISM because the child desires the mother's desire and thus identifies himself (Lacan's GENDERED term) 'with the imaginary object of this desire in so far as the mother herself symbolizes it in the phallus' (1977, 198). Desire is also, according to Lacan, constituted by the hysteric in the very moment of speaking. 'So it is hardly surprising that it should be through this door that Freud entered what was, in reality, the relations of desire to language and discovered the mechanisms of the unconscious' (1979, 12).

Vincent Crapanzano has provided an accessible account of the distinction Lacan makes between desire and need:

Desire, Lacan has written, is 'an effect in the subject of that condition which is imposed upon him through the defiles of the signifier' (Wilden 1968, 185). Need is directed toward a specific object, is unmediated by language, and, unlike desire, can be satisfied directly. (Desire must always be satisfied, insofar as it can be satisfied, by symbolic substitutes for that which it can never possess [Crapanzano 1978].) To become a self, the individual must seek recognition by demanding the other to recognize him-self, or his desire – to acknowledge at least the noun (his name) as a (grammatically) legitimate *Anlage* for the I and the you. The individual must take possession of his own otherness and not be aware simply of the otherness about him. (1992, 89)

It should not surprise anyone who has read this far to discover that FEMINIST critics have displayed both interest in and suspicion towards the concept of desire, variously defined. Catharine A. MacKinnon, for example, states that she has selected 'desire' as a term parallel to 'value' in MARXIST theory, 'to refer to that substance felt to be primordial or aboriginal but posited by the theory as social and contingent' (1982, 2). MacKinnon distances herself forcefully from the use of the term 'desire' to be found both in Jean-Paul Sartre's *Existential Psychoanalysis* and in *Anti-Oedipus: Capitalism and Schizophrenia* by Gilles Deleuze and Félix Guattari. In these works, MacKinnon argues, the concept of desire entails sexual objectification, which for her is 'the primary process of the subjection of women' (1982, 27). To substantiate her case she quotes first Sartre: 'But if I desire a house, or a glass of water, or a woman's body, how could this glass, this piece of property reside in my desire and how can my desire be anything but the consciousness of these objects as desirable?' (Sartre: 1973, 20), and then Deleuze and Guattari's view of man as 'desiring-machine'. She insists: 'Women are not desiring-machines' (1982, 27). Julia Kristeva, however, in her discussion of the ABJECT, has argued that there are lives which are not sustained by desire, 'as desire is always for objects' (1982, 6), which would seem to contradict Lacan's distinction between desire and need (see above).

Robert J. C. Young's 1995 study *Colonial Desire: Hybridity in Theory, Culture and Race* has argued that (specifically sexual) desire is central to racist attitudes and colonial DISCOURSE. Young quotes Ronald Hyam's comment that one thing is certain: 'Sex is at the very heart of racism' (Young: 1995, 97, quoting Hyam: 1990, 203). Young's book provides compelling evidence to support his claim that a furtive and concealed obsession with miscegenation and sexuality is never far away once one examines Victorian writing about race, colonialism and empire. Young's consideration of literary works is generally restricted to brief comments on writers such as Joseph Conrad and Jean Rhys, but his extended discussion of Matthew Arnold should be of interest to students of English.

A similarly historical and socio-political (rather than psychoanalytic) concern with desire can be found in the work of Fredric Jameson, who suggests drily that it 'is not hard to show that the force of desire alleged to undermine the rigidities of late capitalism is, in fact, very precisely what keeps the consumer system going in the first place' (1991, 202).

See also BODY; HYBRIDITY; HOMOSOCIAL; SYNTAGMATIC AND PARADIGMATIC (metonymy as desire).

Destinataire/destinateur See ACT/ACTOR

Determinate absence See ABSENCE

Determinate instance See INSTANCE

Dethroning See CROWNING/DECROWNING

Deviation The more stress is laid upon NORMS and CONVENTIONS in a given theory or approach, the more significance is likely to be accorded to deviation from these norms and conventions. (We can only confidently refer to 'deviates' in a CULTURE in which we have, or think we have, a firm sense of what constitutes normality.) Clearly deviation is closely related to the RUSSIAN FORMALIST concept of DEFAMILIARIZATION, in which the LITERARINESS of language consists in the extent to which it deviates from extra-literary language, or to which it encourages deviation from everyday habits of perception. In the context of the Russian Formalists, then, deviation and DEFORMATION are well nigh interchangeable as terms.

Deviation is also closely related to various usages of the terms DIFFERENCE and DIFFÉRANCE, as a deviation is significant as much (if not more) in terms of what it is *not* as in terms of what it *is*. Deviation has also become an important term in the fields of STYLISTICS and NARRATOLOGY: a style may be constituted at least in part by deviations from a linguistic norm, and according to Gérard Genette, Marcel Proust's *À la Recherche du temps perdu* deviates from then-accepted laws of NARRATIVE by its manipulation of the *singulative* and the *iterative modes* – basing the narrative rhythm of this work not, as in the classical novel, on alternation between the summary and the scene, but on alternation between the iterative and the singulative mode (1980, 143). (For an explanation of these terms see the entry for FREQUENCY.)

Device See FUNCTION

Diachronic and synchronic A diachronic study or ANALYSIS concerns itself with the evolution and change over time of that which is studied: thus diachronic linguistics is also known as historical linguistics, and is concerned with the development of a language or languages over time. A synchronic study or analysis, in contrast, limits its concern to a particular moment of time. Thus Synchronic Linguistics takes a language as a working system at a particular point in time without concern for how it has developed to its present state. One of the main reasons why Ferdinand de Saussure is credited by some with having revolutionized the study of language early in this century is that he drew attention to the possibility of studying language synchronically, and thus established the possibility of a STRUCTURAL linguistics. It is, however, not clearly the case that, as David Lodge has suggested, 'Saussure argued that a scientific linguistics could never be based on such a "diachronic" study but only by approaching language as a "synchronic" system' (1988, 1). Many recent commentators on Saussure's work have made similar claims, but if we turn to the only evidence we have for Saussure's own position – the posthumous reconstruction of his lectures by his students which was published as the *Course in General Linguistics* – we find a more nuanced position. There are strong grounds for attributing a belief in the necessity of both the diachronic and the synchronic study of language to Saussure; at the start of the second chapter of the *Course*, outlining what the scope of linguistics should be, he includes the task of describing and tracing the history of all observable languages (1974, 6), and later on he suggests that

> the thing that keeps language from being a simple convention that can be modified at the whim of interested parties is not its social nature; it is rather the action of time combined with the social force. If time is left out, the linguistic facts are incomplete and no conclusion is possible. (Saussure: 1974, 78)

(It is, additionally, worth mentioning that this comment also tends to the invalidation of another present-day 'Saussurean' myth – that the ARBITRARINESS of language means that words can mean anything one wants them to mean.)

Most conclusively, in the *Course* Saussure speaks directly of the reasons for distinguishing 'two sciences of language', *evolutionary linguistics* and *static linguistics* (1974, 81), which approximate to diachronic and synchronic linguistics.

The extent to which synchronic study really does as it were take a frozen slice of history for study is itself not absolute: to talk of a SYSTEM is necessarily to imply movement and interaction, and movement and interaction can only take place in time. Thus the synchronic studies of complete CULTURES carried out by the anthropologist Claude Lévi-Strauss involved investigation of, for instance, symbolic exchanges which were consecutive rather than simultaneous, so that the element of temporal sequence is still present or implied in such structuralist investigations.

There have been attempts to study literature synchronically (diachronic literary study has, of course, a long pedigree). Roman Jakobson, for example, has argued that the synchronic description of literature concerns itself not just with present-day literary production, but also with that part of the literary tradition which has either remained vital or has been revived (1960, 352). Gérard Genette, taking up this suggestion from Jakobson, suggests that the structural history of literature 'is simply the placing in diachronic perspective of these successive synchronic tables' (1982, 21). This of course leaves unanswered (or unacknowledged) the question of whether there are isolable laws of transformation governing the replacement of one synchronic table by its successor, as to whether, in other words, historical development itself is capable of being analysed in terms of cause and effect. (There is also the question of the interaction between different, co-temporal structures, which may only be observable historically.) The concept of 'structural history', indeed, implies that the fundamental reality is that of the synchronic STRUCTURE, and that history is a secondary reality formed by successive structures.

The NEW CRITICAL treatment of the literary work as object rather than process can be said to resemble synchronic study.

Diacritical Originally an adjective which conveyed the idea of distinguishing or conferring distinction: by extension diacritical marks are those signs added to letters to give them distinction – the cedilla which changes c to ç for instance. By process of association the term has assumed a noun form within the field of Linguistics to signify diacritical marks.

Within STRUCTURALIST usage *diacritical* is granted a slightly different, more general adjectival meaning: to say that language is a diacritical system is to claim that it is a system constituted by significant DIFFERENCES.

Dialect See IDIOLECT

Dialectics From a Greek word meaning debate or argument, dialectics originally referred to the process of revealing the truth by argument or debate – especially when this involved revealing contradictions in one's opponent's arguments. More recently the term has been used to describe (i) a philosophical outlook which considers all things to exist in dynamic relationships and to be possessed of internal tensions and contradictions, and (ii) a method of investigating reality which stresses the dynamic interconnections of things in the world and of their internal tensions and contradictions.

The term is particularly (but not exclusively) associated with MARXISM, especially in the term *dialectical materialism* – a term coined by Plekhanov in 1894 to describe Marx's philosophy. Jorge Larrain points out that although Lenin confidently affirmed that Marx used this term many times to describe his world outlook, neither Karl Marx nor Friedrich Engels actually used precisely this phrase, although both frequently use the term dialectics (1986, 32–3). In his *Dialectics of Nature*, Engels argues that the laws of dialectics are abstracted from the history of nature and human society, and that these laws 'are nothing but the most general laws of these two aspects of historical development, as well as of thought itself' (1964, 63). According to Engels, these laws can be reduced 'in the main' to three:

The law of the transformation of quantity into quality and vice versa;
The law of the interpenetration of opposites;
The law of the negation of the negation. (1964, 63)

Engels claims that Hegel developed these laws idealistically, as laws of thought, but that if they are turned around to apply to historical development and thought, they become 'simple and clear as noonday' (1964, 63). From Hegel come the terms *thesis, antithesis* and *synthesis*, which Marxists have subsequently applied to the course of human history, suggesting that this moves according to these stages.

In practice the three laws summarized by Engels are taken by him and by Marxists following him to mean (i) that slow, regular changes ('quantity') lead to sudden, revolutionary changes ('quality'); (ii) that things that seem utterly separate because opposed to each other very often define one another and interpenetrate (for instance, opposing CLASSES in a given society); and (iii) that negation is the factor which separates old from new: an emergent quality negates that which it replaces, and will itself be negated and replaced in the course of time.

There has been considerable argument about whether Marx fully shared Engels's views about dialectics – particularly as to whether Marx believed that the laws of dialectics applied to the world as such, or merely to a method of investigating this world (the arguments are summarized in Larrain: 1986, 32–8).

The influence of these ideas on the study of literature can be traced in a number of directions. The Marxist refusal to consider the individual WORK of literature in isolation is related to the view that all things in the world can be understood only in terms of their contradictory and dynamic relationships with the rest of social and historical reality. Views of literary history have also been influenced by dialectical views of larger historical change – especially with regard to 'revolutions' such as Romanticism and MODERNISM.

It might seem that a resemblance exists between Marxist views concerning the internal dialectics of things and the NEW CRITICAL emphasis on the literary work's inner tensions and ambiguities. However, the New Critics were not generally sympathetic to Marxism, and in the matter of the work of art's autonomy were directly opposed to Marxist ideas, and so it is unlikely that any direct influence can be claimed here. Marxist critics such as Georg Lukács also stressed the need for the literary work (especially the novel) to reflect the dialectical tensions of society itself, at the level both of form and of content.

Dialogic Along with *dialogue, dialogical,* and *dialogism,* dialogic owes its current technical use to the influence that the writings of Mikhail Bakhtin have had in the West following their translation into English during the 1970s and 1980s. Bakhtin wrote under difficult conditions in the Soviet Union of the 1920s and, especially, the 1930s (his first published work was in 1919 and he was still writing at the time of his death in 1975). As a result of these difficult circumstances it has been claimed (and disputed) that some of his writings were published under the names of his friends V. N. Vološinov and P. N. Medvedev. In what follows I shall attribute opinions to the person whose name was associated with them on initial publication.

Dialogue in its everyday usage means verbal interchange between individuals, especially as represented in literary writing. Vološinov (1986) builds upon this familiar usage in a number of ways. First, he suggests that verbal *interaction* is the fundamental reality of language: both in the history of the individual and also in the history of the human species, language is born not within the isolated human being, but in the interaction between two or more human beings. The recent development of PRAGMATICS – both in Linguistics and Literary Studies – may make this obvious to the present-day reader, but highly influential theories of language have obscured this truth. Second, however, Bakhtin was increasingly to argue that even in DISCOURSE or UTTERANCE which was not overtly interactive, dialogue was to be found. Because all utterances involve the, as it were, 'importing' and naturalization of the speech of others, all utterances include inner tensions, collaborations, negotiations which are comparable to the process of dialogue (in its everyday sense). For Bakhtin, words were not neutral; apart from neologisms (of which he was, not surprisingly, rather fond) they were all second-hand and had belonged to other people, and in incorporating them into his or her own usage the individual had to engage in dialogue with that other person, struggle to wrest possession of them from their previous owner(s). Discussing language, Bakhtin habitually makes use of terms such as 'saturated', 'contaminated', 'impregnated'; a word for Bakhtin is like a garment passed from individual to individual which cannot have the smell of previous owners washed out of it. Spoken or written utterances are like PALIMPSESTS: scratch them a little and hidden meanings come to light, meanings which are very often at odds with those apparent on the surface.

In the 1970s and 1980s Bakhtin's ideas caught the attention of various Western literary critics committed to opposing a view of literature as consisting primarily of individual expression, and engaged in rejecting a view of the AUTHOR as determining origin of and authority concerning the TEXT – or even PRESENCE in the WORK. For such critics even the purest lyric poem is not lonely voice but cacophony of voices, a veritable HETEROGLOSSIA.

Thus the Bakhtinian view of the dialogic connects with the topics of INTER-TEXTUALITY and transtextuality, and with Harold Bloom's concept of the anxiety of influence (see the entry for REVISIONISM). For in using a word or an expression, an author will engage in some sort of dialogue with the text in which he or she first encountered this word, or the text in which the word has had a particular meaning embossed upon it.

It also connects with psychoanalytic theories of the UNCONSCIOUS and with Marxist theories concerning the manner in which HEGEMONY is asserted. Get someone to speak your words, and they may well end up by thinking your thoughts. There are clearly also links to be made here with FEMINIST concerns about SEXIST language.

Bakhtin's view of dialogue as conflictual rather than purely collaborative stands in sharp contrast to certain other conceptions of the term and the activity. We can for example set the following comment from Maurice Merleau-Ponty against Bakhtin's position:

> In the experience of dialogue, there is constituted between the other person and myself a common ground; my thought and his are interwoven into a single fabric, my words and those of my interlocutor are called forth by the state of the discussion, and they are inserted into a shared operation of which neither of us is the creator. We have here a dual being, where the other is for me no longer a mere bit of behaviour in my transcendental field, nor I in his; we are collaborators for each other in consummate reciprocity. Our perspectives merge into each other, and we co-exist through a common world. (1962, 354)

There are both collaborative and shared elements in Bakhtin's conception of dialogue, but there is also a sense of struggle which is absent from Merleau-Ponty's position. The opposite of dialogue for Bakhtin is, logically, *monologue*. According to him,

> Ultimately, *monologism* denies that there exists outside of it another consciousness, with the same rights, and capable of responding on an equal footing, another and equal *I (thou)*. ... The monologue is accomplished and deaf to the other's response; it does not await it and does not grant it any *decisive* force. (Quoted in Todorov: 1984, 107)

Polyglossia is Bakhtin's term for the simultaneous existence of two national languages within a single CULTURAL system; in contrast, *monoglossia* indicates that a culture contains but one national language.

Interest in Bakhtin has sent a number of commentators back to the work of the German Hans-Georg Gadamer, in whose major work *Truth and Method* the concept of dialogue also looms large. Gadamer distinguishes between AUTHENTIC and inauthentic conversation and suggests that a reader's encounter with a text is like authentic conversation – open, two-sided, unegocentric (1989, 385).

See also INTERIOR DIALOGUE.

Dialogue See DIALOGIC

Diaspora literature The word *diaspora* comes from a Greek word meaning dispersal, and was originally applied to the condition of the Jewish people living outside Palestine. With the development of POSTCOLONIALIST theory the term has been extended to cover a range of different CULTURAL and ethnic groups held together by shared cultural or religious commitments and having some sense of exile from a place or state of origin and belonging. Within Cultural Studies, Peter Brooker reports that recent writings 'have proposed that the term be "decoupled" from an actual or desired homeland and understood instead, in more post-structuralist vein, to describe a dynamic network of communities without the stabilizing allusion to an original homeland or essential identity' (1999, 71; Brooker attributes this position to writings by Stuart Hall – see Hall: 1990).

Diegesis and mimesis Both of these terms are to be found in the third book of Plato's *Republic*, in which Socrates uses them to distinguish between two ways of presenting speech. For Socrates, diegesis stands for those cases where the poet himself is the speaker and does not wish to suggest otherwise, and mimesis stands for those cases in which the poet attempts to create the illusion that it is not he who is speaking. Thus a speech spoken by a CHARACTER in the play would represent mimesis, whereas if the writer spoke 'as him or herself' about characters, we would have a case of diegesis. Monika Fludernik has stressed that these terms must be understood in relation to the artistic GENRES and practices from which they emerged and to which they were designed to apply.

> When Plato opposes narration (diegesis) to mimesis (imitation), he does so within a generic contrast of drama (all imitation) versus the dithyramb (all diegesis) and the epic (mixed), and the diegesis is here not simply 'narrative', but very explicitly the author's direct voice. For Plato, of course, does not distinguish between a narrator and the author, which is the only way that the narrator of the epic would become identified with the speaker of elegiac verse. In narrative theory Plato's distinctions have been forgotten, with the result that diegesis has come to signify narration, *per se*, that is to say the *narrator's* rendering of the story in everything except clearly defined discourse not attributable to this enunciator, i.e. the characters' directly quoted speech and thought acts. This schema makes it very difficult to conceptualize action (or, for that matter, description). (1993, 28)

Fludernik illustrates this distinction by means of a diagram taken from Irene de Jong (1989), and explains that

Narrative is here considered 'pure' or 'simple' (*haplè*), i.e. 'single-voiced' speaking, whereas in mimetic narration the narrator impersonates one of the characters, and the discourse therefore becomes double-voiced, dual or double-levelled. (1993, 30)

	diegesis haplè	*mimesis*
the poet speaks as	himself	one of the characters
in the	parts between the speeches	speeches

Aristotle extended use of the term mimesis in his *Poetics* to include not just speech but also imitative actions, and as these could of course be rendered in indirect speech this extension had the effect of blunting Plato's rather sharper distinction.

In his Appendix to Aristotle's *Poetics*, D. W. Lucas (1968) notes that it is clear that not just poetry, painting, sculpture and music are forms of mimesis for both Plato and Aristotle, but so too is dancing. Lucas further adds that the word 'mimesis' has an extraordinary breadth of meaning which makes it difficult to discover just what the Greeks had in mind when they used it to describe what poet and artist do, and he suggests that to translate it we may at different times need to use words such as 'imitate', 'indicate', 'suggest' and 'express', although all of these words are related to human action ('praxis').

Since Aristotle, both terms have been incorporated into different systems of terminology, and their original, clear-cut meanings have been extended into new usages and more complex (and often contradictory and confusing) distinctions. The term 'mimesis' has been pressed into service to describe the more general capacity of literature to imitate reality, and has on occasions accumulated a somewhat polemical edge as a result of its use by those wishing to establish imitation as central or essential to art – by MARXIST critics intent on stressing that literature and art 'reflect' extra-literary reality, for example.

With the growth of modern NARRATIVE theory in recent years, diegesis in particular has been given something of a new lease of life. A number of theorists have equated diegesis and mimesis with telling and showing, a distinction which can be traced back to Henry James, and which was both adopted and simplified by Percy Lubbock. This actually makes rather a large difference in the meaning of diegesis. For in the case of almost any classic novel, what the READER learns he or she acquires through a *telling*, a *narration*, rather than as a result of a PERFORMANCE as in a play. One could thus defend referring to the work *in toto* as an example of diegesis, because even the direct speech of characters is *told* to the reader through a narrating. But any reader of the novel will recognize that such passages in the novel, in which dialogue and character interaction give a dramatic effect, cause the reader to forget about the NARRATOR and to feel as if one is witnessing the characters in dramatic interaction. (Note that we have now moved from a concern with the AUTHOR to a concern with the narrator.) From a Jamesian perspective such passages would be categorized as examples of showing rather than telling, so that if diegesis and mimesis are to be treated as equivalent to telling and showing, then clearly *Pride and Prejudice* is not an example of pure diegesis, but includes both diegetic and mimetic elements. Gérard Genette comments:

> no narrative can 'show' or 'imitate' the story it tells. All it can do is tell it in a manner which is detailed, precise, 'alive,' and in that way give more or less the *illusion of mimesis* – which is the only narrative mimesis, for this single and sufficient reason: that narration, oral and written, is a fact of language, and language signifies without imitation. (1980, 164)

Modern narrative theory has introduced another use of these terms, one which is related to those discussed already, but which actually represents a significant change and extension of their meaning. Instead of relating them to telling and showing, it has equated them with PLOT and STORY, such that the diegetic level is the level of the 'story reality' of the events narrated, while the mimetic level is the level of the 'narrator's life and consciousness'. Both Genette and Rimmon-Kenan, for example, use *diegesis* as 'roughly equivalent to my "story"' (Rimmon-Kenan: 1983, 47). This extension can lead us into some terminological contradictions. For if diegesis is equivalent to story, then *extradiegetic* must mean 'outside the story', and therefore could refer us to the actual *telling* of the story, the comments from a narrator who is not a member of the world of the story. But this is exactly the opposite of what we started with: for Socrates, we may remember, diegesis referred to those cases where the poet himself is the speaker, roughly what we have just termed *extradiegetic*! In narrative theorists such as Shlomith Rimmon-Kenan and Gérard Genette then, an extradiegetic narrator is a narrator who, like the narrator of *Pride and Prejudice*, exists on a different narrative level from the level of the events narrated or the story, whilst an intra-diegetic narrator is one who is presented as existing on the same level of reality as the characters in the story he or she tells: Esther Summerson in Charles Dickens's *Bleak House*, for example. Non-personified narrators introduce an additional problem here, but it is still possible to refer to 'extradiegetic narrative' even in these cases, for the narrative 'knows' things which the characters do not and could not.

To add to the confusion (as he himself admits), in his *Narrative Discourse* Gérard Genette uses the term *metadiegetic* to describe 'the universe of the second narrative', and the term *metanarrative* to refer to 'a narrative within the narrative' (1980, 228n). This is confusing because a METALANGUAGE is a language about a language – in other words, a 'framing' language and not a 'FRAMED' one. For this reason Genette's terminology has not caught on (as can be confirmed by reference to François Lyotard's definition of the postmodern as 'incredulity towards metanarratives', by which he means narratives *about* and not *within* other narratives: see the entry for MODERNISM AND POSTMODERNISM). Indeed, Genette himself is not consistent, and in essays collected in his *Figures of Literary Discourse* he uses a different terminology: he defines a *metalanguage* here as a 'discourse upon a discourse' (he defines criticism as a metalanguage) and a metaliterature as 'a literature of which literature itself is the imposed object' (1982, 3–4). Rimmon-Kenan's alternative term for the level of the EMBEDDED narrative – *hypodiegetic* – avoids these confusions (1983, 92).

A number of recent narrative theorists have suggested that, rather than considering mimesis and diegesis as two mutually exclusive categories, it is more productive to think of them as representing a continuum with minimal narrator colouring at one end and maximal narrator colouring at the other. (For *coloured narrative*, see the entry for FREE INDIRECT DISCOURSE.)

Monika Fludernik, however, has proposed a different use of these terms, such that diegesis 'as invention or projection of a FICTIONAL world...spans all "narrative" genres, all genres that tell a story: drama, fiction, film, epic, jokes', while at the same time those genres in which mimesis relies on the medium of language need to be distinguished from drama and film, 'where the medium by means of which mimesis is achieved is not narration, i.e. a uniformly linguistic act, but a re-enactment of the plot in which the visual presentation dominates' (1993, 29). Her approach to mimesis bases itself upon mimetic *effect*, an effect which may combine a range of quite disparate aspects:

> [F]aithfulness to a putative 'original' reproductiveness; narrative empathy ('directness' as a renunciation of narratorial, evaluative intrusion); the evocation of an *effet de réel*; and particularity, or... 'distinctiveness', creating an effect of a 'full' character whose individuality shows through his or her linguistic performance, idiosyncrasies of style and idiom as well as manners or gestures. (1993, 314)

The terms *homodiegetic* and *heterodiegetic*, coined by Gérard Genette, introduce additional complications. Genette uses these terms to distinguish different types of ANALEPSIS or flashback: whereas a homodiegetic analepsis provides information about the same character, or sequence of events or milieu that has been the concern of the text up to this point, a heterodiegetic analepsis refers back to some character, sequence of events, or milieu *different from* that/those that have been the concern of the preceding text. 'We now have seen John behave so strangely, that some information about his experiences in his childhood needs to be provided', prepares us for a homodiegetic analepsis; 'It is now time to travel back thirty years to meet a character who has not so far appeared in these pages', prepares us for a heterodiegetic analepsis. Both can, however, be used more generally, along with a range of cognate terms. A useful listing of some of these cognate terms can be found in the following comment by Robert Burden about the narratives of the frame narrator and Marlow in *Heart of Darkness*:

> the first [frame] narrator is *extra-diegetic* but also *homo-diegetic* (located outside the main story as narrator, while participating in it as narratee). Marlow...is... *intra-diegetic* and also *auto-diegetic* (located in the main story as narrator while participating in it as its central character or protagonist). (1991, 54)

The terminology here clearly has its function, but is possibly on the edge of being confusing rather than illuminating (as the presence of the explanatory notes in parentheses perhaps acknowledges).

See also INTERTEXTUALITY; DISCOURSE; DOUBLE-VOICED; PALIMPSEST TEXT.

Différance A portmanteau term coined by Jacques Derrida, bringing together (in its French original) the senses of DIFFERENCE and deferment. For Derrida différance is the opposite of and alternative to LOGOCENTRISM; while logocentrism posits the existence of fixed MEANINGS guaranteed by an extra-systemic PRESENCE or origin, différance sees meaning as permanently deferred, always subject to and produced by its difference from other meanings and thus volatile and unstable. Meaning is always relational, never self-present or self-constituted. Derrida uses and discusses the term throughout his writing, but perhaps the most accessible of his discussions is in *Positions* (1981b, 26ff), in which he identifies three main meanings for the term:

> *First, différance* refers to the (active *and* passive) movement that consists in deferring by means of delay, delegation, reprieve, referral, detour, postponement, reserving. ...*Second*, the movement of *différance*, as that which produces different things, that which differentiates, is the common root of all oppositional concepts that mark our language, such as, to take only a few examples, sensible/intelligent, intuition/signification, nature/culture, etc. . . . *Third, différance* is also the production, if it can still be put this way, of these differences, of the diacriticity that the linguistics generated by Saussure, and all the structural sciences modeled upon it, have recalled is the condition for any signification and any structure. ...From this point of view, the concept of *différance* is neither simply structuralist, nor simply geneticist, such an alternative itself being an 'effect' of *différance*. (1981b, 8–9)

Derrida has suggested a number of alternative terms for différance, including (in *Positions*) gram.

It should be apparent from what has been said that the attempt to provide a neat, glossary definition of this term raises certain logical problems. For if one accepts Derrida's argument then the meaning of différance, like that of any other term, is deferred and subject to difference, then there is no firm or fixed presence that can guarantee or underwrite the meaning of the term. If there were, then the theory on which the term depends would be in error.

This has not prevented the writers of many textbooks concerned with DECONSTRUCTION and with the work of Derrida from providing unproblematic and unproblematized glosses on the meaning of différance, however. Of such attempts we can remark, as Antonio comments of Gonzalo's description of his ideal state in Shakespeare's *The Tempest*, a state which will have no sovereignty but of which Gonzalo will be king, 'The latter end of his commonwealth forgets the beginning.' For example, Alan Bass, the English translator of Derrida's *Writing and Difference*, in his Introduction to the volume, states that the meanings of the term are 'too multiple to be explained here fully' (Derrida: 1978a, xvi). This certainly implies a logocentric view of the meanings of a term as in some sense finite and belonging to the term rather than themselves subject to the play of différance.

Difference In an essay on the varied meanings attributed to this term within FEMINIST theory alone, Michèle Barrett expresses surprise at 'what can be fitted into this capacious hold-all of a concept', and admits to a lack of clarity concerning the term's meaning within different contexts (1989, 38). If we seek to explain the rise to prominence of the term in the last couple of decades then the best place to start is with Ferdinand de Saussure's *Course in General Linguistics*. Absolutely fundamental to Saussure's approach is the view that language works as a system of differences – that, as he puts it, 'in a language-state everything is based on relations' (1974, 122). He points out, for example, that the modern French *mouton* and the English *sheep* have the same signification but not the same value, because the single French word is roughly equivalent to *two* English ones: *sheep* and *mutton*. Thus the value of *sheep* is partly conditioned by its being *not-mutton* – by being *different* from *mutton*.

Saussure adds that 'everything said about words applies to any term of language, e.g. to grammatical entities' (1974, 116). It is certainly true of the phonemic system, where it is not necessary that all speakers of a language produce identically sounding phonemes, but that the same set of phonemically significant *differences* between sounds can be recognized. On the syntactical level, Saussure draws attention to the importance of SYNTAGMATIC and PARADIGMATIC choices, thus providing two key axes of meaning-generating difference in the syntax of the sentence.

Given the significance of Saussure's work for the development of important theoretical movements such as STRUCTURALISM, the idea that it is difference rather than identity or PRESENCE that is important has won widespread acceptance in a range of theoretical fields. Jacques Derrida's coinage DIFFÉRANCE is a development of a Saussurean theme – even though one which deconstructs its own parent. The idea that where signification is concerned, what something *is* is dependent upon what it *is not*, that meaning is generated at least in part by a difference from what is *not meant*, has clear points of contact with theories of determinate ABSENCE in the INTERPRETATION of complex TEXTS – including literary ones. MEANING in literary and CULTURAL texts is in part (those who believe that systems of signification are closed would say wholly) generated by paradigmatic exclusions, by a difference from the not-meant. A smart three-piece suit has significance at least in part because of what it is not, as a result of its displayed difference from other possible styles of dress – just as sheep is sheep partly by virtue of being not-mutton.

Jonathan Culler suggests one way in which some of these insights can be applied to literature:

> If in language there are only differences with no positive terms, it is in literature that we have least cause to arrest the play of differences by calling upon a determinate communicative intention to serve as the truth or origin of the sign. We say instead that a poem can mean many things. (1975, 133)

Michèle Barrett's essay, mentioned at the start of this entry, provides some representative examples of the appropriation and development of this term within feminist theory. Barrett isolates three main feminist usages of the concept of difference: (i) the 'sexual difference' position, seen for example in psychoanalytic discussion which invokes an ESSENTIALIST conception of GENDER identity and gendered subjectivity, and which explicitly refuses the sex/gender distinction; (ii) a more Saussurean view of meaning as positional or relational which, in the form of a POST-STRUCTURALIST and anti-MARXIST critique of totality, sees gender, race and CLASS as SITES of difference (rather than, as Barrett points out, sites of the operation of power), and which DECONSTRUCTS the idea of gendered subjectivity; and (iii) a more diffuse usage which stresses plurality and diversity within, say, feminism. Barrett suggests that these different usages may not be reconcilable, and that the use of the same word to cover all three may therefore be unwise.

Différend Following Jean-François Lyotard's usage, the impossibility of translating from one mode of DISCOURSE to another; the autonomy of discourses. In E. Ann Kaplan's words, the '*différend* signals the desire to "know" the Other *and* its impossibility' (1997, 17). The concept is representative of a modern or – more correctly, a POSTMODERN – abandonment of monism and embracing of a universe of multiple realities which are hermetically sealed from one another. At the heart of such solipsism lies a paradox: if it is impossible for us to 'know' the OTHER, then how do we know of it? The Lyotardian rejection of GRAND NARRATIVES is thus incomplete, as to talk of those discourses or NARRATIVES to which we do not have access through a master discourse or metanarrative is, at one and the same time, to engage in a master discourse or metanarrative. Were discourses really to be separated from one another by impenetrable barriers, then the universe of discourses would be like the assemblage of personalities in an individual suffering from absolute multiple personality, in which each personality is locked away from the penetrating GAZE of each other one. In actual fact, cases of multiple personality typically involve at least one meta-personality which has access to all the sub- or dissociated personalities, and it seems logically impossible to claim that there are discourses which are locked away from our scrutiny. Were this the case, we would not have any access to them and thus would not know that we had no access to them. There is, of course, no logical problem in claiming that there may be discourses to which we have no access.

Lyotard's solipsism owes something to Wittgenstein (Lyotard revealingly uses the term 'language games' in *The Postmodern Condition* [1984, 40]), but it is representative of a marked tendency in modern theoretical writing to reject relations of cause-and-effect, hierarchies of influence, and the possibility of relating discourses and ranking their chains of influence and determination. See my (hostile) discussion in Hawthorn: 1996, 19–47.

Digital and analogic communication The distinction between digital and analogic communication is illustrated by Paul Watzlawick *et al.* through reference to the difference between the basic modes of operation of the central nervous system and of the humoral system. In the central nervous system

> the functional units (neurons) receive so-called quantal packages of information through connecting elements (synapses). Upon arrival at the synapses these 'packages' produce excitatory or inhibitory postsynaptic potentials that are summed up by the neuron and either cause or inhibit its firing. (1968, 60)

Thus the central nervous system works by means of the *digitalization* of information via a mass of BINARY possibilities: a neuron either fires or it does not: there are no shades of grey. The humoral system, in contrast, works in a completely different manner, by means of the release of discrete quantities of particular substances into the bloodstream. Releasing either more or less of a particular substance can lead to a significantly different effect. Watzlawick *et al.* point out that these two systems 'complement and are contingent upon each other'.

A more familiar example of the same distinction would be that between the two sorts of loudness indicator on a tape recorder. The traditional moving-needle indicator is an analogue system: each slight variation in noise produces a comparable variation in the position of the needle. In contrast, the LED display relies upon a digital system, upon lights which either fire or do not fire. Modern computer systems are based upon the digitalization of information.

Theories dependent upon the digitalization of information and binary distinction have assumed a considerable importance in Linguistics in recent years. In phonetic systems, for example, research may reveal that different members of a language community may actually produce rather different sounds to represent a particular phonetic unit, but so long as these sounds produce recognizable *oppositions* or binary distinctions, the system works. The Linguistics of Ferdinand de Saussure relies heavily upon the recognition of DIFFERENCES between binary oppositions. In his essay 'Rhetoric of the Image', Roland Barthes notes that in Linguistics, 'communication by analogy', 'from the "language" of bees to the "language" of gesture', is denied the status of a true language, because 'such communications are not doubly articulated, i.e., definitively based on a combinatory system of digital units, as phonemes are' (1991, 21).

It is also Roland Barthes to whom we are indebted for the term *analgon*, which he uses to describe the relation between photograph and that which it depicts. In his essay 'The Photographic Message', Barthes writes:

> ... of course, the image is not the reality, but at least it is its perfect *analgon*, and it is just this analogical perfection which, to common sense, defines the photograph. Here appears the particular status of the photographic image: *it is a message without a code*; a proposition from which we must immediately extract an important corollary: the photographic message is a continuous message.
>
> Are there other messages without a code? At first glance, yes: specifically, all analogical reproductions of reality; drawings, paintings, movies, theater performances. But, as a matter of fact, each of these messages develops in an immediate and evident fashion, beyond the analogical content itself (scene, object, landscape), a supplementary message which is what we commonly call the *style* of the reproduction; here we are concerned with a second meaning... (1991, 5)

It is perhaps worth asking to what extent the filming of a scene in a FICTIONAL film is a 'reproduction of reality'; the actors and scenery are of course real in one sense, but not quite in the same way that a holiday snap is an analogical reproduction of that which is depicted.

The list given by Barthes would seem to exclude literature and literary criticism, although not theatrical PERFORMANCE. But Jonathan Culler has pointed out that the linguistic model has encouraged STRUCTURALISTS to think in binary terms and to search for FUNCTIONAL oppositions in the material they are studying (1975, 14), and this has had a direct influence upon such fields of knowledge as NARRATIVE and literary criticism.

It has, for example, created an awareness that the READER's perception of a set of binary oppositions may play a necessary function in the READING of a WORK of literature,

85

alongside the operation of more subtle, 'analogic' responses. This is true at the macro-level of GENRE and generic classification (for example, the opposition between tragedy and comedy sets up certain either/or expectations which exert a strong influence on our literary responses), and also at micro-levels within particular TEXTS. An example here would be Claude Bremond's narrative theory in which each function allows for two possibilities: ACTUALIZATION or non-actualization.

Certainly in FORMULAIC literature response seems to be conditioned by the operation of simple binary distinctions: 'If this blonde, shy girl is the heroine, then this dark, self-confident girl must be the attractive but treacherous rival.'

Diglossia See HETEROGLOSSIA

Directives See SPEECH ACT THEORY

Disavowal A term from Freudian PSYCHOANALYSIS referring to the way in which a person under analysis will simultaneously affirm and deny something – or will affirm something *by* denying it. According to Sue Thornham, '[i]t was *disavowal* which for Christian Metz characterized the processes of cinematic "belief" (the viewer both recognizes and disavows the absence which characterizes the projected images of the cinema screen, just as the fetishist both affirms and denies the female phallus)' (1997, 125).
See also REPRESSION.

Discourse This word has experienced a relatively sudden rush of fashionability in the past couple of decades in a number of different academic and intellectual fields. Unfortunately, however, the term's popularity in a range of different academic disciplines means that frustrating differences of usage can be encountered. Martin Jay describes discourse as 'one of the most loosely used terms of our time', adding that the term 'has been employed in a host of different contexts, from the communicative rationalism of a Jürgen Habermas to the archaeology of a Foucault; from the computerized Althusserianism of a Michel Pêchaux to the sociolinguistics of a Malcolm Coulthard; from the textual analysis of a Zelig Harris to the ethnomethodology of a Harvey Sacks' (1993, 15). But Jay sees a need to retain the term in his own account of, as the title of his book has it, 'the denigration of vision in twentieth-century French thought':

> Despite these contrary and shifting usages, discourse remains the best term to denote the level on which the object of this enquiry is located, that being a corpus of more or less loosely interwoven arguments, metaphors, assertions, and prejudices that cohere more associatively than logically in any strict sense of the term. Discourse in this usage is explicitly derived from the Latin *discurrere*, which means a running around in all directions. The antiocularcentric discourse that I hope to examine is precisely that: an often unsystematic, sometimes internally contradictory texture of statements, associations, and metaphors that never fully cohere in a rigorous way. (1993, 16; *ocularcentric* = privileging, or based upon, vision)

In Linguistics a renewed reliance upon the term is related to the growth in importance of PRAGMATICS; discourse is language in use, not language as an abstract system. (According to the *OED*, discourse as noun can mean [sense 4] 'Communication of thought by speech', and Samuel Johnson's definition is quoted: 'Mutual intercourse of language.' Interestingly, the use of the noun to mean 'talk' or 'conversation' is described as archaic.) But even within Linguistics there are varieties of meaning. Michael Stubbs comments on the use of the terms TEXT and discourse, and states that this is often ambiguous and confusing. He suggests that the latter term often implies greater length than does the former, and that discourse may or may not imply interaction (1983, 9). Thus if we take an academic seminar, for some linguisticians the whole process of verbal interaction would constitute a discourse, whereas for others an extended statement by one participant would qualify as a discourse. Yet others would be prepared to accept even short statements by individuals as discourses. Moreover, for some linguisticians discourse is uncountable, for others it is not, and for yet others it appears to be countable at some times but not at others. If discourse *is* countable, the next problem is to decide what constitute(s) the defining borders of a single discourse: Michael Stubbs notes that the unity of a particular discourse can be defined in either STRUCTURAL, SEMANTIC or FUNCTIONAL ways (1983, 9). *Critical discourse analysis* is a term used within Linguistics to denote a non-FORMALIST analysis of written or spoken texts which pays attention to issues of social and cultural context.

Gerald Prince isolates two main meanings for the term within NARRATIVE theory: first, the expression plane of a narrative rather than its content plane, the narrating rather than the narrated. Second, following Benveniste, *discourse* is distinguished from *story* (*discours* and *histoire* in the original French) because the former evokes a link between 'a state or event and the situation in which that state or event is linguistically evoked' (Prince: 1988a, 21). Contrast 'John's wife was dead' (story) with 'He told her that John's wife was dead' (discourse). (Compare the distinction between *énonciation* and *énoncé* in the entry for ENUNCIATION.) Some writers on narrative in English prefer to retain *discours* in untranslated form when using the term in Benveniste's sense. Onega and Landa's definition – also from within narrative theory or NARRATOLOGY – is simpler; for them discourse is 'the use of language for communicative purposes in specific contextual and generic situations, called *discourse situations*' (1996, 8). I suspect that this is so broad as to be unhelpful.

The work of Michel Foucault has been highly influential across a number of disciplines so far as the term discourse is concerned. For Foucault discourses are 'large groups of statements' – rule-governed language terrains defined by what Foucault refers to as 'strategic possibilities' (1972, 37), comparable to a limited extent to one possible usage of the term REGISTER in Linguistics. Thus for Foucault, at a given moment in the history of, say, France, there will be a particular discourse of medicine: a set of rules and CONVENTIONS and SYSTEMS of MEDIATION and transposition which govern the way illness and treatment are talked about – when, where, and by whom. Clearly we meet a similar problem here to that mentioned in a different context above: how does one define the boundaries of a particular discourse?

According to Foucault

[w]henever one can describe, between a number of statements, such a system of dispersion, whenever, between objects, types of statement, concepts, or thematic choices, one can define a regularity (and order, correlations, positions and functionings, transformations), we will say, for the sake of convenience, that we are dealing with a *discursive formation* . . . (1972, 38)

All societies, following Foucault, have procedures whereby the production of discourses is controlled, selected, organized and redistributed, and the purpose of these processes of discourse control is to ward off 'powers and dangers' (1981, 52). These procedures govern, variously, what Foucault terms *discursive practices*, *discursive objects*, and *discursive strategies*, such that in all discourses *discursive regularities* can be observed. As Paul A. Bové puts it in his discussion of Foucault's use of the term, discourse 'makes possible disciplines and institutions which, in turn, sustain and distribute those discourses' (Lentricchia and McLaughlin: 1990, 57).

It is not just disciplines and institutions which are enabled by discourse, according to Foucault; his work also suggests that rather than considering discourses as secondary to the brute facts of the world, we should move to seeing such brute facts as in some way produced or enabled by discourses. In *The Archaeology of Knowledge* Foucault argues that what he wishes to do is to

substitute for the enigmatic treasure of 'things' anterior to discourse, the regular formation of objects that emerge only in discourse. To define these *objects* without reference to the *ground*, the *foundation of things*, but by relating them to the body of rules that enable them to form as objects of a discourse and thus constitute the conditions of their historical appearance. To write a history of discursive objects that does not plunge them into the common depth of a primal soil, but deploys the nexus of regularities that govern their dispersion. (1972, 47–8)

If we recall Edward Said's description of ORIENTALISM as the means by which European culture was able to 'manage – and even produce – the Orient politically, sociologically, militarily, ideologically, scientifically, and imaginatively' (1979, 3), then we can, I think, perceive the Foucauldian element within his theorizing.

But Foucault goes further: discourse does not just produce disciplines and institutions and discursive objects – it also produces itself: '[suppose that] we no longer relate discourse to the primary ground of experience, not to the *a priori* authority of knowledge; but that we seek the rules of its formation in discourse itself' (1972, 79).

Lynda Nead argues that Foucault is not consistent in his use of the term 'discourse', and that consequently there is some uncertainty about its precise meaning even as it is used in a single work of his (she cites *The History of Sexuality*) (1988, 4). In *The Archaeology of Knowledge* Foucault is quite open about the flexibility of the term as he uses it.

[I]nstead of gradually reducing the rather fluctuating meaning of the word 'discourse', I believe that I have in fact added to its meanings: treating it sometimes as the general domain of all statements, sometimes as an individualizable group of statements, and sometimes as a regulated practice that allows for a certain number of statements; and have I not allowed this same word 'discourse', which should have served as a boundary around the term 'statement', to vary as I shifted my analysis or its point of application, as the statement itself faded from view? (1972, 80)

Later on in *The Archaeology of Knowledge* Foucault makes another attempt at definition.

[B]y discourse, then, I meant that which was produced (perhaps all that was produced) by the groups of signs. But I also meant a group of acts of formulation, a series of sentences or propositions. Lastly – and it is this meaning that was finally used (together with the first, which served in a provisional capacity) – discourse is constituted by a group of sequences of signs, in so far as they are statements, that is, in so far as they can be assigned particular modalities of existence. And if I succeed in showing, as I shall try to do shortly, that the law of such a series is precisely what I have so far called a *discursive formation*, if I succeed in showing that this discursive formation really is the principle of dispersion and redistribution, not of formulations, not of sentences, not of propositions, but of statements (in the sense in which I have used this word), the term discourse can be defined as the group of statements that belong to a single system of formation; thus I shall be able to speak of clinical discourse, economic discourse, the discourse of natural history, psychiatric discourse. (1972, 107–8)

Discursive here represents the adjective form of discourse, not the adjective meaning 'round-about, meandering'. (John Frow has proposed the term *universe of discourse* as an alternative to discursive FORMATION. He gives as examples of universes of discourse 'the religious, scientific, pragmatic, technical everyday, literary, legal, philosophical, magical, and so on', and distinguishes these from *genres of discourse*, which, after Vološinov, he defines as 'normatively structured clusters of formal, contextual, and thematic features, "ways of speaking" in a particular situation' [1986, 67].)

The work of Mikhail Bakhtin gives us yet further examples of the pressing of the word *discourse* into new services. According to the glossary provided in Bakhtin: 1981, *discourse* is used to translate the Russian word *slovo*, which can mean either an individual word, or a method of using words that presumes a type of authority (1981, 427). This is quite close to the usage argued for by Foucault, and this similarity can also be seen in some cognate terms used by Bakhtin. Thus *authoritative discourse* is the privileged language that 'approaches us from without; it is distanced, taboo, and permits no play with its framing context' (1981, 424). In contrast, *internally persuasive discourse* is discourse which uses one's own words, which does not present itself as 'other', as the representative of an alien power. *Ennobled discourse* is discourse which has been made more 'literary' and elevated, less accessible. Tzvetan Todorov gives a number of brief quotations from Bakhtin which show, however, that even his use of the term (or its Russian near-equivalent) has its variations: 'Discourse, that is language in its concrete and living totality'; '*discourse*, that is language as a concrete total phenomenon'; '*discourse*, that is utterance (*vyskazyvanie*)' (Todorov: 1984, 25). In his *Problems of Dostoevsky's Poetics*, Bakhtin refers to '*discourse*, that is, language in its concrete living totality, and not language as the specific object of linguistics, something arrived at through a completely legitimate and necessary abstraction from various aspects of the concrete life of the word' (Bakhtin: 1984, 181). In the same work, Bakhtin also refers to 'double-voiced discourse', which he claims always arises under conditions of dialogic interaction (1984, 185).

It seems clear that IDEOLOGY, variously defined, is a near neighbour to discourse in both Foucault's and Bakhtin's understanding of the term, and in his own definition Roger Fowler mentions ideology directly:

> 'Discourse' is speech or writing seen from the point of view of the beliefs, values and categories which it embodies; these beliefs (etc.) constitute a way of looking at the world, an organization or representation of experience – 'ideology' in the neutral, non-pejorative sense. Different modes of discourse encode different representations of experience; and the source of these representations is the communicative context within which discourse is embedded. (1990, 54)

If from Fowler's perspective 'beliefs, values and categories' are embodied in discourse, Foucault appears to go further and to suggest that discourses may force these beliefs, values and categories on to others, implying that the rules of particular discourses do not just allow certain things to be said, but impose certain ways of looking upon the world while excluding alternatives. Thus it is not surprising that a MARXIST or quasi-Marxist use of the term has emerged in recent years, one which owes something to some or all of the sources suggested above, but perhaps most to Foucault (who is not, incidentally, a Marxist).

In his article 'The Value of Narrativity in the Representation of Reality', written in 1980/81, Hayden White distinguishes between 'a historical discourse that narrates, on the one side, and a discourse that narrativizes, on the other' (1981, 2–3). According to him the former 'openly adopts a perspective that looks out on the world and reports it', whereas the latter 'feigns to make the world speak itself and speak itself as a *story*' (1981, 3). A narrativizing discourse, moreover, has no narrator; the events are 'chronologically recorded as they appear on the horizon of the story', no one speaks, and the events appear to tell themselves (1981, 3). Monika Fludernik has proposed a meaning for *narrativizing* different from Hayden White's; 'Whereas I use narrativization to describe a reading strategy that naturalizes texts by recourse to narrative schemata, Hayden White uses the term in the sense of storification, a transformation of historical material into narrative shape' (1996, 34).

Not surprisingly, the varied meanings which have accrued to 'discourse' are also active in the term 'discourse analysis'. Robert de Beaugrande (1994) has attempted to gather together some of the varied elements in discourse analysis, suggesting three areas of initial concentration: 'the cross-cultural study of stories and narratives' of the type carried out by Claude Lévi-Strauss, 'the discourse of schooling and education' (such as in the work of Michael Stubbs and others), 'and, with a sociological turn, the organization of conversation' (1994, 207). But as de Beaugrande points out, from the 1970s onwards the picture becomes much more complicated, as 'discourse analysis became a convergence point for a number of trends; "text linguistics" on the European continent; "functional" or "systemic linguistics" in Czechoslovakia, Britain and Australia; "cognitive linguistics," "critical linguistics," "ethnography of communication," "ethnomethodology, and the structuralism, poststructuralism, deconstruction, and feminism emanating from France; along with semiotics and cognitive science, both convergence points in their own right' (1994, 207–8). All human life is truly there so far as discourse analysis today is concerned.

For *monovalent discourse* and *polyvalent discourse* (Todorov), see the entry for REGISTER.

POSTCOLONIALIST theorists have applied the concepts of *master discourse* and *hegemonic discourse* to those ideologically charged ways of looking at and speaking about the world which presuppose and incorporate EUROCENTRIC and racist assumptions. Thus a master discourse is not just the chief among discourses, it is also the discourse of the masters.

See also ARCHAEOLOGY OF KNOWLEDGE; ENUNCIATION; FREE INDIRECT DISCOURSE; GENRE; NEW HISTORICISM AND CULTURAL MATERIALISM; and the discussion of the difference between text and discourse in the entry for TEXT AND WORK. For *double-voiced*, see DIEGESIS AND MIMESIS; DOUBLE-VOICED; PALIMPSEST TEXT.

Discursive practice See DISCOURSE

Disidentification Following Michel Pêchaux, Helen Tiffin uses this term to 'denote a transformation and displacement of the subject position interpellated by a dominant ideology' (Ashcroft *et al.*: 1995, 98 n2).
See also IDEOLOGY; INTERPELLATION.

Disnarrated Those EVENTS which never happened but which are nonetheless narrated, normally as if they *had* happened. See Prince (1988b).

Displacement Within Linguistics, displacement refers to the human ability to refer to things removed from the utterer's immediate situation, either in time or in space. This ability seems to distinguish human beings from other living creatures, and it is language-dependent: it is human language which allows us this unparalleled freedom to refer beyond our geographical, social, CULTURAL or historical here-and-now. Thus a question such as 'Do you remember the nice time we had on holiday in Bulgaria last year?' may appear trivial, but it exemplifies a resource not available in any significant way to other species. Bees may be able to signal the presence and exact location of nectar to other bees when they return to the hive, but only within strict limits: experiments have demonstrated that they cannot, for example, accurately report the location of nectar placed at the top of a mast. (Compare Marx's comment on the difference between the worst of architects and the best of bees, cited in the entry on BASE AND SUPERSTRUCTURE.)

Human beings, in contrast, can talk about the possibility of finding gold on Mars – or on the edge of the known universe (or even beyond it!). They can also talk about the time before the human race emerged, and the time subsequent to its extinction. In other words, our language gives us a power to refer which is unconstrained by our personal or species life-possibilities, and this gives us the freedom to imagine (and plan for or towards) distant possibilities in a way that no other species is capable of.

In one sense literature is one of the most sophisticated exemplifications of this ability: members of other species can sham and mislead, but FICTION seems a specifically

91

human resource (although it is arguably related to play, in both humans and animals). This should perhaps lead us to consider whether or not literature and other imaginative arts actually play a more important role in human development than has sometimes been accorded them. It may also suggest that REDUCTIONIST views of literature as merely a form of reflection of the life-situation of the writer or his or her society are inadequate: clearly what we imagine is based upon what we know, but in important respects it is not limited to it. Our ability to imagine 'what may be the case' or 'what might have been the case' have arguably increased our chances of survival (as well as having given us a much greater ability to endanger ourselves and our future).

   Sigmund Freud's use of this term is rather different: see CONDENSATION AND DISPLACEMENT.

Displayed See DEFAMILIARIZATION

Dispositif A term used by Michel Foucault in a 'conversation' entitled 'The Confession of the Flesh'. Foucault reports that what he is trying to pick out with the term *dispositif* (rendered as *apparatus* in English translation)

> is, firstly, a thoroughly heterogeneous ensemble consisting of discourses, institutions, architectural forms, regulatory decisions, laws, administrative measures, scientific statements, philosophical, moral and philanthropic propositions – in short, the said as much as the unsaid. Such are the elements of the apparatus. The apparatus itself is the system of relations that can be established between these elements. Secondly, what I am trying to identify in this apparatus is precisely the nature of the connection that can exist between these heterogeneous elements. (1980a, 194)

See APPARATUS for the Brechtian meaning of this term, and see also DISCOURSE.

Disruption See DEFORMATION

Dissemination From Jacques Derrida's book *Dissemination* (1981a), the term describes that state of endless seeding and potential growth of MEANING said to characterize the play of SIGNIFIERS in the absence of SIGNIFIEDS. According to Gayatri Chakravorty Spivak, the translator of Derrida's *Of Grammatology*, the term refers to 'the seed that neither inseminates nor is recovered by the father, but is scattered abroad' (Derrida: 1976, xi). Dissemination differs from Empsonian AMBIGUITY to the extent that the flow of new meanings can never be exhausted, nor can these be in any way attached to an AUTHOR: they are the product of language itself.
   Homi K. Bhabha has punned on Derrida's term to produce the neologism DissemiNation, a term which both brings together and juxtaposes 'the lonely gatherings of the scattered people' and 'the cultural construction of nationness' (1994, 139–40) with which we are confronted by the modern world.
   Compare ECHOLALIA.

Dissonant closure See CLOSURE

Dissonant psycho-narration See FREE INDIRECT DISCOURSE

Distance A term used with a range of related meanings in literary criticism, mostly within the theory of NARRATIVE. The most general meaning refers to READER involvement in a literary WORK. Thus whereas readers of Dickens's novels typically became (and become) very involved in the fate of CHARACTERS in the course of reading (gathering on the quay in the United States to meet the latest instalment of *The Old Curiosity Shop* to learn of the fate of Little Nell, for example), much of Joseph Conrad's FICTION encourages the reader to observe characters and events more dispassionately, at more of an emotional distance.

This is not unrelated to more specific usages of the term within narrative theory. The reader of Conrad's 'An Outpost of Progress' feels relatively distanced from the fates of the characters of the work, but this is in part because the NARRATOR also seems detached and, if pitying, at a distance from the characters. Distance can, therefore, refer to the gap between STORY and NARRATION, and this gap can be temporal, geographical, or emotional – or traceable to a clash between the value-systems associated with characters and with the narrative. It can also be attributed to more technical matters: the more anonymous and covert the narration, the less distance there is between story and narration; the more the narrative draws attention to itself as narrative (through, for example, a personified narrator), then the greater the story–narrative distance. It should be remembered, however, that it is possible for the technical distance between narrative and story to be very small without necessarily producing very much reader or NARRATEE involvement in the work on an emotional level. Distance, in other words, can be technical, intellectual, moral, or emotional according to various usages.

Mieke Bal uses distance as a measure of types of ANACHRONY: the more an event presented in an anachrony is separated from the 'present' (that is, the moment at which the story is interrupted by the anachrony), the greater the distance (1985, 59).

See also ANALEPSIS.

Dominant According to the PRAGUE SCHOOL theorist Jan Mukařovský:

> The systematic foregrounding of components in a work of poetry consists in the gradation of the interrelationships of these components, that is, in their mutual subordination and superordination. The component highest in the hierarchy becomes the dominant. All other components, foregrounded or not, are evaluated from the standpoint of the dominant. (1964, 20)

And Roman Jakobson proposes that

> The dominant may be defined as the focusing component of a work of art: it rules, determines, and transforms the remaining components. It is the dominant which guarantees the integrity of the structure. (1971b, 82)

Jakobson goes on to suggest that one may seek a dominant not only in an individual artist's poetic WORK or in the poetic CANON, 'but also in the art of a given epoch, viewed as a particular whole' (1971b, 83), and he suggests that in Renaissance art 'such an acme of the aesthetic criteria of the time, was represented by the visual arts' (1971b, 83).

So far as the individual poetic work is concerned, Jakobson suggests that 'the aesthetic function' be defined as its dominant (1971b, 84). It is arguable that this takes us rather less far than does Mukařovský's above-quoted definition: defining 'the aesthetic function' is itself so problematic that were one able satisfactorily to accomplish it the need for a concept such as that of 'the dominant' would be rather less pressing.

Brian McHale has pointed out that it is thanks to Roman Jakobson that the concept is known today, but that Jurij Tynjanov (Yuri Tynyanov) is probably the person who deserves to be credited with its invention (1987, 6).

Mikhail Bakhtin makes very extensive use of the concept, especially in his study of Dostoevsky (Bakhtin: 1984).

See also CULTURE and TRANSCULTURATION (dominant culture); DEFAMILI-ARIZATION; DEFORMATION; AESTHETIC; HEGEMONY; IDEOLOGY (dominant ideology).

Dominant discourse See DISCOURSE; IDEOLOGY

Dominant ideology See IDEOLOGY

Double articulation See MIMICRY

Double-bind A term from interpersonal psychology. In their book *Pragmatics of Human Communication* Paul Watzlawick *et al.* give the following definition.

A double-bind is a message so structured that it both (1) asserts something, and (2) asserts something about its own assertion with the result that (3) assertion 1 contradicts assertion 2. Furthermore, it is necessary that the recipient of the message be incapable of stepping outside the FRAME of contradiction set up by these conflicting assertions, such that he or she oscillates between them but cannot resolve the contradiction by means of some sort of meta-assertion (1968, 212).

This sounds complex, but relates to a very simple and not uncommon situation. The parent who says to a child, 'If you loved me you wouldn't want to go out,' will double-bind the child if it is incapable of stepping out of the enclosing frame of the double-bind and responding 'My wanting to go out does not affect the fact that I *do* love you.' To give another illuminating example: according to Gilles Deleuze and Félix Guattari in their *Anti-Oedipus: Capitalism and Schizophrenia*, 'the "double bind" is none other than the whole of Oedipus' (1983, 80, their emphasis).

The theory of the double-bind has been made use of by literary critics in two rather different ways. A number of critics have made use of the theory to throw light on what it is claimed are depictions of unhealthy or pathological human relationships. Such analyses have, in other words, concentrated upon literary CHARACTERS and have treated them as if they suffered from the same problems in their relations with others as do real people. Thus in their book *Families under Stress* (1975), Tony Manocchio and William Petitt use a number of psychological concepts including that of the double-bind to analyse family relations in WORKS by Terence Rattigan, Shakespeare, Eugene O'Neill, Arthur Miller and Edward Albee. The experiment has points of interest for students of literature, but the failure fully to take account of the FICTIONAL and artistic aspects of the works studied leads to a number of shortcomings in the analyses.

A rather different use can be found in Harold Bloom's *The Anxiety of Influence*, in which Bloom invokes the double-bind concept to characterize 'the paradox of the precursor's implicit charge to the ephebe'. For Bloom, what the precursor's poem says to its descendant poem (here Bloom shifts the ground of his argument a little), is, 'Be like me but unlike me' (1973, 70). The EPHEBE's relation to his precursor, then, is for Bloom essentially neurotic and pathological in nature.

For a more detailed account of Bloom's position see the entry under REVISIONISM.

Double chronology See NARRATIVE

Double colonization A form of subjugation experienced by women in colonized countries, who are on the receiving end both of colonial power in general and also of colonial and domestic PATRIARCHAL oppression.

See the entry for SUBALTERN.

Double consciousness A term originally associated with the divided allegiances of African Americans who found it hard or impossible to reconcile or relate their identities as African Americans and as Americans. Sometimes applied more generally to the split allegiances experienced by other subordinate or MARGINALIZED groups.

Compare CODE SWITCHING.

Double focalization See PERSPECTIVE AND VOICE

Double-voiced Presenting two VOICES (normally, in an IDEOLOGICAL sense) either simultaneously or alternating with each other. Compare overt and COVERT PLOTS, and also more traditional views of the function of irony and paradox in poetry. Now often used in connection with the intrusion of DOMINANT ideas into the DISCOURSE of a minority or MARGINAL writer. Also used as a synonym for DIALOGIC, as in a *double-voiced text*.

For further discussion of *double-voiced* see DIEGESIS AND MIMESIS, DISCOURSE and PALIMPSEST TEXT, and compare FREE INDIRECT DISCOURSE and INTERTEXTUALITY.

Doxa See DEFAMILIARIZATION

Drag In (slang) colloquial use, applied to the wearing of (normally) women's clothes by (normally) men. The term has assumed a new importance in discussions of GENDER formation; as Judith Butler argues:

> Drag constitutes the mundane way in which genders are appropriated, theatricalized, worn, and done; it implies that all gendering is a kind of impersonation and approximation. If this is true, it seems, there is no original or primary gender that drag imitates, but *gender is a kind of imitation for which there is no original*; in fact, it is a kind of imitation that produces the very notion of the original as an *effect* and consequence of the imitation itself. (1991, 21)

Dragnet theory

Or as Carole-Anne Tyler puts it, '[o]nce masculinity is seen as a put-on, mere style, its phallic imposture is exposed as such and so delegitimated, according to proponents of drag' (1991, 32).

See also CROSS-DRESSING; MASQUERADE; MIMICRY; PHALLOCENTRISM; TRANS-GENDER.

Dragnet theory A dismissive term for recent crude forms of positivism. From the 1950s American TV series in which Sergeant Joe Friday always seemed to be saying, 'The facts, Ma'am, just give me the facts.'

Dramatic theatre See ALIENATION EFFECT

Dubbing From the technique of dubbing a new soundtrack on to a film so as to represent the characters speaking in a language different from that in which the film was made. The term has some currency in FEMINIST and POSTCOLONIAL discussion, where it is used to describe a (frequently but not necessarily) subversive or oppositional re-presentation of the literature of a dominant power or IDEOLOGY. Thus feminist retellings of traditional fairy-tales can be treated as a form of recuperative (see INCORPORATION) dubbing.

See also INTERTEXTUALITY; MASQUERADE; MIMICRY.

Duration In NARRATIVE theory, duration can refer either to the time covered by the STORY or part of it (an EVENT), or to the 'time' allotted to either by the TEXT (story-time and text-time). As Rimmon-Kenan points out, the latter concept is a highly problematic one as 'there is no way of measuring text-duration' (1983, 51). On a very rough basis it is possible to note that three years of story-time may be covered by three pages of text, while further on in the same text one hour of story-time may occupy fifty pages. But 'pages' do not give a particularly reliable measure: not only do some READERS read more quickly than others, the same reader will read more or less quickly depending upon such factors as textual complexity, reader involvement and tension, and so on. Gerald Prince points out that as a result many writers on narrative find *speed* or *tempo* more fruitful concepts in the analysis of narrative texts (1988a, 24).

In film and other PERFORMANCE arts, of course, 'text-time' can be very precisely measured. Seymour Chatman has noted that while the basic convention in film is 'the "literal" correspondence of discourse-time to story-time, Genette's "scenic" mode', editing in the classic Hollywood movie can be used to adjust the pace of story-time to mood: 'the cuts in a suspense thriller are taut and rapid, those in a moody melodrama languorous and slow, with the dissolve much favored over the straight cut' (1990, 50).

In some usages 'represented time' and 'representational time' are terms used to describe 'time-in-the-story' and 'time-it-takes-to-tell-the-story'.

According to Gérard Genette, the four basic forms of narrative movement are ELLIPSIS, pause, scene and summary. These constitute four different ways of varying duration (1980, 94).

See also ISOCHRONY; SLOW-DOWN.

Durative anachrony See ANACHRONY

Dysphoric text See EUPHORIC/DYSPHORIC TEXT

E

Echolalia A term intended to convey the ceaseless echoing back and forth between SIGNS whose significance is determined only relationally and not by any overriding PRESENCE or fixed authority.
Compare DISSEMINATION.

Ecological validity A claim or procedure which lacks ecological validity is one that is based on too narrow or artificial a set of assumptions or test procedures. The term is used to indicate that laboratory experiments may not accurately duplicate or replicate those conditions in 'real life' for which the experiment in question is designed.
Thus for example early behaviourist experiments into the 'effects' of TV programmes which asked schoolchildren a set of questions to determine attitudinal orientation, and then repeated the same questions after the viewing of a TV programme, can be said to lack ecological validity, as the way TV alters attitudes is far more subtle than is presupposed by such experiments.
Within literary criticism and theory the term is most used in the study of READERS AND READING. Attempts to determine how 'Common Readers' read are plagued with problems relating to artificial test situations. Ordinary reading is relatively unselfconscious and it intermeshes with a range of other quotidian activities; as soon as an individual is asked questions concerning his or her reading these conditions may be altered in a way that makes the results of such an investigation unreliable.

Economism In traditional MARXIST usage, the term economism carries with it the accusation of REDUCTIONISM and always has a pejorative edge to it. It is used to refer to a too-mechanical relating of all CULTURAL, historical or social elements to economic factors or forces, with no provision made for complex processes of MEDIATION.

Écriture French-English dictionaries give 'writing' as the equivalent of écriture, and in an article on DECONSTRUCTIVE criticism M. H. Abrams has glossed écriture as 'the written or printed text' (1977, 428), but the fact that many critics writing in English continue to use the French term suggests that this equivalence is very incomplete. We need to understand that the contemporary critical use of this term dates from Roland Barthes's extension of the meaning of the French term in his *Le Degré zéro de l'écriture*, which was published in 1953. The English translation (Barthes: 1967b) has what, given the following comments, is arguably the misleading title *Writing Degree Zero*. In an article on écriture, Ann Banfield has named other 'landmark texts' which have contributed to the establishment of this term: Maurice Blanchot's 'The Narrative Voice' (1981); Michel Butor, 'L'Usage des pronoms personnels dans le roman' (1964), and Michel Foucault, 'What is an Author?' (1980b) (Banfield: 1985, 2). Barthes's translators point out in a note that although in everyday French *écriture* normally means only 'handwriting', or 'the art of writing', '[i]t is used here in a strictly technical sense to denote a new concept' (Barthes: 1967b, 7). This 'new concept' has to be explained by reference to Barthes's setting of écriture in opposition to *littérature*, a distinction related to that which he makes between *lisible* and *scriptible* or, as rendered in English translation, READERLY AND WRITERLY TEXTS. As Banfield points out, the distinction between écriture and *littérature* is the more striking in French because prose FICTION in French has appropriated to itself certain *grammatical* characteristics which distinguish it from other forms of writing, notably the *passé simple* and the third-person NARRATIVE (Banfield: 1985, 4). If *littérature* is characterized by these overt grammatical markers, and by less overt and related IDEOLOGICAL ones, écriture seeks to escape from 'LITERARINESS' by a 'zero style' first, and most strikingly, seen in the French novel in Albert Camus's *L'Étranger*, a novel told in the first and not the third person, and using not the *passé simple* but the *parfait composé*, a grammatical choice which has (or had) a shock effect in French which is lost in English translation. For Barthes, 'writing degree zero' is a 'colourless writing, freed from all bondage to a pre-ordained state of language' (1967b, 82), it represents an attempt 'to go beyond Literature by entrusting one's fate to a sort of basic speech, equally far from living languages and from literary language proper' (1967b, 83).

What, then, is the significance of this for non-French readers? Banfield argues that although the grammatical markers of écriture are not so apparent in English, nonetheless the term points to a writing characterized by ABSENCE, an absence of the marks of literature, of human agency, which is not limited to French language or CULTURE. Écriture as substantive, says Banfield, 'is a product now divorced from the person and activity of its producer', it is 'the name for the coming to language of a knowledge which is not personal' (1985, 13), and she links it with the use of *style indirecte libre*, or FREE INDIRECT DISCOURSE in the novel.

The same loss of complexities can accompany the translating of Jacques Derrida's use of the term 'écriture' by the English term 'writing'. In an interview with Henri Ronse, published in *Positions*, Ronse puts a case for this complexity to Derrida, who does not reject Ronse's argument.

> *Ronse*: In your essays at least two meanings of the word 'writing' are discernible: the accepted meaning, which opposes (phonetic) writing to the speech that it allegedly represents (but you show that there is no purely phonetic writing), and a more radical meaning that determines writing in general, before any tie to what glossematics calls an 'expressive substance'; this more radical meaning would be the common root of writing and speech. The treatment accorded to writing in the accepted sense serves as a revelatory index of the repression to which archi-writing is subject. (Derrida: 1981b, 7–8)

For *archi-writing*, see the entry for ARCHE-WRITING. It seems clear that for Derrida, the terms *écriture* and *arche-writing* can on occasions perform almost interchangeable roles.

Theories of écriture clearly appealed to STRUCTURALISTS who were keen to stress the depersonalized systematics of LANGUE and eager to reject views which saw language always in terms of (normally individual) human origins or PRESENCE. So far as literature is concerned, adoption of the term seems typically to stem from impulses similar to those which lie behind a belief in the death of the AUTHOR, and its use often betokens a commitment to a writer-less writing, or to a writing seen as intransitive and self-referring.

See also ÉCRITURE FÉMININE.

Écriture féminine According to Elaine Showalter, 'the inscription of the feminine body and female difference in language and text' (1986, 249). Showalter's discussion of the concept is worth consulting in its entirety. The term was coined by French FEMINISTS, and represents more a description of an ideal, future achievement than of a particular type of writing of which there already exist many examples.

The name most frequently associated with the term is that of Hélène Cixous, although those described as practitioners of écriture féminine have, themselves, rarely used the term. Nor can one expect a tidy definition or theorization of the term from Cixous; as she writes in one of her best-known pieces, 'The Laugh of the Medusa':

> [i]t is impossible to *define* a feminine practice of writing, and this is an impossibility that will remain, for this practice can never be theorized, enclosed, coded – which doesn't mean that it doesn't exist. But it will always surpass the discourse that regulates the phallocentric system; it does and will take place in areas other than those subordinated to philosophico-theoretical domination. It will be conceived of only by subjects who are breakers of automatisms, by peripheral figures that no authority can ever subjugate. (1981, 253)

The concept has interesting forebears. Take the following comment from Virginia Woolf's essay 'Women and Fiction', which was first published in 1929.

> But it is still true that before a woman can write exactly as she wishes to write, she has many difficulties to face. To begin with, there is the technical difficulty – so simple, apparently; in reality, so baffling – that the very form of the sentence does not fit her. It is a sentence made by men; it is too loose, too heavy, too pompous for a woman's use. (1966b, 145)

Woolf concludes that a woman must 'alter and adapt' the current sentence until she can write one that 'takes the natural shape of her thought without crushing or distorting it' (1966b, 145).

In another essay she makes it clear that it is not just the shape of a woman's thought but the reality of her BODY that manifests itself as a problem of writing for her. In 'Professions for Women', which was first read as a paper to the Women's Service League, she pictures for her listeners a girl sitting with pen in hand, and notes that the image that this picture brings to mind is that of a fisherman 'lying sunk in dreams on the verge of a deep lake with a rod held out over the water'.

> Now came the experience that I believe to be far commoner with women writers than with men. The line raced through the girl's fingers. Her imagination had rushed away. It had sought the pools, the depths, the dark places where the largest fish slumber. And then there was a smash. There was an explosion. There was foam and confusion. The imagination had dashed itself against something hard. The girl was

roused from her dream. She was indeed in a state of the most acute and difficult distress. To speak without figure, she had thought of something, something about the body, about the passions which it was unfitting for her as a woman to say. (1966a, 287–8)

More recent feminist accounts of *écriture féminine* suggest that this sense of one's own body may become the source from which the new writing must stem. Madeleine Gagnon, for example, after noting that she has to take over a language which, although it is hers, is foreign to her, argues that there is an alternative: '[a]ll we have to do is let the body flow, from the inside; all we have to do is erase, as we did on the slate, whatever may hinder or harm the new forms of writing; we retain whatever fits, whatever suits us' (1980, 180). Some feminist commentators have, however, suggested that the process may not be so easy as is here assumed, pointing out that women's sense of their own bodies may already be saturated with IDEOLOGICALLY foreign elements: what flows from the inside of the body may thus be more than body alone. Thus Kadiatu Kanneh has described the 'privileging of the body in the writing of Cixous and Irigaray as the focal point for a radical subversion' as, in many ways, 'a dangerous political move', and has pointed out that although it is crucially important to 'revalorize the female body, to rescue it from the vilification which, for centuries, has been practised against it through oppressive codes and institutions', a belief in 'determinism through body language' relies upon a (false) belief in a pre-linguistic reality (quoted in Mary Eagleton: 1996, 31–2).

A similar and forceful objection to proposals that 'place the body at the center of a search for female identity' is voiced by the Editorial Collective of *Questions Féministes* in an article entitled 'Variations on Common Themes'.

To advocate a 'woman's language' and a means of expression that would be specifically feminine seems to us equally illusory. First, the so-called explored language extolled by some women seems to be linked, if not in its content at least in its style, to a trend propagated by literary schools governed by male masters. This language is therefore as academic and as 'masculine' as other languages. Secondly, it is at times said that women's language is closer to the body, to sexual pleasure, to direct sensations, and so on, which means that the body could express itself directly without social mediation and that, moreover, this closeness to the body and to nature would be subversive. In our opinion, there is no such thing as a direct relation to the body. To advocate a direct relation to the body is therefore not subversive because it is equivalent to denying the reality and the strength of social mediations, the very same ones that oppress us in our bodies. At most, one would advocate a different socialization of the body, but without searching for a true and eternal nature, for this search takes us away from the most effective struggle against the socio-historical contexts in which human beings are and will always be trapped. (Quoted in Mary Eagleton: 1996, 338)

Ego See TOPOGRAPHICAL MODEL OF THE MIND

Eidetic A term taken from the Greek *eidos* meaning form, or type, and used by the German philosopher Edmund Husserl to describe his method of abstracting universals from the flux of images given to us in consciousness. In the words of Maurice Merleau-Ponty, '[t]he eidetic method is the method of a phenomenological positivism which bases the possible on the real' (1962, xvii). The method is supposed to be able to find what is constant and invariable in the objects of our consciousness, such that universals can be built up from a series of images giving, necessarily, only partial knowledge. Applied to literature, the method would involve our abstracting what is local and adventitious in all literary experiences of – say – *Hamlet*, so as to be able to arrive at the universal *Hamlet*, one which is the play itself in all its specificity and concreteness. A problem soon encountered in such an application of the method to literature, however, is what one does with contradictory and irreconcilable elements in different experiences of the same WORK.

Ellipsis Alternatively *gap*. The omitting of one or more items in a NARRATIVE series: any gap of information in a temporal or other sequence. We never learn anything concrete, for example, of Heathcliff's history prior to his discovery in Liverpool by Mr Earnshaw, nor of what he does to become rich between the time of his disappearance and re-appearance in *Wuthering Heights*. In this case the ellipsis is relatively *unmarked* (or implicit), as it covers information not known to the personified NARRATORS. But when in Charles Dickens's *Bleak House* Esther Summerson seeks to explain why she finds Mrs Woodcourt irksome, and breaks off with the words, 'I don't know what it was. Or at least if I do, now, I thought I did not then. Or at least – but it don't matter', then we have a clearly *marked* (or explicit) ellipsis: the READER's attention is drawn to the fact that something that is known to the narrator is withheld from him or her. (See the entry for MARKEDNESS.) Few readers are concerned to ask the above question about Heathcliff in reading *Wuthering Heights*, and L. C. Knights, in a famous article, certainly thought that a correct response to Shakespeare's *Macbeth* should *not* lead one to ask how many children Lady Macbeth had. Examples of the FANTASTIC, in contrast, draw readers' attention to certain explanatory gaps which cause them to hesitate between natural and supernatural explanations of events.

Gérard Genette characterizes certain ellipses as *hypothetical*; these are those ellipses which are impossible to localize or – on occasions – to place in any spot at all, but which are revealed after the event by an ANALEPSIS (1980, 109).

Ellipses can be permanent or temporary: in most detective novels certain marked gaps are sustained until the end of the WORK only to be filled in during the final pages.

In a related but different sense, theorists such as Roman Ingarden and Wolfgang Iser have drawn attention to the gaps and indeterminacies necessarily possessed by literary works, gaps and indeterminacies which must be filled in or fleshed out and, as it were, CONCRETIZED by readers.

See also ABSENCE; DURATION (narrative movements); PARALIPSIS.

Embedded event See EVENT

Embedded narrative See FRAME

Embedding Alternatively *nesting* or *staircasing*. In general terms, embedding involves the enclosing of one unit in a larger unit – a clause in a sentence, a sub-clause in a clause, and so on. Within different branches of Linguistics the terms *embedding* and *nesting* may be given varying meanings, often relating to the extent to which the enclosed unit either determines or modifies the enclosing one.

Similarly, in NARRATIVE embedding refers in its simplest form to what is often called 'a story within a story': Dickens's *The Pickwick Papers* contains a succession of embedded tales told by Sam Weller. But certain narrative theorists use the term only when, as above, the enclosed unit (which may not be a complete story) either determines or modifies the enclosing unit in some way. Thus Shlomith Rimmon-Kenan uses embedding to translate Claude Bremond's term *enclave*, and she points out that he uses this term to indicate where one narrative sequence is 'inserted into another as a specification or detailing of one of its functions' (Rimmon-Kenan: 1983, 23).

See also EVENT (embedded event) and FRAME (embedded frame).

Emotive See FUNCTIONS OF LANGUAGE

Empirical/empiricism See SOLUTION FROM ABOVE/BELOW

Empirical reader See READERS AND READING

Empiricist fallacy See NORM

Emplotment A term much used within NEW HISTORICIST writing which refers to the textualizing of historical 'facts' or 'events' to create a PLOT or NARRATIVE. Just as a novelist may create any amount of novels from a given set of CHARACTERS and events, so too (certain radical historians have argued) a given set of historical data can be emplotted in innumerable manners, all of which will present that material in different ways.

Those who use the term often draw on the distinction between STORY and plot to be found in narrative theory, and suggest that just as we can get at a story only through a plot, so too it is an illusion to believe that the raw facts of history can be directly apprehended, as they too can be apprehended only in one emplotted form or another. What such writers argue is that the process of emplotment should be made visible, that historians should come clean about the principles behind their structuring of narratives.

In their most extreme form such arguments espouse highly idealistic positions which deny the existence of historical facts or events as such, and argue that all the historian has is a set of different emplotments which cannot be judged against a reality that each claims to represent or reproduce, but which is actually produced and re-produced by these emplotments. Put simply: in such a view reality is not the basis for history, but histories create (varied) realities. Here Jacques Derrida's notorious claim that there is nothing outside the TEXT (1976, 158) is taken to a logical extreme. I have myself claimed that such a position can be found in the work of the historian Hayden White, and have argued against it (Hawthorn: 1996, 36–47).

Not all of those who argue that emplotment comes between the reader of history and the events and characters of history adopt such extreme positions, however, and many are concerned that by drawing attention to the inevitability of forms of emplotment the reader of history may better be able to distinguish between what actually happened and how this is presented.

Enchained event See EVENT

Enclave See EMBEDDING

Energetics/geometrics The BINARY opposition between energetics and geometrics can be related to the more established distinction between DIACHRONIC AND SYNCHRONIC. While energetics is concerned with *forces* which exist within a particular ensemble, geometrics rests upon a spatial metaphor that views relations between components in a system cartographically. Thus an outlook such as MARXISM is premised upon certain oppositions (primarily those which lead to class struggle) that lead to change, whilst STRUCTURALISM sees forces and relations in suspension as it were, mapped along a network of geometrical paths which together constitute a single, balanced SYSTEM. The distinction has enjoyed some currency among NARRATIVE theorists. Andrew Gibson, for example, has argued that it was 'precisely a geometrisation of textual space . . . that underlays attempts to establish narrative grammars, like Todorov's grammar of the *Decameron*' (1996, 3).

Energy Otherwise *social energy*. A term associated with the NEW HISTORICISTS and especially with Stephen J. Greenblatt, who provides an account of the origin and significance of this term in 'The Circulation of Social Energy' (Greenblatt: 1988, 1–20).

According to Greenblatt, he wished to find out why in Renaissance England cultural objects, expressions and practices – and, especially, plays by Shakespeare – acquired compelling force. Turning to English literary theorists of that period he found that they needed a new word for this force,

> a word to describe the ability of language, in Puttenham's phrase, to cause 'a stir to the mind'; drawing on the Greek rhetorical tradition, they called it *energia*. This is the origin in our language of the term 'energy,' a term I propose we use, provided we understand that its origins lie in rhetoric rather than physics and that its significance is social and historical. We experience that energy within ourselves, but its contemporary existence depends upon an irregular chain of historical transactions that leads back to the late sixteenth and early seventeenth centuries. (1988, 4–5)

This does not mean that when modern spectators feel the force of an Elizabethan play they are experiencing what a contemporary of the playwright would have experienced. Continuous processes of NEGOTIATION and EXCHANGE have reformulated this aesthetic force anew for each succeeding generation; the play's social energy is still active, but transformed in its effects from what these were several centuries ago. Indeed, one of the things which characterizes art is that its social energy can survive transplantation to new social and historical contexts:

Whereas most collective expressions moved from their original setting to a new place or time are dead on arrival, the social energy encoded in certain works of art continues to generate the illusion of life for centuries. I want to understand the negotiations through which works of art obtain and amplify such powerful energy. (1988, 7)

In practice it seems fair to say that New Historicism in general and the work of Greenblatt in particular focus less on contemporary renegotiations of, say, the aesthetic force of Shakespeare's plays, than these comments might suggest. Such study is associated far more with the British cultural materialists than with the New Historicists (see NEW HISTORICISM AND CULTURAL MATERIALISM).

English This has long been considered to be an ideologically loaded or, at least, coloured word by those who have argued that the tendency within and outside Britain to substitute it for the often more accurate *British* compromises its use as a neutral descriptive term in other contexts (the 'English language', for example).

This suspicion of the word seems to have been at least partly responsible for the emergence of a new usage, current in British rather than American contexts, which can be summed up as that complex of attitudes and exclusions which accompanies the role played by English language and literature in the educational system, and which functions as a part of the dominant ideology. Thus in an article from 1989 entitled 'Towards Cultural History – in Theory and Practice', Catherine Belsey writes that 'I start from the assumption that English as it has traditionally been understood, as the study of great literary works by great authors, has no useful part to play in a pedagogy committed to a politics of change' (Ryan: 1996, 82).

The usage owes much to Louis Althusser's theory of the Ideological State Apparatuses (see the entry for IDEOLOGY), and has been backed up by arguments which appeal to the evidence of public examinations and the syllabuses and teaching associated with them. Such arguments typically involve reference to the ideologically determined element in CANON-formation. The usage can be confusing – especially, it seems, to non-British users – as it is often difficult to tell whether the word is intended as a neutral, descriptive term or as a term with a specifically political thrust behind it.

Enigma See DEFERRED/POSTPONED SIGNIFICANCE

Énoncé/Énonciation See ENUNCIATION

Enthymeme According to V. N. Vološinov, 'every utterance in the business of life is an objective social enthymeme. It is something like a password known only to those who belong to the same social purview' (1976, 101).

John Frow has developed this argument using Althusser's concept of INTER-PELLATION. According to Frow the concept of presupposition is central to a theory of how implied SUBJECT positions are locked into implied structures of meaning, and Vološinov's conception of 'the *enthymematic* structure of discourse defines the logic of self evidence which is an important consequence of generic norms'. For Frow, the 'free' or implicit information in a statement is often more important than its 'tied' or overt information, as this 'free' information 'anchors the statement to a context other than the immediate one' (Frow: 1986, 77–8). A GENRE may, accordingly, carry with it important IDEOLOGICAL constraints and determinations.

Entrapment See INCORPORATION

Entropy See REDUNDANCY

Enunciatee See ENUNCIATION

Enunciation Along with cognate words such as *enunciatee, enunciator* and *enunciated,* enunciation has now begun to replace the French loan-word *énonciation* and its cognates. However such translations often fail to carry the more specific meanings of the French originals. (The translator of Roland Barthes's article 'To Write: an Intransitive Verb?', for example, regularly includes the French original terms alongside the English translation, and *énonciation* is translated on one occasion as *utterance* and on another as *statement*. Umberto Eco, in contrast, renders *énoncé* and *énonciation* as *sentence* and *utterance* [1981, 16].)

What is central to use of the various French terms is a distinction between the particular, time-bound *act* of making a statement, and the *verbal result* of that act, a result which escapes from the moment of time and from the possession of the person responsible for the act. We can note that the important distinction between *utterance* and *statement* is that the former term links that which is uttered to its human originator, whereas the latter term concentrates attention on to the purely verbal result. When *énonciation* is used in French it more usually has the meaning we attribute to *utterance*, that is to say, it calls to mind the *act* of producing a form of words which involves a human SUBJECT. In contrast, when *énoncé* is used the intention is normally to consider a form of words independently from their context-bound association with a human subject.

In addition, the French terms generally include the idea of a human target or audience (whereas a statement or UTTERANCE can be made in the absence of these). Thus some writers in English prefer to translate the term *énonciateur* as *addresser*, a usage which inevitably perhaps also brings with it *addressee* – the person at whom an utterance is aimed. When one meets with the term *enunciation* in English care should therefore be taken. This may refer to that act-in-a-context which produces a person-orientated utterance, but it can also have a more restricted reference: the internal *evidence* that an utterance stems from a *subject's act-in-a-context*.

See also the distinction between DISCOURSE and STORY in the entry for discourse. For *enunciative field* see FIELD.

Ephebe According to the *OED*, in Classical Greece a young citizen aged between 18 and 20 years who was chiefly involved in garrison duty. The term has been pressed into new service by Harold Bloom to describe the 'young citizen of poetry' or 'figure of the youth as virile poet' (1973, 10, 31). Bloom's ephebe, it should be said, seems to be engaged more in storming the paternal garrison than in defending it (see REVISIONISM).

Epic theatre See ALIENATION EFFECT

Episodic narrative See STRING OF PEARLS NARRATIVE

Épistémè (Sometimes written *epistēmē* or without accents.) A term coined by Michel Foucault and based on the Greek for knowledge. Foucault defines it thus:

> By *episteme*, we mean, in fact, the total set of relations that unite, at a given period, the discursive practices that give rise to epistemological figures, sciences, and possibly formalized systems; the way in which, in each of these discursive formations, the transitions to epistemologization, scientificity, and formulization are situated and operate; the distribution of these thresholds, which may coincide, be subordinated to one another, or be separated by shifts in time; the lateral relations that may exist between epistemological figures or sciences in so far as they belong to neighbouring, but distinct, discursive practices. (1972, 191)

The term has been widely used by, among others, Jacques Derrida. In some usages it seems to refer to a given historical period during which the above-mentioned relations and laws of transformation are constant and stable. Thus *épistémè* has points of contact with Marx's *ruling ideas* and with the MARXIST sense of IDEOLOGY, but it has a more all-embracing, totalizing sense: an *épistémè* leaves no room – or attempts to exclude the space – for any ways of producing or arranging knowledge apart from its own. As Richard Harland points out, one problem caused for Foucault by the theory of the *épistémè* is that the theorist of the concept (i.e. Foucault himself) must be part of the *épistémè* if indeed the *épistémè* is all-embracing (Harland: 1987, 123). A further set of problems involves the reason why – and manner whereby – one *épistémè* gives way to and is replaced by another.

See also the entries for PARADIGM SHIFT and PROBLEMATIC, for comparable concepts. For *discursive practice* see DISCOURSE.

Epistemological break Epistemology is the theoretical study of knowledge – its nature, how it is to be studied or achieved, what its grounds are. The concept of the *epistemological break* is associated with the theories of the French MARXIST philosopher Louis Althusser, who developed it initially to describe what he saw as the significance of the changes reflected by 'the confrontation between Marx's Early Works and *Capital*' (1969, 13). For Althusser, this confrontation involved a major opposition, the opposition that separates science from IDEOLOGY. Althusser's definition of these two terms is not uncontroversial, and has been subjected to considerable criticism in recent years. It involves, among other things, attributing to science a self-validating role which, as Terry Eagleton has pointed out, runs counter to most traditions of Marxist thought (1991, 137–8).

For Althusser, the concept of the epistemological break does not just have a historical application: science is separated from ideology by such a break on the theoretical as well as the historical plane. To move from ideology to science always involves such a break: there is no smooth path or ordered logical progression from ideology to science: 'what we are dealing with in the opposition science/ideologies concerns the "break" relationship between a science and the *theoretical* ideology in which the object it gave the knowledge of was "thought" before the foundation of the science' (1969, 13).

All of this is reminiscent of other theories of fundamental revolutions of thought, and indeed Althusser compares Marx's epochal (and, he claims, unprecedented) break-through to scientific knowledge, to the birth of Platonic philosophy 'induced' by the foundation of mathematics by Thales, and to the birth of Cartesian philosophy 'induced' by Galileo's foundation of physics (1969, 14; Althusser's inverted commas). This, in other words, can be seen as a variant on the metaphor of the COPERNICAN REVOLUTION to which a number of theorists have had recourse in recent years; it also has something in common with Thomas Kuhn's theory of PARADIGM SHIFTS, although for Kuhn such a shift involves a change from like to like, which is clearly not the case for Althusser with the shift from ideology to science.

In recent common usage all three concepts – the paradigm shift, the Copernican revolution, and the epistemological break – have assumed a less technical and more metaphorical meaning, such that their original distinguishing features have been lost, and such that the three terms are often more or less interchangeable. Accordingly Slavoj Žižek is able to refer to the films made by Alfred Hitchcock before *The Thirty-Nine Steps* as 'Hitchcock before his "epistemological break"' (1992, 3).

See also *ÉPISTÉMÈ*; PROBLEMATIC.

Epoché In PHENOMENOLOGICAL criticism, that suspension of all pre-existing beliefs and attitudes which must precede the analysis of consciousness. *Bracketing* is sometimes used as a synonym. According to Gérard Genette, 'when the semiologist has operated the semiological reduction, the *epoché* of meaning on the object-form, he is presented with a matte object, cleansed of all the varnish of dubious, abusive significations, with which social speech had covered it, restored to its essential freshness and solitude' (1982, 39).The term(s) and the concept can usefully be related to Samuel Taylor Coleridge's reference in *Biographia Literaria* (written 1808–15) to 'that willing suspension of disbelief' which he saw as the aim of his endeavours in his contribution to the *Lyrical Ballads* (1798) written jointly with William Wordsworth.

Erasure In recent theoretical usage, normally associated with a practice popularized by Jacques Derrida and the bane of typesetters and proofreaders, of leaving deleted words 'under erasure' (*sous rature*) in his writings – that is, of leaving them crossed out but not removed. By so doing Derrida enjoys a certain simultaneous having and eating of his cake: he makes use of words and terms which he feels to be inadequate but for which he finds no viable alternatives. Derrida apparently adopted the practice after noting Martin Heidegger's use of it. The erasure marks thus act in a manner similar to what are known colloquially as scare quotes; that is, quotation marks placed round a word with the similar intention of drawing attention to its inadequacy or questionable validity.

The term is sometimes given a more general meaning in discussion of MODERNIST and POSTMODERNIST techniques whereby achieved verisimilitude or REALISM is subsequently denied. Thus an erased CHARACTER would be a character accepted by the reader as 'real' according to realist CONVENTIONS, but who was shown later to be not-real in some sense, either within the achieved world of the FICTION or by a transference of the character from this world to the extra-fictional world of the text. (See the discussion in McHale: 1987, 64–6, and compare CANCELLED CHARACTER.)

Certain FEMINIST writers have extended the term to describe the way in which women are rendered invisible by PATRIARCHAL accounts which effectively treat them as non-existent or unworthy of serious attention. In his Introduction to a special issue of the journal *The Conradian* concerned with 'Conrad and Gender', for example, the editor, Andrew Michael Roberts, refers to a reference-book summary of the plot of *Lord Jim* which omits all mention of the female character Jewel – a character already MUTED in her relations with other characters in the novel (Roberts: 1993, vi).

See also the entry for ARCHE-WRITING.

Erlebte Rede See FREE INDIRECT DISCOURSE

Erotics The study of sexual love. In recent, especially FEMINIST, usage erotics is concerned to trace the formation of the erotic by socio-historical and CULTURAL, as well as biological, forces. Literature is an especially important source material for such study, as literary WORKS not only depict the erotic and very often set it in a larger genetic context, but literary works are often an important MEDIATING element in the formation of the erotic in modern times. Comparative study of the erotic element in literature thus offers a valuable way into the changing sources and developing nature of the erotic.

Errance See BROWSING

Essentialism The belief that qualities are inherent in objects of study, and that therefore the contexts in which these exist or are studied are of no relevance. Essentialism is therefore to be distinguished from DIALECTICAL, contextual or relational theories and approaches. The term often carries with it the implication that the qualities of objects of study are self-evident and do not themselves need to be sought for or explained (see Cameron: 1985, 187).

The charge of essentialism (the term nowadays is generally used pejoratively) has been laid at the door of the NEW CRITICS, with a certain justice in some cases. But essentialist elements are to be found in any theory which sees the individual literary WORK to be possessed of some core of fixed and unchanging meaning – a position associated with, among others, E. D. Hirsch.

HUMANISM is often accused of essentialism by its critics (see the entry for this term), and Alan Sinfield argues that

> [t]he essentialist-humanist approach to literature and sexual politics depends upon the belief that the individual is the probable, indeed necessary, source of truth and meaning. Literary significance and personal significance seem to derive from and speak to individual consciousnesses. But thinking of ourselves as essentially individual tends to efface processes of cultural production and, in the same movement, leads us to imagine ourselves to be autonomous, self-determining. (1992, 37)

The opposite of essentialism is RELATIVISM, but it is possible (indeed, it is probably normal) for both of these terms to be used pejoratively. To be critical of essentialism is not necessarily to accept that one is a relativist. This seems to be because many believe that there are certain absolutes (which is denied by strict relativism), but that this does not commit one to being an essentialist. The term 'relationism' is sometimes used as a non-pejorative alternative to relativism.

In an article entitled 'Sexual Skirmishes and Feminist Factions: Twenty-five Years of Debate on Women and Sexuality', Stevi Jackson and Sue Scott make some telling points about the dangers of essentialism.

In the first place, it rests on something unknowable, a hypothesised 'natural' sexuality somehow uncontaminated by cultural influences. As a result, it cannot adequately explain cultural and historical variations in human sexuality – differential repression is too crude a concept to capture the complexities of such variations. Furthermore, it conceptualises the social regulation of sexuality as a negative force and hence does not allow for the productive deployment of power in the shaping of sexuality. It cannot allow for differences in masculine and feminine sexuality except in terms of 'natural' differences or differential repression. (In Jackson and Scott: 1996, 11).

A term associated with Gayatri Chakravorty Spivak is *strategic essentialism*; the term carries the belief that the use of essentialist categories may be strategically necessary in the fighting of certain battles. See Spivak: 1984–5.

Pierre Bourdieu's term 'substantialist' appears to have much the same force as 'essentialist'.

Estrangement (effect) See ALIENATION EFFECT

Ethnoscope Arjun Appadurai's term to encompass that 'landscape of persons who constitute the shifting world in which we live: tourists, immigrants, refugees, exiles, guestworkers and other moving groups and persons constitute an essential feature of the world and appear to affect the politics of (and between) nations to a hitherto unprecedented degree' (1990, 7).

Euphoric/dysphoric text A distinction introduced in Nancy K. Miller's book *The Heroine's Text: Readings in the French and English Novel, 1722–1782* (1980). A euphoric text is one similar to Daniel Defoe's *Moll Flanders* or Samuel Richardson's *Pamela*, in which the heroine's course in life follows a trajectory of ascent in society with final integration. A dysphoric text, in contrast, ends with the heroine's death in the flower of her youth.

Compare PAMISSA.

Eurocentric Perceived from the PERSPECTIVE of Europe. The term almost always refers to the viewpoint of a set of beliefs or attitudes rather than simply from a perspective in the geographical sense; it thus has a predominantly IDEOLOGICAL force. Very often the implication is that the perspective has been NATURALIZED, and is thus believed to represent a neutral or value-free outlook or point of view. At the same time, the assumption is that Europe represents a standard that the non-European can aspire to but cannot exceed or replace.

Compare Dipesh Chakrabarty (1992) on European history as master narrative:

> [I]nsofar as the academic discourse of history – that is, 'history' as a discourse produced at the institutional site of the university – is concerned, 'Europe' remains the sovereign theoretical subject of all histories, including the ones we call 'Indian,' 'Chinese,' 'Kenyan,' and so on. There is a peculiar way in which all these other histories tend to become variations on a master narrative that could be called 'the history of Europe.' (In Ashcroft *et al.*: 1995, 383)

Compare GRAND AND LITTLE NARRATIVES (master narrative); MALE-AS-NORM; WEST.

Event According to Mieke Bal an event is 'the transition from one state to another state' in a NARRATIVE (1985, 5). It is conventional in NARRATOLOGY to distinguish between 'existents' (those things that are, such as CHARACTERS, settings, etc.), and 'events' (the things that are done or which occur).

Steven Cohan and Linda M. Shires distinguish between *kernel* and *satellite* events, a distinction first propounded by Seymour Chatman in his *Story and Discourse: Narrative Structure in Fiction and Film* (1978). Kernel events 'advance or outline a sequence of transformations' while satellite events 'amplify or fill in the outline of a sequence by maintaining, retarding, or prolonging the kernel events they accompany or surround' (Cohan and Shires: 1988, 54). Further, events are *enchained* when they are found in back-to-back succession with each other, whereas it is, alternatively, possible for one event to be *embedded* in another (1988, 57; such EMBEDDING is also called *staircasing*). Finally, they point out that an event can be *singular*, *repeated*, or *iterative* (1988, 86; for *iterative*, see the entry for FREQUENCY).

Roland Barthes (1975) makes a similar distinction between *catalyses* and *nuclei*: the former denotes events that are not logically essential to the narrative, and the latter those that are.

Compare *kernel function* in the entry for FUNCTION.

Exchange A term used by the NEW HISTORICIST writer Stephen J. Greenblatt to describe the manner whereby works of art *negotiate* new forms of social ENERGY as they enter the life of social and cultural contexts different from those in which they were created. Talking about such negotiations in his book *Shakespearian Negotiations* (1988), Greenblatt describes his search for 'an originary moment' in which 'the master hand shapes the concentrated social energy into the sublime aesthetic object'. The search yields no such moment, however.

> In place of a blazing genesis, one begins to glimpse something that seems at first far less spectacular: a subtle, elusive set of exchanges, a network of trades and trade-offs, a jostling of competing representations, a negotiation between joint-stock companies. (1988, 7)

Many commentators have drawn attention to the fact that Greenblatt's metaphor-kitty seems here to rely very heavily on the stock market, and some have argued that with these metaphors Greenblatt imports a set of values and assumptions that lead to one sort of EMPLOTMENT rather than another.

Compare TRAVELLING THEORY.

Exchange value See FETISHISM

Exegesis Stemming from a tradition of Biblical study, exegesis traditionally involved a range of activities from the elucidation of textual cruces and difficulties through commentary on the implications and applications of textual meanings. The Roman *exegetes* had as official function the interpretation of such things as dreams, laws, omens and the pronouncements of the Oracle, so that in some usages exegesis is more or less interchangeable with INTERPRETATION. In current usage, however, the term is normally reserved for more careful commentary or *close reading* which stays near to the words on the page.

Tzvetan Todorov distinguishes between *literal exegesis*, which seeks to elucidate the meanings or words, supply references to allusions, and so on; and *allegorical exegesis*, which seeks a further meaning for a TEXT or part of a text which already has one (1984, xxii).

Existent See EVENT

Exotopy The word suggested in the English translation of Tzvetan Todorov's *Mikhail Bakhtin: The Dialogical Principle* (1984) to represent a coinage of Bakhtin's which describes an AUTHOR's movement outside of and away from his or her CHARACTER subsequent to an earlier, initial stage of identification and empathizing with the character.

Both movements are important to Bakhtin: the novelist must understand his or her character from within, as it were, but in order to understand the character fully it must be perceived as OTHER, as apart from its creator and in its distinct ALTERITY. Moreover, DIALOGUE is only possible with an 'other': one can only talk to oneself if one estranges oneself from part of oneself and treats this part as other.

Compare CANCELLED CHARACTER, and see the discussion in OPAQUE AND TRANSPARENT CRITICISM.

Expressive(s) See FUNCTIONS OF LANGUAGE; SPEECH ACT THEORY

Extent See ANALEPSIS

Exteriority In Michel Foucault's usage, rejecting the procedure whereby the investigator proceeds from DISCOURSE to its 'interior, hidden nucleus, towards the heart of a thought or a signification supposed to be manifested in it', and instead, adopting the alternative procedure whereby the investigator proceeds on the basis of discourse itself, 'its appearance and its regularity, [and moves] towards its external conditions of possibility, towards what gives rise to the aleatory series of these events, and fixes its limits' (1981, 67; for *aleatory*, see the entry for ALEATORY TECHNIQUE).

Externalizer

This recommendation ties in with a number of movements in recent theory which reject the search for a hidden, inner, CENTRE or PRESENCE and instead seek to explain the object of study in terms of the possibilities engendered by its existence in a complex of shifting relations. In literary criticism an analogous movement would be represented by the rejection of ESSENTIALIST views of the literary TEXT in favour of a study of the literary text's 'conditions of possibility' in different READING or INTERPRET[AT]IVE COMMUNITIES.

See also RADICAL ALTERITY for Jacques Derrida's use of this term.

Externalizer According to Barbara Korte, 'externalizers, as distinct from emotional displays, are those forms of [non-verbal communication] which convey information about a character apart from his or her temporary emotions: relatively stable mental conditions (such as psychopathological states, attitudes, opinions, values, personality traits), but also mental and intellectual activities and conditions' (1997, 41).

Compare *non-verbal leakage* in the entry for LEAKAGE.

Extimate According to Tom Cohen, the 'proto-psychotic encounter with radical exteriority' (1998, 149).

Extradiegetic See DIEGESIS AND MIMESIS

Extrinsic criticism See INTRINSIC CRITICISM

F

Fabula See STORY AND PLOT

Fabulation See METALANGUAGE; MODERNISM AND POSTMODERNISM

Face-threatening acts (FTAs) See POLITENESS

Faction A portmanteau word (fact + FICTION) coined by the American author Truman Capote to describe works such as his *In Cold Blood* in which novelistic techniques are used to bring actual historical events and personages to life. A work of faction lies on the borderline between fact and fiction: the people and events described are non-fictional, but the corroboratory detail is often imagined so as to bring the READER closer to them.

Faghag/fagstag character In Gay slang a faghag is a (normally heterosexual) woman who prefers the company of homosexual men, while a fagstag is a heterosexual man who prefers the company of homosexual men. Such preferences may be related (especially for women) to the need to escape from sexual predation, or to an affinity with aspects of Gay CULTURE. Literary CHARACTERS may thus be portrayed as sharing such preferences, although such portrayals may in the past only have been fully understood by Gay or Lesbian READERS. Literary OUTING might thus involve revealing that a character had to be understood as, for example, a faghag.

False consciousness See IDEOLOGY

Fantastic Recent years have seen a marked growth of interest in fantasy and the fantastic, partly associated with a more general concern with POPULAR literature and partly as accompaniment to a more questioning attitude towards too simplistic accounts of REALISM. If this explanation is correct it is perhaps not surprising that an earlier concern with the fantastic can be found in the work of the RUSSIAN FORMALISTS. In his essay 'Thematics', for example, Boris Tomashevsky quotes an interesting passage from Vladimir Solovyev's Introduction to Alexey Tolstoy's novel *The Vampire*, which Tomashevsky describes as 'an unusually clear example of fantasy'. According to Solovyev, the distinguishing characteristic of the genuinely fantastic is that it is never,

> so to speak, in full view. Its presence must never compel belief in a mystic inter-
> pretation of a vital event; it must rather point, or *hint*, at it. In the really fantastic, the
> external, formal possibility of a simple explanation of ordinary and commonplace
> connections among the phenomena always remains. This external explanation,
> however, finally loses its internal probability. (Tomashevsky: 1965, 83–4)

A major point of controversy among more recent commentators concerns the extent to which the fantastic constitutes an independent GENRE, and, if so, what the defining characteristics of this genre are. Perhaps the most influential contribution to the view that the fantastic constitutes such an independent genre is Tzvetan Todorov's *The Fantastic: A Structural Approach to a Literary Genre* (1975). Christine Brooke-Rose has made a useful summary of the three conditions which Todorov believes to be more or less standard components of the 'pure' fantastic. The READER must hesitate between natural and supernatural explanations of what happens in the WORK up to its conclusion; this hesitation may be represented – that is, it may be shared by a leading CHARACTER in the work (this, according to Todorov, is normal but not essential); and the reader must reject both a poetic and an allegorical reading of the work, as both of these destroy the hesitation which is fundamental to the pure fantastic (Brooke-Rose: 1981, 63). If there is no hesitation, then either we are in the realm of some variant of the *uncanny* (the events are seen by the reader to have a natural explanation), or of the *marvellous* (the events are seen by the reader to have a supernatural explanation). There would seem here to be full agreement with Solovyev's above-quoted definition. (For the uncanny, see Sigmund Freud's essay 'The Uncanny' [1955], in which he relates the uncanny [or *unheimlich*] to 'that class of the frightening which leads back to what is known of old and long familiar' [1955, 220], but which has become alienated from the mind through the process of repression [1955, 241]. Through an analysis of E. T. A. Hoffmann's tale 'The Sandman', Freud reaches the conclusion that a major component of the uncanny is the fear of castration.)

Brooke-Rose points out that Todorov's demanding conditions leave us with very few examples of the pure fantastic – that is, works in which a hesitation between natural and supernatural explanations lasts until the very end of the STORY. She suggests that the pure fantastic is 'not so much an evanescent *genre* as an evanescent *element*' (1981, 63), which of course makes the fantastic a much more widespread literary phenomenon.

Kathryn Hume, in her *Fantasy and Mimesis* (1984), provides an extended discussion of the problems of defining the fantastic, and in her summary of attempted definitions she categorizes these as either one-, two-, three-, four-, or five-element definitions. The elements involved range from the choice of subject matter, the changing of 'ground-rules' as with Alice's discovery of the new rules governing Wonderland (Erik Rabkin), the 'persuasive establishment and development of an impossibility' (W. R. Irwin), satisfying readers' desire for recovery, escape, consolation (J. R. R. Tolkien), and tracing 'the unsaid and the unseen of culture: that which has been silenced, made invisible' in a way that is fundamentally subversive (Rosemary Jackson) (Hume: 1984, 13–17).

Some commentators make an overt or implied distinction between *fantasy* and *the fantastic*. Thus Anne Cranny-Francis uses *fantasy* as an umbrella term containing three different sub-types: 'other-world fantasy', 'fairy-tale', and 'horror' (1990, 77). It is clear that in this usage fantasy is different from (but related to) the fantastic.

Faultline By analogy with the physical faultlines around which earthquakes take place because of the pressure between two opposing land plates – any structural weakness or contradiction in an IDEOLOGY or a society from and around which disturbances can be expected. Laura Mulvey has argued that '[n]o ideology can ever pretend to totality: it searches for safety-valves for its own inconsistencies' (1989, 39). These safety-valves can be traced as fissures or faultlines.

The term is associated with Alan Sinfield, whose book *Faultlines: Cultural Materialism and the Politics of Dissident Reading* (1992) sets itself the task of exploring a number of such specific faultlines, mainly from the early modern period. Sinfield provides a good example of what he means by the term in a discussion of Shakespeare's *Macbeth*.

> In *Macbeth*, Duncan has the legitimacy but Macbeth is the best fighter. Duncan cannot but delegate power to subordinates, who may turn it back upon him – the initial rebellion is that of the Thane of Cawdor, in whom Duncan says he 'built/An absolute trust.' If the thought of revolt can enter the mind of Cawdor, then it will occur to Macbeth, and others; its source is not just personal (Macbeth's ambition). Of course, it is crucial to the ideology of absolutism to deny that the state suffers such a structural flaw. (1992, 40)

Much of Sinfield's discussion involves the way in which authority tries to conceal such faultlines while dissidence attempts to expose them – often in transposed or disguised forms.

Felicity conditions See SPEECH ACT THEORY

Female See FEMINISM

Female affiliation complex A term proposed by Sandra M. Gilbert and Susan Gubar in *The War of the Words*, the first volume of their study *No Man's Land* (1988). They build on Freud's model of the family ROMANCE as outlined in his 'Female Sexuality' (1963; first published 1931). In this work Freud suggests that the growing girl may follow one of three lines of development when, as she enters the Oedipal phase, she definitively confronts the fact of her FEMININITY. Either she can turn her back on sexuality altogether, or she can cling in obstinate self-assertion to her threatened masculinity, or, she can arrive at the ultimate normal feminine attitude in which she takes her father as love-object and thus arrives at the Oedipus complex in its feminine form.

Gilbert and Gubar compare the situation of Freud's 'growing girl' to that of the woman writer in the twentieth century, who confronts both a matrilineal and a patrilineal inheritance. Her reaction to these two 'parents' can take three forms similar to those faced by the 'growing girl', but whichever path she chooses, according to Gilbert and Gubar, she will have to struggle with a *female affiliation complex*. Very often the woman writer will oscillate between more than one of the available options, but whatever she does she will experience anxiety about her choice. For this reason, they argue, what is needed is 'a paradigm of ambivalent affiliation, a construct which dramatizes women's intertwined attitudes of anxiety and exuberance about creativity' (1988, 170). To this paradigm they give the name 'female affiliation complex'.

See also AFFILIATION, and the discussion of the 'anxiety of influence' in the entry for REVISIONISM.

Femaling A term denoting a conscious attempt to counter SEXIST and male-dominated bias in political, social or CULTURAL contexts by assertively requiring that women's experiences and perspectives be recognized and acknowledged.

Femininity See FEMINISM

Feminism Toril Moi makes a useful distinction between three cognate terms which provides a good starting point: *feminism* is a political position, *femaleness* a matter of biology, and *femininity* a set of CULTURALLY defined characteristics (1986b, 204). It should be recognized, of course, that Moi's suggested definitions here have a political edge: she is as much arguing for how these terms *should* be used as describing an actual, existing usage. Phrases such as 'the eternal feminine' make it clear that non-feminist usages can define femininity in universal, biological rather than cultural terms – nor is it that uncommon to find 'female' used to refer to culturally acquired characteristics. (The *OED* definitions of femininity make interesting reading in this context.)

However good a starting point this is it is not unproblematic – not least because Elaine Showalter, in her *A Literature of Their Own*, suggests a different way of using these three terms in the narrower field of women's writing. For Showalter, the feminine stage of women's writing involves a prolonged phase of imitating the prevailing modes of the dominant tradition and internalizing its standards of art; the feminist stage involves the advocacy of minority rights and values; and the female stage is the phase of self-discovery and search for identity (1982, 13).

Of the three terms, feminism is probably the most complex. The (original) *OED* described the word as 'rare', and defined it as 'the qualities of females', giving an example from 1851. But from the end of the nineteenth century the word comes increasingly to be applied to those committed to and struggling for equal rights for women – including men: in Joseph Conrad's *Under Western Eyes* (first book publication 1911), for example, the CHARACTER Peter Ivanovitch is repeatedly referred to (ironically) as a feminist. Moreover, not all those women fighting for women's rights accepted the term. In Virginia Woolf's *Three Guineas*, first published in 1938, Woolf writes

> What more fitting than to destroy an old word, a vicious and corrupt word that has done much harm in its day and is now obsolete? The word 'feminist' is the word indicated. That word, according to the dictionary, means 'one who champions the rights of women'. Since the only right, the right to earn a living, has been won, the word no longer has a meaning. (1977, 117)

Woolf goes on to describe a symbolic burning of the 'dead' and 'corrupt' word, and declares that once this has been done the air is cleared, and that we can see men and women working together for the same cause. Woolf argues, too, that the word *feminist* was one which was applied to those fighting 'the tyranny of the patriarchal state', 'to their great resentment' (1977, 118) – in other words, that the word was imposed on rather than chosen by women fighting for the rights of women. Luce Irigaray's objection to the word in a 1982 interview was that *feminism* 'is the word by which the social system designates the struggle of women. . . . I prefer to say the struggles of women, which reveals a plural and polymorphous character' (Todd: 1982, 233)

Such arguments have not been successful in burying the word in question, however, and to a very large extent women (and men) fighting for women's rights have been happy to call themselves, and be called, feminists. But doubts about the term have remained. In an interview published in the *Guardian*, 18 May 1987, Margaret Atwood responds as follows when her interviewer suggests that in her book *Bluebeard's Egg* she seems mellower about men than in her other books.

> 'It depends how you count. (I was in market research,' she adds, very deadpan.) 'If we all vote if women have souls, I vote on that side, if it's kill all the men, I'm not for it. I don't know what feminism means.' (Nadelson: 1987, 10)

Such doubts are probably more testimony to the health of the women's movement than the opposite, however. As the movement expands and develops, discussion about such a key descriptive term inevitably takes on a political character, and different interest groupings engage in struggle to impose their own MEANINGS on any term which has become a very important rallying point. To have feminism defined in such a way as to reflect one's own political objectives clearly does one's own political position and/or grouping no harm. It is perhaps worth recalling that Karl Marx was reported (by Engels) to have declared, 'all I know is that I am not a Marxist' when exasperated by some of his younger 'followers' (see the discussion in Draper: 1978, 5–11). What is indisputable is that feminism is a broad church, one within which many different emphases and persuasions (by no means necessarily opposed to one another) can be found. In the index entry for 'feminism' in the second edition of Mary Eagleton's *Feminist Theory: A Reader* (1996) one can find a representative list of sub-entries: academic/activist; bourgeois;

cultural; cyberfeminism; French; international; Marxist; materialist; negative; object-relations; radical; separatist; socialist. Such diversity is a sign of health and energy.

In general usage the term feminist is usually treated as an umbrella term to describe those (normally women but sometimes also men) who disagree with Virginia Woolf that there are no more rights to be achieved for women, and who think that it is necessary to struggle against the oppression of women on a number of different planes: social, economic, and IDEOLOGICAL. Such struggle takes varied forms and has differing objectives: if one can make the comparison with Marx and MARXISM again, one finds in both cases more unity over what is to be fought against than what is to be fought for (although in neither case should the disagreements be exaggerated or allowed to obscure the significant area of agreement).

Feminism as socio-political movement experienced a resurgence in the late 1960s and early 1970s, especially in Western Europe and the United States, a resurgence which continues and which has established a number of seemingly permanent changes in the developed countries – and which has not been without an effect in the developing world. (See the entry for SECOND-WAVE FEMINISM.)Since that time feminism has become more and more of an international movement, with increasing contacts between activists and sympathizers in different parts of the world. From the start of this movement, the role of literature was considerable. This is partly because literary writing was less closed to women than most of the other arts, and other forms of writing, but also because the literature of the past written (especially) by women offered itself as a record and analysis of the past oppression of women. It should also be remembered that the modern resurgence of feminism had one of its most important sources in the universities and colleges of the developed world, amongst a group of widely read women.

Radical feminism is a term still current but perhaps more in use in the 1960s and 1970s. It is in its insistence upon the fundamental and all-embracing significance of GENDER differentiation that radical feminism's radicalness is normally taken to consist – along with (often but not always) a rejection of most or all forms of collaboration with men or with organizations containing men. Radical feminism is often (but again, not always) associated with a commitment to Lesbianism (as a moral-political commitment as much as a sexual orientation), and if it is possible for a man to be a feminist it seems impossible (or at the very least extremely difficult) for one to be a radical feminist. Radical feminism tends to be universalizing rather than to focus upon the socially, culturally, and historically specific characteristics of PATRIARCHY, although to this it needs to be added that radical feminists have led important campaigns against specific forms of oppression. Eve Kosofsky Sedgwick has commented, in criticism of radical feminism, that it

> tends to deny that the meaning of gender or sexuality has ever significantly changed; and more damagingly, it can make future change appear impossible, or necessarily apocalyptic, even though desirable. Alternatively, it can radically oversimplify the prerequisites for significant change. In addition, history even in the residual, synchronic form of class of racial difference and conflict becomes invisible or excessively coarsened and dichotomized in the universalizing structuralist view. (1993, 13)

117

Fetishism

Against such a view, in their own discussion of radical feminism Andermahr, Lovell and Wolkowitz stress the fact of some 'commitment to the goals of socialism' in the early stages of the radical feminist movement, a belief that 'the whole gender order in which people, things and behaviour are classified in terms of the distinction between masculine and feminine is socially constructed and has no basis in natural differences between the sexes', and a desire to annihilate sex-roles as important aspects of radical feminism (1997, 222–3). This suggests that the universalizing side of radical feminism is only part of the story, and indeed in their introductory essay 'Sexual Skirmishes and Feminist Factions: Twenty-five Years of Debate on Women and Sexuality', which is the first piece in their *Feminism and Sexuality: A Reader*, Stevi Jackson and Sue Scott claim that radical feminists 'are often misrepresented as essentialist, as believing in an essential female nature and female sexuality'. While Jackson and Scott concede that the criticism may be true of some radical feminists, they insist that most do not hold such views, and they point to the example of Andrea Dworkin, who 'is on record as being fundamentally opposed to the idea that women are innately "better than men" ... yet she is frequently labelled essentialist' (1996, 7).

Of perhaps most specific interest to students of literature has been the radical feminist analysis of patriarchal and SEXIST elements in language. Representative radical feminists are Adrienne Rich, Mary Daly and Shulamith Firestone.

See RECRUITIST for the distinction between transparent, recruitist and fragmented relations between feminism and women, and see too the entry for ESSENTIALISM.

Fem(me) See QUEEN/BUTCH

Fetishism Broadly speaking, as Laura Mulvey notes, fetishism 'involves the attribution of self-sufficiency and autonomous powers to a manifestly "man"-derived object' (1996, 7; the comment indicates that there are important points of contact between fetishism and ESSENTIALISM). This, Mulvey adds, means that the fetish is always supremely CULTURALLY specific, and it is 'always haunted by the fragility of the mechanisms that sustain it' (1996, 8).

In the MARXIST sense of the term, fetishism is closely linked to Karl Marx's distinction between *use value* and *exchange value*. Marx distinguishes between the value a commodity has, measured in terms of what it can be exchanged for (exchange value), and measured in terms of its use to whoever possesses it (use value). Fetishism for Marxists thus involves a confusion between the two: the miser hoards his or her gold as if it had value in itself, not realizing that it is valuable only in terms of what it can be exchanged for. For Marx, *commodity fetishism* is a form of fetishism in which the value given to commodities within a system of exchange – a set of relationships – is incorrectly believed to be intrinsic to the commodity itself (again, this can be seen as a variant form of essentialism). The terms have frequently been brought into discussions of literary value by Marxist critics, especially in the context of discussions of the way in which literature itself becomes a commodity in the eighteenth and nineteenth centuries.

Fetishism plays a rather different role in Freudian theory. According to Juliet Mitchell, Freud's theory of fetishism was a long time in the making, for although a number of its crucial aspects are pinpointed quite early in his work, the synthesis comes only in 1927 (1974, 84–5). For Freud, fetishism is connected to the *castration complex* which, according to Freud, follows the boy child's shock at the sight of his mother's genitals. As Mitchell puts it:

> Instead of acknowledging this evidence of castration they set up a fetish which substitutes for the missing phallus of the woman, but in doing this the fetishists have their cake and eat it: they both recognize that women are castrated and deny it, so the fetish is treated with affection and hostility, it represents the *absence* of the phallus and in itself, by its very existence, asserts the *presence* of it. (1974, 85)

Thus in Freudian theory the fetish is there *to disguise a lack*. Roland Barthes applies this to the literary TEXT: the text itself is a fetish object which disguises the lack of the author (1976, 27). The author is of course, as Barthes has already told us, dead: see AUTHOR.

Marjorie Levinson, in a difficult but interesting passage, has suggested ways in which Marxist and Freudian fetishism can be distinguished from each other.

> Our everyday use of the word 'fetish' tends less to emphasize the naturalization of historically constituted objects, than the secondary alienation which, in Marx's account, occupies the final moment of the process: the moment of consumption. This is also the dimension which Freud focuses by *his* concept of fetishism: where an inanimate object, associated with a living human ensemble or part of that ensemble, is invested with a vividness stolen from the objective totality and with the subject's own cathexis. The logic is that of metonymy or synecdoche (a superimposition of the whole upon the attribute or part), whereas the Marxian fetish emphasizes *metaphoric* dimension of the abstractive process: substitution and displacement. The accent in Freud's discussion is not, as it is in Marx, on de-animation (naturalization), but rather on the *re-animation* of the isolated part. (1988, 288)

Laura Mulvey, in her major study *Fetishism and Curiosity* (1996), notes that both the Freudian and the Marxist conceptions of fetishism involve a refusal or inability to understand a symbolic system of value, but that the differences between the two are more significant than their similarities.

> One, the Marxist, is derived from a problem of inscription. How, that is, does the sign of value come to be marked onto a commodity? It is in and around the difficulty of establishing the exchange value of actual objects produced under capitalism that commodity fetishism flourishes, while the Freudian fetish, on the other hand, flourishes as phantasmatic inscription. It ascribes excessive value to objects considered to be valueless by the social consensus. (1996, 2)

For a useful study of fetishism in literature, David Simpson's *Fetishism and Imagination: Dickens, Melville, Conrad* (1982) can be consulted.

See also REIFICATION.

Fiction Literary critics have traditionally used the term *fiction* to denote imaginative WORKS (normally written NARRATIVES) which occupy a category distinct both from writing which purports to be true and also from forms of deceit and lying. The fact that certain early works now defined as novels were passed off on their initial readers as historical and true accounts complicates but does not invalidate this usage.

In recent years the word has been yoked into more extended applications by literary and CULTURAL critics. One of the first to comment upon this extension was Gerald Graff, who entitled Chapter 6 of his *Literature Against Itself* (1979) 'How Not to Talk About Fictions'. Graff summarized the extension of MEANING given to the term as follows: not just the action and PLOT of literary works, but the ideas, beliefs and themes embodied in the action or plot and the 'message' or 'world view' conveyed in their presentation were often now described as fiction by those critics whose position Graff was concerned to attack (generally speaking STRUCTURALIST and POST-STRUCTURALIST and New Left sympathizers). Nor was this the end of the matter, Graff added:

> Going a step farther, critics now sometimes suggest, by a kind of tautology, that literary meanings are fictions because *all* meanings are fictions, even those of nonliterary language, including the language of criticism. In its most extreme flights, this critical view asserts that 'life' and 'reality' are themselves fictions. (1979, 151)

Graff further suggests that the use by Jonathan Culler of the term MYTH is very close to the (mis)use of the term fiction with which he is concerned (1979, 153).

Fictogram See FICTOGRAPH

Fictograph Also *fictogram*. A term coined by the Nigerian writer Wole Soyinka to describe a false picture of (in this case African) society which has been culled from a (mis)READING of works of FICTION. Soyinka argues that 'certain European critics proceed from the abyss of ignorance on which they must erect a platform', and that these construct a *BRICOLAGE* which has the fictogram as its basic unit. As example he cites the critic Gerald Moore,

> late developer currently knocking at the portals of the Nigerian leftocracy . . . [who] takes one look at the following lines –

> I watch my dreams float vaguely through the streets, lie at the bulls' feet.
> Like the guides of my race on the banks of Gambia or Saloum.

> – and, from them, constructs this 'fictograph' of an African world-view: 'Senghor, in any case, has expressed unforgettably *the classical view* of the dead as the principal force *controlling* the living, benevolent and watchful.' (Soyinka: 1984, 45, Soyinka's emphases)

Field Introducing Pierre Bourdieu's *The Field of Cultural Production* (1993), Randall Johnson provides the following gloss on this particular term.

> Agents do not act in a vacuum, but rather in concrete social situations governed by a set of objective social relations. To account for these situations or contexts,

without, again, falling into the determinism of objectivist analysis, Bourdieu developed the concept of field (*champ*). According to Bourdieu's theoretical model, any social formation is structured by way of a hierarchically organized series of fields (the economic field, the educational field, the political field, the cultural field, etc.), each defined as a structured space with its own laws of functioning and its own relations of force independent of those of politics and the economy, except, obviously, in the cases of the economic and political fields. Each field is relatively autonomous but structurally homologous with the others.

In other words, the field's structure *refracts*, much like a prism, external determinants in terms of its own logic, and it is only through such refraction that external factors can have an effect on the field. The degree of autonomy of a particular field is measured precisely by its ability to refract external demands into its own logic. (1993, 6, 14)

The concept has been put to use in, for example, the study of post-colonial literature. Thus in an article entitled 'Post-colonial Literatures and Counter-discourse' which was first published in 1987, Helen Tiffin suggested that 'Post-colonial literatures/cultures are thus constituted in counter-discursive rather than homologous practices, and they offer "fields" [. . .] of counter-discursive strategies to the dominant discourse' (In Ashcroft *et al.*: 1995, 96).

Michel Foucault uses the concept of the 'associated field': this, in his view, 'turns a sentence or a series of signs into a statement' (1972, 98). For him such a field includes:

- the series of other formulations within which the statement appears and forms one element
- all the formulations to which the statement refers (implicitly or not)
- all the formulations whose subsequent possibility is determined by the statement, and which may follow the statement as its consequence, its natural successor
- all the formulations whose status the statement in question shares [= , I think, an enunciative field, *J. H.*] (Adapted from 1972, 98–9).

Compare AFFILIATION and cultural and ideological CAPITAL, and also DISCOURSE, and contrast the more material APPARATUS.

Figuralization/reflectorization A distinction introduced by Monika Fludernik in her 1996 study *Towards a 'Natural' Narratology*. For Fludernik

[The term *figuralization* describes] the evocation of deictic centre of subjectivity in a reflector-mode narrative that has no ruling figural consciousness attached to it. I use the word *figuralization* because the linguistic signals evoke a perceiver and experiencer, a consciousness (or SELF) on the story level. This figure (hence *figuralization*) operates as a reflector character . . . but it can develop into a teller with speaker functions in its own right. (1996, 197, small capitals in original; for *deictic* see DEIXIS)

This 'teller', however, 'cannot be aligned with a character on the story level' (1996, 202). *Reflectorization*, in contrast,

> can be defined as the *ironic* echoing of figural discourse well beyond free indirect discourse into the very opinions voiced by the narrative itself. The term . . . is therefore retained for cases where, besides a character whose consciousness is invoked, there is also a conspicuous narrative presence that triggers *either* the (ironic) assumption of the character's perspective by the narrator . . . *or* the juxtaposition of narratorial and figural perspectives, resulting in a dual voice that can be both dissonant . . . and empathetic . . . or may remain ambiguous between empathetic and ironic readings . . . (1996, 217)

The difference between the two, then, is that

> Figuralization renders perspectivizations of story matter that – within the reflectoral mode of narration – remain divorced from a specific focalizer; reflectorization, on the other hand, on account of the authorial mode of presentation, thematizes a clash between authorial language and a definite character's (or a group of characters') outlook and perspective. (1996, 202)

We can compare Fludernik's *figuralization* with Seymour Chatman's use of Bertrand Russell's term *sensibilia* – that is, 'those objects which have the same metaphysical and physical status as sense-data, without necessarily being data to any mind' (quoted by Chatman 1990, 138). Figuralization, then, provides the reader (or film viewer) with sensibilia to the extent that what it offers is not data to any mind *in the story* – any INTRA-DIEGETIC consciousness.

Chatman argues that much that the film viewer sees on screen is of this order: information about things that are there in the world of the film but not perceived by any consciousness within that world. Fludernik's *figuralization* does perhaps involve rather more of a sense of a subjectivity.

See also FREE INDIRECT DISCOURSE; DIEGESIS AND MIMESIS; NARRATIVE SITUATION; PERSPECTIVE AND VOICE; UNCLE CHARLES PRINCIPLE.

Figure According to Gérard Genette, there is a *gap* between what the poet has written and what the poet has thought. Like all gaps, Genette continues, this gap has a form, and the form is called a figure (1982, 47). Genette thus relates the term to some of the traditional concerns of rhetoric; indeed, he rejects the term *figure of thought* on the ground that a figure pertains not to *thought* but to *expression* (1982, 54; compare the more idiomatic English expression *figure of speech*).

See also ABSENCE; FIGURE AND GROUND.

Figure and ground Experiments have confirmed that the process of visual perception typically involves a sorting of the information received by the brain from the eye into two categories, which psychologists name figure and ground. This process of sorting prevents the brain from being swamped by too much information, and allows for concentration upon certain aspects of incoming messages at the expense of other aspects.

R. L. Gregory has cited the Dane, Edgar Rubin, as the psychologist whose name is associated with the first experiments involved with figure/ground reversal. In 1915 Rubin published a study, *Synopplevende Figurer* (roughly translated: 'figures that excite the sight'), describing his use of line drawings which were ambiguous and could be perceived in two ways: the best-known example of these (much pirated for book jackets!) is that of the picture which can be seen either as an elegant urn or vase, or as two human faces turned towards each other. Gregory points out that such trick pictures tell us something about the active nature of perception and of the principles on which the brain sorts out incoming information (1970, 15–18). What is achieved by Rubin's pictures, or a conjuror's sleight-of-hand, is a disturbing of the perceptual process either in the interests of illustrating some of the principles which govern it, or of trickery.

According to Irvin Rock, the essence of the figure/ground concept

> is not, contrary to popular opinion, that one or another region stands out from the background (although that is true) but that the contour dividing two regions ends up *belonging to* the region that becomes figure. It therefore gives that region rather than the other a specific shape. (1983, 65)

Both Rubin and Rock are concerned with the processes of visual perception, but many recent commentators on the RUSSIAN FORMALIST concepts of FOREGROUNDING and DEFAMILIARIZATION (which have, potentially, a much wider application) have associated both with figure/ground separation, just as we pay only passing attention to what we perceive as 'ground', reserving our attention and concern for what we single out as 'figure', so too there are things – concepts, ideas, attitudes as much as objects – which we perceive as STEREOTYPES in a 'familiarized' manner. And just as Rubin's diagrams upset the fixed categories with which the brain sorts information received from the eye, so literary defamiliarization upsets other fixed categories that allow us to skip over certain information without scrutinizing it at length or in detail. Many MODERNIST and POSTMODERNIST writers have attempted to disturb READERS' familiar responses in comparable ways: breaking those artistic rules and CONVENTIONS which are dominant at any given period.

One of the reasons why some literary WORKS give new READING experiences time and time again may well be that we make different figure/ground distinctions on successive readings. Experimental psychologists have demonstrated that although there may be some innate predispositions in the making of figure/ground distinctions, personal and CULTURAL experience, motivation, and varying needs are also powerful factors. Thus as a reader's background and experience alter, his or her figure/ground distinctions will also change. Especially in the reading of a long novel, the reader will not pay equal attention to everything that happens, to every page of NARRATIVE; we sort out an element or set of elements on which we concentrate. But these elements will not necessarily be the same ones the next time we read the same work.

See also ALIENATION EFFECT; FRAME.

Filiation See AFFILIATION

Filters See PERSPECTIVE AND VOICE

First-person See NARRATIVE SITUATION

Flâneur A (normally male) idler who wanders along crowded city streets and observes without involvement. The term is associated with the French poet Charles Baudelaire who popularized the figure, but other, later writers – most notably the German MARXIST Walter Benjamin – seized upon it as expressing something essential about modern life and the modern artist which was captured in MODERNIST art: the sense of semi-lonely detachment in the midst of the crowded urban scene.

In an essay entitled 'Rear-View Mirror: Hitchcock, Poe, and the Flaneur in America', Dana Brand has suggested that Jeffries, a photographer and the main male character of Hitchcock's 1954 film *Rear Window*, is a sort of flâneur.

> Jeffries's spectatorship, like that of the flaneur, is a form of dismemberment. He sees little pieces of people's lives and imagines that these pieces are the whole. This process is characteristic of his profession, which tries to pass off striking images of something at a particular dramatic moment as a representation of the totality of what is being photographed. It is clear, from early on in the film, that Jeffries is only concerned with the pieces into which he can fragment the world. (Brand: 1999, 125)

See also CRUISING ZONE.

Flashback See ANALEPSIS

Flashforward See PROLEPSIS

Flicker The effect achieved by a certain sort of AMBIGUITY, in which rather than having two clear alternatives between which to choose, the READER is disturbed by flashes of alternative MEANINGS. The term is Brian McHale's, and he relates it to Roman Ingarden's concept of *iridescence* or *opalescence*, found where two alternative worlds are struggling for supremacy in a TEXT but neither is capable of achieving it (1987, 32).
See also FANTASTIC.

Flip-flop According to Bernard Dupriez, a term which has a range of MEANINGS involving symmetrical substitution. This can be at a syntactical level, in which two elements having the same FUNCTION are exchanged in two syntactically identical sequences: Dupriez illustrates this with a quotation from Jacques Prévert's *La Pluie et le beau temps*:

> Yes I have a glass leg
> and I have a wooden eye.

The term can also be used in NARRATOLOGY, and Dupriez gives the example of an O'Henry story in which a young servant girl pretending to be a millionairess meets an extremely rich heir who is pretending to be a waiter (Dupriez: 1991, 193).

Focalization/focalizer See PERSPECTIVE AND VOICE; REFLECTOR (CHARACTER)

Folk See POPULAR

Force In his 1996 book *Postmodern Narratology* Andrew Gibson has a useful discussion of the way in which the concept of force has been adopted and developed by a range of writers who, like himself, have 'misgivings about the fixity of structuralist and narratological models of the text' (1996, 41). He cites Peter Brooks to the effect that force is a concept that may 'help us move beyond the static models of much formalism' (Brooks: 1984, 47). Gibson also cites Derrida's essay 'Force and Signification', and Deleuze and Guattari's use of a distinction between 'segmentarity' and 'lines of force' in narrative texts in their analysis of Henry James's 'In the Cage' in their *A Thousand Plateaus* (1988). Building also on M. Serres's 1974 study of Jules Verne, Gibson stresses that form 'is always relational, a function of the relation between text and reader, text and context etc' (1996, 46).

The adoption of this term by a number of NARRATIVE theorists can be seen as one of a number of modifications to STRUCTURALIST narratology which seek to preserve the analytical power of the approach while introducing some sense of tension or movement into it. *Force* can thus be seen as one of a number of attempts to reintroduce a DIACHRONIC or historical perspective into the SYNCHRONIC world of structuralist theory. Compare the discussion in the entry for ALWAYS-ALREADY; see also NARRATOLOGY.

Foregrounding See DEFAMILIARIZATION

Foreshadowing See PROLEPSIS

Formalism See FUNCTIONALIST CRITICISM; NEW CRITICISM; PRAGUE SCHOOL; RUSSIAN FORMALISM

Formation Louis Althusser was fond of this word, especially in compounds such as social formation, ideological formation, theoretical formation, and so on. The following quotation from 'Marxism and Humanism' (in *For Marx*) is helpful in establishing the force of the term:

> So in every society we can posit, in forms which are sometimes very paradoxical, the existence of an economic activity as the base, a political organization and 'ideological' forms (religion, ethics, philosophy, etc.). *So ideology is as such an organic part of every social totality*. It is as if human societies could not survive without these *specific formations*, these systems of representations (at various levels), their ideologies. (1969, 232; Althusser's emphases)

The term seems to be a way of smuggling SYNCHRONIC distinctions into the historicity of MARXISM; the formation is a *level*, a semi-autonomous area of linked practices which are determined, if at all, only indirectly by other levels. There seems little doubt that the concept allows for a dilution of the element of economic determinism in Marxism – something that becomes apparent once one sees how close an Althusserian formation can be to, say, a Foucauldian DISCOURSE in certain usages. However, given that the term 'relative autonomy' as used by Marxists can be traced back to Engels, Althusser's usage may be less REVISIONIST than I have suggested.

Formulaic literature A concern with the formulaic element in art and literature during the twentieth century is closely connected with investigations into POPULAR and folk art, but has spread beyond the boundaries of such investigations. A key figure here is that of the Russian Vladimir Propp, whose *Morphology of the Folktale* was first published in Russian in 1928. Propp based his work on the study of a corpus of nearly two hundred Russian folk tales, and attempted to abstract common elements from these, elements which he named FUNCTIONS. Propp's work was ground-breaking, but it focused attention on to what is rather an obvious point, that folk tales rely very heavily on elements that recur from tale to tale – formulae. (Think how many fairy tales begin with 'Once upon a time' and end with 'And they lived happily ever after'.) We are led to speculate upon two again obvious and related questions: where does this heavy reliance upon formulae come from, and what function does it perform?

There is conclusive evidence to substantiate the claim that *oral* PERFORMANCE typically involves a heavy reliance upon the formulaic, and that the advent of writing leads to a lessening of the verbal artist's reliance upon formulaic elements. Just as those who must frequently speak in public without notes in our own time tend to rely upon formulaic expressions (think of politicians and the tellers of jokes), so too the oral poet or story-teller needed formulae to act as props to the memory, while his or her listeners also found them useful as they injected familiar elements into that which could not be read a second time and thus made it easier to assimilate. To use a technical term we can say that a reliance upon formulaic elements increases the REDUNDANCY rate, and it is a fact that both the production and the generation of speech require a higher redundancy rate than does writing, which is one reason why popular film and TV is often highly formulaic. This does not mean to say that formulaic elements have no AESTHETIC significance; as Max Lüthi puts it,

> [t]he esthetics of production and the esthetics of reception are parallel, just as mnemetic technique, the basis of oral narration in general, and esthetic effect are connected to one another. ... Formulas are memory props and transition aids for the narrator. They are useful to him and comfortable, but they are additionally agreeable to him – just as the hearer is also delighted – when they turn up time and again, because he feels the organizing effect they have, and also simply because they are familiar to him. (1984, 44)

It is possible to add that in a situation in which an audience is very familiar with a range of formulae, the slightest variations in these will be perceived by the audience. This provides the opportunity for very subtle aesthetic effects based on such variation.

The research carried out by Propp and others into material which was unambiguously either oral in nature or closely related to oral material led, however, to an interest in formulaic elements in non-oral productions. The classic film Western, popular romantic FICTION (see the entry for ROMANCE), and television soap operas certainly appeared to rely more heavily upon formulaic elements than did CANONICAL literature. Put crudely, we know what will happen on the last pages of a Barbara Cartland novel

126

before we have started it, but even three-quarters of the way through *Wuthering Heights* on a first reading we will be in doubt as to its final conclusion. It is of course true that even canonical literature often contains formulaic elements which may be invisible to modern READERS and which it is the function of research and scholarship to reveal to them. But beyond this it is apparent that the REPETITION of familiar elements, of recurrent patterns, plays a greater role in some literary WORKS than in others, and that it appears to be associated more with popular than with 'high' art.

John Cawelti has defined a formula as a 'combination or synthesis of a number of specific cultural conventions with a more universal story form or archetype' (1977, 181; quoted in Yanarella and Sigelman: 1988, 7). Cawelti finds a particular CULTURAL significance in such formulae because through many repetitions they become the conventional way in which particular IMAGES, symbols, MYTHS and THEMES are represented, and from which inferences concerning collective fantasies can be hazarded.

This perhaps suggests that formulaic elements involve an IDEOLOGICAL element through an association with STEREOTYPES: the reader or TV viewer faced with a familiar formula is released from the need to confront a problem but merely swallows a pre-formed 'truth' without examining it. This seems to be true of certain formulaic elements in popular literature, but Max Lüthi argues, interestingly, that the formula's lack of individualization and concretization – what he calls its 'quasi-abstract generality' – actually leaves the reader's imagination more free to plump out the bare bones of the formula as he or she wishes (1984, 21). (Compare Umberto Eco's argument in the entry for OPEN AND CLOSED TEXTS.) This leads to the unusual idea that formulaic literature and art may actually allow for greater rather than lesser reader creativity. The negative side of such freedom, however, may be that the work offers fewer aesthetically productive constraints to the reader's fantasizing.

Any investigation into the formulaic needs to be set in the more general context of the way in which elements of the familiar are used to FRAME, form and guide literary RESPONSE. Such an investigation would necessarily overlap with the study of GENRE and form.

Fort/da From Freud's discussion in *Beyond the Pleasure Principle* (and also noted earlier in *The Interpretation of Dreams*) of the sound 'o – o – o – o' made by his grandson at the age of eighteen months. Freud interpreted the sound as the child's attempt to pronounce the German word 'fort' (gone) and he claimed to have substantiated this when he witnessed the child throw a wooden reel on a piece of string over the end of his cot and repeat the sound, then pull it back into sight and repeat the word 'da' ('there'). For Freud this game represented the child's attempt SYMBOLICALLY to represent – and thus to gain symbolic mastery over – the unpleasant experience of his mother's regular separation from him. The game thus involved, for Freud, the symbolic representation of ABSENCE.

Jacques Lacan sees this game as manifesting the *primordial symbolization* which inaugurates the conception of the signifying chain (1977, 215), and he claims that Freud's study of it exposed the origin of the REPETITION compulsion.

Frame This is a term with a very wide variety of meanings in different discipline contexts. Andrew Gibson attributes a useful way of categorizing different sorts of usage within NARRATIVE theory to Ian Reid's 1992 book *Narrative Exchanges*:

Reid distinguishes four kinds of narrative framing. The first is circumtextual, and a question of the physical adjuncts to the narrative, like title, footnotes, epigraph and so forth. The second is extratextual: the framing information, expectations and preoccupations that a reader brings to a text. The third is intratextual, taking place directly on the page itself. The fourth and last kind is intertextual, and a matter of the relationship between a narrative and other texts. (Gibson: 1996, 218)

More widely, Manfred Jahn claims that recent reference works (including earlier editions of this book) list more than ten uses within literary theory alone (1997, 441). I list below those usages with which I am acquainted.

1. According to Mieke Bal, 'the space in which the CHARACTER is situated, or is precisely not situated, is regarded as the *frame*' (1985, 94).

2. In her book *Reading Frames in Modern Fiction* (1985) Mary Ann Caws applies the term *frame* to the experience that many READERS have of finding that certain passages in works of prose FICTION 'stand out' from their surroundings. These passages are as it were *framed* by the surrounding TEXT, and this framing has important effects upon the manner in which they – and the WORK as a whole – are read. Caws suggests that such framing assumes an especial form in MODERNIST fiction as the idea of framing is called attention to or, we might say, FOREGROUNDED in modernist fiction (1985, xi).

3. Following Erving Goffman's *Frame Analysis* (1974) the term is also used to denote various ways in which works of art (among other things) are AESTHETICALLY bounded and, thus, require or invite a range of different possible relationships with the art consumer, with other works of art, or generally with extra-artistic reality. Manfred Jahn's definition is similar: 'a frame will be understood as in Perry (1979) to denote the cognitive model that is selected and used (and sometimes discarded), in the process of reading a narrative text' (1997, 441–2). Jahn draws on Artificial Intelligence research, and quotes from Marvin Minsky's presentation of 'the essence of frame theory':

> When one encounters a new situation (or makes a substantial change in one's view of a problem), one selects from memory a structure called a frame. This is a remembered framework to be adapted to fit reality by changing details as necessary. (Jahn: 1997, 442, quoting Minsky: 1979, 1–2)

The adaptation or discarding of frames will be resisted or delayed by that principle of conservatism or inertia known by narratologists as OBSTINATION. Compare also the movement between rival systems outlined within *polysystem theory* (see the entry for SYSTEM).

4. A framed (or nested) narrative is either a 'narrative within a narrative', as in Henry James's *The Turn of the Screw*, or any narrative containing different narrative levels. With reference to such a work the term *frame narrator* refers to the NARRATOR of the outer narrative (alternatively, the term *outer narrator* is often used). Inner, or framed narratives are also known as *embedded narratives* or *Chinese Box narratives*, and where multiple EMBEDDING occurs it is sometimes known as *staircasing*.

5. Umberto Eco adopts definitions from Eugene Charniak and Michael Riffaterre in order to suggest a distinction between common frames – which are the rules for

practical life possessed by ordinary individuals – and INTERTEXTUAL frames, which are existing literary *topoi* or narrative schemes (1981, 21). (For *topoi* see TOPOS.)

In P. N. Furbank's *Reflections on the Word 'Image'* there is an interesting discussion of what Furbank sees as the peculiarly modern tendency of 'abolishing the frame', a tendency he relates to a revolt against the idea of standards of REFERENCE and to an egalitarian desire to oppose the isolation of art in separated-off compartments (1970, 128–9).

6. In his *Framing the Sign*, Jonathan Culler explains why he prefers the term *frame* to the more conventional *context*. Most important, perhaps, is the argument that whereas the assumption is that a context is given, he avers that the truth is that 'context is not given but produced', and that

> [t]he expression *framing the sign* has several advantages over *context*: it reminds us that framing is something we do; it hints of the frame-up . . . , a major use of context; and it eludes the incipient positivism of 'context' by alluding to the semiotic function of framing in art, where the frame is determining, setting off the object or event as art, and yet the frame itself may be nothing tangible, pure articulation. (1988, ix)

7. In his introductory comments to an essay by Barbara Johnson, Robert Young discusses briefly Jacques Derrida's use of the terms *parergon* (a term Derrida finds in Kant) and *ergon* as substitutes for *frame* and *work*.

> In the visual arts, the parergon will be the frame, or drapery, or enclosing column. The parergon could also be a (critical) text, which 'encloses' another text. (1981, 226)

He goes on, however, to note that Derrida's terms are connected by a more complex relationship than that of a simple inside/outside dichotomy, a complexity (we may add) which relates to Derrida's interest in the paradoxical nature of MARGINALITY.

According to Brian McHale, *frame-breaking* is characteristic of much POST-MODERNIST fiction: as, for instance, the statement of the narrator of John Fowles's *The French Lieutenant's Woman* that 'This story I am telling is all imagination. These characters I create never existed outside my own mind' (McHale: 1987, 197). In like vein, John Frow argues that the task of the reader interested in coming to terms with a text's stored-up symbolic value who is also concerned with a reflexive integration of his or her situation, cannot be that of a 'correct' interpretation of the text:

> Rather than reproducing the text's official value, the reader must undertake a negative revalorization by 'unframing' it, appropriating it in such a way as to make it subversive of its own legitimacy and so *useful* in the class struggle. (1986, 228)

See also CLOSURE; EMBEDDING; FIGURE AND GROUND; OBSTINATION; SCRIPT (frame theory).

Frankfurt School The term generally applied nowadays to those individuals and works associated with the Frankfurt School of Critical Theory. The School grew out of the Frankfurt Institute of Social Research, which was founded in 1923, and especially out of Max Horkheimer's directorship of the Institute. Horkheimer's own work, and that of others such as Herbert Marcuse, Theodor Adorno, and Erich Fromm, established itself as an important development (or revision, depending upon one's perspective) of MARXISM, and is generally seen as a founding element in what is now referred to as Continental Marxism. The School was pro-MODERNIST and anti-Stalinist (especially in its view that the industrial working class of advanced countries was no longer a revolutionary force), and was sympathetic to an open attitude towards PSYCHOANALYSIS. In spite of its name the School was not always located in Frankfurt; its members regrouped in the United States during the Nazi period, but reopened in Frankfurt in 1950.

During the 1960s and 1970s the ideas of the Frankfurt School seemed to offer a non-Stalinist application and development of Marxism to issues of CULTURE and IDEOLOGY, and in 1977 Fredric Jameson was able to write that the Frankfurt School had transmitted 'fundamental themes and concerns' from debates around Marxism in the 1930s to 'the student and anti-war movements of the 1960s' (Bloch *et. al.*: 1977, 197).

The standard study of the Frankfurt School is Martin Jay's *The Dialectical Imagination: A History of the Frankfurt School and the Institute of Social Research 1923–50* (1973). For students of literature, Adorno's contributions to the debates collected in the volume *Aesthetics and Politics* (Bloch *et. al.*: 1977) – including letters to Walter Benjamin and a critique of the work of Georg Lukács – are of abiding interest.

See also CRITICAL THEORY.

Free Direct Discourse See FREE INDIRECT DISCOURSE

Free Indirect Discourse Also *Free Indirect Speech* or *Style*; *Narrated Monologue*; *Erlebte Rede*; *Style Indirecte Libre*; *Quasi-Direct Discourse* or *Substitutionary Narration*. In some usages these all represent the same general NARRATIVE technique, subdivisions within which are indicated by distinguishing between *Narrated Speech* and *Narrated Thought*, or between *Free Indirect Speech* and *Free Indirect Thought* (thus making the former phrase slightly ambiguous as it can either represent the umbrella term or a subdivision within it).

Usages do vary, however, and some commentators use *narrated monologue* to refer to a variety of Free Indirect Discourse in which there is indirect quotation of the words used in a CHARACTER's speech or thought. This would mean that non-verbalized thought processes could not be represented by means of narrated monologue, and thus another term is called for: *psycho-narration*. According to Steven Cohan and Linda M. Shires, psycho-narration can be either *consonant* (following a character's own self-apprehension), or *dissonant* (moving back from a character's own perspective) (1988, 100).

The traditional way of defining what we can refer to as FID makes use of grammatical or linguistic evidence. This involves seeing FID as a midway point between Direct, and Indirect (or Reported) Discourse (DD and ID), or as a combination of the two which blends their grammatical characteristics in a distinctive mix. Thus Shlomith Rimmon-Kenan provides the following example, in which one can note that the third example retains the third person 'he' and past tense from ID, but in its truncation resembles the words in inverted commas in the DD example.

DD: He said, 'I love her'
ID: He said that he loved her
FID: He loved her   (1983, 111)

FID often resembles ID minus the normal accompanying tag phrases (e.g. 'he suggested', 'she thought'). The standard grammatical/linguistic signs of FID are taken to be such things as DEICTICS referring to the character's own time or place (e.g. 'Tomorrow was Christmas'), the use of colloquialisms, etc. unlikely to have been used by the NARRATOR, abridgement such as is found in spoken but not, normally, written language, and the back-shift of tenses to be found in ID. When many of these characteristics are found together then a passage can be unambiguously FID, but FID may appear without any linguistic markers, such that only the semantic content of the passage in question can be adduced as evidence that one is dealing with FID.

More recent studies have exhibited increasing scepticism about approaches to FID that rely upon grammatical definitions. Richard Aczel, for example, argues

(1) that FID, though grammatically analyzable is above all contextually identifiable, and (2) that FID is not a 'transformational' phenomenon that can be linguistically derived from direct discourse according to a series of generative rules.

. . . most accounts would now seem to agree that FID *can* be grammatically marked, but is not in any final sense grammatically *identifiable*. That is to say the linguistic definition of FID is accurate but not sufficient. (1998, 477–8)

Dorrit Cohn suggests that FID 'may be most succinctly defined as the technique for rendering a character's thought in their own idiom while maintaining the third-person reference and the basic tense of narration' (1978, 100). As already suggested, however, it is not just thought that can be represented, but also speech and, furthermore, attitudes, IDEOLOGICAL presuppositions, and so on. And the speech and thought can be either particular acts or ITERATIVE examples, or even thoughts that are potential in a character but unactualized. Moreover, the thought may either be verbalized or unverbalized.

Monika Fludernik has said that with the exception of certain ambiguous Middle English examples, to her knowledge Aphra Behn is the first writer in English to employ free indirect discourse for the representation of consciousness (1996, 155).

A matter of some contention has been that of the 'dual voice' hypothesis, with Pascal (1977) and Banfield (1982) taking up positions for and against the suggestion that FID involves the combination of two VOICES, those of the narrator and the character. Richard Aczel's position here is that 'dual voice can . . . be posited at a level beyond the free indirect utterance itself' (1998, 478). In other words, the actual UTTERANCE represented in FID belongs to only one voice, but the act of representation of this utterance is that of another voice, and indeed Aczel suggests that FID can productively be considered as 'a form of quotation' (1998, 479).

The general advantage gained from a use of FID is probably that of an apparently dramatic and intimately direct access to a character's thoughts or speech without the

131

distracting presence of a narrator signalled by tag-phrases such as 'he thought' or 'she said'. By mixing FID, DD and ID an AUTHOR can achieve very considerable narrative flexibility.

A related term noted by Wales (1989, 77), who attributes it to Graham Hough, is *coloured narrative*. In this case, as Wales points out, the narrative is seen to be 'coloured' by the speech of a character, whereas in FID it is, in a sense, the speech which is coloured by the narrative voice. Very similar to colouring is *mind style*, in which a passage which is not directly attributed to a character gives us, nevertheless, his or her style of thinking or speaking, or understanding. See also UNCLE CHARLES PRINCIPLE.

Free Direct Discourse (or Speech or Thought or Style) is Direct Discourse represented without tags such as 'she thought' and 'he said'. Thus '"I'm tired", he said' would be Direct Speech, while 'I'm tired' (the inverted commas may be omitted altogether) is Free Direct Speech.

See also OBSTINATION.

Frequency Following Genette, the numerical relationship between events in a PLOT (or *sjužet*) and events in a STORY (or FABULA). This relationship can vary as follows:

1. a singular event which is narrated once (*singulative narration*)
2. an event which occurs x times and is narrated x times (*multiple narration*)
3. an event which occurs once but is narrated more than once (*repetitive narration*)
4. a repeated event which is narrated only once (*iterative narration*).

A writer or NARRATOR's skill in varying frequency can play a crucial role in the telling of a story: stories which consist only of examples (1) and (2) above can give a mechanical and unvarying impression, whereas the skilled use of REPETITION – especially forms of repetition with significant variation – can contribute to the achieving of an impression of depth and multiple PERSPECTIVE. Some writers (Genette draws particular attention to Proust) have made effective use of iterative narration to suggest underlying consistencies and patterns in a CHARACTER or situation.

It will be noted that examples (2), (3) and (4) are all forms of repetition, although only (3) is a form of *narrative* repetition. Repetition is probably one of the most common and most effective ways of building up patterns of meaning in a NARRATIVE.

Movement from frequencies (1) or (2) to frequencies (3) or (4) in a narrative can be one of the means whereby an AUTHOR manipulates such things as DISTANCE, perspective, and dramatic involvement.

Generally speaking, although frequency is a concept that has developed within narrative theory, it is less easy to apply to PERFORMANCE arts such as film or theatre – 'film narrative' is arguably 'told' only in a metaphorical sense, or at least in a very different sense from literary narrative. But frequency effects are certainly possible in, say, film. Thus Dana Brand has argued that the opening frames of Alfred Hitchcock's 1954 film *Rear Window* offer us sight of 'a process that we imagine is the same every single morning' (1999, 125). This of course is very close to what in a work of written narrative would be termed the *iterative* mode. Gérard Genette uses the term *pseudo-iterative* to describe passages of narrative which claim to be iterative but which provide extended detail or include elements which by their very nature must be unique, and the effect of the opening frames of Hitchcock's film is very similar to this.

FTAs (face-threatening acts) See POLITENESS

Function The word 'function' has been used by a number of NARRATIVE theorists to distinguish a range of proposed 'fundamental narrative units'. Shlomith Rimmon-Kenan has suggested that the attraction of the term to NARRATOLOGISTS is probably twofold: first the general sense of an activity which is proper to something, and second the logico-mathematical use which denotes ' "a variable quantity in relation to others by which it may be expressed" (*OED*)' (1983, 21). Probably the most important usage in its relevance for Literary Studies is that to be found in Vladimir Propp's *Morphology of the Folktale*. Here Propp defines a narrative function as 'an act of a character, defined from the point of view of its significance for the course of the action' (1968, 21). Propp argued that, although folk tales contain an extremely large number of different CHARACTERS, they contain a relatively small number of functions, functions which constitute the 'fundamental components' of the folk tale (1968, 21).

Propp's approach is STRUCTURALIST to the extent that it assumes a GRAMMAR of the folk tale. From this perspective, functions play a role in an individual folk tale analogous to that played by parts of speech in a well-formed sentence. Thus just as the same word can perform different grammatical functions in different sentences (compare 'I set the table' with 'You win the first set'), so too can the same ACT perform a different narrative function in different folk tales (the appearance of a dragon could represent struggle in one tale, pursuit in another).

We find a similar distinction in the work of the RUSSIAN FORMALISTS between *function* and *device*. Of the two terms, device is the more neutral, and has a general reference independent of the context of a single TEXT. Thus Viktor Shlovsky writes of the device of eavesdropping in Dickens, which performs different functions in his works (Šklovskij: 1971, 221). The distinction is perhaps clarified by reference to another term used by the Russian Formalists – that of *motivation*. According to Yuri Tynyanov, 'Motivation in art is the justification of some single factor vis-à-vis all the others...Each factor is motivated by means of its connections with the remaining factors' (Tynjanov: 1971, 130). (Contrast the definition of *motivation* given in the entry for ARBITRARY.) This resembles Barthes's comments, referred to below, on the *chaining* of sequences of actions to form functions. For the Russian Formalists, device and function were both involved in the concept of DEFAMILIARIZATION: a device could perform the function of defamiliarization at one time, but as it became familiar to readers it lost this ability.

Propp limited the number of functions to 31, and argued that these appear in the individual folk tale in a sequence which is fixed and invariable – although, of course, not all functions appear in every tale. As with the governing of the choice and order of words in a sentence, the choice of alternative functions in a given STORY was seen to be governed by SYNTAGMATIC and PARADIGMATIC rules.

To the extent that modern narrative theory is associated with the structural analysis of narratives, Propp's work can be taken to have established a new discipline, and it has unquestionably been highly influential. But it has not been without its critics. Arguments about just how many functions there are, about the rules governing their selection and use, and about which function(s) particular acts represent, soon began to suggest that even the relatively simple narratives with which Propp was concerned might resist the systematized analysis that he brought to bear on them. In general Propp's work has been more fruitful for the study of FORMULAIC LITERATURE than for more CANONICAL works, although it is clear that even in the canonical works of high literary CULTURES structural analysis on the basis of functions may have *some* validity.

In Claude Bremond's (1966 and 1973) development and modification of Propp's work, functions group together in threes to form sequences within which they punctuate three logical stages: possibility, process, outcome. For Bremond, each function opens a potentiality which can be ACTUALIZED or non-actualized.

In the work of Roland Barthes we find a further variation in the use of this term. In his 'Introduction to the Structural Analysis of Narrative' (1975), Barthes argues that a narrative can be seen as a large sentence and a sentence as, in some sense, a small narrative. He proceeds to isolate basic narrative units, and distinguishes between the *function* and the *index*. If the narrative units can be chained in sequences of actions they are termed functions, while if they perform a less structured role in the story they are termed indices. Jonathan Culler has suggested that Barthes's use of the term *function* in this essay is not a happy one, and that Barthes would have done better to have stuck to the term *lexie* (in the English translation: *lexia*) used in *S/Z* (Culler: 1975, 202). In *S/Z* a lexia is a minimal unit of reading, a passage which has an isolable effect on the reader which can be distinguished from the effect of other passages (Barthes: 1990, 13–14).

Gérard Genette uses the word in a different sense when he argues that 'there is no literary object strictly speaking, but only a *literary function*, which can invest or abandon any object of writing in turn' (1982, 4). Genette here uses *function* as equivalent to 'system-determined set of rules' in a structuralist sense. Thus if one played chess with stones, one would be (according to this view) investing the stones with the chess function, a function which would subsequently abandon them if they were thrown away after the game.

A *kernel* function or type, according to some recent theorists of narrative, is one of the basic or essential components of a PLOT – or alternatively an element in a story that advances the action. (Compare HINGE, and see also *kernel event* in the entry for EVENT.)

See also ATTRIBUTE/FUNCTION; FUNCTIONS OF LANGUAGE; LINGUISTIC PARADIGM.

Functionalist criticism Edward Said's term for criticism which has the critic 'talking about what a text does, how it works, how it has been put together in order to do certain things, how the text is a wholly integrated and equilibrated system'. Said clearly regards the NEW CRITICISM as the predominant example of such functionalist criticism, and he pays it the tribute that 'it has done away with empty rhetorical testimonials merely proclaiming a work's greatness, rhetorical worth, and such', and has 'made it possible for critics to talk seriously and technically and precisely about the text' (1984, 144).

Functions of language In 1934, in his book *Sprachtheorie* (*Theory of Language*), Karl Bühler suggested an elegant way of classifying the different semantic functions performed by the linguistic SIGN. He distinguished between the linguistic sign's *symbolic* function, which arose from its relation to things and states of affairs, its *symptomatic* function, which arose from its dependence upon its sender, whose inner states it expressed, and its *signalling* function, which rested upon its appeal to the listener, whose external or internal attitudes it directed much like a traffic sign. As Anders Pettersson (who refers to Bühler's distinctions) points out, Roman Jakobson's classification of the functions of language is 'a well-known further elaboration of Bühler's' (1990, 73).

Jakobson's rather more influential account is to be found in his essay 'Linguistics and Poetics', in which he claims that before the 'poetic function' is discussed, its place amongst the other functions of language must be defined. To do this, he argues, the constitutive factors in any act of verbal communication must first be surveyed. In a much-quoted passage he proceeds to do just this.

> The *addresser* sends a *message* to the *addressee*. To be operative the message requires a *context* referred to ('referent' in another, somewhat ambiguous, nomenclature), seizable by the addressee, and either verbal or capable of being verbalized; a *code* fully, or at least partially, common to the addresser and addressee . . . ; and, finally a *contact*, a physical channel and psychological connection between the addresser and the addressee, enabling both of them to enter and stay in communication. (1960, 353; small capitals in original replaced by italics)

Jakobson then moves to claim that each of these six factors determines a different function of language. An orientation towards the context involves the *referential function*, which he sees as the leading task of numerous messages. The *emotive or expressive function* is focused upon the addresser, and an example of the emotive function in a rare, pure form would be interjections such as 'Tut! tut!' The *conative function* involves an orientation towards the addressee, typically in the vocative or imperative modes, and this function is distinguished by the fact that it is not liable to a truth test. The *phatic function* includes messages designed purely to 'keep the line open', to maintain communicative contact without actually communicating any information other than that needed to remain in such contact. The *metalingual function* involves checking that the same CODE is being used, where, for example, we ask a conversational partner to explain what he or she means by a particular word. Finally, a focusing on the message itself for its own sake, leads us to the *poetic function* of language.

Jakobson's analysis has been influential but it has not escaped criticism. Referring to the passage quoted above, R. A. Sharpe delivers the acid verdict that banality does not preclude falsehood, and he goes on to argue that Jakobson's ignoring of the role played by INTERPRETATION in the literary arts is fundamental to what is wrong with his terminology (1984, 15). It is clear that to define the poetic use of language as a focusing upon the message itself, for its own sake, rather than on any of the other 'constitutive factors' he lists, takes us near to some very familiar FORMALIST arguments – that the literary work refers only to itself and neither comments upon the world nor communicates between human beings. It would seem to be the case that much literature encourages the READER to scrutinize the language it uses; much turns the reader's attention to specific issues in human history and perennial problems of human conduct; much directs the reader's attention to the writer of the WORK; and, finally, much leads the reader to think of him or herself. Literature, in other words, seems to straddle all of Jakobson's functions apart from, perhaps, the phatic. Robert Scholes has explicitly adapted the diagrammatic rendering of Jakobson's functions so as to describe the reading of a literary text, as follows.

contexts
text

author ———————————————— reader

medium
codes

The term 'addressee' has been given a pair of sub-categories – 'superaddressee' and 'loophole addressee' – by Mikhail Bakhtin. Starting with the addresser as 'first party' and the addressee as 'second party', Bakhtin continues:

> But in addition . . . the author of the utterance, with a greater or lesser awareness, presupposes a higher *superaddressee* (third), whose absolutely just responsive understanding is presumed, either in some metaphysical distance or in distant historical time (the loophole addressee). In various ages and with various understandings of the world, this superaddressee and his ideally true responsive understanding assume various ideological expressions (God, absolute truth, the court of dispassionate human conscience, the people, the court of history, science, and so forth). (1986, 126)

According to Lynne Pearce, who refers to Bakhtin's comments, the notion of a loophole addressee 'is exemplified by a text like Margaret Atwood's *The Handmaid's Tale* . . . in which the heroine directs her address not only to her lost communicants of the past (mother, husband, friends) but also to one outside the present Giladean time: a superaddressee who will understand all that she says' (Pearce: 1994, 76).

See also the entry for the SHANNON AND WEAVER MODEL OF COMMUNICATION, in which it is suggested that renderings of Jakobson's argument in diagrammatic form are much influenced by the Shannon and Weaver model, and also the entry for *S'ENTENDRE PARLER*.

G

Gap See ABSENCE; ELLIPSIS; FIGURE; PHENOMENOLOGY

Gatekeeping In some ways comparable to AGENDA-SETTING, the concept of gatekeeping comes from MEDIA STUDIES and, more particularly, from studies of the attitude-forming effects of the news media. Just as a literal gatekeeper will prevent you getting through the door to talk to an important person, metaphorical gatekeepers prevent certain news items, or opinions, or INTERPRETATIONS from reaching a larger public. As with the agenda-setter, the gatekeeper has power that is wide-ranging and largely invisible, and there is a disproportion between the gatekeeper's overt and covert authority.

A splendid literary example of this is the figure of ex-Pfc Wintergreen in Joseph Heller's satirical novel *Catch-22*, who has been demoted so many times that he is not even a private any longer, but who, because he is the radio operator, can decide which messages are sent and which are not. It can be argued that the formation and defence of a CANON can have a gatekeeping function, and that gatekeepers work with certain IDEOLOGICAL presuppositions that help them to carry out their function – as much in university departments of literature as on TV news desks.

Gay Criticism An umbrella description rather than the name of a homogeneous and unified 'school'. To a certain extent Gay Criticism has been put under the shadow of more fashionable umbrellas such as GENDER Studies and Lesbian theory, and of more apparently radical groupings such as QUEER THEORY. In most usages what distinguishes Gay Criticism is not just an interest in gender formation but a moral impulse which opposes HOMOPHOBIA and uses this opposition as a springboard to launch into wider CULTURAL and political issues.

Gaze The concept of the gaze is widespread in current theoretical writing, but the term does not have a fixed or standard meaning from usage to usage. This is partly because of its origins in diverse fields, from psychoanalysis to social psychology, and partly because of its currency in a range of subjects from Film Studies to POSTCOLONIALISM.

The concept constitutes an important if opaque element in Jacques Lacan's theories concerning the formation of SUBJECTIVITY. In his *The Four Fundamental Concepts of Psychoanalysis* he states that

> [t]he gaze is presented to us only in the form of a strange contingency, symbolic of what we find on the horizon, as the thrust of our experience, namely, the lack that constitutes castration anxiety.
>
> The eye and the gaze – this is for us the split in which the drive is manifested at the level of the scopic field.
>
> . . .
>
> In our relation to things, in so far as this relation is constituted by the way of vision, and ordered in the figures of representation, something slips, passes, is transmitted, from stage to stage, and is always to some degree eluded in it – that is what we call the gaze. (1979, 72–3)

Elsewhere, Lacan subjects Sartre's view of the gaze to critical scrutiny (1979, 84, 89, 182), insisting (if I understand aright) on the necessarily reflexive nature of his own conception of the gaze. (For Sartre's discussion of the concept, see his *Being and Nothingness* [1969, 258–300].)

The concept has been more utilized in film than in literary criticism, and especially by FEMINIST critics who have used it to explore the element of DESIRED (but perhaps denied) power in the voyeuristic male utilization of the gaze in the cinema. The classic text here is Laura Mulvey's 'Visual Pleasure and Narrative Cinema', first published in 1975. Mulvey points out that

> [i]n a world ordered by sexual imbalance, pleasure in looking has been split between active/male and passive/female. The determining male gaze projects its fantasy onto the female figure, which is styled accordingly. In their traditional exhibitionist role women are simultaneously to be looked at and displayed, with their appearance coded for strong visual and erotic impact so that they can be said to connote *to-be-looked-at-ness*. (1989, 19)

This world of sexual imbalance finds a comfortable home in the cinema.

> At first glance, the cinema would seem to be remote from the undercover world of the surreptitious observation of an unknowing and unwilling victim. What is seen on the screen is so manifestly shown. But the mass of mainstream film, and the conventions within which it has consciously evolved, portray a hermetically sealed world which unwinds magically, indifferent to the presence of the audience, producing for them a sense of separation and playing on their voyeuristic fantasy. Moreover, the extreme contrast between the darkness in the auditorium (which also isolates the spectators from one another) and the brilliance of the shifting patterns of light and shade on the screen helps to promote the illusion of voyeuristic separation. Although the film is really being shown, is there to be seen, conditions of screening and narrative conventions give the spectator an illusion of looking in on a private world. Among other things, the position of the spectators in the cinema is blatantly one of repression of the exhibitionism and projection of the repressed desire onto the performer. (1989, 17)

As a result, in the typical Hollywood film, the male viewer is able to identify with the main male protagonist, 'so that the power of the male protagonist as he controls events coincides with the active power of the erotic look, both giving a satisfying sense of omnipotence' (Mast *et al.*: 1992, 751). Women are both looked at in the film *and* in the cinema, and in both cases the gaze is in the possession of men, thus depriving women of power and of self-determined subjectivity. Women are to be looked at, not to look; their alienation from the gaze is an aspect of their passivization and REIFICATION.

In her 1997 book *Looking for the Other: Feminism, Film, and the Imperial Gaze*, E. Ann Kaplan makes a distinction between the gaze and the look. She explains that

> I will reserve the term 'look' to connote a process, a relation, while using the word 'gaze' for a one-way subjective vision. ... Looking will connote curiosity about the Other, a wanting to know (which can of course still be oppressive but does not have to be), while the gaze I take to involve extreme anxiety – an attempt in a sense *not* to know, to deny, in fact. (1997, xvi–xvii)

Moreover, 'the subject bearing the gaze is not interested in the object per se, but consumed with his (*sic*) own anxieties, which are inevitably intermixed with desire' (1997, xviii; Kaplan's interpolation), so that 'process' or interaction is not possible.

As I warned, however, there are many variations of usage that have to be contended with so far as the gaze is concerned, and Kaja Silverman has proposed an alternative distinction: 'unlike the gaze, the look foregrounds the desiring subjectivity of the figure from whom it issues, a subjectivity that pivots upon lack, whether or not that lack is acknowledged' (1994, 286). A further distinction is provided by Martin Jay who, following David Michael Levin, distinguishes between the

> 'assertoric' and 'aletheic gaze.' The former is abstracted, monocular, inflexible, unmoving, rigid, ego-logical and exclusionary; the latter is multiple, aware of its context, inclusionary, horizontal, and caring. (Jay: 1993, 275, quoting Levin: 1988, 68)

Kaplan's book is clearly written in the wake of POSTCOLONIALIST discussions of the way in which inequalities of power at the political level become translated into oppressive interpersonal relations.

> The imperial gaze reflects the assumption that the white western subject is central much as the male gaze assumes the centrality of the male subject. As noted before, anxiety prevents this gaze from actually seeing the people gazed at.

> The gaze of the colonialist thus refuses to acknowledge its own power and privilege: it unconsciously represses knowledge of power hierarchies and its need to dominate, to control. Like the male gaze, it's an objectifying gaze, one that refuses mutual gazing, mutual subject-to-subject recognition. It refuses what I am calling a 'looking relation.' (1997, 78, 79)

Thus when white western males 'gaze' at non-white, non-western females – as in Hollywood representations of 'native women' – two forms of dehumanizing and de-personalizing observation come together.

This is not just an academic matter: in his 1963 book *Behavior in Public Places*, Erving Goffman pointed out that at that time in certain southern US states there were definite rules about how much a Black man was allowed to look at a White female, before a sexual offence punishable by law was committed, and in the same book he described the 'hate stare' used by Whites to demonstrate and enforce power over Blacks (quoted in Argyle and Cook: 1976, 63, 74). More recently the African American writer bell hooks has argued that a space of black agency can be opened up by 'an oppositional gaze' (1992: 116).

Work such as Mulvey's and Kaplan's opens up important perspectives for literary criticism, not least in the tracing of larger power inequalities down to the writer's choice of PERSPECTIVE AND VOICE in novels and short stories. Is the READER encouraged to gaze or to look at the CHARACTERS presented to us in a work of fiction? Is the vantage-point of our observation white, western and male?

See Doane (1988) for further discussion of this topic, and the entries for VOYEURISM and SCOPOPHILIA.

Gender In current FEMINIST usage, *gender* is used to refer to those characteristics of socio-cultural origin which are attributed to the different biological sexes. Within Linguistics this usage is sometimes varied in order to avoid confusion with linguistic gender, but generally speaking feminist influence has succeeded in establishing that *gender* involves society and or CULTURE and *sex* involves biology. There are thus two sexes, but many different genders. In their article 'Sexual Skirmishes and Feminist Factions: Twenty-five Years of Debate on Women and Sexuality', Stevi Jackson and Sue Scott confirm the history of this distinction, but note that it is by no means uncontroversial.

> The term 'gender' was adopted by feminists to emphasise the social shaping of femininity and masculinity, to challenge the idea that relations between women and men were ordained by nature. Sometimes a distinction is made between 'sex' as the biological differences between male and female and 'gender' as the cultural distinction between femininity and masculinity along with the social division between women and men. Not all feminists accept this distinction. Some think that it denies the importance of the physical body, while others argue that our understanding of the anatomically sexed body is itself socially constructed. We ourselves endorse the latter view. (Jackson and Scott: 1996, 2)

A *genderlect* is a term used to describe linguistic characteristics which in a given society or culture are specific to members of one gender. (Compare IDIOLECT; SOCIOLECT.)

See also TRANSGENDER.

Genderlect See GENDER

Genealogy A term associated with Michel Foucault, who applies it to 'the union of erudite knowledge and local memories which allow us to establish a historical knowledge of struggles and to make use of this knowledge tactically today' (1980a, 83). He adds that

> [b]y comparison, then, and in contrast to the various projects which aim to inscribe knowledges in the hierarchical order of power associated with science, a genealogy should be seen as a kind of attempt to emancipate historical knowledges from that subjection, to render them, that is, capable of opposition and of struggles against the coercion of a theoretical, unitary, formal and scientific discourse. It is based on a reactivation of local knowledges – of minor knowledges, as Deleuze might call them – in opposition to the scientific hierarchisation of knowledges and the effects intrinsic to their power: this, then, is the project of these disordered and fragmentary genealogies. (1980a, 85)

Geneva School See PHENOMENOLOGY

Genotext and phenotext A distinction associated with Julia Kristeva, who reports in *Séméiotiké* (1969) that she borrowed it from the Russian linguists Saumjan and Soboleva. It was popularized in English as a result of its use by Roland Barthes, among others. According to Kristeva, the phenotext is 'the verbal phenomenon as it presents itself in the structure of the concrete statement', while the genotext 'sets out the grounds for the logical operations proper to the constitution of the subject of the enunciation'; it is 'the place of structuration of the phenotext'; it is a heterogenous domain: at the same time verbal and of the nature of drives ('pulsionnel') (it is the domain 'where signs are cathected by drives'). (Barthes: 1981b, 38, quoting from an interview with Kristeva published in 1972)

As can be seen, the distinction is not an easy one to gloss, but a key element seems to reside in the final quotation given by Barthes: whereas the phenotext is the purely verbal element contained in and constituting a particular UTTERANCE, the genotext is that complex of genetic forces where the non-verbal meshes with and expresses itself in the verbal.

The distinction has enjoyed a limited circulation amongst literary critics engaged in theorizing literary genesis.

Genre The traditional sense of genre as a literary type or class survives in the present day, with the term *form* sometimes confusingly used interchangeably with that of genre. Generic debates have become less heated during a time in which it is more generally accepted that genres have a CONVENTIONAL rather than an intrinsic justification, but the role of genres in forming audience and READER expectations and responses has been considered by a number of recent theorists and critics. Discussion of the FORMULAIC and of the INTERPRET[AT]IVE COMMUNITY have not infrequently impinged upon the topic of generic attribution, and an interest in new ways of categorizing literary WORKS, for example FANTASTIC and POPULAR literature, almost inevitably leads to discussion of the theory of genres.

John Frow uses the term in a way that is very close to what sociolinguists and others have called REGISTER, as can be seen in the following comment:

[A] genre such as prayer is unified by a specific pattern of address (second-person oral to an absent but omnipotent superhuman superior), by grammatical and syntactic structures (vocatives, subjunctives, request structures) corresponding to this authority situation, and by an appropriate decorum, including, in many varieties of prayer, an archaized vocabulary and a reliance on formulaic constructions. (1986, 69)

Anne Cranny-Francis argues that study of the FEMINIST use of generic literary forms confirms that genre is a social practice as well as a literary or linguistic practice, and although her definition of *genre* bases itself in TEXTUAL attributes (conventions, formulae, format) its study leads her into social, historical and IDEOLOGICAL issues. She quotes tellingly from Tzvetan Todorov's (1984) study of Bakhtin: 'Genre is a sociohistorical as well as a formal entity. Transformations in genre must be considered in relation to social changes' (Cranny-Francis: 1990, 16–17).

Gest John Willett's translation of the German term *gestisch*, used by the playwright Bertolt Brecht to bring together the meanings *gist* and *gesture* and suggesting an epiphanic item of behaviour (verbal or non-verbal) which somehow reveals or gives forth the essence of the whole of which it is the part – the whole person, the whole social situation, and so on. John Willett points out that the term can be traced back not just to Brecht's collaborator Kurt Weill, but to Lessing's *Hamburger Dramaturgie*, entry for 12 May 1767 (Willett: 1964, 42).

Willett states that in translating Brecht's German term he chose the archaic English word *gest* (meaning 'bearing, carriage, mien', *Shorter Oxford English Dictionary*), as the 'nearest manageable equivalent' (1964, 42).

See also MOMENT.

Gestalt *Gestalt* is German for 'pattern' or 'configuration', and a group of psychologists operating in Germany during the early years of the twentieth century became known as the Gestalt psychologists because they presented experimental evidence to substantiate the claim that the brain organizes stimulus patterns into wholes on the basis of certain principles which are more the result of genetic inheritance than CULTURAL influence. The word Gestalt is accordingly often used in connection with the claim that in matters of perception or INTERPRETATION the whole is greater than the part.

Ghettoization/deghettoization The word *ghetto* was originally applied to that section of a town to which Jews were confined. Its recent metaphorical extension in Literary Studies has normally to do with separatist and secretive CULTURES associated with Lesbians and Gays (see the entry for CLOSET). Ghettoization is thus seen as a tendency related to persecution in which Gay and Lesbian cultural expression is directed inward and denied encounter with public culture except through licensed and token forms such as that of CAMP. Deghettoization is thus a movement to make public the cultural (and political, social, etc.) life of Gay and Lesbian people.

For *pink ghetto*, see the entry for LAVENDER CULTURE/LANGUAGE/SEX.

Glissement See SLIPPAGE

God trick See CENTRE

Gothic See ROMANCE

Gram See DIFFÉRANCE

Grammar Widespread reliance upon the LINGUISTIC PARADIGM has resulted in the term *grammar* being applied in non-linguistic areas. A good example is found in the title of Tzvetan Todorov's *The Grammar of the Decameron* (published in French, 1969). Central to this sort of metaphorical extension is the idea that as grammars enable the *generation of utterances*, by extension, then, a 'grammar' for *The Decameron* should allow us to understand how tale after tale can be 'generated' by Boccaccio. But the extension of meaning to non-linguistic areas is not exclusively contemporary: thus John Smith (of Pocahontas fame) published *A Sea Grammar: With the Plaine Exposition of Smiths Accidence for Young Sea-Men*, in 1627.

Compare ENERGETICS/GEOMETRICS.

Grammatology In *Of Grammatology* Jacques Derrida attributes this term to Littré, from whom he quotes: 'A treatise upon Letters, upon the alphabet, syllabation, reading, and writing.' Derrida notes that to his knowledge the word has been used in the twentieth century only by I. J. Gelb in *A Study of Writing: The Foundations of Grammatology* (1952), which book, Derrida claims, 'follows the classical model of histories of writing' (Derrida: 1976, 323 n4). Derrida uses the word to indicate a 'science of writing' that is, he believes, showing signs of liberation all over the world (1976, 4). This should not, however, be understood in terms of a full-formed science the basic principles of which are established and final, but – he implies – a science in which everything is questioned, including its own basis and history (1976, 28). For Derrida's use of the word ÉCRITURE ('writing') see the separate entry.

In 'Linguistics and Grammatology' Derrida suggests that the word grammatology should replace the word SEMIOLOGY in the programme set out in Ferdinand de Saussure's *Course in General Linguistics,* as this will give the theory of writing the scope needed to counter LOGOCENTRIC repression and the subordination to linguistics.

Grand narratives and little narratives From the French terms *grand récit* and *petit récit. Grand récit* is sometimes rendered as *master narrative.* The terms have been given widespread currency by Jean-François Lyotard's book *The Postmodern Condition: A Report on Knowledge* (1984; first published in French, 1979). Lyotard distinguishes the modern by its association with what he calls grand narratives:

> I will use the term *modern* to designate any science that legitimates itself with reference to a metadiscourse of this kind making an explicit appeal to some grand narrative, such as the dialectics of Spirit, the hermeneutics of meaning, the emancipation of the rational or working subject, or the creation of wealth. (1984, xxiii)

A grand narrative, then, is a means for EMPLOTTING a life or a CULTURE; to give one's actions or one's life meaning one pictures oneself as a CHARACTER within an already-written narrative, one whose final conclusion is assured in advance.

In popular usage the term is typically applied to IDEOLOGICAL systems such as MARXISM or religious outlooks such as Christianity or Islam. In Lyotard's view the day of such all-embracing, totalizing systems of belief has passed. From now on we have to derive meaning from little narratives, from local justifications:

> The narrative function is losing its functors, its great hero, its great dangers, its great voyages, its great goal. It is being dispersed in clouds of narrative language elements – narrative, but also denotative, prescriptive, and so on. (1984, xxiv)

To describe this great shift from the time of the grand narrative to that of the little narrative, Lyotard argues that the society of the future falls less within the province of a Newtonian anthropology such as STRUCTURALISM or SYSTEMS theory, and more with a PRAGMATICS of language particles, a world of many language games (1984, xxiv).

However modern Lyotard claims this to be, it can sound dangerously like cultivating one's own garden – something that (as the origin of the phrase bears witness) the great age of reason and of the grand narrative of the Enlightenment knew all about. Bruce

Henricksen echoes such misgivings when he fastens upon a comment from Lyotard's *Just Gaming*. Lyotard asks how one can conduct a DISCOURSE in the absence of founding truths and grand narratives, and how one can judge without criteria.

> His answer, certain to be unsatisfactory to many, is that one begins with 'a feeling, that is all.' *Transcendent interpretation*, based on a presumably immutable set of norms – norms provided by Marxist, Christian, or some other grand narrative – is no longer valid, according to Lyotard. But what, one might ask in response, makes *immanent interpretation* anything more than the most juvenile celebration of spontaneity? (1992, 166; the quotation is from Lyotard: 1985, 15)

David Forgacs has also pointed out that the rejection of grand narratives by Lyotard and others involves itself in the paradoxical position of being itself another grand narrative claiming for itself the status of a transcendental truth, and he adds that a 'still more significant weakness in these accounts is their tendency to flatten out the contradictions of modernity and present it as all of a piece' (1995, 13).

See also EUROCENTRIC (European history as a master narrative).

Ground See FIGURE AND GROUND

Gyandry See ANDROGYNY

Gynecocratic See GYNOCRATIC

Gynema See GYNESIS

Gynesis Coined by Alice A. Jardine in her 1985 book *Gynesis: Configurations of Woman and Modernity*. Jardine explains that she suggests the term as

> what I hope will be a believable neologism: gynesis – the putting into discourse of 'woman' as that process diagnosed in France as intrinsic to the condition of modernity; indeed, the valorization of the feminine, woman, and her obligatory, that is, historical connotations, as somehow intrinsic to new and necessary modes of thinking, writing, speaking. The object produced by this process is neither a process nor a thing, but a horizon, that toward which the process is tending: a gynema. This gynema is a reading effect, a woman-in-effect that is never stable and has no identity. Its appearance in a written text is perhaps noticed only by the feminist reader – either when it becomes insistently 'feminine' or when women (as defined metaphysically, historically) seem magically to reappear within the discourse. (In Mary Eagleton: 1996, 261)

The process with which Jardine is concerned is not necessarily FEMINIST, although it is of interest to feminists, representing in many cases a nervousness on the part of male authors who seek to re-establish or resituate challenged concepts of the FEMININE or the female.

Gynocentric See ANDROCENTRIC

Gynocratic/gynecocratic That which is ruled by women. Thus a gynocratic society would be one in which women held power, in contrast to an ANDROCRATIC society, in which power would be – and has been – in the hands of men.

Gynocritics According to Elaine Showalter the term gynocritics is an invention of hers to describe that FEMINIST criticism which studies women *as writers*, 'and its subjects are the history, styles, themes, genres, and structures of writing by women; the psycho-dynamics of female creativity; the trajectory of the individual or collective female career; and the evolution and laws of a female literary tradition' (1986, 248).
　　See also ÉCRITURE; ÉCRITURE FÉMININE; FEMINISM.

H

Habitus A term associated with the work of Pierre Bourdieu. Randall Johnson, in his excellent Introduction to Bourdieu's *The Field of Cultural Production*, quotes from Bourdieu's own definition in his *The Logic of Practice*:

> [D]urable, transposable dispositions, structured structures predisposed to function as structuring structures, that is, as principles which generate and organize practices and representations that can be objectively adapted to their outcomes without presupposing a conscious aiming at ends or an express mastery of the operations necessary in order to attain them. Objectively 'regulated' and 'regular' without being in any way the product of obedience to rules, they can be collectively orchestrated without being the product of the organizing action of a conductor. (Bourdieu: 1993, 4, quoting Bourdieu: 1990, 54)

According to Johnson's account, 'the notion of habitus was conceived as an alternative to the solutions offered by subjectivism (consciousness, subject, etc.) and a reaction against structuralism's "odd philosophy of action" which reduced the agent to a mere "bearer"... or "unconscious" expression (for Lévi-Strauss) of structure' (1993, 4–5). Johnson notes further that Bourdieu 'compares the notion to Chomsky's generative grammar, in that it attempts to account for the creative, active and inventive capacities of human agents, but without – and here he distances himself from Chomsky – attributing it to a universal mind' (1993, 5).
　　Rather more accessible is Johnson's suggestion that habitus can be looked on as

> a 'feel for the game', a 'practical sense' (*sens pratique*) that inclines agents to act and react in specific situations in a manner that is not always calculated and that is not simply a question of conscious adherence to rules. Rather, it is a sense of dispositions which generate practices and perceptions. The habitus is the result of

a long process of inculcation, beginning in early childhood, which becomes a 'second sense' or a second nature. According to Bourdieu's definition, the dispositions represented by the habitus are 'durable' in that they last throughout an agent's lifetime. (1993, 4)

Hard-wired From computer technology. That which is hard-wired into a SYSTEM cannot be changed, as can software programs. The term is used metaphorically to suggest anything structured into a system (such as an IDEOLOGY or a TEXT) that cannot be altered.

Hegemony A term used by MARXISTS to describe the maintenance of power without the use, or direct threat, of physical force; normally by a minority CLASS whose interests are contrary to those over whom power is exercised. The English term has been invoked to translate comparable terms in German, Russian and Italian, and its use can be traced back to early translations of Marx, Engels and Lenin. Its modern use, however, stems from the work of the Italian communist Antonio Gramsci, whose most influential work was written while he was incarcerated by Mussolini's fascists, and published in various collections after the Second World War. Although Gramsci recognized the importance of the use of force by Italian fascism, he was more preoccupied with what he saw as the ' "spontaneous" consent given by the great masses of the population to the general direction imposed on social life by the dominant fundamental group; this consent is "historically" caused by the prestige (and consequent confidence) which the dominant group enjoys because of its position and function in the world of production' (Gramsci: 1971, 12). The concept of hegemony became of increasing interest to Marxists concerned to theorize the apparent acceptance of class society by those of its members who should, according to a Marxist analysis, have been in revolt against their exploitation.

The term is frequently encountered in recent Marxist literary criticism for three main reasons. First, because some recent Marxists have seen literature itself as one of the more important means whereby the IDEOLOGY of the dominant or ruling class is established, disseminated and perpetuated. Some have argued that the very establishment of a CANON which confers the title 'literature' on certain works, thus giving them a certain status and also encouraging a particular way of reading them, is part of a process of hegemonic control. From this perspective either literature, or particular uses of literature, have the function of contributing to the hegemonic domination of one class by another. Thus, for example, many orthodox communists in the 1930s argued that a work such as James Joyce's *Ulysses* encourages the READER to see life in terms of consumption rather than production, of distanced perception rather than of engaged action, and although the word 'hegemony' was infrequently used in such attacks, modern reformulations of them do have frequent access to it.

Second, because other Marxist literary critics have argued that literary texts often give the reader a valuable portrayal of the ways in which hegemony is achieved. (Some such arguments have also used Joyce's novel, and have drawn attention to the way in which *Ulysses* depicts Ireland as in thrall to both the political power of Britain and the ideological power of the Roman Catholic Church.)

And third, because other Marxist literary critics have argued that an oppressed or subordinate class or group can use the writing or INTERPRETING of literature in the battle for hegemony.

Some FEMINIST literary critics and theorists have also had recourse to the term in discussion of the way in which certain PATRIARCHAL or PHALLOCENTRIC ideas or ways of thinking are reproduced and renewed in literature or in the literary INSTITUTION.

For *hegemonic discourse*, see the entry for DISCOURSE.

Helper See ACT/ACTOR

Hermeneutic code See CODE

Hermeneutics Within Anglo-American literary-critical circles the term hermeneutics has often been used as a loose synonym for INTERPRETATION, and indeed its primary reference is to the understanding of TEXTS and the understanding of understanding – especially with relation to the discipline of Theology.

More recently, however, use of the term has generally implied specific reference to the German hermeneutic tradition, a tradition which has become better known in Britain and America during the past couple of decades through the work of E. D. Hirsch and Wolfgang Iser. One of the reasons why the German hermeneutic tradition was generally neglected in the 1970s and 1980s within Anglo-American theory can be traced back to the importance of a historical perspective to this tradition, a perspective which accorded ill with such SYNCHRONIC and anti-historicist approaches as STRUCTURALISM and (to a certain extent) DECONSTRUCTION.

The undisputed founding fathers of the German hermeneutic tradition are Friedrich Schleiermacher (1768–1834) and Wilhelm Dilthey (1833–1911), although both built on the work of German Protestant theologians of the seventeenth century whose development of methods of Biblical interpretation had a clearly theological imperative. It is to Schleiermacher that we owe the concept of the hermeneutical circle (see below), although it was Dilthey who gave it its name.

The philosopher and historian Wilhelm Dilthey, according to a useful discussion by Ian Maclean,

> sought to make hermeneutics the equivalent in relation to the human sciences (*Geistewissenschaften*) of the scientific method of the natural sciences (*Naturwissenschaften*). For him, explanation was the appropriate mode of intelligibility for the natural sciences, whereas understanding was that of the human sciences. Understanding has to do with the experience of other subjects and minds than our own; it relies on the meaningfulness of all forms of expression in which experience is couched (but especially written expression); this meaningfulness is bestowed on expression by interpretation. (1986, 124–5)

Three other very important names in the German hermeneutic tradition are those of Edmund Husserl (1859–1938), Martin Heidegger (1889–1976), and Hans-Georg Gadamer. Husserl's development of PHENOMENOLOGY had a number of very important implications for theories of interpretation, especially in terms of the active and 'completing' role that the act of consciousness has in CONCRETIZING its incompletely perceived objects of perception. Heidegger's main contribution to hermeneutical theory is, arguably, his anti-individualistic and historicist view of the process of interpretation.

The word hermeneutics is etymologically related to the name of the messenger-God Hermes, who, as Richard E. Palmer points out in his book *Hermeneutics*, is, significantly, 'associated with the function of transmuting what is beyond human understanding into a form that human intelligence can grasp' (1969, 13). Palmer points out that hermeneutics has traditionally had two main focuses of concern: 'the question of what is involved in the event of understanding a text, and the question of what understanding itself is, in its most foundational and "existential" sense' (1969, 10). Hermeneutics thus has often had a dual identity, being treated on the one hand as a philosophical study with the aim of understanding (rather than changing) the practice of interpretation, and on the other hand as the search for a set of correct principles and methods that will enable correspondingly correct interpretations to be arrived at.

At different times this dual identity has led to disagreements concerning the 'true' role and function of hermeneutics. It is arguable that this tension can be traced back to the development of hermeneutics within Biblical scholarship and EXEGESIS. Richard Palmer certainly argues for the existence of *two* hermeneutic traditions:

> There is the tradition of Schleiermacher and Dilthey, whose adherents look to hermeneutics as a general body of methodological principles which underlie interpretation. And there are the followers of Heidegger, who see hermeneutics as a philosophical exploration of the character and requisite conditions for all understanding.
>
> . . .
>
> Gadamer, following Heidegger, orients his thinking to the more philosophical question of what understanding itself is; he argues with equal conviction that understanding is an historical act and as such is always connected to the present. (1969, 46)

Perhaps the aspect of the hermeneutic tradition which is best known in Anglo-American circles is that rendered by the term 'the hermeneutic circle'. The term is used to express the seeming paradox that the whole can be understood only through an understanding of its parts, while these same parts can be understood only through an understanding of the whole to which they belong. Allan Rodway suggested back in 1970 that the way we escape from such situations is by 'edging out', 'tacking from evidence to hypothesis to further evidence to renewed hypothesis' (1970, 94) – although it is arguable that such a solution to the problem of the hermeneutic circle is already implicit in the work of both Dilthey and Schleiermacher.

E. D. Hirsch is the theorist who has done most to bring the work of the German hermeneuticists to the attention of Anglo-American readers. Indeed, in his essay 'Objective Interpretation' (first published in 1960 and reprinted in *Validity in Interpretation* [1967]), Hirsch states that 'my whole argument may be regarded as an attempt to ground some of Dilthey's hermeneutic principles in Husserl's epistemology and Saussure's linguistics' (1967, 242, n30). In his subsequent book, *The Aims of Interpretation* (1976), Hirsch describes his relationship to the German hermeneutic tradition in more detail. Like Richard Palmer, he sees two main 'lines' within this tradition, although these he defines in a rather different manner from Palmer:

In this book I write as a representative of general hermeneutics. In the history of the subject, the important distinction between local and general hermeneutic theories has served to define the tradition of Schleiermacher over against more narrowly conceived hermeneutical traditions. Within this line of general hermeneutics stemming from Schleiermacher can be found Boeckh, Dilthey, Heidegger, and Gadamer in a direct, unbroken lineage. (Just as Heidegger was a student of Dilthey's, so was Gadamer a student of Heidegger's.) But the tradition is by no means a uniform one. The relativism of Heidegger and Gadamer runs counter to the objectivism of Boeckh and Dilthey, so that my own objectivist views can be considered a throwback to the 'genuine' or 'authentic' tradition of Schleiermacher. But whether one takes an objectivist or relativist position, certain arguments favoring general hermeneutics over local hermeneutics seem to me very strong. (1976, 17)

It is for Gadamer that Hirsch reserves his strongest criticisms, focusing on his *Truth and Method* in an essay entitled 'Gadamer's Theory of Interpretation', first published in 1965 and reprinted as an appendix to *Validity in Interpretation. Truth and Method* was first published as *Wahrheit und Methode* in Tübingen in 1960; the English translation (1975, revised 1989) is of the second edition, published in Tübingen in 1972.

Hirsch sees Gadamer's book as a 'polemic against that nineteenth-century preoccupation with objective truth and correct method' that is represented by August Boeckh's *Encyclopädie und Methodologie der philologischen Wissenschaften* (1877), to the title of which Gadamer's own work's title responds (Hirsch: 1967, 245). According to Hirsch, Gadamer's 'primary concern is to attack the premise that textual meaning is the same as the author's meaning' (1967, 247). Hirsch is also extremely critical of Gadamer's argument that the author's PERSPECTIVE and the interpreter's perspective must be fused in a fusion of horizons (*Horizontverschmelzung*), asking, 'How can an interpreter fuse two perspectives – his own and that of the text – unless he has somehow appropriated the original perspective and amalgamated it with his own?' (1967, 254)

Hirsch's own distinction between MEANING AND SIGNIFICANCE has been seen by more than one commentator as an attempt to break the then-current orthodoxies of NEW CRITICAL anti-contextualism by going back to the origins of the German hermeneutic tradition – and, in particular, to the work of Friedrich Schleiermacher. Schleiermacher believed that the process of understanding reversed the process of composition, for instead of starting with the AUTHOR's mental life and proceeding to textual embodiment or projection it started with the text and worked its way back to its originating mental life. It is easy to see how Hirsch's insistence on equating *meaning* with authorial INTENTION builds on such a view.

At a time when the death of the author was being confidently announced one can readily understand that this particular position did not meet with general acceptance. T. K. Seung has offered a representative objection to Hirsch's position:

If authorial intention were available for direct inspection and observation by readers, it could readily be used for settling the claims of competing interpretations.

> Unfortunately, authorial intention can be reached only through textual interpretations. (1982, 13)

We are back to another vicious circle. In this case, however, the argument that authorial intention can be reached only through textual interpretation seems unnecessarily limiting, and arguably lands us back in a sort of New Critical formalism (which is not to suggest that Hirsch's own views are unproblematic: see the entry for MEANING AND SIGNIFICANCE).

If the historicist emphases of the German hermeneutic tradition militated against its catching the interest of many Anglo-American theorists during the heyday of structuralism and deconstruction, two new developments may help to change this situation. The first is the rise of the NEW HISTORICISM, which has helped to make the historicist emphases of the hermeneutic tradition much less unfashionable, and the second is the fact that the popularity of a Bakhtinian emphasis on the DIALOGIC may, similarly, make some of the arguments of Hans-Georg Gadamer sound a little more relevant to Anglo-Saxon ears.

In 1984 Iain Wright argued persuasively for a far more positive consideration of Gadamer's work than had E. D. Hirsch. Wright claimed that Gadamer was unjustly neglected in Anglo-Saxon circles – a neglect which Wright explained in part by the fact that his major work, *Truth and Method*, was available in English only in a translation which was 'woefully inadequate' (since Wright wrote it has been revised [1989]).

Even so, Wright argues, Gadamer offers modern theory of interpretation a middle way between 'doctrinaire objectivism versus doctrinaire subjectivism, pure intentionalism versus pure anti-intentionalism, slavish "homage to the truth of the past" versus "intelligibility for our time", ultra-Rousseauism versus ultra-Nietzscheanism, the rights of the text versus the rights of the reader' (1984, 93). It is here, according to Wright, that the idea of dialogue comes in. For Gadamer insists on the tension between past and present, and the need to resolve this through dialogue.

> A false dialogue is one-sided. A true one (and Gadamer's ideal touchstone is the Platonic dialogue) involves a mutual learning-process in which each interlocutor retains his or her identity but is prepared to learn from the other. (1984, 95)

It seems likely that a fruitful interplay between the (very fashionable) ideas of Bakhtin and the (far less fashionable) ideas of Hans-Georg Gadamer is now possible within Anglo-American theoretical circles.

Jacques Lacan has suggested that hermeneutics and interpretation represent two quite separate activities. His distinction is not altogether clear to me, but it appears that for him hermeneutics is a less active process than interpretation.

> [In the] human sciences, one sees emerging, as it were, beneath the feet of whoever finds, what I will call the *hermeneutic demand*, which is precisely that which seeks – which seeks the ever new and the never exhausted signification, but one threatened with being trampled under foot by him who finds.
>
> Now, we analysts are interested in this hermeneutics, because the way of developing signification offered by hermeneutics is confused, in many minds, with

what analysis calls *interpretation*. It so happens that, although this interpretation cannot in any way be conceived in the same way as the aforementioned hermeneutics, hermeneutics, on the other hand, makes ready use of interpretation. In this respect, we see, at least, a corridor of communication between psycho-analysis and the religious register. (1979, 7–8)

Other theorists who have been particularly influenced by the German Hermeneutic tradition are Roman Ingarden, Paul Ricoeur, the members of the Geneva School of Criticism (see the entry for PHENOMENOLOGY) and those of the German RECEPTION THEORY school.

See also the entry for HORIZON. For 'hermeneutics of suspicion', see OPPOSITIONAL READING.

Heterobiography The earliest published use of this term of which I am aware is in Daphna Erdinast-Vulcan's article 'On the Edge of the Subject: The Heterobiography of Joseph K. Conrad' (1995). This article appears as one chapter in Erdinast-Vulcan: 1999.

In personal correspondence Erdinast-Vulcan has told me that the term may be a coinage of her own, although she is not sure of this. She further comments that the term 'as I use it in this context, is a hybrid coinage inspired by the work of both Derrida and Bakhtin on the question of borderlines. It is an attempt to negotiate the rift between the textual and the historical subject, to diagnose the irreducible psycho-cultural specificity of the author's presence (though not his/her sovereign status) in the text'.

In the published article, Erdinast-Vulcan suggests that heterobiography 'revolves on the experience of liminality in more than one way'. She explains that

[t]he first swerve offered by the term . . . is a Derridanean conception of a 'text without edges,' a probing of the jurisdiction of frames and borderlines, where 'the supposed end and beginning of a work, the unity of a corpus, the title, the margins, the signatures, the referential realm outside the frame' are no longer hermetically sealed off from each other.

. . .

Hence the second swerve offered by 'heterobiography,' the suspicious quotation marks around subjectivity itself. While 'autobiography,' as traditionally conceived, aspires to a territorial closure of the self, 'heterobiography' points to the inevitable a-topia of subjectivity, to the permiability of its borderlines. (1995, 303, 304; the quotations from Derrida in the first quoted paragraph are from Derrida: 1979, 83–4)

Erdinast-Vulcan's article exemplifies the workings of heterobiography in its following of 'an isomorphic relationship spiralling across or spilling over the edges of both text and subject: between Bakhtin and Dostoevesky; between Conrad's *Under Western Eyes* and Dostoevsky's *Crime and Punishment*; between Razumov and Haldin; between the narrator of *Under Western Eyes* and Razumov; between Conrad and Dostoevsky' (1995, 304; Razumov and Haldin are characters in Conrad's novel *Under Western Eyes*). Heterobiography, then, traces a 'life' while transgressing or ignoring CONVENTIONAL distinctions between CHARACTER and AUTHOR, self and other, and so on.

Clearly the term and the new attitudes towards 'writing a life' that it reflects and represents can be seen as an aspect of that process of 'decentring the subject' associated with both POSTMODERNISM and POST-STRUCTURALISM; see the entries for CENTRE and SUBJECT.

For more on 'borderlines', see the entry on LIMINALITY.

Heterodiegesis See DIEGESIS AND MIMESIS

Heteroglossia In the writing of Mikhail Bakhtin, that multiplicity of social voices linked and interrelated DIALOGICALLY which enters the novel through the interplay between authorial speech, NARRATOR speech, 'inserted genres', and CHARACTER speech (1981, 263).

The glossary provided in Bakhtin's *The Dialogic Imagination* notes that heteroglossia is determined both contextually and extra-linguistically as well as intra-linguistically: 'all utterances are heteroglot in that they are functions of a matrix of forces practically impossible to recoup' (1981, 428).

In Bakhtin's usage, according to the same source, *polyglossia* refers more specifically to the co-existence of different national languages within a single CULTURE. *Diglossia*, in contrast, is a term used within Linguistics to denote the co-existence of two languages within one culture – normally where one of these languages enjoys greater status and authority.

See the longer entries for DIALOGIC and POLYPHONIC.

Heteronomous objects See CONCRETIZATION

Heteroplasty A *heteroplasm* is a biological term for a tissue growing where it does not normally occur. This appears to be the basis of the term *heteroplasty*, used in NARRATOLOGY to describe a narrative form or MODE which is found in a position where it would not CONVENTIONALLY be expected.

Heterosexism See HOMOPHOBIA

Heuristic reading See MEANING AND SIGNIFICANCE

Hinge 1. Mieke Bal uses the term *hinge* in the context of a discussion of FOCALIZATION, suggesting that it can be applied to passages of NARRATIVE with either a double or an ambiguous focalization.

2. Jacques Derrida's *Of Grammatology* (1976) contains a section entitled 'The Hinge [La Brisure]', which builds upon a suggestion from Roger Laporte that the word *brisure* (meaning joint, break) can serve to designate both difference and articulation (1976, 65). Derrida comments that the hinge (*brisure*) 'marks the impossibility that a sign, the unity of a signifier and a signified, be produced within the plenitude of a present and an absolute presence' (1976, 69). In English translations of Derrida's writing, *brisures* are often rendered as *hinge-words*, although Maud Ellmann has suggested the alternative translation of *cleavage* (Ellmann: 1981, 192). These hinge-words contain, following Derrida, a paradoxical logic which must be explored by DECONSTRUCTIVE

analysis. Commenting upon Derrida's use of this term, Robert Young suggests that the effect of such hinge-words 'is to break down the oppositions by which we are accustomed to think and which ensure the survival of metaphysics in our thinking' (1981, 18).

3. What Roland Barthes refers to as *nuclei* are sometimes described as *hinge-points* in English: see the entry for EVENT.

4. Clemens Lugowski uses the term to refer to a 'crucial point in the action' of a narrative (1990, 56).

Historicism See NEW HISTORICISM

Hommelette Jacques Lacan's coinage, combining the senses of 'little man' and omelette, and by which he seeks to describe the pre-Oedipal psychic condition of the child. The child is a little man (the GENDER bias is impossible to avoid) in as much as it contains *in posse* the whole of the later adult, but in diffused and undistinguished form (the child has no clear sense of self distinct from non-self). Lacan refers to the term as a 'jokey' alternative to the more technical 'lamella' (1979, 197).

Homocommunicative and heterocommunicative See NARRATOR

Homodiegetic See DIEGESIS AND MIMESIS

Homology Also *isomorphism* or *structural parallelism*. A correspondence or similarity which establishes a significant pattern or structural REPETITION. This can either be within a given literary WORK, or (in STRUCTURALIST theory) between the STRUCTURE of a language and the structure of, for instance, the human UNCONSCIOUS. Structuralists have also argued for the existence of homologies between the language SYSTEM and other systems, from kinship relationships to literature, claiming that literature (seen as a total system of relations) is itself structured like a language.

Similarly, in NARRATIVE theory, structuralist theorists have argued that there is a homology between the syntax of a grammatical sentence and the larger narrative 'syntax' of a literary work, and have used terms from linguistics to describe particular narrative functions (e.g. MODE). Tzvetan Todorov has suggested that we think of a literary CHARACTER as a noun and an action as a verb, and their combination as the first step towards narrative (1969, 84). (See the entry for LINGUISTIC PARADIGM.)

The Romanian-French MARXIST critic Lucien Goldmann has made considerable use of the concept in his work, suggesting homologies between CLASS situation, world view, and artistic form.

Fredric Jameson has implied that homology should be distinguished from MEDIATION, for whereas homology involves resemblance at a structural level, mediation involves a connective relationship which has an element of dependence or causality between the different elements linked by mediation (1981, 43). Usage tends to be less tidy than this, however, and although Jameson's suggested distinction makes good sense it does not reflect the way the terms are actually used. For example, the traditional Marxist discussion of BASE AND SUPERSTRUCTURE is often said to involve a homology between these two elements which is generated by reflection, and a sophisticated version of this essential position would be that which sees POSTMODERNISM as reflective of the new set of relations which characterize 'late capitalism' or 'post-Fordist capitalism'. But clearly such arguments propose causal or connective/reflective relationships and not just a parallelism of independent structures. Moreover, Jameson's own discussion of Goldmann's work takes issue with the sort of historical relationship Goldmann finds between the different homologous elements in his study, which suggests that more than just structural parallelism is implied by the term.

Homonymy Following Brian McHale, the reappearance of an entity from one FICTIONAL world in another, but with essential changes. The extent of these changes is important: to count as a case of homonymy there must be variants in essential properties – the main CHARACTERS of Samuel Richardson's *Pamela* and of Henry Fielding's PARODIC *Shamela*, for example.

Where the changes involve only accidental qualities, then we have a case of quasi-homonymy. And where a character is arguably unchanged, as with the character Cordelia in Shakespeare's *King Lear* and Nahum Tate's rewritten version of the same play, then we have a case of *transworld identity* (McHale: 1987, 35–6).

Homophobia Fear (and hatred) of homosexuals. In his discussion of the term, Jeffrey Weeks notes that the popularization of the concept is generally attributed to George Weinberg (1972), who, according to Weeks, argued that 'the real problem was not homosexuality but society's reaction to it' (Wright: 1992, 155).

The term has been important in literary-critical discussion of a range of writers. Eve Kosofsky Sedgwick has commented that the word is etymologically nonsense, presumably because it suggests fear of human beings rather than of homosexuals. She adds that

> [a] more serious problem is that the linking of fear and hatred in the '-phobia' suffix, and the word's usage, does tend to prejudge the question of the cause of homosexual oppression: it is attributed to fear, as opposed to (for example) a desire for power, privilege, or material goods. (1993, 219, n1)

She notes that the term *heterosexism* offers a possible alternative, but chooses to go on using homophobia for a number of reasons, one of which is that the IDEOLOGICAL and THEMATIC treatments of male homosexuality which she is interested in discussing do combine fear and hatred in a way that is appropriately called phobic (1993, 219, n1).

Since 1985, when Sedgwick's book was first published, use of the term *heterosexism* has become more widespread. It has a somewhat different emphasis from homophobia, fastening attention more on the *ignoring* or MARGINALIZING of Gay or Lesbian experience and identity in favour of a universalized heterosexual NORM or set of norms. But it does also carry with it the idea of prejudice against and oppression of homosexuals.

See also HOMOSOCIAL; SEXISM.

Homosocial A term adopted and popularized by Eve Kosofsky Sedgwick in her book *Between Men: English Literature and Male Homosocial Desire* (1993, first published 1985). According to Sedgwick, 'Homosocial' is a word occasionally used in history and the social sciences, where it describes social bonds between persons of the same sex; it is a neologism, obviously formed by analogy with 'homosexual,' and just as obviously meant to be distinguished from 'homosexual.' In fact, it is applied to such activities as 'male bonding,' which may, as in our society, be characterized by intense homophobia, fear and hatred of homosexuality. To draw the 'homosocial' back into the orbit of 'desire,' of the potentially erotic, then, is to hypothesize the potential unbrokenness of a continuum between homosocial and homosexual – a continuum whose visibility, for men, in our society, is radically disrupted. (1993, 1–2)

The term has entered into more general use to describe those social relationships – and the NORMS, habits, and IDEOLOGIES engendered by them – which are overtly and aggressively single-sex (normally male) and heterosexual. One of the attractions of the term has been that, as Sedgwick demonstrates, behind an overt HOMOPHOBIA concealed homosexual or homo-erotic impulses may often be found, and *homosocial* manages to suggest the possibility of such a combination.

Homosocial exchange builds on the basic term, and denotes that economy of giving and barter (including the giving and bartering of women and access to women) by which men order and structure a CULTURE.

See also DESIRE.

Horizon Members of the group around Mikhail Bakhtin (P. N. Medvedev, V. N. Vološinov, and Bakhtin himself) regularly used this term to suggest the borders of possibility (normally) constraining a READER. Thus we come across terms such as *ideological horizon, socio-linguistic horizon*, and *axiological horizon* (i.e. the limit of possible evaluative acts) in their work. The usage has something in common with theories concerning the manner in which IDEOLOGICAL situations restrict INTERPRE-T[AT]IVE possibility, and also with Michel Foucault's view of the way in which the ARCHIVE of possible DISCOURSES limits an individual's access to knowledge. See the discussions in Todorov (1984).

The entry for HERMENEUTICS should be consulted for Hans-Georg Gadamer's theory of the 'fusion of horizons'. For 'horizon of expectations', see the entry for RECEPTION THEORY.

Hot and cool media According to Marshall McLuhan, there is a basic principle which distinguishes hot media such as radio and film from cool media such as the telephone and TV.

A hot medium is one that extends one single sense in 'high definition.' . . . Telephone is a cool medium, or one of low definition, because the ear is given a meager amount of information. And speech is a cool medium of low definition, because so little is given and so much has to be filled in by the listener. (1964, 22–3)

McLuhan argues that hot media do not leave so much to be filled in or completed by the audience, whereas cool media require the receiver of the information to fill in much. Hot media, therefore, are low-participation media, whilst cool media are high-participation media.

McLuhan's assimilation of technology and message raises a number of problems here – problems which have led to his being accused of TECHNOLOGICAL DETERMINISM by many commentators. For clearly although the telephone gives a meagre amount of information compared to a film *in a purely technical or quantifiable sense*, the information given in a telephone conversation can be semantically very rich indeed. It is nonsense, surely, to say that a monophonic record requires more audience participation than does a stereophonic one, or that a black-and-white film requires more participation from viewers than does a colour film – and both assertions would seem to follow logically from McLuhan's premises.

Compare READERLY AND WRITERLY TEXTS, noting the difference that emphasis on a medium and emphasis on a TEXT makes.

Humanism This is a term that has undergone a marked change of fortunes during the last two or three decades. Michèle Barrett has pointed out that this is particularly true in the field of culture, 'to the extent that in some circles *it is assumed that* "humanist" is a derogatory term' (1991, 93).

The current attribution of a peculiarly pejorative force to this term within Anglo-American (and especially Anglo) literary theory can probably be dated from the publication of Louis Althusser's *For Marx* (1969; first published in French, 1966). Althusser declares at the beginning of this work that his aim is to oppose 'Marxist humanism' and the '"humanist" interpretation of Marx's work' (1969, 10). In his essay 'Marxism and Humanism' (1963; included in *For Marx*), Althusser makes clear that a key opposition for him is that between the insistence on the end of *class* exploitation (the MARXIST goal), and the attainment of human freedom (which, he implies, is the goal of humanism) (1969, 221). Althusser locates a non-Marxist humanism in the works of the early Marx, in which, according to Althusser, 'the proletariat in its "alienation" represents the human essence itself, whose "realization" is to be assured by the revolution' (1969, 221–2). For Althusser this positing of a human essence lies at the heart of humanism, and many subsequent theorists have accepted his emphasis. For them such a posited human essence is beyond history and beyond society, and thus is essentially idealist rather than REALIST, often involving the projection of the characteristics of one form of society on to human beings at large (thus one often finds reference to *bourgeois humanism* or *liberal humanism*). Furthermore (the argument continues), humanism typically situates the human essence in individual human beings rather than in social structures or CULTURAL formations: humanism is thus idealistic, ahistorical, and individualistic.

Althusser's view of the early Marx is not uncontroversial. In the early *Economic and Philosophical Manuscripts of 1844* Marx does, it is true, refer to 'man's' (by which he means the human individual's) '*essential* being', but he also says that this is what man makes from his 'life activity'. He also argues that man is a being that treats its species as its own essential being – that treats itself 'as a species being' (Marx: 1970b, 113). None of these arguments, it will be noted, posits an essence that is outside of history, and indeed Pauline Johnson has gathered evidence to suggest that Marx's theory of a human essence does not imply any 'natural' human attributes, but 'refers specifically to the process of transformation and development which characterizes the history of the species' (1984, 36). Johnson claims that this is certainly how both Lukács and Adorno interpreted Marx's 'human essence' (1984, 100).

Nonetheless, anti-humanist views spread from Althusserian Marxism to a range of other theoretical positions, and it is only comparatively recently that a number of commentators have begun to question them. One such careful reconsideration, by Francis Mulhern, is worth citing in full. It comes from his editorial Introduction to *Contemporary Marxist Literary Criticism* (1992).

> The nostrum of 'anti-humanism' calls for particular attention. 'Anti-humanism' is confident in rejecting the notion of a human essence (its principal definition) and the putatively bourgeois conception of the subject as self-transparent originator of meaning (its longest-running theme); yet as a contributor to radical social thought, it belongs to a broad historical tradition that affirms the possibility and value of human self-development, and is in that sense 'humanist'. This ambiguity is more than superficial and more than contemplative; it bespeaks theoretical deficiency and promotes practical confusion. The critique of essentialism, pursued unilaterally, is itself idealist, denying our common and relatively stable reality as a natural species; and too-euphoric a dissolution of the humanist subject may reduce all programmes of emancipation to a Babel in which ideas of 'need' and 'right' are merely positional gambits. 'Anti-humanism' is defiantly 'historical' – but historical understanding is practised whole or not at all. Human time is complex, syncopated but also regular, rapid but also unobservably slow; and even if our history does not move towards a preinscribed *telos*, it does not follow that all ideas of development are 'modern' fictions. (1992, 33, n32)

There is in fact a strong case to be made for the argument that, as Mulhern suggests, much recent anti-humanism throws various babies out with the idealist and ESSENTIALIST bathwater. One recurrent problem is that the term is used as if it were unproblematic, but in fact a number of different usages lurk behind this assumption. As Elizabeth Deeds Ermarth has commented,

> the term 'humanism' means widely different things. If humanism is synonymous with Judeo-Christian morality, causality, and historical time as these were constructed between (roughly) 1500 and 1900, then perhaps humanism is in deep trouble, but I am not persuaded that either the problem or so-called crisis has yet been fully conceived. (1992, 123)

Michèle Barrett argues that to assume that the term can and should be dispensed with

> is historically a great injustice, in that it ignores the immensely progressive role that humanism – as an 'ideology' – has played. In particular, one can point to the honourable tradition of humanism as a secularising force and, indeed, to its enormously important role in contemporary politics. (1991, 93)

There is, moreover, a humanist tradition in the twentieth century which builds on and extends Marx's historicist and non-essentialist emphases. Thus Arnold Kettle, in his essay 'The Progressive Tradition in Bourgeois Culture' (first published 1954, reprinted in Kettle: 1988), argues that the positives in Shakespeare's work are neither the feudal values nor the bourgeois ones, nor are they the values of the masses, which at this time do not yet constitute a conscious class. What then are these positive values? Kettle concludes: 'I can only say that they are the values of *humanity*.' This, he recognizes, is a problematic statement.

> There is, I know, a danger in thus formulating humanity as the positive value behind the plays. Humanity, abstracted from actual situations, becomes an idealistic conception of no validity. Humanity does not exist in the abstract; Man is always a particular man. What I mean then by humanity in this context is *man in his fullest aspirations realizable in the concrete situation of England of the sixteenth and seventeenth centuries*, remembering always that England of the sixteenth and the seventeenth centuries is the England not only of the feudal landowners and the Puritan businessmen but of Sir Thomas More and Francis Bacon and the New Model Army. (1988, 25–6)

The same essential point is expressed in Alan Sinfield's comment that, according to CULTURAL MATERIALISM, 'our "humanity" is not an essential condition towards which we may aspire, but what people have as a consequence of being socialized into human communities' (1992, 291). In his 1992 article 'The Postcolonial and the Postmodern', Kwame Anthony Appiah underscores the fact that contingency and moral worth are not incompatible:

> [W]hat I am calling humanism can be provisional, historically contingent, anti-essentialist (in other words, postmodern) and still be demanding. We can surely maintain a powerful engagement with the concern to avoid cruelty and pain while nevertheless recognising the contingency of that concern. (In Ashcroft *et al.*: 1995, 123)

These debates may seem abstract but they have rather important consequences. The rejection of humanism has involved a rejection of the idea that 'the human' can constitute a fixed reference point, and thus the rejection of humanism is very much tied up with the loss of a determining CENTRE and the free play of the signifier. But if a non-essentialist humanism can be established then the situation is somewhat changed, and the free play of the signifier may be, if not arrested, at least slowed down. Even if 'the human' is not a fixed or a unitary reference point, it may denote certain relatively stable (if contested) reference points, whose history, movements and conflicts can be plotted.

A closing comment. Louis Althusser is not the only recent anti-humanist with a strongly Catholic upbringing, and I suspect that he is not the only one with Marxist pretensions to have actually imported a number of points of Catholic doctrine into his definition of humanism. This would explain why, when there clearly *is* a humanist tradition which does not depend upon a belief in a human essence (or, when it does, does not necessarily situate that essence outside history), he and others have nonetheless strenuously asserted that this belief is integral to the humanist project.

Hybrid/hybridization According to Mikhail Bakhtin,

> [w]hat we are calling a hybrid construction is an utterance that belongs, by its grammatical (syntactic) and compositional markers, to a single speaker, but that actually contains mixed within it two utterances, two speech manners, two styles, two 'languages,' two semantic and axiological belief systems. We repeat, there is no formal – compositional and syntactic – boundary between these utterances, styles, languages, belief systems; the division of voices and languages takes place within the limits of a single syntactic whole, often within the limits of a simple sentence. (1981, 304–5)

Bakhtin analyses a number of PARODIC/ironic passages in Charles Dickens's *Little Dorrit* as examples of hybrid UTTERANCES (1981, 302–7; see also FREE INDIRECT DISCOURSE).

Following Bakhtin, a *hybrid text* can be one formed by cutting two other TEXTS together – in either a planned or a random manner. The term hybrid text can also be used to describe a text in which two separate, and often opposed, elements can be detected, on a thematic or an IDEOLOGICAL level.

It is, however, since the rise of POSTCOLONIALIST theory and criticism that the concept of hybridity has experienced its fullest upsurge of popularity. According to Homi K. Bhabha, for example, in his highly influential 1985 article 'Signs Taken for Wonders: Questions of Ambivalence and Authority Under a Tree Outside Delhi, May 1817',

> [h]ybridity is the sign of the productivity of colonial power, its shifting forces and fixities; it is the name for the strategic reversal of the process of domination through disavowal (that is, the production of discriminatory identities that secure the 'pure' and original identity of authority). Hybridity is the revaluation of the assumption of colonial identity through the repetition of discriminatory identity effects. It displays the necessary deformation and displacement of all sites of discrimination and domination. It unsettles the mimetic or narcissistic demands of colonial power but reimplicates its identifications in strategies of subversion that turn the gaze of the discriminated back upon the eye of power. For the colonial hybrid is the articulation of the ambivalent space where the rite of power is enacted on the site of desire, making its objects at once disciplinary and disseminatory – or, in my mind a mixed metaphor, a negative transparency.
> . . .
> If the effect of colonial power is seen to be the *production* of hybridization rather than the noisy command of colonial authority or the silent repression of native traditions, then an important change of perspective occurs. (In Ashcroft *et al.*: 1995, 34–5)

What such usages do is to take the idea of ideological dialogue, accommodation, or coercion that is contained in Bakhtin's usage, and to apply it to the way in which the coercive and HEGEMONIC imposition of alien meanings in the colonialist context is worked through at the level of language.

Developing such usages, Helen Tiffin (1987) has argued that 'Post-colonial cultures are inevitably hybridised' (in Ashcroft *et al.*: 1995, 96); Kumkum Sangari (1987) has argued that 'the hybrid writer is already open to two worlds and is constructed within the national and international, political and cultural systems of colonialism and neocolonialism' (in Ashcroft *et al.*: 1995, 144); and André Lefevere (1983) has written of a 'hybrid poetics' in which European publishers have been willing to publish 'anything that came out of Africa', and which 'has produced its hybrid patronage: the canonization of works and writers that is now going on, is not the work of Africans only: it is also carried out in London, in various centers in the United States and in Europe' (in Ashcroft *et al.*: 1995, 469–70).

As a result the term *hybridization* is often now encountered: it means 'the fusion of cultural forms, often as a result of inequalities of commercial or political power'.

Compare NOMAD.

Hymen Derrida's use of this term has been taken up by a number of theorists interested, as Andrew Gibson puts it, in benefiting from those ambiguities and slippages with which it is associated. Accordingly, use of the term 'consciously seeks to avoid the purity of absolute separation, of clear polarity' (Gibson: 1996, 127). Gibson builds on Derrida's discussion in his *Positions* (1981b), in which the hymen is 'a figure for the principle of interdependence or interinvolvement, of inseparability' (Gibson: 1996, 117). Described thus, the appeal of the term seems to reside in its ability to suggest a relationship between entities not possessed of clearly demarcated or fixed identities.

Compare LIMINALITY and see also LEAKAGE.

Hyperspace A term used to suggest those new experiences engendered by the architecture of POSTMODERNISM. Thus, discussing his experience of the Westin Bonaventure Hotel, built in downtown Los Angeles by architect and developer John Portman, Fredric Jameson writes:

> I am tempted to say that such space makes it impossible for us to use the language of volume or volumes any longer, since these are impossible to seize. Hanging streamers indeed suffuse this empty space in such a way as to distract systematically and deliberately from whatever form it might be supposed to have, while a constant busyness gives the feeling that emptiness is here absolutely packed, that it is an element within which you yourself are immersed, without any of that distance that formerly enabled the perception of perspective or volume. You are in this hyperspace up to your eyes and your body; and if it seemed before that that suppression of depth I spoke of in postmodern painting or literature would necessarily be difficult to achieve in architecture itself, perhaps this bewildering immersion may now serve as the formal equivalent in the new medium. (1991, 43)

Compare *hyperreality*, in the entry for PRECESSION, and VIRTUAL REALITY.

Hypertext Fundamental to the idea of the hypertext is the replacement of linear and unidirectional progression between two fixed points ('beginning' and 'end') with a very large number of potential journeys through a TEXT-mass which is continually being added to, amended, and re-signposted and re-mapped. Hypertext is a child of the electronic media, and there are few below the age of 30 in the developed world who are unfamiliar with the experience of surfing the net by following a succession of links.

A conventional literary text such as a play by Shakespeare or a novel by Dickens can be made part of a hypertext by being linked electronically with such things as linguistic information about words and grammatical formations in the work, biographical information about the AUTHOR, contextual information about the author's time, generic information about the literary traditions within which the author was working, and so on.

The electronic hypertext can be seen to realize some of the formal aspirations of certain experimental writers, who wished to break out of or away from the strict linearity and unidirectionality of the printed text. Laurence Sterne, for example, at one point in *Tristram Shandy* (1759–67), advises an imagined female reader to go back and reread an earlier passage in the book, while B. S. Johnson's novel *The Unfortunates* (1969) was published in a box of 27 stapled gatherings, which could be read in any order. And there is a sense in which any footnote or reference in an academic book invites the reader to move to another text. Genuine hypertextuality, however, had to await the resources of the electronic media.

Compare IF.

Hypodiegetic See DIEGESIS AND MIMESIS

Hypostatization See REIFICATION

Hypotaxis In Linguistics, (normally syntactical) subordination. The term is apparently somewhat old-fashioned in the field of Linguistics, but the term and cognates such as *hypotactic* appear every now and then in fields such as NARRATOLOGY.

Hypothesis-driven See SOLUTION FROM ABOVE/BELOW

I

Icon Traditionally an image, especially painted and adhering to fixed CONVENTIONS, representing a holy figure or subject and itself considered to be holy. The introductory note on the title of his book *The Verbal Icon* by W. K. Wimsatt provides a useful summary of the more modern meaning given to the term:

> The term *icon* is used today by semeiotic writers to refer to a verbal sign which *somehow* shares the properties of, or resembles, the objects which it denotes. ... The verbal image which most fully realizes its verbal capacities is that which is not

merely a bright picture (in the usual modern meaning of the term *image*) but also an interpretation of reality in its metaphoric and symbolic dimensions. (1970, x)

Wimsatt is not quite correct to state that modern SEMIOTIC writers restrict icons to *verbal* signs; generally speaking, an icon for such writers is any SIGN which bears an extra-SYSTEMIC resemblance to that for which its stands. Modern semiotic usage stems from C. S. Peirce's tripartite distinction between what he saw as the three essential forms of sign: icon, INDEX, and SYMBOL.

Jonathan Culler points out (1981, 23) that this is the only one of Peirce's very many taxonomic speculations concerning signs which has had lasting influence, and he expresses the relationship in a technically more correct manner when he writes that while all signs consist of a *signifiant* and a *signifié*, an icon 'involves actual resemblance between *signifiant* and *signifié*: a portrait signifies the person of whom it is a portrait not by arbitrary convention only but by resemblance' (Culler: 1975, 16). To this one should add that in many accounts this resemblance needs to be intended: the lump of rock which the elements have shaped to a resemblance of a real person is not according to these accounts an icon, because the shaping has not been intentional.

Wimsatt's use of *icon* is often treated as exemplary of the NEW CRITICAL habit of treating the literary WORK as object or thing, as is Cleanth Brooks's similar use of *well wrought urn* (itself a quotation from John Donne) to describe the poem. For the New Critics, certain literary and (particularly) poetic patterns and relations are HOMOLOGOUS of patterns and relations in the extra-literary world.

New Critical views of the iconic properties of language also tend to underscore a view of poetic or literary language as self-reflective; the painted icon may resemble a saint, but it is worshipped as holy object itself. In like manner, the New Critics suggested, the literary work may resemble aspects of extra-literary reality but it is valued for what it is in itself, not primarily because of the force or extent of these resemblances.

Id See TOPOGRAPHICAL MODEL OF THE MIND

Ideal reader See READERS AND READING

Ideation The process whereby propositions or REFERENCES (concerning either the outer or the inner world) are formed and expressed. Thus the use of language for ideation is to be distinguished from the use of language to cement interpersonal bonds.

Because some very influential theorists have suggested that literature is non-propositional and is characterized by its non-referential use of language, the claim that the writing or READING of literature is at least partly ideational is controversial.

Compare FUNCTIONS OF LANGUAGE.

Ideogram See DEFORMATION

Ideologeme According to Fredric Jameson, 'the smallest intelligible unit of the essentially antagonistic collective discourses of social classes' (1981, 76). Formed by analogy with such terms as *phoneme* – the smallest intelligible unit of significant sound in a language.

Compare SEMEME, STYLEME, kineme (the smallest significant unit in kinesics or 'body language'), narreme (the smallest significant unit in narrative), and other such coinages.

See also the more detailed entry for IDEOLOGY.

Ideological horizon See HORIZON

Ideological State Apparatuses (ISAs) See IDEOLOGY

Ideology No definition of this term can hope to provide a single and unambiguous meaning; instead a cluster of related but not always compatible meanings have to be indicated. What nearly all commentators agree upon is that the present-day use of the term refers to a *system of ideas*: according to some usages an ideology may include contradictory elements, but if so these elements are somehow brought into a functioning relationship which obscures these contradictions for the person or people by whom the ideology is lived. An ideology is thus a way of looking at and INTERPRETING – of 'living' – the world. A further point of agreement is that ideologies are *collectively held*; a purely personal system of ideas would not normally be called an ideology.

Alternative present-day usages of the term differ on a number of other points, however: whether an ideology is necessarily a form of false consciousness or whether it can give a true and objective insight into reality (probably the most important area of disagreement or variation of usage); and whether an ideology represents the interests of a particular social CLASS – and if so, how. In his book *Ideology: An Introduction*, Terry Eagleton suggests six broad definitions of the term: (i) 'the general material process of production of ideas, beliefs and values in social life'; (ii) 'ideas and beliefs (whether true or false) which symbolize the conditions and life-experiences of a specific, socially significant group or class'; (iii) 'the *promotion* and *legitimation* of the interests of such social groups in the face of opposing interests'; (iv) such promotion and legitimation when carried out by a 'dominant social power'; (v) 'ideas and beliefs which help to legitimate the interests of a ruling group or class specifically by distortion and dissimulation'; (vi) similar false and deceptive beliefs which arise 'not from the interests of a dominant class but from the material structure of society as a whole' (1991, 28–30).

Ideology as concept has flourished in particular within the MARXIST tradition, although even here no single and unambiguous usage can be charted. Raymond Williams points out that at the time that Marx and Engels wrote their *The German Ideology* the term (in a range of language variants) was generally taken to mean 'abstract, impractical or fanatical theory' (1976, 126). *The German Ideology* was written in 1845 and 1846, but failed to find a publisher on completion and was, as Marx put it, abandoned to 'the gnawing criticism of the mice'. C. J. Arthur, editor of the modern English translation of the text, points out that this comment turned out to be literally true, and the text of the work had to be reconstructed from a damaged manuscript (Marx and Engels: 1970, ix).

There is no doubt that the whole thrust of *The German Ideology* is towards seeing ideology as a form of false consciousness. The following words of the Preface give a reliable indication of the tone and attitude of the subsequent pages.

The first volume of the present publication has the aim of uncloaking these sheep [the German Young Hegelian philosophers], who take themselves and are taken for wolves; of showing how their bleating merely imitates in a philosophic form the conceptions of the German middle class; how the boasting of these philosophic commentators only mirrors the wretchedness of the real conditions in Germany. (Marx and Engels: 1970, 37)

Here we see an important complex of assumptions central to one Marxist usage of the term ideology: (i) an ideology reflects the ideas, living conditions, or interests of a particular social class; (ii) those in the grip of the ideology are not aware of this, but think that their ideas are correct because they seem to accord with reality, not realizing that the reality in question is particular not general, and that it has itself created the seemingly true ideas; (iii) the ideology may be lived by, and may control, individuals other than those whose interests it reflects or expresses.

The term *false consciousness* is derived, incidentally, from a letter written by Engels to Franz Mehring, dated 14 July 1893. In this letter Engels states that

[i]deology is a process accomplished by the so-called thinker consciously, it is true, but with a false consciousness. The real motive forces impelling him remain unknown to him; otherwise it simply would not be an ideological process. (Marx and Engels: 1962 [2], 497)

According to the earlier *The German Ideology*,

[i]f in all ideology men and their circumstances appear upside-down as in a *camera obscura*, this phenomenon arises just as much from their historical life-process as the inversion of objects on the retina does from their physical life-process. (1970, 47)

The implication is clearly that just as effective visual perception requires that the brain reinvert the image on the retina, so effective understanding of one's social, material and historical reality requires that one reinvert the distorted images produced by the particularities of one's living conditions: in short, de-ideologize one's view of reality by starting with facts rather than ideas.

[W]e do not set out from what men say, imagine, conceive, nor from men as narrated, thought of, imagined, conceived, in order to arrive at men in the flesh. We set out from real, active men, and on the basis of their real life-process we demonstrate the development of the ideological reflexes and echoes of this life-process. (1970, 47)

This advice involves us in the potential paradox, of course, that it assumes that 'we' see 'real, active men' and not just what we 'say, imagine [or] conceive': everyone else is in the grip of ideology but us. The paradox is, however, only potential if we assume that for Marx and Engels an ideology is never as all-embracing as is, for example, Michel Foucault's ÉPISTÉMÈ; if so, one can always escape from the grip of an ideology by grounding one's inquiries in the investigation of 'real life-processes'.

In Marx's Preface to *A Contribution to the Critique of Political Economy*, at a point where he is talking about the way in which changes in the economic foundation lead to changes 'of the whole immense superstructure', he warns:

> In studying such transformations it is always necessary to distinguish between the material transformation of the economic conditions of production, which can be determined with the precision of natural science, and the legal, political, religious, artistic or philosophic – in short ideological forms in which men become conscious of this conflict and fight it out. Just as one does not judge an individual by what he thinks about himself, so one cannot judge such a period of transformation by its consciousness, but, on the contrary, this consciousness must be explained from the contradictions of material life... (Marx: 1971, 21)

The argument here has much in common with that contained in the previous passage quoted, but the two arguments are not identical in their view of ideology. The second quotation might suggest that at certain historical periods an ideological view of reality *is* all-encompassing and inescapable, and can be broken out of only from the perspective of a later age, but it also seems to leave open more of a possibility that an ideology might not necessarily give a *false* view of things, merely an indirect, SUPERSTRUCTURAL one. Certain Marxists who have developed these ideas have extended some of the hints and possible implications in these and other comments. For these later commentators, an ideology can be so all-embracing that escaping from it by looking at 'real, active men' is not so easy: indeed, such commentators would argue, even when one looks at real, active men one may still see them in the light of one's inescapable ideological assumptions.

This, at any rate, is very reminiscent of the arguments of the French Marxist philosopher Louis Althusser, and even more of some of his followers. For Althusser the ideas of the ruling class are imposed both by means of force and also through the imposition of these ideas on to those ruled. Indeed, in *The German Ideology* itself we can read that

> [t]he ideas of the ruling class are in every epoch the ruling ideas, i.e. the class which is the ruling *material* force of society, is at the same time its ruling *intellectual* force. The class which has the means of material production at its disposal, has control at the same time over the means of mental production, so that thereby, generally speaking, the ideas of those who lack the means of mental production are subject to it. (Marx and Engels: 1970, 64)

When Marxists refer to the 'dominant ideology' or to the 'dominant discourse' they are often using such terms as replacements for 'the ruling ideas', although to complicate matters, Jorge Larrain has argued that

> [h]istorical materialism identifies a specific form of distorted consciousness which conceals contradiction and is called *ideology*. Ideology should not be confused with ruling ideas. Not all ruling ideas necessarily mask contradictions. (1986, 123)

For Althusser, class societies are maintained as much by a consensus produced ideologically, through what he calls Ideological State Apparatuses (ISAs), as by repression through Repressive State Apparatuses (RSAs). The ISAs include the educational ISA, the family ISA, the legal ISA, the political ISA, the trade-union ISA, the communications ISA and the cultural ISA. Althusser's short definition of ideology is that it is 'a "representation" of the imaginary relationship of individuals to their real conditions of existence' (1971, 152); for him ideology is always a distortion of reality, in contrast to science, which is not.

It is worth comparing Althusser's ISA with the way in which Foucault defines a DISCOURSE, and indeed Terry Eagleton has pointed out that Foucault and his followers effectively abandon the concept of ideology altogether and replace it with 'the more capacious "discourse"'. Eagleton notes, however, that such a substitution relinquishes a useful distinction, as '[t]he force of the term ideology lies in its capacity to discriminate between those power struggles which are somehow central to a whole form of social life, and those that are not' (1991, 8).

Althusser notes that the family has functions other than those associated with being an ISA, and that the Law is both RSA and ISA (1971, 136–7). This clearly could be taken to mean (and *has* been taken to mean by some) that the educational system of a capitalist society has the exclusive function of disseminating bourgeois ideology: indeed, Althusser states that

[i]f the ISAs 'function' massively and predominantly by ideology, what unifies their diversity is precisely this functioning, insofar as the ideology by which they function is always in fact unified, despite its diversity and its contradictions, *beneath the ruling ideology*, which is the ideology of 'the ruling class'. (1971, 139)

In her *Psychoanalysis and Feminism* Juliet Mitchell has suggested an interesting link between an essentially Marxist concept of ideology and the Freudian concept of the UNCONSCIOUS.

The patriarchal law speaks to and through each person in his unconscious; the reproduction of the ideology of human society is thus assured in the acquisition of the law by each individual. The unconscious that Freud analysed could thus be described as the domain of the reproduction of culture or ideology. (1974, 413)

Let us pause at this moment to ask what all this has – or might be argued to have – to do with literature. We can start off by observing that Althusser's list of ISAs is very reminiscent of Marxist descriptions of the superstructure, and that literature has been categorized as superstructural by certain Marxists. From this perspective, to say that Marx sees literary works as part of 'a larger ideological superstructure' (Forgacs: 1986, 170) might suggest that Marx held literature to be entrapped by its function of disseminating the ideas of the current ruling class – and this clearly REDUCTIVE view has found its adherents (although not, it should be pointed out, David Forgacs himself).

A rather more optimistic application of these ideas to literature would proceed along the lines recommended by Marx and Engels in *The German Ideology*. Rather than taking literary works at their own estimation these need to be read in the light of 'the contradictions of material life' as lived by the AUTHOR and his or her contemporaries. This is probably the most important and representative element in the various forms of Marxist literary criticism that have developed in the twentieth century and is the Marxist version of genetic criticism.

For some Marxists, however, literature is valuable precisely because it allows READERS a unique form of access to ideology or ideologies. According to Terry Eagleton,

> Marxist criticism is part of a larger body of theoretical analysis which aims to understand *ideologies* – the ideas, values and feelings by which men experience their societies at various times. And certain of these ideas, values and feelings are available to us only in literature. (1976b, 8; it should be added that Eagleton's later book *Ideology: An Introduction* [1991] tackles the relationship of literature to ideology in a far more detailed and sophisticated manner)

Notice here that literature is not explicitly limited to ideology, although as Marxist criticism is apparently limited to understanding ideologies one could be forgiven for believing that this was Eagleton's position. And although Eagleton does not state here that ideologies are necessarily false, he does argue that literature is important because it reveals to us the ideas, values and feelings which have been held by writers about their societies, while he does *not* tell us that literature is important because it reveals – or can reveal – *truths* to us.

In like vein John Frow argues that 'one must stress that aesthetic judgment is always a judgment about the determinate ideological force to be attached to an utterance in a particular historical conjuncture' (1986, 187). This tends more or less to collapse the aesthetic into the political, to the extent that – if accepted – one can hardly make a strong case for retaining the term 'aesthetic'.

Other Marxists have chosen two rather different ways of granting literature a somewhat higher status than some of these approaches might imply: either by denying that literature is part of the superstructure and that it can correctly be characterized as ideology (see the entry for BASE AND SUPERSTRUCTURE), or by seeing ideologies as the SITES of struggle and as capable of providing truth. Thus whereas Althusser sees a Chinese wall dividing ideology and science, the official Soviet handbook *The Fundamentals of Marxist-Leninist Philosophy*, written to circulate and support an orthodoxy that no longer exists, makes a distinction between 'scientific ideology, which is an accurate reflection of material social relations, and ideology that reflects these relations in an illusory, distorted and even fantastic form' (Konstatinov *et al.*: 1974, 474). This position is based upon a view of ideologies as systems of ideas which reflect a particular class viewpoint: to the extent that it is in a class's interests to develop and propagate an accurate view of reality then to that extent is the ideology emanating from that class capable of producing truth. Thus the Soviet handbook defines an ideology as 'a system of views and ideas directly or indirectly reflecting the economic and social peculiarities of society, expressing the position, interests and aims of a definite social class and designed to preserve or change the existing social structure' (Konstatinov *et al.*: 1974, 475).

The term has entered into much more general use in recent years, and a person who talks about ideology certainly need not be a Marxist or be appealing to a set of Marxist assumptions. In such general usage ideology can mean something as general as a system of ideas, either true or false. Thus Gunther Kress and Robert Hodge write:

> [We define ideology] as a systematic body of ideas, organized from a particular point of view. Ideology is thus a subsuming category which includes sciences and metaphysics, as well as political ideologies of various kinds, without implying anything about their status and reliability as guides to reality. (1979, 6)

The tendency, however, is for the term to be used pejoratively rather than neutrally, and for it to imply a partisan commitment to a set of ideas that are not held in a disinterested manner.

One result of a much-increased concern with the topic of ideology on the part of literary theorists and critics has been that both have become rather more aware that a critic may be prevented even from asking certain questions as a result of the pressure of what, to be uncontroversial, can be named prevailing attitudes. Thus Cynthia Ozick has reported on a letter written to her by Lionel Trilling, in which Trilling admitted that he had realized that E. M. Forster was homosexual only years after he had completed his book on Forster's work; 'It wasn't an issue in the society at the time he was writing' (Plimpton: 1989, 295). Today it seems almost unbelievable that one could write on Forster without at least considering the possibility of his homosexuality, but the dominant ideology (or ideologies) of the society in which the critic as much as the writer lives necessarily has an AGENDA-SETTING function, and things that are not on the agenda may not even get considered.

For Roland Barthes's attempt to link connotation to ideology via rhetoric, see the entry for CONNOTATION AND DENOTATION. See also FORMATION; INCORPORATION.

Idiolect A term used by linguisticians to describe the features of a particular person's language which mark out him or her *individually* from others. An idiolect is thus distinguished from a *dialect*, which refers to the language characteristics marking out a *community* (geographical, social, educational) from others. Linguisticians normally restrict the primary reference of both terms to speech, but they are also applied by extension to written language as well.

Thus a writer's achievement in giving a particular literary CHARACTER a distinctive idiolect can be an important aspect of that writer's success in characterization. Linguistic analysis of Jane Austen's FICTION has confirmed that one of the reasons why readers find her characters to be possessed of such convincing independent life is that she is very adept at granting them distinctive idiolects.

A writer has, of course, to represent both dialect and idiolect in writing, and although this may present few problems in certain areas (vocabulary, syntax) it requires the use of special CONVENTIONS of notation in others (pronunciation, for example). Additional problems stem from the symbolic weight accorded by readers to divergences from the conventions of standard written English: as Leech and Short point out, 'non-standard language often implies remoteness from the author's own language, and hence from the central standards of judgement in a novel' (1981, 170).

Roland Barthes suggests, following Jakobson, that the concept of idiolect is a problematic one as, in Jakobson's words, 'private property in the sphere of language does not exist'. This objection notwithstanding, Barthes is prepared to use the concept to describe either (i) the language of the aphasic, (ii) the style of a writer, and even (iii) the language of a linguistic community (Barthes: 1967a, 21).

Compare *genderlect* in the entry for GENDER; and SOCIOLECT.

IF A standard abbreviation for Interactive Fiction. Interactive fiction allows for the possibility of revising and expanding a TEXT by means of the incorporation of reader feedback. The electronic media offer the most fully developed possibilities for such interaction, both with regard to speed and to the number of participants, but the GENRE or sub-genre apparently predates the computer.

In common with the HYPERTEXT, IF challenges certain traditional and CONVENTIONAL qualities of the text, such as autonomy, linearity, and a sharp distinction between AUTHOR and READER.

See also FICTION.

Illocutionary act See SPEECH ACT THEORY

Image This is a term which has become much less fashionable since the heyday of the NEW CRITICS, in whose criticism it frequently played a central and crucial role. One reason for this decline may be that doubts were raised concerning the extent to which it referred to something clear and unambiguous; P. N. Furbank's book *Reflections on the Word 'Image'* presented these doubts in a clear and polemical manner at an opportune time. Its central argument was that the 'trouble with "imagery" is that it appears to refer to some technical feature in literature – like "rhythm" or "stanza" or "metaphor" – yet it is hard to discover *what*' (1970, 60). Furbank established that the term was used with very varied and even contradictory meanings, ranging from 'mental picture' to METAPHOR, simile, or symbol. Ironically, he was able to use the weapons of the New Critics against one of their own favourite terms: to abstract patterns of imagery from a work was, he argued, to ignore one of the more important principles established by modern criticism – that literary works are 'integral wholes and that the various elements composing them only have significance as a part of the whole' (1970, 12).

In spite of this loss of fashionability critics still make considerable use of *image* and *imagery* today. The terms retain the breadth of meaning pointed out by Furbank, being used to refer to figurative language in general or to those elements of literary works to which the word CONCRETE rather than *abstract* seems suited, and which appear to have a certain *sensuousness* – that is, that cause one sensuously to experience the taste, feel, smell, sound or appearance of something strongly and in a particularized way.

In recent years *image* has begun to be used within Media Studies as a term which is distinguished from *picture*. Usage is by no means fixed, but it seems that *picture* is conventionally associated with representationality and thus with REALISM, whereas *image* does not carry any necessary implication of the representational, and has thus been favoured by anti-realists. (Compare the distinction between TEXT AND WORK.)

Imaginary/symbolic/real A tripartite distinction found in the works of Jacques Lacan. Michèle Barrett gives an elegant short account of the force these three terms have in Lacan's writings:

The 'imaginary order' includes images and fantasies, both conscious and unconscious; it is a key register of the ego and its identifications, evolving from the mirror stage but continuing in adult relationships; it particularly includes material from pre-verbal experience. The 'symbolic order', on the other hand, is the domain of symbolisation and language, and it is through the social and cultural processes of this symbolic order that the subject can represent desire and thus be constituted. The 'real' is defined as that which exists outside symbolisation, and outside the analytic experience which is necessarily contained by the limits of speech: it is that which is formally outside the subject. (1991, 102; Barrett notes that she bases her definition on Lacan's translator's [Alan Sheridan's] note [see below] and on Benvenuto and Kennedy: 1986, 80–82. For MIRROR STAGE, see the separate entry)

Martin Jay notes that Lacan's Imaginary, 'the dimension or realm of images, perceived or imagined, conscious or not, is a constant dimension of the human psyche, which can never permit unimpeded access to "the Real," the realm of raw, unpresentable fullness prior to the organization of the drives'. There is, nonetheless,

> a difference between normal and psychotic behavior which depends on the partial transition from the Imaginary to a further stage, which Lacan termed 'the Symbolic.' Coincident with the resolution of the Oedipus complex, the Symbolic meant the child's entry into language. (1993, 349–50)

For a more extended discussion of these three 'orders', see the separate entries in Wright (1992). See also Vincent Crapanzano's 'The Self, the Third, and Desire', Chapter 3 of Crapanzano (1992). The translator of Lacan's work, Alan Sheridan, also includes a useful commentary on these linked terms in a note at the end of Lacan's *The Four Fundamental Concepts of Psychoanalysis* (1979, 279–80).

Andrew Gibson reports that there is a specifically Bachelardian concept of the imaginary,

> as a complex of what [Bachelard] calls 'unconscious values' haunting the discourse of a given *savoir*. In the case of scientific discourse, Bachelard sees these values as unhelpful and a weakness. He wants to see them disempowered and dissolved. (1996, 2)

He notes that the Bachelardian concept of the imaginary has been noted and developed by the French feminist philosopher Michèle le Dœuff.

Imagined community A term which originates with Benedict Anderson's 1983 book *Imagined Communities: Reflections on the Origin and Spread of Nationalism*. An imagined community is a group of human beings whose sense of commonality is not necessarily coterminous with the limits of a nation-state at a single point in time. The term has been much discussed by theorists of POSTCOLONIALISM, who have found it useful in mapping CULTURES and shared IDEOLOGIES which bind peoples together across state boundaries. At the same time it has been subject to criticism for paying too little attention to the multiple, antagonistic and mutually contradictory forms of 'belonging' experienced by (especially) subject peoples. As Padmini Mongia has put it, postcolonial theory 'problematizes the nation-state and its ideologies and reveals the difficulty of conceiving the nation even as an "imagined community"' (1996, 5).

Immasculation According to Judith Fetterley, '[t]hough one of the most persistent of literary stereotypes is the castrating bitch, the cultural reality is not the emasculation of men by women, but the *immasculation* of women by men' (1978, xx). By immasculation Fetterley means that process whereby 'as readers and teachers and scholars, women are taught to think as men, to identify with a male point of view, and to accept as normal and legitimate a male system of values, one of whose central principles is misogyny' (1978, xx). Thus the title of her book, *The Resisting Reader: A Feminist Approach to American Fiction* (1978) proposes such resistance on the part of the READER as a necessary counter to the pressure of immasculation.

See also FEMALING; STEREOTYPE.

Implicature (conversational) See SPEECH ACT THEORY

Implied author See AUTHOR

Implied reader See READERS AND READING

Incorporation In Freudian theory, that process of internalizing a lost or dead person as a way of coping with separation or (especially) bereavement. To the extent that that which has been internalized starts to exert power, incorporation may turn into possession. Elements of both incorporation and possession may be traced in the depicted relationship between Norman Bates and his mother in Alfred Hitchcock's film *Psycho*.

Within MARXIST political discussion the term is used to refer to the manner whereby opposition is neutralized by being incorporated into the dominant structures of power. Thus – the argument runs – the freedom enjoyed by speakers at Speakers' Corner in London is often paraded as evidence of the existence of free speech in Britain, whereas the relative ineffectiveness of speaking to a small gathering of persons in the age of the mass media suggests that this is a form of incorporation: the free speech is of more use in advertising the benefits of British democracy than it is in actually achieving anything that the free speakers want. Incorporation is, then, a form of 'If you can't beat them, get them to join you'. This is what has been called the 'licensed-jester syndrome', whereby licensed attacks on ruling authority give those making the attacks the idea that they are making a real challenge, whereas in practice they are strengthening that same authority.

A number of the CULTURAL MATERIALISTS have explored the concept and the issues it raises, although not always using the term 'incorporation'. Alan Sinfield's preferred terms are 'entrapment and containment'. Sinfield credits NEW HISTORICISTS with having developed the 'entrapment model' of IDEOLOGY and power, 'whereby even, or especially, maneuvers that seemed designed to challenge the system help to maintain it' (1992, 39), although he notes that entrapment is a concept found also in functionalism, STRUCTURALISM and Althusserian Marxism.

Containment, of course, is what an adversary who knows that victory is impossible seeks to achieve to avoid defeat. If you can't put out the forest fire then try to contain it.

Yet another related term is *recuperation*; this is a term used to describe a strategy whereby controlling authorities concede certain ideological positions to oppositional forces, but only so as to be able to incorporate these in a larger system of beliefs which reflects the interests of the controlling authorities.

What all of these concepts are concerned with is the way in which dissidence can be managed. If you cannot stamp out all opposition, then encourage it in its most harmless form, or in a form that actually underpins the existing order.

Cultural materialists such as Sinfield have argued that New Historicist arguments for successful containment very often exaggerate the extent to which dissidence is successfully managed. And these arguments are very directly concerned with the social and political function performed by literary works. Like their mentor, Raymond Williams, the cultural materialists have rejected the arguments of those who have interpreted all oppositional or dissident elements in literature as examples of containment.

The term *appropriation* has a similar force to incorporation, but the implied 'take-over' is more complete. Whereas an argument which is incorporated may retain some of its integrity, one which is appropriated becomes the total property of the appropriating authority. Some writers have proposed that the term *abrogation* be used as an antonym for *appropriation*, especially in the context of a refusal of the categories of an imperial(ist) culture. See Ashcroft *et al.* (1989, 38–9). Certain postcolonialist writers have taken a cue from Gayatri Chakravorty Spivak (1991) and have adopted the term *catachresis* (originally denoting a perverted or improper use of words) to refer to the way in which a subordinate group can adopt and redefine a term taken from the language of the oppressor (compare the entries for DUBBING and MIMICRY).

Finally (the multiplicity of terms bespeaks either the widespread nature of the described phenomenon or mass paranoia), Gerald Graff introduces yet another near synonym in his interesting article entitled 'Co-optation' (1989) in which he discusses many of the issues touched on above. He makes the interesting point that 'the problem with the co-optation argument as often wielded by the Left is that it tends to cast an attitude of disapproval on success without *making clear the conditions under which success might be legitimate*' (1989, 172), and he notes that this problem lies at the root of many Marxist and Leftist objections to Foucault. He makes the shrewd point that the sort of refusal to play the role of university intellectual seemingly recommended by Foucault can itself become yet another NORMATIVE posture in its turn, 'the normative posture of a new type of universal intellectual modeled along the lines of Foucault' (1989, 172).

See also *articulation* in the entry for MEDIATION.

Indeterminacy See ELLIPSIS

Index Edmund Leach distinguishes between an index and a signal as follows. Both are forms of SIGN, but whereas with an index the relationship involved is 'A indicates B', that with a signal is 'A triggers B'. Thus shivering is a signal produced by fever, whereas the word 'fever' is an index of the physical condition (1976, 12–13). For Leach a *natural index* is one in which the association is a natural (or MOTIVATED) one, but has been chosen by human beings to perform a signifying function (for example, smoke as an index of fire).

Along with ICON and SYMBOL, *index* represents one of C. S. Peirce's three essential forms of the sign, and Peirce's definition of an index is somewhat different from Leach's, and is, confusingly, very similar to Leach's definition of a signal. Robert Scholes glosses Peirce's view as follows: for Peirce, 'a sign is indexical to the extent that there is a phenomenal or existential connection between the sign and what it signifies' (1982, 144). Thus Robinson Crusoe takes Friday's footprint in the sand as an index of the fact that another man has been on his island, or, as Scholes puts it, 'Involuntary facial and bodily gestures are taken to be indices of emotional states and therefore truer than mere verbal reports on them (symbols)' (1982, 144).

These varying definitions have had some relevance to debates concerning literary INTERPRETATION. It is obvious that certain elements in a literary WORK have an indexical force in Peirce's sense, inasmuch as they could not be there did not the AUTHOR have a certain knowledge or experience. Details relating to cooking and pastry-making in the plays of Arnold Wesker, or of seamanship in the FICTION of Joseph Conrad, act as indices of the lives these authors lived prior to their writing careers. But this does not necessarily mean that their interpretative significance can be read off from the significance that such matters had in the lives of the individuals concerned.

Authors typically seek to create what one can call false indices in their work – that is, they provide details which they hope will lead READERS to assume a 'phenomenal or existential connection' with particular experiences, such that a narrator or CHARACTER seems to come from a particular background or milieu.

Influence See REVISIONISM

Inscribed reader See READERS AND READING

Inside/outside view In NARRATIVE, a distinction that allows us to specify whether a narrative takes us 'inside a character's head' or, alternatively, presents us only with that which a human being would be able to observe were the narrated events real. 'View' needs to be understood broadly: an inside view can involve thoughts and mental reflections as well as sensory information which is not thought about or analysed by the CHARACTER concerned.

Instance In his essay 'Ideology and Ideological State Apparatuses' Althusser refers to the revolutionary character of Marx's conception of the 'social whole':

> Marx conceived the structure of every society as constituted by 'levels' or 'instances' articulated by a specific determination: the *infrastructure*, or economic base (the 'unity' of the productive forces and the relations of production) and the *superstructure*, which itself contains two 'levels' or 'instances': the politico-legal (law and the State) and ideology (the different ideologies, religious, ethical, legal, political, etc.). (Althusser: 1971, 129)

Thus Althusser divides up all *social formations* into three 'instances': the IDEOLOGICAL, the economic and the political. The term is often used by Althusser in connection with Marx's reference to the determination in the last instance by the (economic) mode of production (cited in Althusser: 1969, 111). It should be noted that this is a somewhat different use of the word 'instance'.

Althusser also uses the term *determinant instance* – in other words, that force (ideological, economic, or political) that is DOMINANT and decisive in a particular CONJUNCTURE.

Institution According to certain recent theorists, the literary WORK is 'an institutional object' and can only fully be understood in the light of this fact. As Stein Haugom Olsen puts it,

> the specifically artistic features of a literary work are defined by the institutional conventions and have no existence independently of the institution; ...therefore the literary work has no objectively given institutional features, but...these features are a product of a set of descriptive and classificatory possibilities created by the institution. (1987, 22)

In common with a number of different recent theories, then, such an approach rejects the NEW CRITICAL view that literary qualities are *intrinsic* to a work, although it retains the possibility of arguing that certain works are more fruitfully treated as institutional objects than are others (in other words, that we cannot make anything a literary work by institutional means in the way that more or less any object can be treated as a chess piece). On the other hand, certain critics who have incorporated 'institutional' elements into their approaches have left open the possibility that works not written with the intent of being considered literature may, by being absorbed into the institution, become literary: as Terry Eagleton has remarked, some texts are born literary, some achieve LITERARINESS, and some have literariness thrust upon them (1983, 8–9).

Olsen's own position here has something in common with the idea of the INTERPRET[AT]IVE COMMUNITY; it differs inasmuch as whereas he tends to describe the literary institution in cross-cultural and cross-historical terms, a multitude of different and differing interpret[at]ive communities has been posited, even within particular CULTURES at particular times. A further difference is that whereas Olsen claims that 'the characteristic purpose of the institutional transaction which constitutes a literary work is aesthetic significance' (1987, 23), those arguing for the existence of interpret[at]ive communities have seen these to be characterized by varied and on occasions non-AESTHETIC purposes.

Intellectuals The Italian MARXIST Antonio Gramsci makes a useful distinction between *traditional* and *organic* intellectuals: according to him an organic intellectual is one who remains a member of and committed to his or her CLASS of origin – a working-class leader, for example – whereas a peasant who leaves his class to become a Jesuit priest becomes a traditional intellectual because such a move takes him out of his class of origin. See the chapter entitled 'The Intellectuals' in Gramsci (1971).

The distinction has been invoked in arguments about working-class writing, especially with regard to the question as to whether a member of the working class who becomes a writer can remain an organic intellectual, can claim the same relationship to the working class as, say, an industrial worker, or whether becoming a writer necessarily ALIENATES the individual from his or her class of origin.

Intended reader See READERS AND READING

Intention Matters relating to AUTHORS' intentions have probably been argued about since the beginnings of literature, but intention has been an especially problematic and contentious issue in literary criticism and, especially, with regard to literary INTERPRETATION, since the publication in 1946 of the article 'The Intentional Fallacy' by W. K. Wimsatt and Monroe Beardsley. Wimsatt and Beardsley define intention as 'design or plan in the author's mind', and argue that although 'the designing intellect' might be the *cause* of a poem it should not be taken as the *standard* 'by which the critic is to judge the worth of the poem's performance'. Moreover, they add, if 'the poet succeeded in doing [what he tried to do], then the poem itself shows what he was trying to do. And if the poet did not succeed, then the poem is not adequate evidence, and the critic must go outside the poem – for evidence of an intention that did not become effective in the poem' (Wimsatt: 1970, 4).

The position outlined in 'The Intentional Fallacy' by Wimsatt and Beardsley soon became Holy Writ for the NEW CRITICS and for those influenced by them; indeed, whereas Wimsatt and Beardsley's article clearly treats as legitimate the use of evidence of authorial intention drawn from the literary WORK itself (rather than from extra-textual material such as letters from the author), and although they also allowed evidence of contemporary linguistic usage to aid interpretation, in the 1950s and 1960s use of the word 'intention' alone was sufficient to make many critics reach for their revolvers.

In spite of this there were many who rejected the arguments of Wimsatt and Beardsley, and it is fair to say that the New Critical party line on this issue never commanded universal support – either among critics or literary theorists. It has also become apparent that the term 'intention' is used to cover a number of distinct elements in the author's creative process: Quentin Skinner has distinguished, usefully, between 'motives for writing' and 'intention in writing', which are clearly very different (albeit, possibly, intermingled) things.

Generally speaking, theorists have been less interested in intention during the last three decades – partly perhaps as a reaction against New Critical orthodoxies, and partly because the concept has, logically, little force if one accepts Roland Barthes's case that the author is (or should be treated as) dead. A significant exception is found in the work of the American critic E. D. Hirsch, whose attachment to the importance of the concept is linked to the influential distinction he makes between MEANING AND SIGNIFICANCE. Hirsch has remained committed to the position that '[a] determinate verbal meaning requires a determining will' (1967, 46), and to the belief that to abandon the concept of intention is to plunge Literary Studies and, especially, literary interpretation, into an anarchic free-for-all in which there is no criterion to distinguish correct from incorrect interpretations. At the same time, Hirsch has made his view of authorial intention more and more sophisticated, so that (for example) he can include in the concept elements logically entailed by the author's original intention, but of which the author was unconscious or unaware. Such a revision of his position has brought Hirsch quite close to the standpoint of the PRAGUE SCHOOL theorist Jan Mukařovský, who, in an article on intentionality and unintentionality in art published in 1943, argued that 'intentionality makes the work [of art] be felt as a sign, non-intentionality as a thing' (cited by O'Toole and Shukman: 1977, §23, 22). On the other hand, as Mukařovský's fellow Prague School member, Yuri Tynyanov, had pointed out in an article written in 1927, the author's intention can be no more than the yeast in baking; '[o]nce equipped with some specific literary material, the author retreats from his original intention and submits to the material' (cited by O'Toole and Shukman: 1977, §89, 36).

For *intentionality*, see the entry for PHENOMENOLOGY.

Intercalated narration See INTERPOLATION

Interior dialogue Alternatively (in Mikhail Bakhtin's usage) *internal dialogue* or *micro-dialogue*. A DIALOGUE between two well-defined voices within the single consciousness of a literary CHARACTER (or, in a wider usage, of a real human being), and the NARRATIVE representation of this process.

Interior dialogue involves more than the representation of a character's verbalized thought processes in which questions are asked and answered. To count as genuine interior dialogue the questions and answers must stem from two voices which represent different and as it were *personified* attitudes, beliefs, or characteristics. A good example occurs towards the beginning of the tenth chapter of Charlotte Brontë's *Jane Eyre*, in which we have represented a long dialogue between different and personified aspects of Jane Eyre's personality or identity. Mikhail Bakhtin gives another example from Book 11 of Part 4 of Feodor Dostoevsky's *The Brothers Karamazov* (Bakhtin: 1984, 255).

Vincent Crapanzano provides a comparable concept with his term *shadow dialogue*. According to him the term refers to

> those dialogues that one partner to the primary dialogue has with an interlocutor, real or imaginary, who is not present at the primary dialogue. Such dialogues are 'silent,' 'mental,' 'quasi-articulate,' 'beneath consciousness' though capable, at least in part, of becoming conscious. They are analogous to thought when it is conceived as a conversation. (Crapanzano: 1992, 214; he refers to Vygotsky: 1986, in the last quoted sentence)

Crapanzano distinguishes between two types of shadow dialogue: one which takes place during the primary dialogue, and one afterwards. It will be seen that for Crapanzano a shadow dialogue is parasitic on what he refers to as the primary dialogue – a normal person-to-person discussion. One can either hold imaginary discussion with the shadow interlocutor while talking to one's primary interlocutor, or after the primary dialogue is over. (In his autobiographical *A Personal Record*, discussing childhood arguments about whether he should become a seaman, Joseph Conrad reports: 'I catch myself in hours of solitude and retrospect meeting arguments and charges made thirty-five years ago by voices now for ever still; finding things to say that an assailed boy could not have found, simply because of the mysteriousness of his impulses to himself' [1946, 121]. The staging of arguments with the dead, the absent, or the FICTIONAL seems to be a natural part of our imaginative lives.)

Crapanzano's suggestion is an interesting one, and perhaps more widespread than he suggests. (Does there have to be a primary dialogue for shadow dialogue to take place?) I suspect that it is integral to much READING of fiction, as the reader engages in imaginary discussions with characters or author either during the reading or after the book has been put down. Moreover, much literary writing takes the form of a dialogue with an imagined participator or interlocutor (not necessarily a human one – think for example of Keats's 'Ode to a Nightingale'). Perhaps imaginary or shadow dialogue is (as Vygotsky suggests) a central part of our development of an adult imagination.

Internal dialogue See INTERIOR DIALOGUE

Internally persuasive discourse See DISCOURSE

Interpellation According to the French MARXIST philosopher Louis Althusser, all IDEOLOGY *'hails or interpellates concrete individuals as concrete subjects*, by the functioning of the category of the subject' (1971, 162). Althusser (possibly as a result of the influence of Lacan) is making use of a technical term used to describe what happens when the order of the day in a governmental chamber is interrupted so as to allow a Minister to be questioned. The implication is that, like the Minister, individuals are interrupted and called to account – but in this case, by different ideologies. As ideology calls them – so the argument goes – so they think that they recognize who they are. ('Think that', because actually they are being *told* who they are.) In other words: individuals come to 'live' a given set of ideological assumptions and beliefs, and to identify these with their own selves, by means of a process whereby they are persuaded that that which is presented *to* them actually represents their *own* inner identity or self. For Althusser, then, the SUBJECT is the *concrete individual* after interpellation, that is, after a sort of ideological 'body snatching'. However, Althusser believes that bodies are ALWAYS-ALREADY snatched; he adds that individuals *'are always-already subjects'*; even before being born 'an individual is always-already a subject' (1971, 164). According to Althusser, the only way for an individual to change this is for him or her, 'from within ideology', 'to outline a discourse which tries to break with ideology, in order to dare to be the beginning of a scientific (i.e. subject-less) discourse on ideology' (1971, 162).

Fredric Jameson has described the concept as 'somewhat outmoded', arguing that it was 'a group-oriented theory to begin with, since class as such can never be a mode of interpellation, but rather only race, gender, ethnic culture, and the like'. For Jameson, 'class consciousness as such . . . marks the moment in which the group in question masters the interpellative process in a new way . . . such that it becomes, however momentarily, capable of *interpellating itself* and dictating the terms of its own specular image' (1991, 345–6).

On the theoretical level, the discussion by Etienne Balibar and Pierre Macherey in 'Literature as an Ideological Form' (1978) should be consulted. Some literary critics have applied Althusser's concept of interpellation to the way in which a reader adopts the 'subject' of a literary NARRATOR or CHARACTER as the consciousness through which the literary WORK or events in it are experienced and assessed. Thus Roger Webster refers to the reader's experience of Leo Tolstoy's *Anna Karenina*: 'The reader is drawn towards Levin and becomes through him the experiencing centre of the novel's organic vision: unless we resist such positioning by reading against the grain, it is hard to avoid the process' (1990, 82–3; for AGAINST THE GRAIN, see the separate entry). The term has been of use not just to Marxist critics, but also to FEMINIST critics and to those exploring the ways in which, for example, a literary work can force a reader from a subject group to adopt a READING POSITION which positions him or her in such a manner as to force acceptance of his or her own oppression.

Not to be confused with INTERPOLATION. See also ENTHYMEME.

Interpolation To interpolate is to make insertions in something, and the term has been used in different ways by recent literary critics and theorists. The term *interpolated narration* (sometimes referred to as *intercalated narration*) is used to describe passages of NARRATIVE which come between two moments of action. Prince (1988a, 44) points out that the epistolary novel provides many examples: letters are normally written in between dramatic events rather than during them, although *Shamela*, Henry Fielding's parody of Samuel Richardson's *Pamela*, suggested that Richardson's CHARACTERS wrote letters at times and in situations when they would not have been written in real life.

In an essay on Virginia Woolf entitled 'Virginia's Web', Geoffrey Hartman (1970) argues that Woolf's subject is the activity of the mind, and he defines that activity as a work of interpolation: the mind is perpetually filling in gaps and adding explanatory information.

Not to be confused with INTERPELLATION.

Interpretation Because interpretation was central to many crucial literary-theoretical debates during and after the time when the NEW CRITICISM held sway, the term itself has been subject to continuous critical scrutiny since the 1940s. Literary critics have always argued about specific interpretations, but in the 1980s the focus of dispute shifted to the nature of interpretation itself. A revealing comment is to be found in an influential article by Steven Knapp and Walter Benn Michaels, 'Against Theory': 'By "theory" we mean a special project in literary criticism; the attempt to govern interpretations of particular texts by appealing to an account of interpretation in general' (1985, 11). The comment is revealing because of its assumption that literary theory is involved *only* with interpretation(s), and because of its implication that literary criticism itself is centrally concerned with the act (and principles) of interpretation. Jonathan Culler has seen the 'fundamental assumption' that 'the production of new interpretations is the task of literary study, the *raison d'être* of all writing about literature', as a legacy of the New Critics, and has himself argued for the more 'tendentious position' that

> while the experience of literature may be an experience of interpreting works, in fact the interpretation of individual works is only tangentially related to the under-standing of literature. To engage in the study of literature is not to produce yet another interpretation of *King Lear* but to advance one's understanding of the conventions and operations of an institution, a mode of discourse. (1981, 5)

In contrast to the post-New Critical expansion of interpretation to the point where it is almost synonymous with literary criticism itself, earlier critics and theorists have often seen interpretation as less important or less problematic. In 1929 in his *Practical Criticism*, for example, I. A. Richards notes early on in confident vein that there are two ways of interpreting all but a very few UTTERANCES: either we consider *what seems to be said* or the *mental operations* of the person who said it (1964, 6), and this is the sum total of his *theoretical* discussion of interpretation. John Wain's Introduction to the collection of essays which he edited under the title *Interpretations* in 1955 spends no time discussing what interpretation *is*; it is equated with the ANALYSIS of (in this case) poems, and treated as, theoretically, relatively unproblematic. Again symptomatic is the fact that the volume ends with an essay by G. S. Fraser 'On the Interpretation of the Difficult Poem', in which it is the poem (and perhaps its interpretation) rather than the concept of interpretation itself which is considered difficult (Wain: 1961, 211–37).

Yet as Wain and his contributors were writing, the foundations of this confidence were already being undermined, and partly by a reaction for which they themselves were responsible. T. S. Eliot refers to *Interpretations* in his essay 'The Frontiers of Criticism' (first published in 1956), and this essay was influential in changing attitudes to what interpretation involved or entailed. Eliot suggested that one danger which the book might bring with it was that of assuming that there must be just one interpretation of the poem as a whole, that must be right, and went on to suggest 'the meaning [of the poem] is what the poem means to different sensitive readers' (1961, 126).

However, it is probable that no single factor was more influential in making modern critics and theorists unhappy with the assumption that interpretation, while often difficult in practice, presented few *theoretical* problems, than the debates around the concept of authorial INTENTION which stemmed from W. K. Wimsatt and Monroe Beardsley's influential article 'The Intentional Fallacy' (1946). Previous to this debate literary critics in Great Britain and the United States were confident that to interpret a literary WORK was to reveal its MEANING by analysis, paraphrase, comparison, or more general discussion – just as to interpret *any* verbal message was to reveal its meaning by these or other means. But the implication of 'The Intentional Fallacy' was that literary works were not like other verbal messages. These *could* be interpreted by seeking to isolate the intention which gave rise to them (along with a regard to other CONVENTIONAL elements), but literature was now a case apart. And so although the immediate aim of new critics such as Wimsatt and Beardsley was actually to clarify and simplify the task of interpretation – one should pay attention to 'the words on the page' and ignore irrelevant information – the actual effect of their arguments was to make literary interpretation problematic because it was unlike non-literary interpretation.

On the European continent the greater influence on Literary Studies of the HERMENEUTIC tradition meant that the awakening from innocence perhaps came as less of a shock, but in Britain and the United States one of the notable characteristics of recent theory and criticism is that it treats interpretation as a problematic rather than a transparent concept. If it is agreed that to interpret is 'to seek the meaning of' (and this is not itself universally agreed), then to problematize *meaning* is necessarily to problematize *interpretation*. And many recent theories have so problematized the concept of meaning. Partly, but not exclusively because the dependence of meaning on intention is no longer taken for granted, the *source* or *defining authority* for meaning is now matter for debate. If the New Critics no longer allowed the AUTHOR's intention to determine meaning, other theorists denied what the New Critics asserted, that 'the words on the page' of a great work of literature generated a clear (if complex) meaning of their own. DECONSTRUCTIONISTS were very happy to confirm what critics of Wimsatt and Beardsley had averred, that with the death of the author literary works (along with all verbal formulations) were dispossessed of any fixity of meaning they might once have been believed to have. The unceasing play of SIGNIFIERS produced an unceasing stream of varying (and equally valid because there is nothing to be valid *to*) meanings.

Some of these issues are traceable back to the term *interpretation* itself. When we talk of an actor's interpretation of the role of Hamlet we are using the word in a rather different sense from that which survives in the cognate term *interpreter* (at the United Nations, for example). These variations can be found in the *OED* definitions of the term, which include 'to elucidate', 'to explain', 'to translate' (obsolete except in the cognate term 'interpreter'), and 'In recent use: to give one's own interpretation of (a musical composition, a landscape, etc.)'. In between interpretation as translation (from author to READERS, for example), and interpretation as 'one's own', there is clearly a wide gap. Recent debates have oscillated between these two extremes: the literary interpreter as the translator, conveying the author's meaning as accurately as possible, and the interpreter as performer from a SCRIPT written by the author. The interpreter as midwife, helping the author's meaning into the world, and the interpreter as parent.

Thus whereas a critic such as E. D. Hirsch defines interpretation as the recovery of authorial meaning, others have been happy to accept T. S. Eliot's assertion that there is not just one correct interpretation of a poem, for the meaning of a poem is what it means to different sensitive readers. More radically, others have followed the lead of the French theorist Pierre Macherey in denying that the critic should be primarily concerned with interpretation, but rather with the literary work's ABSENCES, with what neither the work nor the author knows.

The term *interpretant* comes from the SEMIOTIC theory of C. S. Peirce; according to Peirce, when a SIGN is understood a new sign is created in the mind of the interpreter, and this second sign is the interpretant of the first (see Scholes: 1982, 145).

See also DEFAULT INTERPRETATION.

Interpret[at]ive communities The notion of the interpretive community stems from the American critic Stanley Fish; British critics have sometimes adopted the term and modified it to *interpretative* communities so as to conform with more usual British English usage. Fish's view of the interpretive community is bound up with a related concept: that of the *interpretive strategy*:

> it is interpretive communities, rather than either the text or the reader, that produce meanings and are responsible for the emergence of formal features. Interpretive communities are made up of those who share interpretive strategies not for reading but for writing texts, for constituting their properties. In other words these strategies exist prior to the act of reading and therefore determine the shape of what is read rather than, as is usually assumed, the other way round. (1980, 14)

From this perspective an interpretive community is rather like a speech community – unified around adherence to a common set of rules which enable meaning trans- formations and MEDIATIONS. An interpretive strategy is thus comparable to the transformations made possible by the rules of GRAMMAR and syntax: its possession by a group of people means that they will all share a common relation to a TEXT or an UTTERANCE because all of them will bring the same transformational/interpretative procedures to bear on the text-to-be-interpreted or the utterance-to-be-understood.

This leads Fish to claim that when READERS interpret a text in either the same or in varying ways this is because

> members of the same community will necessarily agree because they will see (and by seeing, make) everything in relation to that community's assumed purposes and goals; and conversely, members of different communities will disagree because from each of their respective positions the other 'simply' cannot see what is obviously and inescapably there. This, then, is the explanation for the stability of interpretation among different readers (they belong to the same community). It also explains why there are disagreements and why they can be debated in a principled way: not because of a stability in texts; but because of a stability in the makeup of interpretive communities and therefore in the opposing positions they make possible. (1980, 15)

It will be seen that there is a potentially dangerous circularity here. Any group of individuals which reaches agreement concerning ground rules necessary for the discussion of a text belongs by definition to the same interpretive community, while any group which disagrees about these ground rules consists of members from different interpretive communities. This becomes more of a problem when we remember that two readers may reach such agreement with regard to one text while failing to do so with regard to another. Moreover, it is hard to see what might disprove the theory: if two readers share a common interpretation then they belong to the same interpretive community; if they disagree but can talk about their disagreement then they still belong to the same community; but if they cannot even find a common ground on which to talk about a difference then they belong to different interpretive communities.

In a section dealing with Fish's theory of the interpretive community, in his book *Textual Power* Robert Scholes indicates other problems: only those who belong to the same community can discuss interpretive disagreements – but as they belong to the same community they shouldn't have any such disagreements to discuss. Thus only those who have no disagreements can settle them in a principled way! Scholes also points out that the inevitable multiplicity of interpretive communities (see my comments above) means that the interpretive community cannot be equated with Thomas Kuhn's PARADIGM or Michel Foucault's *ÉPISTÉMÈ* (Scholes: 1985, 154–6).

Fish's argument does focus a necessary attention on to the formation of writers and readers by pre-existing CONVENTIONS, but it lacks a suitably sophisticated underpinning in the form of a detailed theory of communities – where they come from, why they change, what their internal contradictions and tensions are, and how their members communicate with and influence one another. It also seems to condemn readers to imprisonment within the conventions of the reading community to which they belong:

as Fish puts it, 'in other words, there is no single way of reading that is correct or natural, only "ways of reading" that are extensions of community perspectives' (1980, 16).

The concept ties in with STRUCTURALIST and other notions of literary COMPETENCE, although it perhaps suggests a greater degree of homogeneity in the community than does the former approach.

Interrogate A term which came into use in the 1970s to describe a more aggressive and adversarial manner of dealing with TEXTS (literary or non-literary) than CONVENTIONAL READING or more traditional methods of INTERPRETATION or ANALYSIS. The term was associated in particular with MARXIST and other attempts to avoid acceptance of the text's underlying IDEOLOGY, and involved challenging the text and the presuppositions it demanded of the READER rather than accepting the terms it seemed to lay down. It is now used more generally whenever there is question of more aggressive and less participatory forms of reading or criticism.

See also AGAINST THE GRAIN; OPPOSITIONAL READING.

Intersubjectivity Used to suggest that SUBJECTIVITY is not specific to the individual but – because it is formed by common forces – is a collective phenomenon. In recent literary theory often associated with the view that the reader's experience of a TEXT is actively internalized through INCORPORATION in his or her self rather than passively adopted or 'taken over'. As a result, a READER's view of a WORK becomes, in part, a view of him or herself: the work has been structured into the reader and is no longer something 'external'. Such a view gives the reader more of a creative role than he or she is accorded by a number of other theories, in which textual MEANING is received rather than received/constructed.

In his essay 'Right in the Eyes', Roland Barthes builds upon Jacques Lacan's definition of imaginary intersubjectivity in his *Seminar 1* as a three-term structure: '(1) I see the other; (2) I see him seeing me; (3) he knows I see him'. Barthes argues that in the relation of lovers (1) and (2) apply, but the lover 'cannot (or will not) recognize that the other knows I see him' (1991, 240–41).

Intertextuality A relation between two or more TEXTS which has an effect upon the way in which the *intertext* (that is, the text within which other texts reside or echo their PRESENCE) is READ. In some usages the term *transtextuality* is reserved for more overt relations between specific texts, or between two particular texts, while *intertextuality* is reserved to indicate a more diffuse penetration of the individual text by memories, echoes, transformations, of other texts. Gérard Genette has also coined the terms *hypertext* and *hypotext* to refer to the intertext and the text with which the intertext has some significant relation. Thus the relationship between James Joyce's *Ulysses* and Homer's *Odyssey* is that of hypertext to hypotext.

It is possible to argue that any system of GENRES, of generic distinctions or requirements, carries with it the idea that the individual text is read in a manner determined by its relations with other texts, and indeed commentaries on literary WORKS from the earliest times have generally involved cross-references to other texts which have served as models or contrasts. Even during the heyday of the NEW CRITICISM, when a commitment to the autonomy of the individual text was almost a *sine qua non* in certain circles, it was still common and accepted to INTERPRET individual literary works in terms of their intertextual relations with others.

More recently, however, specific attention has been paid to the various forms that intertextuality can take. One of the most influential presences here has been that of Mikhail Bakhtin. His insistence upon the DIALOGIC element in all UTTERANCES, and the range of different dialogues to be traced in literary works, undoubtedly sparked a more overt interest in the issue of intertextuality. A good example here is his extended discussion of 'the problem of quotation' in his essay 'From the Prehistory of Novelistic Discourse' (in Bakhtin: 1981). He pays particular but not exclusive attention to such forms as parody and travesty, and develops a theory of the linguistic HYBRID to cover them, pointing out in passing parallels with the use of parody and travesty in the modern novel (1981, 77).

Bakhtin seems himself to be an intertextual presence in Roland Barthes's and Julia Kristeva's development of theories of intertextuality. In her *Desire in Language* Kristeva defines the text as 'a permutation of texts, an intertextuality: in the space of a given text, several utterances, taken from other texts, intersect and neutralize one another' (1980, 36). Commenting upon the concept of intertextuality in his Introduction to *Desire in Language*, Leon S. Roudiez claims that it has been generally misunderstood. According to him, intertextuality has nothing to do with matters of influence of one writer upon another or with the sources of a literary work, but, rather, involves

> the components of a *textual system* such as the novel, for instance. It is defined in [Kristeva's] *La Révolution du Langage Poétique* as the transposition of one or more *systems* of signs into one another, accompanied by a new articulation of the enunciative and denotative position. (Kristeva: 1980, 15)

Roland Barthes seems partly in agreement with this position, at least so far as the distinction between intertextuality and influence is concerned. But his usage seems significantly more diffuse and all-embracing than Kristeva's. According to him, all texts are intertexts.

> Any text is a new tissue of past citations. Bits of code, formulae, rhythmic models, fragments of social languages, etc. pass into the text and are redistributed within it, for there is always language before and around the text. Intertextuality, the condition of any text whatsoever, cannot, of course, be reduced to a problem of sources or influences; the intertext is a general field of anonymous formulae whose origin can scarcely ever be located; of unconscious or automatic quotations, given without quotation-marks. (1981b, 39)

Of course, if 'any text whatsoever' is an intertext, then the term becomes tautologous and can be dispensed with.

John Frow has made a number of thought-provoking points about intertextuality which help to demonstrate how much more complex it is than some accounts have implied. His approach reminds us that intertextuality is not restricted to genesis, and that each new reading may involve a different set of intertextual relations: 'any particular construction of a set of intertextual relations is limited and relative – not to a reading subject but to the interpretive grid (the regime of reading) through which both the subject position and the textual relations are constituted' (1986, 155). Most interesting of all, he argues that 'the text has not only an intertextual relationship to previous texts (in the case of the classics this is usually effaced) but also an intertextual relationship to itself as canonized text' (1986, 230–31). Intertextuality has thus to be seen in association with the whole complex issue of the reader's varied expectations as formed by IDEOLOGICAL, generic, and other factors. It must also be seen, according to Frow's view, not as something which is just handed to the reader on a plate, as it were congealed into the text, but as something which to at least a certain extent the reader can control and change.

'The intertextual strategy' is a phrase which has been used to describe the process of rewriting classic or CANONICAL texts so as (normally) to subvert or APPROPRIATE their ideological force. Compare DUBBING.

See also PALIMPSEST TEXT, and discussion of the term *double-voiced* in the entries for DIEGESIS AND MIMESIS, DISCOURSE, and DOUBLE-VOICED.

Intertitle Following Gérard Genette (1997, 294), a title which is internal to a WORK (in contrast to the title *of* a work). Thus the titles of chapters, sections, 'books' within a larger work are all intertitles.

Intra-diegetic See DIEGESIS AND MIMESIS

Intrinsic criticism A general description of those critical theories which countenance, and those critical methods which attempt to practise, a criticism which attends primarily or exclusively to the evidence of the individual literary WORK itself. The term is normally set in opposition to *extrinsic criticism*: criticism which does not limit itself to what is to be found 'inside' the work but which goes outside it and brings for example historical, biographical, or sociological evidence to bear upon the READING and INTERPRETATION of the work. The opposition has points of similarity with that between ESSENTIALIST and DIALECTICAL or relational positions.

The intrinsic/extrinsic opposition was much in vogue during and immediately after the period in which the NEW CRITICS had most influence, and its use is linked to their arguments against a literary-critical reliance upon *extrinsic* evidence. But in recent years the terms have fallen out of fashion, partly because a number of critics have argued that it is very difficult to decide what is or is not intrinsic or extrinsic. Frank Cioffi, for example, refers to the distinction made between internal and external evidence by W. K. Wimsatt and Monroe Beardsley in their very influential essay 'The Intentional Fallacy' (1946), and argues that it is misconceived from the start because a reader's response to a poem will vary according to what he or she knows, and that deciding whether a remark is a critical comment about a poem or a biographical one about the AUTHOR is not the simple matter that Wimsatt and Beardsley assume it to be (1976, 63–4).

Introjection See PROJECTION CHARACTERS

Intrusive narrator A NARRATOR who breaks into the NARRATIVE to comment upon a CHARACTER, EVENT or situation – or even to introduce opinions not directly related to what has been narrated. The term is often reserved for situations in which the intrusion is felt to break into an established narrative tone or illusion, although it is also used in a purely technical sense to describe 'own voice' comments from a narrator which may hardly be remarked by the READER because of their homogeneity with the rest of the narrative.

Iridescence See FLICKER

Isochrony Borrowed by recent NARRATIVE theorists from a term used to describe poetic rhythm, isochrony denotes an *unvarying* or an *equal* relationship between NARRATING-time and STORY-time. The two are not the same: if a story covers three hours and each hour is narrated by means of five thousand words, then the relationship between narrating-time and story-time is unvarying. But if a story covers three hours and each hour of the story takes approximately an hour to read, then the relationship between narrating-time and story-time can be said to be equal. It should be clear that whereas the former relationship can be measured with some degree of precision, the latter cannot. (Different readers read at different speeds, and one's speed of reading varies according to a number of factors – level of textual difficulty or interest, for example.) Mieke Bal reminds us that real isochrony (of the second type) cannot be determined precisely, although we may 'assume that . . . a dialogue without commentary takes as long in TF [FABULA-time] as it does in TS [story-time]' (1985, 70–71). Isochrony is, of course, capable of precise determination in the PERFORMANCE arts (film, drama).

The opposite of isochrony is *anisochrony*: either a varying or an unequal relationship between narrating-time and story-time – normally the former.

See also DURATION.

Isotopy See TOPIC

Iterative See FREQUENCY

J

Jouissance To the surprise of many English-speaking people, this word can be found in the *OED*, although classified as obsolete and with examples cited from, among others, Carew and Spenser. Of the two main meanings given, that which is nearer to the current usage found amongst critical theorists is the second: Pleasure, delight; merriment, mirth, festivity. This sounds very innocent, and is clearly different from the current usage – loaned from the French – that involves, among other things, *sexual* PLEASURE. The first meaning concerns the possession and use of something affording advantage, as in the *enjoyment* of a right, and jouissance is etymologically related to the word enjoyment.

Leon S. Roudiez dates the renewed critical interest in this term from the publication of Jacques Lacan's discussion of it in his 1972–3 seminar, which in its French publication sported a cover picture of the *Ecstasy of St Theresa*, suggesting the prominent part played by sexual orgasm in jouissance. For Lacan, Roudiez claims, jouissance 'is sexual, spiritual, physical, conceptual at one and the same time' (Kristeva: 1980, 16). Julia Kristeva states that jouissance alone causes the ABJECT to exist as such. 'One does not know [the abject], one does not desire it, one joys in it [*on en jouit*]. Violently and painfully. A passion' (1982, 9).

In Roland Barthes's *The Pleasure of the Text* jouissance is translated as *bliss*. Barthes claims that to judge a TEXT according to pleasure means that it is impossible to say either that it is good or that it is bad, because the text is 'too much *this*, not enough *that*' (1976, 13). This suggests that textual jouissance is an orgasmic experience in which the reader is so enrapt (or enwrapped) that that objectivity and distance necessary for judgement is impossible.

See also *RAVISSEMENT*.

K

Kenosis See REVISIONISM

Kernel event See EVENT

Kernel function See FUNCTION

Kernel word or sentence In STYLISTICS, any word possessed of such stylistic emphasis as to colour the stylistic force of a textual unit, however defined.

Kink See STRAIGHT

L

Lack See ABSENCE

Lamella See HOMMELETTE

Language acquisition device See ARCHE-WRITING

Langue and parole Perhaps the most important – and influential – distinction introduced by Ferdinand de Saussure in his *Course in General Linguistics*. It is now common to use the French words to represent these paired concepts in English, but one can find attempts to render them in English, with langue represented by *language* (sometimes *a* or *the* language, as in the English translation of Roland Barthes's *Elements of Semiology*, or as *language-system*), and parole as *speaking, speech, language-behaviour*, or, on occasions, phrases such as *the sum of all actual (possible) utterances*.

For the sake of clarity, where other terms are used in the following quotations, I will replace them with either 'langue' or 'parole' – in square brackets so that the substitution is MARKED.

According to Saussure,

> [i]f we could embrace the sum of word-images stored in the minds of all individuals, we could identify the social bond that constitutes [langue]. It is a storehouse filled by members of a given community through their active use of [parole], a grammatical system that has a potential existence in each brain, or, more specifically, in the brains of a group of individuals. For [langue] is not complete in any speaker; it exists perfectly only within a collectivity. (1974, 13–14)

A number of points need to be stressed here. First, that as the reference to 'a given community' makes clear, Saussure's mention of the minds of 'all individuals' should be taken to refer to all individuals within a particular language community. Second, that langue is supra-individual: were Martians to kidnap a single English speaker they could not extract the langue of English from him or her alone. Third, that langue is a *system*, and one that has generative power ('potential existence'). Thus, if those same Martians were able to gather every example of English speech and feed them into a super computer they still could not end up with our langue, for langue is that set of rules, that SYSTEM, that is able not just to generate all those acts of English speech, but also all the *potential but as yet unuttered acts of speech* that *could* be generated by it. (However, Saussure argues [1974, 15] that although we no longer speak dead languages, we can gain access to their linguistic systems [langues]; this suggests that langue *can* be said to be accessible even to those without the ability to *generate* paroles, so long as they can understand all previously generated paroles.) Fourth, it is also the system that allows native speakers to *understand* all the acts of speech correctly generated (in other individuals) by itself.

Saussure stresses that langue is not a function of the individual speaker: it is passively assimilated by the individual and does not require premeditation (contrast speaking in a *foreign* language). Parole, on the other hand, he insists is 'an individual act' which is wilful and intellectual (1974, 14).

We can use an old parallel here, and compare langue to the rules of chess, and parole to individual games of chess or 'chess acts'. Clearly chess is more than just all the games of chess that have ever been played: it is all the games of chess that the rules allow to be played (including those that may, or will, never be played, because a given game of chess has meaning partly because of the games that it is not, games that may never actually be played). And while one chess game in a sense 'belongs' to the players who play it, chess itself is supra-individual and social in nature: it is the possession of the chess community. (Whether one extends this to a supra-historical chess community is a moot point: both chess and langue are clearly the product of historical processes, but Saussure's stress is on the system seen SYNCHRONICALLY, as it exists supra-individually at a certain moment of time.)

187

Langue and parole

During the early years of the current revival of interest in the work of Saussure both Roland Barthes (1967a) and Jonathan Culler (1975) pointed out that deciding what was language and what was parole was not unproblematic, but the over-arching distinction between rule and rule-generated ACT has proved extremely fertile in a range of different contexts. It may well be that the growth of interest in PRAGMATICS marks the end of a rather uncritical use of the distinction: in our post-pragmatics age there are rather fewer who are prepared unreservedly to accept Saussure's contention that the 'science of language is possible only if the other elements [of parole] are excluded' (1974, 15). Culler assumes the possibility of a relatively unproblematic relating of langue and parole to Chomsky's COMPETENCE AND PERFORMANCE (1975, 9), and he seems to use these terms (here and elsewhere) relatively interchangeably.

In literary criticism this distinction has been most influential as a model. The use of the LINGUISTIC PARADIGM by STRUCTURALIST critics has led to a succession of attempts to find parallels to langue and parole in the 'system of literature'. In an essay entitled 'Structuralism and Literary Criticism' (first published in French in 1964), Gérard Genette suggested that

> literary 'production' is a *parole*, in the Saussurian sense, a series of partially autonomous and unpredictable individual acts; but the 'consumption' of this literature by society is a *langue*, that is to say, a whole the parts of which, whatever their number and nature, tend to be ordered into a coherent system. (1982, 18–19)

One of the more interesting attempts to develop this analogy is to be found in a number of successive attempts by Jonathan Culler to distinguish between a general LITERARINESS and the specific acts of literary READING this enables. Culler does not always refer directly to Saussure but sometimes to the distinction between competence and performance. However, given the comments made above this should not be too significant.

Culler argues that just as Linguistics has changed its focus with the realization that description of a finite set of sentences is no longer enough, and that 'linguistics must instead describe the ability of native speakers, what they know when they know a language', so too the study of literature must 'become a poetics, a study of the conditions of meaning' (1980, 49), and abandon the attempt merely to 'analyse a corpus of works' (1980, 50). This argument is linked to a view of literature as INSTITUTION: 'Just as sequences of sound have meaning only in relation to the GRAMMAR of a language, so literary works may be quite baffling to those with no knowledge of the special conventions of literary discourse, no knowledge of literature as an institution' (1980, 49). According to Culler, 'the conventions which make literature possible, are the same whether one adopts the reader's or the writer's point of view', and he suggests that 'as a reader oneself, one can perform all the experiments one needs' (1980, 50, 51).

Here some caveats become necessary. We seem to have moved a long way from Saussure's supra-personal system (langue) to a competence to which anyone can obtain access by means of a process of introspection that would hardly have been challenged by the NEW CRITICS. Moreover, a clear difference between linguistic and literary competence would appear to be that whereas the former normally involves *both* the generation *and* the understanding of all grammatical sentences within one's native language, literary competence for most people is limited to understanding rather than production of literary works. Furthermore, whereas langue (as Saussure pointed out – see above) is automatically and unselfconsciously assimilated by the individual and does not require a self-conscious learning effort, literary 'competence' seems on the evidence to require an educational system to raise it to a certain level. Certainly the lowest common denominator of literary competence would appear to be a good deal lower than that of linguistic competence in our CULTURE.

Genette and Culler are by no means the only theorists to attempt to apply the langue/parole distinction to literature. In his *Introduction to Poetics* Tzvetan Todorov clearly defines poetics as the study of the literary equivalent of langue.

> It is not the literary work itself that is the object of poetics: what poetics questions are the properties of that particular discourse that is literary discourse. Each work is therefore regarded only as the manifestation of an abstract and general structure, of which it is but one of the possible realizations. Whereby this science is no longer concerned with actual literature, but with a possible literature in other words, with that abstract property that constitutes the singularity of the literary phenomenon: *literariness.* (1981, 6–7)

There is no doubt that this shift of emphasis has had many beneficial results. It has directed more attention to the reader and the reading process, it has obliged us to consider whether there are invariant rules of literary reading or INTERPRETATION which constitute, wholly or partially, the institution of literature, and it has thus shifted some debates from being primarily about the interpretations of individual TEXTS to being primarily about the principles underlying literary interpretation(s). In so doing it has almost (often unintentionally) shifted attention to the cultural and IDEOLOGICAL determinants of literary reading and interpretation.

But there have been problematic aspects to the attempt to apply these concepts to the study of literature or literariness, some of which have been indicated. One more should perhaps be mentioned: it would seem that whereas Culler sees the literary equivalent of parole to be the *analysis* of individual texts, Todorov sees these texts (he actually refers to WORKS rather than texts) *themselves* as if they were acts of literary parole – while Genette has suggested that it is the *production* of literature that constitutes the literary parole (see above). Onega and Landa, too, have made a comparable comment.

> Structuralists often hesitate, however, when it comes to deciding the level at which the analogy [between language and literature, *J. H.*] should work: is it literature as a whole that works as a language, or is it the individual work that does so? Each work may be argued to constitute a *langue* of its own, may be seen as a self-regulating structure, since it creates, up to a point, the conditions for its own meaning and helps define the language in which it is interpreted. (1996, 5)

These differences – and the fact that there can be such differences – suggest that the literary assimilation of the langue/parole distinction may be a little less straightforward than has sometimes been suggested.

Lavender culture/language/sex Stevi Jackson and Sue Scott report that 'Betty Friedan, a prominent member of NOW [= the National Organization of Women], dubbed [Lesbians who joined this body] the "lavender menace", provoking a demonstration of lesbians at the second NOW congress in 1970' (1996, 13). I have been unable to discover why Friedan should have associated Lesbians with lavender – nor do I know whether she had the colour or the flower in mind. (The association between Gays and Lesbians with the colour pink can be attributed to the fact that the Nazis made homosexuals wear a pink triangle. Janice A. Radway attributes the term 'pink ghetto' to Catherine Kirkland [Radway 1991, 18, 244], but the term seems to be associated not with Lesbianism but with cultural ghettos for women in general.)

Subsequent to Friedan's attack, *lavender* appears to have been one of a number of originally derogatory terms which have been commandeered and used aggressively by those originally attacked through their use. Thus in 1978 a volume edited by K. Jay and A. Young entitled *Lavender Culture* appeared. But the term should be used with care as its original derogatory force still clings to it, and I have heard the phrase 'lavender language' used dismissively comparatively recently.

Compare VANILLA SEX.

Leakage Much modern theory is suspicious of mechanistic models which posit relationships between fixed and autonomous entities (see, for example, the entries for HYMEN and LIMINALITY). *Leakage* is one of a number of terms that help to destabilize such models without actually rejecting concepts such as identity or relationship altogether.

Non-verbal leakage occurs when a person's non-verbal behaviour (posture, gesture, facial expression) betray feelings, thoughts or attitudes which the person wishes to conceal. (Compare the entry for EXTERNALIZER.)

Legitimation A process whereby a state, government, individual, action, or whatever, is *legitimated*, that is to say, made to appear to conform with the rules or principles of the existing or DOMINANT order, or made to seem *natural*.

The term is often used in recent literary criticism to suggest that one of the roles of literary works is to present the ruling order or its values in such a light as to legitimize it. Thus Graham Holderness suggests that E. M. W. Tillyard's study *Shakespeare's History Plays* (1944), reproduces Shakespeare's plays

> as parables of order, or what contemporary criticism would prefer to call 'strategies of legitimation', cultural forms by means of which the dominant ideology of the Tudor state validated its own moral and political power, through the intervention of a loyal and talented subject, Shakespeare. (1992, 21–2)

Leitmotif See THEME AND THEMATICS

Lexia/lexie See FUNCTION

Lexicon In his essay 'Rhetoric of the Image' Roland Barthes poses the (appropriately) rhetorical question: 'What is a lexicon?' He answers: 'It is a portion of the symbolic level (of language) which corresponds to a body of practices and techniques' (1991, 35).

Liminal The *OED* provides the following definition: 'of or pertaining to the threshold or initial stage of a process', and classifies the word as 'rare'. The recent growth of interests in thresholds and boundaries associated especially with POSTCOLONIALIST theory has brought the word back into common usage in literary-critical and CULTURAL-theoretical circles. Part of the current postcolonialist interest stems from the POST-STRUCTURALIST concern to reject BINARY distinctions and the black/white categories which go along with them, but a more general interest in the MARGINAL has also led to a greater reliance upon the term. Here for example is Dominick LaCapra: 'The most engaging, if at times perplexing, dimensions of interpretation exist on the margin, where these two meanings are not simply disjoined from one another, for it is at this liminal point that the dialogue with the past becomes internal to the historian' (1983, 18).

Some FEMINISTS have found the term useful as a way of locating women in an (appropriately named) 'no-man's land' between nature and culture.

See also FRAME; PARATEXT.

Line fiction Publishers' term for FICTION sold to a mass market on the basis of non-varying generic characteristics. A classic example is that of ROMANCE paperbacks. Those READERS who are loyal to one such 'line' are known as 'category readers'.

Linguistic paradigm Ferdinand de Saussure established a number of extremely influential analytical distinctions in his work which, while originally applied by him to the study of language, have subsequently been extended metaphorically to other areas. Concepts such as SYNTAGMATIC AND PARADIGMATIC relations, LANGUE AND PAROLE, and SIGNIFIER AND SIGNIFIED have all been pressed into service by theorists concerned with a range of non-linguistic phenomena.

All of these extensions of linguistic distinctions involve treating other SIGN-systems as if they were fundamentally similar to language: language, in other words, is taken as a *paradigm* for the study and analysis of other sign-systems.

Jonathan Culler gives an extended account of two such uses of the linguistic paradigm in his *Structuralist Poetics*: Claude Lévi-Strauss's structural analysis of MYTHOLOGY and Roland Barthes's of fashion (Culler: 1975, 32–54). But once one has grasped the essential idea, the method has a potentially unending set of applications. Thus for example one can treat a meal with several courses like a sentence composed of several words: in a given CULTURE there are all sorts of different dishes that can be chosen as the first course, but once chosen these constrain what is chosen as the second course – and so on.

Within the field of literary criticism one can refer to the way in which terminology and distinctions taken from the GRAMMAR of verbs have been applied to the study of NARRATIVE by Gérard Genette. Hence he uses *tense* to designate temporal relations between narrative and STORY; MOOD to designate forms and degrees of narrative 'representation'; and *voice* to designate the narrative situation or its instance (1980, 30–31). (See the entry for PERSPECTIVE AND VOICE.)

Jacques Lacan's claim that the UNCONSCIOUS is structured like a language represents a more global use of language as explanatory paradigm; other theorists have taken Noam Chomsky's distinction between COMPETENCE AND PERFORMANCE and applied it to literature: readers of literature are said to possess (perhaps to different

191

degrees) a fundamental competence *vis-à-vis* the READING of literary WORKS, a competence which results in certain specific performances – that is, specific readings of literary works.

In addition to applying particular distinctions originating in the study of language to non-linguistic sign-systems, those influenced by Saussure and other linguisticians have tended to place great significance on the fact of BINARY opposition itself: a fondness for binary distinctions is one of the MARKS of those using, or influenced by, the linguistic paradigm.

See also *BRICOLEUR*; HOMOLOGY; SEMIOTIC.

Lisible See READERLY AND WRITERLY TEXTS

Literariness In his essay 'The Theory of the "Formal Method"' Boris Eichenbaum quotes tellingly from Roman Jakobson's 'Recent Russian Poetry, Sketch 1', first published in Prague in 1921. In the extract quoted, Jakobson makes the polemical claim that

> [t]he object of study in literary science is not literature but literariness – that is, that which makes a given work a work of literature. Until now literary historians have preferred to act like the policeman who, intending to arrest a certain person, would, at any opportunity, seize any and all persons who chanced into the apartment, as well as those who passed along the street. The literary historians used everything – anthropology, psychology, politics, philosophy. Instead of a science of literature, they created a conglomeration of home-spun disciplines. (Eichenbaum: 1965, 107; for an alternative translation see Èjxenbaum: 1971a, 8)

Eichenbaum comes back to this point in his essay 'Literary Environment': 'Literary-historical fact is a complex construct in which the fundamental role belongs to *literariness* – an element of such specificity that its study can be productive only in immanent-evolutionary terms' (Èjxenbaum: 1971b, 62). It is arguable that it is this insistence upon the specificity of literature and, thus, of the specificity of the *study* of literature, which is one of the key reasons why RUSSIAN FORMALISM is formalist.

The insistence served to distinguish the study of literature not just from other disciplines such as those listed by Jakobson, but also from the study of other art-forms. This insistence upon the *specificity* and distinctiveness of literature, and of the need for it to be studied in a specific and distinctive manner, often tipped over into an insistence upon the *autonomy* of literature and of the irrelevance to Literary Studies of all references to, as Jakobson put it, environment, psychology, politics, and philosophy. It should be stressed that such developments were criticized by leading Russian Formalists. Thus Jakobson himself stated that neither he, nor Tynyanov, Shklovsky or Mukařovský ever declared that art was a closed sphere, that they had emphasized not the separation of art but 'the autonomy of the aesthetic function' (Tynyanov *et al.*: 1977, 19).

See also CODES OF READING; LANGUE AND PAROLE.

Literary mode of production (LMP) A term proposed by Terry Eagleton in his *Criticism and Ideology* (1976a). Eagleton here attempts to apply and refine the orthodox MARXIST concept of 'Mode of Production'. In the orthodox view each major period of world history is characterized by a dominant mode of production such as the feudal mode or the capitalist mode (Marx also mentioned the Asiatic mode of production, and of course looked forward to the socialist one). A mode of production is defined – again in the orthodox view – in terms of its *forces of production*, and of its *relations of production* (otherwise referred to as the control or ownership of the *means of production*). Thus the capitalist mode of production would involve the revolutionizing of the forces of production through industrialization, alongside the private ownership of the means of production – meaning that the relations of production are between two main groups: the owners of CAPITAL, and those who own nothing but their labour power.

Traditional Marxist literary criticism attempted to relate literature (seen as part of the SUPERSTRUCTURE) to society's economic BASE, understood in terms of its mode of production. What Eagleton attempts to do is to make this process more receptive to local 'relative autonomies', STRUCTURES which MEDIATE between base and superstructure. According to him, a number of distinct modes of literary production will exist and co-exist in any literate society, and some of these may be 'survivals', that is to say they may have arisen in one society (with its own distinctive general mode of production), and have survived so as to be found in a subsequent society possessed of a different general mode of production. He notes that

> [a] classical instance of such survivals is typically to be found in the historical mutation from 'oral' to 'written' LMPs, where the social relations and kinds of literary product appropriate to the 'oral' LMP normally persist as significant constituents of the 'written' LMP itself, both interactive with and relatively autonomous of it. (1976a, 45)

Locutionary act See SPEECH ACT THEORY

Logic of the same A term which has entered into FEMINIST discourse in English from the writings of the French writer Luce Irigaray. It describes a process of argumentation whereby x is treated as equivalent to y and thus effectively subsumed into the value-scheme of y. The foremost example of this is the PATRIARCHAL assumption that the male represents a standard, and that the female is thus necessarily less than this standard, or formed in response to it. In her *Speculum of the Other Woman* (published in English in 1985), she argues that woman is forced into a subjectless position by this patriarchal logic of the same: Freud models his account of the little girl's development on his account of the little boy's development, thus presenting female sexuality as 'the negative response to the male's desire' (Millard: 1989, 159).

More widely, the logic of the same is typically seen in the sort of argument that runs 'x is like y, let us consider x as if it were y, x is y'. Discussions of literary influence are particularly prone to this variant form of SLIPPAGE.

Compare FEMALING; FEMALE AFFILIATION COMPLEX; IMMASCULATION.

Logocentrism Jacques Derrida's coinage (sometimes used interchangeably with *phonocentrism*). Logocentrism refers to systems of thought or habits of mind which are reliant upon what Derrida, following Heidegger, terms the metaphysics of PRESENCE – that is, a belief in an extra-systemic validating presence or CENTRE which underwrites and fixes linguistic meaning but is itself beyond scrutiny or challenge. For Derrida, such a position is fundamentally idealist, and he argues that the dismantling of logocentrism is simultaneously the DECONSTRUCTION of idealism or spiritualism 'in all their variants' (1981b, 51).

In his 'Writing Before the Letter' (with which *Of Grammatology* opens), Derrida claims that the *history of metaphysics* has 'always assigned the origin of truth in general to the logos: the history of truth, of the truth of truth, has always been...the debasement of writing, and its repression outside "full" speech' (1976, 3). Logocentrism, then, is associated by Derrida with the making of écriture subject to speech (the English translation of écriture as 'writing' may be misleading: see the entry for ÉCRITURE).

Derrida's much-quoted assertion that '*there is nothing outside of the text*' (1976, 158), which can also be rendered in English as 'there is no outside-text', has to be read in the light of his attack on logocentrism: the TEXT cannot be assigned a MEANING that is underwritten by an origin, a presence, which resides in self-validating isolation beyond the confines of the text.

See also DIFFÉRANCE.

Logos Richard Harland provides the following useful gloss on Jacques Derrida's use of this term:

> [A] Greek word that illuminatingly brings together in a single concept the inward rational principle of verbal texts, the inward rational principle of human beings, and the inward rational principle of the natural universe. Even more illuminating, 'logos' combines all these meanings with a further meaning: 'the Law'. For 'logos' as an inward rational principle serves to control and take charge of outward material things. (1987, 146)

It should be added that in Derrida's view the sense of security provided by a belief in logos is illusory: there are, from his perspective, no such inward rational principles.

See also PRESENCE.

Look See GAZE

Loophole addressee See FUNCTIONS OF LANGUAGE

Ludism From a Latin root meaning to play, *ludism* and *ludic* are used interchangeably in English with *play* and *playful* in DECONSTRUCTIONIST writing or by writers influenced by deconstructionist ideas. More recently *play* and *playful* have perhaps been more favoured, probably because their use allows reference to a wider range of meanings.

The central idea behind all these usages is that once the illusion of PRESENCE has been dispensed with, READING and INTERPRETATION no longer involve a decoding that is subject to the firm discipline of some CENTRE of authority that has access to the CODE book; instead the READER can observe and participate in the free play of SIGNIFIERS endlessly generating a succession of MEANINGS none of which can claim superiority or authority. The main senses of 'play' involved here are: play as in 'to play a game', and play as in 'to play a fish' or 'to play a hose'. In other words there is a combined sense of the absence of discipline alongside the almost aestheticized experiencing of interrelated tensions and forces. Vicki Mistacco expresses it as follows:

> 'Ludism' may be simply defined as the open play of signification, as the free and productive interaction of forms, of signifiers and signifieds, without regard for an original or an ultimate meaning. In literature, ludism signifies textual play; the text is viewed as a game affording both author and reader the possibility of producing endless meanings and relationships. (1980, 375)

This view is closely related to a belief in the (metaphorical) death of the AUTHOR, the stern parent who would restrict the child's play.

Recent discussions of POSTMODERNISM have suggested that one important way in which it can be distinguished from MODERNISM is by reference to its more playful and unserious tone. Instead of a view of the loss of centre in the contemporary world as tragic, the postmodernist views this as a justification of playfulness – exploring the potentialities of SIGNIFICATIONS without an irritable searching after final truths or unified meanings.

It should be noted that in such uses the fact that games often have *rules*, and that playing, among both animals and humans, is often the way in which the player is prepared for life in the non-ludic world, is not generally accorded much importance.

M

Magic realism In his book *Magic Realism Rediscovered, 1918–1981* (1983), Seymour Menton notes that although this term has been used with increasing frequency since 1955 to describe post-Second World War Latin American FICTION (1983, 9), it was in 1925 that Franz Roh first formulated the term and described its characteristics (1983, 13). Menton associates the term's juxtaposition of 'magic' and 'realism' with the psychological-philosophical ideas of Carl Jung, and suggests that the oxymoron 'captures the artists' and the authors' efforts to portray the strange, the uncanny, the eerie, and the dreamlike – but not the fantastic – aspects of everyday reality' (1983, 13). Menton's insistence that magic realism can be found both in painting and in literature is worth noting. (Jean Weisgerber's *Le Réalisme magique* [1988] adds cinema to the list.) Among the magic realist painters Menton discusses are Henri Rousseau, Giorgio de Chirico, Carel Willink, Carlo Mense, Anton Räderscheidt, Carl Grossberg, and Camille Bombois.

Not all would agree with Menton that magic realism cannot involve the FANTASTIC, and current usage generally bestows the term on works in which a blending of the fantastic – or at least the extraordinary – with REALISM, takes place. The term is, as Menton notes, particularly associated with certain Central and South American novelists such as Gabriel García Márquez and Isabella Allende but it is being applied more and more liberally to a range of writers and works from many different periods and cultures, including, especially, a number of recent female and FEMINIST European novelists.

In an essay in Jean Weisgerber's *Le Réalisme magique*, Jeanne Delbaere-Garant discusses 'Le Domaine anglais'. She admits that the term excites little Anglo-Saxon excitement, and that for the English the juxtaposition of 'magic' and 'realism' seems incongruous. Nevertheless, as she points out, an interest in the supernatural and the marvellous does coexist with realism in the history of the English novel from Defoe and Richardson onwards, and she reminds us, usefully, that in the nineteenth century the work of Dickens, Kingsley, Lewis Carroll, and Ruskin involved both elements (1988, 155). If to these one adds other works mentioned by her, such as Wilde's *The Picture of Dorian Gray,* Stevenson's *The Strange Case of Dr Jekyll and Mr Hyde*, and even Joseph Conrad's 'The Secret Sharer', then it becomes less problematic to talk of something approaching a tradition. The most recent novelists mentioned by Delbaere-Garant are John Cowper Powys, William Golding, and Muriel Spark. Her article is a useful reminder that many of the characteristics associated with magic realism did not spring into existence in Britain with the fiction of Angela Carter, and the specifically female use of the mode can be associated with Virginia Woolf's *Orlando*, and even with certain aspects of the female Gothic novel.

In its current usage, magic realism seems typically to involve the sudden incursion of fantastic or 'magical' elements into an otherwise realistic PLOT and setting. In the years since Delbaere-Garant wrote (*Le Réalisme magique* was published in 1988, but from the evidence of its editor's Preface it seems to date from 1983) the Anglo-Saxons seem to have caught up: it is indisputable that a recent leading exponent of the GENRE is the British novelist Angela Carter. According to Paulina Palmer, in her earlier work Carter 'exploited this mode to evoke the individual's experience of anxiety, estrangement and isolation (the kind of emotions discussed by Freud in his essay on "The Uncanny")', in her more recent work 'she uses it as a vehicle for the expression of emotions which have a liberating effect', such as pleasure and wonder (Palmer: 1987, 182). It is arguable that the word 'realism' is justifiably included in the term because behind all the fantastic elements to be found in magic realist WORKS, a realist impulse can be detected: the main concern of the novelists involved is to explore what they see as contemporary reality, rather than to provide an alternative to it.

Male-as-norm The (normally NATURALIZED and unmeditated) assumption that that which is male represents a (or more often the) standard, from which all other possible PERSPECTIVES (especially that which is female) represent divergences and failures to measure up to the NORM.
 Compare EUROCENTRIC; FEMALING.

Manner (maxims of) See SPEECH ACT THEORY

Marginality Literary criticism has focused a certain amount of attention on the way in which AUTHORS from the earlier part of the twentieth century occupying marginal or ambiguous positions *vis-à-vis* social or national identity were often able to see beyond the accepted or CONVENTIONAL attitudes and beliefs of their time, as their marginality made it difficult for them to be – or feel – fully incorporated in any dominant system of values. MODERNIST literature in particular is characterized by its relation not only to authors who occupied various forms of marginal position, but also by its overt concern with marginality as representative of something central to modern existence. Thus we can point to the large number of major early twentieth-century authors who were (to quote the title of a book by Terry Eagleton) exiles or émigrés – caught on the margins between different CULTURES.

More recently, FEMINIST writers have focused attention on the way in which PATRIARCHY marginalizes female experience and thus makes male experience the determining and dominating NORM. Some feminist writers have seen this process as two-edged: on the one hand, it serves to invalidate female experience and to consolidate patriarchal power through the social, cultural and political disenfranchisement of women, but on the other hand, it opens women's eyes to aspects of the functioning of patriarchy, as marginalization typically confers insight. (The person who does not belong is the person who perceives most clearly what it is to which he or she does not belong.) It is, for example, noteworthy that the most important British writer of the early twentieth century who is not an exile or an émigré in the conventional sense is Virginia Woolf; her experience of marginality involves GENDER rather than culture.

An important point to stress is that that which is defined as marginal is normally done so from a perspective of 'power-as-centre'; thus Linda Hutcheon has quoted Rick Salutin's telling comment that Canadians are marginal, not 'because of the quirkiness of our ideas or the inadequacy of our arguments, but because of the power of those who define the centre' (Salutin: 1984, 6).

Jacques Derrida's concept of *supplementarity* is sometimes associated with marginality. The logic behind such an association appears to be that if all representation and INTERPRETATION requires a supplementary element – can never feed merely upon that which is to be represented or interpreted – then attention is necessarily drawn to the margins of that which is to be either interpreted or represented, to the borderline between the thing itself and that which is brought to supplement it. Derrida makes the point with regard to writing:

> Writing is dangerous from the moment that representation there claims to be presence and the sign of the thing itself. And there is a fatal necessity, inscribed in the very functioning of the sign, that the substitute make one forget the vicariousness of its own function and make itself pass for the plentitude of a speech whose deficiency and infirmity it nevertheless only *supplements*.
>
> . . .
>
> 'The sign is always the supplement of the thing itself'. (1976, 144, 145)

Marjorie Levinson has offered her own supplement to Derrida, arguing that

> Derrida has taught us that the supplemental or additive character of masturbation is also its substitutive character. Derrida's word, *'le supplément'*, describes that which adds its own difference and subtractiveness: masturbation, writing. (1988, 26)

See also FRAME; HYBRID; LIMINAL; NOMAD; PRESENCE.

Markedness In Linguistics a marked signifier is one which is qualified or added to in such a way as to focus or adapt its meaning. Thus *bananas* is a marked form of *banana*.

The term has been adapted in discussion of IDEOLOGICALLY charged terms. Thus to use the term 'female poet' – a marked form of 'poet' – reveals that one's concept of 'poet' involves maleness (no one ever refers to Shelley, the well-known male poet).

Marvellous See FANTASTIC

Marvellous realism A term which in its general use predates the not dissimilar but unrelated MAGIC REALISM by several decades. The Haitian writer Jacques Stephen Aléxis, in his 'Of the Marvellous Realism of the Haitians' (1956) lists what he takes to be the features of this particular literary mode or movement.

1. To sing the beauties of the Haitian motherland, its greatness as well as its wretchedness, with the sense of the magnificent prospects which are opened up by the struggles of its people and the universal and the profound truth of life;
2. To reject all art which has no real and social content;
3. To find the forms of expression proper to its own people, those which correspond to their psychology, while employing in a renovated and widened form, the universal models, naturally in accordance with the personality of each creator;
4. To have a clear consciousness of specific and concrete current problems and the real dramas which confront the masses, with the purpose of touching and cultivating more deeply, and of carrying the people with them in their struggles. (In Ashcroft *et al.*: 1995, 198)

Marxist literary theory and criticism The singular term is perhaps misleading: there have been a number of variants of Marxist literary theory, and even today not all who call themselves Marxist literary theorists (or critics) would be able to reach more than a very general agreement concerning their fundamental beliefs. We can perhaps dispense with the clumsy 'Marxist literary theory and criticism': one thing that does distinguish Marxist literary criticism (unlike, say, the criticism of F. R. Leavis), is that it is and sees itself to be theory-dependent. Marxism constitutes a general philosophical outlook, one which differs from other such outlooks in important ways but which is characterized by its monist view of reality. Like all such monist beliefs, therefore, its adherents feel that it has something to say about everything: even if the details of particular fields of study may have to be worked out in the course of applied study, the direction of this study is in part laid down by pre-existing fundamental principles.

Marxism is a MATERIALIST philosophy, one which insists upon the primacy of material living conditions rather than ideas or beliefs in the life of human beings. It sees history as, in Marx's words, 'the history of class struggle' – the history of struggle for control of the material conditions upon which life rests. It is on the basis of these material conditions, and in response to the struggle for them, that ideas, philosophies, mental pictures of the world, develop – as secondary phenomena. These secondary phenomena may provide human beings with an accurate picture of reality, including themselves and their situation, but they may not. IDEOLOGIES are all related to CLASS positions and thus, in turn, to material conditions and the struggle for their control, but this is not to say that they provide a reliable picture of these. Traditional Marxists have laid great stress upon the distinction between BASE (or basis) and SUPERSTRUCTURE, seeing the social base as essentially economic in nature, and the superstructure as constituting the world of mental activities – ideas, beliefs, philosophies, and (in the opinion of some but not all Marxists) art and literature.

For Marxists, all is in movement, and – because there is no separate or pure realm of ideas, or values, or spiritual phenomena – all is interconnected, however complex and MEDIATED the interconnections turn out to be. The complexity of these interconnections takes, according to Marx, a characteristic form: a DIALECTICAL rather than a mechanical and purely hierarchical one. And this opens up the possibility for human beings to gain at least partial control over their life-circumstances: Marxism has traditionally been an active and interventionist philosophy, not a spectatorial or passive one, although this may be changing with a growing suspicion of the dangers of too partisan an attitude to theory.

Marxist ideas about literature have a long history. Marx himself was extremely well read in classical and contemporary literature, and literary allusions and references abound in his work. A number of early Marxists sought to apply Marx's ideas to literature: both in terms of the INTERPRETATION and evaluation of existing literary works, and also in terms of advice to writers and those with (or seeking) political power about what sort of literature should be encouraged. The active and interventionist nature of Marxism has recurrently led to attempts to *use* literature for social or political ends: some of these have gained a bad press in the reviews of history, as in the case of Soviet Socialist Realism; others have received a more positive response, as in the case of Brecht's attempt to use his political theatre in the interests of social revolution. It should be noted that Marxism did not introduce the political use of art and literature to the world; there is a long tradition of such attempts – one which it is fair to say the modern academic study of literature consistently underplays and undervalues.

Early Marxist writings on literature and art tended to be of a generalizing nature, seeking to explain why large bodies of writing took the form that they did by relating them to the social and economic conditions of their emergence. Thus G. V. Plekhanov's essay *Art and Social Life* (first published in 1912) has a long opening section on 'French Drama and Painting of the Eighteenth Century' which attempts to relate the class STRUCTURE of eighteenth-century France with the more general characteristics of the drama and painting of the period. To a large extent this sort of impulse has remained central to Marxist literary criticism, although it can take a crude 'vulgar Marxist' form in which art is seen directly and unproblematically to mirror or reflect a society's class structure or economic base, or it can take a more sophisticated form in which increased attention is paid to complex processes of mediation between a society and its art and literature. A good example of the latter would be the work of the Romanian-French critic Lucien Goldmann – sometimes referred to as a 'genetic STRUCTURALIST' – whose attempt to relate the literature of seventeenth-century France to the society from which it emerged makes use of a number of important concepts which see this relationship in terms of forms of complex mediation, such as 'mental structure' and 'world-view'.

Marxist literary criticism has had two periods of significant influence: in the 1930s, and in the 1960s. In both periods this influence has been related to a more general interest in and commitment to Marxist ideas. Undoubtedly the most influential and important Marxist literary critic of the 1930s (and after) was the Hungarian Georg

Lukács, associated in particular with a strong defence of the REALISM to which he believed his Marxism committed him, alongside a concomitant hostility on the artistic and the political level to all forms of MODERNISM. Lukács's relationship to Stalinism is complex: on the one hand, his general position *vis-à-vis* realism and modernism was in tune with the 'line' of Stalin and Socialist Realism, although this line tended to be played down as the period of the Popular Front developed. But Lukács's own position was a lot more sophisticated than that of Stalin or his henchman Zhdanov, and Lukács's very positive view of the high art of the bourgeoisie was not really equatable with Zhdanov's belief that the greatest literature in the world was then being written in the Soviet Union. In Lukács's defence it has too to be pointed out that his criticism, although generalizing in many ways, attempts to grapple with the particularities of individual works of literature in a way that was not common at this time amongst Marxist critics – although it is also true of the British critic Alick West, whose *Crisis and Criticism* was published in 1937.

Since 1960 Marxist literary criticism has reflected the diversities of Marxism in the modern world, and in certain usages today a point is made of dropping the capital 'M' so as to indicate less dependence upon the particular historical individual whose name is borrowed for the term. As a generalization we can say that the less contentious it has become to see literary works in the context of their emergence and subsequent life, the more Marxist ideas have penetrated literary criticism in general. Committed modern Marxist critics are more likely than their predecessors to be engaged in the study of mediating processes: ideology, the 'political unconscious' of the American Marxist Fredric Jameson, the LITERARY MODES OF PRODUCTION of the British Marxist Terry Eagleton, and the STRUCTURE OF FEELING of the Welsh cultural theorist and novelist Raymond Williams (who is more difficult to situate with regard to Marxism). They are also less likely to be happy with a straightforward relegation of literature to the realm of the superstructure. The influential French Marxist Pierre Macherey's *A Theory of Literary Production* (first published in French in 1966), for instance, by seeing the writing of literature as a form of production necessarily sees it as more than the simple reflection of economic facts that vulgar Marxism attributed to literature.

A group of Russian theorists and critics grouped around the figure of Mikhail Bakhtin has been particularly influential over the past two decades, during which time their writings from the inter-war period have reached Western European and American readers in translation for the first time. In addition to Bakhtin himself the names of P. N. Medvedev and V. N. Vološinov should be mentioned: whether Bakhtin wrote the works published under their names is still under discussion. The extent to which these writers were Marxist is also a matter for discussion: given their situation in the Soviet Union of the 1920s and the 1930s they had to pay at least lip-service to Marxist ideas, and Bakhtin appears to have retained a Christian belief all of his life. But their writings unquestionably engage productively with Marxist ideas, seeing literature and art in its genetic socio-historical context, but paying close attention to matters of linguistic, CULTURAL and aesthetic detail and often applying Marxist principles more rigorously than the official watchdogs of Soviet art and culture were doing. They were anti-formalists (cf. Medvedev's and Bakhtin's *The Formal Method in Literary Scholarship*, first published in 1928), but did not confuse this with a belief that formal issues were unimportant.

Since the 1970s one is likely to find literary critics or theorists describing themselves as 'Marxist-FEMINISTS', or 'structuralist-Marxists', or seeking to combine or relate Marxism and POST-STRUCTURALISM. What we can call monolithic Marxism seems very much a thing of the past, and after the collapse of communism in Eastern Europe it seems unlikely to make a particularly strong comeback.

'Mascon' words In an 'Overview' printed as an Introduction to his 1973 book *Understanding the New Black Poetry*, Stephen Henderson draws attention to 'a curious and very important aspect of Black speech' in the USA. 'Certain words and constructions seem to carry an inordinate charge of emotional and psychological weight, so that whenever they are used they set all kinds of bells ringing, all kinds of synapses snapping'. Henderson explains that he is thinking of words such as 'rock', 'roll', 'jelly', 'bubber', 'jook', and so on. He suggests that such words have levels of meaning that seem to go back to the earliest grappling with the English language in a strange and hostile land undergone by African Americans.

> These words... are used in complex associations, and thus form meaningful wholes in ways which defy understanding by outsiders. I call such words 'mascon' words, borrowing from (of all places!) the National Aeronautics and Space Administration. NASA invented the acronym to mean a 'massive concentration' of matter below the lunar surface after it was observed that the gravitational pull on a satellite was stronger in some places than in others I use it to mean *a massive concentration of Black experiential energy* which powerfully affects the meaning of Black speech, Black song, and Black poetry ... (1973, 44).

He gives as example the line from the hymn 'Hold to His hand, God's unchanging hand', and relates it to the blues line 'If you don't want me, baby, give me your right hand' and to Faye Adams's song from the 1950s, 'Shake a Hand, Shake a Hand'. Contrary to the assertions of White critics, such expressions are not, according to Henderson, clichés. While White people can sense only the 'outside', the morphology of the expression, 'Black people have used these expressions over and over because they are rooted in an apparently inexhaustible reality, in this case, a highly compressed secular/sacred experience' (1973, 45).

Compare CONNOTATION AND DENOTATION.

Masquerade Alternatively *parade*. Recent FEMINIST theorists of GENDER have gone back to Joan Riviere's 1929 theorizing about the behaviour of successful intellectual women who adopted a 'masquerade' of exaggerated feminine flirtatiousness when interacting with men. Women thus successful in traditionally male roles used womanliness as a mask or masquerade to hide the possession of 'masculinity' and to deflect the negative reactions that would stem from it.

More recent theorists of gender have extended the term to cover the male assumption of different forms of 'masculinity'. Thus Norman Bryson, in his essay 'Géricault and "Masculinity"' writes:

To be a subject constructed as a male involves a necessary masquerade, the masquerade of the masculine. Although the mechanisms for producing the gender masquerade are necessarily different for each gender position . . . what is held in common is the strain of that continuous production. The masquerade is interminable, not least because of the sanctions against those who would try to escape it. By a system of 'cross-censorship,' the same codes of masculine identity that the subject introjects into his own case he projects outwards onto all other males as a continuous injunction to maintain the codes. (Bryson, Holly and Moxey: 1994, 231)

See also MIMICRY; PAMISSA (masquerade as a type of PLOT); and TRANS-CULTURATION.

Master narrative See GRAND NARRATIVES AND LITTLE NARRATIVES

Master discourse See DISCOURSE.

Materialism In 1937 the British MARXIST literary critic Ralph Fox defined materialism as a belief in 'the primacy of matter and that the world exists outside of us and independently of us', leading to the view that 'being determines consciousness' (1979, 26). This of course leaves one with the problem of defining what matter (not to say being) itself is. Terry Lovell has pointed out that one of the reasons why the term materialism has suffered from 'considerable loss of definition in recent years' is that those using it have taken their lead from the natural sciences. As it has appeared that the term 'matter' has become far less precise within the natural sciences – to the extent that nowadays it is sometimes used synonymously with the word 'real' – so the consequence has been that materialism has lost that sharply defined meaning which it previously possessed.

Lovell suggests that to equate 'matter' with 'real' is unhelpful, for although it is arguable that ideas are certainly real, to define them as a *material* reality leads only to confusion. She suggests that materialism 'is more usefully restricted to an assertion of the relationship between different levels of reality, where reality is conceived on the realist model of a multi-layered structure with different levels, or depths' (1980, 26). Commitment to such a hierarchically layered reality in which certain levels are privileged and dominant in causal terms seems to be more fundamental to materialism than is any particular definition of what matter consists of. Even Fox recognized 'all matter as changing', and accordingly noted a historical development within materialism as well (1979, 27). Raymond Williams has accepted Sebastiano Timpanaro's definition of materialism in which 'we understand above all acknowledgment of the priority of nature over "mind", or if you like, of the physical level over the biological level, and of the biological level over the socio-economic and cultural level; both in the sense of chronological priority [. . .] and in the sense of the conditioning which *still* exercises on man and will continue to exercise at least for the foreseeable future' (Williams: 1980, 106, quoting Timpanaro: [1975], 34).

Within Literary Studies a materialist position has generally indicated a belief that literary works are created and read by means, and have to be explained in terms, of pressures and influences in contrast to which the works are in some sense or other secondary rather than primary. This, it should be stressed, is a *causal* and definitely not an *evaluative* judgement. (Bricks and mortar clearly come before, and are thus primary to, houses, but this does not mean that they are more valuable than houses.)

Thus a crude materialism would be one in which it was believed that physical objects were more important than ideas or CULTURAL artifacts, but this is certainly not a belief to which adherents of more sophisticated varieties of materialism are committed – although they might well argue that while physical objects can exist without ideas and cultural artifacts, ideas and cultural artifacts cannot exist independently of physical objects (broadly defined).

See also NEW HISTORICISM AND CULTURAL MATERIALISM (cultural materialism).

Matriarchy Government by women – either within the family or in society at large, with authority descending through the mother. Significant in recent criticism mainly as an implied rather than actualized alternative to PATRIARCHY; there have, however, been claims for the past existence of fully matriarchal CULTURES. Rather than seeing it as a form of patriarchy with women playing the roles previously played by men, most FEMINISTS see matriarchy as embodying a very different set of alternative (and better) values.

In literature matriarchies frequently occur in feminist imaginative FICTIONS such as utopias and science fiction.

Meaning and significance Use of the word *meaning* has been associated with literary-critical discussion for a very long time, although certain theoretical arguments have made it a rather more contentious term today than it has been in the past (see below). The pairing of *meaning* with *significance*, however, is very much associated with one particular theorist: the American critic E. D. Hirsch. In his book *Validity in Interpretation* Hirsch defines these two terms in ways that are matched and complementary:

> *Meaning* is that which is represented by a text; it is what the author meant by his use of a particular sign sequence; it is what the signs represent. *Significance*, on the other hand, names a relationship between that meaning and a person, or a conception, or a situation, or indeed anything imaginable. (1967, 8)

The definition has to be seen in the light of increasing debate about the respective roles and authority of AUTHOR and READER in the INTERPRETATION of literary WORKS, for it proposes a clear separation of powers: the author is responsible for meaning while significance comes from the interaction of this meaning with that which lies outside the work. Thus if Milton was telling the truth when he claimed that by his use of the 'particular sign sequence' that is 'Paradise Lost' he meant to justify the ways of God to man (interpreting this as a shorthand expression of a larger and more complex intention), then this is what the meaning of 'Paradise Lost' *is*. But if a particular reader is reminded of his or her own religious conversion when reading the poem, because an earlier READING was instrumental in effecting that conversion, then that is (part of) the work's *significance* for him or her.

A rather similar distinction is made by Michael Riffaterre, whose view of the two-stage nature of the reading process also uses these terms. According to Riffaterre, 'before reaching the significance the reader has to hurdle the mimesis', and thus the first stage in 'decoding the poem' starts with a *heuristic reading* which is where the first interpretation takes place, 'since it is during this reading that *meaning* is apprehended'. Riffaterre's second stage is that of a *retroactive reading* during which the second interpretation takes place, and this is the truly HERMENEUTIC reading (1978, 4–5). For Riffaterre, 'units of meaning may be words or phrases, or sentences, [while] *the unit of significance is the text*' (1978, 5–6).

For Hirsch, significance does not have to be either personal or idiosyncratic, but it is important to stress that it is not completely unconstrained either: if the paper of the first edition in which I read 'Paradise Lost' was yellow, such that every time I read the poem I think of bananas, this would *not* constitute significance on Hirsch's definition, because it is not a relationship between authorial *meaning* (as he defines it) and something else. So that for Hirsch the author exerts control over both meaning and significance, it is just that this control is more MEDIATED and less complete with regard to the latter.

The distinction certainly has the great virtue that it provides something for the individual who believes that the death of the author has not yet taken place, but who also believes that personal elements enter into a literary work's reading and that readers – individually or collectively – donate something to the artistic and AESTHETIC experiences associated with the work, which are not all placed in the work by the author like CODES placed in a computer program by its designer.

Hirsch's distinction has not escaped criticism, however. It is clearly unacceptable to those who accept the arguments of 'The Intentional Fallacy' (Wimsatt and Beardsley: 1946) and who believe that the literary work is cut off from its author at birth and contains its meaning in itself and not in terms of what its author intended. It is also unacceptable to those who believe that the author is dead, and who see Hirsch's argument as still in thrall to the metaphysics of presence (see PRESENCE), wanting a fixed CENTRE to arrest the free play of the SIGNIFIERS in the work.

But it has also come under attack from other directions. In spite of Hirsch's subsequent attempts to modify his position so as to take into account the *implications* of authorial intention that were not – and perhaps could not be – apparent to the author at the time of writing, Hirsch's reliance upon authorial intention has worried some commentators. Others have felt that his concentration upon meaning is itself fundamentally misplaced, for literary works (the argument runs) do not have meanings in the way that UTTERANCES do: they are objects for interpretation or for APPRECIATION. From this PERSPECTIVE it is as misleading to ask what a literary work means as it is to ask what a Grecian urn or a dip in the sea means: literary works are not utterances but aesthetic objects. (See the arguments in Stein Haugom Olsen's essay, 'The "Meaning" of a Literary Work' [1987, 53–72].)

These arguments have important implications with regard to interpretation, for if one believes that a literary work has a (note the singular) meaning which is dependent upon what the author meant by his or her use of a set of SIGNS, then interpretation is, simply, the attempt to ascertain what the author meant by his or her 'use of a particular sign sequence'. 'Simply' refers, of course, to the level of theory: in practice such an attempt will certainly be far from simple and will often be impossible, but the interpreter will at least have no doubts about what it is that he or she is trying to do. But if the interpreter believes either that the author is dead or at least very poorly, or that he or she is a SITE rather than an origin so far as the literary work is concerned, then interpretation will be problematic on a theoretical as much as a practical level. And from some perspectives this may lead to a belief that interpretation itself is a misguided activity, for if literary works need to be seen as much in terms of their ABSENCES and gaps, or of their insertion into systems of meaning by forces apart from themselves or their authors, then the search for meaning cannot find its primary field of activity within the work or the author's intention. Those who *do* believe this have not generally been happy to accept that they are concerned with the work's *significance* – as defined by Hirsch – because this carries with it the implication that they accept Hirsch's definition of *meaning*.

See also DEFERRED/POSTPONED SIGNIFICANCE.

Méconnaissance In the work of Jacques Lacan, applied to the infant's *misrecognition* of its image seen in the mirror, misrecognition because, as Michèle Barrett puts it, the reflected image 'offers a *false* reflection of a whole body *Gestalt* and thus transcends the infant's own knowledge of physical dependence and psychic frustration' (1991, 103). Lacan also uses the term to refer to Freud's apparent misrecognition of 'everything that the ego neglects' (1977, 22), as well as in a more general sense. Sometimes translated as *misprision* (see REVISIONISM for Harold Bloom's use of this term).

See also BODY; GESTALT; MIRROR STAGE.

Mediascape Taken by E. Ann Kaplan from Arjun Appadurai's 1990 essay 'Disjuncture and Difference in the Global Cultural Economy'. Kaplan reports that she finds Appadurai's term useful and cites his description of mediascapes as

'image-centered, narrative-based accounts of strips of reality' which offer to peoples experiencing and transforming them globally 'a series of elements (such as characters, plots and textual forms) out of which scripts can be formed of imagined lives, their own as well as those of others living in other places' which may lead to the desire of acquisition and movement. (1997, 13, quoting Appadurai: 1990, 9)

See also SCRIPT.

Media Studies The rise of the academic study of the press, radio, and – in particular – television and film, has been especially marked in the last four decades in Britain, although this area of study started earlier in the United States. This development has been of particular importance for the academic study of literature in perhaps two ways. First, because the academic study of media content, especially with regard to motion pictures, used theories and traditions from Literary Studies which were thus tested out and scrutinized in a different context from that in which they had been developed. Second, because new theories and traditions arising in Media Studies have been exported back to Literary Studies, and have often been of significant influence there.

As a generalization, we can say that two academic disciplines in particular contributed to the establishment and development of Media Studies: Literary Studies (especially in ENGLISH departments, so far as Britain was concerned), and Sociology. Historically, again so far as Britain is concerned, the academic study of film often borrowed more extensively from Literary Studies in its early years: *Auteur* theory, to take a striking example, came to Film Studies in Britain from the attempt of a group of French theorists to treat the Director of a film as if he or she were like the AUTHOR of a literary work, and to see all his or her films as having something in common in much the same way as all the novels by, say, Henry James can be seen to share common features and elements. The academic study of television, in contrast, very often owed its greatest academic debt to Sociology, and in its early years often concentrated less on what was seen as the impressionistic content analysis or INTERPRETATION of the literary critic, and much more on the study of *institutions* and *audiences*: who owned or controlled the organizations that produced TV programmes; what effects did these programmes have on those who followed them. Where TV content was analysed – again in the early years of the development of the academic subject – the analysis was likely to draw on traditions taken from American behaviourist psychology: testing viewers' attitudes before and after watching a particular TV show, for example.

This outline history is of course an oversimplification. But it is certainly the case that one of the crucial functions performed by Media Studies in the 1960s and after was as a SITE on which traditions emanating from Literary Studies and Sociology could engage in mutual criticism. The results of this process of interdisciplinary discussion and cross-fertilization has been extremely valuable for both Literary Studies and for Sociology. If literary critics were able to suggest that sociological analyses of programme content and audience responses were often crude and unreliable, and failed to confront complex processes of MEDIATION, response and interpretation, sociologists were able to counter by suggesting that a failure on the part of literary critics to engage with the wider issues of social control beyond that of the author him- or herself meant that an AESTHETIC force or motive was often attributed to TEXTUAL features which needed to be understood and explained in a completely different way.

Beyond this, the rise of Media Studies undoubtedly contributed to students of literature taking a far more critical attitude to the notion of the CANON. Study of film or television inevitably confronted academics with the issue of the POPULAR, an issue that had been of concern to MARXIST literary critics in an earlier period, but which in the 1940s and 1950s was a matter for relatively little critical concern in Britain and the United States. If students following Media Studies courses could engage in serious study of soap operas, then why could not students taking degrees in, say, English not study popular FICTION? And such questions inevitably raised issues connected with IDEOLOGY: not just the ideology contained in the texts studied, but the ideology or ideologies which lay behind choices about what was to be studied and how it was to be studied.

Other examples of cross-fertilization are more specific. The study of NARRATIVE, for example, can today hardly be confined to literary narrative. So much that is important in narrative theory involves analysis of film that the literary student ignores it at his or her peril.

Mediation A stress on the highly mediated nature of human interaction and communication is common to many recent theories. Such a stress militates against simple (or simplistic) views of direct transference or copying such as are attributed by their critics to so-called *reductive* or *mechanistic* views. Central to processes of mediation are systems of *transformation*, and this means that a point at one end of a chain of complex mediations can never be accurately recaptured by an unproblematic 'reading-off' at the other.

This is clearly relevant to efforts to reach social or historical insights through the READING of literary WORKS (or to the attempt to understand literary works by means of social or historical investigations), as all sorts of mediating factors such as IDEOLOGY or literary CONVENTION have to be taken into account if these efforts and investigations are to bear fruit.

In his *The Political Unconscious* Fredric Jameson's discussion of this concept draws attention to its two-sidedness: mediation is both something the investigator *does*, by a process of *transcoding* or inventing a set of terms 'such that the same terminology can be used to analyze and articulate two quite distinct types of objects or "texts", or two very different structural levels of reality' (1981, 40), and it is also the *uncovering* of relationships independent of the work of the investigator: '[w]hat is crucial is that, by being able to use the same language about each of these quite distinct objects or levels of an object, we can restore, at least methodologically, the lost unity of social life, and demonstrate that widely distant elements of the social totality are ultimately part of the same global historical process' (1981, 226).

In summary: the investigator both *mediates* between different levels or instances, and also *uncovers mediations* between these same levels or instances. *Both* of these elements should be borne in mind with reference to the following comment by Jameson: '[m]ediation is the classical dialectical term for the establishment of relationships between, say, the formal analysis of a work of art and its social ground, or between the internal dynamics of the political state and its economic base' (1981, 39). 'Establishing of relationships' should perhaps be understood both as 'establishing that there are relationships' and also as 'creating relationships'.

In various contexts the term *articulation* is given a very similar meaning to that allotted to *mediation*. What articulation typically carries with it is that sense of struggling to express something in terms that are not natural to it. For this reason, articulation is often used when one set of meanings, practices, or beliefs is as it were translated and expressed in a way that 'fits' another. Articulation thus often carries a strong sense of incorporation, appropriation, or recuperation (see the entry for INCORPORATION for all these terms).

See also HOMOLOGY.

Mediation reading See OPAQUE AND TRANSPARENT CRITICISM

Mémoire involontaire See AURA

Message See FUNCTIONS OF LANGUAGE; TEXT AND WORK

Metacriticism 'Criticism of criticism': in other words, critical theory which has as its subject literary (or other) criticism, and which attempts to analyse and categorize examples of critical practice and to establish generally applicable principles for it. In contemporary usage the term is often replaced by *literary theory*, although this can have a rather wider meaning.

Metafiction See METALANGUAGE

Metalanguage Technically, any language used to describe or refer to another language: 'a language about a language'. One of the characteristics of human word language is that it can function as its own metalanguage; we can discuss our language in that same language (as I am doing now). This is a characteristic not shared by animal communication systems: dogs cannot bark about barking.

This has a bearing on literature and literary criticism precisely because both exploit this resource. Gérard Genette suggests a version of the LINGUISTIC PARADIGM in which the literary WORK is compared to a language and literary criticism to a metalanguage (1982, 29). However, literature can itself serve as its own metalanguage, as in *metafiction* (see below). One consequence of this is that the play of *levels* in a literary work can be very complex, and recent study of NARRATIVE in particular has performed an important function in making our awareness of the specificity and interrelations of different narrative levels much sharper.

A *metanarrative* can thus be either a narrative which talks about other, EMBEDDED narratives, or a narrative which refers to itself and to its own narrative procedures. Metanarratives can play an extremely important role *vis-à-vis* the establishment of a particular IDEOLOGICAL position in a work of FICTION: Anne Cranny-Francis has pointed out, for example, how recent FEMINIST rewritings of fairy-tales can problematize the READER's relationship to familiar tales by means of metanarratives which change this relationship from a passive to an active one (1990, 89).

Metafiction is, literally, fiction about fiction. To a certain extent the term overlaps with *metanarrative* because any work of fiction which contains a metanarrative will contain a metafictional element. It is generally used to indicate fiction which includes any *self-referential element* (not necessarily resulting from a metanarrative: thematic patternings can also contribute to the formation of a metafictional effect in a work). In their Introduction to an extract from Linda Hutcheon's *Narcissistic Narrative: the Metafictional Paradox* (1980), Onega and Landa suggest that

> Hutcheon's narcissistic narrative is more or less equivalent to such terms as Robert Scholes's 'fabulation', William H. Gass's 'metafiction', Raymond Federman's 'surfiction' and Ronald Binn's 'anti-novel', all of which were coined to account for the widespread tendency to introversion and self-referentiality of much postmodernist fiction. (Onega and Landa: 1996, 203)

Metafiction typically involves games in which levels of narrative reality (and the reader's perception of them) are confused, or in which traditional REALIST CONVENTIONS governing the separation of MIMETIC and DIEGETIC elements are flouted and thwarted. The term is generally used with reference to relatively recent POSTMODERNIST writing, but it can have wider applications to far older work in which elements of self-observation and self-commentary can be found. The 'play within a play' in *Hamlet*, for example, inevitably introduces a metafictional element into the work, for even though there is no overt introduction of a metacommentary the audience is encouraged by Hamlet's comments on the players' PERFORMANCE to think about the process of dramatic illusion. The comments above on the ideological role of metanarrative can also be applied to metafiction, and Anne Cranny-Francis further suggests that feminist metafictions can deconstruct the GENDER ideology of POPULAR texts (1990, 99).

See also the entry for DIEGESIS AND MIMESIS (in which some variations in Genette's definition of a number of the terms mentioned here are discussed), and the entry for FRAME.

Metalepsis According to Gérard Genette, any transgressing of NARRATIVE levels, such as when Laurence Sterne (or his NARRATOR) implores the READER of *Tristram Shandy* to help the CHARACTER Mr Shandy get back to his bed (1980, 234).

Metalingual See FUNCTIONS OF LANGUAGE

Metanarrative See DIEGESIS AND MIMESIS; METALANGUAGE

Metaphor See SYNTAGMATIC AND PARADIGMATIC

Metaphysics (of presence) See PRESENCE

Metonymy See SYNTAGMATIC AND PARADIGMATIC

Microdialogue See INTERIOR DIALOGUE

Mimesis See DIEGESIS AND MIMESIS

Mimicry A concept which has played an important role in both FEMINIST and POST-COLONIALIST theory in recent years. Clearly the central usefulness of the concept involves the subversive potential contained in the forced and (often overtly) half-hearted adoption of the *style* or *conventions* of a DOMINANT authority – whether national-CULTURAL or GENDER-political. The concept also carries with it some of the associations of 'poking fun' – a sort of body-language equivalent of parody. In mimicking you I stick to the letter of your authority but I attempt to signal – if only to myself – my rejection of its spirit.

In his 'Of Mimicry and Man: The Ambivalence of Colonial Discourse', Homi K. Bhabha starts his discussion of mimicry with a quotation from Lacan: 'The effect of mimicry is camouflage' (Lacan: 1979, 99), but moves on to suggest that this is only the beginning.

> Mimicry is, thus, the sign of a double articulation; a complex strategy of reform, regulation and discipline, which 'appropriates' the Other as it visualizes power. Mimicry is also the sign of the inappropriate, however, a difference or recalcitrance which coheres the dominant strategic function of colonial power, intensifies surveillance, and poses an immanent threat to both 'normalized' knowledges and disciplinary powers. (Bhabha: 1994, 86)

From this PERSPECTIVE, it will be seen, mimicry is not just a weapon of the oppressed but also of the oppressor. Jenny Sharpe (1989) has drawn attention to this double-edged aspect of colonial mimicry, suggesting that the 'mimic man is a contradictory figure who simultaneously reinforces colonial authority and disturbs it' (Ashcroft *et al*.: 1995, 99). Bhabha's discussion is interesting, especially for the student of literature: it takes in (inevitably) V. S. Naipaul's *The Mimic Men*, but also a literary CHARACTER such as Decoud in Conrad's *Nostromo*.

Luce Irigaray (1985) has suggested that the feminine is something which women have to adopt by mimicry, but again fastens upon the subversive potential contained in the activity: 'One must assume the feminine role deliberately. Which means already to convert a form of subordination into an affirmation, and thus to begin to thwart it' (in Mary Eagleton: 1996, 317).

Compare MASQUERADE, and Bakhtin's concept of ASSIMILATION.

Minoritizing/universalizing An opposition between those who define GENDER in exclusive or even ESSENTIALIST terms and who accordingly may seek a separatist political expression of their gender commitments, and those who stress the unstable, plural, and historically volatile nature of gender characteristics, and who accordingly seek to achieve broader alliances in their politics. The actual term appears to date from Eve Kosofsky Sedgwick's *The Epistemology of the Closet* (1991), but the opposition is much older, and has its parallels in almost all political and social movements.

Mirror stage In his essay 'The Mirror Stage as Formative of the Function of the I as Revealed in Psychoanalytic Experience', first delivered as an address in 1949 and reprinted in his *Écrits*, Jacques Lacan argues for this *conception* (his term) as necessary to a full understanding of 'the formation of the *I*' (1977, 1). Lacan compares the behaviour of children and chimpanzees when confronted with their own image in a mirror; even at the age at which the child is outdone by the chimpanzee in instrumental intelligence, it can recognize its own image in a mirror. But whereas this act of recognition 'exhausts itself' for the chimpanzee, the child gives forth a series of gestures in which the relation between the real and the mirrored movements is played. This, Lacan suggests, leads to the creation of an 'Ideal-I' (from Freud's *Ideal-Ich*) which 'situates the agency of the ego, before its social determination' (1977, 2).

Lacan's further discussion of the conception is complex, but what it seems to stress is that the I is thus fixed in a fictive format: our conception of ourselves is necessarily a FICTION which we are then put to defend against the onset of the real. The ego should not then be regarded as centred on what Lacan calls the *perception-consciousness system*, or as organized by the 'reality principle', but on the function of *MÉCONNAISSANCE* (1977, 6).

Mirror-text See *MISE-EN-ABYME*

Mise-en-abyme From the French meaning, literally, thrown into the abyss. The term is adapted from heraldry, and in its adapted form generally involves the recurring internal duplication of images of an artistic whole, such that an infinite series of images disappearing into invisibility is produced – similar to what one witnesses if one looks at one's reflection between two facing mirrors. Mieke Bal recommends the term *mirror-text* for literary examples of *mise-en-abyme*, as in verbal examples it is not the whole of the WORK which is mirrored but only a part. For Bal, when the primary FABULA and the

EMBEDDED fabula can be paraphrased in such a manner that both paraphrases have one or more elements in common, 'the subtext is a *sign* of the primary text' (1985, 146; see the entry for SUB-TEXT). The possibilities for reflexivity and self-reference opened up by such repetitions are not limited to MODERNIST art and literature, but have been utilized by artists and writers over many centuries.

For a detailed study of *mise-en-abyme* which covers both the fine arts and literature, see Lucien Dallenbach (1989).

The term is sometimes used by DECONSTRUCTIONIST writers to invoke the sense of vertigo produced by that instability of MEANING resulting from the endless play of SIGNIFIERS in a TEXT.

Misprision/misreading See AGON; *MÉCONNAISSANCE*; REVISIONISM

Mode Apart from serving as a general synonym for 'type', *mode* enters into recent critical vocabulary mainly in connection with NARRATIVE theory. A usage associated with the linguistician M. A. K. Halliday equates mode with what can be termed the 'medium' of a TEXT or 'channel of communication'. Thus a telephoned message is in a different mode from a written one.

Alternatively, modifications of narrative DISTANCE can be said to produce different modes; thus a sudden shift into irony on the part of a NARRATOR involves a change of mode.

In Gerald Prince's definition, MOOD (see also the entry for PERSPECTIVE AND VOICE) consists of two sub-categories: *perspective* (or point of view) and *distance* (or mode) (1988a, 54). In other words: one determines the mood of a narrative by finding out (i) what perspective on CHARACTERS and events the narrative has and (ii) how close to or distanced from these characters and events the narrative is.

It is fair to say that none of these usages is sufficiently well established to be dominant or authoritative.

Modernism and postmodernism Both of these terms reach beyond national-cultural and generic boundaries; they describe artistic and cultural artifacts and attitudes of (mainly) the twentieth century which are possessed of certain family resemblances. The term *postmodernism* can, further, be used to refer not just to art and CULTURE but also more comprehensively to a wide range of aspects of modern society.

It is not easy to define modernism and postmodernism independently because the boundaries between the two terms vary according to different usages. Andreas Huyssen, for example, points out that the

> amorphous and politically volatile nature of postmodernism makes the phenomenon itself remarkably elusive, and the definition of its boundaries exceedingly difficult, if not per se impossible. Furthermore, one critic's postmodernism is another critic's modernism (or variant thereof), while certain vigorously new forms of contemporary culture (such as the emergence into a broader public's view of distinct minority cultures and of a wide variety of feminist work in literature and the arts) have so far rarely been discussed *as* postmodern. . . . (1988, 58–9)

Indeed, as Ihab Hassan points out, this indeterminacy can draw in other terms such as *avant-garde*:

> Like other categorical terms – say poststructuralism, or modernism, or romanticism for that matter – postmodernism suffers from a certain *semantic* instability. That is, no clear consensus about its meaning exists among scholars. . . . Thus some critics mean by postmodernism what others call avant-gardism or even neo-avant-gardism, while still others would call the same phenomenon simply modernism. (1985, 121)

In like vein, David Harvey has suggested that there is more continuity than difference in the movement from modernism to postmodernism, and that the latter represents a crisis within the former in which fragmentation and ephemerality are confirmed while the possibility of the eternal and the immutable is treated with far greater scepticism (1989, 116). Similarly, Alex Callinicos (1989) has argued that there is no sharp distinction between modernism and postmodernism, and that the belief that there is can be explained by reference to the particular political and cultural disappointments of the generation of 1968 in Western Europe and the United States.

Of the terms so far mentioned, perhaps the least problematic is *avant-garde*. The term comes from military terminology, and refers to the (normally small) advance guard which prepares the way for a larger, following army – what later became known as shock-troops. In the context of cultural politics the term was used in the early part of the twentieth century to refer to movements which had the aim of assaulting CONVENTIONAL standards and attitudes – particularly but not exclusively in the field of culture and the arts. Thus Cubism, Futurism, Dadaism, Surrealism and Constructivism are all conventionally described as avant-gardist in essence. It is striking that the avant-garde is normally discussed in terms of *movements*, whereas modernism is normally discussed in terms of individual artists and WORKS. This may be at least partly because avant-garde movements typically saw their cultural task as a part of a larger cultural-political campaign dedicated to the destruction of bourgeois standards, and it is the overtly political and activist element in many avant-garde movements that is frequently used as one of the criteria for distinguishing between avant-gardism and modernism. The very name *avant-garde* implies a concern for what will follow after, whereas many modernist artists were often profoundly pessimistic or resigned about the likelihood that their work might inspire any form of wider social or cultural change. The standard works on the avant-garde are Poggioli (1971) and Bürger (1984).

The term *modernism* has achieved a more stable meaning during the past two decades, although the attempt to, as it were, 'backdate' postmodernism to apply to works of art previously described as modernist has shaken this stability somewhat. (Thus works such as Virginia Woolf's *The Waves* and James Joyce's *Finnegans Wake* have been confidently described as *modernist* for some years, but during the last decade or so the term *postmodernist* has begun to be applied to them by some critics.) In general usage, though, modernism describes that art (not just literature) which sought to break with what had become the dominant and dominating conventions of nineteenth-century art and culture. The most important of these conventions is probably that of REALISM: the modernist artist no longer saw the highest test of his or her art as that of verisimilitude. This does not mean that all modernist art gave up the attempt to understand or represent the extra-literary world, but that it rejected those nineteenth-century standards of realism which had hardened into unquestioned conventions. Instead, the modernist art-work is possessed, typically, of a *self-reflexive* element: we may lose ourselves in the FICTIONAL 'world' of, say, *Pride and Prejudice* when reading Jane Austen's novel, but when reading James Joyce's *Ulysses* or Virginia Woolf's *The Waves* we are made conscious that we are reading a novel. (Just as we might look at a painting by Claude Monet and lose ourselves in the scene depicted, while a painting by Picasso thrusts its 'paintingness' upon our attention.)

Daphna Erdinast-Vulcan has argued that although 'the modernist novel' is of course a critical construct, during the first three decades of the twentieth century 'a new generic paradigm, a mutation of the "classical" novel', does seem to emerge. 'This new paradigm involves a discarding of narratorial omniscience, a plurality of partial perspectives, a conscious problematization of the relationship between language (the symbolic) and experience (the real), and – most notably and disturbingly – a frustration of narrative framing or closure' (1994, 144).

John Frow has asserted that while the modernist AESTHETIC is characterized by attention to the status of the UTTERANCES it produces, this does not usually extend to 'a political awareness of the social and institutional conditions of enunciation' (1986, 117). We can compare the attack on perspective in the visual arts and on tonality in music with the attempt of various modernist writers to escape the constraints of traditional views of CHARACTER and PLOT.

In a major contribution to the history and theory of modernism David Forgacs has isolated six qualities which, according to him, make modernism 'all of a piece':

First, it is, or was, about novelty: it was a set of artistic practices which shared a commitment to 'make it new', in Pound's phrase. ... Second, and this is a corollary of the first point, many modernist artists – those at any rate who took an interest in politics – envisaged political change in terms of a radical and often violent break. ... Third, modernism, it is claimed, cut for itself a separate path from mass culture. It could – and frequently did – cite kitsch, ephemera and popular entertainments, but it did not want to merge with these or be confused with them. They remained modernism's other, the torn other half of a whole freedom, in Adorno's famous phrase. ... Fourth, it has been argued that modernism – in this respect like the realism to which in other ways it was diametrically opposed – was an art of 'depth' not of 'surfaces', in that the modernist art work, even at its most abstract, always signified something that was not itself a representation: for example Mondrian's grid compositions explored the essence of colour and geometric form. ... Fifth, large areas of modernism have been subjected to political critique by feminism and anti-racism. ... Sixth, and finally, there has been a critique of the status which modernism has acquired in cultural history (including art history, literary history and so forth). The notion, implicit in much Western scholarship and the teaching of the arts since around 1950, that modernism constitutes the most significant tradition, the leading-edge movement in the twentieth century, has been contested. (1995, 9–12)

Against such common features, however, Forgacs insists that it is important not to lose sight of those 'conflicts within modernism which constituted its inner dynamic' (1995, 15). His article is rich in the discussion of particular AUTHORS and works and is strongly recommended.

Modernism announces itself as a break with the past similar, in some ways, to the assault on traditional values associated with romanticism. One of the qualities which distinguishes modernism from romanticism, however, is a generally more pessimistic, even tragic view of the world. Generalization is dangerous here, and it seems that British literary modernism (which, revealingly, was contributed to by many non-Britons) is perhaps more pessimistic than Continental modernism. But the work of T. S. Eliot, Ezra Pound, D. H. Lawrence, Franz Kafka, Knut Hamsun – to take some representative names – is typically characterized by a pessimistic view of the modern world, a world seen as fragmented and decayed, in which communication between human beings is difficult or impossible, and in which commercial and cheapening forces present an insuperable barrier to human or cultural betterment.

In general, modernists are hostile towards, or at least suspicious of, developments in contemporary science and technology. This is not universally the case: it is not true, for example of Vladimir Mayakovsky or of the Italian Futurists. But it is revealing that the latter have often been described as avant-garde rather than modernist. This suspicion of science and technology, in many cases directly attributable to revulsion from the use of technology to slaughter millions in the First World War, and often associated with a disgust at commercialism, is one of the clearest ways of distinguishing modernism from much postmodernism.

Here one needs to point out that an involvement in a cultural and artistic revolution does not necessarily imply political progressiveness: the work of Knut Hamsun, T. S. Eliot, Ezra Pound, Luigi Pirandello, D. H. Lawrence, and W. B. Yeats is central to modernism, but the social and political vision which can be extracted from it is more backward- than forward-looking, more conservative than progressive in political terms. This is not true of all modernism, but it serves to demonstrate that artistic and cultural experimentation, innovation, and anti-traditionalism could well go along with political traditionalism, conservatism, or even fascism: Pound's and Hamsun's fascist commitment was of long duration, and (at least according to some accounts) unshaken by the revelations of Nazi atrocities which followed the Second World War. In contrast, an important modernist writer such as Virginia Woolf maintained a consistent liberalism which shaded into support for the Labour Party during the 1930s, and, like many other important modernist writers, Woolf had no truck with fascism at any time.

Mention of Woolf prompts the observation that the development of modernism seems to be associated with a certain 'masculinization' of art: in contrast to the dominant position of women novelists in the nineteenth century, women take a long time to regain this supremacy subsequent to the modernist revolution. Part of the explanation may relate to the association of modernism with social and geographical mobility, and the adoption of a bohemian lifestyle – much more difficult for women than for men, as Woolf pointed out (in the course of a different argument) in her *A Room of One's Own*. On the other hand, part of this masculinization may well lie in the eye of the (male) beholder, and interesting work is being done at present to rediscover neglected women modernists.

Behind much modernist pessimism lies not just the empirical discovery that full communication between human beings is difficult in the modern age, but a more philosophical belief that although the world may be single and knowable, it is knowable only in small pieces at once. David Harvey has argued that modernism took on multiple PERSPECTIVISM and RELATIVISM as its epistemology for revealing 'what it still took to be the true nature of a unified, though complex, underlying reality (1989, 30). (Post-modernism, in contrast, tends to retain the relativism while abandoning the belief in the unified underlying reality, and David Harvey quotes Jean-François Lyotard's definition of the postmodern as 'incredulity towards metanarratives' [1989, 45] – a definition which is itself, paradoxically, something of a METANARRATIVE; the resemblance between post-modernism and DECONSTRUCTION is strongly apparent at this point.) For the modernist, therefore, human beings are doomed to exist in a state of social – and even existential – fragmentation, while yearning (unlike the postmodernist) to escape from this situation. Here the influence of Freud is probably important, for Freud turned the attention of many writers inward, towards SUBJECTIVE experience rather than the objective world. On the one hand, this led to the development or refinement of important new techniques: Joyce's and Woolf's development of internal monologue and stream-of-consciousness, Eliot's refinement of the dramatic monologue. But it also tied in with a pessimistic belief in the unbridgeability of the gap between subjective experience and an objective world, the belief that 'It is impossible to say just what I mean!' ALIENATION becomes close to a cliché in modernist literature, and it is typically associated with *urban* landscapes: we can hardly imagine T. S. Eliot's 'The Waste Land' or James Joyce's *Ulysses* set in the middle of the countryside.

Furthermore, this alienation also leads to – or is associated with – a problematizing of human individuality and identity. 'Who am I?' asks Virginia Woolf's Bernard, in her experimental novel *The Waves*, and his question is emblematic of a recurrent problem for modernist artists. Thus one of the conventions attacked by modernist novelists is that of character, where this is taken to represent a unified, stable and coherent person, knowable both to him- or herself as well as to others. Just as Bernard is not sure who he is, so in Kafka's *The Castle*, K. finds that he can obtain no stable description of Klamm, who is seen in different ways by different people, or by the same people at different times. This dependence of identity upon the observer is pursued to perhaps its farthest extreme in modernist literature in some of the plays of Luigi Pirandello, and clearly ends up in varieties of solipsism. It should be added that in this respect a work such as James Joyce's *Ulysses* seems relatively conventional.

Ihab Hassan has traced the term *postmodernism* back to Frederico de Onis's use of the term *postmodernismo* in his *Antología de la Poesía Española e Hispanoamericana* (1934), but a letter from Charles Jencks to the *Times Literary Supplement*, 12 March 1993, points out that it was used by the British artist John Watkins Chapman in the 1870s, and in 1917 by Rudolf Pannwitz. In the same letter Jencks adds, perhaps ironically, that one of the great strengths of the word is that it implies that one has gone beyond the 'clearly inadequate' world-view of modernism, but without specifying where we are going. He also notes that as the term 'modernism' was apparently coined in the third century then perhaps 'postmodernism' was first used then too (Jencks: 1993, 15).

The term *postmodernism* only enters Anglo-American critical DISCOURSE in the 1950s, and only in a significant way in the 1960s. At first it seems to indicate a new

215

periodization: postmodern art or culture is that art or culture which, in the years after the Second World War, extends or even breaks with modernist techniques and conventions without reverting to realist or pre-modernist positions. But before long critics start to use the term to refer to particular cultural, artistic – or even social – characteristics irrespective of when they manifested themselves. The use of the word 'social' is significant: *postmodernism* is typically used in a rather wider sense than is *modernism*, referring to a general human condition, or society at large, as much as to art or culture (a usage which was encouraged by Jean-François Lyotard's book *The Postmodern Condition: A Report on Knowledge* [English translation, 1984]). *Postmodernism*, then, can be used today in a number of different ways: (i) to refer to the non-realist and non-traditional literature and art of the post-Second World War period; (ii) to refer to literature and art which takes certain modernist characteristics to an extreme stage; and (iii) to refer to aspects of a more general human condition in the 'late capitalist' world of the post-1950s which have an all-embracing effect on life, culture, IDEOLOGY and art, as well as (in some usages) to a generally more welcoming attitude towards these aspects.

Thus those modernist characteristics which may produce postmodernism when taken to their most extreme forms, would include the rejection of representation in favour of self-reference – especially of a 'playful' and non-serious, non-constructive sort; the willing, even relieved, rejection of artistic AURA and of the sense of the work of art as organic whole (although David Harvey has argued that modernist [unlike postmodernist] art is essentially auratic [1989, 22]); the substitution of confrontation and teasing of the reader for collaboration with him or her; the rejection of 'character' and 'plot' as meaningful or artistically defensible concepts or conventions; even the rejection of MEANING itself as a hopeless delusion, a general belief that it is not worth trying to understand the world – or to believe that there is such as thing as 'the world' to be understood. Postmodernism takes the subjective idealism of modernism to the point of solipsism, but rejects the tragic and pessimistic elements in modernism in the conclusion that if one cannot prevent Rome burning then one might as well enjoy the fiddling that is left open to one. This and other broad definitions of postmodernism allow for the possibility of dubbing many literary and artistic works of the early part of the twentieth century, or even of previous centuries, as to a greater or lesser extent postmodernist: the fiction of Franz Kafka, Knut Hamsun's *Hunger*, Ezra Pound's 'Cantos', and even Laurence Sterne's *Tristram Shandy*. They also open the way to seeing postmodernist elements in the work of various POST-STRUCTURALIST and deconstructive critics such as Jacques Derrida, Michel Foucault, and Jacques Lacan. Satya P. Mohanty's statement that 'I use "poststructuralist" to refer to the dominant strand of postmodernist theory, whose focus is on language and signifying systems but whose claims are basically epistemological' (1997, 28, n4) is representative of a widespread attitude.

David Lodge has singled out five techniques typical of postmodernist fiction, although he notes that these indicate only 'some of the possibilities' (1977, 228). It is worthy of note that many of Lodge's examples are taken from the work of Samuel Beckett, who for many critics represents the pinnacle of modernism rather than post-modernism: to write about postmodernism is to get involved in a variety of problematic issues relating to boundaries and definitions. The five techniques are *contradiction* (Lodge quotes a passage from Samuel Beckett's *The Unnamable* which 'cancels itself out as it goes along' [1977, 229]); *permutation*: postmodernist writers typically incorporate 'alternative narrative lines in the same text' (1977, 230); *discontinuity*: Beckett, according to Lodge, 'disrupts the continuity of his discourse by unpredictable swerves of tone, metafictional asides to the reader, blank spaces in the text, contradiction and permutation' (1977, 231); *randomness* or a discontinuity produced by composing 'according to a logic of the absurd' (1977, 235); and finally *excess*: taking 'metaphoric or metonymic devices to excess [and testing them] to destruction' (1977, 235).

Other commentators have suggested that postmodernism is characterized by a more welcoming, celebrative attitude towards the modern world. That this world is one of increasing fragmentation, of the dominance of commercial pressures, and of human powerlessness in the face of a blind technology, is not disputed. But whereas the major modernists reacted with horror or despair to their perception of these facts, in one view of the issue it is typical of postmodernism to react in a far more accepting manner. David Harvey argues that postmodernism is mimetic of social, economic, and political practices in the societies in which it appears, and he compares the superimposition of different but uncommunicating worlds in many a postmodern novel with 'the increasing ghettoization, disempowerment, and isolation of poverty and minority populations in the inner cities of both Britain and the United States' (1989, 113). Harvey also makes very suggestive comparisons between the new organizational structures of post-Fordist capitalism (productive dispersal alongside CAPITAL concentration) and postmodernist ideology.

In our third possible usage of the term there is also a perception that the world has changed since the early years of the twentieth century. In the developed ('late capitalist') countries the advances of the communications and electronics industries have (it is argued) revolutionized human society. Instead of reacting to these changes in what is characterized as a Luddite manner, the postmodernist may instead counsel celebration of the present: celebration of the loss of artistic aura that follows what Benjamin (one of the most important prophets of postmodernism) calls 'mechanical reproduction'. Thus the paintings of an Andy Warhol or a Roy Lichtenstein (often categorized as Pop Art but arguably also postmodernist) force us to look more carefully and less dismissively at aspects of the commercial culture of our age, arguably carrying on the earlier work of Marcel Duchamp who, in 1919, could exhibit a mass-produced urinal as if it were a sculpture. In common with some much earlier avant-gardists, many postmodernists are fascinated with rather than repelled by technology, do not reject 'the POPULAR' as being beneath them, and are very much concerned with the immediate effect of their works: publication is more a strategic act than a bid for immortality. Alex Callinicos has, however, pointed out that such accounts tend to under-represent the relations between many of the 'high modernists' and popular culture, and he instances T. S. Eliot's interest in Music Hall and Stravinsky's indebtedness to Ragtime (1989, 15).

Slavoj Žižek claims that the break between modernism and postmodernism affects the very status of interpretation. Modernist works typically shock on first acquaintance, and the interpreter must work to help us integrate this shock, such that 'interpretation is the conclusive moment of the very act of reception' (1992, 1). Postmodernism, in contrast, presents us with objects or art-works which have mass-appeal, and the interpreter must then work on these apparently unproblematic entities 'to detect in them an exemplification of the most esoteric theoretical finesses of Lacan, Derrida or Foucault'. In the first case interpretation normalizes the shocking, in the second it defamiliarizes the ostensibly simple. Žižek further suggests that if 'there is an author whose name epitomizes this interpretive pleasure of "estranging" the most banal content, it is Alfred Hitchcock' (1992, 2). But note that this is not necessarily to suggest that Hitchcock's films are postmodernist, but rather that it is a particular sort of interpretative engagement with such popular and unproblematic works that is constitutive of post-modernism.

It is fair to say that there is far more debate around the term *postmodernism* than there is around the term *modernism*. The title of Allan Megill's 1989 article 'What Does the Term "Postmodernism" Mean?' poses a question that has been repeated by many others. One of the most powerful critiques of the term and the concept can be found in John Frow's essay 'What Was Postmodernism?' Frow argues that the concept is 'incoherent' for two reasons: first that no one can agree who actually was a post-modernist, and second that no one can agree about *when* postmodernism occurred or is occurring.

> If I think postmodernism means Olson and Heissenbüttel and Pynchon and catas-trophe theory, and you think it means MTV, fashion advertisements, political sound-bites, and the excremental vision, and someone else thinks it's hypertext, *trompe-l'œil* façades, 'Oprah', and *Blue Velvet*, then we're probably talking right past each other, since the definition of the concept shifts with the object taken to exemplify it. (1997, 27)

> It is clear, I think, that for both Jean-François Lyotard and Jean Baudrillard the concept of the postmodern is set against the 'modernity' of nineteenth-century capitalism, and thus includes most *modernist* aesthetic production. Jameson, by contrast, dates the postmodern from around the 1960s, but as Mike Davies notes, Mandel's concept of 'late capitalism', with which Jameson correlates post-modernism, extends through the post-war period and *ends* with the slump of 1974–5. (Frow: 1997, 29)

Frow accordingly suggests an alternative way of conceptualizing the various social, cultural and artistic changes that these varied terms are attempting to encompass, proposing that we distinguish

> between three conceptual moments: those of *modernism* (an adversary aesthetic culture); of *modernization* (an economic process with social and cultural implications); and of *modernity* (which overlaps with the modernization process, but which I understand as a philosophical category performatively designating the temporality of the post-traditional world). The same distinction of ontological levels holds good, *mutatis mutandis*, for postmodernism, postmodernization, and postmodernity. (1997, 34)

John Urry has conceded that 'it is difficult to address the topic of postmodernism at all', and that it 'seems as though the signifier "postmodern" is free-floating, having few connections with anything real, no minimal shared meaning of any sort' (1990, 83). But he argues for a new understanding of the terms based upon the idea that whilst modernism involves a differentiation of cultural spheres, postmodernism involves a de-differentiation, leading to

> a breakdown in the distinctiveness of each of these spheres of social activities, especially the cultural. Each implodes into the other, and most involve visual spectacle and play. This is seen most clearly in so-called multi-media events but much cultural production, especially via the central role of TV, is difficult to categorise and place within any particular sphere. (1990, 84)

It is probably fair to say that *modernism* as concept and term is relatively firmly established in present-day intellectual debate, but that the (generally left-wing) criticisms of theorists such as Callinicos and Frow have made *postmodernism* a rather more controversial term. Even so, it is probably relatively common to call the following writers and their works postmodernist: John Barth, John Ashberry, Thomas Pynchon, Donald Barthelme, William Burroughs, Walter Abish, Alain Robbe-Grillet, Peter Handke, Carlos Fuentes, and Jorge Luis Borges.

Two related terms describing postmodernist fiction are *fabulation* and *surfiction*. Both terms imply an aggressive and playful luxuriation in the non-representational, in which the writer takes delight in the artifice of writing rather than in using writing to describe or make contact with a perceived extra-fictional reality.

See also *BRICOLEUR*.

Moment During the 1920s and 1930s the word *moment* was given a particular meaning in Virginia Woolf's writing, one similar to James Joyce's *epiphany*. A Woolfian moment typically involved the sensation of time pausing, of a number of human and/or non-human factors coming together in a unity which was unique but which also had the power to 'speak' an inner truth or set of inner truths, both of the participants and components and to the observer. This observer of the Woolfian moment will thus simultaneously discover something fundamental about that which is observed and, at the same time, about him- or herself, something profound, complete, and of visionary intensity. Woolf admired Thomas De Quincey's ability to isolate such moments in his writing: in her 'De Quincey's Autobiography' she notes that the earlier writer 'was capable of being transfixed by the mysterious solemnity of certain emotions; of realizing how one moment may transcend in value fifty years' (Woolf: 1967, 6–7).

During the past two decades a rather different meaning of *moment* has emerged, one which shares an emphasis upon the self-speaking intensity that may suddenly flash out from the coming together of a number of separate elements, but which focuses upon social-CULTURAL and historical as well as individual and subjective forces. The 'moment' of *Left Review*, then, is that particular concatenation of forces – social, political, cultural – which provides both the impetus to found the journal and also the audience and context to APPRECIATE and form it.

Used thus the term shares much with the rather more technical *conjuncture*, which has a somewhat more mechanical sense of social and political forces coming together like railway lines to a junction. *Conjuncture* seems to have risen and fallen in concord with the changing authority of Louis Althusser, and although it is still encountered, the mechanistic connotations of its rigorously Latinate etymology have something of a 1970s flavour to them. (This was a time when the human SUBJECT had to be excluded from the heady realms of theory.)

Moment has suffered less of a decline, perhaps partly because this term seems to allow more space for the human and the experiential than does *conjuncture*.

Compare GEST; PROBLEMATIC.

Monoglossia/monologic See DIALOGIC

Monovalent discourse See REGISTER

Montage The combination of elements taken from different sources so as to produce a new whole, but (normally) one in which the origin of the component parts is clearly discernible. The *OED* relates the term to the cinema, but as Dawn Ades points out in her book *Photomontage*, 'manipulation of the photograph is as old as the photograph itself, which makes photomontage (a term invented by Dadaists in Berlin after the First World War) older than cinematic montage' (Ades: 1976, 7). Literary montage is associated in particular with MODERNISM, although if one wishes to use the term loosely then it can, for example, be applied to a work such as Laurence Sterne's *Tristram Shandy*, which includes various 'found texts' in its pages – including a page resembling a marbled book cover. Montage uses one of the most fundamental of all literary procedures: that of juxtaposition. What Samuel Johnson said of the metaphysical poets – 'The most heterogeneous ideas are yoked by violence together; nature and art are ransacked for illustrations, comparisons, and allusions' (in his 'Life' of Abraham Cowley) – is extended by the writer of montage to include not just ideas but a gamut of linguistic (and often non-linguistic) elements.

Montage occupied a central role in debates about REALISM and modernism in the 1930s, especially in what has become known as the 'Brecht–Lukács debate'. As this debate was only published in full after the Second World War, and in English translation only in 1977, its effect was felt some time after it took place. The Hungarian Marxist Georg Lukács included montage among the sins of Expressionism and modernism in his defences of realism during this period. For Lukács montage represented the pinnacle of the symbolist movement and was, he thought, to be set firmly in the centre of modernist literature and thought (Bloch *et al.*: 1977, 43). Brecht, in contrast, while admitting that a certain type of *anarchistic montage* succeeded only in reflecting the symptoms of the surface of things (Bloch *et al.*: 1977, 72), testified to the importance of montage technique to his own work, and remarked drily that in writing his recent play he had learned more from the paintings of the peasant Breughel than from treatises on realism (Bloch *et al.*: 1977, 70).

Lukács makes some rather grudging positive noises about photomontage, probably prompted by the success of those of the German anti-fascist John Heartfield. Heartfield's work also had considerable influence after the Second World War, and confirmed that seal of left-wing approval on montage which Lukács had attempted to deny it.

The same year in which the documents of the Brecht–Lukács debate were published in English translation, David Lodge's *The Modes of Modern Writing* appeared. Lodge refers to Roman Jakobson's characterization of montage as METAPHORIC but himself argues that montage can be either metaphoric or METONYMIC depending upon context

(1977, 84), a point he develops in the context of a discussion of the opening of Dickens's *Bleak House*. This piece of writing, he suggests, becomes a kind of metaphorical metonymy, and if filmed would have to be transposed into filmic montage (1977, 100).

Mood According to Gérard Genette, 'one can tell *more* or tell *less* what one tells, and can tell it *according to one point of view or another*; and this capacity, and the modalities of its use, are precisely what our category of *narrative mood* aims at' (1980, 161–2). The term is borrowed from grammatical mood, and its adoption by Genette is a good example of the reliance by NARRATOLOGISTS upon the LINGUISTIC PARADIGM.

> See also MODE; PERSPECTIVE AND VOICE.

Morphing In various forms of experimental writing and science FICTION, CHARACTERS are able to transform themselves (or are subject to be transformed) such that they can exist in a range of different states, each of which has different characteristics, powers of vision, and possibilities of interaction with the universe(s) of the fiction. Such transforming processes are known as *morphing*.

M/Other See OTHER

Motif See THEME AND THEMATICS

Motivated See ARBITRARY; FUNCTION

Move According to Thomas G. Pavel, 'the choice of an action among a number of alternatives, in a certain strategic situation and according to certain rules' (1986, 17). The term has currency in various DISCOURSES, including that of NARRATIVE theory.

> Compare SCRIPT.

Multivalent In chemistry, the valency of a substance is measured by its ability to combine with or displace a standard hydrogen atom. Used metaphorically, the term thus indicates an ability to combine with or displace other elements so as to create something new. In literary-critical DISCOURSE the term *multivalent* normally indicates that a TEXTUAL element assumes a variety of different sorts of significance as it combines with other textual or extra-textual elements (e.g. INTERPRETATIVE techniques or READINGS).

> See also AMBIGUITY.

Mundanes A dismissive term apparently used by certain groups of fans (such as those who follow the *Star Trek* series) to refer to outsiders or non-initiates.

Muted In current usage applied particularly to non-dominant groups or individuals who are denied the right of and the means to expression – especially self-expression. FEMINISTS have drawn attention to the way in which women typically constitute a muted group, unable to express their real situation and thus experiencing it as an individual deviation from a proclaimed NORM rather than as the common experience which it in fact is.

Elaine Showalter credits two essays by the Oxford anthropologist Edwin Ardener with the establishment of this term. According to him, she reports, muted groups must

221

'mediate their beliefs through the allowable forms of dominant structures' (1986, 261). Particularly important is Edwin Ardener's belief that women's beliefs and experience find expression through ritual and art, and can be deciphered by the ethnographer. Muting, in other words, is not silencing; it involves the partial silencing and suppression of valid expression, but not to the extent that this cannot be brought to the surface by the right investigator. Not surprisingly, the concept has been used by feminist literary critics as an indication of the sort of READING that should be given to literary WORKS written by women in male-dominated societies.

See also ERASURE.

Myth Two of the most influential of contemporary thinkers – Claude Lévi-Strauss and Roland Barthes – have helped to revivify the concept of myth in recent times. Lévi-Strauss's discussion of myth in *The Savage Mind* helped to establish the idea of myth as *a kind of thought*, one, as he puts it, based on elements that are 'half-way between percepts and concepts' (1972, 18). This is very different from the traditional view of myth, conveniently defined by Robert Scholes and Robert Kellogg as 'a traditional plot which can be transmitted' (1966, 12).

This shift of emphasis from myth as a sort of PLOT to myth as a way of thinking with close resemblances to (along with some differences from) IDEOLOGY, can also be found in Roland Barthes's highly original *Mythologies*. Barthes's great achievement was to bring myths home to contemporary life, to make present-day European READERS aware that myths were not just something that other people (remote African tribes, Russian peasants, the ancient Greeks) believed in and created – but were part of the stuff and fabric of everyday modern life in the West. *Mythologies* includes brief studies of such diverse topics as wrestling, soap powders, the face of Greta Garbo, steak and chips, and striptease. Barthes explained that for him the notion of myth explained a particular process whereby historically determined circumstances were presented as somehow 'natural', and that it allowed for the uncovering of 'the ideological abuse' hidden 'in the display of *what goes without saying*' (1973, 11). Myth, for Barthes, thus performs a NATURALIZING function, one which can be likened to an inversion of DEFAMILIARIZATION. *Mythologies* was a very influential book, leading directly to a British book entitled *Television Mythologies* (Masterman:1984) and indirectly to a rather different usage of the word 'myth'.

If Lévi-Strauss sees myth as a kind of thought, for Barthes it is 'a type of speech', and his emphasis is very similar to that of Lévi-Strauss: 'Myth is not defined by the object of its message, but by the way in which it utters this message' (1973, 109), it is 'depoliticized speech' (1973, 142).

In recent usage, then, the concepts of myth and of ideology are interlinked: myths perform an ideological FUNCTION while ideologies function by means of myths. This shift away from more traditional meanings is perhaps what led the poet Basil Bunting, responding to a questionnaire for a special issue of the journal *Agenda* on myth in 1977, to claim that arguments about what the devil myth meant were unprofitable, because the word does not seem to mean anything in particular.

Clemens Lugowski's *Form, Individuality and the Novel*, first published in German in 1932 and only recently published in English, makes use of the concept of the *mythic analogue* in a way reminiscent of, though predating, the work of Barthes and Lévi-

Strauss. Introducing the modern reissue of Lugowski's work, Heinz Schaffler notes that 'Lugowski's inquiry implies that while the original vitality of myth has faded, the remnants of mythic thought have gone over into aesthetic structures', and this remnant Lugowski dubs the mythic analogue (1990, xiii). (Although Lugowski is unlikely to have been influenced by Marx, this argument has much in common with Marx's comments on myth in what has become known as the Introduction to the *Critique of Political Economy*, in which Marx relates the achievement of Greek art to Greek mythology.) As with Barthes and Lévi-Strauss, myth for Lugowski involves a way of representing reality. By reference to the *Decameron* he suggests that the mythic analogue involves a 'view of the world as a form of timeless, static existence' (1990, 42) – which reminds us of Barthes's view of myth as a transformation of history into a sort of common sense.

See also *BRICOLEUR*; ARCHETYPAL CRITICISM; ROMANCE.

N

Nachträglichkeit From the German of Sigmund Freud: delayed effect or after-experience. Central to much of Freud's work is the belief that reactions to disturbing experiences (witnessing the sexual act of one's parents, for example) are not immediate but long term and highly MEDIATED. Both Jacques Derrida and Jacques Lacan draw on this concept (in, for instance, the former's 'Freud and the Scene of Writing' and the latter's 'The Function and Field of Speech and Language in Psychoanalysis'). An insistence upon the long-term and indirect nature of chains of cause and effect is central to much recent theory – compare the entries for MEDIATION and OVERDETERMINATION.

Naked ape-ism See BIOLOGISM/BIOLOGICAL DETERMINISM

Name-of-the-Father According to Jacques Lacan 'the attribution of procreation to the Father can only be the effect of a pure signifier, of a recognition, not of a real father, but of what religion has taught us to refer to as Name-of-the-Father' (1977, 199). He further argues that Freud linked this signifier of the Father 'as author of the Law, with death, even to the murder of the Father – thus showing that if this murder is the fruitful moment of debt through which the subject binds himself for life to the Law, the symbolic Father is, in so far as he signifies this Law, the dead Father' (1977, 199). According to Lacan the child enters language during the Oedipal phase, and it is at this time that language as it were INTERPELLATES him or her – to use a somewhat anachronistic term. The Name-of-the-Father constitutes the child's authority, and comes with the acquisition of language, but it is simultaneously an authority that is dead.

More loosely, the term is used to refer to any (normally PATRIARCHAL) external and unchallenged source of authority.

Narcissistic narrative See METALANGUAGE

Narrated monologue See FREE INDIRECT DISCOURSE

Narratee The 'target' at whom a NARRATIVE is directed. A narratee is not just the individual by whom a narrative is received; there has to be some evidence that the narrative is actually intended for a particular goal for it to count as the (or a) narratee. This leads Prince (1988a) to argue that the narratee must be inscribed in the TEXT. He argues that there is a difference between a narratee and both the READER and the IMPLIED READER. In the final section of James Joyce's *Ulysses* therefore, if we follow Prince on this matter, the narratee is Molly Bloom herself (she aims her comments at herself), but the implied reader is rather a person who can, for example, pick up the classical analogies contained within the text of *Ulysses* as a whole, with the real reader being anyone who actually reads the novel.

Some NARRATOLOGISTS distinguish between *intra-fictional (or intra-diegetic) narratees* (such as Molly Bloom, or Lockwood in *Wuthering Heights*), who are FICTIONAL personae within the works concerned as well as having a narrative addressed to them, and *extra-fictional (or extra-diegetic) narratees*, who are not.

Narratees may be single or multiple, personified or non-personified. Thus in a complex WORK such as Joseph Conrad's *Heart of Darkness*, those sitting and listening to Marlow's account are the narratees of his narrative, but they are not the narratees of the FRAME narrative. Translating all this into a less technical form, we can say that whereas Marlow talks to certain personified individuals who are CHARACTERS within the novel, the anonymous frame narrator directs his (or her) comments to an unpersonified, non-specific and somewhat diffuse narratee who exists within the novel as narratee and nothing else.

One should add that, of course, a well-defined narratee exerts considerable influence on the formation of the implied reader as well as on the attitudes and behaviour of the real reader.

Narration This is a rather slippery term in contemporary NARRATIVE theory, and is given different weight by different theorists. By some it is used as a synonym for narrative, by others as the act or process whereby a narrative is produced. The second of these is the definition chosen by Shlomith Rimmon-Kenan, for whom narration is both (i) the *communication* process in which the narrative as message is transmitted and (ii) the *verbal* nature of the medium used to transmit the message (1983, 2). For Rimmon-Kenan the communication process involved in narration is a double one, both contained in the TEXT (Marlow narrates his STORY to those listening to him in *Heart of Darkness*) as well as involving the text (Joseph Conrad is engaged in narration when writing *Heart of Darkness* for READERS to read) – although for her the former of these processes is the more important (1983, 3).

Michael J. Toolan discusses a number of alternative usages, and suggests his own: narration is 'the individual or "position" we judge to be the immediate source and authority for whatever words are used in the telling' (1988, 76).

Compare the distinctions listed in the entry for ENUNCIATION and its cognates.

Narrative A term which is much used but about which there is limited consensus when it comes to defining its meaning.

Gerald Prince defines this term as 'the recounting of one or more real or fictitious events' but as 'product and process, object and act, structure and structuration' (1988a, 58). For Onega and Landa, narrative can be defined in a wider, Aristotelian sense as '"a work with a plot" (e.g. epic poetry, tragedy, comedy)' or in a narrower sense as '"a work with a narrator" (epic poetry, but not, in principle, drama or film)' (1996, 1). They compare the difference between their wider and narrower senses to the difference between TELLING AND SHOWING (1996, 2), and further define the term in a way that impinges on certain definitions of 'plot' (see STORY AND PLOT):

A narrative is the semiotic representation of a series of events meaningfully connected in a temporal and causal way. Films, plays, comic strips, novels, newsreels, diaries, chronicles and treatises of geological history are all narratives in this wider sense. (1996, 3)

Seymour Chatman claims that there is no particular reason why 'to narrate' should mean *only* 'to tell', and he suggests that once 'we decide to define Narrative as the composite of story and discourse (on the basis of its unique double chronology), then *logically*, at least, narratives can be said to be actualizable on the stage or in other iconic media' (1990, 114). By double chronology Chatman means that a narrative contains two time-scales: that of the story and that of the narrating (telling, enacting, displaying) of that story; again, see the entry for STORY AND PLOT.

Gérard Genette points out that the word *narrative* (in French, *récit*) can refer to three separate things: either the oral or written narrative statement that undertakes to tell of an EVENT or events; or the succession of real or fictitious events that are the subject of the DISCOURSE, with their varied relations; or, finally, the act of narrating (1980, 25–6). In his own usage he reserves the word narrative for the first of these three, while the second he refers to as STORY or DIEGESIS and the third as *narrating*. This makes good sense, but others have suggested alternative usages and one should be prepared for the possibility that the term may be used in any one or more of the three alternatives suggested by Genette.

On two points there is, however, general agreement. First that a narrative must involve the recounting of an event or events, otherwise it is not a narrative but a description. And second that these events can be either real or fictitious. The person telling the TV News what happened in an accident in which he or she was involved, is as much delivering a narrative as is the person telling a joke, or the Marlow of Joseph Conrad's *Heart of Darkness*.

In an article entitled 'Narrative Comprehension', Carol Fleisher Feldman, Jerome Bruner, Bobbie Renderer and Sally Spitzer have attempted to distinguish between two types of 'narrative version': 'conscious' and 'unconscious'. In order to substantiate this distinction they first differentiate between what they term a 'landscape of action' and a 'landscape of consciousness'. The former is 'a temporally patterned sequence of action events reported in the third person with minimal information about the psychological states of protagonists', while the latter 'is devoted precisely to how the world is perceived or felt by various members of the cast of characters, each from their own perspective' (1990, 2). On the basis of this differentiation, they suggest that two different types of narration – conscious and unconscious – can be constructed. They argue that conscious narrative versions (i.e. retellings of stories heard) involve the reordering of basic plot events, and the evocation of more detail. Whereas conscious versions tend to focus upon psychological information, unconscious versions tend to concentrate upon possible actions. They conclude as follows.

> We may suppose then that we have found two kinds of narrative thinking. The first is triggered by the conscious version. It is meta-cognitive as well as interpretive and is organized in a temporal pattern around the psychological state of the protagonist. The second is triggered by the nonconscious version, is also interpretive, and is organized in a static pattern around matters of literary form. The first seems to be a psychologically richer form of narrative thinking; the second seems more richly literary. Both modes are generative in permitting subjects to go beyond the information given, but the mode triggered by the conscious version is more generative. (1990, 21)

See also FUNCTION; REGISTER.

Narrative levels See STORY AND PLOT

Narrative movements See DURATION

Narrative situation Used by Mieke Bal in a technical sense, and fixed according to the answers evinced by a set of typical questions. Is the NARRATOR a CHARACTER or not? Does the narrator exist within the world of the STORY? Is the NARRATIVE FOCALIZED through the narrator? (1985, 126). In other words, narrative situation has nothing to do with whether the narrative is ostensibly delivered in Paris or Rome, or whether the narrator narrates in a sitting or standing position, but is defined according to the narrator's relationship to the narrative and the story. From this perspective the narrative situations in Joseph Conrad's *Heart of Darkness* and Woody Allen's film *Broadway Danny Rose* have certain striking similarities, even though the setting, story, and action of the two WORKS have precious little in common.

Compare the discussion of *narrative levels* in the entry for STORY AND PLOT.

Narrativizing discourse See DISCOURSE

Narratology A term which, according to Richard Macksey (1997, xiii), was coined by Tzvetan Todorov in 1969. Onega and Landa claim that as the term was popularized in the 1970s by a number of STRUCTURALIST writers, 'the definition of narratology has usually been restricted to structural, or more specifically structuralist, analysis of narrative'. And indeed, Gerald Prince suggests that narratology can refer to the structuralist-inspired theory which studies the functioning of NARRATIVE in a medium-independent manner, and he attempts to define both narrative COMPETENCE as well as what narratives have in common and what enables them to differ from one another (1988a, 65).

Onega and Landa add, however, that narratology 'now appears to be reverting to its etymological sense, a multi-disciplinary study of narrative which negotiates and incorporates the insights of many other critical discourses that involve narrative forms of representation', and that today narratology 'studies the narrative aspects of many literary and non-literary genres and discourses which need not be defined as strictly narrative, such as lyrical poems, film, drama, history, advertisements' (1996, 1).

Narrator Whereas Gerald Prince describes the narrator as 'the one who narrates' (1988a, 65), and Katie Wales as 'a person who narrates' (1989, 316), Mieke Bal stresses that for her the narrator is the narrative agent, 'the linguistic subject, a function and not a person, which expresses itself in the language that constitutes the text' (1985, 119). The tension between these two approaches pinpoints a problem: whereas the term evokes a sense of a human individual for most people, many NARRATIVES do not stem from recognizably human or personified sources, but from a SUBJECT position within the text, although Claude Bremond (1966) has claimed that 'where there is no implied human interest (narrated events neither being produced by agents nor experienced by anthropomorphic beings), there can be no narrative, for it is only in relation to a plan conceived by man that events gain meaning and can be organized into a structured temporal sequence' (Onega and Landa: 1996, 63–4). On this account the 'Time Passes' section of Virginia Woolf's *To the Lighthouse* might not qualify as narrative.

Monika Fludernik has argued for reserving the term *narrator* for 'those instances of subjective language that imply a *speaking* subject: the personal pronoun *I*, addresses to the narratee, metanarrative commentary and evaluation' (1993, 443), but many theorists continue to use the term, as does Bal, to indicate a narrative agent of any form, personified or not. Richard Aczel accepts that the issue involved in such questions is at least partly terminological.

> If one chooses to restrict the term 'narrator' to an identifiable teller persona, then there ostensibly are narratorless narratives. This does not, however, address the problem of to whom one attributes functions of (nonpersonified) selection, organization, and comment. I prefer to see the 'narrator' as an umbrella term for a cluster of possible functions, of which some are necessary (the selection, organization, and presentation of narrative elements) and others optional (such as self-personification as teller, comment, and direct reader/narratee address). (1998, 492)

An alternative way round these problems is to reserve the term *covert narrator* for those instances in which a telling is delivered from a non-personified and non-intrusive source which does not address a NARRATEE.

The issues involved become clearer when we remember that in some theoretical systems the narrator must be distinguished not just from the real author, but also from the implied author. This is most obvious in the case of a *personified narrator*: Charles Marlow, whom we encounter in four of Joseph Conrad's FICTIONS, is neither Joseph Conrad nor that AUTHORIAL presence and CENTRE that we sense (according to some commentators) in each complete fiction of Conrad's, and which some prefer to name the implied author. (Gérard Genette uses the term *authorial* rather more loosely: '*authorial* is to be understood, henceforth, as meaning authentic and assumptive' [1997, 196].)

A similar point can be made about the narrator of George Eliot's *Middlemarch*, who is neither George Eliot (or Marian Evans!) nor the 'sense of an author' we get when reading *Middlemarch*. (Although narrator and implied author are more difficult to distinguish in *Middlemarch* than they are in, say, Conrad's *Lord Jim*. See the discussion of the term *career author* in the entry for AUTHOR.) But if the narrator of *Middlemarch* is not a real or implied author, it does not follow that he/she is (as Wales has it) 'a person' – otherwise I would not be driven to the awkwardness of a formulation like 'he/she'. That unwillingness to refer to the narrator of *Middlemarch* as 'he' or 'she' – or, come to that, as 'it' – reveals that although many narrators assume certain human characteristics, they must sometimes be distinguished from human individuals. Indeed, it may be argued that (like literary CHARACTERS) they need to be distinguished from human individuals even when they are personified and appear most human – as with, for example, Charles Marlow. Moreover, even if a narrator may be personified, he or she may still be relatively anonymous. The FRAME narrator of Henry James's *The Turn of the Screw* is so anonymous that there is no firm evidence as to whether we are dealing with a male or a female.

Level of personification is thus one important element in distinguishing between narrators, but it is not the only one. Other important elements are: *narrative level* (does the narrator belong to the same 'reality' as the characters, or is he/she *extradiegetic*? (See the entries for DIEGESIS AND MIMESIS and STORY AND PLOT.) So far as this particular issue is concerned, Monika Fludernik has introduced two related terms: 'In my terminology, an "existential" continuity between the communicative (narrator–narratee) level and the story level is defined as *homocommunicative*, whereas a complete discontinuity between these existential levels is characterized as *heterocommunicative*' (1996, 245).

Does the narrator *participate in the story* fully, partially, or not at all? (The narrator may be fully personified and portrayed on a REALISTIC level, but merely recounting a story which he/she observed without personal involvement.) Is the narrator *perceptive or obtuse*? *Wuthering Heights* has one (relatively) perceptive narrator and one obtuse one; *Huckleberry Finn* and *Gulliver's Travels* have narrators who are at times perceptive, at times obtuse. Is the narrator *overt or covert*? In other words, are we aware of a narrating subject or does the TEXT seem transparent, giving us a view of character and action which so occupies our attention that we are not conscious of any narrator? Is the narrator *reliable or unreliable*? Do we believe everything that the narrator tells us, or suspect that either deceit or obtuseness on his/her part requires us to see more than he or she does?

Narreme See IDEOLOGEME

Nation/nationalism The rise of POSTCOLONIALIST theory and criticism has led to a certain problematizing of the concept of the nation, such that the standard term 'national literature' is increasingly seen to beg many questions. Recent, pre-postcolonialist usage has defined a nation as a political unit which may consist of a number of separate peoples and CULTURES, but the *OED* definition singles out settlement within a defined geographical territory as of primary importance. Very often such usage equated nation and state (witness the term nation-state), although the concept of a state is more tightly defined in politico-economic terms. (Thus Britain is a state but England is not.) All of these terms are subject to the play of political pressures and forces and can thus be contested. There may be no disagreement that those people who live in Ireland belong to two states, but there is unlikely to be agreement as to whether they constitute one or two nations. This is because the term *nation* is sometimes approximated to state, and at other times to other terms and concepts such as *people* or even culture.

A single individual in the developed world is likely to be a member (willing or unwilling) of one state, but membership of nation, people or culture may in each case be contested or multiple.

In their discussion of this term, Bill Ashcroft, Gareth Griffiths and Helen Tiffin have drawn attention to the fact that the idea of the nation is a relatively recent one, and that the instability of nations is nothing new (1998, 149). Their extended discussion is valuable and recommended.

These problems of definition have impacted on the study of literature quite regularly, and not just subsequent to the rise of postcolonialist theory and criticism. As the entry for ENGLISH points out, the term 'English literature' can imply either a common language or the literature of a particular people or nation. At the same time, literary WORKS have very often formed an important element in *nationalist* movements – that is to say, movements that attempt to transform national aspirations into a representative nation-state.

Nationalist See AFRICANIST/NATIONALIST

Nativism According to Gĩtahi Gĩtĩtĩ, 'the idea that "true African independence requires a literature of one's own," that is a literature or literatures in indigenous African languages' (1994, 6–7). Benita Parry discusses the concept in relation to, among other things, the NÉGRITUDE movement in her 1994 article 'Resistance Theory/Theorizing Resistance or Two Cheers for Nativism.'

More generally, the term is given a pejorative force and used to refer to any sentimentalizing or semi-paternalistic valorization of 'unspoilt' CULTURES, or to attempts by oppressed people to sentimentalize or glamorize their cultural heritage in such a way as to conceal divisions and conflicts within it. The pejorative MARXIST term 'workerism', used to describe a sentimental admiration for the working class in capitalist society, has a comparable force.

See also RELEXIFICATION for a related but more specifically linguistic term.

Naturalization See DEFAMILIARIZATION

Negotiation See EXCHANGE

Négritude A neologism coined by the Martinique writer Aimé Césaire in his *Cahier d'un retour au pays natal* (*Notes on a Return to the Land of My Birth*) in 1939. The French term is now generally used in English, although when Frantz Fanon's *Les Damnés de la terre* (1961) was first translated into English as *The Wretched of the Earth* in 1967, the term was translated as 'Negro-ism'.

One of the definitions of the term provided by Césaire is simple and all-embracing: '*Négritude* is the simple recognition of the fact that one is black, the acceptance of this fact and of our black destiny, our history, and our culture' (Kesteloot: 1968, 80). Following Césaire, the term was applied to a movement of Black (mainly African) writers resident in Paris, and was in conscious opposition to the French colonial policy of integrating colonial peoples and their cultures into French CULTURE. The Senegalese writer Léopold Sédar Senghor was an influential figure in the movement.

The term was taken up by some Black American writers in the 1960s, for whom it became a shorthand way of celebrating Blackness and Black culture. During this time its use generally betokened an anti-rational, anti-colonialist standpoint, the associations its use by Black writers in Paris had gathered by the time that visiting Black American writers encountered it. It suggested the anti-rational inasmuch as its use went hand in hand with a rejection of the rational in favour of more mystical, collective and emotional forms of understanding; and anti-colonialist inasmuch as Black Americans identified their own situation as oppressed group in the United States with that of Black Africans fighting against European domination. Much Black American writing of the 1960s and 1970s used these associations to label and LEGITIMIZE a sort of writing that broke with what were seen as culturally alien forms of expression. It had its critics, however, who argued that many negative STEREOTYPES of Black people were perpetuated by the term.

With the rise of POSTCOLONIALIST theory the term has been subjected to renewed analysis. Benita Parry's 1994 article 'Resistance Theory/Theorizing Resistance or Two Cheers for Nativism' attempts a balanced assessment by placing the movement in its historical context.

> Négritude's moment of articulation and reception – before the nationalist movements in Africa and the Caribbean had gained momentum, but after Marxist critiques of colonialism had been developed within the Indian independence struggle – may testify to both its originality as a cultural-political position and its limitations as an ideology. Many of the contemporary objections to Négritude came from those who had welcomed its inception, and were delivered from a Marxist standpoint. These can be arranged into the following categories: systemised mystification construing 'black being' as irrational and 'black culture' as genetically determined, unified and transnational, thus fostering the universalising myth of a unified black identity in the face of its multiplicity and diversity; political error in failing to represent the anti-colonial struggle as the national liberation of all classes, or to acknowledge the specificities of each national culture in the colonised world and, in the case of the Caribbean, in driving a wedge between African and other oppressed communities; theoretical error in distorting African world-views and overlooking that the synthesising of indigenous with foreign elements in the colonised world had issued in complex and particularised modes of *mestizaje* or creolisation – sometimes, though rarely, this fusing being differently represented as the reconciliation of the African with the western, or even complete cultural acclimatisation to the west. (Mongia: 1996, 92)

The mention of 'mystification' is important; subsequent attacks on the movement frequently accused it of both mystification and mysticism, and such attacks generally came from intellectuals who took exception to its claimed anti-rational or anti-intellectual elements. Parry is probably right, however, to stress the historical context; as with many popular movements, its initially positive and progressive elements (asserting Black and African pride and confidence at a time when these needed to be asserted and built up) became overshadowed by other elements at a later stage of history. Parry quotes, tellingly, from Césaire's 1967 interview with the Haitian writer and political activist René Depestre:

> We adopted the word *négre* as a term of defiance... We found a violent affirmation in the words *négre* and *négritude*... it is a concrete rather than an abstract coming to consciousness... We lived in an atmosphere of rejection, and we developed an inferiority complex... I have always thought that the black man was searching for his identity. And... if what we want is to establish this identity, then we must have a concrete consciousness of what we are – that is the first fact of our lives: that we are black; that we were black and have a history. ... [that] there have been beautiful and important black civilizations... that its values were values that could still make an important contribution to the world. (In Mongia: 1996, 94, quoting Césaire: 1972, 74, 76)

Neo-Tarzanism According to Judie Newman,

> [w]riting in 1975, Wole Soyinka coined the term 'Neo-Tarzanism' in order to characterise the poetics of pseudo-tradition. Soyinka was responding to three African literary critics, the 'troika' of Chinweizu, Onwuchekwa Jemie and Ihechukwu Madubuike, whose views (subsequently expanded in *Toward the Decolonization of African Literature*) emphatically rejected European universalism. Known also as 'bolekaja', meaning 'come down and fight', the troika denounced the standards used to evaluate contemporary African literature as Eurocentric and inappropriate, particularly in the imposition of realist norms upon the novel. They argued for a return to African traditions and a revalorisation of earlier African orature, as a first step to the decolonisation of African literature. (1995, 108; see Soyinka: 1975)

See also BOLEKAJA CRITICS; EUROCENTRIC; ORATURE.

Nesting See EMBEDDING

New Criticism The New Criticism is much referred to, and rarely in a way that suggests that there might be any problem in identifying what it is or was, or who its members were. However, in an article entitled 'In Search of the New Criticism', Cleanth Brooks – whose name is almost always mentioned in the list of those who are presumed to have been New Critics – states that 'the New Criticism is not easy to describe or locate' (1983, 41). Brooks points out that the name comes from a book by the poet and man of letters John Crowe Ransom entitled *The New Criticism*, published in 1941. Brooks continues:

> In it [Ransom] discussed the critical aims and methods of Yvor Winters as the 'logical' critic, T. S. Eliot as the 'historical' critic, and Ivor A. Richards as the 'psychological' critic. He mentions more briefly R. P. Blackmur, William Empson, and a few others. Though Ransom treated all with respect, he put on record his reservations and disagreements. He neither defined an entity called the New

Criticism nor did he attempt to promote it. In fact, his last chapter is entitled: 'Wanted: An Ontological Critic.' (1983, 41)

Brooks suggests that the belief that there was a group of critics called 'The New Critics' stems from people who either had not read Ransom's book or had misread it, and who assumed that Ransom was the primal New Critic and that his former students and friends were the others.

Other accounts of the emergence and development of the group (or the belief that there was such a group) take a different starting point. Jonathan Culler suggests that it originates in debates about the nature of poetry in T. S. Eliot's *The Sacred Wood* (1920), and was continued by a group of poets meeting at Vanderbilt University under the tutelage of John Crowe Ransom who published – from 1922 to 1925 – a review called *The Fugitive*. Culler sees a collection of political essays published by this group under the title of *I'll Take My Stand* (1930) as an important ancestor of the New Criticism. The essays defended the Southern way of life against those who, following the Scopes 'monkey' trial, denigrated it: 'Contrasting the agrarian with the industrial, the traditional and the organic with the alienated and the mechanistic, the contributors celebrated the life of yeoman farmers in small communities and argued for a spiritual superiority of subsistence farming over cash crop farming and industrial manufacture (1988, 9). According to Culler, as a result of a lack of success on the political front the writers concerned (known as the Agrarians) abandoned the cause of the autonomous, self-sufficient farm for that of the self sufficient poem. Whether or not we accept this account, the political element introduced by Culler is an important one, and explains why a number of commentators (normally but not always American ones) have included the English critic F. R. Leavis in their list of New Critics. There are certainly passages in which Leavis sings the praises of the 'organic community' which are very reminiscent of the political arguments of the Agrarians – especially when taken in conjunction with Leavis's own brand of insular conservatism.

Another important father figure for the New Criticism is undoubtedly I. A. Richards, although he is infrequently named as a New Critic himself – perhaps because by the time the term came into common use Richards was pursuing interests very different from those associated with New Criticism. If the Agrarians are important IDEOLOGICAL forebears of the New Criticism, Richards's main importance lies more on the practical level, in the *method* he bequeathed to the New Critics. On the ideological plane many of Richards's ideas were taken (sometimes in a rather unmodified form) from contemporary psychology, something which strikes the modern reader of his *Principles of Literary Criticism* (1924) rather forcibly. Much more influential was *Practical Criticism* (1929), which not only popularized a term now firmly established in the vocabulary of Literary Studies and the syllabuses of innumerable schools, colleges and universities, but also established a particular way of approaching the critical reading of poems which, with modifications, became central to what with some justification can be termed the ideology of the New Criticism. Richards's aim was in fact pedagogical: he was shocked by how badly his Cambridge students read and understood poems, and adduced as evidence for this sorry state of affairs a set of READINGS given by these students on the basis of 'unseen' TEXTS – that is to say, texts of poems the students had not previously read, presented with no information about AUTHOR, date of composition, publishing history, socio-historical context, and so on. It should be stressed that Richards was not suggesting that readings of poems should ideally be based on such a context-free approach to naked texts, but rather that the *teaching* of literature should be such as to enable students to read poems carefully and intelligently even when such contextual information was lacking. But a process of historical transformation led first to the study of the unseen text becoming a part of many Eng. Lit. syllabuses, and in the most extreme forms of the New Criticism to an actual embargo upon the use of such contextual information in the INTERPRETATION or ANALYSIS of poetry or other literature.

Brooks points out that Ransom's *The New Criticism* also mentions the English critic William Empson, who often figures on lists of prominent New Critics. Empson's *Seven Types of Ambiguity* (1930) was extremely influential by virtue of what many saw as a continuation of the lessons of *Practical Criticism* (and Richards was Empson's tutor at Cambridge). *Seven Types of Ambiguity* was full of close and detailed *analytical* readings of poetry which – unlike the biographical criticism of a previous age or the MARXIST criticism of a slightly later one – kept the reader's attention firmly and consistently upon matters of textual detail. Empson was certainly a very important influence on those American critics who became known in the 1940s and 1950s as the leading New Critics: an essay written by Cleanth Brooks for the journal *Accent* and entitled simply 'Empson's Criticism' singles out what Brooks sees as the most important elements in Empson's criticism: 'the significance of Empson's criticism is this: his criticism is an attempt to deal with what the poem "means" in terms of its structure *as a poem*' (1946, 498). This, Brooks goes on to argue, is radically different from what 'the critic in the past' had attempted to do: either to find the goodness of the poem in terms of its prose argument and its 'truth' – thus making poetry compete with philosophy or science – or else trying to find the poetry in the charm of the decorative elements. For Brooks, Empson's great virtue as critic is that he moves beyond such positions, showing how poem after poem ' "works" as a complex of meanings', with metaphor playing a functional (not decorative) role, metrics also performing a function, corroborating the play of meaning throughout the poem, and connotations no longer seen as hints of decorative, mysterious beauty, 'but active forces in the development of the manifold of meanings that is the poem' (1946, 498).

If we go back to 1938, when Brooks and Robert Penn Warren had published a book entitled *Understanding Poetry* (revised edition, 1958), we can see that both Empson and Richards must have had a profound influence upon the writing of this book, a book that was perhaps *the* most influential in establishing a new set of critical principles and practices. According to Brooks's 1983 essay, he and Warren faced a similar problem to that faced by Richards: their students were 'bright enough young men and women', but 'very few of them had the slightest conception of how to read a short story, let alone a poem' (1983, 42). *Understanding Poetry* contained a 'Letter to the teacher' which noted that there were three substitutes for the poem as object of study: paraphrase of logical and narrative content; study of biographical and historical materials; inspirational and didactic interpretation. These three substitutes were to be avoided, although paraphrase was allowable as a necessary preliminary step in reading a poem.

'The teacher', then, (who was typically hard-pressed and faced with the problem of how to interest his or her pupils) was handed the perfect pedagogical recipe: concentrate upon the poem as poem; study the words on the page; use the poem as your teaching material – it can be read in class, and analysed and discussed there and then, with no need for extra study or information.

By the end of the Second World War the stage was thus set for the confirmation on the theoretical plane of what was seen by critics such as Brooks to be a new set of working practices for critics. Key documents here are the two essays 'The Intentional Fallacy' and 'The Affective Fallacy', written by critic W. K. Wimsatt and aesthetician Monroe Beardsley, and published respectively in 1946 and 1949. These elevated the pedagogical/polemical technique of Richards, and Brooks and Warren, and what was perceived to be the working practice of a critic like Empson, to the level of a set of theoretical injunctions. The poem had to be treated as poem not as anything else; it had to be read and analysed 'in itself'; criticism that contained references to the author's intention or the poem's 'affects' in the reader was deemed illegitimate.

In the 1940s and the 1950s the new doctrine spread like wildfire in schools and establishments of higher education, and there are many educated in the 1950s and 1960s who can remember red lines through paragraphs in essays which dared to bring in biographical or socio-historical information, or to make use of words such as 'intention'. The rise to HEGEMONY of what were seen to be New Critical principles was certainly helped by the fact that this was the period of the Cold War and one of the consistent targets of the then practitioners of New Criticism was that of MARXIST criticism.

What is interesting, however, is that the remarkable degree of consensus concerning the New Critical principles in the 1950s and 1960s, at all levels of the educational systems of Britain, the United States, and many Western European countries, does not actually match with the actual beliefs, theories, and even practice of many of the revered father figures. Richards's psychologism, Empson's lifelong commitment to the use of biographical information and speculation in poetic analysis (only noticed by many when books such as *Milton's God* and, especially, *Using Biography* appeared, and when Empson started to criticize the intentional fallacy loudly and sarcastically) – even Brooks's use of paraphrase as a critical tool at much the same time as he rejected it on the theoretical plane – none of these seemed to have disturbed the still waters of New Critical consensus too much for at least a couple of decades. And this suggests that the New Criticism took its nourishment as much sideways (from contemporary non-literary ideology) as it did from the past and the father figures. The consensus, in other words, seems to have been established between the followers of the father figures more than between the father figures themselves.

To quote just one from many possible examples. The Cambridge University Press's series of introductory critical studies entitled 'British Authors' had as General Editor in the 1970s Robin Mayhead, whose own *Understanding Literature* (1965) declared a clear indebtedness to the criticism and teaching of F. R. Leavis. In spite of its title, the series was not primarily biographical in orientation, and volumes in it included a one-page General Preface written by Mayhead which contained the following statement:

> The general critical attitude implied in the series is set out at some length in my *Understanding Literature*. Great literature is taken to be to a large extent self-explanatory to the reader who will attend carefully enough to what it says. 'Background' study, whether biographical or historical, is not the concern of the series.

Apart from noting that the 'general critical attitude' outlined seems to come perilously close to rendering even introductory 'critical studies' unnecessary, we can see how Leavis's heritage could merge in with more general New Critical attitudes seemingly unproblematically here. It is doubtless partly for this reason that many confidently name Leavis himself as a New Critic.

I would suggest, then, that the New Criticism presents us with the paradoxical picture of a remarkable hegemonic consensus overlaying what (as Brooks quite rightly points out in his 1983 essay) was a much more pluralistic set of critical practices. Was, and is. In 1981, Jonathan Culler wrote that: 'Whatever critical affiliations we may proclaim, we are all New Critics, in that it requires a strenuous effort to escape notions of the autonomy of the literary work, the importance of demonstrating its unity, and the requirement of "close reading"' (1981, 3). It is in particular the analytical *methods* of the New Criticism which are perhaps its most valuable gift to its successors: even a Marxist literary critic today will ignore the need for close attention to textual detail at his or her peril, and it seems impossible for us to return to the sort of criticism whose inadequacies brought the New Criticism into being.

It should be noted that the French term *nouvelle critique* is not to be confused with the New Criticism, although it is sometimes rendered into English as the (French) New Criticism. It was brought to the attention of a larger public through a polemical attack on Roland Barthes's book *Sur Racine* (1963) entitled *Nouvelle critique ou nouvelle imposture?*, written by Raymond Picard and published in 1965. *Nouvelle critique* was a term Picard adopted from the critics he was attacking (Barthes served as the main focus of his rage), and which he attempted to turn against them. Picard represented a highly conservative form of criticism, and he saw the work of critics such as Barthes, Lucien Goldmann, Georges Poulet, Jean Starobinski and Jean-Pierre Richard as a threat to the fundamental values of scholarly criticism. (It is worth noting in passing that it is only from the extremely traditionalist standpoint occupied by Picard that it is possible to lump the named individuals so unproblematically together.) Picard attacked Barthes in particular for failing to enter into the author's (Racine's) intention, of relying upon illegitimate psychoanalyses, of dragging in sexuality everywhere in his discussion of Racine – and so on. (For a full discussion of Picard's attack, and of the *nouvelle critique* in general, see Doubrovsky: 1973.)

See also AESTHETIC; COHERENCE; FUNCTIONALIST CRITICISM.

New Historicism and cultural materialism Victor Shea has pointed out that Wesley Morris used the term 'New Historicism' in 1972 'to designate a mode of literary criticism derived from German historicists such as Leopold von Ranke and Wilhelm Dilthey, and American historians such as Vernon L. Parrington and Van Wyck Brooks' (1993, 124). Kiernan Ryan has suggested that the term is foreshadowed even earlier, in the title of Roy Harvey Pearce's 1969 book, *Historicism Once More*, but he concedes that 'it is Stephen Greenblatt who gets the credit for slipping the term into circulation in its current sense in his Introduction to "The Forms of Power and the Power of Forms in the Renaissance", a special issue of *Genre* (15 1–2 [1982]) devoted to what was already billed as a fresh departure in critical practice' (Ryan: 1996, xiii).

Nowadays the term is restricted to this later usage stemming from Greenblatt, and describing groupings of critics and theorists who have rejected the synchronic approaches to CULTURE and literature associated with STRUCTURALISM and who have attempted to provide more adequate answers to various problems associated with the tensions between aesthetic, cultural, and historical approaches to the study of a range of different sorts of TEXT.

Most of those known as New Historicists (some of whom have gone on record with their preference for the term 'cultural poetics') are from North America, while cultural materialism is by and large a British phenomenon. On occasions, however, New Historicism is used as an umbrella term to include members of both groupings.

The writings of Michel Foucault and Raymond Williams constitute a major influence on the New Historicists, who have succeeded in defining (or suggesting) new objects of historical study, with a particular emphasis upon the way in which causal influences are mediated through discursive practices (see the entry for DISCOURSE).

Stephen J. Greenblatt is certainly a key figure in the rise of the New Historicism, and in his collection of essays *Learning to Curse* (1990) he admits that for him the term describes not so much a set of beliefs as 'a trajectory that led from American literary formalism through the political and theoretical ferment of the 1970s to a fascination with what one of the best new historicist critics [Louis A. Montrose] calls "the historicity of texts and the textuality of history" ' (1990, 3). Elsewhere he describes the New Historicism as a practice rather than a doctrine (1990, 146). Greenblatt sees the New Historicism's creation of 'an intensified willingness to read all of the textual traces of the past with the attention traditionally conferred only on literary texts' (1990, 14) to be central to its value. Thus in a study of a design by Dürer for a monument to commemorate the defeat of peasants involved in protest and rebellion, Greenblatt notes that intention, genre and historical situation all have to be taken into account, as all are social and IDEOLOGICAL and must be involved in any 'reading' of the design (1990, 112). He continues:

> The production and consumption of such works are not unitary to begin with; they always involve a multiplicity of interests, however well organized, for the crucial reason that art is social and hence presumes more than one consciousness. And in response to the art of the past, we inevitably register, whether we wish to or not, the shifts in value and interest that are produced in the struggles of social and political life. (1990, 112)

The New Historicist, in other words, has as much to say about the READING of texts as about their composition.

For those who like negative definitions, Greenblatt cites three definitions of the word 'historicism' from *The American Heritage Dictionary*, all of which he sees to be counter to the practice of New Historicists:

1. The belief that processes are at work in history that man can do little to alter.
2. The theory that the historian must avoid all value judgments in his study of past periods or former cultures.
3. Veneration of the past or of tradition. (Quoted in Greenblatt: 1990, 164)

Although Greenblatt and other New Historicists pay tribute to the work of various POST-STRUCTURALISTS, the anti-formalist element in their work clearly distances them from important aspects of post-structuralism.

The term 'historicist' is sometimes used in a pejorative sense which is unconnected with New Historicism. Historicist in this sense implies the view that human, social or cultural characteristics are determined in an absolute sense by historical situation; historicism in this sense is thus a form of REDUCTIONISM as the human, the social and the cultural are collapsed back into the historical. Thus the title of an essay by Louis Althusser, 'Marxism is not a historicism', rests on such a definition of historicism (the essay is included in Althusser and Balibar: 1977).

Graham Holderness has produced a useful checklist of what he considers to be the differences between the (mainly British) cultural materialism and the (mainly North American) New Historicism. According to him, cultural materialism

> is much more concerned to engage with contemporary cultural practice, whereas New Historicism confines its focus of attention to the past; cultural materialism can be overtly, even stridently, polemical about its political implications, where New Historicism tends to efface them. Cultural materialism partly derives its theory and method from the kind of cultural criticism exemplified by Raymond Williams, and through that inheritance stretches its roots into the British tradition of Marxist cultural analysis, and thence into the wider movement for socialist education and emancipation; New Historicism has no sense of a corresponding political legacy, and takes its intellectual bearings directly from 'post-structuralist' theoretical and philosophical models. . . . Cultural materialism accepts as appropriate objects of enquiry a very wide range of 'textual' materials [. . . whereas] New Historicism concerns itself principally with a narrower definition of the 'textual': with what has been *written* . . . (1991, 157)

Clearly, then, both terms denote relatively loosely defined schools which approach literary (or other) TEXTS contextually.

Faith Nostbakken has pointed out that the term 'cultural materialism' emerges independently in two different academic contexts. As she explains, 'Marvin Harris applied the name "cultural materialism" to a scientific method of studying the interaction between social life and material conditions (*The Rise of Anthropological Theory* 1968)' (1993, 21). In Literary Studies, however, the term has a rather different ancestry from this, as it owes not just its theory and method to Raymond Williams, but also its name. In his essay 'Notes on Marxism in Britain since 1945', Williams gives an interesting account of the intellectual journey which culminated in cultural materialism for him.

> It took me thirty years, in a very complex process, to move from that received Marxist theory [= cultural theory from Engels and through Plekhanov, Fox, Caudwell, West, and also Zdhanov, *J. H.*] (which in its most general form I began by accepting) through various transitional forms of theory and inquiry, to the position I now hold, which I define as 'cultural materialism'. The emphases of the transition – on the production (rather than only the reproduction) of meanings and values by specific social formations, on the centrality of language and communication as

formative social forces, and on the complex interaction both of institutions and forms and of social relationships and formal conventions – may be defined, if anyone wishes, as 'culturism', and even the old (positivist) idealism/materialism dichotomy may be applied if it helps anyone. What I would now claim to have reached, but not necessarily by this route, is a theory of culture as a (social and material) productive process and of specific practices, of 'arts', as social uses of material means of production (from language as material 'practical consciousness' to the specific technologies of writing and forms of writing, through to mechanical and electronic communication systems). (1980, 243)

If the model presented here is one of the relatively gentle evolution of cultural materialism from Marxism, elsewhere Williams suggests that more of a sharp break took place.

What is actually latent in historical materialism is not, in Lukács's categorical sense, a theory of art, but a way of understanding the diverse social and material production (necessarily often by individuals within actual relationships) of works to which the connected but also changing categories of art have been historically applied. I call this position cultural materialism, and I see it as a diametrically opposite answer to the questions which Lukács and other Marxists have posed. (1989, 273)

Cultural materialism's relations with Marxism today are by no means simple or uniform, however, and many cultural materialists would distance themselves from the position(s) of theorists such as Lukács less forcefully than does Williams. John Higgins has commented that in Williams's work cultural materialism looks two ways: 'As *cultural* materialism, it is the name Williams gave to his distinctive version of Marxist theory, but, as cultural *materialism*, it refers to his response to the theory and practice of literary analysis at work in the existing institutions of English studies' (1999, 125). Put another way: the word *culture* represents a challenge to traditional Marxists, whereas the word *materialism* represents a challenge to the apolitical tradition of English literary criticism.

Much that Williams puts forward in the former of the two quotations given above has entered into cultural materialist orthodoxy. What Williams does not mention overtly, though, is the now-typical cultural materialist insistence upon situating cultural artifacts and art-works in the varied and successive contexts of their 'consumption' or interactive enjoyment. Thus according to Alan Sinfield, the 'rough programme' of cultural materialism involves the placing of a text in its (plural) contexts: 'a strategy [which] repudiates the supposed transcendence of literature, seeking rather to understand it as a cultural intervention produced initially within a specific set of practices and tending to render persuasive a view of reality; and seeing it also as re-produced subsequently in other historical conditions in the service of various views of reality, through other practices, including those of modern literary study' (1992, 22).

In his book *Shakespeare Recycled* (1992), Graham Holderness suggests that the New Historicists have preferred to 'reproduce a model of historical culture in which dissent is always already suppressed, subversion always previously contained, and opposition always strategically anticipated, controlled and defeated' (1992, 34). By implication, therefore, the cultural materialists see a culture far more as a battlefield: riven with struggles, tensions, and contradictions on a number of different planes. Alan Sinfield, the title of whose important cultural-materialist book *Faultlines: Cultural Materialism and the Politics of Dissident Reading* (1992) is itself indicative of this view, agrees with Holderness in tracing this crucial difference back to the work of Raymond Williams: 'Much of the importance of Raymond Williams derives from the fact that at a time when Althusser and Foucault were being read in some quarters as establishing ideology and/or power in a necessarily unbreakable continuum, Williams argued the co-occurrence of subordinate, residual, emergent, alternative, and oppositional cultural forces alongside the dominant, in varying relations of incorporation, negotiation, and resistance' (1992, 9). Thus while we can picture the New Historicist standing safely on the shore and gazing at the sea of history (at least this is how the cultural materialist sees the matter), the cultural materialist believes that his or her head is already under water, that a historical approach requires that the investigator take full account of his or her historical location and of the historical life of literary WORKS (including their life in the present time of the investigator), not just the historical situation of the work's creation and composition. It should be added that although a New Historicist such as Greenblatt has also acknowledged an important intellectual debt to the work of Raymond Williams, this debt has (at least according to the cultural materialists) carried with it less of a political imperative than it has for the cultural materialists.

A good example of such a cultural materialist approach, then, would be Holderness's chapter on E. M. W. Tillyard's *Shakespeare's History Plays* (1944) in his *Shakespeare Recycled*. Holderness suggests that this and other works all 'derive from a common problematic: the ideological crisis of British nationalism precipitated by the events of the 1930s and 1940s: the Depression, the crisis of Empire and particularly of course the Second World War' (1992, 22). He implies, too, that the continued life of such criticism can be understood only in the context of continued ideological crisis and struggle. One could say that for the cultural materialist the focus of study is not the text, but the birth and life of the text in culture and history.

The following scholars have been associated with New Historicism: Stephen Greenblatt, Louis Montrose, Jonathan Goldberg, Leonard Tennenhouse, Stephen Mullaney, and Hayden White. The best-known cultural materialists are Jonathan Dollimore, Alan Sinfield, Lisa Jardine, Graham Holderness, Catherine Belsey, and Francis Barker.

See also CHIASMUS; CIRCULATION; EMPLOTMENT; EXCHANGE; NEGOTIATION; RESONANCE.

New Readers Coined by M. H. Abrams and used during the earlier days of debate about POST-STRUCTURALISM and DECONSTRUCTION to refer to such individuals as Jacques Derrida, Stanley Fish, and Harold Bloom – and their followers.

Nomad Chapter 12 of *A Thousand Plateaus: Capitalism and Schizophrenia* by Gilles Deleuze and Félix Guattari is entitled '1227: Treatise on Nomadology – the War Machine'. For Deleuze and Guattari the nomads are of interest because the war machine is their invention, and because nomadic existence 'necessarily effectuates the conditions of the war machine in space' (1988, 380). They continue:

> The life of the nomad is the intermezzo. Even the elements of his dwelling are conceived in terms of the trajectory that is for ever mobilizing them. The nomad is not at all the same as the migrant; for the migrant goes principally from one point to another, even if the second is uncertain, unforeseen, or not well localized. But the nomad goes from point to point only as a consequence and as a factual necessity; in principle, points for him are relays along a trajectory. (1988, 380)

For Deleuze and Guattari nomads are 'vectors of deterritorialization' (1988, 382), and nomad space 'lies between two striated spaces: that of the forest . . . and that of agriculture' (1988, 384). The nomad thus enters the paradoxical position of being in the fashionable category of falling between categories. The POSTMODERNIST interest in boundaries and MARGINS in a more abstract sense, and the POSTCOLONIALIST interest in actual geographical/political boundaries and of the gaps and divisions they generate in the minds of human beings have both ensured that the nomad has suddenly become chic.

That would be to express the matter in a negative manner. Taking a less jaundiced view one can say that the concept of nomadity has generally been used metaphorically rather than literally so as to underwrite and valorize flexible and shifting modes of thought and habits of categorization. Thus Deleuze and Guattari's 'deterritorialization' can be seen as advocating an abandonment of that 'native earth' that carries with it NATURALIZED opinions and habitual modes of thought.

Clearly the nomadic offers an alternative to the HYBRID; both respond to the contradictory claims of rival cultural, political or ideological power-centres, but one responds by movement betwixt and between, to and fro, while the other responds in terms of MIMICRY and mixing, disguises and camouflages.

A number of FEMINIST critics have found *nomad* and *hybrid* to present interesting possibilities, both in terms of potential goals and in terms of the description of existing female experience. Take the following comment from Rosi Braidotti's 1994 book *Nomadic Subjects*: 'The starting point, for my scheme of feminist nomadism, is that feminist theory is not only a movement of critical opposition of the false universality of the subject, it is also the positive affirmation of women's desire to affirm and enact different forms of subjectivity' (in Mary Eagleton: 1996, 411). Lynne Pearce quotes from Robert Stam's *Subversive Pleasures: Bakhtin, Cultural Criticism, and Film*, in which he refers to the title character from Woody Allen's film *Zelig* who, he suggests, 'exemplifies the contemporary condition of what Lawrence Grossberg has called "nomadic subjectivity"'. Further, the self 'in this sense, forms a kind of shifting hybrid sum of its discursive practices' (Pearce: 1994, 98, quoting from Stam: 1989, 214). The bringing together of 'nomadic' and 'hybrid' in the space of two sentences is clearly not fortuitous. It is also worthy of note that in his following sentence Stam goes on to refer to Bakhtin's concept of ASSIMILATION.

See also ROOT/RADICLE/RHIZOME; SCHIZOANALYSIS.

Nominalism According to the *OED*, the doctrine that universals or abstract concepts are mere names. In current theoretical usage, the belief that names signify nothing fixed or consistent. Linda Alcoff (1988) links the revived interest in the term with POST-STRUCTURALIST theories of linguistic non-referentiality:

[T]he post-structuralist's view results in what I shall call nominalism: the idea that the category 'woman' is a fiction and that feminist efforts must be directed towards dismantling this fiction. 'Perhaps . . . "woman" is not a determinable identity. Perhaps woman is not some thing which announces itself from a distance, at a distance from some other thing. . . . Perhaps woman – a non-identity, non-figure, a simulacrum – is distance's very chasm, the out-distancing of distance, the interval's cadence, distance itself.' (In Mary Eagleton: 1996, 378; the quotation is from Jacques Derrida: 1978b, 49)

Norm According to Jan Mukařovský, the basic prerequisite for an aesthetic norm is not its statability, 'but the general consensus, the spontaneous agreement, of the members of a certain community that a given esthetic procedure is desirable and not another' (1964, 44). Clearly this can be generalized: *all* norms and not just aesthetic ones, are characterized, in their own sphere, by general consensus and spontaneous agreement rather than by an agreed statement or formulation. Members of the PRAGUE SCHOOL such as Mukařovský thus use *norm* in a manner which is very close to 'CONVENTION'; certainly Mukařovský's account of the way in which breaking norms involves DEFAMILIARIZATION, is very close to Roman Jakobson's (1971a) account of the way in which too rigidified a system of conventions leads to AUTOMATIZATION of response.

Felix Vodička suggests that the literary critic needs to reconstruct the relevant literary norms in order to READ a work of literature written in a context in which norms different from those of his or her own culture flourish. He argues that the norms are contained, 'in the literature itself, that is, in the works that are being read and liked, and by which are measured and evaluated new, or additional, literary works' (1964, 74). He adds, further, that normative poetics or literary theories allow us to know only the rules which a period believes *should* guide literary composition. Thus for him, the richest source of evidence for literary norms is to be found in evaluative statements about contemporary literature. Vodička does not consider literary norms to be totally isolated from contemporaneous, non-literary norms, but sees these two fields in interactive relationship (1964, 75).

The *normative fallacy*, according to Pierre Macherey, is apparent when criticism attempts to modify a literary WORK in order that it may be more thoroughly assimilated, 'denying its factual reality as being merely the provisional version of an unfulfilled intention'. For Macherey, the normative fallacy is a variety of a more fundamental fallacy, the *empiricist fallacy*, which we witness whenever criticism 'asks only how to *receive* a given object' (1978, 19).

Normative fallacy See NORM

Nouvelle critique See NEW CRITICISM

Nucleus See EVENT

O

Object-relations theory/criticism According to Nancy Chodorow:

> Object-relations theory, rooting itself in the clinical, requires by definition attention to the historically situated engagement with others as subjects, an attention to the processes of transference and counter-transference that constitute the clinical situation and do so by bringing each person's relational history to it. This theory argues, through clinical example, that people are fundamentally social, even that there is a fundamental social 'need'. (1989, 148)

The theory is post-Freudian to the extent that its proponents feel a need to re-emphasize that concern with object-relations which, it is claimed, is to be found in Freud's work but that has subsequently been denied or ignored. It should be clear that the emphasis upon SUBJECT construction through social relations rather than as a result of instinctual drives and forces is also un-Freudian.

The objects in object-relations theory are those with which the human infant engages during its first year of life, a year in which mother-child relations are of paramount importance. A key figure in the theorizing of the infant's object-world is Melanie Klein, to whose work object-relations theory is largely indebted. Klein argues that

> [t]he development of the infant is governed by the mechanisms of introjection and projection. From the beginning the ego introjects objects 'good' and 'bad', for both of which the mother's breast is the prototype – for good objects when the child obtains it, for bad ones when it fails him. But it is because the baby projects its own aggression on to these objects that it feels them to be 'bad' and not only in that they frustrate its desires: the child conceives of them as actually dangerous – persecutors who it feels will devour it, scoop out the inside of its body, cut it to pieces, poison it – in short, compassing its destruction by all the means which sadism can devise. (1988, 262)

Object-relations theory has been of particular interest to FEMINISTS as it has offered an alternative to such posited Freudian universals as penis-envy and the castration complex; Melanie Klein's work suggests an initial delight in the female on the part of both male and female infants, and her concentration on mother-child bonds has also been of great significance to object-relations criticism, particularly in its tracing of female-female relations in literary works. Also important has been its provision of a model for the internalization and objectification of interpersonal relationships.

Carole-Anne Tyler has volunteered the criticism that '[o]bject-relations theorists assume masculinity and femininity are there from the start, rather than produced through the resolution of the castration complex and the separation from the mother in which it results' (1991, 49).

Lynne Pearce has perceived a DIALOGIC element in the emphasis placed by object-relations theorists upon the intersubjective nature of subject acquisition, 'and on the social contextualization of any such exchange' (1994, 90). Pearce also draws attention to Nancy Chodorow's point that 'since each child's (male or female) primary attachment is to the mother, boy children will find the process of individuation easier because it is based upon *difference*' (Pearce: 1994, 90).

Some literary critics associated with object-relations theory are Elizabeth Abel, Joan Lidoff, Marianne Hirsch, and Margaret Homans.

Objet a/Objet A   Otherwise *Objet petit a/Objet grand A*. Coinages of Jacques Lacan. According to Lacan's translator Alan Sheridan, Lacan insisted that these terms should not be translated and refused to comment on them, 'leaving the reader to develop an appreciation of the concepts in the course of their use'. Sheridan does provide the information that the little 'a' stands for *autre* or OTHER, a concept developed out of the Freudian 'object', and that 'the "*petit a*" (small "a") differentiates the object from (while relating it to) the "*Autre*" or "*grand Autre*" (the capitalized "Other")' (Lacan:1977, xi). For Lacan,

> [t]he *object a* is something from which the subject, in order to constitute itself, has separated itself off as organ. This serves as a symbol of the lack, that is to say, of the phallus, not as such, but in so far as it is lacking. It must, therefore, be an object that is, firstly, separable and, secondly, that has some relation to the lack. (1979, 103)

According to Ellie Ragland-Sullivan, 'the *objet a* is any filler of a void in being, which, because of its indispensable function in filling up that void, quickly provides a consistency, palpable in repetitions' (Ragland-Sullivan: 1992a, 58). In another context she adds that the '*objet a* – a plus value or excess in *jouissance* – enters the fantasy as "*the object which causes the desire of a subject and limits its jouissance*"' (Ragland-Sullivan: 1992b, 175; the quotation is from Brousse: 1987, 116; for JOUISSANCE, see the separate entry.)

A rather fuller definition is provided by Martin Jay, who explains that the *objet a*

> was Lacan's term for the object of lack or the missing object that will seemingly satisfy the drive for plenitude, 'a' being the first letter of the French word for 'other' (*l'autrui*). At its most fundamental level, it is the phallus which the child (of whatever sex, according to Lacan) wishes to be in order to make up for the mother's alleged lack, her apparent castration. It can then be transformed into the Symbolic register as the metonymic object of desire which motivates the split subject's interminable search for a unity it can never achieve. But it operates as well in the realm of the Imaginary, where 'the object on which depends the phantasy form from which the object is suspended in an essential vacillation is the gaze .... From the moment that this gaze appears, the subject tries to adapt himself to it, he becomes

that punctiform object, that point of vanishing being with which the subject confuses his own failure.' (1993, 361)

Slavoj Žižek, writing about Alfred Hitchcock's term the *McGuffin* (that plot device consisting of a puzzle that intrigues the audience and moves the action along, but which is essentially of little importance and is generally forgotten by the end of the film), has suggested (apparently seriously) that the McGuffin 'is clearly the *objet petit a*, a gap in the centre of the symbolic order – the lack, the void of the Real setting in motion the symbolic movement of interpretation, a pure semblance of the Mystery to be explained, interpreted' (1992, 8).

For other terms mentioned above, see the entries for GAZE and PHALLOCENTRISM (phallus).

Obstination According to Monika Fludernik, Paul Ricoeur's translation of a term used by Harald Weinrich to indicate the READER's tendency to continue to frame a passage of NARRATIVE in a consistent manner (e.g. as FREE INDIRECT DISCOURSE) unless prompted by TEXTUAL or contextual features to shift to a new frame.

See also the comments on frame-shifting in the entry for FRAME, and those on the movement between different systems postulated by *polysystem theory* (entry for SYSTEM).

Ontological status Ontology is that branch of metaphysics concerned with the essence of things or with their level or state of being, and so to discuss the ontological status of something is to discuss to which level of reality or type of existence it belongs.

So far as the discussion of literary WORKS is concerned, this bears most frequently on those things – CHARACTERS, places, actions – which are in some sense referred to in literary works. What sort of existence do they have? Can a literary work refer to things that exist in the real world? To what level of reality does a literary character such as David Copperfield belong?

Opalescence See FLICKER

Opaque and transparent criticism Terms coined by A. D. Nuttall in his *A New Mimesis* to distinguish what he terms two languages of criticism: 'the first "opaque", external, formalist, operating outside the mechanisms of art and taking those mechanisms as object, the second "transparent", internal, realist, operating within the "world" presented in the work' (1983, 80). Thus a statement such as 'In the opening of *King Lear* folk-tale elements proper to narrative are infiltrated by a finer-grained dramatic mode' involves the use of opaque critical language, whereas 'Cordelia cannot bear to have her love for her father made the subject of a partly mercenary game' involves the use of transparent critical language (Nuttall's own examples).

In an article about the meanings of TV documentary John Corner and Kay Richardson suggest a pair of comparable terms: *mediation reading* and *transparency reading*. A mediation reading is one in which the READER is conscious of the intention or motivation behind what is being read, whereas a transparency reading is one in which 'comments are made about the depicted world as if it had been directly perceived reality' (Corner and Richardson: 1986, 149).

For the use of *transparent* in FEMINIST discussion, see RECRUITIST.

Open and closed texts The theorist who has done most to popularize the idea that TEXTS can be either open or closed is Umberto Eco. His formulation is, however, quite complex, and he defines 'open' and 'closed' in rather unexpected ways. As a result, the terms are often used in a sense that is the reverse of what he recommends.

The problem is very clear in the following discussion by Eco of texts such as Superman comic strips and novels by Ian Fleming (the creator of 'James Bond'). For Eco, such texts are closed precisely because they are open to any sort of READING:

> Those texts that obsessively aim at arousing a precise response on the part of more or less precise empirical readers . . . are in fact open to any possible 'aberrant' decoding. A text so immoderately 'open' to every possible interpretation will be called a *closed* one. (1981, 8)

In contrast, where the AUTHOR of the text has envisaged the role of the READER at the moment of generation, according to Eco the text is, paradoxically, open to successive INTERPRETATIONS. These interpretations and reinterpretations, according to Eco, echo one another, and operate within certain textually imposed constraints (unlike responses to what he calls closed texts): 'You cannot use the [open] text as you want, but only as the text wants you to use it. An open text, however "open" it be, cannot afford whatever interpretation' (1981, 19). At the root of Eco's argument here lies a relatively traditional belief in the possibility of distinguishing between correct and incorrect interpretations of a certain sort of valued text: 'it is possible to distinguish between the free interpretative choices elicited by a purposeful strategy of openness and the freedom taken by a reader with a text assumed as a mere stimulus' (1981, 40).

The theory thus depends upon two sorts of distinction: between different sorts of texts, and between different sorts of response to, or interpretation of, texts. As I have said, there are strongly traditional elements here in spite of the new terminology, and indeed, at one point in his essay 'The Poetics of the Open Work' Eco stops talking about *texts* and refers to *works of art*:

> A work of art, therefore, is a complete and *closed* form in its uniqueness as a balanced organic whole, while at the same time constituting an *open* product on account of its susceptibility to countless different interpretations which do not impinge on its unadulterable specificity. Hence every reception of a work of art is both an *interpretation* and a *performance* of it, because in every reception the work takes on a fresh perspective for itself. (1981, 49; compare the entry for PERFORMANCE)

For Eco, open texts, works of art, are thus *in movement*, another coinage of his by which he seeks to describe their power to generate a never-ending series of new but valid reading experiences and interpretations.

245

Oppositional reading

Eco's discussion is thought-provoking and fruitful, but the complexities of a terminology that requires us to remember that a closed text is open to any sort of response and that an open text constrains what the reader does to it, have ensured that his suggested definitions have not obtained wider popularity – even though the terms *open* and *closed* are regularly and loosely used in discussions of literary and other texts.

Beyond this, it may be that the suggested distinction between these two sorts of text is perhaps too absolute, that *all* texts attempt to constrain how the reader makes use of them, and that all readings may choose to accept such constraints to a greater or a lesser extent.

See also FORMULAIC LITERATURE; READERLY AND WRITERLY TEXTS.

Opponent See ACT/ACTOR

Oppositional reading A reading which rejects and seeks to undermine the terms overtly or implicitly proposed by a given TEXT for acceptance by the READER prior to and during its own reading. Thus an oppositional reading of Mark Twain's *Huckleberry Finn* might consciously seek to read the closing section dealing with the boys' treatment of 'Nigger Jim' in a way that the text tries to exclude: as an attempt to conciliate those racist views which the novel has earlier attacked. An oppositional reading of Henry James's *The Turn of the Screw* might view this text as reflective of STEREOTYPED views of women as hysterical, unreliable, mysterious, corrupted by repressed passion, and so on.

The term 'hermeneutics of suspicion', which is associated with Paul Ricoeur, denotes a very similar process, although it lays more stress on interpretation than on the reading process and focuses attention on the unsaid rather than the said. (Compare the entry for ABSENCE.)

See also AGAINST THE GRAIN; HERMENEUTICS; INTERPRETATION; INTERROGATE.

Optimal reader See READERS AND READING

Orality A term used to denote an extended complex of elements associated with oral CULTURES – that is, cultures either unaffected by literacy and the written word or only marginally affected by them. One of the most influential (and accessible) theoretical contributions to the study of orality is Walter J. Ong's *Orality and Literacy* (1982), in which Ong argues that in a predominantly oral culture thought differs from the thought typical of a culture characterized by universal or near-universal literacy. The thought and expression of an oral culture, according to Ong, are *additive rather than subordinative, aggregative rather than analytic, redundant or 'copious', conservative or traditionalist, close to the human lifeworld, agonistically toned* (that is, polemical and emotive), *empathetic and participatory rather than objectively distanced, homeostatic,* and *situational rather than abstract* (1982, 37–57). Following Ong, a distinction is sometimes made between primary orality (orality in pre-literate societies) and secondary orality (orality in literate societies in which new technologies reintroduce forms of orality).

Ong's arguments have not gone unchallenged, and there is a growing literature concerned with debates around the concept of orality. These are of relevance to Literary Studies in a number of ways. For example: it seems clear that poetry emerged in an oral

246

culture, and that some of its inherited characteristics owe something to the thought patterns of an oral culture. Understanding more about an oral culture may help us to understand more about the poetry of both the distant past and also of more recent periods.

See also ORATURE.

Orature By extrapolation from *literature*: a body of works of art transmitted in oral rather than written form and stored in memory rather than in writing, along with the conventions and techniques associated with oral transmission and memorial storage.

See also ORALITY.

Orchestration In the work of Mikhail Bakhtin, part of an analogy between musical and novelistic STRUCTURE (see also POLYPHONIC). The varied VOICES active in a given CULTURE at a given time can be orchestrated so as to reveal different aspects alone and in harmony/disharmony with one another.

Order Both the temporal succession of events in a STORY and also the placing in linear succession of EVENTS in a NARRATIVE.

See also ACHRONY; ANACHRONY; ANALEPSIS; PROLEPSIS.

Organic intellectuals See INTELLECTUALS

Organicism In literary criticism, particularly during the heyday of the NEW CRITICS, it came to be an item of faith that the work of literature (or art) had to be treated as an *organic* STRUCTURE – that is, having the qualities of a living unit with its parts organically rather than mechanically related.

During the same time F. R. Leavis extended the analogy from the individual literary work to literature as a whole; in his essay 'Literature and Society' he argues that a 'literature . . . must be thought of as essentially something more than a separation of separate works: it has an organic form, or constitutes an organic order, in relation to which the individual writer has his significance and his being' (1962a, 184). Leavis goes on to argue that this approach is to be distinguished from that of the MARXIST, in that it stresses not economic and material determinants but intellectual and spiritual ones, and that although it accepts that material conditions have an enormous importance, 'there is a certain measure of spiritual autonomy in human affairs' (1962a, 184). Leavis also made much of the concept of 'the organic community', most notably in *Culture and Environment* which was written with Denys Thompson and first published in 1933, although directly comparable ideas can be found in the essay 'Literature and Society' (and in many other places in Leavis's writing) as well. The conservative-nostalgic concept of the organic community in Leavis's work owes much to T. S. Eliot. It represents a lost unity in sharp contrast to the alleged disintegration and divisions of modern urban society, a unity both among human beings and between human beings and their environment, in which a CULTURE shared by all the community's members and interwoven with the realities of their daily lives could be found.

It is necessary to fill in this historical sketch of earlier usages of *organic* because it is in reaction to these that a more recent usage is based. Representative is a discussion by Christopher Hampton of the passage quoted above from Leavis's 'Literature and

Orientalism

Society'. Hampton's objection to Leavis's position centres upon the fact that as a result of the terms he uses, 'history vanishes; and with it the influence of the changing conditions of material existence which determine not only the ways in which people's lives are shaped but also the cultural products of their thinking, including literature' (1990, 50). Hampton's critique is sharper and less conciliatory than that of others – notably Raymond Williams in a number of his studies – but it sums up a particular sort of reaction against certain of Leavis's ideas. And in so doing it also sums up what is meant by the current, pejorative use of the term *organicist*: viewing either literature, or art, or culture, or social life as organic unities superior to material or economic determinants and untroubled by inner fissures, dissent, or tension.

Orientalism A term given new meaning by Edward Said in his highly influential study of the same name (1979; first published 1978). Traditionally, an Orientalist was a scholar devoted to the study of 'the Orient' or the East. In this traditional usage the term had positive connotations – devotion to scholarship, a commitment to unearthing the secrets of another CULTURE, and so on.

Said's development of the term attempts to draw out its concealed political allegiances – the fact that Orientalists were complicit with imperialism and that they effectively provided Europe with 'one of its deepest and most recurring images of the Other' (1979, 1; see the entry for OTHER). This statement suggests a certain Lacanian element in Said's development – or DECONSTRUCTION – of this term, but there are also Foucauldian elements too, in spite of Said's view of Foucault's own EUROCENTRISM (see his essay on Foucault in Said: 1984). The following comment certainly suggests a Foucauldian influence:

> Orientalism can be discussed and analyzed as the corporate institution for dealing with the Orient – dealing with it by making statements about it, authorizing views of it, describing it, by teaching it, settling it, ruling over it: in short, Orientalism as a Western style for dominating, restructuring, and having authority over the Orient.
> . . .
>
> My contention is that without examining Orientalism as a discourse one cannot possibly understand the enormously systematic discipline by which European culture was able to manage – and even produce – the Orient politically, sociologically, militarily, ideologically, scientifically, and imaginatively during the post-Enlightenment period. (1979, 3)

Said makes it clear that he is interested in Orientalism as a set of ideas that are regulated more to achieve internal coherence than to achieve 'any correspondence, or lack thereof, with a "real" Orient' (1979, 5). This is not, however, to say that Orientalism is merely a fantasy with no relationship to the real; Said insists that over many generations it involved 'considerable material investment', and that it serves as a sign of 'European-Atlantic power over the Orient' (1979, 6).

Orientalism is, moreover, 'premissed upon exteriority' according to Said: that is to say, it always involves a non-oriental doing the studying; 'the Orientalist is outside the Orient, both as an existential and as a moral fact' (1979, 20, 21).

Said's views have aroused heated debate and violent rejoinders, many accusing him of simplifications of which a careful reading of *Orientalism* shows him not to be guilty. Whatever one's views, he has certainly succeeded in changing the resonances of the word Orientalism, to the extent that its neutral or innocent use is now very difficult.

See also the entry for WEST.

Ostension According to Umberto Eco, in his 1977 article 'Semiotics of Theatrical Performance':

> Ostension is one of the various ways of signifying, consisting in de-realizing a given object in order to make it stand for an entire class. But ostension is, at the same time, the most basic instance of performance.
>
> You ask me, 'How should I be dressed for the party this evening?' If I answer by showing my tie framed by my jacket and say, 'Like this, more or less', I am signifying by ostension. (Walder: 1990, 117)

Other To characterize a person, group, or institution as 'other' is to place them outside the system of normality or CONVENTION to which one belongs oneself. Such an activity is referred to by some theorists by means of a verb form: *othering*. Processes of exclusion by categorization are central to certain IDEOLOGICAL mechanisms. If woman is other, then that which is particular to the experience of being a woman is irrelevant to 'how things are', to the defining conventions by which one lives. If members of a given racial group are collectively seen as other, then how they are treated is irrelevant to what humanity demands – because they are other and not human.

What lies behind use of this term is the perception that when we divide up reality into separate components these are typically seen in a sort of FIGURE/GROUND manner, with one component representing a norm and other components representing divergences from this norm.

When granted a capital letter the term invokes Jacques Lacan's theory of the way in which the SUBJECT seeks confirmation of itself in the response of the Other. As he puts it in one of his less opaque pronouncements in 'The Agency of the Letter in the Unconscious or Reason Since Freud',

> If I have said that the unconscious is the discourse of the Other (with a capital O), it is in order to indicate the beyond in which the recognition of desire is bound up with the desire for recognition.
>
> In other words this other is the Other that even my lie invokes as a guarantor of the truth in which it subsists. (1977, 172)

Also illuminating is Lacan's comment in 'On a Question Preliminary to any Possible Treatment of Psychosis', that the Other is, 'the locus from which the question of [the subject's] existence may be presented to him' (1977, 194).

According to Anthony Wilden,

> Lacan's Other represents the patrocentric ideology of our culture. The Other is only theoretically *ne-uter*, for it is not pure 'Otherness'. It is the principle of the locus of

> language and of the signifier, which for Lacan, is naturally the phallus . . . (1972, 261)

Without its capital letter, 'other' in Lacan's usage designates the other, imaginary self, which is first formed during the MIRROR STAGE when the infant confronts his or her own reflected image.

A recent coinage is that of the M/Other, often in the term 'the phallic M/Other'. As the formulation suggests, we are here dealing with a situation in which a child's or individual's mother represents the threatening Other, often by virtue of her allegedly having assumed PATRIARCHAL power or authority and having thus become a PHALLIC figure.

Lynne Pearce's term *textual other* she defines as

> whoever or whatever causes us to engage with a text in a manner that is *beyond the will-to-interpretation*. It is what, in terms of my own metaphorical conceit, causes us to both 'fall in love', and endure the sequel of our falling, in what is often an incredibly intense roller-coaster of emotional experience. (1997, 20)

See also AGAINST THE GRAIN (contrapuntal reading); *DIFFÉREND*; *OBJET A/OBJET A*; STEREOTYPE.

Outing No longer exclusively something recreative and innocent involving a tour of picturesque scenery, but also the act of revealing a person's (normally non-heterosexual) GENDER identity against their will. From the metaphor of 'coming out of the closet', meaning abandoning the pretence of heterosexuality and declaring one's homosexuality. Diana Fuss cites Michelangelo Signorile's report that the use of *outing* in its new sense was initiated by *Time* magazine (Fuss:1991, 9 n11).

By extension, *literary outing* thus involves revealing or arguing that a particular writer or literary CHARACTER was or is homosexual or bisexual. Given that much if not most literature has been written at times and in cultures hostile to what was typically characterized as 'sexual deviance', it is clear that openness on such matters has rarely been easy, and that much reference to homosexuality or bisexuality in literature and by writers has necessarily been covert or coded.

See FAGHAG/FAGSTAG CHARACTER; PASSING; QUEER THEORY.

Overcoding See CODE

Overdetermination From the work of Sigmund Freud: if a symbol is the result of several separate or related causes then it is described as overdetermined. Freud saw the dream symbol as overdetermined because its full explanation could not involve merely one source or MEANING but had to take account of several interrelated sources and meanings. Writing of one of his own dreams, Freud suggests that certain elements are to be seen as 'nodal points' 'upon which a great number of dream-thoughts converged, and [which] had several meanings in connection with the interpretation of the dream' (1976, 388). In the same passage, however, Freud goes on to suggest a slightly different meaning for the term: 'each of the elements of the dream's content turns out to have been "overdetermined" – to have been represented in the dream-thoughts many times over' (1976, 388–9).

It is with the former sense of 'many determining forces fused into one resultant symbol (or event, or state of affairs)' that the term has entered into more general currency, however. A clear implication is that if something is overdetermined, then its ANALYSIS and explication will require a sort of exploding into component parts or sources: the commentary will be much longer than the symbol because the symbol is so concentrated. Both dream analyses and analyses of poetic symbols are invariably much more extensive than the symbols themselves.

The term achieved some fashionability in the 1960s following its use by the French Marxist philosopher Louis Althusser in his essay 'Contradiction and Overdetermination' (in Althusser: 1969, 87–128). The use ushered in by Althusser was more historico-political: a range of different social forces could result in a single, overdetermined event such as a political revolution. According to Althusser, he was 'not particularly taken' by the term, but used it 'in the absence of anything better, both as an *index* and as a *problem*, and also because it enables us to see clearly why we are dealing with something *quite different from the Hegelian contradiction*' (1969, 101). What Althusser seems most concerned with here is to use the concept as a means of arguing against a crude economic determinism; as he argues,

> [overdetermination] is *universal*; the economic dialectic is never active *in the pure state*; in History, these instances, the superstructures etc. – are never seen to step respectfully aside when their work is done or, when the Time comes, as his pure phenomena, to scatter before His Majesty the Economy as he strides along the royal road of the Dialectic. From the first moment to the last, the lonely hour of the 'last instance' never comes. (1969, 113)

Thus overdetermination as concept served to warn against simplistic cause-and-effect views in a range of disciplines. It reminded the investigator that just as it was unlikely that the analysis of symbol or event could be completed by reference to a single cause, so too a single cause would be unlikely to lead unproblematically to an isolated event. And, moreover, that as overdetermination involved a play of interrelated and opposed forces, the result of this play could be very different from what might be predicted because of the diversions imposed by successive and complex MEDIATIONS. As T. S. Eliot put it: 'History has many cunning passages.' We can compare an earlier comment of Frederick Engels:

> [H]istory is made in such a way that the final result always arises from conflicts between many individual wills, of which each again has been made what it is by a host of particular conditions of life. Thus there are innumerable intersecting forces, an infinite series of parallelograms of forces which give rise to one resultant – the historical event. This may again itself be viewed as the product of a power which works as a whole, *unconsciously* and without volition. For what each individual wills is obstructed by everyone else, and what emerges is something that no one willed. (Marx and Engels: 1962 [1], 489. The comment comes in a letter to J. Bloch, September 1890)

The analysis of literary symbols, unlike that of dream symbols during psychoanalysis, has never focused to such a great extent on *causal* or *genetic* factors. Nevertheless the introduction of the concept of overdetermination to Literary Studies has had the effect of ruling out many crude or simplistic attempts to relate literary WORKS or aspects of literary works to 'origins' in unproblematic ways.

P

Paleofiction FICTION which is set in a prehistoric or primeval world.

Palimpsest text A TEXT in which hidden or repressed meanings can be found between the lines or under the surface. Compare overt and COVERT PLOTS and DOUBLE-VOICED. See also INTERTEXTUALITY.

Pamissa One of five main plot types identified by Helen McNeil in Mills and Boon FICTION of the 1970s. The 'Pamissa' plot gets its name from Samuel Richardson's two novels, *Pamela, or Virtue Rewarded* (1740) and *Clarissa Harlowe* (1747), and centres on a desirable but lower-status heroine who has to resist the hero's advances until he has proposed marriage. Nickianne Moody lists McNeil's other plot types as follows:

> 'Cinderella': a fantasy of class and derivation of the governess plot found in Brontë's *Jane Eyre* (1847).
> 'Rebecca': named after Daphne du Maurier's pre-war novel, is also a fantasy of class. The second wife or girlfriend is a quiet mousy type who has to live up to the sexual aggression of her predecessor.
> 'Masquerade': the heroine finds herself in a situation where she pretends to be married/engaged to her social superior.
> 'Bartered Bride': the heroine is traded, usually by her father, to a man she hates but eventually comes to love and respect. (Based on Moody: 1998, 145, quoting Helen McNeil: 1991)

See also EUPHORIC/DYSPHORIC TEXT; MASQUERADE; STORY AND PLOT.

Panoptism/panopticism A concept which descends from Jeremy Bentham through Michel Foucault. Foucault's *Discipline and Punish: The Birth of the Prison* (first published in French, 1975) contains a chapter entitled 'Panopticism', in which reference is made to Bentham's *Panopticon*. Bentham's proposal was for a prison built on a circular pattern by means of which each prisoner was uninterruptedly available to surveillance, but without ever knowing when or whether he or she was being watched. Foucault sees this proposal – which actually influenced the design of prisons and other institutions – as a staging-post in the growth of surveillance. Such surveillance is built upon the belief that citizens must be made to internalize the belief that they are, or might be, being watched by someone in authority at all times. As Foucault expresses it in an interview (in which the term is translated slightly differently into English),

> [b]y the term 'Panoptism', I have in mind an ensemble of mechanisms brought into play in all the clusters of procedures used by power. Panoptism was a technological invention in the order of power, comparable with the steam engine in the order of production. This invention had the peculiarity of being utilised first of all on a local level, in schools, barracks and hospitals. This was where the experiment of integral surveillance was carried out. (1980a, 71)

The concept has been much referred to in discussion of theories of the GAZE, especially in Film Studies. Central to its importance is the fact that it relates looking, and unequal relationships of looking, to the exercise of power.

Parabolic text A coinage of Barbara Herrnstein Smith which draws on the two meanings of *parabolic*: 'displaying the infinitely open curve of a parabola, and forming parables for an infinite number of propositions' (1978, 144). A parabolic text, then, is *open* rather than *closed*, receiving and transforming varied approaches to it as a parabolic dish antenna 'captures' a range of different signals, but it also has the quality of a parable, supporting a succession of never-ending applications.

See also OPEN AND CLOSED TEXTS.

Parade See MASQUERADE

Paradigm shift A term introduced by Thomas S. Kuhn in his *The Structure of Scientific Revolutions* (1970; first published 1962). Kuhn suggested that particular learned communities or specialities rested upon acceptance of 'a set of recurrent and quasi-standard illustrations of various theories in their conceptual, observational, and instrumental applications'. These, he proposed, are the community's *paradigms*, which can be found revealed in its 'textbooks, lectures, and laboratory exercises' (1970, 43). Kuhn (as his title suggests) was particularly interested in how changes take place in scientific thinking, and his concept of the paradigm plays a central role in his explanation. Kuhn's paradigms are not just the illustrations he mentions but also the assumptions which are to be found behind, and constituted by, these illustrations. In other words, a paradigm is constituted by a set of beliefs which both enables and constrains research: a framework or scaffold which can underpin or support further work but which of necessity also excludes a range of possibilities.

Readers of Kuhn's book from the Humanities were much struck by his account of cases of scientific evidence which was not recognized as such because it did not fit into known and accepted paradigms. Michel Foucault's account of the reception of Mendel's work is presented in the context of Foucault's own concept of the DISCOURSE, but it could equally well exemplify the alleged inability of those located on different sides of a paradigm shift to communicate.

> People have often wondered how on earth nineteenth-century botanists and biologists managed not to see the truth of Mendel's statements. But it was precisely

because Mendel spoke of objects, employed methods and placed himself within a theoretical perspective totally alien to the biology of his time.

. . .

Mendel spoke the truth, but he was not *dans le vrai* (within the true) of contemporary biological discourse: it was simply not along such lines that objects and biological concepts were formed. (1972, 224)

Such accounts had more than a passing resemblance to then-influential theories of IDEOLOGY, and ideas about self-enclosed paradigms attracted much attention outside the realms of the philosophy of science.

In particular, Kuhn's view of the necessity for a *paradigm shift* to enable major advances in scientific theory to take place seemed to have something (but only something) in common with what Louis Althusser was saying concerning the need for the theorist to move from ideology to science. The difference is that for Kuhn there is no promised land of science; paradigm succeeds paradigm like the succession of blinkered generational views with which Philip Larkin's poem 'High Windows' presents us, each seeming as if it represents an advance but each with its own inevitable limitations.

Kuhn's concept of the paradigm shift attracted criticism, however, because of its 'inwardness': the shift was engendered and triggered by the pressure of internal contradictions rather than by (as in traditional MARXIST views) the pressure of external forces which, in Darwinian mode, excluded theories which could not adapt to new external needs. The term has entered into literary-critical vocabulary in relation, very often, to arguments about the CANON (a WORK is only recognized as major when new literary paradigms allow it to be understood or appreciated), and in relation to arguments about INTERPRETATION (we interpret the evidence of a TEXT differently when our literary paradigms change, just as the scientist reinterprets the evidence provided by an experiment when his or her scientific paradigms change).

For comparable concepts, see also CONVENTIONALISM; COPERNICAN REVOLUTION; *ÉPISTÉMÈ*; EPISTEMOLOGICAL BREAK; PROBLEMATIC.

Paradigmatic See SYNTAGMATIC AND PARADIGMATIC

Paralanguage See PARATEXT

Paralepsis According to Gérard Genette, the presenting of more information in a NARRATIVE than is authorized by the attribution of focus (1980, 195; see the discussion of *focalizer* in the entry for REFLECTOR [CHARACTER]).

Thus in Joseph Conrad's novel *Under Western Eyes* the NARRATOR (the 'Teacher of Languages') claims to base his account on the written report of the CHARACTER, Razumov. And yet after Razumov has finished this report and has wrapped it up, the Teacher of Languages continues to describe Razumov's actions and experiences.

Such anomalies bother Courts of Law more than they do literary critics, although they do help us to explore from what direction (IDEOLOGICAL as well as technical) an AUTHOR situates him- or herself in relation to his or her narrative. See the more extended discussion in PERSPECTIVE AND VOICE.

Not to be confused with PARALIPSIS.

Paralipsis Gérard Genette suggests this term for an ELLIPSIS which is created not by missing out a temporal unit in the NARRATIVE succession, but by omitting a constituent element or elements in a period of STORY-time that is covered in the narrative.

Not to be confused with PARALEPSIS.

Paraliterature See CANON

Parataxis Within Linguistics, a (now outmoded) term meaning coordination. Sometimes used by theorists of NARRATIVE to refer to the coordination of different narrative elements (e.g. so that the viewpoints of different CHARACTERS coincide). Experimental writers may wish to challenge parataxis – by means of ANACHRONY, for example.

Paratext A coinage of Gérard Genette, used in his work *Seuils* (1987; English translation *Paratexts: Thresholds of Interpretation* [1997]). According to Richard Macksey the term refers to 'those liminal devices and conventions, both within the book (*peritext*) and outside it (*epitext*) that mediate the book to the reader: titles and subtitles, pseudonyms, forewords, dedications, epigraphs, prefaces, intertitles, notes, epilogues, and afterwords – all those framing devices that so engaged Sterne' (1997, xviii). Thus as Genette explains, '*paratext = peritext + epitext*' (1997, 5). He also points out that of course something only qualifies as a paratext if 'the author or one of his associates accepts responsibility for it' (1997, 9).

> More than a boundary or a sealed border, the paratext is, rather, a *threshold*, or – a word Borges used apropos of a preface – a 'vestibule' that offers the world at large the possibility of either stepping inside or turning back. It is an 'undefined zone' between the inside and the outside, a zone without any hard and fast boundary on either the inward side (turned toward the text) or the outward side (turned toward the world's discourse about the text), an edge, or, as Philippe Lejeune put it, 'a fringe of the printed text which in reality controls one's whole reading of the text.' (1997, 1–2)

Genette argues that a TEXT without a paratext does not exist, and never has, but stresses that the 'ways and means of the paratext change continually, depending on period, culture, genre, author, work, and edition, with varying degrees of pressure, sometimes widely varying' (1997, 3). The term is presumably applied on the model of *paralanguage*: paralinguistic features are those non-verbal accompaniments to a verbal UTTERANCE: grunts, facial expression, hand gestures and BODY movements, and so on.

Paratextual features are of particular interest to those interested in challenging belief in the transcendent and self-sufficient nature of the literary text or WORK. A good example of such a utilization is to be found in Jerome J. McGann's *The Textual Condition* (1991).

See also BIBLIOLOGY; LIMINAL; PREPUBLICATION/POSTPUBLICATION READING.

Parergon See FRAME

Parody See MIMICRY

Partial synonymy See SENSE AND REFERENCE

Passing 'Passing for white' was something that those classified as non-White in racist societies were able to do if their physical appearance was sufficiently Caucasian. The term was moved sideways and adopted by Gays who used it to denote those homosexuals who 'passed' as straight, or heterosexual.

See also CLOSET CRITICISM; MASQUERADE; OUTING.

Patriarchy Technically, government by men – either within the family or in society at large – with authority descending through the father. In Lacanian theory, patriarchy is the internalization of the law of the father (see the entry for NAME-OF-THE-FATHER), which takes place when the individual enters human CULTURE through the Oedipus complex. In recent usage the term has been used to point both to the actual exercise of power and also to the IDEOLOGICAL system – the ideas and attitudes – used to bolster, justify, and protect this power. Patriarchy thus has political, economic, social and ideological dimensions.

Much recent FEMINIST literary criticism has aimed to uncover patriarchal ideas in WORKS of literature as well as in the systems surrounding these works: education, publishing, journalism, reviewing, and the general 'systems of literary production' specific to different cultures and societies.

Pause See DURATION

Pejoration Attributing negative qualities to persons, actions, words, or indeed anything. Most normally used in FEMINIST accounts of the way in which certain words are associated with women or the female and are thereby given negative associations.

Contrast 'MASCON' WORDS.

Pentad From Kenneth Burke's *A Grammar of Motives* (1969), in which Burke noted that – at a minimum – NARRATIVE requires an ACTOR, an action, a goal or INTENTION, a scene, and an instrument. (For scene see DURATION; see also GRAMMAR.)

Performance The distinction between the performing and the non-performing arts has always been important in Literary Studies, and has normally been recognized as such – although critics who spend too much time with the printed page are liable to neglect it. (The NEW CRITICS, among others, have on occasions been criticized for studying plays more as TEXTS than as scripts for a performance.) It is important to remember that poetry was originally a performing art: the silent and individual READING of a poem is historically recent when seen in the context of the total lifespan of poetry. More recently a number of theorists have argued that it can be illuminating to see any reading or INTERPRETATION as a form of performance: even the silent reader of a novel 'performs' the text in his or her mind in the course of a single reading, and just as no two performances are exactly the same nor are any two readings of a given literary WORK. Seeing a reading in these terms highlights certain things: the particular, concrete life that is given to the text in performance represents a choice among many possibilities, a choice to which both the performer and the AUTHOR and his/her text contribute in partnership (or in conflict).

See also the discussion of *performatives* in the entry for SPEECH ACT THEORY, and the entries for COMPETENCE AND PERFORMANCE and OSTENSION.

Performatives See SPEECH ACT THEORY

Perlocutionary act See SPEECH ACT THEORY

Perspective and voice The distinction made by Gérard Genette between MOOD and VOICE is perhaps the best way into a topic which was once conceptualized in relatively unproblematic terms under the rubric of *point of view*, but which with the advances in NARRATIVE theory of recent years has become a much more complex topic known by a range of terms, the most accepted of which is probably *perspective*.

Genette has drawn attention to the importance of a long-neglected distinction between *who sees?* and *who speaks?*. As a lot of this entry is concerned with problems of terminology, it is important to stress that behind differences of terminology there is broad agreement concerning the importance of this distinction. Thus, for example, although the narrative voice in Joseph Conrad's *Under Western Eyes* is that of the personified NARRATOR, the English 'Teacher of Languages', what is observed (in both senses of the word) frequently goes beyond his actual consciousness, and the reader is told things which he (the narrator) could not possibly know if he were a living human being rather than a FICTIONAL character/narrator. (See the entry for PARALEPSIS.)

A comparable distinction can be made in film narrative, although here the sees/speaks distinction is not appropriate. But when Elisabeth Weis argues that Alfred Hitchcock's 1954 film *Rear Window* 'quintessentially presents a subjective point of view within an apparently realistic style', and that only 'at the end of the film do we realize that we have shared the hero's dangerously distorted perception of events (it is mere accident that in one case his assumption is correct); and we are forced to reinterpret everything that has gone before (including our complicity in the hero's voyeurism) in a new light' (1982, 107–8), we are being invited to make a similar distinction between two points of view in the traditional sense. (We do not have to accept the invitation: my own view is that the hero is not presented as having a 'dangerously distorted perception of events'.)

In Genette's terminology the distinction between *who sees?* and *who speaks?* is expressed in terms of the opposition between mood and voice (1980, 30). According to him, the category of mood gathers together the problems of DISTANCE which American critics have traditionally discussed in terms of the opposition between *telling and showing*, and he suggests that these terms represent a resurgence of the Platonic terms DIEGESIS AND MIMESIS. *Voice*, in contrast, he reserves to describe the way the NARRATIVE SITUATION, along with the narrator and his or her audience, is implicated in the narrative (1980, 29–31). To summarize: *mood* operates at the level of connections between STORY and narrative, while *voice* designates connections both between narrating and narrative, and narrating and story (1980, 32).

There are as I have suggested complications of terminology here, however, and what Genette here calls *mood* he elsewhere refers to as *focalization*, while other theorists such as Franz Stanzel have used the term *mode* (see the discussion in Fludernik: 1996, 344). Others following Genette have preferred to replace *mood* by *perspective*, as the pair 'perspective and voice' matches up more neatly with 'who sees/who speaks'. (In Mieke Bal's terminology, perspective covers both the physical and psychological points of perception in a narrative, but it does not involve the actual *agent* performing the act of narration [1985, 101].)

In what follows I will adopt this terminology, and use 'perspective' to indicate 'who sees' and 'voice' to indicate 'who speaks'. I do so in spite of the fact that some narrative theorists object to any such use of the term *voice*; Andrew Gibson, for example, states that *voice* as represented by NARRATOLOGY is actually always a metaphor for INTENTION, MEANING and totality, and that when narrative theorists have referred to the voice in narrative, they have never really meant voice at all (1996, 169). Those interested in pursuing this debate should consult Richard Aczel's excellent article 'Hearing Voices in Narrative Texts' (1998). Aczel agrees that in the study of narrative discourse, voice is a complex and problematic category, and that its use raises questions of ONTOLOGY and metaphoricity (1998, 467). His article makes very useful suggestions regarding the significance of the work of Mikhail Bakhtin for the study of voice, specifically with regard to Bakhtin's 'treatment of narrative discourse as an essentially quotational form where the quoting instance is not unitary and monological, but a configuration of different voices or expressive styles organized into an "artistic" whole by means of identifiable rhetorical principles' (1998, 483; see the entry for POLYPHONIC for more on Bakhtin's conception of voice).

Both Genette and Bal use the term *focalization*, and this term is now widely accepted. Accordingly, a narrative which has zero focalization is one in which it is impossible to fix the perspective in terms of which the narrated characters, events and situations are being observed and presented. Many works of fiction which were traditionally described as characterized by an *omniscient* point of view are described by modern narratologists as having a zero focalization. One could suggest that a novel such as George Eliot's *Middlemarch* was characterized by zero-focalization – which does not of course mean that the reader associates no set of values or attitudes, or even traces of personification – to the narrating of the work. A related term is *camera-eye narrative*, which is generally taken to imply some sort of neutrality in the narrative determinations – as if a camera were left in a room to record anything that took place in front of it. Those familiar with the complexities of film narrative have tended to react against the somewhat simplistic assumptions lying behind the usage.

The term *focalized narrative* can also be rendered as *internal perspective*: the story is told from the perspective of a point (normally a consciousness) which is internal to the story, or *intra-diegetic*. (Sometimes the term *intra-fictional* is preferred to intra-diegetic.) Thus a *focalizer* is a character or consciousness *in* a work who or which offers the reader 'positions' from which that which is narrated can be experienced.

Focalized narratives can be *fixed*, as in Jean Rhys's *After Leaving Mr Mackenzie* where everything we learn comes from the heroine/narrator Julia Martin, *variable*, as in Emily Brontë's *Wuthering Heights* in which some events are presented from the perspective of Mr Lockwood, some from that of Mrs Dean, and some from that of Isabella (in the long letter she writes), or *multiple* as in Tobias Smollett's *Humphry Clinker* in which the epistolary technique allows the same events to be presented more than once from different and contrasting perspectives. It will be clear that the distinction between variable and multiple perspective is not always so very easy to establish. The term *double focalization* is normally used to indicate the simultaneous or co-terminous (rather than just consecutive or alternating) presentation of two narrative 'points of view'.

External focalization denotes a focalization that is limited to what, were the story true, the observer could actually have observed 'from the outside'; in other words, it involves no accounts of characters' thoughts, feelings, and emotions unless these are revealed in external behaviour or admitted to by the characters. According to Genette, external focalization involves a perspective which is intra-diegetic but outside that of the characters. In his Introduction to Genette's *Narrative Discourse*, Jonathan Culler has referred to the criticism made by Mieke Bal of Genette's distinction between *internal focalization* and *external focalization*. Culler notes that Bal claims that the two terms refer to rather different cases, for whereas '[i]n what Genette calls *internal focalization* the narrative is focussed *through* the consciousness of a character, . . . *external focalization* is something altogether different: the narrative is focussed *on* a character, not through him' (Genette: 1980, 10). An alternative way of referring to types of focalization is by means of reference to varieties of narrative *vision*.

Seymour Chatman has distanced himself from Genette's and Bal's use of the term *focalization* and has proposed '*slant* to name the narrator's attitudes and other mental nuances appropriate to the report function of discourse, and *filter* to name the much wider range of mental activity experienced by characters in the story world – perceptions, cognitions, attitudes, emotions, memories, fantasies, and the like' (1990, 143). For further discussion of *focalizer*, see REFLECTOR (CHARACTER).

Because of these variations in usage care needs to be exercised in the use of these terms. See also CENTRE; ENUNCIATION; FRAME; INSIDE/OUTSIDE VIEW; NARRATIVE SITUATION.

Petit récit See GRAND NARRATIVES AND LITTLE NARRATIVES

Phallic criticism See PHALLOCENTRISM

Phallocentrism A term dating from recent FEMINIST theory and used to refer to interlocking social and IDEOLOGICAL systems which accept and advance a PATRIARCHAL power symbolically represented by the phallus. 'Phallus' has to be understood as a *cultural* construction attributing symbolic power to the *biological* penis. Thus Carole-Anne Tyler has argued that some women do 'have' the phallus in our culture because it is not just the penis but all the other signs of power and privilege, which stand in a metaphoric and metonymic relation not only to 'penis' but also to 'white' and 'bourgeois' – the signs of a 'proper' racial and class identity (1991, 58).

The concept clearly builds upon artistic and CULTURAL representations of the penis which, in both ancient and modern societies, have been incorporated into ideological justifications of male power. The transformation of penis to phallus has a clear ideological colouring: a penis is one of a pair of matched sexual organs both of which are necessary for reproduction, while a phallus is seen as *prime* source of biological fruitfulness and thus can be used to underwrite the domination of one GENDER by the other. (Jacques Derrida, incidentally, sees such a view of the phallus as an example of a transcendental signifier: see the entry for TRANSCENDENTAL SIGNIFIED.)

In contemporary feminist usage, phallocentric patterns of thought consciously or unconsciously assume and advance a view of the masculine as natural source of power and authority, and of the feminine as naturally subject to this. Thus man is PRESENCE, woman ABSENCE, and this absence is symbolically underwritten by overt or concealed reference to the absent phallus. For some feminists, the phallus has an even more all-embracing set of symbolic meanings; Madeleine Gagnon, for example, writes that

> [t]he phallus, for me at this time, represents repressive capitalist ownership, the exploiting bourgeoisie, the higher knowledge that must be gotten over; it represents an erected France that watches, analyzes, sanctions. The phallus means everything that sets itself up as a mirror. Everything that erects itself as perfection. Everything that wants regimentation and representation. That which does not erase/efface but covets. That which lines things up in history museums. That which constantly pits itself against the power of immortality. (1980, 180)

The term seems to have entered contemporary feminism through the Lacanian critique of Freud. Lacan's essay 'The Signification of the Phallus', based upon a lecture delivered in 1958 and first published in French in 1966, is by no means feminist in orientation. But in exploring the phallus as signifier in this and other writings, Lacan opened the way to a feminist appropriation of the term which used, initially, a STRUCTURALIST conceptual framework.

Phallocratic denotes, literally, rule by the phallus – on the model of democratic, autocratic, and so on, and is used in feminist DISCOURSE to indicate a system of power and authority which is based upon phallocentric values.

Phallic criticism is criticism which not only abides by and furthers phallocentric values, but which also uses methods associated with the exercise of phallocentric power and is backed by the institutional resources of phallocentrism.

Phallocratic See PHALLOCENTRISM

Phallogocentrism A portmanteau term combining PHALLOCENTRISM and LOGOCENTRISM, coined by Jacques Derrida in his critique of Jacques Lacan in 'The Purveyor of Truth' (1975). For Derrida, Lacan's reading of Edgar Allan Poe's *The Purloined Letter* is guilty of phallogocentrism because Lacan sees the letter unproblematically as phallus, rather than recognizing that meaning cannot exist in such unproblematic one-to-one relationships.

Although the term was intended to imply criticism it has appealed to FEMINISTS and others eager to imply a connection between male, PATRIARCHAL authority, and systems of thought which LEGITIMIZE themselves by reference to some PRESENCE or point of authority prior to and outside of themselves. The hidden, legitimizing presence, in other words, is always, at root, that of the Father, whose authority is a starting point or unconsidered assumption rather than something that can be justified or admitted. The term implies that both phallocentrism and logocentrism have in common that they are both monolithic systems built round a single, ultimate determining CENTRE (the phallus, the word), a centre which ends indeterminacy and play and imposes meaning by the imposition of its unchallengeable authority.

David Lehman's explanatory note to a short poem by himself, published in the *Times Literary Supplement* for 18–24 May 1990, attributes to Benjamin Krull the following definition of phallogocentrism: 'what happens when you eliminate the space between the second and third words of the sentence *the pen is mightier than the sword*' (1990, 524). This suggests that the term's meaning has undergone a shift from that which Derrida originally intended (which would, presumably, neither surprise nor dismay him).

It is hard to see Martin Jay's variant 'phallogocularcentrism' (Jay: 1993, 494) gaining general currency. The term appears to combine the senses of phallocentrism and logocentrism with a privileging of sight over the other senses. As the sub-title of Jay's book (*The Denigration of Vision in Twentieth-Century French Thought*) suggests, such a privileging has come under strong attack in much modern French theory.

See the useful extended discussion of phallogocentrism by Paul Julian Smith (1992).

Phallogocularcentrism See PHALLOGOCENTRISM

Phatic See FUNCTIONS OF LANGUAGE

Phenomenology. Phenomenology originates in the writing of the German Edmund Husserl, whose philosophy takes as its starting point the world as experienced in our consciousness. It thus rejects the possibility of considering the world independently of human consciousness, but seeks rather to get back to concrete reality through our experience of it. For Husserl, consciousness is always *consciousness of something*: it is directed outwards rather than inwards – even if it is directed on to something imagined. It is thus too simple to describe phenomenology as idealist, for although it posits the impossibility of our gaining a knowledge of the world which is untouched by our perception of that world, it does suggest that through an EIDETIC method we can build up a successively more and more accurate understanding of the objects of our consciousness by filtering off accidental and personal elements in our perception of them. In order so to analyse our consciousness we must suspend all preconceptions about the objects with which it is concerned (see the entry for *EPOCHÉ*). Terry Eagleton comments that although

> Husserl rejected empiricism, psychologism and the positivism of the natural sciences, he also considered himself to be breaking with the classical idealism of a thinker like Kant. Kant had been unable to solve the problem of how the mind can really know objects outside it at all; phenomenology, in claiming that what is given in pure perception is the very essence of things, hoped to surmount this scepticism. (1983, 56–7)

It is not hard to understand the interest that such ideas aroused amongst students of art and literature, for whom the pseudo-objectivity of positivism seemed no more applicable to the study and appreciation of art-works than did variants of Kantianism which too soon could end up in solipsism and an abandonment to unfettered personal 'taste'. A range of literary theorists and aestheticians found in Husserl's ideas something upon which they felt they could build. One of the earliest was the Polish aesthetician

Roman Ingarden, who argued that a READING of a WORK of literature CONCRETIZES it (much as the PERFORMANCE of a play concretizes the written TEXT).

The Geneva School of criticism owes its largest debt to Husserl and phenomenological ideas. Its members were mostly associated with the University of Geneva, and have on occasions been referred to collectively as the 'Critics of Consciousness'. J. Hillis Miller, who was for a time closely identified with the school, has written a useful survey-account of the school which is reprinted in his book *Theory Then and Now* (1991). According to Miller, for the Geneva critics literature is a form of consciousness (1991, 14), while criticism is

> fundamentally the expression of a 'reciprocal transparency' of two minds, that of the critic and that of the author, but they differ in their conceptions of the nature of consciousness. From the religious idea of human existence in [Marcel] Raymond and [Albert] Béguin, to the notion in [Georges] Poulet's criticism that what counts most is 'the proof, the living proof, of the experience of inner spirituality as a positive reality,' [Jean] Rousset's belief that the artist's self-consciousness only comes into existence in the intimate structure of his work, the unquestioning acceptance of an overlapping of consciousness and the physical world in [Jean-Pierre] Richards's criticism, and the fluctuation between incarnation and detachment in the work of [Jean] Starobinski, these six critics base their interpretations of literature on a whole spectrum of dissimilar convictions about the human mind. (1991, 29)

This is criticism that is a long way away from the death of the AUTHOR; the idea of writing as self-expression or self-projection is central to the work of Jean Rousset, and according to Miller, Georges Poulet believes that

> [c]riticism must therefore begin in an act of renunciation in which the critic empties his mind of its personal qualities so that it may coincide completely with the consciousness expressed in the words of the author. His essay will be the record of this coincidence. The 'intimacy' necessary for criticism, says Georges Poulet, 'is not possible unless the thought of the critic *becomes* the thought of the author criticized, unless it succeeds in re-feeling, in re-thinking, in re-imagining the author's thought from the inside ... ' (1991, 15)

READER-RESPONSE CRITICISM owes an important debt to phenomenology and the Geneva School, particularly in the person of the German critic Wolfgang Iser. Iser's essay 'The Reading Process: a Phenomenological Approach' (reprinted in Iser: 1974) is a good example of the creative development of a number of aspects of phenomenology – and, too, of the way in which phenomenology leads naturally to some of the preoccupations of reader-response critics. Take, for example, the first sentence of the essay: 'The phenomenological theory of art lays full stress on the idea that, in considering a literary work, one must take into account not only the actual text but also, and in equal measure, the actions involved in responding to that text' (1974, 274). Iser then moves on to discuss Ingarden's theory of artistic concretization, and concludes that the literary work has two poles: the artistic pole (the text created by the AUTHOR), and the AESTHETIC pole (the realization accomplished by the READER) (1974, 274). The argument is an interesting one, although the proposed nomenclature is perhaps odd, suggesting as it does that there is nothing aesthetic about the author's created text and nothing artistic about the reader's realization.

Iser stresses in particular the work's *virtuality*: like the text of a play which can be produced in innumerable ways, a literary work can lead to innumerable reading experiences. (Compare Derrida's argument that 'reading is transformational' [1981b, 63].) He also makes use of Husserl's argument that consciousness is *intentional*, that it is directed and goal-seeking rather than random and all-absorbing. So far as the reading of literature is concerned, this allows Iser to place a high premium not just upon the reader's 'pre-INTENTIONS' – what he or she goes to the text with – but also upon the intentions awakened by the reading process itself (and, indirectly, by the text). One of the best-known of Iser's arguments involves the literary work's 'gaps'. According to him, no literary work is, as it were, complete: all have gaps which have to be filled in by the reader, and all readers and readings will fill these in differently (1974, 280; Iser makes similar points in a number of other essays). Iser's gaps bear a close relationship to Roman Ingarden's 'spots of indeterminacy': see the entry for CONCRETIZATION.

It will be seen that such a position offered a good base for the mounting of a counter-offensive against the NEW CRITICAL anathematizing of the Affective Fallacy: it showed how readers' responses could be taken account of without giving the individual reader absolute freedom to do with the text as he or she wished: the reader has licence to fill in only the gaps.

See also ABSENCE (gaps); AFFECT; SUB-TEXT.

Phenotext See GENOTEXT AND PHENOTEXT

Phonocentrism See LOGOCENTRISM

Pidgin See RELEXIFICATION

Pink/pink ghetto See LAVENDER CULTURE/LANGUAGE/SEX

Play See LUDISM

Pleasure The attitude of literary critics towards pleasure can perhaps be compared to that of MARXISTS towards sartorial fashion: during the twentieth century they seem never to have been quite sure whether or not they approve of it, but on balance they do not. There is a wonderfully evocative sub-heading in Laura Mulvey's very influential 1975 essay 'Visual Pleasure and Narrative Cinema', which is reprinted in her 1989 book *Visual and Other Pleasures*. The sub-heading reads: 'Destruction of Pleasure is a Radical Weapon'. In spite of the forbidding nature of this declaration, Mulvey's essay (and indeed her book) includes much fascinating discussion of Freud's theories concerning SCOPOPHILIA – for Freud one of the component instincts of sexuality, which involves the taking pleasure from subjecting others to a 'controlling and curious gaze' (Mulvey: 1989, 16) and 'using another person as an object of sexual stimulation through sight' (1989, 18). To do Mulvey some justice, of course, what lies behind the sentiment expressed in her title is the belief that forms of pleasure NATURALIZE all sorts of conservative political attitudes and beliefs.

According to Freud the *pleasure principle* dominates the new-born infant, but in the maturing or mature individual it is placed under the sway of the *reality principle*, regaining its sway only in fantasy or day-dreaming (see the discussion in Mitchell: 1974, 13). Pleasure for Freudians is thus infantile, temporary, not to be confused with the adult experiences offered by literary WORKS – although to the extent that the READING of literature is seen to be regressive and comparable to dream-experiences then pleasure may enter into it.

In the 1930s and 1940s the premium placed upon a stern moral experience and evaluation of literature by F. R. Leavis and his followers seemed on occasions to consign words such as *pleasure* to the vocabulary of the literary dilettante. In his *The Great Tradition* Leavis's comparison of Conrad and Dickens is (to use one of his own favoured words) representative:

> We may reasonably, too, in the same way see some Dickensian influence in Conrad's use of melodrama, or what would have been melodrama in Dickens; for in Conrad the end is a total significance of a profoundly serious kind.
>
> The reason for not including Dickens in the line of great novelists is implicit in the last phrase. (1962b, 29)

The final judgement comes a couple of lines later: Dickens may have been a great genius, but his genius 'was that of the great entertainer'.

However much Common Readers may have gone on using terms such as *pleasure* and *enjoyment* with reference to their reading of literary works, within modern movements in literary criticism during the twentieth century these have generally had something of a thin time. In 1975, however, Roland Barthes's *Le Plaisir du texte* was published (translated as *The Pleasure of the Text* in 1976), and pleasure suddenly became much more respectable amongst literary critics and theorists. Barthes's *plaisir* is difficult to translate into English, and has a generally more indulgent and more specifically sexual/sensual force than its more staid English counterpart. Barthes distinguishes between *pleasure of the text* and *texts of pleasure*: the former can be spoken, whereas the latter are perverse and are outside any imaginable finality (1976, 51–2). *The Pleasure of the Text* is, however, not an easy work to summarize or describe, and perhaps its most important effect was to bring the issue of reader gratification through the reading experience back into the forefront of critical attention. A recent work which uses Barthes's study in the exploration of reading processes is Lynne Pearce, *Feminism and the Politics of Reading* (1997).

The issue of pleasure has also been taken up by recent FEMINIST theorists, some of whom have argued along the same lines as Mulvey's title that pleasure has been naturalized in particular ways within PATRIARCHAL societies, ways which devalue, MARGINALIZE or ignore specifically female forms of pleasure. Thus not only are descriptions or definitions of pleasure at the content level of literary works to be held up to renewed scrutiny, but also the pleasures to be obtained by women from the writing and reading of literary works have to be reconsidered from non-patriarchal perspectives.

Plot See STORY AND PLOT

Plurisignification See AMBIGUITY

Poetic See FUNCTIONS OF LANGUAGE

Point de capiton Slavoj Žižek provides an illustration of how this concept from Jacques Lacan can be utilized in the ANALYSIS of a TEXT. He is writing about a scene in Alfred Hitchcock's 1940 film *Foreign Correspondent*. In a scene from this film which is set in Holland, the hero notices that the arms of one of a number of windmills is rotating in a different direction from those of the others. Žižek comments:

> Here we have the effect of what Lacan calls the *point de capiton* (the quilting point) in its purest: a perfectly 'natural' and 'familiar' situation is denatured, becomes 'uncanny,' loaded with horror and threatening possibilities, as soon as we add to it a small supplementary feature, a detail that 'does not belong,' that sticks out, is 'out of place,' does not make any sense within the frame of the idyllic scene. (1991, 88)

See also DEFAMILIARIZATION; FANTASTIC (for *uncanny*); MARGINALITY (for *supplement*). Also worth considering is Barthes's distinction between *studium* and *punctum* (in the entry for STUDIUM/PUNCTUM); Barthes's punctum has something in common with the *point de capiton*.

Point of view See PERSPECTIVE AND VOICE

Politeness In a useful article entitled 'The Politeness of Literary Texts' Roger Sell traces the application of this term from 'the zenith of its lofty meaning' in the eighteenth century when it 'embraced intellectual enlightenment and civilization as prized by the Augustans', through to the way in which the term has been redefined by anthropological linguists (1991, 208). It is this most recent usage that has established the term's current process of redefinition: 'the strategies, linguistically realized, by which human beings hold their own or grasp for more' (Sell: 1991, 211; after Brown and Levinson: 1978 and 1987).

Sell details a number of recent attempts on the part of scholars interested in a *rapprochement* of Linguistics and Literary Studies to connect the concept of politeness with literary TEXTS, particularly with regard to the way in which these – or their AUTHORS – handle face-threatening acts (FTAs) in the language of authorial personae and CHARACTERS. (A face-threatening act is an act which challenges or endangers an individual's 'face', or public esteem. Thus to be bawled out by one's boss is one thing, but to have it done in front of one's colleagues threatens not just one's relation to him or her, but one's whole reputation and esteem. It is possible to criticize a person without threatening their face – for example, by pretending that an action was a mistake rather than done deliberately. Pragmatic skill normally involves avoiding either delivering or receiving FTAs whenever possible.)

Sell's own approach, however, is wider than that mentioned above: he sees all interaction, and all language, as operating within politeness parameters (1991, 215), a position that he associates with Mikhail Bakhtin's view that all language use is DIALOGIC, and thus to some extent engages with those others who hear or read it. In Bakhtin's circle it is clear that issues relevant to the later concept of politeness were discussed; P. N. Medvedev's *The Formal Method in Literary Scholarship* (attributed, not uncontroversially, in its current English translation, to both Medvedev and Bakhtin), includes a discussion of 'speech tact', which

> has a practical importance for practical language communication. The formative and organizing force of speech tact is very great. It gives form to everyday utterances, determining the genre and style of speech performances. Here tact . . . should be understood in a broad sense, with politeness as only one of its aspects. Tact may have various directions, moving between the two poles of compliment and curse. Speech tact is determined by the aggregate of all the social relationships of the speakers, their ideological horizons, and, finally, the concrete situation of the conversation. (Medvedev/Bakhtin: 1978, 95)

For Sell politeness is 'a matter of choice and co-operativeness in interpersonal relations' (1991, 221), more a form of helpfulness than the purely selfish manoeuvring for personal advantage some other theorists view it as. He distinguishes between *selectional* and *presentational* politeness, the former involving the avoidance of anything 'threatening the readers' positive or negative face' and the latter observing 'the co-operative principle at all costs, so that his readers would never be in the slightest doubt as to what was happening, what he meant, or why he was saying what he was saying' (1991, 221, 222).

As this makes clear, the concept owes a lot to, or has much in common with, aspects of both SPEECH ACT THEORY and PRAGMATICS. It can be added that once one starts to talk about the politeness of literary texts the way is open to talk about their impoliteness. Just as impoliteness can be a technique for getting one's own way in interpersonal relations, so too an author may challenge and manipulate a reader's expectations and responses through, for example, making it very difficult for him or her to understand what is happening, what is meant, or why what is being said is being said. Much early MODERNIST literature can be said to have recourse to impoliteness of this sort.

Political unconscious See UNCONSCIOUS

Polyglossia See HETEROGLOSSIA

Polyphonic Literally, many-voiced. The term is associated with the theories of Mikhail Bakhtin, especially with his idea of the *polyphonic novel*. In his study of Dostoevsky Bakhtin argues that Dostoevsky was the creator of the polyphonic novel:

> *A plurality of independent and unmerged voices and consciousnesses, a genuine polyphony of fully valid voices is in fact the chief characteristic of Dostoevsky's novels.* What unfolds in his works is not a multitude of characters and fates in a single objective world, illuminated by a single authorial consciousness; rather a *plurality of consciousnesses, with equal rights and each with its own world,* combine but are not merged in the unity of the event. (1984, 6)

Bakhtin uses the word *voice* in a special way, to include not just matters linguistic but also matters relating to IDEOLOGY and power in society. *Voice* for Dostoevsky refers not just to an originating person, but to a network of beliefs and power relationships which attempt to place and situate the listener in certain ways. As Bakhtin puts it,

> [l]anguage is not a neutral medium that passes freely and easily into the private property of the speaker's intentions; it is populated – overpopulated – with the intentions of others. Expropriating it, forcing it to submit to one's own intentions and accents, is a difficult and complicated process. (1981, 294)

That process is the means whereby *language* is transformed into a *voice*.

Bakhtin's view that the polyphonic novel was born with Dostoevsky has been challenged, and he himself seems sometimes to have accepted that polyphonic elements can be found in many novels in many CULTURES and times. But his work on Dostoevsky has drawn attention to a representative lack of a single CENTRE of authority in the modern (or MODERNIST) literary WORK. And this can be said to relate to arguments about the death of the AUTHOR, for if there is no authorial PRESENCE in a novel, no centre of authority established by the author, but the author's is only one voice (or several voices), then clearly in a certain traditional sense of the term the author is no more.

Bakhtin's views here take up and extend a number of more traditional views relating to the literary use of personae.

Brian McHale points out that a rather different use of the concept can be found in the work of the Polish PHENOMENOLOGIST Roman Ingarden. According to Ingarden,

> the literary artwork is not ontologically uniform or monolithic, but *polyphonic*, stratified. Each of its layers has a somewhat different ontological status, and functions somewhat differently in the ontological make-up of the whole. (McHale: 1987, 30)

For Ingarden there are four such strata: that of word-sounds, that of meaning-units, that of 'presented objects' (which are distinguished from 'real-world objects'), and that of 'schematized aspects'. ('Presented objects' do not have the same determinacy as 'real-world objects', and they are inevitably schematic – which is why it bespeaks a failure to approach the art-work as art-work if one asks questions such as 'How many children had Lady Macbeth?') (Based on McHale: 1987, 33)

See also DIALOGIC; HETEROGLOSSIA; and compare PERSPECTIVE AND VOICE.

Polysemy See AMBIGUITY

Polysystem theory See SYSTEM

Polyvalent discourse See REGISTER

Polyvocality See POLYGLOSSIA

Popular Dissatisfactions with the literary CANON, along with the impact of interdisciplinary ventures involving not just literature but also other art-forms and the products of the mass media, have led to a renewed interest in the issues raised by the word *popular*. Raymond Williams points out that the word stems from a legal and political term meaning 'belonging to the people', but that in the historical shifts towards the widespread modern usage of 'well liked' there has been a strong pejorative streak relating to the implication the word carries of 'setting out to gain favour' (1976, 198).

In current critical usage terms such as *popular culture*, *popular literature* and *popular art* typically cover the senses both of '*for* the people' and '*of* the people'. Williams suggests that this is a relatively recent development, as previously a term such as 'folk culture' was reserved for usages involving the CULTURE produced by people for themselves. We can suggest, however, that the etymological relation between *popular* and *people* inevitably leads the former word to respond to shifts of attitudes and meaning attached to the latter one – especially of a socio-political nature. Thus during 1938 Bertolt Brecht's polemics against the anti-MODERNIST positions of Georg Lukács included interesting proposed definitions (working definitions in the sense that they were intended to be put to work in specific cultural practices) of both *popular* and culture. The link between views of 'the people' (both the term and the reality to which the term refers) and views of the *popular* are clear in Brecht's comments:

> Our concept of what is popular refers to a people who not only play a full part in historical development but actively usurp it, force its pace, determine its direction. We have a people in mind who make history, change the world and themselves. We have in mind a fighting people and therefore an aggressive concept of what is *popular*.
>
> Popular means: intelligible to the broad masses, adopting and enriching their forms of expression / assuming their standpoint, confirming and correcting it / representing the most progressive section of the people so that it can assume leadership, and therefore intelligible to other sections of the people as well / relating to traditions and developing them / communicating to that portion of the people which strives for leadership the achievements of the section that at present rules the nation. (Bloch *et al*.: 1977, 81)

Brecht's comments only reached English-speaking readers in any significant way in 1977, and they chimed in with a more general move against assigning purely pejorative associations to the term *popular* within the context of literary or artistic discussion. Even with regard to pulp literature – that which previously had been seen as the most blatant example of material foisted on the people by others for financial or IDEOLOGICAL reasons – attempts were made to discover elements of the 'genuine', that is to say, elements which expressed something valid about their lives and experiences to the consumers of this material themselves.

The very considerable influence of the work of Mikhail Bakhtin during the 1980s also involved a renewal of interest in the concept of the popular, directing attention towards traditions of expression and resistance both within and outside canonical literature and art.

See also CULTURE; DIALOGUE; IDEOLOGY.

Popular culture See CULTURE; POPULAR

Pornoglossia According to Deborah Cameron, 'since the word *pornography* means "pictures of prostitutes", perhaps *pornoglossia* would be a good name for the language which reduces all women to men's sexual servants' (1985, 77). Pornoglossia, then, is a use of language to describe women purely in terms of their sexual usefulness, availability, or attractiveness to men.

Position/positionality See READING POSITION

Postcolonialism At the time of writing probably the most fashionable, varied, and rapidly growing of critical or theoretical groupings. 'Critical or theoretical' sums up one of the issues: the term can be used in a relatively neutral descriptive sense to refer to literature emanating from or dealing with the peoples and CULTURES of lands which have emerged from colonial rule (normally, but not always, relatively recently), but it can also be used to imply a body of theory or an attitude towards that which is studied. Exactly how precise a descriptive term *postcolonialism* is is a matter of some debate; Georg M. Gugelberger claims of 'Postcolonial Studies' that it 'is not a discipline but a distinctive problematic that can be described as an abstract combination of all the problems inherent in such newly emergent fields as minority discourse, Latin American studies, African studies, Caribbean studies, Third World studies (as the comparative umbrella term), *Gastarbeiterliteratur*, Chicano studies, and so on, all of which participated in the significant and overdue recognition that "minority" cultures are actually "majority" cultures and that hegemonized Western (Euro-American) studies have been unduly privileged for political reasons' (1994, 582).

As many different commentators have noted, both parts of the term are problematic. Does the 'post' imply temporal supersession or IDEOLOGICAL rejection? (If the latter, then clearly one can have postcolonial literature in lands which are still experiencing colonial rule.) So far as 'colonialism' is concerned, should one extend this to lands such as Australia, Canada, and the United States – which after all did emerge as independent nations after periods of colonial rule? Should 'colonialism' include 'neo-colonialism' – in other words that pursuance of the political objectives of colonial rule by means which (at least not overtly) do not involve the exercise of direct political sovereignty backed up by military might?

Many commentators have admitted that the term has caught on in part because it raises fewer hackles than do terms which contain words such as 'imperialism' or 'Third World', because it is more potentially all-embracing than are terms such as 'Commonwealth literature', and because it carries with it no fixed ideological baggage as does ORIENTALISM. It is hard, after all, to be opposed to postcolonialism, in large part precisely because of the term's ambiguities and vagueness. As Judie Newman puts it, there are advantages to the term.

It is not as specific as a national identity and therefore allows resemblances between cultures to be perceived. It foregrounds the history of oppression without undue euphemisation. It is politically charged but not prescriptive, unlike 'resistance literature' which rather confines its practitioners to the binarism of opposition.

269

> When colonialism ends, writers must have the right to write about trees or love. 'Third World' or 'Fourth World' tends to perpetuate an image of potbellied starvelings (the 'Oxfam baby' victim syndrome). 'Commonwealth' (drily amended to 'common poverty' by Diana Brydon) is antiquated, never includes Britain (the absent yardstick), ignores the difference between old and new Commonwealth, and tends to foster an image of happy families rather than acknowledging the realities of domination. 'Terranglian' has never found a following. 'Postimperial' has more resonance for the colonising than for the colonised power. Pragmatically speaking, 'postcolonialism' allows for the formation of an adjective – as opposed to its alternatives . . . (1995, ix–x)

Whatever the case, the term has created institutional space for the study of a wide variety of non-CANONICAL literatures, and has given academics (and, let us admit it, publishers) a focus for the development of new areas of study. Moreover, while, as I have said, the term carries no specific ideological baggage with it, a body of theoretical work is associated with the field and a range of terms associated with it can now be listed.

Postmodernism See MODERNISM AND POSTMODERNISM

Post-structuralism A term that is sometimes used almost interchangeably with DECONSTRUCTION while at other times being seen as a more general, umbrella term which describes a movement of which one important element is deconstruction. As I point out in my entry on POSTMODERNISM, Satya P. Mohanty's statement that 'I use "poststructuralist" to refer to the dominant strand of postmodernist theory, whose focus is on language and signifying systems but whose claims are basically epistemological' (1997, 28 n4) is representative of a widespread attitude.

Richard Harland suggests that the post-structuralists fall into three main groups: the *Tel Quel* (a French journal) group of Jacques Derrida, Julia Kristeva and the later Roland Barthes; Gilles Deleuze and Félix Guattari (authors of the influential *Anti-Oedipus: Capitalism and Schizophrenia*, [published in French in 1972]) and the later Michel Foucault; and (on his own) Jean Baudrillard (Harland: 1987, 2). Whether Jacques Lacan is a structuralist or a post-structuralist (or both) is a matter for continuing debate.

The degree of uncertainty that surrounds the use of this term can, however, be suggested by noting that Alex Callinicos proposes a rather different division of post-structuralism into two main strands of thought. The first of these is what Richard Rorty has dubbed TEXTUALISM, while the second is one in which the master category is Michel Foucault's 'power-knowledge'. This 'worldly post-structuralism', as Callinicos calls it, using a term of Edward Said's, involves an 'articulation of "the said and the unsaid", of the discursive and the non-discursive' (Callinicos: 1989, 68). Callinicos argues that whereas the textualists see us as imprisoned in TEXTS, unable to escape the discursive (or unable to see any reality unmediated by DISCOURSES), 'worldly post-structuralism' leaves open the possibility of contact with a reality unmediated by or through discourses. If one accepts this division, then it has to be said that at least part of Foucault's work seems to belong with the textualists. It also has to be said that post-structuralism in its textualist version has had a far more significant impact upon Literary Studies than has the worldly variant, although many of Foucault's ideas have been taken up for criticism and development by FEMINIST critics.

'Textualist' post-structuralism represents at the same time both a development and a deconstruction of STRUCTURALISM – a demonstration of its argued inner contradictions. A classic example of this is to be found in an early (1968) interview of Derrida by Julia Kristeva, published in *Positions*. Derrida here takes issue with what he claims is Saussure's maintenance of a rigorous distinction between 'the *signans* and the *signatum*, [and] the equation of the *signatum* and the concept', which, he argues, 'inherently leaves open the possibility of thinking a *concept signified in and of itself*, a concept simply present for thought, independent of a relationship to language, that is of a relationship to a system of signifiers...' (1981b, 19).

Within Saussure's revolutionary view of language as a system of DIFFERENCES with no positive forms, that is, Derrida argues that one can discover (by deconstructing Saussure's argument) a relic of the old ideas, an extra-systemic entity, a TRANSCEN-DENTAL SIGNIFIED. By pursuing the implications of Saussure's arguments as far as possible one is able to go beyond them: the rigorous structuralist thus stands like Keats's Cortez, staring at the Pacific of post-structuralism (although his or her wild surmise is hardly silent).

Derrida's own position is best followed through certain key terms such as *deconstruction*, LOGOCENTRISM, DIFFÉRANCE, *transcendental signified*, METAPHYSICS OF PRESENCE, and so on – which to avoid repetition I will not reconsider here. Suffice to say that central to his endeavour (as he himself admits) has been a commitment to the rooting out of a belief in absolute and extra-systemic determinants of meaning. Thus central to the post-structuralist impact on literary theory and criticism has been its argument that the play of SIGNIFIERS cannot be stopped or made subject to the sway of any extra-textual authority: there is, as Derrida infamously puts it, nothing outside the text (1976, 158). Post-structuralism is therefore implicated in the death of the AUTHOR, and in consistently opposing any textual INTERPRETATION laying claim either to finality or undeconstructable authority. It has also contributed to a suspicion of any argument or position which grants the individual human SUBJECT powers of self-determination or of historical causation: Louis Althusser's long-lasting attack on HUMANISM prefigures many later post-structuralist attempts to see the subject as SITE rather than CENTRE.

Power In NARRATIVE theory, that which either allows a SUBJECT to reach, or prevents it from reaching, its object. A power can be an individual CHARACTER, or it can be an abstraction such as fate, age, nature, and so on (see Bal: 1985, 28).

The issue of power has entered into recent discussion of literature mainly in connection with issues loosely related to IDEOLOGY. Literature is often subject to control (through censorship, restrictions on literacy, use of powers associated with the ownership of libraries, publishing houses, reviewing media) precisely because it can challenge existing authorities – or because these at least believe that it can.

Pragmatics From two important early theorists of SEMIOTICS, Charles Morris and Charles Peirce, has come a useful tripartite distinction between *syntactics* (SIGNS and their relations to other signs), *semantics* (signs and their relations to the 'outside world'), and *pragmatics* (signs and their relations to users). The distinction has been most fruitful within the realm of Linguistics, where it has enabled theorists such as Ferdinand de Saussure and those who followed his example to isolate different systems of formal rules (syntactic and semantic) from language in its actual, day-to-day use (its pragmatic existence). Saussure and his disciples argued that language at the pragmatic level was subject to too many random and unquantifiable pressures to constitute a proper object of study. To be studied it had to be reduced to an ideal state untouched by the accidents and casual pressures of everyday usage.

Ignoring the pragmatic aspect of language use in this way made life much simpler for linguisticians, and during the time of Saussure's greatest influence was seen by some to be a precondition for the formal study of language. At the same time, during the 1960s and 1970s, the theories of the American linguist Noam Chomsky also argued for a linguistic object of study which could be set apart from the pragmatic use of language.

But in recent years more and more disquiet has been expressed at the banishing of the realm of the pragmatic from the concern of the theorist of language, and pragmatics, which has its primary origin within the discipline of Linguistics, involves a certain reaction against the ideas and practices of Saussure and Chomsky. Thus Stephen C. Levinson, in his *Pragmatics*, suggests that the growth of interest in pragmatics owes much to a reaction against Chomsky's treatment of language as an abstract device or mental ability which is dissociable from the uses, users, and functions of language (1983, 35). He adds, however, that this is not the whole story:

> Another powerful and general motivation for the interest in pragmatics is the growing realization that there is a very substantial gap between current linguistic theories of language and accounts of linguistic communication. . . . For it is becoming increasingly clear that a semantic theory alone can give us only a proportion, and perhaps only a small if essential proportion, of a general account of language understanding. (1983, 38)

This development in Linguistics has its parallels in other disciplines, including Literary Criticism. A collection of essays edited by Roger Sell and entitled *Literary Pragmatics* contains a number of attempts to transpose some of the more general principles of pragmatics to a literary context. Central to such a project is a commitment to moving away from the study of literary WORKS as closed or purely formal structures of TEXT to a recognition of them as MEDIATING elements in chains of communication.

> Literary pragmatics takes for granted that no account of communication in general will be complete without an account of literature and its contextualization, and that no account of literature will be complete without an account of its use of the communicative resources generally available. In effect, it reinstates the ancient linkage between rhetoric and poetics . . . (1991, xiv)

Perhaps paradoxically, such emphases can take us back to formal systems. It is well known that ancient rhetoric tended to generate these: in its modern variants attempts to isolate the sets of rules and CONVENTIONS that bind writers to READERS, and which can be seen as the forces which choreograph actual readings of works of literature, can lead straight into SYSTEMS as formal and formalized as GRAMMARS.

Literary pragmatics typically tries to bring together CENTRIFUGAL AND CENTRIPETAL movements: moving into the text and isolating pragmatic techniques (implicature, presupposition, persuasion), and relating these to forces outside the text in the worlds of writer and reader, such as power relations, CULTURAL traditions, systems of publishing and distribution, censorship, and so on, with a stress throughout on *particular* pragmatic conjunctions and interactions.

Even in abridged form this begins to look like an ambitious project, and literary pragmatics seems to enjoy greatest success in attempts to isolate relatively isolated pragmatic mechanisms, often in highly localized studies.

Not to be confused with Pragmatism, a philosophical doctrine which recommends a concentration upon that which is of practical concern for human beings and which avoids the consideration of more absolute or abstract issues.

See also DISCOURSE; LANGUE AND PAROLE.

Prague School Alternatively *Prague (Linguistic) Circle*. A group of theorists writing in Prague from the late 1920s through to the German invasion of Czechoslovakia and a little beyond, some of whom were émigrés from the Soviet Union (the best-known amongst whom was Roman Jakobson, who moved to Prague in 1920 and was a founder member of the group at its inception in 1926). The best-known members of the group, apart from Jakobson, were René Wellek, Felix Vodička and Jan Mukařovský.

According to many commentators the Prague School writers constitute a clear bridge between RUSSIAN FORMALISM and modern STRUCTURALISM – a claim which can be confusing to the uninitiated as English translations of Prague School writings often have their authors describing their own position as structuralist. The structuralism of the 1960s and later is, however, somewhat (but not completely) different from the structuralism of the Prague School. What the two have in common is a significant debt to the writings of Ferdinand de Saussure, and an attempt to extend the application of Saussure's theories beyond language. The subtitle of *A Prague School Reader*, Paul L. Garvin's useful collection of some of the more important non-linguistic Prague School texts, 'On Esthetics, Structure, and Style', helpfully indicates the extent to which their work moved beyond Linguistics as such (see Garvin: 1964). The starting point may be Saussure and language, but the work of the Russian Formalists, upon which the Prague writers built, is at least as important a source as is the work of Saussure. Much of the work of the group had a specifically linguistic focus – working with phonetics, phonology and semantics and attempting to define such concepts as 'phoneme', 'distinctive/redundant feature', and so on, but from this base the members of the group moved into a number of cognate areas, including those of literature and aesthetics. But none of this work was untouched by formalism and formalist ideas: Mary Louise Pratt argues that although the School's members made a point of calling their linguistics 'functional', like Saussure they were concerned almost uniquely 'with the function of elements within the linguistic system rather than with the functions the language serves within the speech community' (1977, 7), although she adds that in the pre-Second World War period the poeticians of the group *were* concerned with this latter issue – as can, incidentally, be seen from the essays in Garvin's *Reader*. This, she adds, meant that from the publication of the important Prague School Theses of 1929, an opposition between poetic and non-poetic language is built into the group's pronouncements on the social function of

273

language. The position is clearly expressed in Jan Mukařovský's essay 'Standard Language and Poetic Language' (reprinted in Garvin: 1964).

We can trace this distinction right through to Roman Jakobson's much later, and no less influential, argument about the different FUNCTIONS OF LANGUAGE. The poetic function, as defined by Jakobson, involves 'a focussing on the message itself for its own sake'. This is a definition which, although it maintains the Prague School commitment to a distinction between poetic and ordinary language, effectively denies literature any significant social role and can be seen as a step away from some of the pre-Second World War positions of the group's members concerning literature. It is not surprising, following this, to find Mukařovský arguing a standard formalist case in 'Standard Language and Poetic Language': 'the question of truthfulness does not apply in regard to the subject matter of a work of poetry, nor does it even make sense' (1964, 22–3).

It is fair to say that one item of Prague School belief which has not stood the test of time well is that of the existence of a separate 'poetic language' which can be distinguished from 'ordinary language', and whose function 'is that of the maximum of foregrounding of the utterance' (Mukařovský: 1964, 19).

With the movement of René Wellek to the United States another important link – between the Prague School and Anglo-American NEW CRITICISM – can also be traced. *Theory of Literature* by René Wellek and Austin Warren first appears in the United States in 1949, at the beginning of the period of the New Criticism's greatest influence (perhaps a more accurate word would be HEGEMONY) in that country. Garvin's *Reader* prints as frontispiece a statement of Josef Hrabák's which was first published in 1941 in *Slovo a slovesnost*, the journal of the Linguistic Circle of Prague, and which can serve to indicate the common ground between these different critical schools and movements:

> Structuralism is neither a theory nor a method; it is an epistemological point of view. It starts off from the observation that every concept in a given system is determined by all other concepts of that system and has no significance by itself alone; it does not become unequivocal until it is integrated into the system, the structure, of which it forms part and in which it has a definite fixed place. ...For the structuralist, there is an interrelation between the data (facts) and the philosophic assumptions, not a unilateral dependence. ... In one word, the entire structure is more than a mechanical summary of the properties of its components since it gives rise to new qualities. (1964, vi)

Here we see the Saussurean emphasis on relation (or DIFFERENCE) instead of self-identity, but within the individual SYSTEM rather than in language in general. And for the Prague School the individual system so far as literature is concerned tends to be the individual literary WORK rather than LITERARINESS in general although, as the above quotation demonstrates, there is a generalizing impulse in Prague School theory which helps to prevent it from being imprisoned in pre-existing categories such as 'the work'.

At any rate, a view of the literary work as a STRUCTURE which had to be seen as a whole generated by the dynamic relationships between its component parts (a view which probably also owes a lot to GESTALT psychology), encouraged ANALYSIS of these dynamic relationships. Thus Prague School theories can be said to have contributed to the already existing emphasis upon close reading made by the New Critics. And it is fascinating to read Felix Vodička's 1942 essay 'The History of the Echo of Literary Works' in conjunction with W. K. Wimsatt's and Monroe Beardsley's highly influential 'The Intentional Fallacy' and 'The Affective Fallacy'. Two brief quotations from Vodička's essay must suffice to make this point:

> The literary work, upon being published or spread, becomes the property of the public, which approaches it with the artistic feeling of the time.
> : . . .
>
> Subjective elements of valuation, stemming from the momentary state of mind of the reader or his personal likes and dislikes, must in the historical criticism of sources be separated from the attitude of the times, because the object of our cognition are those features which have the character of historic generality. (1964, 71)

It is probably fair to say that, in common with the Russian Formalists, the Prague School theorists responded to critical pressure from orthodox MARXIST critics by stressing the internal relationships in the literary work at the expense of its external relationships with AUTHOR, READER, or socio-historical reality, although at the same time a writer such as Mukařovský was able to incorporate talk about the literary work's internal DIALECTIC in a way which suggested some absorption of Marxist ideas.

So far as literary theory and criticism are concerned, the development of the Russian Formalist concept of DEFAMILIARIZATION into the similar concept of FOREGROUNDING represents perhaps the most influential of Prague School theoretical contributions, especially within the fields of NARRATOLOGY and STYLISTICS. There are strong points of resemblance between the Prague School concept of foregrounding and certain aspects of Bertolt Brecht's theories concerning the ALIENATION EFFECT, although it seems unlikely that any direct influence can be traced here.

Praxis The Greek and German word meaning *practice*, praxis is associated in particular with MARXIST and neo-Marxist theorists who argued against abstract philosophizing on the ground that understanding arose only when linked to attempts to change the world through active engagement in social and political movements.

Precession In standard English a term relating to the earlier occurrence of the equinoxes in each successive sidereal year, but used in English translations of Jean Baudrillard to mean 'that which precedes', especially with regard to his argument that the simulacrum (IMAGE or representation) precedes that which it represents. His argument can be categorized as an extreme form of POSTMODERNIST anti-REALISM, as the following quotation perhaps reveals:

> Abstraction today is no longer that of the map, the double, the mirror or the concept. Simulation is no longer that of a territory, a referential being or a substance. It is the generation by models of a real without origin or reality: a hyperreal. The territory no longer precedes the map, nor survives it. Henceforth it is the map that precedes the territory – **PRECESSION OF SIMULACRA** – it is the map that engenders the territory . . . (1983, 2; Baudrillard's emphasis)

Hyperreality can thus be seen as an extreme version of HYPERSPACE, taking its solipsistic and idealistic tendencies to an extreme.

Such a position can be seen as an (again extreme) version of linguistic relativism or linguistic determinism (see the entry for SAPIR-WHORF HYPOTHESIS), according to which it is the language that we speak that determines the reality that we see or inhabit. Such positions normally have difficulty in explaining why different peoples speak different languages, and where these languages come from, and in like manner Baudrillard's position is weakened by its inability to explain where the maps which define our territories come from.

Having said that, it should be admitted that Baudrillard's concerns are related to the problems of a modern world in which the AGENDA-SETTING powers of the mass-media seem at times to have grown to the point at which the media create the reality on which they ostensibly report, and which READERS and viewers inhabit.

Prefiguring See PROLEPSIS

Prehistory In her article 'Virginia Woolf and Prehistory', which was first published in 1984, Gillian Beer gives a succinct account of three different meanings relevant to literature and criticism which are associated with this term.

> In recent years 'prehistory' has become a useful technical term for describing those conditions of production and of reception which determine the relationship between text and reader. (What do we know about the conditions of production and how does this knowledge define our reading?) The term 'prehistory' is also sometimes used to describe the means by which a work of fiction creates its own past, suggesting a continuity between an unrecorded previous existence for the characters and the language of the text that makes them be. That is, it can be used as a way of claiming a non-linguistic, prior presence for people whom we simultaneously know to be purely the verbal products of a particular act of writing. But there is a further sense of the term which seems particularly apt to Virginia Woolf's work: prehistory implies a pre-narrative domain which will not buckle to plot. Just as Freud said that the unconscious knows no narrative, so prehistory tells no story. It is time without narrative, its only story a conclusion. That story is extinction. (1996, 9)

Prepublication/postpublication reading Adopted by Jerome J. McGann from John Sutherland's account of,

> on the one hand, the 'English' model of postpublication reading via the traditional reviewing institutions; and, on the other, the 'American' model of prepublication reading via early promotional apparatuses, advance printing and purchase orders, and various peripheral schemes for disseminating (not necessarily the text but) the presence of the text. (McGann: 1991, 125)

McGann's adoption of the terms is in line with his interest in the way in which extra-textual factors affect the READING and reception of a literary WORK.

See also PARATEXT.

Presence According to Jacques Derrida in the early and influential article 'Structure, Sign and Play in the Discourse of the Human Sciences', 'all the names related to funda-mentals, to principles, or to the center have always designated an invariable presence – *eidos, archē, telos, energeia, ousia* (essence, existence, substance, subject) *alētheia*, transcendentality, consciousness, God, man, and so forth' (1978a, 279–80). All of these represent extra-SYSTEMIC entities, points of reference or CENTRES of authority which escape from that play of DIFFERENCE which, following Saussure, Derrida believes to be the sole source of MEANING. The *metaphysics of presence*, then, is a LOGOCENTRIC belief in and reliance upon some such extra-systemic point of authority.

See also COPERNICAN REVOLUTION.

Presentism On the model of racism, sexism, etc.: the imposition of the standards, values and attitudes of the present on the past (and, on occasions, the future). Presentism universalizes the present and refuses to perceive other times in their particularity and their movement.

Brook Thomas points out that those of the left and the right object to presentism for rather different reasons: their disagreements often involve what is meant by a sense of historicity.

> For conservatives it too often implies a somewhat pious attitude toward and knowledge of the past. For leftists it is not an attitude toward the past but toward the present, an awareness that the present itself is a moment of history, an awareness dependent upon a historical consciousness. (1991, 18)

Primal scene See PRIMARY PROCESS

Primary process In *The Interpretation of Dreams* Sigmund Freud posits the existence of two psychical forces (or currents, or systems), one of which constructs the wish which is expressed by the dream whilst the other exercises a CENSORSHIP upon the dream-wish and forcibly brings about a distortion of its expression (1976, 225). These two forces have come to be known as the primary and the secondary processes in discussion of Freud's theories.

Juliet Mitchell has glossed the *primary process* as 'the laws that govern the workings of the unconscious' (1974, 8) and the primary process is characterized by the free and unrestrained nature of its operation. Of interest to literary critics has been the suggestion that the primary process has a significant or dominating responsibility with regard to artistic and literary composition. The construction of a literary WORK is seen to be analogous in important ways to the construction by the UNCONSCIOUS of a dream, and not surprisingly the INTERPRETATION of both thus requires comparable techniques. Some critics have even suggested that the secondary process comes into play in READING and criticism: the reader is unwilling to accept the forces unleashed in the literary work, but has to disguise and deny their presence. More usually, however, the secondary process is also seen by Freudian critics to come into play at the creative stage: the artist or writer has to disguise the free workings of the unconscious in the finished work just as the dream-content is censored by the secondary process.

Not to be confused with the *primal scene*, which in Freudian terminology is the child's witnessing of its parents' copulation.

Privilege The verb *to privilege* and cognate noun and adjectival forms are frequently used by recent theorists to indicate a hierarchical structuring of causal factors. To privilege GENDER in a consideration of CLASS and gender in historical change, then, is to suggest that gender is more influential than class in historical causality.

When NARRATIVE theorists talk of privilege, however, they generally refer to the possession of information which is either exclusive to a particular NARRATOR or to some form of understanding which is not shared by some or all of the CHARACTERS in the narrative.

Proairetic code See CODE

Problematic Problematic as noun came into the vocabulary of Anglo-Saxon theorists through Louis Althusser's *For Marx*, first published in English translation in 1969. According to Althusser he borrowed the concept from Jacques Martin, 'to designate the particular unity of a theoretical formation and hence the location to be assigned to this specific difference' (1969, 32).

Although Althusser assigned the term to *theoretical* formations it is often used to designate IDEOLOGICAL ones as well; any complex of beliefs which (whatever their implicit or explicit contradictions) hangs together in a self-supporting unity may be referred to as a problematic by recent theorists. It is probably too late to alter this drift of meaning, but Althusser's usage does have the virtue of fitting in with his concept of the EPISTEMOLOGICAL BREAK, that is, of a shift from one problematic to another such as he claimed to discover in the writings of Karl Marx.

The term can be used in a way that makes it appear similar to Foucault's concept of the *ÉPISTÉMÈ*, in as much as it may be believed that a particular problematic represents what is 'thinkable' for those in its grip, and beyond which thought cannot venture.

See also PARADIGM SHIFT for another comparable concept.

Projection See PROJECTION CHARACTERS

Projection characters CHARACTERS into whom an AUTHOR projects (often contradictory) aspects of him- or herself. The term *projection* is taken from the work of Sigmund Freud, who used it to describe a process in which impulses or beliefs unacceptable to the ego are attributed to someone else.

The opposite of projection is *introjection*, in which an individual as it were internalizes things from outside him/herself and looks on them as his or her own. According to Nicola Diamond (1992, 177), the term was coined by Sandor Ferenczi in 1909 (see Ferenczi: 1909), but was adopted and developed by Freud. The process described by the term has interesting points of contact with claims made by members of the Bakhtin circle and by the Russian L. S. Vygotsky (1986) concerning the internalization of the VOICES of others. (See the entry for INTERIOR DIALOGUE.)

Of course, when we take the relationship between a real-life author and his/her characters, it may be difficult to distinguish between projection and introjection. (An author may cause a character to introject voices from other extra-FICTIONAL characters, while simultaneously projecting his or her own unacceptable beliefs on to the character[s] in question.)

Prolepsis Also, following Prince (1988a), *anticipation, flashforward* or *prospection*. Any narrating of a narrative EVENT before the time in the STORY at which it will take place has been reached in the NARRATIVE. Some theorists, including Genette, have argued that the term be extended to the *evocation* (as well as the narrating) of such 'future' events. If this is accepted, it will follow that many prolepses cannot be recognized as such on first reading of a narrative: the story of the 'gringos' who disappear looking for silver at the opening of Joseph Conrad's *Nostromo* is proleptic of the final fate of many other CHARACTERS in the novel, but the evocation of these fates by this early account can take place only in the READER's memory or upon a second reading of the novel. Prolepses would thus be either overt or implied. As I have argued with reference to ANALEPSIS, there is perhaps a case for restricting the term prolepsis to more overt cases, while examples such as that cited above can be described as 'proleptic of' later events rather than as clear examples of prolepsis. An alternative solution is to use terms such as *prefiguring* and *foreshadowing* for the evocation of future events, and to reserve prolepsis for more overt narrative references to such events.

It should be added that even overt prolepses may be difficult to recognize as such on first reading of a narrative; they may initially be read as examples of ACHRONICITY.

A *completing prolepsis* is one which is needed to achieve a full chronological coverage because of a later omission in the narrative; a *repeating prolepsis* or *advance notice* supplies information that will be provided afresh later on in the narrative.

Gérard Genette distinguishes between *internal prolepses*, which are sited within the time-span of the story, and *external prolepses*, which are sited outside of the story's temporal limits (1980, 68–71).

Prospection See PROLEPSIS

Prototype theory Monika Fludernik provides the following useful explanation:

> Prototype theory stresses how whole/part relationships and back/front, right/left, up/down orientations (as well as a host of other concepts) not only play a crucial role for our immediate body experience but from there are apt to infect our categorial thinking and effect repercussions even on the level of entirely 'abstract' areas of reasoning. (1996, 18)

Psychoanalytic criticism Perhaps the most striking difference between the literary criticism influenced by or based upon psychoanalytic theories of the pre-Second World War period, and that based upon psychoanalytic theories of the past few decades, is that the latter is unlikely to be built purely upon such psychoanalytic theories. Freudian literary criticism of the 1920s and 1930s, for example, generally presented a rather exclusivist appearance: distinguishing itself from other literary criticism and relying very little upon theorists other than Freud or his followers. In contrast, the modern literary critic or theorist who relies heavily upon the writings of, say, Jacques Lacan, is likely also to exhibit a more general interest in DECONSTRUCTIONIST and POST-STRUCTURALIST theory.

An extremely useful and accessible introduction to and overview of psychoanalysis and psychoanalytic criticism can be found in E. Ann Kaplan's editor's Introduction to her 1990 book *Psychoanalysis and Cinema*, entitled 'From Plato's Cave to Freud's Screen'. Kaplan differentiates the following six different aspects of psychoanalysis:

1. Psychoanalysis as a 'talking' cure. (Kaplan divides this into two parts: the analytic scene, and 'the theory of human development ... found in Freud's basic concepts'.)
2. Psychoanalysis used to *explain* literary relationships, actions, motives, and the very existence itself of the text.
3. Psychoanalysis as *structurally* an aesthetic discourse. (Kaplan refers here to narrative theory, and notes that '[t]he analyst and the analysand are seen to construct "fictions" in the course of their interaction that are not dissimilar from literary use of language'.)
4. Psychoanalysis *in* a narrative discourse – used as the subject of literary or film texts.
5. Psychoanalysis as an historical, ideological, and cultural discourse.
6. Psychoanalysis as a specific process or set of processes, that the literary or film critic uses as a *discourse* to illuminate textual processes and reader/spectator positions *vis-à-vis* a text. (Abridged/adapted from Kaplan: 1990, 12–13)

Kaplan's account of the emergence of psychoanalytic literary methods in Germany in the 1930s, and of their development in the United States in the 1940s and subsequently is an ideal starting point for anyone wishing to pursue this topic.

Lacan is the psychoanalytical theorist who has been most influential on literary theory and criticism in recent years, particularly with regard to his development of the theories of both Freud and Saussure. Lacan's assertion that the Unconscious is structured like a language involves an extension of the LINGUISTIC PARADIGM into the realms of psychoanalysis, and has been seen to have important implications for our understanding of the concept of the SUBJECT and of language itself. In terms of studies of particular literary TEXTS it is harder to point to a great influence on Lacan's part. His study of Edgar Allan Poe's short story *The Purloined Letter* is less a piece of literary criticism and more the use of a literary text to exemplify certain psychoanalytic issues, and although it has inspired a number of subsequent studies it is doubtful to what extent the student of Poe will find too much of local interest in these.

Since the 1980s psychoanalytical theory has typically entered Literary Studies in company with FEMINISM. Stevi Jackson and Sue Scott point out that the centrality of the concept of repression to psychoanalysis has encouraged both MARXIST and socialist feminists to use psychoanalysis in their exploration of female sexuality (1996, 7), and many feminist literary-critical appropriations of psychoanalysis have been concerned with issues of GENDER formation, repression, and sexuality. For Jackson and Scott, the attraction of a perspective on Freud mediated through Lacan, 'is its emphasis on the cultural and linguistic structures in which we are positioned in becoming sexed subjects, and its representation of feminine sexual identity as a precarious accomplishment'.

Laura Mulvey has explained the considerable influence of Lacan's writings within Film Studies and feminism as follows.

His influence broadened and advanced ways of conceptualising sexual difference, emphasising the fictional, constructed nature of masculinity and femininity, the results of social and symbolic, not biological, imperatives. From a political point of view, this position has an immediate attraction for feminists: once anatomy is no longer destiny, women's oppression and exploitation can become contingent rather than necessary. The Lacanian account of the Oedipus complex pivots on the relation of the Father to law, culture and symbolisation, so motherhood under patriarchy gains an important psychoanalytic dimension. (1989, 165)

She adds, however, a note of warning.

But, in the last resort, the theory and the politics remain in tension. The Lacanian representation of sexual difference (defined by the presence or absence of the Phallus) leaves woman in a negative relation, defined as 'not-man' and trapped within a theory that brilliantly describes the power relationships of patriarchy but acknowledges no need for escape. (1989, 165)

The sceptical note is also struck by Stevi Jackson and Sue Scott, who note that many feminists 'remain sceptical of the entire psychoanalytic enterprise', since the 'universalistic theory of subjectivity' which it offers is 'very difficult to reconcile with historical understandings of sexuality as changing over time' (1996, 10).

Another very useful critical overview of psychoanalytic literary criticism is to be found in Peter Brooks's essay 'The Idea of a Psychoanalytic Criticism', which is one of the essays (originally lectures) in his 1994 book *Psychoanalysis and Storytelling*. In this essay Brooks admits that an initial and basic problem is that 'psychoanalysis in literary study has over and over again mistaken the object of analysis' (1994, 20), concentrating upon either the AUTHOR, the READER, or the FICTIVE persons of the text as objects of ANALYSIS. Brooks proposes an alternative:

I believe that the persistence, against all the odds, of psychoanalytic perspectives in literary study must ultimately derive from our conviction that the materials on which they exercise their powers of analysis are in some basic sense the same: that the structure of literature *is* in some sense the structure of mind – not a specific mind, but what the translators of the *Standard Edition* of Freud's Works call 'the mental apparatus' ... a term which designates the economic and dynamic organization of the psyche, to a process of structuration. ... We continue to dream of a convergence of psychoanalysis and literary criticism because we sense that there ought to be, that there must be, some correspondence between literary form and psychic process, that aesthetic structure and form, including literary tropes, must somehow coincide with the psychic structures and operations they both evoke and appeal to. (1994, 24–5)

This is clearly the statement of a man who feels himself swimming against the current: 'against all the odds', 'in some sense', 'dream', 'sense', 'that there ought to be, that there must be', 'some correspondence', 'somehow coincide' – Brooks's argument is hardly brimming with confidence, and itself invites the sort of analysis that is popularly thought of as psychoanalytic.

Brooks himself rehearses two of the major criticisms of psychoanalytic criticism, first 'that psychoanalysis imperialistically claims to explain literature' and second the 'more subtle (and contemporary) charge that psychoanalysis may be nothing *but* literature, and the relations of the two nothing more than a play of intertextuality, or even a tautology' (1994, 36). Psychoanalytical criticism, in other words, after being attacked early on for being outside the text and unresponsive to its subtleties and uniqueness, now has to adapt to a world of post-structuralist doubt in which many believe that there is no longer anything at all outside the text.

In another essay collected in the same volume, 'Changes in the Margin: Construction, Transference, and Narrative', Brooks takes a rather different tack, focusing not on parallels between literature and mind, but on parallels between telling stories to an analyst and telling stories to a literary reader. He notes that 'there appears to be increasing agreement, even among psychoanalysts themselves, that psychoanalysis is a narrative discipline'. The psychoanalyst is concerned with the stories told by 'his' patients, which typically suffer from a 'faulty syntax', full of gaps, contradictions in chronology, and screen memories concealing repressed material (1994, 47). The analyst must therefore reconstruct this narrative DISCOURSE, along with the analysand (1994, 54), and in doing so with the help of concepts such as transference and construction, Brooks suggests, in perhaps his boldest move in the essay, that psychoanalysis may 'suggest a properly dynamic model of narrative understanding that allows us to recapture, beyond a formalist "narratology," a certain referential function for narrative, where reference is understood not as a naming of the world, and not as the sociolect of the text, but as the *movement of reference* that takes place in the transference of narrative from teller to listener, and back again' (1994, 72).

Brooks is an interesting and thought-provoking critic, but the essays gathered together in *Psychoanalysis and Storytelling* do rather suggest a theory in some crisis.

See also OBJECT-RELATIONS THEORY/CRITICISM.

Psycho-narration See FREE INDIRECT DISCOURSE

Punctual anachrony See ANACHRONY

Punctuation Punctuation in its traditional sense has been of considerable concern to literary scholars and critics; the task of establishing a reliable TEXT has always included a responsibility with regard to its punctuation – often no easy job, as writing and publishing CONVENTIONS regarding punctuation are not stable. The imposition of modern punctuation conventions on literature originally published with very sparse and free punctuation is a difficult and controversial matter, and I. A. Richards suggested anecdotally that William Empson's interest in AMBIGUITY in literature stemmed from his reading of a discussion of the unpunctuated form of Shakespeare's 'The Expense of Spirit in a Waste of Shame' by Laura Riding and Robert Graves.

More recent theorists in a range of different disciplines have given a metaphorical meaning to this term, extending its coverage to include more than just the insertion of stops or divisions in written (or spoken) language for the purpose of refining MEANING and limiting ambiguity. Social psychologists, for example, have drawn attention to the way in which conflicting views of the same process of interpersonal process can be explained by reference to the manner in which the participants involved punctuate the interaction differently. (In a classic version: 'I drink because she nags me'; 'I nag him because he drinks'.)

Punctuation, in other words, involves the imposition of order and causality on a set of otherwise discrete facts by means of boundary-setting and grouping. It is not just the syntax of sentences that can be established by punctuation, but the syntax of relationships – and of literary WORKS. AUTHORS can impose a certain amount of punctuation on their works by means of chapter and other divisions: anyone who feels that this is not the case should read a work such as Joseph Conrad's *The Shadow-Line* both in its manuscript form (in which there are no divisions) and in its published version (in which the work is divided into numbered sections). The difference may seem merely formal, but such merely formal elements can have a very significant effect on the READER's experience of a work, and Conrad knew this: in a very interesting letter which he wrote to the publisher of his novel *Lord Jim*, he makes it quite clear that in imposing such divisions upon his text he has the effect on the reader very much in mind.

In an original essay on James Joyce's *A Portrait of the Artist as a Young Man*, Maud Ellmann has devoted considerable attention to the issue of punctuation in the work, showing how the growth and maturing of the hero, Stephen, involves experimentation with punctuation activities, and that these are to be seen both as attempts to master the world and as the unwitting imposition of intermittency upon himself (1981, 197–8).

In the work of Jacques Derrida the term *espacement*, normally translated as *spacing*, seems to mean something very similar to punctuation in its broader sense.

The term *segmentation* carries a comparable force within Linguistics, where it refers to the way in which language is 'chunked' or divided into segments. Segmentation is most frequently discussed at the level of intonation, and it is well known that a change in intonation can alter the meaning of an utterance. (Some of the humour in Peter Sellers's parodic version of the Beatles' *A Hard Day's Night*, which imitates Sir Laurence Olivier's 'Richard the Third' delivery, depends upon re-segmentation of the well-known lyrics.) Segmentation can also, however, be applied to written language. Where written language is concerned it is clear that segmentation and punctuation (in the traditional sense) are not necessarily synonymous. Punctuation marks may be taken as the visual indicators of a sort of internal or ideal intonation, but they are not just that nor do they exert complete control over such sense-determining 'intonation'. According to Geoffrey Leech and Michael Short, segmentation is, along with sequence and salience, one of the three main factors of textual organization (1981, 217). (Salience involves 'significant prominence' – for example, as caused by 'end focus', or the principle that we notice that which comes last in a sequence.) For sequence, see the entry for FUNCTION.

See also STUDIUM/PUNCTUM.

Punk Although this is a term which assumed a widespread and very public meaning in the late 1960s and 1970s to describe a form of raw, oppositional music and the sub-culture of (typically) unemployed young people associated with it, older meanings stretching back many centuries seem never to have disappeared entirely, and still occasionally resurface in current usage. The *OED* gives as its first meaning for the term 'a prostitute', and Gordon Williams's *A Glossary of Shakespeare's Sexual Language* (1997) gives examples of this usage in *The Merry Wives of Windsor* and *Measure for Measure*. In the early twentieth century the term had a specifically homosexual resonance, although such meanings could be concealed by the fact that a standard non-sexual American usage (a derogatory term for a young male) also existed.

Thus although the dominant meaning is still concerned with the music of groups such as the Sex Pistols and the Clash, and the clothing and oppositional behaviour of those who followed these groups, there are some signs that older sexual meanings are still associated with the term. Generally speaking such sexual associations come from Gay culture, within which the term suggests a young sexually available male.

For *cyberpunk*, see CYBER/NETICS/PUNK/SPACE.

Q

Quality (maxim of) See SPEECH ACT THEORY

Quantity (maxim of) See SPEECH ACT THEORY

Queen/butch As a result of the growing importance of QUEER THEORY within CULTURAL STUDIES and literary criticism, a number of terms from Gay and Lesbian sub-cultures have entered into more general usage in these academic areas, very often as shorthand ways of characterizing literary CHARACTERS or AUTHORS. Among such terms are the following.

A queen is an 'effeminate' Gay male. Butch refers to a person of either sex displaying physical and behavioural characteristics CONVENTIONALLY associated with the masculine. A fem(me) is a Lesbian or a Gay man who displays physical and behavioural characteristics conventionally associated with the feminine. The abbreviation r. g. stands for real girl, used to distinguish a female displaying physical and behavioural characteristics conventionally associated with the feminine from either a queen or a butch.

Queer theory The RECUPERATION of the term *queer* – originally a term of abuse aimed at homosexuals, but reclaimed by them to announce their pride in their identity as Gays and Lesbians – can be dated from the formation of the American group Queer Nation. As Ian Lucas reports, Queer Nation dates from March 1990, when after divisions amongst the ACT UP movement in New York, activists began to develop a new grouping.

> Queer Nation built activism based on sexual identity – not just lesbian, gay or bisexual, but *queer*. Queer was used as an in-your-face catch-all designer label. Its shocking tone caught some of the violence shown against lesbian and gay communities in America, and threw it right back. It was also a call to queer nationalism – a community that confronted homophobia and had collective responsibility for dismantling the power of 'the closet'. (Lucas: 1998, 14)

Following the widespread publicity achieved by Queer Nation, the term *queer* entered more and more into the vocabulary of Gay and Lesbian activism. According to an anonymous leaflet entitled 'Queer Power Now', distributed in London a year after the formation of Queer Nation, in 1991, and cited by Stevi Jackson and Sue Scott in their essay 'Sexual Skirmishes and Feminist Factions: Twenty-five Years of Debate on Women and Sexuality', 'Queer means to fuck with gender'. Jackson and Scott themselves go on to provide a rather less succinct definition.

> Among Left academics in particular, disillusionment with traditional Marxism rendered poststructuralist and postmodernist perspectives attractive. Once appropriated by feminists and gay theorists, and applied to sexuality, this tendency ultimately led to the development of Queer theory. Rather than setting up categories such as 'lesbian' as the basis of political identities, Queer sought to destabilise the binary oppositions between men and women and straight and gay. Such identities were not to be seen as authentic properties of individual subjects, but as fluid and shifting, to be adopted and discarded, played with and subverted, strategically deployed in differing contexts . . . . Radical lesbian perspectives were regarded as essentialist in that they cast lesbianism as a fixed point outside of, and in opposition to, patriarchal relations. Politically the aim of Queer theory is to demonstrate that gender and sexual categories are not given realities but are 'regulatory fictions', products of discourse. Here Queer theory converges with Queer politics, in the latter's playing out of parodic performances at street level, for example holding public 'kiss-ins' and mock weddings, and the notion of 'gender-fuck' – challenging gender categories through dress and transgressive sexual performance. (Jackson and Scott: 1996, 15)

Jackson and Scott express some reservations about this development, noting that 'much of the blurring of gender categories within gay culture is occurring at the level of style rather than politics' and allowing themselves the tart observation that they 'doubt whether wearing a tutu with Doc Martens will bring patriarchy to its knees' (1996, 16).

Catherine Grant (1994/5) is more guarded, noting that although 'Queer' has come to mean different things to different people it

> generally denotes the application of poststructuralist and postmodern ideas to interdisciplinary studies of the historical formations of lesbianism and homo-sexuality, and of the relationship between these formations and those of heterosexuality. It implies a shift from the consideration of lesbianism and homosexuality as discrete identities to one of homosexualities as kinds of discursive construct. 'Queer' theorists also often advocate the disruption or destruction of traditional categories of sex and gender. (In Jackson and Scott: 1996, 166)

As we can see, the term 'Queer' can invoke both high theory as well as a relatively unintellectualized activism, but at its heart is an anti-discriminatory view of GENDER as unfixed and certainly more complex than our neat BINARY distinctions would suggest. In his essay 'True love in queer times: romance, suburbia and masculinity', David Oswell has suggested that the 'notion that identity is not fixed but can be played with and

contested has been a central element within the recent formation of "queer politics"'
(1998, 161). He adds, however, that the practices associated with queer politics are 'far
from unified', and that 'there is clear disagreement about the meaning of the term
"queer"' (1998, 162). In spite of this he finds the term useful:

> Although the term 'queer' is used to articulate a range of political positions, it has
> clearly come to signify an assault both on 'straight' sexual discourses and practices
> and on an earlier moment in lesbian and gay sexual 'identity politics' which called
> upon individuals to express the truth of their self. ... [T]he queer politics of the late
> 1980s and 1990s has been deployed against the binary divide between heterosexual
> and homosexual and in favour of an enunciation of the pluralisation of sexual
> identities.
>
> . . .
>
> Likewise it has also come to define a wider articulation of 'perverse' sexual
> identities, communities, and practices. Sex-workers, lesbian and gay identified men
> and women, practitioners of S&M, body piercers and so on are articulated within
> the category of 'queer'. In this sense the politics of queer is neither assimilationist
> nor separatist. (1998, 163; S&M = sadism and masochism)

Oswell's article provides useful evidence of the way in which the term and the concept
can be useful within literary criticism: it is devoted to a study of Hanif Kureishi's *The
Buddha of Suburbia* (1990). The article is recommended as an excellent introduction to
Queer studies.

Various coinages involving plays on the similarity of *queer* and *query* are popular
at present. Thus *queer(y)ing* suggests that a queer READING of a literary WORK can serve
to raise questions about conventional reading, and about conventions in general.

Quest narrative In Anne Cranny-Francis's definition, a linear NARRATIVE in which
temporal sequence is taken to signify material causation. She sees this as the dominant
STRUCTURE in nineteenth- and twentieth-century Western writing, a structure which
carries a particular IDEOLOGICAL and political charge, for it PRIVILEGES linear sequence
rather than, say, seasonal cycles, and thus underwrites DOMINANT DISCOURSES in our
CULTURE (1990, 10, 11).

There are significant differences in the way in which heroes and heroines experience
the quest in traditional (non-FEMINIST) narrative. The hero is active in his quest,
overcoming difficulties and aided by helpers, whereas the heroine is passive (is often the
object of quest), has to endure suffering and humiliation, and rather than overcoming the
world has to learn to adapt to its demands (as these are MEDIATED by men).

R

Radial reading See READERS AND READING

Radical alterity A term used to describe that belief in the essential self-ALIENATION of the SIGNIFIER from itself that can be found in the writing of Jacques Derrida. The following comment illustrates the concept without actually using the term.

> The *representamen* [which we can render as *signifier*] functions only by giving rise to an *interpretant* that itself becomes a sign and so on to infinity. The self-identity of the signified conceals itself unceasingly and is always on the move. The property of the *representamen* is to be itself and another, to be produced as a structure of reference, to be separated from itself. (1976, 49–50)

In other words, signifiers are never themselves alone. Derrida accuses the Linguistics of Saussure of concealing a self-identical signified within what, on the surface, appears to be a relational SYSTEM based on DIFFÉRANCE. In fact, he claims, behind this overtly differential system lies the concealed PRESENCE of a signifier the identity of which is prior to différance. In opposition to this he argues for the recognition of the signifier's radical alterity – or essential 'difference-from-itself'.

Although Derrida's insistence on the radical alterity of the signifier appears to reject the metaphysics of presence in favour of a system based on différance, it will be noted that the posited process is completely internal to language; it allows for no way in which the signifier can function other than by means of interaction with other signifiers. It is possible to argue that it is through PRAXIS that the signifier functions, and that one avoids the infinite regress described by Derrida only by rejecting a 'prison-house' view of language as a totally closed system and allowing for a linguistic engagement with non-linguistic reality. (It is only from within the relatively closed systems of certain contemporary theories that such a proposition appears questionable and proof that one is trapped within the metaphysics of presence.)

Derrida's use of the term *exteriority* invokes many of the same issues as does the term radical alterity. According to Derrida,

> [t]he exteriority of the signifier is the exteriority of writing in general, and...there is no linguistic sign before writing. Without that exteriority, the very idea of the sign falls into decay.
> . . .
> Thus, within this epoch, reading and writing, the production or interpretation of signs, the text in general as fabric of signs, allow themselves to be confined within secondariness. (1976, 14)

See also EXTERIORITY for Michel Foucault's use of this term.

The point can be expressed another way: language is not to be compared with a dictionary in which all words are defined in terms of other words in the dictionary; it is a system which interlocks with human practice. Only at a late stage in language acquisition and in exceptional circumstances do *some* individuals learn the use of (meanings of) words in the mother tongue through the use of a dictionary. This knowledge and skill is, on the contrary, acquired by (at the risk of a tautology) *using* words: putting them to work (and not just putting them to work on other words).

This argument has important consequences for theories relating to literary INTERPRETATION, for the influence of the LINGUISTIC PARADIGM in recent years has meant that when once it has been decided that *language* is a closed system, it takes very little time before this decision is extended to other fields, and we find ourselves with 'literature' (in general) seen as a comparably closed system, or back with the closed individual literary WORK that previous formalisms such as that of the NEW CRITICS have argued for.

See also SIGN.

Radical feminism See FEMINISM

Radicle See ROOT/RADICLE/RHIZOME

Ravissement A term which Lynne Pearce attributes to Roland Barthes and which she applies to those 'sexual/textual pleasures' which have to do with 'the emotional field associated with that euphoric first connection between "self" and "other" in which the amorous subject (reader) is swept away on a tide of abandonment, joy and devotion to the loved object (text)' (1997, 85).

See also JOUISSANCE.

Reach See ANALEPSIS

Readerly and writerly texts Translated from Roland Barthes's coinages *lisible* and *scriptible* in his *S/Z* (1990, 4–5). Barthes uses the terms to distinguish between traditional literary WORKS such as the classical novel, with their reliance upon CONVENTIONS shared by writer and READER and their resultant (partial) fixity or CLOSURE of meaning, and those works produced especially in the twentieth century which violate such conventions and thus force the reader to work to produce a meaning or meanings which are inevitably other than final or 'correct'. Thus

> [t]he writerly text is a perpetual present, upon which no *consequent* language (which would inevitably make it past) can be superimposed; the writerly text is *ourselves writing*, before the infinite play of the world (the world as function) is traversed, intersected, stopped, plasticized by some singular system (Ideology, Genus, Criticism) which reduces the plurality of entrances, the opening of networks, the infinity of languages. (1990, 5)

Readerly texts, in contrast, are products rather than productions, and they make up the enormous mass of our literature (1990, 5).

Behind these comments lies a polemical element: Barthes, as he himself admits, is concerned to challenge the conventional division of labour between producers and consumers, between writers and readers. The writerly text involves such a challenge, for it forces the reader to engage in the process of writing – that is, it forces him or her to be creative in the manner traditionally reserved to the writer function. '[T]he goal of literary work (of literature as work) is to make the reader no longer a consumer, but a producer of the text' (1990, 4). This ties in with Barthes's comments on the death of the author – see the entry for AUTHOR.

A comparable distinction is that provided by Umberto Eco in his *The Role of the Reader* (1981) between OPEN AND CLOSED TEXTS.

Reader-response criticism See READERS AND READING

Readers and reading According to the American critic Stanley Fish, in a book published in 1980: 'Twenty years ago one of the things that literary critics didn't do was talk about the reader, at least in a way that made his experience the focus of the critical act' (1980, 344). Since the time about which Fish was writing, however, more and more attention has been devoted to the identity, role and function of readers of literature, and this has led to the coining of a range of new terms. Some of this attention has stemmed from a number of different critical theories and approaches which are often collectively described as *reader-response criticism*, but some of it can best be seen in relation to the loosening of NEW CRITICAL dogmas. Once appeal to the INTENTIONAL and AFFECTIVE fallacies lost its force, curiosity about the reader faced no interdiction. A sure indication of this sense of new-found freedom is the gradual movement away from talk of 'the reader' towards reference to 'readers' – a movement accompanied by the willingness of critics to say 'I' rather than 'we', which in its turn has to be related to a growing awareness of the dangers of ethnocentricity and parallel GENDER and CLASS biases. For this reason it may be a little misleading to think of reader response criticism as a school: the term gathers together a range of attempts to theorize about readers and to study them and the reading process, and Terry Eagleton's joke description 'The Reader's Liberation Front' catches some of the diversity in the reality described. Indeed, not all criticism categorized as reader-response criticism is actually concerned with readers' response(s); much of it is concerned with other issues: readers' COMPETENCE, the reading process *in toto*, the TEXT's formation of the reader, and so on.

Perhaps not surprisingly, much of the criticism described as reader-response criticism is concerned with the novel. We are much more conscious of reading as a process when reading a novel than when reading a poem – especially a lyric poem which can be held as a finished unit more easily in the memory. Wayne Booth's 1961 book *Rhetoric of Fiction* popularized the notion of the IMPLIED AUTHOR, and by extension the term 'implied reader' was coined to describe the reader which the text (or the author through the text) suggests that it expects. Booth himself talks of the *postulated* or *mock* reader; another very similar term – *extrafictional* or *authorial voice* – is suggested by Susan Sniader Lanser:

> The authorial voice is an *extrafictional* entity whose presence accounts, for example, for organizing, titling, and introducing the fictional work. This extra-fictional voice, the most direct textual counterpart for the historical author, carries all the *diegetic authority* of its (publicly authorized) creator and has the ontological status of historical truth ... (1981, 122; quoted by Aczel: 1998, 474)

It should be noted that this term, like all other terms with the form 'the X reader', although singular, actually has the purpose of describing a group or category of reade*rs*.

289

Jacques Derrida has argued that all reading is transformational, and in the same comment warned against reading (in this case the classic texts of MARXISM) 'according to a hermeneutical or exegetical method which would seek out a finished signified beneath a textual surface' (1981b, 63). Although Derrida is not normally thought of as a reader-response critic, the same insistence upon those transformational and creative aspects of reading which we associate with this group of critics can be found in his work.

Closely related to the implied reader is the *inscribed reader*, that is, the reader whose characteristics are actually there to be discovered in the text itself, waiting for the actual reader to slip on like a suit of clothes. Umberto Eco has introduced the similar concept of the *model reader*; he argues that '[t]o make his text communicative, the author has to assume that the ensemble of codes he relies upon is the same as that shared by his possible reader (hereafter Model Reader) supposedly able to deal interpretatively with the expressions in the same way as the author deals generatively with them' (1981, 7). This may be taken to imply that the model reader is external to the text, but later in the same chapter of his book Eco makes it clear that for him the concept is more intra-textual in nature and that the model reader is thus also to be understood to be inscribed in the text:

> [T]he Model Reader is a textually established set of felicity conditions ... to be met in order to have a macro-speech act (such as a text is) fully actualized. (1981, 11; for *felicity conditions* see SPEECH ACT THEORY)

Rather different is the *intended reader*, because here the evidence may be either intra- or extra-textual: an author's comment in a letter that a WORK of literature was written to be read by a particular person or group of people can be used as evidence substantiating a case for a particular intended reader, but clearly not for a particular inscribed reader. Again related but slightly different are the *average* and the *optimal* or *ideal reader* (sometimes translated as *super-reader*). Super-reader comes from Michael Riffaterre (he later replaces it with *archi-lecteur* or composite reader), and describes (paradoxically) as much readings as readers, in other words, the responses engendered in different readers by particular textual elements. Riffaterre has also coined the term *retroactive reading* to describe a second-stage, HERMENEUTIC reading which comes subsequent to an initial, *heuristic reading* or reading-for-the-meaning process (1978, 5; see the entry for MEANING AND SIGNIFICANCE).

Different again is *symptomatic reading*: if we define a SYMPTOM as a non-intentional SIGN then it follows that a symptomatic reading treats a work much as a doctor examines a patient for symptoms. The doctor (in the exemplary situation) does not ask the patient what is wrong with him or her, but looks for clues which the patient is unable to recognize or interpret. A symptomatic reading, then, seeks to use such clues in a work as a way into the secrets of the author, or of his or her society or CULTURE, or whatever.

Jerome J. McGann has coined the term *radial reading* for the sort of reading that 'puts one in a position to respond actively to the text's own (often secret) discursive acts'. As an example he refers to the two volumes which comprise the first edition of Ezra Pound's first 27 cantos, each of which 'makes a clear historical allusion not only to William Morris and the bibliographical face of the late nineteenth-century aesthetic movement, but also to the longer tradition which those late nineteenth-century works were invoking: the tradition of the decorated manuscript and its Renaissance bibliographical inheritors' (1991, 122).

The *optimal/ideal reader* is a term used to refer to that collection of abilities, attitudes, experience, and knowledge which will allow a reader to extract the maximum value from a reading of a particular text. (For some commentators, the maximum *legitimate* value.) It should be noted that whereas for some critics the optimal/ideal reader is a universal figure, for most he or she is particular to given texts: the ideal reader for *Humphry Clinker* may not be the ideal reader for 'My Last Duchess'. Closely related again is the *informed reader*, a term given currency by Stanley Fish. According to Fish

> [t]he informed reader is someone who (1) is a competent speaker of the language out of which the text is built up; (2) is in full possession of 'the semantic knowledge that a mature . . . listener brings to his task of comprehension,' including the knowledge (that is, the experience, both as a producer and comprehender) of lexical sets, collocation probabilities, idioms, professional and other dialects, and so on; and (3) has *literary* competence. That is, he is sufficiently experienced as a reader to have internalized the properties of local discourses, including everything from the most local of devices (figures of speech, and so on) to whole genres. (1980, 48)

In spite of the fact that all of these terms have sprouted on the grave (or the sick-bed) of the New Criticism, it can be argued that all of them except the intended reader retain a certain text-centredness. Rather different is the *empirical reader*, used to describe those actual human beings who read a given literary work in varied ways and get varied things out of their readings. This concept arises perhaps more from the sociology of literature than from literary criticism as such, but study of the empirical reader and of empirical readings can have important implications for literary criticism. In particular, confirmation that one literary work can generate a range of different reading experiences, over time, between cultures or groups (or within them), and even for the same individual, leads necessarily to the question of the status and authority of these different reading experiences. If there is an optimal reader is there also an optimal reading, or is it a characteristic of major literature that it can generate a succession of new reading experiences as the individual reader or his or her culture changes? It has to be said that study of empirical readings is at a very early stage; Norman N. Holland's *5 Readers Reading* (1975) contained interesting material, but it could more accurately have been entitled *5 Readers Remembering What They Read*. Lynne Pearce's *Feminism and the Politics of Reading* (1997) combines empirical study of her own and other reading processes with a view of the reader–work relationship as a form of ROMANCE, a romance which proceeds through a set of standard phases which Pearce borrows from Roland Barthes's *The Pleasure of the Text* (1976).

It is important to distinguish the reader or readers from the NARRATEE or narratees, although in very special circumstances (a lyric poem addressed to and read only by a given person) the two roles may be filled by one and the same person.

For *mediation reading* and *transparency reading* see OPAQUE AND TRANSPARENT CRITICISM. For *category readers* see LINE FICTION.

See also COMPETENCE AND PERFORMANCE; NEW READERS; READERLY AND WRITERLY TEXTS; RECEPTION THEORY.

Reading as a woman/like a woman See READING POSITION

Reading community See INTERPRET[AT]IVE COMMUNITY

Reading position According to Anne Cranny-Francis, the concept of reading position helps us to understand how an audience is constructed by a literary TEXT. For her, a reading position is 'the position assumed by a reader from which the text seems to be coherent and intelligible' (1990, 25). Put another way: the text *situates* the READER in certain ways. Just as we have to get into a certain position to see certain physical objects, so too in order to read Jane Austen's *Pride and Prejudice* the reader has to adopt a stance with regard to the values and procedures of the NARRATIVE, unless a decision is made to give the WORK an OPPOSITIONAL READING. In the words of Coleridge's much earlier formulation, the reader has to undergo a *suspension of disbelief*, and perhaps the reason why this particular phrase has fallen somewhat out of fashion is that recent critics have been more interested in the IDEOLOGICAL situating of the reader by the text than was Coleridge. As we know from the realm of public politics, merely to agree to negotiate with someone may involve some sort of concession; those who talk of reading positions or of the way the text situates the reader are concerned to stress that merely to start reading a literary work (as a literary work) may involve certain concessions which are not always consciously granted by the reader.

On the other hand, reading positions have very often to be negotiated between reader and work. As Lynne Pearce puts it: 'While I, the reader, exist in dialogic relationship with the text (any text), I am nevertheless *positioned by it*, and the challenge and excitement of the reading process depends upon my not knowing, in advance, if it will embrace me or reject me, position me as an ally or as an antagonist. (1997, 49).

Two related concepts are those of reading as a woman and reading like a woman. Evelyne Keitel distinguishes between the two as follows.

> 'Reading as a woman' rests on the (tacit) assumption that gender is the decisive factor in all human activity: women *are* different from men, therefore they *read* differently – reading is seen to be grounded in biology. Its second assumption is that there must be an obvious and *viable* continuity between all female experience . . .
> For women to read 'like a woman' requires an intentional and voluntary act of 'unlearning', an act of 'defamiliarization' with their gender roles. (1992, 371, 372)

Real See IMAGINARY/SYMBOLIC/REAL

Realism Debates around the concept of realism go back a long way, and recent arguments need to be seen as the latest attempts to grapple with certain perennial problems. (There is an excellent historical account of the development of this term – not limiting itself to literary or artistic usages – in Raymond Williams's *Keywords* [1976].) David Lodge has pointed out that, as with the term 'literature', '[realism] is used sometimes in a neutrally descriptive sense and sometimes as an evaluative term', and he reminds us that 'the particular instances to which it is applied will vary from one period to another... and it is not exclusively aesthetic in application' (1977, 22).

Discussions of realism recur at regular intervals, and tend to reflect dominant concerns of the time and place in which they occur. Of particular interest to students of literature are perhaps the following cases.

The Brecht–Lukács debate dates from the 1930s, but Brecht's contributions were not made known to Lukács at that time nor were they published until much later. In his published writings the Hungarian MARXIST Georg Lukács had, by the mid-1930s, arrived at a definition of realism which placed a high premium upon the artist's (i) portraying the *totality* of reality in some form or other, and (ii) *penetrating beneath* the surface appearance of reality so as to be able to grasp the underlying laws of historical *change*. For Lukács, then, the artist's task is similar to that set for himself by Marx: to understand world history as a complex and dynamic totality through the uncovering of certain underlying laws. In practice this led Lukács to place a supreme value upon certain works of classical realism in the novel – the names of Tolstoy, Balzac and Thomas Mann are frequently on his lips or at the tip of his pen – and to wage an unceasing campaign against different aspects of what he classified as MODERNISM. At the end of his *The Historical Novel* (written 1936–7) Lukács refers to the 'misunderstanding' of his position that 'we intended a formal revival, an artistic imitation of the classical historical novel' (1969, 422), but even so many commentators have seen his opposition to modernism to be so all-embracing that this is actually what would have been needed to satisfy his requirement that a literary WORK be 'realistic'.

So that when Brecht, writing about the concept of realism, states that we 'must not derive realism as such from particular existing works' (Bloch *et al.*: 1977, 81), the unstated target is clearly Lukács (especially as he goes on to refer to Balzac and Tolstoy). Brecht's argument is, in a nutshell, an anti-ESSENTIALIST one. In other words, realism for him is not INTRINSIC to a literary work, coded into it for all time like the genetic code in a living being, but a function of the role the work plays or can play in a given society at a particular historical moment. To simplify, we can say that whereas for Lukács a work is realistic or not depending upon whether it portrays a socio-historical totality in terms of its underlying laws of transformation, for Brecht a work is realistic not once and for all, but by reference to its ability at a particular time and place to allow individuals to understand and to change the conditions of their existence. As he says, reality changes and in order to represent reality modes of representation must also change (Bloch *et al.*: 1977, 82). Brecht's realism focuses not on questions of form or content, but of function.

Realistic means: discovering the causal complexes of society / unmasking the prevailing view of things as the view of those who are in powe r / writing from the standpoint of the class which offers the broadest solutions for the pressing difficulties in which human society is caught up / emphasizing the element of development / making possible the concrete, and making possible abstraction from it. (Bloch *et al.*: 1977, 82)

Not surprisingly, then, Brecht's view of the formal experimentation associated with modernism is far more favourable than is Lukács's.

Interestingly, too, Brecht's views on this issue have something in common with those expressed by Roman Jakobson in his 1921 essay 'On Realism in Art' (1971a). Both stress the need for continuous formal regeneration and transformation in order to prevent AUTOMATIZATION, although it has to be said that Brecht's position has a practical-political element which Jakobson's lacks.

If the crudities of some theories of socialist realism inherited from the Soviet Union of the 1930s and 1940s led to a movement away from any concern with realism on the part of more recent theorists, the women's movement and associated FEMINIST theories have placed it back on the agenda even when the term itself is not used. Recent feminist literary criticism and theory tends to be sharply distinguished from a range of other contemporary theories which either deny that the literary work reflects (and reflects upon) non-literary reality, or which express uninterest in such processes if indeed they take place. The essential point in this context was made in an article by Cheri Register dating from the early years of contemporary feminist literary criticism: 'Feminist criticism is ultimately cultural criticism' (1975, 10). Feminist literary critics are interested in literary works not 'in themselves' but in relation to a reality they reflect, distort, form and change. Thus even if the term 'realism' is infrequently encountered in feminist criticism, realism in a broad sense as an assumption lies behind much of it.

Mieke Bal (1993) has usefully isolated six different 'conceptions' associated with the concept of realism, and her examples are usefully indicative of some current theoretical concerns associated with the concept.

1. Realism serves the interests of dominant moral and political structures: ... what is real translates into what is acceptable; *vraisemblance* is decency.
2. Realism serves the illusion of iconicity, based on a grave misreading of that concept in the work of Charles S. Peirce.
3. Realism promotes the use of art, politically biased as it is, to serve as documentary.
4. Realism serves the interest of mystification in what it conceals and obscures. Thus it reveals not only what is 'there' but also what is not there.
5. Realism is even more aggressively political than that, specifically in its preference for details: it serves what Barthes termed an *effect of the real*, a mode of interpretation that willingly neglects the content of a representation in order to instill the notion that 'this is reality.'
6. The complicity between realism and colonialism makes the conjunction of the two in the sixteenth and seventeenth, and again in the nineteenth, centuries, a suspicious coincidence. (Adapted from 1993, 388–90, omitting Bal's discussion of each conception.)

Bal's discussion of these conceptions is very rewarding and is recommended.
See also DEFORMATION; SYNTAGMATIC AND PARADIGMATIC.

Rear-mirrorism Following Marshall McLuhan, the tendency of new media to be constrained by the limits of existing media when first introduced, and to take time to find their potentialities fully exploited. (We are always looking in the rear-view mirror to see what is behind us, rather than looking ahead.)

Recall See ANALEPSIS

Receiver See SHANNON AND WEAVER MODEL OF COMMUNICATION

Reception theory A term generally used in a relatively narrow sense to describe a particular group of (mainly German) theorists concerned with the way in which literary WORKS are 'received' by their READERS over time, but also sometimes used in a looser sense to describe any attempt to theorize the ways in which art-works are received, individually and collectively, by their 'consumers'. The names most frequently mentioned as core members of the particular group of theorists are Hans Robert Jauss, Wolfgang Iser, Karlheinz Stierle and Harald Weinrich.

The translators of an article by Karlheinz Stierle entitled 'The Reading of Fictional Texts' suggest that the German term *Rezeption* as used by those known as 'reception theorists', 'refers to the activity of reading, the construction of meaning, and the reader's response to what he is reading' (Stierle: 1980, 83 n1). In analysing the activity of reading, reception theorists make considerable use of a concept defined by Hans Robert Jauss – along with Wolfgang Iser the most important founder-member of the group. In an early and influential essay entitled 'Literary History as a Challenge to Literary Theory', Jauss singles out three ways in which a writer can anticipate a reader's response which seem to represent his view of the component parts of the reader's *horizon of expectations*:

> first, by the familiar standards or the inherent poetry of the genre; second, by the implicit relationships to familiar works of the literary-historical context; and third, by the contrast between history and reality. . . . The third factor includes the possibility that the reader of a new work has to perceive it not only within the narrow horizon of his literary expectations but also within the wider horizon of his experience of life. (1974, 18)

All of these elements may fuse into a single if complex tradition which a TEXT accumulates as it becomes well known, a tradition with which its reader has to contend or grapple as he or she reads and responds to it. A well-known text, in other words, raises more specific expectations for the reader than one that has accrued no such tradition. (The implication of the last-quoted sentence above is that the reader of an *old* work does *not* have to perceive it within the wider horizon of his or her experience of life, and this implication perhaps reveals a certain formalist element in the theory.)

An important part of the theory as it has developed and matured involves a view of literary texts as partially open, and of the responses engendered by them to be (again partly) the creation of their readers. Thus in a much-quoted example, Wolfgang Iser sees the sense a reader actively *makes* of a literary text to be contained within certain limits imposed by the text itself.

> In the same way, two people gazing at the night sky may both be looking at the same collection of stars, but one will see the image of a plough, and the other will make out a dipper. The 'stars' in a literary text are fixed; the lines that join them are variable. (1974, 282)

This argued element of textual containment has, incidentally, led the American critic Stanley Fish to distinguish his own concept of the INTERPRET[AT]IVE COMMUNITY from the reception theorists' horizon of expectations: for Fish the text is itself constituted by the pre-existing CONVENTIONS of the interpret[at]ive community.

Reception theory is distinguished by a certain interdisciplinarity, and its exponents make use of elements from AESTHETICS, Philosophy, Psychology, and (particularly) from PHENOMENOLOGY.

Reconstructionism The attempt to rebuild or expand the accepted CANON of literary works, normally by seeking to reduce or remove ethnocentric, SEXIST, or PRESENTIST bias or by countering such bias with oppositional bias(es).

Recruitist Within FEMINIST debate and discussion this term is increasingly used to describe (and criticize) an attitude and goal within feminist research 'in which the goal is to make "them" (ordinary women) more like "us" (feminists)' (Thornham: 1997, 77). Sue Thornham attributes the term to Angela McRobbie (1982), but also refers to Charlotte Brunsdon's identification of three phases in the shifting relationship between *feminism* and *women*:

> The first is the *transparent*, in which an unproblematic identification of the two is assumed. The second is the *hegemonic* or 'recruitist', in which the feminist writer manifests 'the impulse to transform the feminine identifications of women to feminist ones'. The third is the *fragmented*, in which no necessary correspondence between the two is assumed. (1997, 173; quotations are from Brunsdon: 1993, 313)

Recuperation See INCORPORATION

Reductionism A pejorative description of any form of explanation which allegedly ignores higher-level qualities in whatever is being studied and reduces the object of study to certain or all of its lower-level qualities. An example would be 'all flesh is grass', but only if the statement is interpreted literally rather than metaphorically; perhaps a better one would be that which reduces human beings to the physical composition of their BODIES in a form which has accrued no metaphorical meaning.

'Literature is just words' is reductionist (the word 'just' is often a giveaway), for literature is more than words (or language, or marks on paper, and so on). Literature involves also the *arrangement* and *presentation* of words in particular ways which draw their force from CONVENTIONS established within different CULTURES, communities and traditions. To make an obvious point, it is not a verbal characteristic of the sonnet that it has 14 lines: it is a formal one; nor is it a verbal characteristic of the novel that the reader starts at the beginning and reads through to the end (which one does not do with all forms of writing – holiday brochures, for example). These are trivial examples, but they serve to establish an important point.

Redundancy Information theorists define redundancy as the degree of relative predictability of a message, as against the degree of unpredictability of a message, which is known as *entropy*. A message with a high degree of redundancy is one from which a large amount can be lost without the message being rendered incomprehensible. Newspaper headlines and telegrams tend to have a very low degree of redundancy: the loss of one word can often completely alter their meaning – or cause it to vanish irretrievably. Ordinary person-to-person conversation, in contrast, tends to have a relatively high degree of redundancy – something that can be attributed not just to the message itself but to other, extra-linguistic and contextual factors which make certain meanings more likely than others. Written communication tends to have a lower redundancy rate, as it is easier to read twice what one does not understand than to keep asking someone to repeat what they have said. Not surprisingly, then, forms of literature which are more nearly related to spoken forms very often show a greater level of redundancy – REPETITIONS, use of predictive aids such as rhyme and metre, and so on.

But to describe such elements purely in terms of technical redundancy is clearly unsatisfactory; in the best literature they fulfil certain AESTHETIC functions which render them, in the everyday sense of the word, far from redundant. For this reason the use of information theory to analyse literature has been seen as a form of REDUCTIONISM, and its relevance to DISCOURSE about literary or aesthetic value has been questioned – by, among others, Sharpe (1984).

However, it is possible to make more careful use of terms such as redundancy and entropy when dealing with literature. It seems to be one characteristic of FORMULAIC literature that it is far more predictable, and of MODERNIST and POSTMODERNIST literature that it is far less predictable, than what one can posit as a literary NORM. Such variations in level of redundancy cannot be mechanically linked with aesthetic or other significance, however, although they may have relevance in discussion of different INTERPRETATIONS and of interpretation in general. On the other hand, the high redundancy level of the cliché is, except in ironic use, almost invariably accorded negative aesthetic value.

What should be remembered above all is that literature is valued other than for its usefulness in imparting information, other than for its MEANING(s). Repetition (as, for example, in the closing lines of James Joyce's *The Dead*) may convey no new 'information', but it has aesthetic force and works on the READER in complex ways.

See also OPEN AND CLOSED TEXTS; READERLY AND WRITERLY TEXTS.

Reference To refer is to point or allude to, and thus to assert the existence or nature of. In literary criticism from a very early time the term has been associated with controversies about whether literary WORKS make reference to extra-literary or extra-textual reality, and, if so, how. Many influential recent theories (and especially those associated with STRUCTURALISM and POST-STRUCTURALISM) have argued that literature is non-referential, that statements in literary works cannot be either true or false because they claim no reference to anything that really exists – a position that can be traced back to Sir Philip Sidney's *An Apology for Poetry* (1595) and beyond. Such positions sometimes also argue that literary works can refer only to themselves, that they represent closed spheres within which referential statements are locked and unable to escape.

Those committed to some form of REALISM, in contrast, believe literary works (and/or their AUTHORS by means of these works) to be capable of referring to an extra-literary reality.

A *referent* is that which has been referred to, and considerable argument can take place as to what the referent(s), if any, of a literary work are. The *referential fallacy* is the belief that every semiotic entity must be underwritten by an actual 'fact' or state of the world.

J. Hillis Miller uses the term 'head referent' in a rather special sense, equating it with what DECONSTRUCTIONISTS call the (missing) CENTRE which would stop the play of SIGNIFIERS and which would allow the MEANING of the TEXT to be fixed if it existed (which they deny). Thus for Miller the head referent in Emily Brontë's *Wuthering Heights* is that 'original literal text' of which all the other texts that are in, and that constitute, *Wuthering Heights*, are figures. The reader of the novel searches for this head referent, according to Miller, in order to 'still the wandering movement from emblem to emblem, from generation to generation, from Catherine to Catherine, from Hareton to Hareton, from narrator to narrator' in the novel (1982, 67).

See also INTERTEXTUALITY; SENSE AND REFERENCE.

Referent See REFERENCE

Referential See FUNCTIONS OF LANGUAGE

Referential code See CODE

Reflector (character) Alternatively *focalizer*. Following Henry James, the central consciousness or intelligence in a work of FICTION. More generally, a CHARACTER whose perception of events plays an important unifying or AESTHETIC role in a NARRATIVE. According to Jahn *et al.*, there is a simple test to find out who the focalizer is in a given passage: 'Since s/he is the grammatical subject that belongs to the verbs that express thought, feeling, and perception, one only has to ask: Who thinks?, feels, sees, hears, remembers, etc. whatever is being narrated in a given passage?' (1993, 16).

Very often (although not invariably) such a character's perceptions and responses will be authoritative for the READER and will encourage reader identification. Sometimes used in a wider sense to describe any consciousness or character used by an AUTHOR to present things to the reader which would otherwise go unperceived.

See also PERSPECTIVE AND VOICE for more discussion of focalization.

Refraction In the writings of Mikhail Bakhtin, according to the editor of *The Dialogic Imagination*, the INTENTIONS of the writer of prose are subject to refraction through 'already claimed territory' (Bakhtin: 1981, 432). As the written word proceeds from writer to READER its direction is changed as a light-ray changes direction when it hits a prism. The metaphorical prisms in question exist both within the WORK (the other VOICES that the AUTHOR inhabits as the TEXT unfolds), and also outside the work: usages and associations in the reader's or critic's CULTURE through which the author's words have to struggle before making contact with the reader – in whose consciousness yet other refractions may take place.

Register The concept of register comes originally from the study of music, where it refers to the compass of a musical instrument or of a human voice. From here a succession of metaphorical adaptations takes it to Phonetics where it is used to refer to the pitch of speech UTTERANCES, and to Linguistics in general in which it is used (with variations) to refer to context-dependent linguistic characteristics – either spoken or written, and encompassing any set of choices which are made according to a conscious or unconscious notion of appropriateness-to-context (vocabulary, syntax, GRAMMAR, sound, pitch, and so on). If, for example, one switches on a commercial radio station it is normally immediately apparent if an advertisement is being broadcast, for broadcast sound advertisements generally conform to particular register characteristics that make them immediately distinguishable as such, even if one hears them so badly that the actual words used are indistinguishable. There are, similarly, accepted (if changing) registers for church sermons, academic lectures, political speeches, declarations of undying love, and so on. An A-level examination answer on Thomas Hardy's novel *Jude the Obscure*, marked by a friend of mine, which started 'What a miserable bugger Jude Fawley was!', albeit undeniably accurate and dramatic, does not conform to the register to which such answers are normally expected to conform.

From Linguistics the concept has, by a further metaphorical leap, been adopted within literary criticism and NARRATOLOGY. Tzvetan Todorov, for example, in his *Introduction to Poetics*, lists a number of categories by which different *registers of DISCOURSE* may be recognized. These include the discourse's *concrete or abstract* nature, the ABSENCE or presence of *rhetorical figures*, the presence or absence of *reference to an anterior discourse* (giving, respectively, *polyvalent* and *monovalent* discourse), and, finally, the extent to which the language involved is characterized by 'subjectivity' or 'objectivity' (1981, 20–27). According to Gérard Genette, the 'chief advantage of the [footnote or endnote] is . . . that it brings about local effects of nuance, or sourdine, or as they say in music, of *register*, effects that help reduce the famous and sometimes regrettable linearity of discourse' (1997, 328; *sourdine*: damper in a piano).

It seems clear that the work done by the concept of register in Literary Studies to some extent duplicates that done by the concept of GENRE, and Mikhail Bakhtin's essay 'The Problem of Speech Genres' does in fact define what Bakhtin calls 'speech genres' in a way that brings together both 'register' and 'genre' as they are used today. Bakhtin argues that thematic content, style, and compositional STRUCTURE are linked to the whole of an utterance 'and are equally determined by the specific nature of the particular sphere of communication'.

> Each separate utterance is individual, of course, but each sphere in which language is used develops its own *relatively stable types* of these utterances. These we may call *speech genres*. (1986, 60)

Bakhtin further distinguishes been primary (simple) and secondary (complex) speech genres.

> Secondary (complex) speech genres – novels, dramas, all kinds of scientific research, majors genres of commentary, and so forth – arise in more complex and comparatively highly developed and organized cultural communication (primarily written) that is artistic, scientific, sociopolitical, and so on. During the process of their formation they absorb and digest various primary (simple) genres that have taken form in unmediated speech communion. These primary genres are altered and assume a special character when they enter into complex ones. For example,

rejoinders of everyday dialogue or letters found in a novel retain their form and their everyday significance only on the plane of the novel's content. They enter into actual reality only via the novel as a whole, that is, as a literary-artistic event and not as everyday life. (1986, 62)

Put another way, a 'complex speech genre' for Bakhtin is a genre that has swallowed and transformed a range of simple registers, recruiting them all to its complex artistic or other purpose.

Reification According to the *OED*, the mental conversion of a person, process, or abstract concept into a thing. In more recent usage the term has been applied to the procedure whereby relationships or processes are 'frozen' and treated as objects, and the usage resembles Marx's use of the term FETISHISM to describe the way in which a commodity is treated as a thing rather than as the visible point of a process of MEDIATION between groups or individuals.

In translations of Mikhail Bakhtin's work the term has been used to refer to that process of objectification which causes words to be treated as things with fixed meanings, rather than as mediators which gather new significance from use in varied contexts.

In literary-critical usage the term has been applied to the misconception, of which the NEW CRITICS were allegedly guilty, whereby the TEXT is fetishized at the expense of the shifting complex of relationships on which, it is argued, it depends.

Another very closely related term is *hypostatization*, meaning to reduce a process to a static substance; to turn a complex movement into a thing or object. The term thus has something in common with fetishism and reification, and the British literary theorist Christopher Caudwell tended to use it in his MARXIST writings in the 1930s in a way that was very close to Marx's use of the concept of fetishism.

Relation (maxim of) See SPEECH ACT THEORY

Relationism See ESSENTIALISM; RELATIVISM

Relativism The belief that standards, meanings, or truths, have no absolute force, but one which is relative to their circumstances, contexts, or relationships. Generally speaking the term has a pejorative ring, and for this reason those wishing to defend a belief that all knowledge is of relations rather than of absolutes have preferred terms such as *relational*, DIALECTICAL, or the more modish DIFFERENCE.

Theoretical approaches such as STRUCTURALISM and DECONSTRUCTION have, many recent critics are agreed, met with problems when their essentially relational epistemologies have been extended from the realm of the abstract to that of more practical realms such as politics. Playing with TEXTS does not seem a morally adequate response to accounts of the holocaust.

One way round such problems has involved distinguishing between *cultural relativism* and *epistemological relativism*. While the claims of the former tend to be more modest, insisting merely upon the need to understand that different CULTURES predispose their members to perceive the world, themselves, and their relation to it in different ways, the latter is more universalistic and all-embracing, arguing that our differential relation to reality makes communication impossible and denying that we have access to a shared world or a common experience. Cultural relativism has roots in sociology and anthropology and has been encouraged by much work in POSTCOLONIAL theory, whilst epistemological relativism is more likely to be traced back to abstract philosophical reasoning.

For *linguistic relativism*, see SAPIR-WHORF HYPOTHESIS. See also ESSENTIALISM; HUMANISM.

Relexification Chantal Zabus (1991) distinguishes between *relexification* which, following Loreto Todd, involves using English vocabulary but indigenous structures and rhythms in order to simulate the African language in the Europhone text, and 'nativism' or 'Africanism', which refer to an English (or, presumably other European language's) construction that reflects the structural properties of a text in an African (or, presumably, any other non-European) language (Ashcroft *et al.*: 1995, 314–17). (See the separate entry for an alternative meaning of NATIVISM.) A further term mentioned is *auto-translation*: the translation of a work by its own AUTHOR.

Another related term is *creolization*, which originally referred to that process whereby two (sometimes more than two) languages merged to form a new language over a period of time. A creole is to be distinguished from a *pidgin* which, as Jean Aitchison has it, 'is a language in embryo, a foetus with the potential to become a full language, but not yet capable of fulfilling the entire communication needs of a human'. However, Aitchison continues, at the point at which an individual learns a pidgin as his or her first language, it has become a creole, 'from the French *créole* "indigenous", borrowed in turn from the Spanish *criollo* "native"' (1991, 190).

All of these usages are affected by a confusing multiplicity of meanings attached to the word *creole* in its non-linguistic sense. Dictionary definitions list the major meanings as: (1) a person of 'mixed blood', (2) a person of European descent born in the West Indies or South America, (3) a West African freed slave or his/her descendant, (4) a person of French descent living in the southern states of the United States.

As a result, *creolization* has had its meaning extended from the linguistic sphere to that of CULTURE in general, and generally implies cultural or ethnic mixing. Thus Afro-Caribbean immigrants to Britain took with them a culture which, through interaction with British culture, has arguably evolved into a culture which is both Afro-Caribbean and British, and which has therefore been creolized.

Repertoire Often used in more specific ways in recent theory, as in 'cultural repertoires', 'symbolic repertoires', and so on. A person's CULTURAL repertoires would accordingly be composed of those cultural TEXTS, objects and practices to which he or she has expressive or participatory access. Thus were the British Queen to enter a working-class pub she would probably find much that was outside her cultural repertoire.

See also SYSTEM for the particular meaning *repertoire* has in polysystem theory.

Repetition The use of repetition is obviously central to a number of literary effects, and in consort with other elements such as metre, stress and rhythm in poetry it is a key means whereby the technical rate of REDUNDANCY is increased in a WORK. So far as poetry is concerned this can be related to ORALITY and the origins of poetry in oral PERFORMANCE:

we repeat things more in spoken than in written communication to guard against mistakes. It would be a mistake to stop here, however, for repetition in literature has crucial AESTHETIC significance, and performs far more important functions than that of guarding against errors in transmission. The use of repetition can contribute to the formation of *patterns* in a literary work – THEMATIC, symbolic, and STRUCTURAL.

An influential study of the importance of repetition to FICTION is J. Hillis Miller's *Fiction and Repetition*, which includes studies of seven central fictional TEXTS from *Wuthering Heights* to *Between the Acts*. Miller distinguishes between two types of repetition, a distinction which he bases on Gilles Deleuze's opposition of Nietzsche's concept of repetition to that of Plato. Deleuze summarizes the distinction in two formulations: 'only that which resembles itself differs', and 'only differences resemble one another' (Miller: 1982, 5). Homi K. Bhabha has reminded us that we are drawn to repetition because of the security which it offers us: ' "Play it again, Sam", which is perhaps the Western world's most celebrated demand for repetition, is still an invocation to similitude, a return to the eternal verities' (1994, 182).

So far as NARRATIVE is concerned, Mike Bal reminds us that

> [t]he phenomenon of *repetition* ... has always had a dubious side. Two events are never exactly the same. The first event of a series differs from the one that follows it, if only because it is the first and the other is not. Strictly speaking, the same goes for verbal repetition in a text: only one can be the first. . . . Obviously, it is the onlooker ... who remembers the similarities between the events of a series and ignores the differences. (1985, 77)

Bal places repetition under the general heading of FREQUENCY, and the entry for this item should be consulted for information about types of repetition in narrative.

See the entry for FORT/DA for Freud's concept of the *repetition compulsion*.

Representatives See SPEECH ACT THEORY

Represented and representational time See DURATION

Represented speech and thought See FREE INDIRECT DISCOURSE

Repression A key concept in Freudian theory, first used by Sigmund Freud in *Studies on Hysteria*, which he co-wrote with Joseph Breuer. The concept is linked to that of CENSORSHIP: repression involves the censorship of material such that the conscious mind becomes unaware of it, or is aware of it only indirectly (in jokes, dreams, 'slips', and so on). What is important is that the material is not lost, nor is it completely without effect upon the consciousness involved; its effect is indirect and unperceived.

In *Studies on Hysteria* Freud cites the example of 'those cases in which the patients have not reacted to a physical trauma because the nature of the trauma excluded a reaction, as in the case of the apparently irreparable loss of a loved one or because social circumstances made a reaction impossible' (Freud and Breuer: 1974, 61). A typical example thus might be the case of a person whose much-loved parent dies, who represses the reaction of relief at the death (the parent was senile, the child could no longer look after the parent, and so on). The act of repression is not conscious, but it is intentional; the censorship will not allow the conscious mind access to the sense of relief. The repressed material, typically, *returns*; not directly, or overtly, but in censored form. Thus, Freud argues, it is precisely distressing things of this kind that, under hypnosis, are found to be behind hysterical phenomena (1974, 61).

The relevance of the concept to literature and literary criticism lies in the frequent suggestions by Freudians and neo-Freudians that art or literature have much in common with dreams and other activities which evade the censorship and release repressed material – either for the writer in the course of composition or for the READER during the reading process. A writer may not be able to recognize his or her own relief at the death of a parent, but may be able to express (and thus, to some extent, neutralize) the repressed material in disguised form in his or her writing. Such a theory clearly LEGITIMIZES (or hopes to legitimize) attempts to INTERPRET a literary work by means of a PSYCHOANALYTIC investigation of the AUTHOR.

Alternatively, a reader's responses to a literary work may be, according to some, traced back to his or her repressions. We would thus be able to express our emotions in uncensored form while reading a literary work. ANALYSIS of our literary responses, then, would – like analysis of our dreams – help us to discover and identify our otherwise inaccessible repressions.

See also ARCHE-WRITING; DISAVOWAL.

Resonance A term used by the NEW HISTORICIST writer Stephen J. Greenblatt in preference, he explains, to 'allusion' – a term which he finds inadequate because it seems to imply a 'bloodless, bodiless thing' in contrast to the 'active charge' suggested by 'resonance' (1990, 163). What is being alluded to is the complex set or sequence of living MEANINGS that a CULTURAL artifact, or activity (for example), can generate or release when introduced into the right situation. We are close here to issues discussed by Raymond Williams in connection with his term STRUCTURE OF FEELING, and Greenblatt's acknowledged indebtedness to Williams may be relevant in discussion of his meta-phorical use of the term 'resonance'.

According to Greenblatt, the New Historicism 'obviously has distinct affinities with resonance; that is, its concern with literary texts has been to recover as far as possible the historical circumstances of their original production and consumption and to analyze the relationship between these circumstances and our own' (1990, 170).

See also CIRCULATION.

Retroactive reading See MEANING AND SIGNIFICANCE

Retrospection/retroversion See ANALEPSIS

Revisionary ratios See REVISIONISM

Revisionism In current literary-critical usage this term is mainly associated with the theories of the American critic Harold Bloom. The more traditional MARXIST usage established in the writings of Lenin, in which the term refers to attempts to revise

Marxism in such a way as to dilute or negate its revolutionary impetus, appears now to have disappeared.

In Harold Bloom's writings *revisionism* is used in a non-pejorative sense to indicate a general theory or set of theories concerning the manner in which the poet (Bloom uses this word in a wide sense) revises the work of his (Bloom's use of the female GENDER is very sparing) precursors. Thus, for Bloom, poetic influence 'is part of the larger phenomenon of intellectual revisionism' (1973, 28). Bloom sees this 'larger phenomenon' in terms of concepts much influenced by Freud; thus the poet's relation to these precursors is highly Oedipal in character: the struggle against them is the struggle of the son against the father (or, to stress PATRIARCHAL authority, the Father). Just as Oedipus has to kill his father, the aspirant poet has somehow to destroy the power of his precursors, and, normally, of one especially potent patriarchal precursor, while simultaneously absorbing and transforming his strength and authority. The *strong* poet is the poet who succeeds in this task, and in his *The Anxiety of Influence* Bloom restricts himself to the strong poets, those who have the persistence to wrestle with their major precursors, 'even to the death' (1973, 5). Bloom's insistence upon the *anxiety* associated with influence is consistent with this view: the poet's attitude to his precursors is characterized by the same anxious mixture of love and rivalry to which the Freudian term *Oedipus complex* has been assigned. Bloom's use of Freud here thus shifts the literary-critical use of the Oedipal theme from the level of literary content in the narrower sense to a more all-embracing level. For Bloom, the poet suffers always from a sense of *belatedness*, a sense that he or she has come after important things have been said, and after they have been said in ways which constrain the poet and against which he or she has to struggle.

This leads Bloom to a rather different view of the process of READING. Restricting himself initially to the question of how the strong poet reads his precursor, Bloom asserts that poetic influence '*always proceeds by a misreading of the prior poet, an act of creative correction that is actually and necessarily a misinterpretation*' (1973, 30; Bloom's italics). But having argued for this position, Bloom is soon ready to extend it to the readings of the Common Reader and the literary critic, which he requires to be no less Oedipal than those of the strong poet. He argues challengingly that most 'so-called "accurate"' INTERPRETATIONS of poetry are worse than mistakes, and suggests that 'perhaps there are only more or less creative or interesting mis-readings', because every reading is necessarily a *clinamen*: Bloom's term for a poetic misreading – what he terms a misprision 'proper' (1973, 43).

Clinamen is the first of six 'revisionary ratios' outlined in *The Anxiety of Influence*. The others are as follows.

Tessera, or completion and antithesis. 'A poet antithetically "completes" his precursor, by so reading the parent-poem as to retain its terms but to mean them in another sense, as though the precursor had failed to go far enough.'

Kenosis, or a breaking device and movement towards discontinuity with the precursor, in which the poet's humbling of himself actually also empties out his precursor.

Daemonization, in which

[t]he later poet opens himself to what he believes to be a power in the parent-poem that does not belong to the parent proper, but to a range of being just beyond that precursor. He does this, in his poem, by so stationing its relation to the parent-poem as to generalize away the uniqueness of the earlier work.

Askesis, or a movement of self-purgation in which the poet yields up part of his own self-endowment so as to separate himself from others, including the precursor (but see below for an additional usage).

Apophrades, or the return of the dead, in which the poet holds his work so open to that of the precursor that the impression is given that the work of the precursor was actually written by the poet (1973, 14–16).

The extent to which these categories are available to use by critics other than Bloom is probably limited, but in more general terms *The Anxiety of Influence* has been Bloom's most influential work, and terms such as *revisionism, misprision*, and, especially, *misreading* have entered into current critical usage.

Bloom's theories have been given a specifically FEMINIST emphasis by Sandra M. Gilbert and Susan Gubar, who use Bloom's theories concerning the male author's anxiety about his forebears to highlight the very different situation of the female writer. Asking how such a female writer fits in to Bloom's 'essentially male literary history', Gilbert and Gubar reply, 'we find we have to answer that a woman writer does *not* "fit in"'; the female writer

must confront precursors who are almost exclusively male, and therefore significantly different from her. Not only do these precursors incarnate patriarchal authority...they attempt to enclose her in definitions of her person and her potential which, by reducing her to extreme stereotypes (angel, monster) drastically conflict with her own sense of her self – that is, of her subjectivity, her autonomy, her creativity. (1979, 48)

Accordingly, for the woman writer, ' "the anxiety of influence" that a male poet experiences...is felt as an even more primary "anxiety of authorship" – a radical fear that she cannot create, that because she can never become a "precursor" the act of writing will isolate or destroy her' (1979, 48–9).

The term *askesis* has, following Michel Foucault's use of it, also assumed a certain importance within GENDER studies. Joseph Bristow's book *Sexuality* (1997) reports on Foucault's granting of his seal of approval to 'classical models of *askesis*: an ancient Greek word signifying a form of self-questioning that requires the male citizen to reflect upon his sexual weaknesses, strengths, and potentialities'. Bristow also notes that Foucault found especially attractive the fact that this model of 'ethical subjectivity' presented 'the possibility to enjoy types of sexual pleasure not dominated by an exterior law' (1997, 196). Foucault's position has, as Bristow also reports, been attacked by Terry Eagleton in his *The Ideology of the Aesthetic* (1990), in which Eagleton argues that askesis is a characteristic of the ruling classes in both ancient and modern cultures (Bristow: 1997, 194, following Eagleton: 1990, 394–5).

See also AGON; DOUBLE BIND; EPHEBE; *MÉCONNAISSANCE*. For REVISIONIST HISTORY see next entry.

Revisionist history A term used when referring to a loose grouping of generally traditional historians who, to quote Richard Dutton, 'concentrate on such matters as aristocratic factions and the processes of patronage in propounding a view of Tudor and early Stuart politics (especially the politics of the court) very different from earlier accounts, both Whig and Marxist, which in their different ways had emphasised the corruption, imminent break-down and revolutionary potential of the system'. He notes that the revisionists 'have tended to stress the continuities and pragmatic accommodations within the system as it operated, providing a view of the practical mechanics of politics and power which in many ways is radically at odds with the New Historicist emphasis on ideologically charged structures of authority and subjection' (1992, 221–2). Dutton names as members of this grouping Conrad Russell, Kevin Sharpe, E. W. Ives, Linda Levy Peck, R. Malcolm Smuts, and David Starkey.

R.g. See QUEEN/BUTCH

Rhizome See ROOT/RADICLE/RHIZOME

Romance In Literary Studies the term *romance* has long been used to refer to a particular genre depicting stylized and non-REALISTIC accounts of chivalry or love. The chivalric romance was either in verse or prose and flourished from the twelfth century onwards.

Romance traditions have survived during subsequent centuries in more or less changed forms, and it is arguable that the present-day popular use of the term refers to a GENRE with a long historical pedigree. Recent literary historians and theorists have suggested that to see the Harlequin or Mills & Boon romance as without any generic or historical links to CANONICAL literary WORKS is probably a mistake; a modern pulp romance may bear no comparison with *Wuthering Heights* in terms of the two works' artistic value, but there are clearly FORMULAIC elements which are common to both.

Not surprisingly, FEMINISTS have shown much interest in the modern pulp romance, analysing the role it plays for women through the provision of STEREOTYPED portrayals of love and family relationships. Opinion has differed as to whether the fantasies offered by pulp romance are purely negative, attempting to INTERPELLATE female readers in a way that subordinates them to PATRIARCHY, or whether they provide a literary female space within which values critical of patriarchy can be found. A key text here is Janice A. Radway's *Reading the Romance* (first published in 1984), which bases its conclusion upon extensive interviews with romance readers. For Radway, to 'qualify as a romance, the story must chronicle not merely the events of a courtship but *what it feels like* to be the *object* of one' (1991, 64). Radway argues, further, that 'the story told by all romances can be considered as a myth because every book is dominated by the same set of events resolved in an identical way' (1991, 204). Although Radway found that the READERS she interviewed used their reading of the romance in ways that provided them with personal time and personal space, she also concluded that, as Sue Thornham reports her, '[t]he romance thus functions hegemonically, to represent but ultimately contain women's limited protest, and win their consent to the patriarchal order' (Thornham: 1997, 77).

Radway's book contains useful information on the names given by the publishing industry to sub-genres within the general category of romance. For those readers unable to 'incorporate a more explicit sexuality into the ideology of love' (1991, 16), there is the 'sweet', 'evangelical', or 'inspirational', romance. For those readers requiring a certain amount of ritualized violence and suffering there are the ' "sweet savage romances," "erotic historicals," "bodice-rippers," or "slave sagas," as they were variously known throughout the industry' (1991, 34). Another sub-genre of interest to students of literature is that of the *gothic*. According to Radway, the contemporary gothic owes its origin to Gerald Gross at Ace Books. Gross noted the continuing popularity of Daphne du Maurier's *Rebecca*, and he attempted to locate previously published titles resembling this work. The subsequent list formed the basis of a 'gothic' series, characterized by a heroine who experiences trials and tribulations, and separation from the man she loves, but who ends in his arms on the novel's final page.

In her *Feminism and the Politics of Reading* (1997), Lynne Pearce builds on Roland Barthes's *The Pleasure of the Text* (1976) to suggest that the reader–WORK relationship can be conceptualized as a form of romance.

Root/radicle/rhizome Gilles Deleuze uses these three sorts of root growth to exemplify different types of connective relationship which epitomize contrasting types of connective logic. The classical book is, according to him, the 'root book' which 'endlessly develops the law of the One that becomes two, then of the two that become four... Binary logic is the spiritual reality of the root-tree' (1993, 27, ellipsis in original).

The 'radicle-system, or fascicular root' is the figure of the book to which, he claims, our modernity pays willing allegiance (1993, 28). 'This time, the principal root has aborted, or its tip has been destroyed; an immediate, indefinite multiplicity of secondary roots grafts on to it and undergoes a flourishing development' (1993, 28). Deleuze cites William Burroughs's 'cut-up method' and the writing of James Joyce as productive of radicle-system books (see the entry for ALEATORY TECHNIQUE).

Finally, the 'rhizome' – a subterranean stem such as tubers have – offers a more complex model, one which, according to Deleuze, is also exemplified in the swarming rat-pack. Unlike trees or their roots, 'the rhizome connects any point to any other point, and its traits are not necessarily linked to traits of the same nature; it brings into play very different regimes of signs, and even nonsign states. The rhizome is reducible neither to the One nor to the multiple. . . . It is composed not of units but of dimensions, or rather directions in motion.' The examples Deleuze gives of rhizome structures are not books but, for example, the complex relationship between wasp and orchid ('a becoming wasp of the orchid and a becoming orchid of the wasp' [1993, 33]), and 'Benveniste and Todaro's current research on a type *C* virus, with its double connection to baboon DNA and the DNA of certain kinds of domestic cats' (1993, 33).

See also BINARY/BINARISM; NOMAD; SCHIZOANALYSIS.

Russian Formalism Two related groups of theorists – the Moscow Linguistic Circle and the *Opojaz* group (= Society for the Study of Poetic Language) – are today generally taken to represent what is now seen as a single movement, known as Russian Formalism. The title's connotations are now relatively neutral, but 'formalist' was used in a pejorative sense by the group's contemporaries, especially by those attacking the group from a MARXIST perspective. The most important Russian Formalists were Victor Shklovsky, Boris Eichenbaum, Boris Tomashevsky, Yuri Tynyanov, and Roman Jakobson – who was subsequently involved with the PRAGUE CIRCLE of theorists and eventually moved to the United States. (Different systems of transliterating Russian letters result in there being a number of different spellings of these names.) Vladimir Propp, author of *Morphology of the Folktale*, is not now generally classed as a member of the group, although he was often so classified at various times in the past, and Jakobson's work subsequent to his leaving the Soviet Union is, again, not normally classified as 'Russian Formalist' today.

Russian Formalism developed during the years of the First World War and was, as Victor Erlich has put it, a 'child of the revolutionary period . . . part and parcel of its peculiar intellectual atmosphere' (quoted by Bowlt: 1972, 1). The child was, however, eventually disowned by its parent (or putative parent): Russian Formalism came under increasing pressure in the Soviet Union as a more monolithic and repressive attitude to literary theory developed there, and by 1930 it had been forced into exile.

The first sentence of Eichenbaum's essay 'The Theory of the "Formal Method"' gives a fair indication of its characteristic trajectory: 'The school of thought on the theory and history of literature known as the Formal method derived [Eichenbaum is writing in 1925] from efforts to secure autonomy and concreteness for the discipline of literary studies' (Èjxenbaum: 1971a, 3). Words such as 'autonomy' and 'concreteness' inevitably call to mind the NEW CRITICS, but although it is arguable that both groups can be lumped together under the umbrella of formalism, and although their theories and practices do have elements in common, it would be false to try to impose too close a relationship between them. (And it needs to be noted that only a few of the New Critics – those with Eastern European backgrounds – had any real acquaintance with the work of the Russians.) The autonomy in which the Russian Formalists are interested is less of the individual WORK and more of Literary Studies in general and of literariness; its CONCRETENESS is less what, following F. R. Leavis, we think of as the literary work's local effects and enactments of 'life', and more a matter of the isolation of technical devices and linguistic specificities. But it certainly shares with the New Critics a suspicion of any literary criticism which relies upon biographical details about the AUTHOR or socio-cultural information about his or her age. To this extent it shares with the New Critics a desire to establish Literary Studies as a discipline independent from History, Philosophy, Biography, Psychology, and so on. But in its insistence upon the need for an independent *theory* of literature it stands at some distance from the New Critics and their view of what Literary Studies should be. According to Eichenbaum, opposition to the Symbolists also bequeathed to the group 'the new spirit of scientific positivism that characterizes the Formalists: the rejection of philosophical premises, psychological or aesthetic interpretations, and so forth' (Èjxenbaum: 1971a, 7). The word 'positivism' may jar on the ears of a modern reader, but this ties in with the imperative that concreteness was necessary:

It was time to turn to the facts and, eschewing general systems and problems, to start from the center – from where the facts of art confront us. Art had to be approached at close range, and science had to be made concrete. (Èjxenbaum: 1971a, 7)

As I have said, however, this is not a concreteness to be found in the individual work: Eichenbaum quotes Jakobson to the effect that the object of study in literary science is not literature but LITERARINESS (see the entry for this term), and the Formalists exhibit a good deal less respect for the value and autonomy of the individual work than do the New Critics: indeed, they could often be described as looters, stripping literary works of useful examples to help in the construction of more general theories.

Three important formalistic contributions to Literary Studies need to be mentioned here: first, the belief in a distinction between poetic language and ordinary language – a distinction on which few today would bestow their agreement. Second, the importance of DEFAMILIARIZATION, a concept which has not yet outlived its usefulness. And third, the distinction between *fabula* and *sjužet* (see the entry for STORY AND PLOT), which plays a pivotal role in modern NARRATOLOGY.

One of the most potent critiques of the Formalists was actually first published in the Soviet Union in 1928: P. N. Medvedev's *The Formal Method in Literary Scholarship*, which some have claimed was actually written by Mikhail Bakhtin (Medvedev was a member of Bakhtin's circle). Medvedev's book recognizes the positive elements in the work of the Formalists (his attack should not be equated with the Stalinist suppression of them), but he criticizes their rigid distinction between internal and external factors, and their inability to recognize that an external factor acting on literature can become 'an intrinsic factor of literature itself, a factor of its immanent development' (1978, 67). Medvedev is shrewd in his criticism of some Marxist attacks on the Formalists: it was not that the latter denied that external factors could influence literature, but that they denied that such factors could affect it intrinsically. Medvedev is also effective in his critique of the Formalists' commitment to the existence of a separate poetic language; as he puts it, '[t]he indices of the poetic do not belong to language and its elements, but only to poetic constructions' (1978, 86). However, as one would expect from a member of Bakhtin's circle, Medvedev's strongest criticism is reserved for the ahistoricism of Formalism (1978, 97), and for its failure to recognize that '[e]ven the inner utterance (interior speech) is social; it is oriented toward a possible audience, toward a possible answer, and it is only in the form of such an orientation that it is able to take shape and form' (1978, 126). Finally, he notes that though the Formalists attempted to escape from a psychological subjectivism in their approach to literature, their basic theories (including deautomatization) 'presuppose a perceiving, subjective consciousness' (1978, 149).

S

Salience See PUNCTUATION

Sapir-Whorf hypothesis The belief that any language will fundamentally and inevitably condition the way that those who have it as their mother tongue will perceive the social and material world. The name comes from the two American linguisticians, Edward Sapir and Benjamin Lee Whorf, and particularly from Whorf's studies of American Hopi Indians in the 1930s. Also known as linguistic RELATIVISM, the theory is an early example of the belief in – as the title of a much later book by Fredric Jameson has it – 'the prison-house of language'.

Satellite event See EVENT

Scene See DURATION

Schizoanalysis The concept is associated with the collaboration between Félix Guattari and Gilles Deleuze, especially in their *Anti-Oedipus: Capitalism and Schizophrenia* (1977) and *A Thousand Plateaus: Capitalism and Schizophrenia* (1980), works which take concepts such as 'desire' from PSYCHOANALYSIS and apply them in novel social and political ways. For Deleuze and Guattari, schizophrenia can be detected not just in individuals but also in societies – preeminently capitalist society. Guattari has described his own project, 'loosely termed schizoanalysis', as something other than a self-enclosed field, arguing that what interests him is

> the shift of the analytical problematic away from systems of *enunciation* and of preformed subjective structures, and towards *assemblages of enunciation* that are capable of fashioning new coordinates for reading and for 'bringing to life' hitherto unknown representations and propositions.
>   Schizoanalysis, then, perforce will be ex-centric to other professionalized 'psy' practices with their corporations, societies, schools, didactic initiations, etc. Its provisional definition would thus be: *the analysis of the incidence of assemblages of enunciation among semiotic and subjective productions within a given, problematic context.* (1998, 433)

Deleuze's and Guattari's work is riddled with analogies taken from a wide range of disciplines (see, for example, the entries for NOMAD and ROOT/RADICLE/RHIZOME), and this cross-disciplinary search for analogy betokens a belief that a system such as capitalism does not constitute a logical unity structured according to simple mechanistic, linear or sequential principles. Given the schizophrenic nature of capitalism and its CULTURES, it and they can be analysed only by means of an approach which recognizes this fact: schizoanalysis.

Scientism A form of REDUCTIONISM which examines all social and CULTURAL phenomena according to (normally pre-Einsteinian) scientific principles.

Scopophilia/scopophobia In his *The Fear of Looking, or Scopophilic-Exhibitionistic Conflicts* (1974), David W. Allen quotes the definition of *scopophilia* from Webster's dictionary: a 'desire to look at sexually stimulating scenes especially as a substitute for actual sexual participation that constitutes a partial or component instinct often sublimated (as in a desire for learning)'. Allen notes, however, that within psychiatry the term is defined somewhat differently, and he quotes from Hinsie and Campbell's *Psychiatric Dictionary* (1960): 'Sexual pleasure derived from contemplation or looking. It is a component-instinct and stands in the same relation to exhibitionism as sadism does to masochism' (1974, 1). Allen notes that both active and passive looking are implied in

310

the word 'scopophilia', and he accordingly proposes that ' "scopophobia' be rescued from obscurity and be used to mean a fear of looking as well as a fear of being looked at' (1974, 6).

In recent theoretical debate the renewal of interest in these terms – and especially of *scopophilia* – owes much to Laura Mulvey's highly influential essay 'Visual Pleasure and Narrative Cinema', first published in 1975. Mulvey notes that

> [o]riginally, in his *Three Essays on Sexuality*, Freud isolated scopophilia as one of the component instincts of sexuality which exist as drives quite independently of the erotogenic zones. At this point he associated scopophilia with taking other people as objects, subjecting them to a controlling and curious gaze. (1989, 16)

Mulvey then proceeds to argue that the scopophiliac instinct, which in extreme form 'can become fixated into a perversion, producing obsessive voyeurs and Peeping Toms whose only sexual satisfaction can come from watching, in an active controlling sense, an objectified other' (1989, 17), can also be seen to be a component element in the pleasure experienced by the cinema audience (see the quotation given on page 138). Mulvey's argument rests in part upon her contention that while scopophilia can begin with 'pleasure in using another person as an object of sexual stimulation through sight', it can then develop 'through narcissism and the constitution of the ego' into an 'identification with the image seen' (1989, 18). What is more, Mulvey argues, in a world in which pleasure in looking has been split between active/male and passive/female, the 'determining male gaze projects its fantasy onto the female figure, which is styled accordingly' (1989, 19).

Mulvey's article made an enormously important contribution to the development of PSYCHOANALYTIC film theory, although in recent years it has been attacked for ignoring the situation of the female viewer.

David W. Allen's discussion of scopophobia includes the comment that:

> [a]s Ernest Jones has shown, the play within a play also captures the epitome of the oedipal conflict underling Hamlet's agonizing scopophilic-exhibitionistic vacillations. . . . Hamlet watches or looks and is obsessively unable to commit himself to action or to show his hand until forced by events to do so. (1974, 56)

See also GAZE.

Scotomization Explained by Martin Jay as follows:

> Scotomization was a term first borrowed by Charcot from ophthalmology in the 1880s to describe hysterical vision, and then revived by the French analysts René Laforgue and Edouard Pichon in the 1920s. Technically referring to a retinal lesion producing a visual blindspot, the term (from the Greek *skotos* for darkness) was used by them to designate a mode of psychotic unawareness that was different from repression as Freud had defined it. Whereas repression meant denying an instinct or its mental derivative any access to consciousness, scotomization was 'a process of psychic depreciation, by means of which the individual attempts to deny

everything which conflicts with his ego. ... Contrary to what happens in normal repression, the mind in spite of outward appearances is really simply trying to evade a situation in which it has to endure frustration and which it apprehends as a castration.' (1993, 353–4)

Script Monika Fludernik attributes this term to FRAME Theory, instituted by Roger C. Schank and Robert P. Abelson in their book *Scripts, Plans, Goals and Understanding* (1977), and developed by Fludernik in a specifically NARRATOLOGICAL context.

The theory assumes that familiar events such as, for example, 'eating out' commonly involve a script, or a skeleton outline of what it is normal to report. Thus (unless there are exceptional reasons so to do), when reporting on a meal out one will typically assume that there was a waiter (and so not mention the fact), and will not normally give a description of the protagonists' eating processes (after Fludernik: 1993, 447). Thus NARRATIVE accounts in FICTION can often use particular scripts in deciding what information is redundant, or obvious, or whatever.

Scripts do of course change: before Joyce, accounts of CHARACTERS' BODILY functions did not form a part of the scripts used by most serious writers.

More generally, 'script' as both noun and verb is increasingly used by those who wish to stress the social, historical or CULTURAL (as against the biological or universal) origin of NORMS. Thus Stevi Jackson argues that sexual behaviour is '"socially scripted" in that it is a "part" that is learned and acted out within a social context, and different social contexts have different social scripts' (1978; repr. in Jackson and Scott: 1996, 62). Compare the usage in the entry for MEDIASCAPE, and see also MOVE.

Scriptible See READERLY AND WRITERLY TEXTS

Secondary process See PRIMARY PROCESS

Second-wave feminism Generally used to distinguish the FEMINISM that developed after 1968 from earlier movements, in particular that associated with the battle for female suffrage in the late nineteenth and early twentieth centuries (by extrapolation: first-wave feminism).

Segmentation See PUNCTUATION

Self See SUBJECT

Self-consuming artifact From a book entitled *Self-consuming Artifacts* by Stanley Fish (1972). Literary TEXTS are self-consuming in the sense that AFFECTS produced in the course of a READING of them are destroyed as the reading proceeds. As Fish puts it in a later work,

[t]o read the *Phaedrus*, then, is to use it up; for the value of any point in it is that it gets *you* (not any sustained argument) to the next point, which is not so much a point (in logical-demonstrative terms) as a level of insight. It is thus a *self-*

consuming artifact, a mimetic enactment in the reader's experience of the Platonic ladder in which each rung, as it is negotiated, is kicked away. (1980, 40)

Semantic axis A term coined by Mieke Bal in connection with her proposal for a method to determine which of a CHARACTER's characteristics are of NARRATIVE relevance and which are not. According to Bal, semantic axes are pairs of contrary MEANINGS such as *large* and *small* or *rich* and *poor*. To determine which axes are productive of the most fruitful analytical results one has, Bal suggests, to concentrate upon 'those axes that determine the image of the largest possible number of characters, positively or negatively' (1985, 86).

To a certain extent this proposal formalizes what has long been a stock-in-trade of literary criticism – the recognition that although characters from a literary WORK may be individually very different, they may nonetheless all represent different options along a linear continuum (or along many such continua). Thus the very different characters in Joseph Conrad's *Heart of Darkness* may be grouped along a continuum ranging from 'restraint' at one end to 'abandon or moral collapse' at the other. Whether Bal's proposed formalization of such insights is useful is debatable; the main danger inherent in it would appear to be that of oversimplification or REDUCTIONISM. To group the characters of *Heart of Darkness* as I have (not originally) suggested may be illuminating, but it might be dangerous to see this as an in some way *dominant* or even *exclusive* ordering principle, and although Bal cannot be blamed for misapplications of her proposal it must be said that the diagrammatic example which she gives does lead this reader to fear that the concept may encourage reductionism.

As is the case with other concepts and techniques, this particular one may be more productive and less dangerous when applied to FORMULAIC literature than when applied to more classic or CANONICAL works.

Semantic position A term associated with translations of Mikhail Bakhtin's work, which seeks to convey the fact that a 'voice' is not just a mark of specific human individuality but a commitment (recognized or unrecognized) to a given IDEOLOGICAL persuasion or persuasions. 'Position' here is of course a metaphor, and just as a physical position determines not just what we can see but also how we see what we can see, how we *situate ourselves in relation to the object of our view*, so too our adoption of a certain voice has (the argument runs) comparable implications on the ideological level. ('Voice' here must be given the wider meaning which Bakhtin habitually attributes to it: it is not just that people with, say, a middle-class accent tend to have middle-class views, but that the totality of a person's voice will reflect, imply and entail a set of ways of orientating oneself amongst other people in a particular context or contexts.)

A person's semantic position is supra-individual for another reason: it assumes and expects certain things of other people, and in turn places a certain pressure upon them either to conform to or to resist this placing.

The concept has been found to offer certain fruitful approaches to the analysis of literary DIALOGUE (in the ordinary, non-Bakhtinian sense of the word).

For cross-references to discussion of the concept of voice, see VOICE.

Seme See SEMEME

Sememe A term coined by Umberto Eco to indicate a basic semiotic unit, by analogy with, for example, *phoneme* as the smallest intelligible unit of significant sound in a language. Thus a sememe would represent the smallest independent unit on the SEMIOTIC plane, although the significance of an individual sememe – as with the phoneme – can be refined, altered or disambiguated by processes of selection and combination.

Eco suggests, further, that '*a sememe is in itself an inchoative text whereas a text is an expanded sememe*' (1981, 18).

Eco's use of the term *styleme* represents a similar sort of coinage: a styleme is the smallest independent unit on the *stylistic* plane.

Such terms, and others, represent a good example of the way in which use of the LINGUISTIC PARADIGM generates terms analogous to those in use within the discipline of Linguistics.

The term *seme* is to be found in the English translation of Roland Barthes's *S/Z*, where it is described by Barthes as being more or less interchangeable with the term *signifier* (see the entry for SIGN) on the semantic plane: 'semantically, the seme is the unit of the signifier' (1990, 17).

Compare IDEOLOGEME.

Semic code See CODE

Semiology/semiotics The term *semiotic* was coined at the close of the nineteenth century by the American philosopher Charles Sanders Peirce to describe a new field of study of which he was the founder, and *semiotics* traces its descent from this point. *Semiology* was coined by the Swiss linguistician Ferdinand de Saussure, and in his posthumously edited and published *Course in General Linguistics* he defended the coinage as necessary for the naming of that new science which would form part of social psychology and would study 'the life of signs within society' (1974, 16). This placing of semiology in social psychology, incidentally, was subsequently to incur the wrath of Jacques Derrida, who suggests that it is only by making the phonetic sign the pattern of all other signs (as he does) that Saussure can inscribe general semiology in a psychology – a step Derrida believes to be ill-conceived (1981b, 22).

Today semiology and semiotics are generally used interchangeably, although attempts have been made to give each a distinct meaning; at one time *semiology* seemed generally preferred in Britain (perhaps because French theorists preferred the term *sémiologie*) while *semiotics* was more common in the United States. The latter term now appears to be rather more common in both countries, and I will thus adopt it in what follows. (Both terms are based upon adaptations of the Greek word *sēmeion*, meaning 'sign', and the spelling 'semeiology' is sometimes encountered in older texts.)

Saussure's comments are general and predictive, whereas Peirce's are more detailed and comprehensive in scope, and attempt to present a more integrated and formalized system. (It is Peirce we have to thank for the distinction between ICON, INDEX and symbol: see the entry for SIGN.) W. T. Scott has suggested that it was precisely the 'abstractness, density and range' of Peirce's proposal that militated against its being developed, either by scholars who were neither philosophers nor logicians, or by others with an interest in abstract universals of mind and meaning. In contrast, Scott continues, 'the sketchiness and concreteness of de Saussure's work makes it more approachable', and its association with Linguistics helped to attach semiology to what has been perhaps the most theoretically prestigious of the human sciences during recent decades (1990, 71). Central to this association has been the use by semioticians of the LINGUISTIC PARADIGM.

What is certain is that, between the 1960s and the 1980s, attempts to establish a unified science of signs known as *semiotics* flourished, and that this threw up an extended terminology and set of concepts that have been pressed into use in a very wide range of fields of study – including that of literary criticism. Although Saussure was certainly no narrow formalist, semiotics has often been characterized by a formal-technical approach to the study of signs which, although it may have a place for terms such as *context*, has not emphasized social and CULTURAL determinants. On occasions many of Saussure's terms – SIGNIFIER and SIGNIFIED, LANGUE and PAROLE – have been recruited into the service of more or less acultural and asocial variants of semiotics, often under the aegis of STRUCTURALISM.

In contrast, other versions of semiotics have seen themselves, following Saussure's own suggestion, as a part of the Social Sciences rather than as an abstract, formal and technical discipline, and have seen their work to be closely related to CULTURAL STUDIES. It is significant, for example, that the English translation of Umberto Eco's 1972 essay 'Towards a Semiotic Inquiry into the Television Message' was first published in *Working Papers in Cultural Studies* in Britain, and that although this essay states an initial concern to consider television outputs as 'a system of signs', it also commits itself to a belief in the importance of empirical investigations into how viewers actually 'read' and understand what they see – what they actually 'get' (1972, 104).

For Jonathan Culler, semiotics is not primarily concerned to produce INTER-PRETATIONS, but rather to show how interpretations, or meanings, are generated.

> Semiotics, which defines itself as the science of signs, posits a zoological pursuit: the semiotician wants to discover what are the species of signs, how they differ from one another, how they function in their native habitat, how they interact with other species. Confronted with a plethora of texts that communicate various meanings to their readers, the analyst does not pursue a meaning; he seeks to identify signs and describe their functioning. (1981, vii–viii)

Semiotics is less fashionable today than it was a decade ago, and work which would have been described as belonging to semiotics in the 1970s and 1980s generally receives a rather looser categorization today. Those who do describe themselves as semioticians today are very likely to attach a much greater IDEOLOGICAL significance to the sign than was the case in the 1970s and 1980s. One source of this shift of emphasis is probably the work of Mikhail Bakhtin and his circle, work which reached the English-speaking world only in the 1970s and 1980s, even though much of it was written and/or published in the 1920s and 1930s. V. N. Vološinov's *Marxism and the Philosophy of Language*, for instance, which was first published in Russian in 1929, appeared in English only in 1973. The first chapter of Vološinov's book is entitled 'The Study of Ideologies and Philosophy of Language', and it devotes particular attention to the nature of the *sign*.

> The domain of ideology coincides with the domain of signs. They equate with one another. Wherever a sign is present, ideology is present, too. *Everything ideological possesses semiotic value.* (1986, 10)

The work of Roland Barthes has been influential in both the more formalist and the more culturally orientated variants of semiotics during different stages of his intellectual career. Structuralist semiotics need not necessarily be formalist: the Cultural Anthropology of Claude Lévi-Strauss is structuralist, but can be accused of formalism only to a limited degree.

As suggested above, a use of the linguistic paradigm has often been crucial to semiotic analyses: widely different SYSTEMS such as complete CULTURES (Lévi-Strauss), striptease (Roland Barthes), or the UNCONSCIOUS (Jacques Lacan) are examined as sign-systems operating like a language, and what a component of the system *is* is subordinated to, or explained in terms of, what semiotic function it performs. Not surprisingly, this can take semiotic ANALYSIS close to aspects of traditional literary analysis. Thus Robert Scholes's 'semiotic analysis' of 'Eveline', one of the stories in James Joyce's collection *Dubliners* (Scholes: 1982, 87–104) relies heavily on the codes of reading defined by Roland Barthes in his *S/Z* (see the entry for CODE).

Perhaps because modern literary criticism was long dominated by the need to generate interpretations, semioticians have been less interested in literature than one might have expected, although Jonathan Culler has argued that literature is the most interesting form of semiosis, as it is cut off from the immediate PRAGMATIC purposes which simplify other sign situations, something which allows the 'potential complexities of signifying processes [to] work freely in literature'. Moreover, Culler claims, literature presents us with a difficulty in saying exactly what is communicated at the same time as we are aware that 'signification is indubitably taking place' (1981, 35).

Literary semiotics, like semiotics in general, comes in both formalist and cultural editions (to oversimplify somewhat). Robert Scholes points out that Yuri Lotman's *Analysis of the Poetic Text* (1976) and Michael Riffaterre's *Semiotics of Poetry* (1978), both 'approach poems through conventions and codes but share with the New Critics a sense of the poetic text as largely self-referential rather than oriented to a worldly context', whereas Barbara Herrnstein Smith's *Poetic Closure* (1968), although it also concentrates upon codes and CONVENTIONS as a way into the interpretation of texts, reveals a 'willingness to speak of a poem's "sense of truth"' that links her to other critics concerned with the emotional and intellectual impact of a text on READERS (1982, 12). An interest in the reader, then, is typical of what one can define as non-formalist literary semiotics. An interest in the AUTHOR is much less common among critics of this persuasion, many of them writing when a belief in the death of the author was strongest.

Robert Scholes argues, thought-provokingly, that semiotics has become not so much the study of signs as the study of codes, 'the systems that enable human beings to perceive certain events or entities *as* signs, bearing meaning' (1982, ix).

For Derrida's critique of Saussure's use of the term *semiology* see the entry for GRAMMATOLOGY. The work of Julia Kristeva presents some complications with regard to the terms *semiotics* and *semiotic*. Kristeva has written an essay entitled 'Semiotics: A Critical Science and/or a Critique of Science' (first published in French in 1968, reprinted in Moi: 1986a), in which she defines semiotics as 'the production of models'

(Moi: 1986a, 77) and notes that 'literature' does not exist for semiotics as it 'is *a particular semiotic practice* which has the advantage of making more accessible than others the problematics of the production of meaning posed by a new semiotics, and consequently it is of interest only to the extent that it ("literature") is envisaged as irreducible to the level of an object for normative linguistics (which deals with the codified and denotative word [*parole*])' (Moi: 1986a, 86). But at the same time, in her *Revolution in Poetic Language* (first published in French in 1974), Kristeva distinguishes between 'the semiotic' and 'the symbolic' in a context that is PSYCHOANALYTIC and Lacanian. According to Kristeva she understands the term 'semiotic' in its Greek sense, meaning 'distinctive mark, trace, index, precursory sign, proof, engraved or written sign, imprint, trace, figuration' (Moi: 1986a, 93). The semiotic is connected by Kristeva to 'a precise modality in the signifying process' – 'the one Freudian psychoanalysis points to in postulating not only the *facilitation* and the structuring *disposition* of drives, but also the so-called *primary processes* which displace and condense both energies and their inscription' (Moi: 1986a, 93). The argument is complex, but it seems that for her the semiotic has a subversive role *vis-à-vis* the symbolic, which is connected to the Law of the Father and PATRIARCHAL power. According to Kristeva, the semiotic 'dismantles' the symbolic in poetry (Moi: 1986a, 115).

See also the entry for CHORA.

Sender See SHANNON AND WEAVER MODEL OF COMMUNICATION

Sense and reference The usual way in which a distinction made by the German philosopher Gottlob Frege between *Sinn* and *Bedeutung* is rendered in English, although sometimes *meaning and reference* has been preferred.

In the course of a complex discussion of the issue of what it is that language can be said to refer to, Frege noted that phrases such as 'The Morning Star' and 'The Evening Star' can be said to share the same REFERENCE (that is, the planet Venus) but to be possessed of a different sense (or meaning). It is not just that the one phrase refers to the planet as seen in the morning, and the other to the planet as seen in the evening, but that each phrase has accrued a complex set of CULTURAL and literary associations of its own. Language, in other words, does not just divide up the natural world into segments which can then be referred to; it also encompasses human relations to that natural world along with a set of cultural and human MEANINGS and CONNOTATIONS which are in part created and in part reflected in language.

The distinction has appealed to aestheticians and literary theorists concerned to avoid two polarized responses to the question as to whether WORKS of literature or art can be said to refer to the real world (however defined). Such theorists reject the views that (i) the literary work makes no reference to the real world, but rather creates its own reality, and (ii) the literary work has no meaning independent of its reference to the real world. Instead, they argue that the literary work does have a reference to the real world, but that it also has a sense which is not wholly dependent upon or restricted to its reference. The argument is important, because if accepted it suggests that the literary READER or critic should neither be totally ignorant of nor oblivious to that extra-textual world to which the work in question refers or points, nor should he or she feel that the artistic or aesthetic quality of the work can be reduced to (and thus explained by) that

317

same extra-textual reality. It is thus highly advisable that the reader of – for example – Jane Austen's FICTION should be well informed about her contemporary social world, but the AESTHETIC value of a novel such as *Pride and Prejudice* cannot be 'read off' from the novel's accurate rendering of this social world.

Another term often used to describe words with the same reference but a different sense is *partial synonymy* (see the discussion in Scott: 1990, 108–14).

S'entendre parler A phrase associated with Jacques Derrida which means, literally, 'to hear oneself speak'. Thomas Docherty (1987, 22) suggests that the following quotation from Walter J. Ong's *Orality and Literacy* (1982) is 'a more simple way of explaining the Derridean notion of *s'entendre parler* as fundamental to communication':

> Human communication, verbal and other, differs from the 'medium' model most basically in that it demands anticipated feedback in order to take place at all. In the medium model, the message is moved from sender-position to receiver-position. In real human communication, the sender has to be not only in the sender position but also in the receiver position before he or she can send anything. (Ong: 1982, 176)

Ong explains that by the 'medium' model he means those approaches to communication which focus on 'media' and thus suggest 'that communication is a pipeline transfer of units from one place to another' (1982, 176).

For the medium model see FUNCTIONS OF LANGUAGE and SHANNON AND WEAVER MODEL OF COMMUNICATION.

Sequence See FUNCTION

Sexism Maggie Humm defines sexism as 'a social relationship in which males denigrate females' (1989, 202–3), but this is arguably too restrictive a definition, for a number of reasons. First because in most current usage it is accepted that sexism has an existence on the IDEOLOGICAL plane as well as on the plane of actual social relationships, and second because current usage also often accepts the possibility that women can be guilty of sexism when they adopt PATRIARCHAL attitudes. Having said this, it needs to be admitted that although the term has entered into popular usage, its definition has not attracted as much attention as one might wish. Lynne Segal has referred to Rosalind Coward's argument that we need a more refined way of talking about sexist codes in general. For Coward, 'our descriptions of "sexist", "offensive" and "degrading" remain curiously underdeveloped' (Segal: 1987, 113; Coward's comment was published in 1982).

A broader definition would see sexism as a variant of ESSENTIALISM, concerned with GENDER characteristics and usually relying upon STEREOTYPES, which attributes negative characteristics to women or females and positive characteristics to men or males. Humm's definition does have one very important virtue, however: it reminds us that sexism involves not just a form of insult but a means of repression. The ideology of sexism is thus linked to the practice of patriarchy. (In casual usage the term is often near-synonymous with *patriarchal*.) For this reason I would resist extending sexism to examples of essentialism which attribute negative characteristics to men or males: one might argue that these deserve to be labelled sexist, but in practice this is not representative of current usage so far as I can ascertain.

Many FEMINIST commentators single out Kate Millett's 1970 study *Sexual Politics* for special mention when discussing the way in which the term entered the vocabulary of just about all feminists and many others. Of interest to us is the fact that Millett focused her argument on literary TEXTS, and related the struggle for women's liberation to that sexism which could be uncovered in CANONICAL literary texts and criticism (her treatment of D. H. Lawrence was especially influential).

See also HOMOPHOBIA, which includes discussion of the term *heterosexism*, and HOMOSOCIAL.

Shadow dialogue See INTERIOR DIALOGUE

Shannon and Weaver model of communication In 1948 the American electronic engineer Claude Shannon published two influential essays concerned to propose statistical ways of measuring the information value of a MESSAGE. Part of his argument included a diagrammatic model of the communication process, which has been extremely influential. As these essays were republished in book form in 1949 with an additional essay by Warren Weaver, the model in question has become known as the Shannon and Weaver model.

Shannon and Weaver's model clearly aims at a high level of generality and abstraction, but it is important to remember that its creators were electronic engineers, used to working with information in a technical sense, information that could be *quantified* unproblematically. The model, however, seized the imagination of many working in very different fields, and the development of SEMIOTICS gave it a wider circulation than its creators had probably intended or expected. Its influence can almost certainly be detected in the influential passage in Roman Jakobson's 'Linguistics and Poetics' in which Jakobson attempts to break linguistic communication into its component parts: *addresser, message, addressee, context, code*, and *contact*. Jakobson's suggestion is discussed in the entry on FUNCTIONS OF LANGUAGE, in which the case against using such terms in the study of art or poetry is considered.

The model has been adapted by many who have used it, but generally looks something like this:

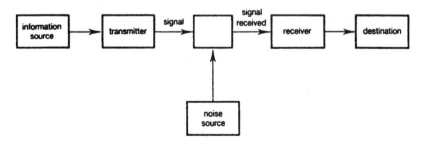

Shannon and Weaver model of communication, 1949

319

Roland Barthes's discussion of the press photograph in his essay 'The Photographic Message' displays the unmistakable influence of Shannon and Weaver's model.

> The press photograph is a message. This message as a whole is constituted by a source of emission, a channel of transmission, and a medium of reception. The source of emission is the newspaper staff, the group of technicians of whom some take the photograph, others select it, crop and compose it, treat it, and then others title it with a caption and a commentary. The medium of reception is the public which reads the newspaper. And the channel of transmission is the newspaper itself, or, more precisely, a complex of concurrent messages of which the photograph is the center but whose environs are constituted by the text, the caption, the headline, the layout, and, more abstractly but no less 'informatively,' the name of the paper itself . . . (Barthes: 1991, 3)

In spite of the insights of Barthes's essay the passage quoted gives a fair basis for understanding the unease that use of Shannon and Weaver's model in the Humanities often evokes. There is, I think, a clear element of Procrusteanism involved in relating complex CULTURAL processes to a model developed to display relationships between components in the mechanical transmission of information. The role of INTERPRETATION in the understanding of art makes this process difficult to equate with the transmission of quantifiable information undertaken by the electronic engineer (compare the discussion in the entry for CODE). The electronic engineer wants his or her 'message' to reach its 'destination' in unchanged form: the poet or novelist – even according to the most pro-INTENTIONALIST of theorists – does not want merely to recreate in the mind of the READER exactly what occurred in his or her mind during the composition of the work. It is probably not irrelevant to note that the word *message* has generally been used in a somewhat pejorative sense in discussions of art.

An adaptation of Jakobson's suggestion to the 'literary system' can be found in Itamar Even-Zohar's *Polysystem Studies* (1990).

INSTITUTION
[context]

PRODUCER   CONSUMER
[addresser] ——————————— [addressee]
('writer')   ('reader')

MARKET
[content/channel]

PRODUCT
[message]

(after Even-Zohar: 1990, 31)

See also the discussion of frame-shifting in the entry for FRAME (third definition).

Perhaps a more successful adaptation of terms which probably originate with Shannon and Weaver can be found in recent NARRATIVE theory. Here a more schematic analysis of what in traditional terminology used to be called *point of view* (discussed in the entry for PERSPECTIVE AND VOICE) has proved to be genuinely illuminating, and in this context terms such as *addresser* and *addressee* serve a useful and generally non-REDUCTIVE function.

See also ACT/ACTOR.

Shifter In Linguistics: a linguistic unit which shifts REFERENCE according to the context in which it appears. Thus 'I', or 'the Pope' can both refer to a range of different historical or FICTIONAL individuals depending upon who utters them, to whom, and in what situation. The term has sometimes been used in discussions of literature.

See also DEIXIS.

Short-circuit In NARRATIVE theory the deliberate and pointed mixing of narrative levels, or the flouting of CONVENTIONS appertaining to narrative levels. Much POSTMODERNIST FICTION indulges frequently in such short-circuiting, as when an author speaks in his own extra-fictional voice about one of his or her created CHARACTERS.

The terms *short-circuit narrative*, or alternatively *Mobius strip narrative*, are used to describe a narrative that forms a seamless circuit, so that one can join it at any point and continue to go round, and round, in an endless loop.

Sign Much modern literary and critical theory has been dominated by or founded on a version of SEMIOTICS – that is, upon a general theory (or 'science') of the nature of the sign and of its life in CULTURE and history. Semiotics is not the child of literary criticism or theory, however, and no theory of the sign can be said to be literature-specific, or directed primarily or exclusively towards literature. Thus a concern with semiotic theories on the part of literary critics and theorists is both the result of a lessening belief in the specificity of literature and what can be clumsily called literary communication, and also the basis for a further search for what literary WORKS and their READING have in common with what one must then refer to as 'non-literary communication'.

A useful starting point is to distinguish between *sign* and *symptom*. The key difference would appear to be that of the *conventional* nature of the sign: a symptom is fixed by and interpreted in the light of nature, a sign by and in the light of CONVENTION. Some theorists would be prepared to see a symptom as a sub-set of sign, while others distinguish sharply between the two. Clearly the issue of INTENTION, or MOTIVATION can be brought in here. (See the entry for SYMPTOMATIC READING in this context.)

The Lacanian use of *symptom* is, not surprisingly, more complex. Rey Chow (1994) quotes from Slavoj Žižek's discussion of the term, a discussion which, according to Chow, uses 'symptom' 'not in the derogatory sense of a dispensable shadow but in the sense of something that gives the subject its ontological consistency and its fundamental structure' (Mongia: 1996, 124). He cites Žižek as follows:

If, however, we conceive the symptom as Lacan did in his last writings and seminars, namely as a particular signifying formation which confers on the subject its very ontological consistency, enabling it to structure its basic, constitutive relationship towards enjoyment (*jouissance*), then the entire relationship [between subject and symptom] is reversed, for if the symptom is dissolved, the subject itself disintegrates. In this sense, 'Woman is a symptom of man' means that man himself exists only through woman qua his symptom: his very ontological consistency depends on, is 'externalized' in, his symptom. (Mongia: 1996, 124, quoting Žižek: 1990, 21)

Probably the theory of the sign which has been most influential so far as literature is concerned is that of the Swiss linguistician Ferdinand de Saussure. It is worth remembering that Saussure's definition is not of the sign as such, but of the *linguistic* sign, although many of his followers have generalized his definition to include non-linguistic signs as well. It should be remembered, however, that when one reads a statement along the lines of 'Saussure defined the sign as . . .', one should bear in mind that this broadening of reference is neither unproblematic nor uncontroversial. (Saussure did, it is true, talk of the then as yet unborn science of semiology, which would study signs in general and their role in social life, but even here he closely associates the laws of semiology with laws applicable in Linguistics.)

Saussure denied the common-sense view that the linguistic sign was a name that could be attached to an object, and argued instead that the linguistic sign was a 'two-sided psychological entity' that could be represented by the diagram reproduced below (1974, 66; some translations have 'sound pattern' rather than 'sound image'). Saussure admits that this goes against then current usage (according to him the term *sign* was normally taken to designate only a sound-image), but argues that to avoid AMBIGUITY three related terms were needed: 'I propose to retain the word *sign* [*signe*] to designate the whole and to replace *concept* and *sound-image* respectively by *signified* [*signifié*] and *signifier* [*signifiant*]' (1974, 67). The English translations of *signifié* and *signifiant* given here have been questioned, and in one suggestion *significance* and *signal* have been proposed as alternatives.

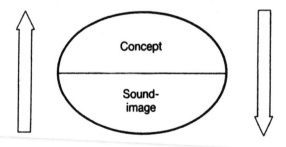

It should be noted that subsequent theorists, Jacques Lacan included, have seen the link between signifier and signified to be far more problematic: shifting, multiple and context-dependent. And Jacques Derrida has seen Saussure's writing about the sign to double back on its own revolutionary insights; according to him, by equating the *signatum* (that which is signified) with the concept, Saussure leaves open the possibility 'of thinking a *concept signified in and of itself*, a concept simply present for thought, independent of a relationship to language, that is of a relationship to a system of signifiers' (1981b, 19). This, Derrida claims, allows Saussure to fall back into the 'classical exigency' of the TRANSCENDENTAL SIGNIFIED (1981b, 19). In other words, the concept is seen to be possessed of an identity separate from the defining system of differences between signifiers: it is seen as extra-systemic and complete in itself. (See the entry for RADICAL ALTERITY.)

It will be noted that what drops out in the movement from what I called the common-sense view to Saussure's definition is the object, or that which represents extra-linguistic reality. This has led many Saussureans to claim that language has no connection with extra-linguistic reality, an assertion that has been advanced especially forcefully by some *literary* critics and theorists concerned to adapt Saussure's theory of the sign to literature. Such assertions have very often brought in Saussure's argument concerning the ARBITRARINESS of the sign in support of this thesis, as well as the claim that Saussure's Linguistics is purely SYNCHRONIC and that it rejects the validity of any DIACHRONIC, or historical, study of language. I have argued elsewhere (Hawthorn: 1987, 52–7) that all of these assertions are incorrect, and that Saussure specifically rejects the basis for all of them in his *Course in General Linguistics*. The acceptance of all or some of these assertions as correct, however, has often provided a theoretical basis for a new formalism since the 1960s, a formalism that involves the isolation of literature from life, and art from society, culture and history. One quotation will perhaps suffice to confirm this; writing about Saussure's theory of the sign in his book *Semiotics and Interpretation* Robert Scholes states confidently that

> Saussure, as amplified by Roland Barthes and others, has taught us to recognize an unbridgeable gap between words and things, signs and referents. The whole notion of 'sign and referent' has been rejected by the French structuralists and their followers as too materialistic and simpleminded. Signs do not refer to things, they signify concepts, and concepts are aspects of thought, not of reality. (1982, 24)

To do Scholes justice it should be said that he goes on to challenge this 'recognition', although he does not challenge the justice of blaming it on Saussure. His summary is otherwise a fair account of an orthodoxy that flourished in the 1970s and 1980s.

A good summary of other important theories of the sign is given by Edmund Leach in the second chapter of his book *Culture and Communication* (1976, 9–16). Leach cites not just Saussure, but also C. S. Peirce, Ernst Cassirer, L. Hjelmslev, Charles Morris, Roman Jakobson and Roland Barthes as influential theorists in this context, but allots the word 'sign' only a limited function in his own terminology, which he represents by means of a complicated grid diagram. (Roland Barthes is driven to the same resort, which I have myself deliberately avoided, in his early work *Elements of Semiology*.) Jonathan Culler has pointed out (1981, 23) that Peirce's influential tripartite distinction between ICON, INDEX and symbol is only one of the many semiotic taxonomies he proposed, and that he finally committed himself to a core 66 classes of sign – a figure which has not been found worthy of adoption by subsequent theorists.

In his later work Roland Barthes has suggested more idiosyncratic definitions for related terms: in *The Pleasure of the Text*, for example, he defines *significance* (*signifiance*) as 'meaning, *insofar as it is sensually produced*' (1976, 61) – a definition that, not surprisingly, has failed to achieve widespread popularity. There is a useful discussion of the use by both Barthes and Julia Kristeva of the French terms *signifiance* and *signification* in Richard Harland's book *Superstructuralism* (1987); Harland suggests that what characterizes this usage is a restriction of the latter term to a fixity and self-identification within a system, and the opening out of this fixity of meaning to a decomposed and more INTERTEXTUAL *signifiance*. Again, such specialist usages have enjoyed only a limited influence in the work of other, non-French writers.

Gérard Genette has suggested an adaptation of Saussure's definition of the sign to the needs of the theory of NARRATIVE; he proposes 'to use the word *story* for the signified or narrative content . . . to use the word *narrative* for the signifier, statement, discourse or narrative text itself, and to use the word *narrating* for the producing narrative action' (1980, 27). The vocabulary proposed is useful, but whether it depends upon the analogy with Saussure's definition of the linguistic sign is debatable.

Jacques Derrida has argued that not a single signified escapes 'the play of signifying references that constitute language'.

> The advent of writing is the advent of this play; today such a play is coming into its own, effacing the limit starting from which one had thought to regulate the circulation of signs, drawing along with it all the reassuring signifieds, reducing all the strongholds, all the out-of-bounds shelters that watched over the field of language. This, strictly speaking, amounts to destroying the concept of 'sign' and its entire logic. (1976, 7)

Others, however, have felt that this obituary is premature.
See also HINGE; SEMEME.

Signal See INDEX

Signifiance/signifiant See SIGN

Significance See SIGN; MEANING AND SIGNIFICANCE

Signification/*signifié***/signified/signifier** See SIGN

Signifying practice In his Introduction to Julia Kristeva's *Desire in Language* Leon S. Roudiez quotes Kristeva's definition of this term from her *La Traversée des signes*:

> I shall call signifying practice the establishment and the countervailing of a sign system. Establishing a sign system calls for the identity of a speaking subject within a social framework, which he recognizes as a basis for that identity. Countervailing the sign system is done by having the subject undergo an unsettling, questionable process; this indirectly challenges the social framework with which he had previously identified, and it thus coincides with times of abrupt changes, renewal, or revolution in society. (Kristeva: 1980, 18)

For Roland Barthes, a signifying practice is 'first of all a differentiated signifying system, dependent on a typology of significations (and not on a universal matrix of the sign)'. This means, he continues, that signification is not produced at the abstract level of LANGUE, but through 'a labour in which both the debate of the subject and the Other, and the social context, are invested in the same movement' (1981b, 36). According to Barthes, this notion restores its active energy to language.

A signifying practice thus involves a struggle for MEANINGS within a social context and against other interests, a struggle which is inseparable from the identity granted or claimed for him- or herself by the individual and by others.

See also DISCOURSE (discursive practice); IDEOLOGY; UTTERANCE.

Simulacrum (Pl. simulacra) An image, representation, or copy. Associated with English translations of the work of Jean Baudrillard, who argues that we now live in a world in which such representations precede, and indeed create, that which they represent.

See the entry for PRECESSION.

Singularization See DEFAMILIARIZATION

Singulative See FREQUENCY

Sinn und Bedeutung See SENSE AND REFERENCE

Sinthom In an essay entitled 'Hitchcockian Sinthoms', Slavoj Žižek explains that he takes this term from the work of Jacques Lacan, where according to him it has to be understood 'as a signifier's constellation (formula) which fixes a certain core of enjoyment, like mannerisms in painting – characteristic details which persist and repeat themselves without implying a common meaning (this insistence offers, perhaps, a clue to what Freud meant by the "compulsion to repeat")' (Žižek: 1992, 126). An alternative definition is provided by Tom Cohen, for whom

> the *sinthom* is a 'symptom' transposed beyond interpretation or the chain of signifiers. While it operates as a sheer manifestation or protrusion, it is also a kind of master-sign that nonetheless grounds or ruptures all signifying chains. One might say that, being opposed to metonymy, it subtly operates as a sort of radical or imploded metaphor without being called such. (1998, 158)

For metaphor and metonymy, see SYNTAGMATIC AND PARADIGMATIC.

Site A word that has accrued a particular polemical force in recent years, although a force that, paradoxically, is linked to a claimed neutrality, IDEOLOGICAL innocence, and lack of proper energy or initiatory force. To describe something as a site has become a favoured way of giving (sometimes exclusive) precedence to external determining forces while playing down or denying the self-initiation of movement or development.

Thus when the SUBJECT is described as site, an attack is being made on views of the subject as in control – or even aware – of its own destiny; a subject is, according to such a view, more or merely a site on which extra-subjective forces clash and resolve their differences. These extra-subjective forces which are given priority can be either language, or history, or ideology, or the CLASS struggle, or whatever. Put simply, the argument thus invoked by the use of *site* denies that the individual is in charge of his or her life, or consciousness, and asserts rather that the subject is constituted by other forces which then proceed either to nest or to fight in it.

Those fond of the term have sometimes come dangerously near to a sort of infinite regress: the subject is a site upon which different ideological forces battle, but then ideology is itself a site on which different class interests war with one another, while class is, in its turn, a site on which different relationships to the forces of production meet in conflict, and so on.

The term is sometimes invoked by those DECONSTRUCTIONISTS arguing for a rejection of any TRANSCENDENTAL SUBJECT or PRESENCE.

In literary criticism the term is often associated with attempts to downgrade the extent to which the AUTHOR is seen to be in control (conscious or otherwise) of his or her creation.

Sjužet See STORY AND PLOT

Skaz A mode or technique of narration that mirrors oral NARRATIVE. A useful alternative definition of the term is given by Ann Banfield, who points out that apart from the epistolary form, *skaz* 'is the only type of literary first person narrative which clearly has a second person' (1982, 172). The term comes from the Russian, as RUSSIAN FORMALIST theorists were the first to tackle the issues raised by *skaz*, but there are many non-Russian examples. For example, from a technical point of view much of Joseph Conrad's *Heart of Darkness* can be described as *skaz*, as much of what we read represents the CHARACTER Marlow's oral address to listeners.

For the Russian Formalist Boris Eichenbaum, *skaz* allots – or can allot – a special role to aspects of a NARRATOR's verbal delivery such as ARTICULATION, miming, and sound gestures. Eichenbaum also distinguishes between the concept of plot and the concept of story-stuff, or, alternatively, between construction and material. *Skaz* for Eichenbaum is important because it is 'the constructional principle of the plotless story' (Èjxenbaum: 1971a, 21; see the entry for STORY AND PLOT).

Mikhail Bakhtin takes issue with this position, claiming that the most important thing about *skaz* is not '*orientation toward the oral form of narration*', but 'orientation toward *someone else's speech*' (1984, 191). Bakhtin's argument seems to be that crucial to *skaz* is not the oral mode of delivery (or its imitation or representation), but the AUTHOR's recruitment of an alternative VOICE (with all the significance that this last word has in Bakhtin's work). Thus Bakhtin would, presumably, argue that Conrad's use of Marlow in *Heart of Darkness* is important not so much because of Marlow's oral delivery, but because of Conrad's use of Marlow's voice, a voice that is 'socially distinct, carrying with it precisely those points of view and evaluations necessary to the author' (1984, 192).

Bakhtin's points are important, but they are probably overstated. Marlow (to continue with this example) is probably important to Conrad because of the voice (in a Bakhtinian sense) which he provides, but the oral manner of delivery is also very important, and carries with it certain possibilities and restrictions which CONVENTIONAL first-person narrative (as, for example, in Charles Dickens's *David Copperfield*) does not, even though such first-person narrative provides an author with the same voice.

Ann Banfield adds a number of other, more complex points. She claims that *skaz* is not actually a form of narration, but 'the imitation of a discourse'. For her, DISCOURSE is characterized by the inseparability of telling from expression, whereas the function of a sentence in narration is 'solely to tell' (1982, 178). Her claim is by no means uncontroversial, and relies upon definitions of *discourse* and *narration* that would not find universal acceptance. She makes one additional, important technical claim: represented speech and thought (see the entry for FREE INDIRECT DISCOURSE) are not found in oral literature, or literature derived from the oral – and this includes *skaz* (1982, 239–40).

Slant See PERSPECTIVE AND VOICE

Slash fandom Defined and described by Constance Penley in her article 'Feminism, Psychoanalysis, and the Study of Popular Culture' (1994). The slash in question is the typographical sign / that is used to separate the names of two FICTIONAL characters drawn from soap operas or science fiction, as in Kirk/Spock (Captain James T. Kirk and Mr Spock from the TV series *Star Trek*). 'Fandom' is the state of being a particular sort of fan. This particular branch of fandom, if Penley's account is anything to go by, involves types of sexual fantasy that my hitherto sheltered life has left me altogether unprepared for. Those interested are referred to the article.

Slippage The term seems to be an anglicizing of the French *glissement*. Vincent Crapanzano suggests, if I read a complex passage aright, that in the work of Jacques Lacan it is applied to that distortion that takes place between the dream and the account given of it by the (woken) dreamer, a distortion which is 'a sliding, a *glissement* of the signified under the signifier, the concept under its acoustic image' (1992, 145).

More loosely: the (normally unconscious) redefinition of terms or commitments in the course of an argument, often as a result of IDEOLOGICAL pressure.

Slow-down The NARRATIVE equivalent to that slow-motion experience which frequently accompanies moments of great danger or tension. A narrative may suddenly provide what seems (in contrast to that which has gone before or that which comes after) a disproportionate number of pages to what takes place in a (relatively) very short span of time. Precisely because the technique does resemble 'slow-motion experience' it suggests by analogy that what is narrated is of great subjective importance either to NARRATOR or CHARACTER, or both.

Compare the (now clichéd) use of filmic slow-motion at moments of high tension in motion pictures: a famous example is the final machine-gunning in *Bonnie and Clyde*.

The obvious justification for slow-down is that its use in the appropriate context creates an impression of psychological REALISM, as at moments of high tension – especially those involving physical danger – human beings do experience events as if they were happening in slow motion. Beyond this, slow-down allows a writer to go more into detail at times when detail is more interesting and of greater significance.

See also DURATION.

Social energy See ENERGY

Socialist realism See REALISM

Sociolect Formed by analogy with *dialect* (compare IDIOLECT and GENDERLECT), and used to denote language (PAROLE rather than LANGUE) which is specific to a particular social group, and which thus carries with it the values and status of the same group. The social group in question can be defined in terms of CLASS (variously understood), age, or GENDER – or a permutation of all three. Sociolects are normally associated with speech, although as lexical, grammatical and syntactical elements can serve to isolate a sociolect it is possible to trace sociolects in written TEXTS. Other defining elements involve aspects of pronunciation: certain sounds are indicative of certain sociolects in British English (the glottal stop, for example).

Many writers have attempted to convey sociolects by means of idiosyncratic spelling, but this is problematic in ENGLISH as the sounds of spoken English are not rendered into writing in a consistent manner (as those learning English as a second language soon discover). Thus use of a spelling such as *wimmin* (for *women*) in the speech of a cockney CHARACTER probably works more by the association 'can't spell – therefore uneducated' than by suggesting cockney pronunciation (*wimmin* is, after all, a spelling that reflects educated pronunciation pretty accurately).

Socio-linguistic horizon See HORIZON

Solution from above/below Also known as 'hypothesis driven' (above) and 'data driven' (below) solutions, and also 'top down (perspective)' and 'bottom up (perspective)'. From the psychology of visual perception: a solution from above is a perceptual INTERPRETATION which has been arrived at as a result of a hypothesis which predates the input of sensory data; a solution from below is a perceptual interpretation which has been prompted by the actual input of sensory data which is itself then interpreted.

'Solution from below' research starts, as the term 'data driven' suggests, from some form of evidence, from what, perhaps misleadingly, can be called 'raw material' – normally raw material that requires some sort of explanation or ordering. In this sort of research, theory is *brought in as part of the solution*. When a couple go to marriage counselling, for example, they are engaged in data-driven research. Hypothesis-driven research, in contrast, takes place independently of or prior to direct contact with the 'raw material' which one wishes to study; it stems from a problem within theory, from pressures at a more abstract and displaced level than the problems that initiate data-driven research. In this sort of research it is *the raw material which is brought in as part of the solution*.

A classic example of such research would be the predictions about planetary movement entailed by Einstein's theories which were eventually confirmed by observation. Classically, the pure sciences work in terms of hypothesis-driven research, while the applied sciences work in terms of data-driven research.

By extension, a literary interpretation which is 'from above' or hypothesis-driven is one prompted by a hypothesis which the WORK itself, or the readings of 'Common

Readers', do not overtly suggest; a literary interpretation which is 'from below' or data-driven is one which is prompted by the work itself.

The distinction seems more straightforward than it is, as what a work 'overtly suggests' is arguably dependent upon the READER's expectations, critical awareness, social and CULTURAL background, and so on. (See, for example, the discussion in the entry for TRANSACTIONAL THEORY OF THE LITERARY WORK on this point.) Nevertheless, the distinction has its merits, especially during the present time when many critical theories propose the need for the critic to step outside a *naturalized* understanding of, or RESPONSE to, the work of literature, and to give it instead an OPPOSITIONAL READING.

As a crude generalization, then, we can say that whereas the period dominated by the ideas and approaches of the NEW CRITICS privileged 'solution from below' readings and interpretations, the past two or three decades have seen the rise of theories and movements committed to arguing for 'solution from above' readings and interpretations, often on the ground that these offer an escape from the IDEOLOGICAL thrall of particular literary works or of particular INTERPRET[AT]IVE COMMUNITIES.

In this context it is worth noting that recent literary theory has often obscured the distinction between *empiricism* (the belief that direct experience or observation is the only source of knowledge), and *empirical* research (which relies upon such direct experience or observation but does not necessarily rest upon the view that such experience or observation is the *only* source of knowledge, or that its significance is self-evident without the application of non-empirical ideas or theories).

For *naturalization* see DEFAMILIARIZATION.

Sous rature See ERASURE

Spacing See PUNCTUATION

Spectatrice Female spectator.

Speech Attempts to render Ferdinand de Saussure's distinction between LANGUE AND PAROLE into English frequently use *speech* as the preferred term for *parole*. However, it is increasingly common to use the original terms in untranslated form, in part because *speech* is a rather unsatisfactory translation of *parole* – something like *the sum of all actual (or possible) UTTERANCES* would probably come nearer to what Saussure seems to have had in mind. An utterance, like *parole*, does not need to be actually spoken: it can be written or expressed to oneself in silent thought.

We can compare the problems associated with translating ÉCRITURE as *writing*, discussed in the entry for this term.

As a general principle, then, it is worth exercising care when one encounters words such as *speech* and *writing* in English translations of French theoretical writing. Jacques Derrida's commitment to the primacy of Writing over Speech, for example (reiterated in a number of his texts) seems less bizarre when his original terms are borne in mind: he is certainly not saying that human speech is historically subsequent to writing in the everyday meanings of these words.

See also SPEECH ACT THEORY; VOICE.

Speech act theory As its name suggests, speech act theory is a theory that attempts to explain exactly what happens when human beings speak to one another. The theory has been influential not just within Linguistics and PRAGMATICS, but also within literary criticism – as a result of books such as Mary Louise Pratt's *Toward a Speech Act Theory of Literary Discourse* (1977). Speech act theory originated with the philosopher John Austin's book *How to Do Things with Words* (1962), in which Austin argues against the philosophical assumptions that verbal statements can be analysed in isolation and in terms only of their truth or falsity.

A number of other philosophers – most notably John Searle but also H. P. Grice and P. F. Strawson – have developed and extended Austin's arguments. They have drawn attention to the manner in which the public UTTERING of statements is governed by rules and CONVENTIONS which have to be understood and abided by on the part of utterers and listeners if effective communication is to take place, and also to the fact that statements not only *say* things, but they typically also *do* things. In Searle (1969) we find a useful distinction between a number of different sorts of verbal act.

5. Uttering words (morphemes, sentences) = performing *utterance acts*.
6. Referring and predicating = performing *propositional acts*.
7. Stating, questioning, commanding, promising, etc. = performing *illocutionary acts*.

Searle's usage is not identical to Austin's: although Searle uses Austin's term 'illocutionary act', for example, he does not accept Austin's distinction between locutionary and illocutionary acts (1969, 23 n1).

Austin distinguishes between *constatives* – utterances which can either be true or false because they claim to report that certain things are the case in certain worlds – and *performatives*, which are utterances used to do something rather than to say that something is the case (e.g. 'I promise to marry you') and of which it makes no sense to claim that they are either true or false. One should add that a constative can also have a performative aspect – by pragmatic implication, for example.

Utterance acts are also referred to as *locutionary acts* if they involve the production of a recognizably grammatical utterance within a language community. *Illocutionary acts* include such things as asserting, warning, promising and so on, and Austin claimed that over a thousand different possible such acts can be performed in English. Searle has suggested that illocutionary acts can be classified into five basic categories: *representatives*, which undertake to represent a state of affairs; *directives*, which have the aim of getting the person addressed to do something; *commissives*, which commit the speaker to doing something; *expressives*, which provide information about the speaker's psychological state, and *declarations*, which bring about the state of affairs they themselves refer to (e.g. 'I now declare you man and wife') (1976, 10–14; compare Roman Jakobson's FUNCTIONS OF LANGUAGE).

Searle has also pointed out that a person who performs an illocutionary act may also be performing what he has dubbed a *perlocutionary act*, in other words, achieving certain intended results in his or her listener. He gives as examples, *get him to do something, convince him (enlighten, edify, inspire him, get him to realize)* (1969, 25).

330

The conventions underlying successful conversation are known as *appropriateness conditions* or *felicity conditions* by speech act philosophers, and together are taken to constitute the *co-operative principle* (a term suggested by H. P. Grice) that governs conversation in ideal situations. They include (i) *maxim of quantity*: (Make your contribution no more or less informative than is required); (ii) *maxim of quality*: (Make your contribution one that is true, and that does not include either false or inadequately substantiated material); (iii) *maxim of relation*: (Be relevant); (iv) *maxim of manner*: (Be perspicuous, avoiding obscurity, ambiguity, unnecessary prolixity). (Based on Pratt: 1977, 130; following Grice.)

On the basis of such maxims, and on their assumed observance by participants in a conversation, statements not immediately interpretable as relevant can be seen to have a particular *implicature* or implication. Take the following exchange between husband and wife: 'Do you want to go home?' 'It's getting rather late.' The second statement may seem to be changing the subject, but its pragmatic meaning or implicature is clearly 'Yes'.

A theory of utterances which reduced the importance of truth REFERENCE and emphasized instead the compact formed between utterer and listener by the mutual adoption of a set of conventions, made literary critics sit up and take notice, for it seemed of far greater potential use in literary criticism than more traditional philosophical approaches to verbal statements had been. An obvious application of such a theory was to the conversations between CHARACTERS in plays and literary NARRATIVES, but there were more interesting and sophisticated ones. In his essay 'The Death of the Author' Roland Barthes suggested that the word *writing* (see ÉCRITURE) no longer designated 'an operation of recording, notation, representation, "depiction",' but rather 'a performative ... in which the enunciation has no other content ... than the act by which it is uttered' (1977, 145–6; see also the entry for AUTHOR). Clearly such an approach could be used as support for the argument that the literary WORK did not say anything about the extra-literary world, but rather performed itself, repeated in endlessly different ways the statement 'I express myself'.

In a very different way the theory of implicature seemed especially promising for literary-critical application. When a writer wrote something that seemed to be irrelevant to what the READER had been led to be interested in, was this not because the writer could rely upon the reader's *searching* for relevance in the TEXT? Do not readers assume that everything that is there in a literary text is there for some purpose, has in other words some implicature? The problem with this use of speech act theory would seem to be that all it did was to give a new name to something about which literary critics and readers had known for a very long time anyway.

Moreover, were not author and reader, and their intercourse, comparable to the participants in a conversation governed by the co-operative principle? Was it not the case that just as a conversation which did not abide by the different Gricean maxims would necessarily be ill-fated and unproductive, so too that any reading of a literary work which did not respect the conventions of literary communication would become pointless and unproductive?

There are a number of possible objections to such an argument. The first is actually a criticism of speech act theory itself, that speech act theory tends to stress co-operation at the expense of struggle and disagreement. Most conversations are not conducted between equals whose interests are identical; they are conducted between individuals who have divergent interests and who either possess, or are subject to the exercise of, social power and authority. Most participants in conversations thus, the argument continues, typically break many of the maxims quoted above to further their own interests, and they expect their fellow conversationalists to do the same. Much the same is true of literary reading: the author and the reader have different interests and are as much trying to outwit as to co-operate with one another. In her poem 'Murder in the Dark' Margaret Atwood (1983) compares the literary process to the party game referred to in her title, with the writer as murderer and the reader as detective, and the NEW HISTORICIST critic Stephen Greenblatt reminds us that Plato's rival Gorgias 'held that deception – *apate* – is the very essence of the creative imagination: the tragic artist's special power is the power to deceive' (1990, 52). (Greenblatt goes on to note that Gorgias did not thereby exclude the power of art to strip away fraud, as 'its successful practitioner is nearer to reality than the unsuccessful, and the man who lets himself be deceived is wiser than he who does not' [1990, 52, quoting from Gorgias].)

Even if one grants this sort of objection, it remains the case that both in conversations and in literary readings, manoeuvrings, battles for position, attempts to further one's interests, take place according to mutually recognized conventions. In Grice's defence it needs to be noted that he never intended the co-operative principle to have a NORMATIVE force. His argument was, rather, that in the absence of evidence suggesting that a conversational partner was knowingly refusing to co-operate, individuals continued to assume that the partner was following the rules, and consequently continued to search for a meaning in what was said that was consistent with that assumption.

The second objection to a literary-critical appropriation of speech act theory is that literary works are not orientated to the achievement of specific goals in quite the way that the typical conversation is. Literary works are objects for APPRECIATION, INTERPRETATION, and (sometimes) PERFORMANCE. They thus have the potentiality to generate new experiences, new SIGNIFICANCE, in a manner quite different from that of a conversation. Moreover, although it is not meaningless to talk of interaction between author and reader, this interaction is nonetheless of a quite different sort from the mutually adjusting and instantaneous reaction involved in ordinary conversation. We can talk back to Emily Brontë as we read *Wuthering Heights*, but this will not change her text or whatever of herself is in that text.

Literary works have, too, an AESTHETIC dimension which conversations lack. This explains why it is that literary works seem actually to be prized to the extent that they break some of the Gricean maxims – that involving AMBIGUITY, for example. Does it always make sense to talk about a writer of literature providing the reader, in an ideal situation, with no more or less information than is required?

Whether one grants such criticisms a certain truth or not, speech act theory has probably had a positive effect upon literary critics inasmuch as it has stressed the importance of mutually accepted conventions in the reading and writing of literature, and it has refocused attention on to the conventional elements implicit in LITERARINESS.

Speed See DURATION

Spots of indeterminacy See CONCRETIZATION

Staircasing See EMBEDDING; EVENT; FRAME

Standpoint theory According to Lynne Pearce, ' "Standpoint theory", as represented by the work of feminist scholars like Dorothy Smith, Nancy Hartsock and Sandra Harding, argues for a "strategic essentialism" which will enable women to analyse their oppression from within the context of their own experience' (1994, 103 n39).

Important essays by these three writers and others can be found in a valuable collection edited by Sandra Harding: *Feminism and Methodology: Social Science Issues* (1987). In her own introductory essay, Harding argues that there is no such thing as a problem without a person or group of persons: 'a problem is always a problem *for* someone or other' (1987, 6). She points out that the adequacy of our total picture is determined at least as much by the questions we ask (or do not ask) as by the answers we receive, and suggests that 'traditional social science' has 'asked only the questions about social life that appear problematic from within the social experiences that are characteristic for men (white, Western, bourgeois men, that is)' (1987, 7, 6).

From this point onwards her own argument itself adopts a more overtly FEMINIST standpoint. For Harding,

> [t]he best feminist analysis . . . insists that the inquirer her/himself be placed in the same critical plane as the overt subject matter, thereby recovering the entire research process for scrutiny in the results of research. That is, the class, race, culture, and gender assumptions, beliefs, and behaviors of the researcher her/himself must be placed within the frame of the picture that she/he attempts to paint. (1987, 9)

She does not accept, however, that this inevitably leads to an espousal of RELATIVISM, and it is perhaps here that the originality of standpoint theory lies, in its bringing together an insistence on the importance of the observer's or researcher's perspective or standpoint, and a rejection of an uncritical relativism or pluralism.

In the same collection, Nancy C. M. Hartsock's essay 'The Feminist Standpoint: Developing the Ground for a Specifically Feminist Historical Materialism', attempts to combine the insights or premises of standpoint theory with a more traditional MARXISM. According to her, 'just as Marx's understanding of the world from the standpoint of the proletariat enabled him to go beneath bourgeois ideology, so a feminist standpoint can allow us to understand patriarchal institutions and ideologies as perverse inversions of more humane social relations' (1987, 159). And as the term 'standpoint' might suggest, just as some physical vantage points allow us a view, or a better view, of certain aspects of a landscape, so too there are some non-physical standpoints which allow us to see certain social, CULTURAL, or IDEOLOGICAL facts more clearly. Furthermore, just as what we see – an appearance – may misrepresent what lies beneath it (as Marx never tired of pointing out), so too some standpoints are better placed to enable us to see things right (here the anti-relativistic element in standpoint theory is again apparent). As Hartsock puts it, a 'standpoint, however, carries with it the contention that there are some perspectives on society from which, however well-intentioned one may be, the real relations of humans with each other and with the natural world are not visible' (1987, 159). This should not be taken to mean that there exist standpoints from which everything is visible, and indeed the thrust of standpoint theory is that although some standpoints allow one to see more than do others, no standpoint allows us to see everything.

None of this makes specific reference to literature or to literary theory, but a comment from Dorothy E. Smith's essay, 'Women's Perspective as a Radical Critique of Sociology', shows perhaps how many of the insights of standpoint theory have potentially interesting and fruitful application to issues raised by NARRATIVE theorists, especially with regard to point of view or PERSPECTIVE AND VOICE.

> Riding a train not long ago in Ontario I saw a family of Indians, woman, man, and three children standing together on a spur above a river watching the train go by. There was (for me) that moment – the train, those five people seen on the other side of the glass. I saw first that I could tell this incident as it was, but that telling it as a description built in my position and my interpretations. I have called them a family; I have said they were watching the train. My understanding has already subsumed theirs. Everything may have been quite other for them. My description is privileged to stand as what actually happened, because theirs is not heard in the contexts in which I speak. If we begin from the world as we actually experience it, it is at least possible to see that we are located and that what we know of the other is conditional upon that location as part of a relation comprehending the other's location also. There are and must be different experiences of the world and different bases of experience. We must not do away with them by taking advantage of our privileged speaking to construct a sociological version which we then impose upon them as their reality. We may not rewrite the other's world or impose upon it a conceptual framework which extracts from it what fits with ours.
>
> . . .
>
> My experience in the train epitomizes a sociological relation. The observer is already separated from the world as it is experienced by those she observes. (1987, 93)

Smith's comments here could well serve as an enlightening point of departure for those interested in investigating crucial issues concerning the relationship between narrative perspective and ideological or moral – not to say epistemological – standpoint. The passage is also interesting in the light of POSTCOLONIALIST theory, which has drawn our attention to the way in which the GAZE of the privileged (western, EUROCENTRIC, male) observer fixes and categorizes the (underprivileged, objectified, 'passified') observed person or persons in terms which reflect and serve the interests of observer rather than observed.

Stereotype Originally taken from a process in printing, the term has become a Standard English phrase for a concept, term, or description that is fixed and unchanging – normally with a pejorative ring, suggesting that oversimplification and prejudice are involved in its formation and use. It has played an important part in recent FEMINIST theory in connection with the description of fixed and, normally, PATRIARCHAL or SEXIST views of GENDER roles and characteristics.

Thus the central third chapter in Mary Ellmann's very influential book *Thinking About Women* (first published 1968) is devoted to 'Feminine Stereotypes', and lists formlessness, passivity, instability, confinement, piety, materiality, spirituality, irrationality and compliancy – along with 'two incorrigible figures': the shrew and the witch.

Stereotyping is not directed only at women, of course: we can isolate stereotypes based on race or CULTURE, on age, on profession, and so on. Moreover, stereotypes may masquerade as positive: thus the beliefs that women are naturally intuitive, or that Black people are always happy and have a wonderful sense of rhythm, are no less stereotypical than more overtly negative views. (It will be noticed that such 'positive' stereotypes typically serve to advance more concealed, negative portrayals.)

Not surprisingly, POSTCOLONIALIST theorists have made much use of the term. Homi K. Bhabha has suggested that stereotypes cannot be understood in isolation, but only as part of a larger system.

> As a form of splitting and multiple belief, the stereotype requires, for its successful signification, a continual and repetitive chain of other stereotypes. The process by which the metaphoric 'masking' is inscribed on a lack which must then be concealed gives the stereotype both its fixity and its phantasmatic quality – the *same old* stories of the Negro's animality, the Coolie's inscrutability or the stupidity of the Irish *must* be told (compulsively) again and afresh, and are differently gratifying and terrifying each time. (1994, 77)

It is arguable that the ability to question, analyse and challenge stereotypes distinguishes important literature from trivial literature. It should be added that according to many theorists a stereotype is only fully effective in disseminating a particular IDEOLOGY when it is not recognized as a stereotype but taken as truth or nature – *naturalized* (see the entry for DEFAMILIARIZATION). Processes of manipulation may involve the conscious use of stereotypes, as in propaganda or media campaigns, but stereotypes may be used unknowingly. Thus when Charles Dickens had it pointed out to him that his portrayal of Fagin in *Oliver Twist* advanced a stereotypical view of Jewish people (the point was not put in these words), he attempted to redress the wrong by means of the CHARACTER Riah in *Our Mutual Friend*.

Stereotypes are, it has been argued, part of the means whereby SUBJECTS are INTERPELLATED by ideological forces.

Stonewall In June 1969, police harassment of the patrons of a Gay bar in New York led to a series of demonstrations (often referred to collectively as 'The Stonewall Riots') from which, according to Eve Kosofsky Sedgwick, 'the modern gay liberation movement dates its inauguration' (1991, 14). The events are seen as a watershed (one meets frequently with the terms 'pre-Stonewall' and 'post-Stonewall'), a watershed which heralded the change from a CULTURE of secrecy and assimilation to one of public affirmation of Gay allegiance along with a public campaign against the persecution of, and discrimination against, Gays. This change affected all aspects of cultural and political life, starting in the United States and spreading to other countries. In literature and literary criticism its changes can be detected in a more open engagement with issues of sexual preference and GENDER orientation, alongside a retrospective concern with the effects of the CLOSET on earlier writers and critics.

The British 'Stonewall Group', according to Ian Lucas, was spearheaded by actors Ian McKellen and Michael Cashman, and established itself during the early months of 1989. The group set itself the task of drafting a Lesbian and Gay rights bill, and was also concerned to focus attention on the debate around an equal age of consent (the then current age for consensual sex between men in Britain was 21) (Lucas: 1998, 9).

Story and plot With this item we are concerned with an essentially very simple distinction surrounded by minefields of confusing vocabulary. A good illustration of the complexities that are here involved can be found in Monika Fludernik's diagrammatic representation of the terminology utilized by different NARRATIVE theorists to represent what she refers to as the different *narrative levels* (more recently Fludernik has used the term 'realms of existence' [1996, 244], which has some overlap with the concept of narrative levels).

	Events in chronological order	Events causally connected	Events ordered artistically	Text on page	Narration as enunciation
Genette	*histoire*		*discours (récit)*		narration (voice + focalization)
Chatman	story	discourse			
Bal	*fabula*	story and focalization		narration (+ language, + voice)	
Rimmon-Kenan	story			text	narration
Prince	narrated			narrating	
Stanzel	–	story		mediation by teller or reflector	mediation by teller or reflector + enunciation if teller figure

(Based on Fludernik: 1993, 62)

The simple distinction is between, on the one hand, a *series of real or fictitious events, connected by a certain logic or chronology, and involving certain ACTORS*, and on the other hand, the NARRATION *of this series of events*. Thus were one to be asked to give the story of *Wuthering Heights*, a suitable response would be to start with the first arrival of the child Heathcliff at Wuthering Heights and then proceed to recount the events of the novel in chronological order until the death of Heathcliff and the (possible) reuniting of him with Cathy. But the plot of *Wuthering Heights* is these events *in the order that they are actually presented in Emily Brontë's novel*. Thus the same story can give rise to many different plots, as FORMULAIC literature reveals very clearly. In an article entitled 'Narrative Time', Paul Ricoeur has suggested a relationship of complex interdependence between three terms: 'A story is *made out of* events to the extent that plot *makes* events *into* a story' (Mitchell: 1981, 167).

Literary critics have long distinguished between major and minor plots, and more recently Cedric Watts (1984) has drawn useful attention to the co-presence of overt and COVERT PLOTS in the same work.

The minefields of which I speak arise from the fact that the same distinction is also referred to by means of the Russian words *fabula* (story) and *sjužet* (plot), and in some translations these are rendered in ways that conflict with the usage associated with story and plot. Mieke Bal, for example, renders our story and plot as *fabula* and *story* (1985, 5), a usage which is also adopted by Onega and Landa (1996), which gives *story* the opposite meaning from that with which we started. Onega and Landa suggest that if we take a work such as *Robinson Crusoe*:

> we will say that the *text* is the linguistic artifact that we can buy and read, written *de facto* by Defoe and supposedly by Robinson. The *fabula* is whatever happened to Robinson in his travels and on his island. The *story* is the precise way in which that action is conveyed, the way the fabula is arranged into a specific cognitive structure of information. (1996, 6; compare the discussion in the entry for TEXT AND WORK)

The usage I have been recommending would, of course require us to say that the *story* is what happened to Robinson in his travels while the *plot* is the precise way in which that action is conveyed.

Meanwhile other translators of RUSSIAN FORMALIST texts have suggested that *fabula* be rendered as *plot* – thus giving *plot* exactly the opposite meaning from that suggested in my 'story and plot'. (Other translators have suggested *fable* and *subject* for *fabula* and *sjužet*, which introduces yet further possibilities of confusion.)

Peter Brooks has proposed that plot 'is the principle of interconnectedness and intention which we cannot do without in moving through the discrete elements – incidents, episodes, actions – of a narrative', and he has gone on to muddy already cloudy waters by observing that plot 'seems to me to cut across the *fabula/sjužet* distinction in that to speak of plot is to consider both story elements and their ordering' (1984, 5, 13).

Speaking as one who has himself trodden on some of these mines, my advice is as follows. When reading these terms always proceed with care and try to confirm what CONVENTION of usage the writer is following. When writing, explain your own convention of usage by making reference to what seems to be the one reliably

Straight

unambiguous term: the paired *fabula and sjužet*. Do not use terms such as *story* or *plot* on their own without making it very clear how you are defining them.

I cannot resist concluding with a comment by the novelist Ivy Compton-Burnett, who I am glad to say follows the usage I recommend in the paragraph preceding:

> As regards plots I find life no help at all. Real life seems to have no plots at all, and as I think a plot desirable and almost necessary, I have this extra grudge against life. (Quoted in Furbank: 1970, 124)

Straight A term that for many years in slang (and one which is by now more or less standard usage) has been used to imply normality and, as Wentworth and Flexner's *Dictionary of American Slang* (1975) has it, 'denotes that the person referred to is not dishonest, not a drug addict, not a homosexual'. Reference works such as Wentworth and Flexner's suggest that such meanings have arisen in opposition to the standard use of *crooked* to mean dishonest, but Partridge's *A Dictionary of Slang and Unconventional English* (1984) points out that *bent* can mean either criminal or homosexual. Once *straight* came to mean normal, other oppositions were possible: straight/kink for example, with its specifically sexual force.

Such BINARY distinctions as straight/bent and straight/kink have met with increasing scepticism from, among others, Queer Theorists, who have argued that GENDER variations and possibilities are more numerous and nuanced than such either/or distinctions can represent. Thus in the entry for QUEER THEORY a quotation from David Oswell puts the word *straight* in inverted commas. It will be noted that what such binary oppositions do is covertly to imply an equation of dishonesty with drug addiction and with homosexuality – all of which share the fact of being 'not straight'.

String of pearls narrative A NARRATIVE that consists of a number of relatively or completely unrelated episodes strung together by a thin thread. The thread can consist of a causal sequence, or the person of an individual CHARACTER, or whatever. Otherwise known as an *episodic* narrative.

Strong poet See REVISIONISM

Strong textualist See TEXTUALIST

Structuralism It is worth starting off by distinguishing between modern structuralism, which is essentially a post-Second World War development, and the structuralism of the Prague School theorists (for which see the entry for PRAGUE SCHOOL). Although these have something in common – notably a central and substantial debt to the work of Ferdinand de Saussure – their differences are such as to justify our treating them separately. The present entry will therefore concentrate upon what we can term modern structuralism, which in its initial phase in the 1950s and 1960s is a largely French phenomenon whose most important figures are probably the anthropologist Claude Lévi-Strauss, and the literary and CULTURAL critic Roland Barthes. Following them, however, many other individuals produced work which has been labelled structuralist. These include a group of MARXIST theorists of differing persuasions within Marxism such as

Louis Althusser and Lucien Goldmann (originally Romanian and known as a 'genetic structuralist'); NARRATOLOGISTS such as Gérard Genette, and Michel Foucault who, for want of a better classification, we can call a historian. We can add that in his insistence that the UNCONSCIOUS is structured like a language, Jacques Lacan also advances a classic structuralist position.

Common to all of these is an interest in structures or SYSTEMS which can be studied SYNCHRONICALLY rather than in terms of their emergence and development through traceable processes of historical causation (this applies even to Foucault, but only with qualifications to Goldmann), and a debt to the theories of Saussure – often involving a commitment to the implications of the LINGUISTIC PARADIGM. Put crudely, structuralism is (at least in its early or 'pure' form) interested rather in that which makes MEANING possible than in meaning itself: even more crudely – in form rather than content.

Not surprisingly, then, many structuralist ideas can be traced back to the RUSSIAN FORMALISTS, either directly or as mediated through the Prague School. A classic early example of a structuralist involvement with literature (or at least with NARRATIVE, depending upon how one defines literature) is to be found in Vladimir Propp's *Morphology of the Folktale*, first published in Russian in 1928. Typical features of Propp's study are its concern to generalize features (or FUNCTIONS) across TEXTS, and thus to concentrate upon a system capable of generating meanings which goes beyond the confines of the individual WORK, and its concomitant lack of interest in the INTERPRETATION of individual works or, even, in their individual specificity. (Roland Barthes's proposed CODES OF READING can be seen to be the direct descendants of Propp's functions.) From this perspective it is as if the work is written not by its AUTHOR (collective or individual), but by the 'GRAMMAR' or system of transformations that pre-exists its creation. A fundamental distinctive feature of structuralism can perhaps be indicated by comparing this to the way in which Lévi-Strauss can treat the system of gift-giving in a culture, or Roland Barthes can treat 'Steak and Chips' or 'Striptease' in his *Mythologies*. What all of these studies have in common is a concern with the pre-existing system which allows individual UTTERANCES to be generated. Indeed, use of the linguistic paradigm means that for the structuralist a particular meal, or giving of a gift, can be treated as a sort of utterance, an example of PAROLE behind which lies a complete LANGUE. When we give a visitor a meal of steak and chips, the meaning which this has for him or her is determined not just by (or not perhaps even primarily by) the actual taste and appearance of the meal, but the grammatical function which 'steak and chips' is allowed to play in the *langue* of meals. How and why this *langue* has developed into the system that exists is a matter of less (or no) interest to structuralism.

Clearly, this downplays the importance of 'the meal itself' and of the individual cook's skill, and thus it is not surprising that when structuralism is applied to literary works, it downgrades or rejects the view that either the 'work itself' or the author determines how the work is to be read. As Genette puts it,

[t]he project [of structuralism], as described in Barthes's *Critique et verité* and Todorov's 'Poétique' (in *Qu'est-ce que le structuralism?*), was to develop a poetics which would stand to literature as linguistics stands to language and which therefore would not seek to explain what individual works mean but would attempt to make

explicit the system of figures and conventions that enable works to have the forms and meanings they do. (1980, 8)

Many structuralists have used Saussurean linguistics as a basis to argue that such structures, like language, are self-enclosed and are neither affected (or caused) by extra-structural pressures (the 'real world'), nor can they change or even refer to an extra-structural reality. My own opinion is that Saussure provides a dubious basis for such an assertion, which seems to me to be as false as the argument that Saussure rejects the historical approach in favour of the synchronic one (in actual fact he argues that both are necessary). Be this as it may, structuralist literary theory and criticism often tend to be characterized by solipsistic and idealistic positions, although in the work of, for example, Roland Barthes, structuralist analyses can also be directed outwards towards social, IDEOLOGICAL and political realities.

Although structuralism has been (and remains) a controversial movement, it has undoubted successes to its credit across a range of disciplines and subject matters. Within literary criticism its most unqualified successes have probably been within the field of narratology. Genette – one of its leading practitioners within this field – has argued that structuralism is more than just a method and needs to be seen as a general tendency of thought or an ideology (1982, 11). Interestingly, Genette sees the concern of structuralism with form at the expense of content as a *corrective* one, as can be seen from his (much-quoted) comment that 'Literature had long enough been regarded as a message without a code for it to become necessary to regard it for a time as a code without a message' (1982, 7). He explains the need for such a corrective shift of focus by characterizing structuralism as a reaction to 'positivism, "historicizing history" and the "biographical illusion",' and sees structuralism as

> a movement represented in various ways by the critical writings of a Proust, an Eliot, a Valéry, Russian Formalism, French 'thematic criticism' or Anglo-American 'New Criticism.' In a way, the notion of structural analysis can be regarded as a simple equivalent of what Americans call 'close reading' and which would be called in Europe, following Spitzer, the 'immanent study' of works. (1982, 11–12)

This broadens structuralism very considerably, as does Genette's claim that 'any analysis that confines itself to a work without considering its sources or motives would, therefore, be implicitly structuralist' (1982, 12).

Structure The concept of structure is not limited to STRUCTURALIST theory. The term is in common use in literary-critical discussion, and, as one might expect, it is used in a number of relatively loose senses. It is usual to make a distinction between a literary work's structure and its plot (see STORY AND PLOT): whereas a work's plot can be seen as the NARRATIVE arrangement of its story, *structure* refers to its total (or total AESTHETIC) organization.

The term tends to be given a SYNCHRONIC, non-historical force, mainly as a result of the influence of structuralist theories which see historical change in terms of the successive replacement of one structure by another (rather than of the modification or development of a single structure), but, as I shall note below, some historians have argued for the term's (and the concept's) indispensability.

A more technical definition developed both from structuralism and Systems Theory is given by Anthony Wilden: 'Structure is the ensemble of laws which govern the behavior of the system' (1972, 242). Moreover, these laws control elements or components which are interchangeable – thus an economic SYSTEM stays the same even though the economic acts which it enables and controls are all unique. This takes us to the structuralist commitment to a set of enabling rules ('LITERARINESS') which remain the same even though the literary WORKS or acts of READING enabled or controlled by the rules change.

The paired terms *deep structure* and *surface structure*, originated by the linguistician Noam Chomsky, denote elements in his Standard Theory. According to this theory, the following sentences would be seen to have the same deep structure, but different surface structures:

The ploughman homeward plods his weary way.
Weary, the ploughman plods his way homeward.
The ploughman plods his weary way homeward.

Surface structure is derived from deep structure by means of transformations: hence transformational GRAMMAR. Chomsky's theory is controversial amongst linguisticians, and amongst non-linguisticians (literary critics, for example) it seems fair to say that the terms *deep structure* and *surface structure* are used only metaphorically. Thus to argue that two of Dickens's novels have the same deep structure is to say only that they share a common theme, or a common concern with certain linked issues, or a common plot. (The fact that one comes up with all these different possible meanings testifies to the fundamentally metaphorical usage to which the Chomskyan distinction is here being put.) After all, from a literary-critical point of view, the example given above would suggest that to concentrate on deep structure in Chomsky's sense would be to cut out a good deal of what literary critics find of value in Thomas Gray's line of poetry.

In an article entitled 'Literary Criticism and the Politics of the New Historicism', Elizabeth Fox-Genovese has argued forcefully for the importance of structure to 'good history'. She distinguishes her use of 'structure' from that of Saussure, Lévi-Strauss, Roland Barthes and Lucien Goldmann, arguing that by *structural* she means 'that history must disclose and reconstruct the conditions of consciousness and action, with conditions understood as systems of social relations, including relations between women and men, between rich and poor, between the powerful and the powerless; among those of different faiths, different races, and different classes'(Veeser: 1989, 217). She notes that her use of the term structure requires justification, and suggests that structure 'has lapsed in fashion in large measure because of our recognition of the multiple ties that link all forms of human activity, including thought and textual production' – in other words, that 'the preoccupation with structure has given way to the preoccupation with system'. She concludes that the 'very notion of textuality in the large sense embodies the insistence on system, interconnection, and seamlessness, and therefore leads inescapably to what Jameson calls totalization' (Veeser: 1989, 218).

See also PRAGUE SCHOOL.

Structure in dominance A term popularized in English by the writings of Louis Althusser, especially his essay 'On the Materialist Dialectic', which is to be found in *For Marx* (1969). Althusser uses the term to introduce a hierarchical element into the set of contradictions which, according to him, constitute a structured unity. This can be seen as a way of escaping one of the problematic elements inherent in the limitation to the SYNCHRONIC which characterizes STRUCTURALISM and neo-structuralism. Because the synchronic by definition excludes development, and because developmental change is the classic way of distinguishing determining from non-determining (or DOMINANT from subservient) influences and forces, structuralism faces the problem that although it can trace relationships it lacks the ability to rank these relationships according to their importance (varyingly defined). The concept of structure in dominance can thus be seen as a reintroduction of the historical to an essentially synchronic schema by Althusser: dominance can only be asserted or revealed on a temporal continuum.

The term has been used on occasions by those advancing a structuralist literary criticism who wish to escape from the wilderness of unhierarchized relationships with which their approach might otherwise leave them.

Compare the discussion in the entry for ALWAYS-ALREADY.

Structure of feeling The term is the coinage of the Welsh CULTURAL theorist and novelist Raymond Williams. In his *Raymond Williams: Literature, Marxism and Cultural Materialism* (1999), John Higgins traces this term in Williams's work from its first appearance in *Drama in Performance* (1954) through to later works and interviews. Higgins argues that in its inception the term was 'used as a deliberate challenge and alternative to the existing explanatory framework of Marxist literary and cultural analysis', although by 'the time of the interviews with the New Left Review team . . . structure of feeling had become known as one of Williams's most characteristic concepts, a keyword of Williams's own vocabulary, and just as shifting and unstable in its conceptual identity as any item in *Keywords* itself' (1999, 37; for the interviews mentioned, see Williams: 1979).

Williams's most extended definitional and explanatory treatment of the term comes in a single chapter of his book *Marxism and Literature*. Williams introduces his discussion by arguing against a reduction of the social to 'fixed forms' and against its separation from the personal (1977, 128, 129). Thus Williams distances himself from what he sees as a tendency in traditional MARXISM to take 'terms of analysis as terms of substance' (1977, 129), and thus to deal with lived experience at at least one remove.

According to Williams, the term is deliberately chosen to emphasize a distinction from more formal concepts such as *world-view* or IDEOLOGY; the reason for this, he states, is that we are 'concerned with meanings and values as they are actively lived and felt', and with 'characteristic elements of impulse, restraint, and tone; specifically affective elements of consciousness and relationships: not feeling as against thought, but thought as felt and feeling as thought: practical consciousness of a present kind, in a living and interrelating continuity' (1977, 132).

The term, Williams adds, represents a cultural hypothesis (1977, 132), and it can be seen as one of a number of attempts to retain Marxism's analytical socio-historical approach while taking it closer to the ways in which people actually experience life.

So far as its relation to literature is concerned, Williams gives a relevant example. He argues that whereas early Victorian ideology specified the exposure caused by poverty, debt or illegitimacy as social failure or deviation, the structure of feeling represented in the works of Dickens, Emily Brontë and others specified exposure and isolation as a general condition, and poverty, debt, or illegitimacy as its connecting instances – a view represented at the ideological level only later (1977, 134). In this view structures of feeling are pre-ideological formations developed almost unconsciously, antagonistic to existing ideological formations, and expressed through (among other things) art and literature. What is important about such a view is that it challenges a belief (very popular at the time Williams was writing) that literature expresses and is in thrall to the dominant ideology.

As John Higgins reports, in the interviews published as *Politics and Letters: Interviews with New Left Review* (1979) Williams's interviewers 'point to difficulties with the point of reference for the term: structure of feeling seems to refer to a generation, and yet at times to have a longer lifespan than any single generation, it seems far too unitary in its expression of social consciousness with its casual reference across classes' (Higgins: 1999, 37, referring to Williams: 1979, 156–62). Higgins suggests that Williams shifts ground under pressure, and that although he defends the term to his interviewers in PRAGMATIC terms as a useful aid to the analysis of actual written works, it is clear that originally the term began 'life very much as a direct challenge to the existing explanatory orthodoxy of Marxist literary criticism', and in particular opposition to the BASE–SUPERSTRUCTURE model (1999, 38, 41).

Studium/punctum A distinction from Roland Barthes's *Camera Lucida* (first published in French in 1980). The distinction can be partially glossed as that between a NATURAL-IZED response to a photograph and a response that is DEFAMILIARIZED and thus more traumatic or moving. Discussing photographs of the horrors of war, Barthes notes:

> Thousands of photographs consist of this field, and in these photographs I can, of course, take a kind of general interest, one that is even stirred sometimes, but in regard to them my emotion requires the rational intermediary of an ethical and political culture. What I feel about these photographs derives from an *average* affect, almost from a certain training. (1993, 26)

Failing to find a French word to account for this kind of human interest, Barthes adopts the Latin *studium*, meaning 'application to a thing, taste for someone, a kind of general, enthusiastic commitment, of course, but without special acuity' (1993, 26).

In contrast is a second element able to 'break (or punctuate) the *studium*':

> [I]t is this element which rises from the scene, shoots out of it like an arrow, and pierces me. A Latin word exists to designate this wound, this prick, this mark made by a pointed instrument: the word suits me all the better in that it also refers to the notion of punctuation, and because the photographs I am speaking of are in effect punctuated, sometimes even speckled with these sensitive points; precisely, these marks, these wounds are so many *points*. This second element which will disturb the *studium* I shall therefore call *punctum*; for *punctum* is also: sting, speck, cut,

little hole – and also a cast of the dice. A photograph's *punctum* is that accident which pricks me (but also bruises me, is poignant to me). (1993, 26–7)

See also PUNCTUATION.

Style and stylistics The noun *style* has a long history and wide set of meanings: the *OED* devotes over six page-columns to its various definitions. It derives from a Latin term meaning stake, or pointed instrument for writing (it shares a broad etymology with *stylus*), and modern meanings involve METAPHORICAL and METONYMIC extensions of this meaning. It is the thirteenth of the *OED*'s definitions that is most relevant to our present concerns: 'The manner of expression characteristic of a particular writer (hence of an orator) or of a literary group or period; a writer's mode of expression considered in regard to clearness, effectiveness, beauty, and the like.'

In the second half of the twentieth century Stylistics grew up as a recognized academic discipline, situated on the borderline between the study of language and of literature (although stylistic ANALYSIS can be and is applied to non-literary TEXTS), and concerned to engage in technical study and analysis of what the *OED* calls 'manners of expression'. It is important for students of literature because – as a result of its close relation to and impingement on Literary Studies – it has brought a number of more specifically linguistic terms and methods of analysis into literary criticism and theory.

Styles can be categorized according to a number of principles: deliverer's intention (a humorous style); receiver's evaluation (an imprecise style); context (an inappropriate style or REGISTER); AESTHETIC (an ornate style); level of formality (a colloquial style); social CLASS (an urbane style) – and so on. For a linguistician these are relatively imprecise categories, of course, and the academic study of style typically involves an attempt to analyse what are perceived impressionistically as distinctive styles in more formal and objective ways, often through the use of statistical analysis directed at syntax, vocabulary, GRAMMAR, and so on. At this level Stylistics involves an attempt to back up the hunches of Common Readers ('Hemingway has a distinctive, plain style') with statistical evidence. At another level, Stylistics can involve an attempt to go beyond the hunches of the Common Reader, detailing significant stylistic differences which may be functional but which are not necessarily noticed by the reader or listener.

At this point the question of purpose must be confronted. According to Geoffrey Leech and Michael Short's *Style in Fiction* (1981), we normally study style, 'because we want to explain something, and in general, literary stylistics has, implicitly or explicitly, the goal of explaining the relation between language and artistic function' (1981, 13). This of course is a central concern of the traditional discipline of Rhetoric, and in many ways Stylistics inherits and develops fundamental concerns of rhetoricians throughout the ages.

Stylisticians have often gone outside the Anglo-American literary-critical tradition for theoretical ideas and approaches. The RUSSIAN FORMALISTS, the PRAGUE SCHOOL, the circle around the Russian Mikhail Bakhtin, the Swiss linguistician Ferdinand de Saussure, the German-American Leo Spitzer – the ideas of these have perhaps been of more interest to stylisticians than has the work of most Anglo-American literary critics: possibly because of the different trajectories taken by the academic study of literature in Britain and the United States on the one hand, and Continental Europe on the other.

What is more, Anglo-American literary critics have frequently expressed reserve or scepticism about the possibility of the 'objective' analysis of literary texts producing results relevant to literary criticism: a good example is the chapter entitled 'Jakobson's Poetic Analyses' in Jonathan Culler's *Structuralist Poetics* (1975).

It is an interesting fact that the contribution of Stylistics to the literary-critical study of prose has been far less controversial, and more influential amongst literary critics, than has its contribution to the analysis of poetry. Even the most traditionalist of literary critics could hardly fail to find much of value and little to take objection to in Leech and Short's *Style in Fiction*; in contrast, Roman Jakobson's analyses of poetry have generally been taken by literary critics much as Culler takes them: as revealing demonstrations of the limits of stylistic analysis. It seems that formal and statistical approaches are more suited to the analysis of NARRATIVE technique than they are to poetic expression – perhaps because many decisions that the writer of narrative has to make involve, at one level, choice from a relatively finite set of alternatives.

For *Affective Stylistics*, see the entry for AFFECTIVE.

Style indirecte libre See FREE INDIRECT DISCOURSE

Styleme See SEMEME

Subaltern The current, widespread use of this term builds upon the work of the Italian communist Antonio Gramsci, whose *Notes on Italian History* open with a section entitled 'History of the Subaltern Classes: Methodological Criteria'. Gramsci's *Notes* were written between 1934 and 1935 while he was in prison in fascist Italy, and as a result many of his comments are guarded and coded in such a way as to allay the suspicions of the censor. Gramsci's focus of concern was on Italian history and, as Quintin Hoare and Geoffrey Nowell Smith (the editors and translators of the English edition of his *Prison Notebooks*) point out, on 'the specific weaknesses of the Italian national state which emerged from the Risorgimento [and which] culminated in the advent to power of Fascism sixty years later' (1971, 45).

Subaltern means, literally, 'of inferior rank', and in Gramsci's study it serves as a coded way of referring to CLASSES such as the peasantry and the working class – social classes other than the ruling class. It is important to note that Gramsci uses the plural form and refers to the subaltern classes; at the beginning of 'History of the Subaltern Classes' he stresses that the subaltern classes, 'by definition, are not unified and cannot unite until they are able to become a "State"'. Further, he directs attention towards both the way in which these groups are called into being by 'developments and transformations occurring in the sphere of economic production', and 'their active or passive affiliation to the dominant political formations' (1971, 52), an issue clearly associated with his unremitting interest in HEGEMONY. His tentative conclusion is that subaltern groups 'are always subject to the activity of ruling groups, even when they rebel and rise up; only "permanent" victory breaks their subordination, and that not immediately' (1971, 55).

Gramsci's theoretical groundwork has contributed significantly to debates in the field of POSTCOLONIALIST studies, in which the issue of the groupings, IDEOLOGICAL commitments, and political effectiveness of those 'of inferior rank' has been seen as crucially important – but it has not contributed alone. Gayatri Chakravorty Spivak's influential article 'Can the Subaltern Speak?' draws more overtly on the work of POST-STRUCTURALIST and DECONSTRUCTIONIST theorists such as Michel Foucault, Jacques Derrida and Gilles Deleuze, and of Karl Marx.

Spivak suggests that 'the phased development of the subaltern is complicated by the imperialist project', and notes that this is a question that has been 'confronted by a collection of intellectuals who may be called the "Subaltern Studies" group'. The group's project, according to Spivak, 'is to rethink Indian colonial historiography from the perspective of the discontinuous chain of peasant insurgencies during the colonial occupation' – what Edward Said has termed 'the permission to narrate' (Spivak: 1988, 283). From this point she moves into a complex discussion of the consciousness of oppressed, MARGINAL, and subordinate groups, building on Pierre Macherey's formula that '[w]hat is important in a work is what it does not say', a focus which, Macherey suggests, may lead to the task of *measuring silences* (Spivak: 1988, 286, quoting from Macherey: 1978, 87; see the entry for ABSENCE). As Spivak adds, when 'we come to the concomitant question of the consciousness of the subaltern, the notion of what the work *cannot* say becomes important' (1988, 287).

For Spivak, there is an element of double oppression for women in the colonial situation: '[if], in the context of colonial production, the subaltern has no history and cannot speak, the subaltern as female is even more deeply in shadow' (1988, 287). (Indeed, at a later stage in her essay Spivak observes wistfully that clearly, 'if you are poor, black, and female you get it in three ways' [1988, 294].) The subaltern's mute and shadowy existence stems from the fact that history is written by the rulers, and the ruled are assigned walk-on (or work-on) parts in a historical play that is not their own. The moral imperative of Subaltern Studies is thus to retrieve the suppressed and erased voices of the subaltern – even if it means measuring silences. Spivak pays considerable attention to the situation of the Western intellectual, and is not unaware of the paradox that measuring silences can involve speaking *for* the subaltern and continuing his or her voicelessness.

See also DOUBLE COLONIZATION; MARGINALITY.

Subject and subjectivity The traditional sense of *subject* as an abbreviation of *the conscious or thinking subject*, meaning the self or ego (*OED*), or individual *cogito*, has been pressed into service in a largely pejorative sense in recent theoretical writing. The main targets for attack in this process have been (i) the view that the human subject is somehow a point of origin for larger historical, social or even personal movements and events, and (ii) the belief that the individual human being is possessed of valid self-knowledge and is self-actuating – in a phrase, in charge and control of him/herself.

A more detailed account of one particular example of this use of *subject* can be found in the entry for INTERPELLATION, in which the position of the French MARXIST philosopher Louis Althusser is outlined. According to Althusser, all IDEOLOGY '*hails or interpellates concrete individuals as concrete subjects*, by the functioning of the category of the subject' (1971, 162). Thus *subject* represents the individual's self-consciousness and consciousness of self after having been 'body-snatched' by ideology. Althusser's position here forms the theoretical basis for a discussion by Etienne Balibar and Pierre

Macherey of the specific role played by literature in this process. According to them, through the endless functioning of its TEXTS,

> literature unceasingly 'produces' *subjects*, on display for everyone. So paradoxically using the same schema we can say: literature endlessly transforms (concrete) individuals into subjects and endows them with a quasi-real hallucinatory individuality. (1978, 10)

These subjects are not just the Readers of literature, but also the Author and his Characters (Balibar and Macherey's capitals). The argument appears in part to be that as subjects are always set in opposition to objects and things, the impression is given that the motor or guiding element in history is the individual self or consciousness, rather than extra- or supra-individual forces. (The subject is active and living: external forces are dead and passive.)

It can be seen that this to a certain extent reflects a traditional Marxist subordination of the role of the individual to extra-individualistic forces. This same form of subordination can also be seen in obituaries for the death of the AUTHOR, except that in the case of Barthes's argument in 'The Death of the Author' it is language rather than the CLASS struggle or the forces of production which is the extra-individual element involved. The individual reappears in this essay in the guise of the READER, however; the dissolution of the subject is perhaps more complete and more consistent in Michel Foucault's 'What is an Author?', and in this essay Foucault stresses that 'it is a matter of depriving the subject (or its substitute) of its role as originator, and of analyzing the subject as a variable and complex function of discourse' (1980b, 158).

Put another way: according to such views the subject is SITE rather than CENTRE or PRESENCE, is where things happen, or that to which things happen, rather than that which makes things happen: extra-individual forces use the subject to exert their sway, the subject does not use them (although it thinks that it does, and this is part of the cunning of the system). Compare, for example, Jonathan Culler's suggestion that as the self is broken down into component systems and is deprived of its status as source and master of meaning, it comes to seem more and more like a construct: 'a result of systems of convention', such that 'even the idea of personal identity emerges through the discourse of a culture: the "I" is not something given but comes to exist as that which is addressed by and relates to others' (1981, 33).

This is the stance generally adopted by POST-STRUCTURALISM, for which a major target is the view of the subject as primary, unified, self-present, self-determining, autonomous, and homogeneous. For post-structuralism the subject is, rather, secondary, constructed (by language, or ideology, for instance), volatile, standing in its own shadow, and self-divided. An important influential theorist here is the French psychoanalyst Jacques Lacan, whose writing on the MIRROR STAGE is much quoted by subsequent theorists concerned to explore the creation of the subject from a rather different angle from that adopted by Althusser.

If we turn to recent FEMINIST theory we find a rather more nuanced attitude to the subject and to subjectivity. During the earlier years of the rebirth of the Women's Movement in the 1960s and 1970s one finds evidence of a far less antagonistic view of the subject – a belief that the subjective might actually provide a rallying point *against*

SEXIST ideas, and against the ideology of PATRIARCHY. In June 1971, for example, Doris Lessing wrote a new Preface to her novel *The Golden Notebook* – a novel which from its first publication in 1962 had been extremely influential in what became known as the Women's Liberation Movement. It is noteworthy that Lessing devotes a lot of attention to the issue of subjectivity in her comments on the novel.

> When I began writing there was pressure on writers not to be 'subjective'. This pressure began inside communist movements, as a development of the social literary criticism developed in Russia in the nineteenth century, by a group of remarkable talents, of whom Belinsky was the best known ... (1973, 12)

Lessing notes, however, that alongside this pressure on the writer to ignore 'stupid personal concerns when Rome is burning', novels, stories, art of every sort, became more and more personal (1973, 13). And finally, she reports, she became aware that the way out of the dilemma with which this confronted the writer was to recognize that 'nothing is personal, in the sense that it is uniquely one's own', and that the way to deal with the problem of subjectivity was to make the personal general by seeing the individual as a microcosm (1973, 13).

Lessing's position here is representative of a widespread tendency in the Women's Movement in the 1960s and 1970s, a tendency to consider (especially a woman's) subjective feelings, responses, beliefs as reliable and worthy of being encouraged and nurtured as a force oppositional to patriarchy. It is true that this went alongside a concern to cleanse sexist ideas out of the subject – through, among other means, CONSCIOUSNESS-RAISING sessions. But this meant that the view of the subject's relationship to what one can refer to as the ideas and beliefs of the dominant ideology was rather different from that of later theorists influenced by Althusser and Lacan.

We can compare the Romantic reaction to the dominant ideas of their Augustan predecessors in Britain. Whereas subjectivity was treated with great suspicion by Augustan writers such as Alexander Pope and Samuel Johnson, for the great Romantics such as Wordsworth and Keats the essential purity of the pre-social self – 'the holiness of the heart's affections' – served as rallying point against what was seen as an artificial order.

Changing attitudes towards the subject inevitably affect both the writer and the critic. If Doris Lessing helped as it were to LEGITIMIZE the personal and the subjective, the theories of Althusser, Lacan and others have placed pressure on the writer and critic to DECONSTRUCT the subject, to take it not as starting point and reliable measure, but as a lumber-room of (mainly or wholly) false ideas stacked there by a range of external forces.

For discussion of decentring the subject, see the entries for CENTRE, COPERNICAN REVOLUTION, and DESIRE, and compare the entry for INTERSUBJECTIVITY.

Substantialist See ESSENTIALISM

Sub-text That which is implied but not directly or overtly stated. The term originates in theatrical usage, and is associated with the so-called *Theatre of Silence* – the normal English translation of the *Théâtre de l'Inexprimé* founded by Jean-Jacques Bernard in the

1920s. The modern dramatist most associated with the term is Harold Pinter, whose plays typically have, critics agree, sub-texts of a violent or sexual nature which is unstated on the surface. The term typically also implies a certain consistency in implied MEANING: thus the sub-text of a given work is unlikely to consist of a sequence of meanings which have nothing in common with one another. Compare *covert plot* in the entry for STORY AND PLOT.

The term has achieved wide usage in recent years, partly because of its points of contact with the influential theory of conversational implicature contained in SPEECH ACT THEORY, and partly because it chimes in with a range of critical theories which, in various ways, argue that literature in particular and language in general often function by means of indirect, hidden, or implied meanings as much as by overt and direct ones.

A related but somewhat different theoretical term that has achieved a much more restricted circulation is that of the *suggestiveness* of literary works. Krishna Rayan's book *Text and Sub-text: Suggestion in Literature* (1987) attempts to establish a link between the two terms, and the attempt is thought-provoking. In general usage, however, *suggestion* and cognate terms, when applied to literary works, normally imply a less consistent or structured series of implications. Rayan does, however, make a useful distinction between two usages: discussing Douglas Bush's and Christopher Ricks's use of the term 'suggestion' in criticism of Milton's *Paradise Lost*, he notes that whereas for Bush the term denotes 'suggestive vagueness', for Ricks it involves 'a notion of suggestiveness as delicate and subtle verbal life, consisting in niceties and nuances of meaning, those more or less specific semantic extensions achieved through word-order, metaphor, word-play, anticipation, echo – even alliteration and punctuation' (1987, 18–20).

As Rayan makes clear, many critics have been aware of the importance of literature's 'suggestive' potential without having made this part of an overt theory. Writers, too, have long known that their task is often more to set the reader's own imagination to work than to tell or impart something to him or her. There is an interesting letter written by Joseph Conrad to his friend Richard Curle in which Conrad objects to Curle's attempt to make specific that which Conrad had deliberately left unspecified. Conrad objects that that which he has, from 'set artistic purpose' laboured to leave 'indefinite, suggestive, in the penumbra of initial inspiration' should be made more explicit, and he insists: 'Explicitness, my dear fellow, is fatal to the glamour of all artistic work, robbing it of all suggestiveness, destroying all illusion' (Curle: 1928, 142).

It should be pointed out that there is a further important distinction between *sub-text* and *suggestiveness* on the theoretical plane. A sub-text is the creation (conscious or unconscious) of the AUTHOR; it can be discovered by READER or audience, but not created by them. But at the heart of the theory of suggestiveness is the idea that the writer encourages the reader to bring his or her creativity into play, and by textual means indicates a direction in which the reader or audience may proceed to explore unstated possibilities. Suggestion, in brief, offers a possible way whereby reader or audience creativity may be theoretically justified and LEGITIMIZED. This is not to say that the author cannot influence the way in which a reader responds to suggestive elements in a work (as the more specifically sexual meaning of the term *suggestive* makes clear, and as Laurence Sterne demonstrated in his *Tristram Shandy*).

Compare the discussion in the entry for READERLY AND WRITERLY TEXTS.

Suggestiveness See SUB-TEXT

Summary See DURATION

Superaddressee See FUNCTIONS OF LANGUAGE

Super-ego See TOPOGRAPHICAL MODEL OF THE MIND

Superstructure See BASE AND SUPERSTRUCTURE

Supplement See MARGINALITY

Surface structure See STRUCTURE

Surfiction See METALANGUAGE; MODERNISM AND POSTMODERNISM

Suspense The everyday meaning of this word has long been applied to the reading of literature, especially FICTION, and to the experience of the spectator of drama. Being in a state of heightened excitement as a result of wanting to know what happens next and what will happen ultimately is one of the forces that keeps the READER turning the pages (or which glues the audience to its seats). Suspense is in part the product of identification and involvement: where we do not care for any of the CHARACTERS or what they represent, we feel little interest in the outcome of the STORY in which they are involved. Suspense is an interesting example of a particular sort of experience which we normally do not like to have in real life, but which we find pleasurable when modelled in our responses to art. It is, therefore, sometimes cited by those arguing that one of the functions of art is to allow us to 'play through' and thereby learn to control, emotions and behaviour patterns which we need to master in everyday life (just as children ask to have frightening stories read to them). The same evidence is, however, used by those wishing to argue against theories which grant literature the ability to reflect or to influence the extra-literary world.

Clemens Lugowski has suggested a useful distinction between 'result-oriented suspense' and 'process-oriented suspense' (1990, 37). The former is where the reader/audience is anxious about *what* will happen; the latter where the anxiety is directed towards *how* it will happen. The reader of a Mills & Boon or Harlequin romance knows that the heroine will be happy in the arms of the hero on the last page of the work, but will experience 'process-oriented' suspense as to how this happy ending will be reached. (A similar point could be made about each of Jane Austen's novels.) The reader of *Great Expectations* will experience 'result-oriented' suspense, wondering whether Pip will marry Estella, who Pip's benefactor is, and so on.

There was an amusing discussion of the distinction between different sorts of suspense in a Tony Hancock TV show from 1960 called 'The Last Page'. Hancock is reading a crime novel entitled *Lady Don't Fall Backwards* by D'Arcy Sarto, and explains to Sidney James how all Sarto's stories end.

Tony	He always keeps you in suspense till the last page, this bloke. (*Reads on, getting excited*) Yes, I thought so, he's invited everybody into his flat. He always does that. He lashes them up with drinks, lights a cigarette and explains who did it. Then the murderer rushes to the window, slips and falls, hits the pavement, and Johnny Oxford turns round to the guests, finishes his Manhattan and says, 'New York is now a cleaner place to live in.' The End. Turn over, a list of new books and an advert for skinny blokes.
Sidney	If you know what's going to happen every time, why bother to read it?
Tony	Because I don't know who it is who's going to hit the pavement. (Galton and Simpson: 1987, 98)

As can be seen, the creation of suspense is often connected to manipulation of FORMULAIC possibilities.

In the realm of POPULAR art and literature, the word *suspense* has assumed a generic force, and shops hiring out video films often use the word as a particular category. As this may suggest, the concept and the experience have often been considered rather unsophisticated or crude, and unworthy of the producers or consumers of high art or literature. Some serious writers have taken pains to avoid creating suspense in their readers, perhaps for this reason. (A good example of this is Joseph Conrad's *Nostromo*, in which many possibilities for the creation of suspense are ignored, and the reader is informed of the outcome of many of the threads of the story well before he or she need be.) The creation of suspense is, however, a crucial element in much major literature, and not just in popular or 'classic REALIST' writers such as Dickens has been alleged to be – it is an important part in much of Kafka's work, for example – although the reaction against suspense is more a feature of MODERNIST literature than of its predecessors. (Given what has been said about Conrad, it is interesting to note that in what is generally taken to be the period of his decline he wrote a novel entitled *Suspense*, which remained unfinished at his death.)

Suture The technical term for the stitching up or joining-together of the lips of a wound has been applied by Steven Cohan and Linda M. Shires to the production of the SUBJECT. According to them the subject is as it were 'stitched' to DISCOURSE by the SIGNIFIER (1988, 162). They base their argument on Jacques-Alain Miller's expansion of a comment by Jacques Lacan. Lacan had referred to suture as the conjunction of the imaginary and the symbolic; Miller develops this suggestion by arguing that suture names the relation of the subject to the chain of its discourse, in which it is said to figure as an element lacking, or stand-in. Cohan and Shires in turn consider the relevance of these ideas to NARRATIVE, and they suggest that reading or viewing narrative 'involves the continuous suturing of a narrated subject whose pleasure is secured, jeopardized, and rescued by a signifier' (1988, 162).

Sometimes applied to the functioning of IDEOLOGY, which is continually splitting opening and (the argument goes) having to be sutured back together by HEGEMONIC practices.

The concept has also achieved an importance within Film Studies, where it is often used to describe the way in which the cinematic viewer is grafted in to the action of the film while simultaneously through his/her viewing melding that action together. As point of view changes in the film narrative, moving (for example in the typical shot/reverse shot chain) sequentially from one camera angle to another, it is only the witnessing of the cinema viewer which ties or sutures all these shots together.

Switchback See ANALEPSIS

Syllepsis A cluster or gathering (of events, circumstances, experiences, etc.) ordered according to some principle other than temporal unity or sequence. 'John told her all the things that had happened in his mother's house' is a syllepsis based on situational coherence. 'Many people fell in love that summer' is a syllepsis based on thematic coherence.

Symbolic See IMAGINARY/SYMBOLIC/REAL

Symbolic code See CODE

Symptomatic reading See READERS AND READING

Synchronic See DIACHRONIC AND SYNCHRONIC

Synecdoche See SYNTAGMATIC AND PARADIGMATIC

Synonymous characters A concept suggested by Mieke Bal, and related to her proposal that one distinguish between a CHARACTER's relevant characteristics and his or her secondary characteristics through a mapping of these characteristics on suitable SEMANTIC AXES. Those characters who end up with exactly the same positive, negative, and unmarked elements after such a mapping are deemed to be synonymous. The concept has much in common with the more traditional term *type*, except that synonymous characters share characteristics which may be specific to a particular WORK whereas types normally have a CONVENTIONAL significance which goes beyond the confines of an individual work. Thus to suggest that characters in different works are synonymous one needs to use a term such as type or FUNCTION (function in the sense in which a writer such as Vladimir Propp uses it, although Propp focuses upon 'action-by-a-character' rather than upon character as such).

Syntagm See SYNTAGMATIC AND PARADIGMATIC

Syntagmatic and paradigmatic According to Saussure's account of language in the *Course in General Linguistics*, '[c]ombinations supported by linearity are *syntagms*', while those 'co-ordinations formed outside discourse' that are 'not supported by linearity' but are 'a part of the inner storehouse that makes up the language of each speaker', 'are *associative relations*' (1974, 123). Present-day usage tends to favour the term *paradigms* over *associative relations*. Thus to construct a grammatical sentence we have to select words according to one set of rules, and combine them according to another set. The first are *paradigmatic* (or *associative*) rules and the second are *syntagmatic* rules. Take the following sentence.

The cat sat on the mat.

Here the first word could be replaced by 'A' or 'No'; the second word could be replaced by 'dog' or 'boy'. The relations between the words within these groups of alternatives (alternative according to the rules of GRAMMAR and syntax, but not, of course, *semantically* interchangeable) are *paradigmatic*; that is to say, they involve rules which govern the *selection* (not the combination) of words used in a sentence. But once one has chosen 'The' as the first word, one's selection of the second word is constrained: it cannot, for example, be 'a'. This is because there are rules governing the *combination* of words in a sentence: *syntagmatic* rules.

Another way of expressing the distinction is as Jonathan Culler puts it: syntagmatic relations bear on the possibility of combination; paradigmatic relations determine the possibility of substitution (1975, 13).

Claude Lévi-Strauss includes an amusing application of the syntagmatic/paradigmatic distinction to a particular literary work in his *The Savage Mind*. Treating Charles Dickens's CHARACTER Mr Wemmick (from *Great Expectations*) as a *BRICOLEUR*, Lévi-Strauss comments as follows on Wemmick's transformation of his suburban house into a fortified castle:

> What, as bricoleur, Mr Wemmick . . . undertook and realized . . . was the establishment of paradigmatic relations between the elements of these two chains: he can choose between villa and castle to signify his abode, between pond and moat to signify the piece of water, between flights of steps and drawbridge to signify the entrance, between salad and food reserves to signify his lettuces.

Wemmick's domestic life, claims Lévi-Strauss, thus

> becomes a succession of ritual actions, the minute repetition of which serves to promote, as the sole reality, the paradigmatic relations between two equally unreal syntagmatic chains: that of the castle which has never existed and that of the villa which has been sacrificed. The first aspect of bricolage is thus to construct a system of paradigms with the fragments of syntagmatic chains. (1972, 150n)

In 1956 Roman Jakobson published an article entitled 'Two Aspects of Language and Two Types of Aphasic Disturbances' which relied heavily upon a distinction between what Jakobson referred to as the metaphoric and the metonymic modes. In traditional usage *metonymy* is a figure of speech in which the name of one item is given to another item associated by *contiguity* to it. Thus 'The pen is mightier than the sword' works by means of metonymy: *pen* and *sword* stand for those activities with which they are closely associated. Under the heading of 'metonymy' Jakobson includes *synecdoche* – that is, the use of a part to represent a whole: 'bloodshed' for war, for example. *Metaphor*, in contrast, relies upon *similarity* rather than contiguity. Thus 'Eddie the eagle' (a strikingly unsuccessful British ski-jumper) was so-called not because he was often in the company of eagles, but because it was suggested (ironically) that a similarity could be observed between his ski-jumping and the flight of an eagle.

Through reference to the varying forms of aphasia experienced by patients with cerebral impairments, Jakobson was able to argue that the metaphoric and metonymic processes were governed by localized brain functions. These different processes (or modes) Jakobson related, in turn, to what he described, following Saussure, as the selection and combination axes of language. Metaphor and metonymy were thus, according to Jakobson, governed by specific brain functions which also governed these two fundamental axes of language. According to Jakobson, all examples of aphasic disturbance consisted of some impairment of either the faculty for selection or of that for combination and contexture.

> The former affliction involves a deterioration of metalinguistic operations, while the latter damages the capacity for maintaining the hierarchy of linguistic units. The relation of similarity is suppressed in the former, the relation of contiguity in the latter type of aphasia. Metaphor is alien to the similarity disorder, and metonymy to the contiguity disorder. (Jakobson and Halle: 1971, 90)

Jakobson did not stop here, but attempted to generalize his discoveries and to claim that although both processes were operative in normal verbal behaviour, the influence of cultural pattern, personality or verbal style could lead to preference being given to one of the two processes over the other. From here, Jakobson then moves to consider literature. He claims that whereas the metaphoric process is primary in Romanticism and Symbolism, metonymy is predominant in REALISM (Jakobson and Halle: 1971, 91–2).

Jakobson's article has itself been very influential; Jacques Lacan refers to it in his essay 'The Agency of the Letter in the Unconscious or Reason Since Freud' (in Lacan: 1977, 146–78), and David Lodge structures his book *The Modes of Modern Writing* (1977) around an attempt to apply and extend what Jakobson says about metaphor and metonymy to the ANALYSIS and INTERPRETATION of literary TEXTS. Roland Barthes has expressed scepticism with regard to Jakobson's opposition between metaphor and metonymy, arguing that 'if metonymy is a figure of contiguity by its origin, it nonetheless functions ultimately as a substitute for the signifier, i.e. as a metaphor' (1991, 39).

Jakobson's work has not been without its critics, however, and in 1998 in an article entitled 'The Naming Disease: How Jakobson's Essay on Aphasia Initiated Postmodern Deceits', James Drake launched an uncompromising frontal attack on Jakobson. Drake claimed that Jakobson distorted the nineteenth-century aphasiologist Hughlings Jackson's work by selective quotation, and he used formulations such as 'Jakobson's frauds'. Referring to Foucault, Drake writes:

> [Foucault's] emphasis on metaphor and linguistics directly echoes Jakobson, and since the validity of Jakobson's theories derives entirely from misrepresentations, lies and distortions, while a similar mendacity has played a role in their post-modernist manifestations, no aspect of postmodernist scholarship is proof of anything except the decline of some university departments into a condition where, like aphasia patients, they wallow in diseased naming. (Drake: 1998, 15)

According to Anthony Wilden, because in Jakobson's theory the metonymic pole of language represents its syntagmatic, connectional or 'concatenated' aspect, 'Lacan states that metonymy *is* desire'. This, Wilden explains, is because for Lacan metaphor is related to being as metonymy is related to non-being, and as the phallus signifies the lack of object in the relation between mother and child, it becomes the representation of a lack or ABSENCE which circulates between human beings in the Symbolic order. 'Consequently, possibly the most fundamental question in the analytic relationship is that both "analyst" and "patient" must recognize ... that one cannot *be* the phallus, for that is to be the desire of the Other' (1972, 29n; see also the entries for DESIRE; OTHER; PHALLOCENTRIC).

In an essay entitled 'The Semantics of Metaphor' Umberto Eco has suggested that metaphor and metonymy are linked at a deeper level, claiming that 'each metaphor can be traced back to a subjacent chain of metonymic connections which constitute the framework of the code and upon which is based the constitution of any semantic field, whether partial or (in theory) global' (1981, 68).

According to Robert Scholes, 'neo-Freudians' such as 'Jacques Lacan and his circle' have reminded us that Jakobson's metaphor and metonymy are very close in meaning to Freud's CONDENSATION AND DISPLACEMENT (1982, 75–6).

System Unlike the term STRUCTURE, *system* tends to be given a number of varied meanings in current theoretical discussion. Perhaps its most precise meaning is to be found in structural Linguistics: here language is seen as a system of relationships based on DIFFERENCE and capable of generating MEANINGS.

Apart from this relatively precise usage the term can be used more or less synonymously with the STRUCTURALIST term *structure* – somewhat confusingly, as a system is typically characterized by its dynamic, goal-seeking impetus, whereas a structure is more usually seen as a succession of over-arching, constant rules (see the separate entry for this term). As Josué Harari puts it, in a discussion of Lévi-Strauss's structural anthropology, 'history' tends to be replaced by 'diachrony', with the former falling under the tutelage of the '*System*' – rather than, we presume, *structure* (1980, 20).

Doubtless it is for this reason that Robert Young insists that for Roland Barthes, *codes of reading* (see CODE) do not constitute 'a rigorous, unified system': they operate simply as 'associative fields', 'a supra-textual organisation of notations which impose a certain idea of structure' (1981, 134).

In Michel Foucault's writing, a discipline (in the sense of an academic discipline), is seen as 'a sort of anonymous system at the disposal of anyone who wants to or is able to use it' (1981, 59).

For Michael Riffaterre, a literary work's system is 'a network of words related to one another around a central concept embodied in a kernel word' (1981, 114).

Polysystem theory is associated with Itamar Even-Zohar, who claims that it was first suggested in works by him published in 1969 and 1970, and that 'its foundations had already been solidly laid by Russian Formalism in the 1920s' (1990, 1). Although the theory is concerned specifically with literature, it 'eventually strives to account for larger complexes than literature', being 'conceived of not as an isolated activity in society, regulated by laws exclusively (and inherently) different from all the rest of the human activities, but as an integral – often central and very powerful – factor among the latter'

(1990, 2). Polysystem theory is overtly 'in opposition to the synchronistic approach', and posits a 'multiplicity of intersections' between systems (1990, 12).

> These systems are not equal, but hierarchized within the polysystem. It is the permanent struggle between the various strata, Tynjanov has suggested, which constitutes the (dynamic) synchronic state of the system. It is the victory of one stratum over another which constitutes the change on the diachronic axis. In this centrifugal vs. centripetal motion, phenomena are driven from the center to the periphery while, conversely, phenomena may push their way into the center and occupy it. However, with a polysystem one must not think in terms of *one* center and *one* periphery, since several such positions are hypothesized. (1990, 14)

In spite of this warning, Even-Zohar goes on to argue that 'the center of the whole polysystem is identical with the most prestigious canonized repertoire,' such that it is 'the group which governs the polysystem which ultimately determines the canonicity of a certain repertoire' (1990, 17). (In this usage, 'repertoire' is conceived of as 'the aggregate of laws and elements... that govern the production of texts' [1990, 17].)

Compare the entry for FIELD to see how close some of these ideas are to those of Pierre Bourdieu.

T

Tain Etymologically related to the term *tin-foil*, the term is used to denote the silver backing of mirrors which causes them to have reflective properties. In the work of Jacques Derrida and his adherents, the term has the force of undercutting any simple or simplistic versions of REALISM which assume or argue that representations are exact copies. Martin Jay refers to 'the Derridean Rodolphe Gasché', who, Jay writes, has emphasized that

> specular or reflective discourses of identity, in which words allegedly mirror thoughts without remainder, have metaphorically forgotten the silver backing, the tain, behind every image. When the tain becomes, as it were, visible, the mirror loses its capacity to reflect; when the materiality of language is foregrounded, signifiers cannot be taken as simple doubles of what they signify: mere transparent vehicles of signification. (1993, 504)

Technological determinism The belief that technological changes and innovations necessarily (and often mechanically) lead to changes in society, CULTURE, and on occasions art. Such a position is normally associated with the belief that all such changes start with technological developments, or (to put it the other way round) that all changes in society, culture or art can be traced back to technology. In the work of Marshall McLuhan, who has been accused of espousing technological determinism in his work, one can also find a related naïvety concerning, for example, the force and influence of economic and political factors.

The term is more in use in MEDIA STUDIES than in connection with the study of literature, for perhaps obvious reasons. But those who have placed too great a premium on such things as developments in printing technology, and book production and distribution, while seeking to explain the rise of the novel, have found themselves accused of technological determinism.

In the field of Media Studies technical determinism is often relatively easy to expose: many leaps forward on the technological plane (such as 'talkies' or TV) have to wait until the right social, political and (not least) economic factors allow their implementation.

Telos See CENTRE

Tempo See DURATION

Tense See LINGUISTIC PARADIGM

Terrorism A term coined by the French writer Jean Paulhan, and made use of by Gérard Genette, to describe a type of writing which refuses to make use of the 'flowers of rhetoric' and which entails a refusal of any of the traditional supports and devices of literature or *belles lettres* (Genette: 1982, 60 n5)

Also used more pejoratively to suggest a method of argumentation that is unprincipled and aggressive (and often SEXIST). Thus Jean-François Lyotard, talking of 'terrorist behaviour', defines terror as

> the efficiency gained by eliminating, or threatening to eliminate, a player from the language game one shares with him. He is silenced, or consents, not because he has been refuted, but because his ability to participate has been threatened (there are many ways to prevent someone from playing). (1984, 63–4)

Tessera See REVISIONISM

Text and work In recent years the distinction between *text* and *work* has played an important part in much theoretical discussion. It has not, however, removed all AMBIGUITY from these terms.

In his essay 'Theory of the Text' Roland Barthes suggests that whereas the work is 'a finished object, something computable, which can occupy a physical space', 'the text is a methodological field', and that '[t]he work is held in the hand, the text in language'. Barthes continues, suggesting that one can put the matter in another way:

> [I]f the work can be defined in terms that are heterogeneous to language (everything from the format of the book to the socio-historical determinations which produced that book), the text, for its part, remains homogeneous to language through and through: it is nothing other than language and can exist only through a language other than itself. In other words, 'the text can be felt only in a work, a production':

that of 'signifiance'. (1981b, 39–40; Barthes's quotation is from his own *Image-Music-Text*; for *signifiance*, see the entry for SIGN)

It is clear that Barthes's view of text and work is related to his belief in the death of the AUTHOR and in the need to grant the READER greater power, status and freedom. If the work is attached to the author by an uncut umbilical cord, the text in contrast assumes a sort of parthenogenetic status, quite free of parental control. (We can contrast the position of Seymour Chatman, who distinguishes a text from non-narrative communicative objects such as paintings or sculptures by drawing attention to the fact that a text *'temporally* controls its reception by the audience' [1990, 7].)

Barthes's distinction suggests a different definition of *work*, at any rate, from that current in most contemporary literary-critical usage. Jerome J. McGann provides us with this more current usage, while giving Barthes credit for having opened up these terms to scrutiny and discussion:

> ['Works'] refer to cultural products conceived of as the issue of a large network of persons and institutions which operate over time, in numbers of different places and periods. 'Texts' are those cultural products when they are viewed more restrictively, as language structures constituted in specific ways over time by a similar network of persons and institutions. Barthes' critique of the concept of the poetical 'work' was a salutary move against the naive idea of poems as stable and defined objects. His related effort to install the concept of 'text' in literary discourse has much less to recommend it, since this concept – while it has promoted certain forms of dialectical thinking in criticism – has also broadened the gap between the empirical and the reflective dimensions of literary studies. (1985a, 20 n27)

In another publication dating from the same year, McGann suggests that speaking of poems as 'texts' invokes two contradictory propositions:

> (1) that a poem is equivalent to its linguistic constitution and (2) that the textual differences in a poem's bibliographical history have no necessary relation to issues of literary criticism as such. The poem-as-text, then, is a critical idea which at once reduces poetry to a verbal construct and inflates it to the level of an immaterial, non-particular pure Idea (the poem as Ideal Text). (1985b, 121)

As against such idealistic (or at least, non MATERIALIST) conceptions, John Frow introduces a tripartite distinction using a historical and materialist form of analysis that relates the terms to social systems and means of production.

> In the case of printed texts we could distinguish between an initial commodification of the material object ('the book'), virtually coeval with the invention of the printing press; a second stage of commodification of the information contained within the material object (and conceptualized in legal doctrine as 'the work'), of which the major historical expression is the development in the eighteenth century of copyright law and the modern system of authorship; and a third, contemporary moment, developed in relation to electronically stored information, which, in

addition to the copyrighted information itself, commodifies access to that information. (1997, 139)

Marjorie Levinson shows that these and other distinctions and definitions can have important implications for critical and interpretative practice:

> What I've attempted is to amplify the silenced voices in Keats's poetry and in the response to that poetry, voices whose tone we catch in the conflict between the material language of the *text*, which cannot *but* speak the truth, and the *poem* – the total form – which can't and won't. (The *work*, we could say, is the compromise between text and poem.) (1988, 34)

In recent years *text* has become the preferred term for referring to a literary or other work (not necessarily linguistic or verbal) stripped of traditional preconceptions about autonomy, authorial control, artistic or AESTHETIC force, and so on. Thus use of the term *text* and its cognates in contemporary literary-critical circles is often associated with an attempt to argue that the traditional distinction between literary and non-literary texts should either be made less absolute, or scrapped altogether. Mieke Bal, for example, defines a text for her purposes as 'a finite, structured whole composed of language signs' (1985, 5) – which could of course apply equally well to both a novel and, for example, a political speech. *Work*, in contrast, has an undeniably more traditional ring to it, and carries with it more traditional implications, and it is revealing that Bal does not bother to define this term in her *Narratology: Introduction to the Theory of Narrative*. Thus one might attempt to summarize by saying that in current literary-critical usage a work stripped of many of its traditional entailments is a text – but then, so are many non-literary (even, in some usages, non-linguistic) productions.

Text Linguistics forms a sub-section of the discipline of Linguistics, and is very close to discourse analysis (which, as the entry for DISCOURSE argues, is itself a term with no clear single meaning). Michael Stubbs (1983) treats text and discourse as more or less synonymous, but notes that in other usages a text may be written while a discourse is spoken, a text may be non-interactive whereas a discourse is interactive (see the quotation from Leech and Short below), a text may be short or long whereas a discourse implies a certain length, and a text must be possessed of surface cohesion whereas a discourse must be possessed of a deeper coherence. Finally, Stubbs notes that other theorists distinguish between abstract theoretical construct and PRAGMATIC realization, although, confusingly, such theorists are not agreed upon which of these is represented by the term *text*.

Text Linguistics is generally taken to be broader than discourse analysis, however, and is normally taken to include, among other things, elements from STYLISTICS and NARRATOLOGY. Geoffrey Leech and Michael Short argue for one way of distinguishing between text and discourse that has already been mentioned:

> Discourse is linguistic communication seen as a transaction between speaker and hearer, as an interpersonal activity whose form is determined by its social purpose. Text is linguistic communication (either spoken or written) seen simply as a message coded in its auditory or visual medium. (1981, 209)

The key phrase here is clearly 'seen simply as a message', an emphasis which is contrasted with 'a transaction between speaker and hearer'. This suggests that the identical words can both constitute a text, if seen simply as a message, but can also be seen as an element in a discourse if seen in terms of their mediating a transaction between speaker and hearer. As we have already noted, this implies that to talk of a text is to concentrate on the language used and to ignore or play down the context in which it is used. The problem comes when one tries to define what is meant by 'seen simply as a message', for some theorists would argue, not illogically, that to see something as a message (even 'simply') one has to posit some sort of a context, for a message is defined as a message not just by its linguistic characteristics, but by the message *function*. 'Get lost' is a message only when used to convey information from a source to a destination: when used to illustrate English spelling it is not a message. (The *OED* starts its definition of *message* as follows: 'A communication transmitted through a messenger or other agency; an oral or written communication sent from one person to another.' This sounds very like 'a transaction between speaker and hearer'.)

Katie Wales quotes the seven criteria for textuality given by de Beaugrande and Dressler in their *Introduction to Text Linguistics* (1981): cohesion and coherence, intentionality, acceptability, situationality, informativity, and INTERTEXTUALITY (1989, 459). These certainly offer a relatively workable definition, and might enable one to use the term *work* as a more specialized sub-set of *text*.

Determining where one text (or work) ends and another begins is an issue that is much less discussed than one might expect. In practice, even those convinced of the death of the author have frequently been prepared to allow the author to decide this. Critics have generally assumed that textual variants produce different texts, but merely modify the same work, although again there is no clear agreement on this, and less theoretical energy has been expended on the issue than one might have expected. (An exception can be found in various interesting discussions of this and related problems in several of Jerome McGann's works.)

See also OTHER (for *textual other*). Compare the discussion in the entry for STORY AND PLOT.

Textualist According to Richard Rorty, 'In the last century there were philosophers who argued that nothing exists but ideas. In our century there are people who write as if there were nothing but texts' (1982, 139). These last Rorty dubs 'textualists'. In his list of textualists Rorty includes the 'so-called "Yale School" of literary criticism', which he claims centres around Harold Bloom, Geoffrey Hartmann, J. Hillis Miller, and Paul de Man; POST-STRUCTURALIST French thinkers such as Jacques Derrida and Michel Foucault, historians such as Hayden White, and social scientists such as Paul Rabinow.

What all of these individuals have in common, according to Rorty, is (i) an antagonistic position to natural science and (ii) the belief that we can never compare human thought or language with 'bare, unmediated reality' (1982, 139). Rorty sees these positions as constituting a textualism which is the contemporary counterpart of idealism, and its practitioners as the spiritual descendants of the idealists (1982, 140).

He goes on to distinguish between what (drawing on Harold Bloom) he terms *weak textualists* and *strong textualists*. He argues that the weak textualist 'thinks that each work has its own vocabulary, its own secret code, which may not be commensurable with that of any other'. The strong textualist, in contrast, 'has his own vocabulary and doesn't worry about whether anybody shares it' (1982, 150).

Rorty's argument clearly uses simplification for ironic and polemical effect, but at the time it appeared it served to rally a number of rather different forces against the growing influence of the individuals described by him as textualists, and it can be seen in retrospect to have constituted an important moment in the development of a counter-movement directed against post-structuralism.

Theme and thematics In traditional literary-critical usage the term *theme* suffers from a certain ambiguity. Whereas for some critics it implies a certain claim, doctrine or argument raised either overtly or implicitly throughout a literary WORK (or by the work as a whole), for others the term *thesis* is used with this meaning, and theme is reserved for what one can better call an issue. Prince suggests the useful distinction that whereas a thesis involves both a question and a proposed answer or answers, a theme 'does not promote an answer but helps to raise questions' (1988a, 97). Disagreement can also be found as to whether thematic elements in a literary work are dependent upon an AUTHOR's conscious and deliberate attempt to raise certain issues, or whether thematic elements can be raised, as it were, unconsciously.

A theme is generally also distinguished from a *motif* (or *leitmotif*) by its greater abstraction: motifs are generally linked to specific, concrete forms of manifestation whereas, for example, one can trace 'the theme of working-class socialization' in Alan Sillitoe's *Saturday Night and Sunday Morning* through a range of very different concrete examples. In contrast, Cedric Watts provides the reader of Joseph Conrad's *Lord Jim* in the Penguin edition with a list of *leitmotifs*, and these are all much more concrete or linked to specific and recurrent forms of words than this: 'butterflies and beetles'; 'dream, dreams'; 'glimpse (of Jim's character) through mist or fog'; '"in the ranks"'; 'jump, leap'; '"nothing can touch me"'; '"one of us"'; 'romance, romantic'; '"under a cloud"'; 'veiled opportunity' (Conrad: 1986, 377). It will be noted that one can *attach* issues to some of these motifs, but they do not raise them overtly, and thus they cannot according to current CONVENTIONS be called either themes or theses.

Prince also relates theme to FRAME, suggesting that a theme has a framing function in a literary work (1988a, 111).

To show how shifting is the use of these different terms, one can note that M. H. Abrams suggests that motif and theme are sometimes used interchangeably, but that theme is more usefully applied to a general claim or doctrine (1988, 111) – which of course is what Prince would dub a thesis.

Some theorists have adopted the term *thematics* in recent years, especially in the study of NARRATIVE. Thematics is distinguished from narrative on a theoretical level although the two are interconnected in practice, narrative technique being one of the ways in which thematics are generated and modified. Thus thematics tends to refer to an end-product: it is the sum of issues raised, normally expressed in a hierarchy of questions and problems, with perhaps some suggested answers. It is not necessarily dependent upon the author's conscious or unconscious INTENTIONS.

Gérard Genette has borrowed 'from certain linguists' the distinction between *theme* (what one talks about) and *rheme* (what one says about it) (1997, 78), thus enabling him to distinguish between thematic and rhematic titles.

361

According to Mieke Bal, *thematic space* refers to a described space in a literary work which assumes a thematic function. In other words, it is not just a SITE on which actions take place, but 'an "acting place" rather than the place of action' (1985, 95).

Thesis See THEME AND THEMATICS

Thick description/thin description The person usually credited with coining this term is the anthropologist Clifford Geertz, but in his 'Thick description: Toward an Interpretive Theory of Culture', the first chapter of *The Interpretation of Cultures* (1973), he attributes the term to two essays by the philosopher Gilbert Ryle: 'Thinking and Reflecting' and 'The Thinking of Thoughts'. Both are reprinted in the second volume of Ryle's *Collected Papers* (1971).

Ryle contrasts the behaviour of two boys, both of whom are rapidly contracting the eyelids of the right eye.

> In the first boy this is only an involuntary twitch; but the other is winking conspiratorially to an accomplice. At the lowest or thinnest level of description the two contractions of the eyelids may be exactly alike.
>
> . . .
>
> [The winker acknowledges] that he had not had an involuntary twitch but (1) had deliberately winked, (2) to someone in particular, (3) in order to impart a particular message, (4) according to an understood code, (5) without the cognisance of the rest of the company . . . (Ryle: 1971, 481)

But Ryle adds another stage of possibility: that of a third boy who to give amusement to his cronies, deliberately PARODIES the first boy's behaviour with a wink of his own. We now have three different 'winks' which, in purely physical terms, are identical, but which in a wider sense are clearly very different. According to Ryle a *thin description* of the winks would see them as identical, whereas a *thick description* of them would recognize their variety. Geertz argues that between such a thin description and such a thick description

> lies the object of ethnography: a stratified hierarchy of meaningful structures in terms of which twitches, winks, fake-winks, parodies, rehearsals of parodies are produced, perceived, and interpreted, and without which they would not (not even the zero-form twitches, which, *as a cultural category*, are as much nonwinks as winks are nontwitches) in fact exist, no matter what anyone did or didn't do with his eyelids. (1973, 7)

According to Geertz, 'ethnography is thick description' (1973, 9–10).

In its extended usage, thick description thus involves essentially INTERPRETATIVE work which tries to burrow down or out to the hidden, CULTURAL meanings of public actions, to the 'ridicule or challenge, irony or anger, snobbery or pride' that is signalled by human behaviour (1973, 10). When applied to literature, it often involves searching out the sort of CONNOTATIONS, cultural significance, PERFORMATIVE force, that might have been apparent or alive in the past but which have become invisible to the modern reader.

This is not so very different from what many literary critics have been used to doing, and indeed Jerome J. McGann has commented that works of *belles lettres* 'can only function through what anthropologists have recently called "thick description", where excess and redundancy flourish' (1991, 14).

However, it is perhaps the development of NEW HISTORICISM that has done most to popularize the use of the term within Literary Studies. Brook Thomas has suggested that in certain New Historicist hands, thick description has degenerated into a sort of ORGANICISM that believes in the possibility of reading of (presumably social or historical) wholes from a (very isolated) part (1991, 10), and he suggests that to demand a thick description of the symbolic world of goods is 'to open up vistas of interpretation that are almost vertiginous in their potential complexity' (1991, 11–12).

Throning/dethroning See CROWNING/DECROWNING

Top down (perspective) See SOLUTION FROM ABOVE/BELOW

Topic Usefully defined by Umberto Eco as the textual operator which is needed to realize all of the relevant semantic disclosures in a DISCURSIVE STRUCTURE (1981, 23).

Eco contrasts this term with Greimas's term *isotopy*, quoting Greimas's definition of this as 'a redundant set of semantic categories which make possible the uniform reading of the story' (1981, 26). The distinction, for Eco, is that whereas the topic governs the semantic properties that can or must be taken into account during the reading of a given TEXT, an isotopy is the actual textual verification of that hypothesis which the topic produces. Put another way: a topic leads the READER to have certain expectations, whereas an isotopy is a READING based upon these expectations.

Topographical model of the mind Topographical means represented by means of a map: topographical models of the mind represent the mind's STRUCTURE through a spatial model which 'maps' its different elements by assigning them different mental 'spaces'. (Note: not different *physical* spaces: one must remember that 'mind' is not the same as 'brain'.)

The best-known of such models is Sigmund Freud's division of the mind into *id* (those instinctual drives arising from the BODY's constitutional needs; *ego* (that agency deriving from and regulating the id and the instinctual drives); and *super-ego* (the mental transformation of social/parental influences on and modifications of the instinctual drives). This particular topography comes later in Freud's career, and replaces a number of earlier models. Jacques Lacan has referred to his own DISCOURSE in which 'each term is sustained only in its topological relation with the others' (1979, 89) – a classic example of the use of the topographical model and one which perhaps betrays the potential dangers of self-enclosure that its use often seems to involve.

This and other models have been used by PSYCHOLOGICAL and PSYCHOANALYTIC literary critics in various ways to 'map' aspects of – for example – the READER's experience of a TEXT.

Topos A traditional term, from the Greek meaning a 'commonplace', often referring to certain CONVENTIONALIZED places or settings consisting of a fixed combination of characteristic and stylized objects – a meadow, a tree, a running stream, for example (Bal: 1985, 96–7). The term is often used in a broader sense to include conventional collocations of MOTIFS, or THEMES, and in some present-day usages is very close to certain usages of STEREOTYPE.

Totalizing discourse Any DISCOURSE which seeks to occupy all the available ground and thus deny any oppositional SITE to those whom it excludes.

Trace See ARCHE-WRITING

Traditional intellectuals See INTELLECTUALS

Transactional theory of the literary work A theory associated with Louise M. Rosenblatt, who outlines it in her book *The Reader, The Text, The Poem* (1978). Rosenblatt takes as her starting point the inadequacy of theories that base themselves on an exclusively active and an exclusively passive component: the READER actively INTERPRETING the literary TEXT, or the text acting upon the reader and producing a response in him or her. According to her, the relation between reader and text is not linear but is a situation, 'an event at a particular time and place in which each element conditions the other' (1978, 16). Rosenblatt states that she adopts the 'transactional' terminology developed by John Dewey and Arthur F. Bentley, a terminology which arises from a philosophical approach with its roots in the thinking of William James and C. S. Peirce. For Dewey and Bentley 'transaction' had certain important advantages over 'interaction'; for them the latter term implied the acting upon each other of 'separate, self-contained, and already defined entities', whereas the former term designated 'an ongoing process in which the elements or factors are ... aspects of a total situation, each conditioned by and conditioning the other' (Rosenblatt: 1978, 17), and she sees her proposed revision of previous views of the READING process to be analogous to the revolution in Linguistics brought about by the shift from UTTERANCE to SPEECH ACT (1978, 19).

Such an approach has, oddly enough, something in common with DECONSTRUCTIVE criticism, for although it uses a different set of terms it does seem to posit a ceaseless play between the different elements involved in the reading process, none of which is fixed in the manner of a TRANSCENDENTAL SIGNIFIED and therefore capable of determining the course taken by any particular reading. In deconstructive criticism, of course, the play is between SIGNIFIERS and is of a rather different nature, but the two approaches share a common view of successive reading acts as the ceaseless generation of something new. For Rosenblatt, this is because all perception is conditioned by interest, expectations, anxieties, and other factors based on past experience (1978, 19), and these must clearly vary not just from reader to reader but also from reading to reading. (My second reading of *Mrs Dalloway* will necessarily be different from my first – and my third – because I will take to it a new set of past experiences, expectations, and so on; the text remains the same only inasmuch as it remains the same collection of signifiers; to the extent that the text's AESTHETIC significance is constituted by interaction between it and a reader, it is in constant process of renewal.)

This takes us to the second important element in Rosenblatt's theory: the distinction between aesthetic and non-aesthetic reading, one which bears resemblances to a number of traditional distinctions (including Roman Jakobson's CODES OF READING). She argues that whereas during a non-aesthetic reading the reader is chiefly concerned with what he or she will carry away from the reading, in aesthetic reading 'the reader's primary concern is with what happens *during* the actual reading event' (1978, 24).

The theory can be seen as one of a number of attempts to move away from one particular element in the practice of the NEW CRITICISM: the treatment of the literary WORK as if it were a fixed, solid object – W. K. Wimsatt's 'verbal icon' or Cleanth Brooks's 'well wrought urn'. (See the discussion in the entry for REIFICATION.) As Rosenblatt puts it,

> [i]nstead of thinking of the structure of the work of art as something statically inherent in the text, we need to recognize the dynamic situation in which the reader, in the give-and-take with the text, senses or organizes a relationship among the various parts of his lived-through experience. (1978, 90)

Rosenblatt pays relatively little attention to the constituting of the reader by forces and elements other than the text (although she does admit its importance in principle, and her theory has room to accommodate this and other 'external' factors), and this distinguishes her position from that of more recent theorists who have more detailed ideas about the constitution of the SUBJECT by social, CULTURAL, and historical forces – as well as by language itself.

Transcendental pretence/signified/subject The influence of Jacques Derrida has radically changed the connotations of the word *transcendental* and its cognates for many. Whereas at one time its associations were mainly positive – 'that which is above all other categories of thing' – since Derrida the word is associated with a belief in fixed, extra-linguistic points of meaning-determination, a view which he characterizes as LOGO-CENTRIC and representative of the METAPHYSICS OF PRESENCE. He points out, incidentally, that those who consider themselves to be MATERIALISTS are just as liable to treat 'matter' as a transcendental signified as those believing themselves idealists are liable to find their own transcendental signified in God or whatever (1981b, 65).

According to Derrida himself, from his very first published work he sought to 'systematize a deconstructive critique precisely against the authority of meaning, as the *transcendental signified* or as *telos*, in other words history determined in the last analysis as the history of meaning, history in its logocentric, metaphysical, idealist...representation' (1981b, 49–50). Alex Callinicos suggests that Derrida believes that 'any attempt to halt the endless play of signifiers, above all by appealing to the concept of reference, must...involve postulating a "transcendental signified" which is somehow present to the consciousness without any discursive mediation' (1989, 74). The implications of such a position for literary criticism are clear: the TEXT is also subject to a totalizing play of linguistic DIFFERENCE which cannot be fixed or organized by any extra-systemic reference-point – AUTHOR, authorial INTENTION, 'Common Reader's' INTERPRETATION, or whatever.

Analogous objections are raised against the transcendental SUBJECT – that is, against the belief that the *ego* is undetermined by and independent of social and CULTURAL forces, and that it constitutes a unity rather than a SITE for the play of contradictions. The transcendental pretence, according to Robert C. Solomon, rests on an IDEOLOGICAL belief that the 'white middle classes of European descent were the representatives of all humanity, and that as human nature is one, then so too must its history be one as well' (1980, xii).

Finally, in *Positions* Derrida points out that it is also possible to believe in a transcendental signif*ier*, and he gives as example the *phallus*, when seen 'as the correlate of a primary signified, castration and the mother's desire' (1981b, 86). (See the entry for PHALLOCENTRISM.)

Transcoding See MEDIATION

Transculturation A term made use of by Mary Louise Pratt in her *Imperial Eyes: Travel Writing and Transculturation* (1992). Pratt notes that ethnographers have used this term 'to describe how subordinated or marginal groups select and invent from materials transmitted to them by a dominant or metropolitan culture' (1992, 6). Pratt also makes use of two other closely related terms – 'autoethnography' and 'autoethnographic expression' – to refer to

> instances in which colonized subjects undertake to represent themselves in ways that *engage with* the colonizer's own terms. ....Autoethnographic texts are not, then, what are usually thought of as 'authentic' or autochthonous forms of self-representation .... Rather autoethnography involves partial collaboration with and appropriation of the idioms of the conqueror. (1992, 7)

Diana Brydon (1991) proposes the rather more challenging term 'contamination' to depict a cross-cultural imagination which constitutes 'not just a literary device but also a cultural and even a political project' (in Ashcroft *et al.*: 1995, 136).

See also CONTACT ZONE (discussion of *contact literatures*); CULTURE; MASQUER-ADE; MIMICRY.

Transference In the work of Sigmund Freud, the transferring of feelings originally associated with an infantile object, childhood trauma or other object of psychoanalytic investigation, from its source to the investigating psychoanalyst. *Studies on Hysteria* provides an early example of Freud's development of the concept. One of Freud's female patients was possessed of a particular hysterical SYMPTOM which he claimed originated in a wish, suppressed because of the fear it caused, that a man with whom she had been talking would take the initiative and kiss her. At the end of a psychoanalytic session the wish re-emerged, with Freud as its object, as a result of which the patient was horrified, spent a sleepless night, and was 'quite useless for work' at the next session. But once the wish was uncovered psychoanalysis proceeded further, and the original, frightening, wish was then revealed (Freud and Breuer: 1974, 390).

Counter-transference, in contrast, is where the analyst's own desires are imposed upon the person undergoing analysis.

In recent literary theory the concept of transference is sometimes broadened to include any process whereby the analyst of a TEXT becomes inextricably involved in the object of his or her ANALYSIS, such that distinguishing between what is 'in' the text and what has been put there by the analyst in the process of analysis, is impossible to determine. (Although readers and critics have not needed psychoanalysts to tell them that distinguishing between these two is no easy matter.)

Such an extension of the concept comes close to some of the positions advanced by recent READER-RESPONSE critics, albeit from a rather different direction. (It should be noted, however, that whereas in Freud's writing it is the person analysed who is responsible for the transference, in the extended concept it is the person doing the analysis who is responsible, so that perhaps counter-transference might be more appropriately invoked here.) It would perhaps be rather closer to Freud's position were we to attribute transference to the third person who sees 'in' the text that which the analyst has actually put there, although again the parallel would not be exact. At any rate, the interest of the concept to theorists of literature is in part that it provides a name for a well-known process: that whereby the analyst or INTERPRETER of a literary WORK can change that work for him or herself and for subsequent readers.

Transgender A term used in a number of ways, but generally suggesting a lifestyle or an identity that mixes or transgresses CONVENTIONAL sex-gender associations. The term can imply that a person is born with the characteristics of both sexes or has had surgery to change his or her physical sexual characteristics. But it may also be used to describe the adoption of dress or behaviour that is conventionally associated with those of a different biological sex.

Much interesting study of CANONICAL literature concerned to show how it explores such challenges to the public GENDER system has resulted from recent work by those within such areas as QUEER THEORY and masculinity studies. In Henry James's short story 'The Death of the Lion', for example, the NARRATOR discovers that a newspaper journalist named Guy Walsingham is actually a woman, while one named Dora Forbes is referred to as 'he'.

> I was bewildered: it sounded somehow as if there were three sexes. My interlocu-tor's pencil was poised, my private responsibility great. I simply sat staring, none the less, and only found presence of mind to say: 'Is this Miss Forbes a gentleman?'
> Mr Morrow had a subtle smile. 'It wouldn't be "Miss" – there's a wife!'
> 'I mean is she a man?'
> 'The wife?' – Mr Morrow was for a moment as confused as myself. But when I explained that I alluded to Dora Forbes in person he informed me, with visible amusement at my being so out of it, that this was the 'pen-name' of an indubitable male – he had a big red moustache. (James: 1948, 89)

John Carlos Rowe suggests that this and other of James's tales have 'been rediscovered as tours de force of a gay aesthetic' (1998, 104), and passages such as the one quoted, which have often been read as examples of James's whimsical humour (which they undoubtedly are), are now being reinterpreted as partly concealed challenges to the dominant gender system, to the idea that the whole of humanity can be divided in BINARY terms between the male and the female. As the READER laughs, he or she is forced to consider the possibility that it is too limiting to assign all of the human race to just two sexes, and as the reader shares first the narrator's and then Mr Morrow's confusion, his or her own certainties regarding sex and gender are rendered less firm and secure.

See also CROSS-DRESSING; DRAG.

Transgredient   According to Tzvetan Todorov's *Mikhail Bakhtin: The Dialogical Principle* (1984), a term which Bakhtin borrowed from Jonas Cohn, *Allgemeine Ästhetik* (Leipzig, 1901). Todorov sees this as a term complementary to *ingredient*, 'to designate elements of consciousness that are external to but nonetheless absolutely necessary for its completion, for its achievement of totalization' (1984, 95).

The implication is that we cannot understand any consciousness purely in terms of its 'ingredients', but only when these are seen in interaction with and complemented by external elements which help to define the consciousness. The term reflects Bakhtin's contextual and DIALOGIC approach.

See also EXOTOPY.

Transgressive strategy   A term sometimes used by POST-STRUCTURALISTS to indicate any way of dealing with a TEXT which attempts to go beyond the assumptions upon which it is based and which (if not challenged) it will reproduce. Transgressive strategies are *denaturalizing* – that is, they prevent us from seeing the text *as* natural or *in* a 'natural' way (a way that does not go AGAINST THE GRAIN of CONVENTION).

See also INTERROGATION; OPPOSITIONAL READING.

Transparency reading/transparent criticism   See OPAQUE AND TRANSPARENT CRITICISM

Transtextuality   See INTERTEXTUALITY

Transworld identity   See HOMONYMY

Travelling theory   Chapter 10 in Edward Said's book *The World, the Text, and The Critic* is entitled 'Traveling Theory'. Said opens the chapter by reminding the reader that like people and schools of criticism, ideas and theories travel, 'from person to person, from situation to situation, from one period to another' (1984, 226). While noting that cultural and intellectual life are usually nourished and are often sustained by this CIRCULATION of ideas, Said points out that there are different kinds of possible movement, and that these may involve both gains and losses. He outlines a four-stage model for such processes: first the point of origin, a set of circumstances in which the idea came to birth or entered DISCOURSE; second the distance traversed, through various contexts in time and space; third a set of 'conditions of acceptance' or resistances which make possible the idea's 'introduction or toleration', and finally 'the now full (or partly) accommodated (or incorporated) idea is to some extent transformed by its new uses, its new position in a new time and place' (1984, 226–7). Said notes that such travelling may take place within and between disciplines: 'there seems nothing inherently literary about the study of what have traditionally been considered literary texts, no literariness which might prevent a contemporary literary critic from having recourse to psychoanalysis, sociology, or linguistics' (1984, 228). But the most interesting part of Said's chapter traces the travels of a particular theoretical concept/complex (that of 'reification and totality') from Georg Lukács through Lucien Goldmann and to Raymond Williams – travels during which the traveller changes in ways that can be seen as forms of adaptation to new circumstances and contexts. Said has interesting things to say about this process, and concludes that

> [t]heory we certainly need, for all sorts of reasons that would be too tedious to rehearse here. What we also need over and above theory, however, is the critical recognition that there is no theory capable of covering, closing off, predicting all the situations in which it might be useful. (1984, 241)

See also SOLUTION FROM ABOVE/BELOW.

True-Real From Julia Kristeva's neologism 'Le vréel' (see Kristeva: 1979). Toril Moi glosses the term as follows, suggesting that it was coined 'in order to account for the modernist revolution in Western thought and art, which [Kristeva] sees as the effort to formulate a truth that would *be* the *real* in the Lacanian sense of the term. . . . The speaking subject in search of the "true-real" no longer distinguishes between the sign and its referent in the usual Saussurian way, but takes the signifier for the real (treats the signifier *as* the real) in a move which leaves no space for the signified.' For Moi, such a 'concretization' of the signifier is typical both of MODERNIST art and also of the DISCOURSE of psychotic patients such as the French modernist writer Antonin Artaud (Moi: 1986a, 214).

U

Uncanny See FANTASTIC

Uncle Charles Principle Monika Fludernik provides an economical account of this term:

> This phenomenon was not discovered in English criticism until Hugh Kenner's response to Wyndham Lewis's remarks on [James] Joyce's sentence: *Uncle Charles repaired to the outhouse* [from *A Portrait of the Artist as a Young Man*]. Lewis had criticized Joyce for slipping into authorial style (ruining the effect of immediacy of presentation, i.e. the reader's illusion of being within Stephen's consciousness throughout the novel). Kenner, by contrast, argues that *repair* in fact echoes Uncle Charles's linguistic preciousness, describing the action in the very terms he might euphemistically have used himself. Kenner then baptized such infection of the narrative by figural language the 'Uncle Charles Principle'. (Fludernik: 1993, 332; she refers the reader to Kenner: 1978, Ch. 2)

The technique might equally well be dubbed the 'Lily Principle', as the first line of Joyce's 'The Dead' exemplifies it equally well: 'Lily, the caretaker's daughter, was literally run off her feet.' Here the misuse of 'literally' echoes Lily's language, and thus infects what is at first sight AUTHORIAL style (i.e. omniscient narrative by a narrator who exists on a different NARRATIVE LEVEL from the CHARACTERS) with something of Lily's.

See also FREE INDIRECT DISCOURSE (*coloured narrative* and *mind style*, both of which overlap very considerably with the Uncle Charles Principle); FIGURALIZATION/REFLECTORIZATION.

Unconscious In an article on rhythm and imagery in English poetry published in 1962, William Empson remarks that four major thinkers – Darwin, Marx, Frazer and Freud – 'gave grounds for the belief that the artist often does not know what he is doing' (1962, 36). The comment is a useful reminder that it is not just Sigmund Freud who has helped to ensure that in comparison with other periods of history the modern age is one in which we are relatively unconvinced of our having conscious access to all that our minds contain. Freud's development of a theory of the Unconscious is part of a general movement of thought that places a great emphasis upon the individual or collective mind's dark or hidden areas. Empson's comment also draws attention to one of the reasons why literary critics have been interested in such ideas: they seem to be confirmed by study of the process of literary composition or creation, in which things happen that are apparently not under the writer's conscious control.

Freud's theory of the Unconscious can be seen emerging in *Studies on Hysteria* – both in the parts of this work written by him and in those written by Joseph Breuer. Both writers were able to draw on a number of important traditions in Psychology in forming a coherent theory, but their actual case-histories also played an important role in this. Much could be written about the Freudian Unconscious, but for our present purposes it is probably most important to indicate the connection between the concept and the idea of *repression*. This has proved very convenient again to literary critics interested in explaining why a given literary work may have a tendency seemingly much at odds with the AUTHOR's expressed or consciously held beliefs and opinions. To quote again from William Empson's article: 'An interpreter of the artwork cannot set out to bring all this to consciousness, where it does not naturally belong; his main function must be to mediate between the unconsciousness of the artist and the unconsciousness of the public he works for' (1962, 36).

Since Freud, various theorists have developed or challenged his theory of the Unconscious. Most influential in literary-critical circles is probably Jacques Lacan, who makes his position clear when he talks of Freud's *discovery* of the Unconscious. Lacan defines the unconscious (he does not grant the term a capital letter) as 'that part of the concrete discourse, in so far as it is transindividual, that is not at the disposal of the subject in re-establishing the continuity of his conscious discourse' (1977, 49), and as 'that chapter of my history that is marked by a blank or occupied by a falsehood: it is the censored chapter' (1977, 50), and it shows us 'the gap through which neurosis recreates a harmony with a real – a real that may well not be determined' (1979, 22). Even so, it can be rediscovered – in monuments, in archival documents such as childhood memories, in semantic evolution, in traditions, and in surviving (conscious) traces (1977, 50). Moreover, the unconscious for Lacan is 'the sum of the effects of speech on a subject, at the level at which the subject constitutes himself out of the effects of the signifier' (1979, 126), and '*the discourse of the Other*' (1979, 131).

Lacan provides a rather more accessible account of the unconscious in his lecture 'Of Structure as an Inmixing of an Otherness Prerequisite to Any Subject Whatsoever', in which he insists that the unconscious has nothing to do with instinct or primitive knowledge or preparation of thoughts in some underground. 'It is a thinking with words, with thoughts that escape your vigilance, your state of watchfulness.' As an illustration he refers to working on his lecture early in the morning:

> I could see Baltimore through the window and it was a very interesting moment because it was not quite daylight and a neon sign indicated to me every minute the change of time, and naturally there was heavy traffic, and I remarked to myself that exactly all that I could see, except for some trees in the distance, was the result of thoughts, actively thinking thoughts, where the function played by the subjects was not completely obvious. In any case the so-called *Dasein*, as a definition of the subject, was there in this rather intermittent or fading spectator. The best image to sum up the unconscious is Baltimore in the early morning. (1970, 189)

Anthony Wilden has drawn attention to Lacan's debt to the work of Lévi-Strauss in arriving at a linguistic model of the Unconscious (in which the Unconscious is seen to be structured like a language). Wilden further draws attention to the fact that Lévi-Strauss has said that his own development of a theory of the Unconscious was influenced both by Freud and Marx – and also by geology! Wilden argues that Lévi-Strauss reformulates the concept of the Unconscious as a locus 'not of instincts, not of phantasies, not of energy or entities, but as a locus of a *symbolic function* – a set of rules governing the possible messages in the system, a sort of syntax or code'. It was this formulation, Wilden argues, that allowed Lacan to declare first (in 1953) that 'The Freudian Unconscious is the discourse of the other', and shortly afterwards that 'The unconscious is structured like a language' (Wilden: 1972, 15).

Fredric Jameson's *The Political Unconscious* attempts to rehistoricize Freud's concept of the Unconscious and to reassign the CENTRE of the Freudian INTERPRETATIVE system (which Jameson sees as wish-fulfilment) to history and society rather than to the individual SUBJECT and individual psychobiology. Thus a number of associated Freudian concepts – repression, censorship, and so on – are resituated in a socio-historical context by Jameson, and thence applied to the reading of literary works. Jameson's historicizing of the concept of the Unconscious can be compared with the earlier use made of Freud by Gilles Deleuze and Félix Guattari in their *Anti-Oedipus: Capitalism and Schizophrenia*. They remark, for example, that 'Women's Liberation movements contain, in a more or less ambiguous state, what belongs to all requirements of liberation: the force of the unconscious itself, the investment by desire of the social field, the disinvestment of repressive structures' (1983, 61). (For a critical FEMINIST view of Deleuze and Guattari, see the entry for DESIRE.)

See also ARCHE-WRITING; CENSORSHIP; CONDENSATION AND DISPLACEMENT; PRIMARY PROCESS; TOPOGRAPHICAL MODEL OF THE MIND.

Unfolding A term used in the English translation of Roland Barthes's *S/Z*. As example Barthes suggests that 'to enter' can be unfolded into 'to appear' and 'to penetrate' (1990, 82). In other words, unfolding involves the semantic, CONNOTATIVE or IDEOLOGICAL unpacking of a term or word.

Unmotivated See ARBITRARY

Use value See FETISHISM

Uses and gratifications A term taken from MEDIA STUDIES, associated especially with a family of theories concerning the way in which television audiences 'use' the programmes they watch to 'gratify' different needs or desires. The theory was developed in the United States and offered a view of TV audiences as more active than the pictures presented by both MARXIST critics and also by more populist 'prophets of doom' pronouncing on the evils of television. McQuail *et al.* (1972), for example, basing their findings upon extensive research into audience responses to TV quiz shows, concluded that 'the typology of media-person interactions' could be divided between four main categories: diversion, personal relationships, personal identity, and surveillance (i.e. keeping in touch with what is happening in the world).

The theory has been criticized for granting too much credence to claims made by TV viewers for active and creative use of television, but in spite of this a major question for students of literature raised by the theory and by the research evidence which it has inspired, is whether research into literature might also find that different READERS take quite different things from READINGS of the same literary WORK: a finding which would be in conflict with the traditional assumption of many literary critics that readers either do, or should, be capable of responding to and INTERPRETING the same literary work in comparable ways.

See the entry for ROMANCE for Janet Radway's discussion of the way in which women readers *use* the reading of romances to create personal time.

Utterance An utterance is generally regarded as a natural unit of linguistic *communication*. In her editorial Preface to her translation of M. M. Bakhtin's *Problems of Dostoevsky's Poetics*, Caryl Emerson claims that the distinction between *utterance* and *sentence*

> is [Bakhtin's] own: a sentence is a unit of language, while an utterance is a unit of communication. Sentences are relatively complete thoughts existing within a single speaker's speech, and the pauses between them are 'grammatical,' matters of punctuation. Utterances, on the other hand, are impulses, and cannot be so normatively transcribed; their boundaries are marked only by a change of speech subject. (Bakhtin: 1984, xxxiv)

In like manner, Jan Mukařovský attributes 'uniqueness and nonrepeatability' to the utterance in his essay 'The Esthetics of Language' (1964, 63).

It should be noted that an utterance can be either spoken or written (or, presumably, expressed in silent thought to oneself).

See also DISCOURSE; ÉCRITURE; ENUNCIATION; LANGUE AND PAROLE; SPEECH.

V

Vanilla sex A dismissive term for CONVENTIONAL heterosexual sexual activity used within Gay and Lesbian circles. Based on the idea that vanilla is the most boring and unexciting flavour of ice cream, and not on any implied use of vanilla-flavoured items as adjuncts to the sexual act.

Verschriftung/Verschriftlichung A distinction attributed by Monika Fludernik to Wulf Österreicher. *Verschriftung* designates the mechanical transcription of oral material into written form, whereas *Verschriftlichung* involves the cognitive reshaping of the oral TEXT into a written format, a structural and cognitive remedialization of the oral story (Fludernik: 1996, 392 n13).

Verfremdungseffekt See ALIENATION EFFECT

Virtual reality Electronically simulated physical spaces and objects, for example those generated by computer games or the simulators used to train pilots.
Compare CYBERSPACE, *hyperreality*, in the entry for PRECESSION, and HYPERSPACE.

Voice See PERSPECTIVE AND VOICE; POLYPHONIC; SEMANTIC POSITION; *SKAZ*. For *double-voiced*, see DIEGESIS AND MIMESIS; DISCOURSE; DOUBLE-VOICED; PALIMPSEST TEXT.

Vorurteil A term from the German HERMENEUTIC tradition referring to the reader's predisposition to INTERPRET in one way rather than another. Howard Felperin points out that whereas Martin Heidegger uses the term in the sense of 'pre-judgement', for Hans-Georg Gadamer it has more the force of 'prejudice' (1992, 110, n11).

Voyeurism See GAZE; PERSPECTIVE AND VOICE; SCOPOPHILIA/SCOPOPHOBIA.

Vraisemblance A French loan-word meaning 'appearance as real', close to the English *verisimilitude*, and used in discussions of REALISM. The term is not new (its use in discussion of art dates from the seventeenth century), but what is new is that it is used in an increasingly pejorative or dismissive sense the more the status of realism has been brought into question.

W

Weak textualist See TEXTUALIST

West The apparently unproblematic nature of the term 'the West' is arguably a classic example of *naturalization* (see the entry for DEFAMILIARIZATION). We use this term to define not just a specific geographical area, but to refer in a covert, half-conscious fashion to a range of assumed values: 'the West' thus *excludes* both communism and post-communist eastern Europe, the 'third world', Islam, and so on. 'The West' sounds like a geographical description, but it often seems to include a strange mix of countries and areas: western Europe, the United States and Canada, Israel, Australia and New Zealand – states and areas that are clearly being yoked together for IDEOLOGICAL and political rather than geographic reasons.

A moment's thought will suffice to confirm that because the world is round, to divide it up into east and west requires that one *assume a standpoint and a perspective*. Thus an unconsidered use of the term 'the West' can be seen in ORIENTALIST terms as BINARY division of the world that pretends to universality but that actually represents the *interests* of certain forces. The term represents a classic example of EUROCENTRISM.

In his *The Invention of the West: Joseph Conrad and the Double-Mapping of Europe and Empire* (1995), Christopher GogWilt argues that the shift from a European to a Western identity at the end of the nineteenth century involves a 'transformation in the nature of cultural hegemony' (1995, 1). GogWilt's argument is complex but rewarding. He claims that as a result of the crossing of imperialist and revolutionary DISCOURSES, the 'ground' of debate about historical and political development was resituated 'from Europe to an idea of "the West" that appears to be greater than Europe, geographically and in political strength, yet at the same time represents only *part* of Europe, its "Western" part, to the exclusion of both eastern and central Europe' (1995, 33). He further suggests that there is 'a powerful connection between the decline of the British Empire and the rise of the West' (1995, 88).

Wild zone A term taken from Elaine Showalter's 1981 essay 'Feminist Criticism in the Wilderness'(Showalter: 1986). A specifically female area of CULTURE, often presented in a utopian or idealized manner for polemical effect.

Work See TEXT AND WORK

Writerly See READERLY AND WRITERLY TEXTS

Writing See ÉCRITURE

Z

Zero (degree writing) See ÉCRITURE

Zero focalization See PERSPECTIVE AND VOICE

Bibliography

This bibliography lists all works from which extracts are quoted, along with some other important works mentioned in entries.

Abrams, M. H. (1977). The limits of pluralism: the deconstructive angel. *Critical Inquiry*, 3, 425–38.

Abrams, M. H. (1988). *A Glossary of Literary Terms* (5th edn). London: Holt, Rinehart & Winston.

Aczel, Richard (1998). Hearing voices in narrative texts. *New Literary History*, 29, 467–500.

Ades, Dawn (1976). *Photomontage*. London: Thames & Hudson.

Agenda (1977). Special Issue on Myth, 15, nos 2–3.

Aitchison, Jean (1991). *Language Change: Progress or Decay?* (2nd edn). Cambridge: Cambridge University Press.

Alcoff, Linda (1988). Cultural feminism versus post-structuralism: the identity crisis in feminist theory. *Signs*, 13(3), repr. in abridged form in Mary Eagleton: 1996, 378–82.

Aléxis, Jacques Stephen (1956). Of the marvellous realism of the Haitians. *Présence Africaine*, 8–10.

Allen, David W. (1974). *The Fear of Looking, or Scopophilic-Exhibitionistic Conflicts*. Bristol: John Wright.

Althusser, Louis (1969). *For Marx* (first published in French, 1966). Brewster, Ben (trans.). London: Allen Lane.

Althusser, Louis (1971). *Lenin and Philosophy and Other Essays*. Brewster, Ben (trans.). London: New Left Books.

Althusser, Louis and Balibar, Etienne (1977). *Reading 'Capital'*. London: New Left Books.

Andermahr, Sonya, Lovell, Terry and Wolkowitz, Carol (1997). *A Glossary of Feminist Theory*. London: Arnold.

Anderson, Benedict (1983). *Imagined Communities: Reflections on the Origin and Spread of Nationalism*. London: Verso.

Anderson, Perry (1969). Components of the national culture. In Cockburn, Alexander and Blackburn, Robin (eds), *Student Power: Problems, Diagnosis, Action*. Harmondsworth: Penguin, 214–84.

Appadurai, Arjun (1990). Disjuncture and difference in the global cultural economy. *Public Culture*, 2(2), 1–17.

Appiah, Kwame Anthony (1992). The postcolonial and the postmodern. *In My Father's House: Africa in the Philosophy of Culture*. London: Methuen.

Argyle, Michael and Cook, Mark (1976). *Gaze and Mutual Gaze*. Cambridge: Cambridge University Press.

Ashcroft, Bill, Griffiths, Gareth and Tiffin, Helen (1989). *The Empire Writes Back: Theory and Practice in Post-Colonial Literatures*. London: Routledge.

Ashcroft, Bill, Griffiths, Gareth and Tiffin, Helen (eds) (1995). *The Post-Colonial Studies Reader*. London: Routledge.

Ashcroft, Bill, Griffiths, Gareth and Tiffin, Helen (1998). *Key Concepts in Post-Colonial Studies*. London: Routledge.

Atwood, Margaret (1983). *Murder in the Dark: Short Fictions, and Prose Poems*. Toronto: Coach House Press.

Austin, John (1962). *How to Do Things with Words*. Oxford: Clarendon Press.

Bakhtin, M. M. (1968). *Rabelais and his World*. Iswolsky, Helene (trans.). Cambridge, MA: MIT Press.

Bakhtin, M. M. (1981). *The Dialogic Imagination: Four Essays*. Holquist, Michael (ed.), Emerson, Caryl and Holquist, Michael (trans.). Austin: University of Texas Press.

Bakhtin, M. M. (1984). *Problems of Dostoevsky's Poetics*. Emerson, Caryl (ed. and trans.). Manchester: Manchester University Press.

Bakhtin, M. M. (1986). *Speech Genres and other Late Essays*. McGee, Vern W. (trans.). Austin: University of Texas Press.

Bal, Mieke (1985). *Narratology: Introduction to the Theory of Narrative*. Van Boheemen, Christine (trans.). Toronto and London: University of Toronto Press.

Bal, Mieke (1993). His master's eye. In Levin, David Michael (ed.), *Modernity and the Hegemony of Vision*. Berkeley: University of California Press, 379–404.

Balibar, Etienne and Macherey, Pierre (1978). Literature as an ideological form. McLeod, Ian, Whitehead, John and Wordsworth, Ann (trans.). *Oxford Literary Review*, 3(1), 4–12.

Banfield, Ann (1982). *Unspeakable Sentences: Narration and Representation in the Language of Fiction*. London: Routledge.

Banfield, Ann (1985). Écriture, narration and the grammar of French. In Hawthorn, Jeremy (ed.), *Narrative: from Malory to Motion Pictures*. London: Arnold, 1–22.

Barrett, Michèle (1989). Some different meanings of the concept of 'difference': feminist theory and the concept of ideology. In Meese, Elizabeth and Parker, Alice (eds), *The Difference Within: Feminism and Critical Theory*. Amsterdam: John Benjamins, 37–48.

Barrett, Michèle (1991). *The Politics of Truth: From Marx to Foucault*. Cambridge: Polity Press.

Barthes, Roland (1967a). *Elements of Semiology*. Lavers, Annette and Smith, Colin (trans.) (first published in French, 1964). London: Cape.

Barthes, Roland (1967b). *Writing Degree Zero*. Lavers, Annette and Smith, Colin (trans.) (first published in French, 1953). London: Cape.

Barthes, Roland (1973). *Mythologies*. Lavers, Annette (ed. and trans.) (first published in French, 1972). Frogmore: Granada.

Barthes, Roland (1975). An introduction to the structural analysis of narrative. *New Literary History*, 6(2), 137–72.

Barthes, Roland (1976). *The Pleasure of the Text*. Miller, Richard (trans.) (first published in French, 1975). London: Cape.

Barthes, Roland (1977). The death of the author. In Heath, Stephen (ed. and trans.), *Image-Music-Text*. London: Fontana, 142–8.

Barthes, Roland (1981a). Textual analysis of Poe's 'Valdemar'. Bennington, Geoff (trans.). In Young, Robert: 1981, 133–61.

Barthes, Roland (1981b). Theory of the text. McLeod, Ian (trans.). In Young, Robert: 1981, 31–47.

Barthes, Roland (1990). *S/Z*. Miller, Richard (trans.) (first published in French, 1973). Oxford: Blackwell.

Barthes, Roland (1991). *The Responsibility of Forms: Critical Essays on Music, Art, and Representation*. Howard, Richard (trans.). Berkeley and Los Angeles: University of California Press.

Barthes, Roland (1993). *Camera Lucida*. Howard, Richard (trans.) (first published in French, 1980, and in English, 1981). London: Vintage.

Baudrillard, Jean (1983). *Simulations*. Foss, Paul, Patton, Paul and Beitchman, Philip, (trans.). New York: Semiotext(e).

Beer, Gillian (1984). Virginia Woolf and prehistory. In Warner, Eric (ed.), *Virginia Woolf: A Centenary Perspective*. London: Macmillan. (Repr. in Beer, Gillian, *Virginia Woolf: The Common Ground*. Edinburgh: Edinburgh University Press, 1996, 6–28.)

Belsey, Catherine (1980). *Critical Practice*. London: Methuen.

Belsey, Catherine (1989). Towards cultural history – in theory and practice. *Textual Practice*, 3(2), 159–68 (repr. in Ryan: 1996, 82–91).

Benjamin, Walter (1973). *Illuminations*. Arendt, Hannah (ed.), Zohn, Harry (trans.) (first published in German, 1955; English trans. first published 1968). London: Collins/Fontana.

Benvenuto, Bice and Kennedy, Roger (1986). *The Works of Jacques Lacan*. London: Free Association Books.

Bhabha, Homi K. (1985). Signs taken for wonders: questions of ambivalence and authority under a tree outside Delhi, May 1817. *Critical Inquiry*, 12(1) (repr. in abridged form in Ashcroft, Griffiths and Tiffin: 1995, 29–35).

Bhabha, Homi K. (1994). *The Location of Culture*. London: Routledge.

Blanchot, Maurice (1981). The narrative voice (the 'he', the neuter). In Davis, Lydia (trans.), *The Gaze of Orpheus and Other Literary Essays*. New York: Station Hill Press.

Bloch, Ernst, Lukács, Georg, Brecht, Bertolt, Benjamin, Walter and Adorno, Theodor (1977). *Aesthetics and Politics*. London: New Left Books.

Bloom, Harold (1973). *The Anxiety of Influence: A Theory of Poetry*. Oxford and New York: Oxford University Press.

Bloom, Harold (1982). *Agon: Towards A Theory of Revisionism*. New York and Oxford: Oxford University Press.

Bodkin, Maud (1934). *Archetypal Patterns in Poetry*. London: Oxford University Press.

Booth, Wayne C. (1961). *Rhetoric of Fiction*. Chicago and London: University of Chicago Press.

Booth, Wayne C. (1988). *The Company We Keep: An Ethics of Fiction*. Berkeley and London: University of California Press.

Bourdieu, Pierre (1990). *The Logic of Practice.* Nice, Richard (trans.). Cambridge: Polity Press.

Bourdieu, Pierre (1993). *The Field of Cultural Production* (ed. and with an Introduction by Randall Johnson). New York: Columbia University Press.

Bowlt, John (1972). Introduction to special issue on Russian Formalism. *20th Century Studies,* 7/8, December.

Braidotti, Rosa (1994). *Nomadic Subjects.* New York: Columbia University Press.

Brand, Dana (1999). Rear-view mirror: Hitchcock, Poe, and the flaneur in America. In Freedman, Jonathan and Millington, Richard (eds), *Hitchcock's America.* New York and Oxford: Oxford University Press, 123–34.

Bremond, Claude (1966). La logique des possibles narratifs. *Communications,* 8, 60–76. Published as 'The logic of narrative possibilities' (Cancalon, Elaine D., trans.) in *New Literary History,* 11 (1980), 387–411, and repr. in abridged form in Onega and Landa: 1996, 61–75.

Bremond, Claude (1973). *Logique du Récit.* Paris: Seuil.

Bristow, Joseph (1989). Being gay: politics, identity, pleasure. *New Formations* 9, 61–83.

Bristow, Joseph (1997). *Sexuality.* London: Routledge.

Brooker, Peter (1999). *Cultural Theory: A Glossary.* London: Arnold.

Brooke-Rose, Christine (1981). *A Rhetoric of the Unreal: Studies in Narrative and Structure, Especially of the Fantastic.* Cambridge: Cambridge University Press.

Brooks, Cleanth (1946). Empson's criticism. In Quinn, Kerker and Shattuck, Charles (eds), *Accent Anthology* (first published 1944). New York: Harcourt Brace.

Brooks, Cleanth (1983). In search of the New Criticism. *The American Scholar,* 53(1), Winter 1983/4, 41–53.

Brooks, Cleanth and Warren, Robert Penn (1958). *Understanding Poetry* (rev. edn; first published 1938). New York: Henry Holt.

Brooks, Peter (1984). *Reading for the Plot: Design and Intention in Narrative.* Oxford: Clarendon Press.

Brooks, Peter (1994). *Psychoanalysis and Storytelling.* Oxford: Blackwell.

Brousse, Marie-Hélène (1987). Des fantasmes au fantasme. In Miller, Gérard (ed.), *Lacan.* Paris: Bordas, 107–22.

Brown, Pamela and Levinson, Stephen (1978). Universals in language usage: politeness phenomena. In Goody, Esther N. (ed.), *Questions of Politeness: Strategies in Social Interaction.* Cambridge: Cambridge University Press, 295–310.

Brown, Pamela and Levinson, Stephen (1987). *Politeness: Some Universals in Language Usage.* Cambridge: Cambridge University Press.

Brunsdon, Charlotte (1993). Identity in feminist television criticism. *Media, Culture and Society,* 15(2), 309–20.

Brydon, Diana (1991). The white Inuit speaks: contamination as literary strategy. In Adam, Ian and Tiffin, Helen (eds), *Past the Last Post: Theorizing Post-colonialism and Post-modernism.* London: Harvester Wheatsheaf (repr. in abridged form in Ashcroft, Griffiths and Tiffin: 1995, 136–42).

Bryson, Norman, Holly, Michael Ann, and Moxey, Keith (1994). *Visual Culture: Images and Interpretations.* Hanover and London: Wesleyan University Press. (Published by University Press of New England).

Bühler, Karl (1990). *Theory of Language: The Representational Function of Language* (first published in German, 1934). (Goodwin, Donald Fraser, trans.). Amsterdam: John Benjamins.

Burden, Robert (1991). *Heart of Darkness*. The Critics Debate. London: Macmillan.

Bürger, Peter (1984). *Theory of the Avant-Garde*. Shaw, Michael (trans.). Minneapolis: University of Minnesota Press.

Burke, Kenneth (1969). *A Grammar of Motives*. Berkeley: University of California Press.

Butler, Judith (1991). Imitation and gender insubordination. In Fuss: 1991, 13–31.

Butor, Michel (1964). L'usage des pronoms personnels dans le roman. In *Répertoire II*. Paris: Les Editions de Minuit.

Callinicos, Alex (1989). *Against Postmodernism*. Cambridge: Polity Press.

Cameron, Deborah (1985). *Feminism and Linguistic Theory*. London: Macmillan.

Cawelti, John (1977). Literary formulas and cultural significance. In Luedke, Luther (ed.), *The Story of . . . American Culture/Contemporary Conflicts*. Deland: Everett/Edwards.

Caws, Mary Ann (1985). *Reading Frames in Modern Fiction*. Princeton: Princeton University Press.

Césaire, Aimé (1972). *Discourse on Colonialism*. New York: Monthly Review Press.

Chakrabarty, Dipesh (1992). Postcoloniality and the artifice of history: who speaks for 'Indian' pasts? *Representations*, 32 (winter), 1–26.

Chatman, Seymour (1978). *Story and Discourse: Narrative Structure in Fiction and Film*. Ithaca and London: Cornell University Press.

Chatman, Seymour (1990). *Coming to Terms. The Rhetoric of Narrative in Fiction and Film*. Ithaca and London: Cornell University Press.

Chinweizu and Jemie, Onwuchekwa and Madubuike, Ihechukwu (1983). *Toward the Decolonization of African Literature*. Volume 1: *African Fiction and Poetry and Their Critics*. Washington, DC: Howard University Press.

Chodorow, Nancy J. (1989). *Feminism and Psychoanalytic Theory*. New Haven: Yale University Press.

Chow, Rey (1994). Where have all the natives gone? In Bammer, Angelika (ed.), *Displacements: Cultural Identities in Question*. Bloomington: Indiana University Press, 125–51 (repr. in Mongia: 1996, 122–46).

Cioffi, Frank (1976). Intention and interpretation in criticism (first published 1964). In Newton-De Molina, David (ed.), *On Literary Intention*. Edinburgh: Edinburgh University Press, 55–73.

Cixous, Hélène (1981). The laugh of the Medusa. In Marks, Elaine and de Courtivron, Isabelle (eds), Cohen, Keith and Cohen, Paula (trans.), *New French Feminisms: An Anthology* (first published in French, 1975; translation is of the revised French version of 1976). New York: Schocken Books, 245–64.

Cleto, Fabio (ed.) (1999). *Camp: Queer Aesthetics and the Performing Subject: a Reader*. Edinburgh: Edinburgh University Press.

Cohan, Steven and Shires, Linda M. (1988). *Telling Stories: A Theoretical Analysis of Narrative Fiction*. London: Routledge.

Cohen, Tom (1998). *Ideology and Inscription: 'Cultural Studies' after Benjamin, de Man, and Bakhtin*. Cambridge: Cambridge University Press.

Cohn, Dorrit (1978). *Transparent Minds: Narrating Modes for Presenting Consciousness in Fiction*. Princeton: Princeton University Press.

Collini, Stefan (1994). Escape from DWEMsville: is culture too important to be left to cultural studies? *Times Literary Supplement*, 27 May, 3–4.

Conrad, Joseph (1946). *A Personal Record: Some Reminiscences* (first published 1912). Dent Collected Edition. London: Dent.

Conrad, Joseph (1986). *Lord Jim*. Hampson, Robert (ed.), Watts, Cedric (Introduction and Notes). Harmondsworth: Penguin.

Corner, John and Richardson, Kay (1986). Documentary meanings and the discourse of interpretation. In Corner, John (ed.), *Documentary and the Mass Media*. London: Arnold, 140–60.

Cranny-Francis, Anne (1990). *Feminist Fiction: Feminist Uses of Generic Fiction*. Cambridge: Polity Press.

Crapanzano, Vincent (1978). Lacan's *Ecrits. Canto*, 2, 183–91.

Crapanzano, Vincent (1992). *Hermes' Dilemma and Hamlet's Desire: On the Epistemology of Interpretation*. Cambridge, MA: Harvard University Press.

Culler, Jonathan (1975). *Structuralist Poetics: Structuralism, Linguistics and the Study of Literature*. London: Routledge.

Culler, Jonathan (1980). Prolegomena to a theory of reading. In Suleiman, Susan R. and Crosman, Inge (eds), *The Reader in the Text*. Princeton: Princeton University Press, 46–66.

Culler, Jonathan (1981). *The Pursuit of Signs: Semiotics, Literature, Deconstruction*. London: Routledge.

Culler, Jonathan (1988). *Framing the Sign: Criticism and its Institutions*. Oxford: Blackwell.

Curle, Richard (ed.) (1928). *Conrad to a Friend: 150 Selected Letters from Joseph Conrad to Richard Curle*. Curle, Richard (Introduction and Notes). London: Sampson Low, Marston.

Dallenbach, Lucien (1989). *The Mirror in the Text*. Whiteley, Jeremy and Hughes, Emma (trans.). Cambridge: Polity Press.

Daly, Mary (1979). *Gyn/ecology: The Metaethics of Radical Feminism*. London: The Women's Press.

Daly, Mary (1984). *Pure Lust: Elemental Feminist Philosophy*. London: The Women's Press.

de Beaugrande, Robert (1994). Discourse analysis. In Groden, Michael and Kreiswirth, Martin (eds), *The Johns Hopkins Guide to Literary Theory and Criticism*. Baltimore: Johns Hopkins University Press, 207–10.

de Jong, Irene I. F. (1989). *Narrators and Focalizers: The Presentation of the Story in the Iliad* (2nd edn). Amsterdam: Grüner.

Delbaere-Garant, Jeanne (1988). Le domaine anglais. In Weisgerber: 1988, 154–79.

Deleuze, Gilles (1993). Rhizome versus tree (repr. in Boundas, Constantin V. [ed.], *The Deleuze Reader*. New York: Columbia University Press).

Deleuze, Gilles and Guattari, Félix (1983). *Anti-Oedipus: Capitalism and Schizophrenia* (first published in French, 1972 and in English, 1977). Minneapolis: University of Minnesota Press.

Deleuze, Gilles and Guattari, Félix (1988). *A Thousand Plateaus: Capitalism and Schizophrenia*. Massumi, Brian (trans.) (first published in French, 1980). London: Athlone Press.

Delphy, Christine (1984). *Close to Home: A Material Analysis of Women's Oppression*. London: Hutchinson.

Derrida, Jacques (1973). Différance. *Speech and Phenomena, and other Essays on Husserl's Theory of Signs*. Allison, David B. (trans.). Evanston: Northwestern University Press.

Derrida, Jacques (1975). The purveyor of truth. *Yale French Studies*, 52, 31–113.

Derrida, Jacques (1976). *Of Grammatology*. Spivak, Gayatri Chakravorty (trans.) (first published in French, 1967). Baltimore: Johns Hopkins University Press.

Derrida, Jacques (1978a). *Writing and Difference*. Bass, Alan (trans.). London: Routledge.

Derrida, Jacques (1978b). *Spurs*. Harlow, Barbara (trans.). Chicago: University of Chicago Press.

Derrida, Jacques (1979). Living on the borderlines. In Bloom, Harold (ed.), *Deconstruction and Criticism*. London: Routledge, 82–4.

Derrida, Jacques (1981a). *Dissemination*. Johnson, Barbara (trans.). London: Athlone Press.

Derrida, Jacques (1981b). *Positions*. Bass, Alan (trans.). London: Athlone Press.

Diamond, Nicola (1992). Introjection. In Wright, Elizabeth: 1992, 176–8.

Doane, Mary Anne (1988). *The Desire to Desire: The Woman's Film in the 1940s*. London: Macmillan.

Docherty, Thomas (1987). *On Modern Authority: The Theory and Condition of Writing: 1500 to the Present Day*. Brighton: Harvester Press.

Doubrovsky, Serge (1973). *The New Criticism in France*. Coltman, Derek (trans.). Chicago and London: University of Chicago Press.

Drake, James (1998). The naming disease: how Jakobson's essay on aphasia initiated postmodern deceits. *The Times Literary Supplement*, issue 4979, 4 September, 14–15.

Draper, Hal (1978). *Karl Marx's Theory of Revolution: The Politics of Social Class*. New York: Monthly Review Press.

Dupriez, Bernard (1991). *A Dictionary of Literary Devices*. Halsall, Albert W. (trans. and adapted) (first published in French, 1984). Hemel Hempstead: Harvester Wheatsheaf.

Dutton, Richard (1992). Postscript. In Wilson, Richard and Dutton, Richard (eds), *New Historicism and Renaissance Drama*. Harlow: Longman, 219–26.

Eagleton, Mary (ed.) (1996). *Feminist Theory: A Reader* (2nd edn). Oxford: Blackwell.

Eagleton, Terry (1970). *Exiles and Émigrés*. London: Chatto & Windus.

Eagleton, Terry (1976a). *Criticism and Ideology*. London: Verso.

Eagleton, Terry (1976b). *Marxism and Literary Criticism*. London: Methuen.

Eagleton, Terry (1983). *Literary Theory: An Introduction*. Oxford: Blackwell.

Eagleton, Terry (1990). *The Ideology of the Aesthetic*. Oxford: Blackwell.

Eagleton, Terry (1991). *Ideology: An Introduction*. London: Verso.

Eco, Umberto (1972). Towards a semiotic inquiry into the television message. Splendore, Paola (trans.) (first read as a paper in Italian, 1965). *Working Papers in*

Cultural Studies, 3, 1972, 103–21. (Repr. in Corner, John and Hawthorn, Jeremy [eds], *Communication Studies: An Introductory Reader*. London: Arnold, 1980, 131–49.)

Eco, Umberto (1977). Semiotics of theatrical performance. *The Drama Review*, XXI (1), (March) (repr. in abridged form in Walder: 1990, 115–22).

Eco, Umberto (1981). *The Role of the Reader: Explorations in the Semiotics of Texts*. London: Hutchinson.

Eichenbaum, Boris (1965). The theory of the 'formal method' (first published in Ukrainian, 1926; this translation from the Russian version, 1927). In Lemon, Lee T. and Reis, Marion J. (eds and trans.), *Russian Formalist Criticism: Four Essays*. Lincoln, NE: University of Nebraska Press.

Èjxenbaum, Boris M. (1971a). The theory of the formal method (first published in Russian, 1927). In Matejka, Ladislav and Pomorska, Krystyna (eds), Titunik, I. R. (trans.), *Readings in Russian Poetics: Formalist and Structuralist Views*. Cambridge, MA. and London: MIT Press, 3–37. See also previous entry.

Èjxenbaum, Boris M. (1971b). Literary environment (first published in Russian, 1929). In Matejka, Ladislav and Pomorska, Krystyna (eds), Titunik, I. R. (trans.), *Readings in Russian Poetics: Formalist and Structuralist Views*. Cambridge, MA. and London: MIT Press, 56–65.

Eliot, T. S. (1920). *The Sacred Wood*. London: Methuen.

Eliot, T. S. (1922). *The Waste Land*. London: Hogarth Press.

Eliot, T. S. (1961). *On Poetry and Poets*. New York: Noonday Press.

Ellmann, Mary (1979). *Thinking about Women* (first published 1968). London: Virago.

Ellmann, Maud (1981). Disremembering Dedalus: *A Portrait of the Artist as a Young Man*. In Young, Robert: 1981, 189–206.

Empson, William (1961). *Seven Types of Ambiguity* (3rd edn; first edn. published 1930). Harmondsworth: Peregrine.

Empson, William (1962). Rhythm and imagery in English poetry. *British Journal of Aesthetics*, 2(1), 36–54.

Empson, William (1965). *Milton's God* (rev. edn; first edn. published 1961). London: Chatto & Windus.

Empson, William (1984). *Using Biography*. London: Chatto & Windus/Hogarth Press.

Engels, Frederick (1964). *Dialectics of Nature* (3rd rev. edn). Dutt, Clemens (trans.). London: Lawrence & Wishart.

Erdinast-Vulcan, Daphna (1994). Narrative, modernism, and the crisis of authority: a Bakhtinian perspective. *Science in Context*, 7(1), 143–58.

Erdinast-Vulcan, Daphna (1995). On the edge of the subject: the heterobiography of Joseph K. Conrad. *Genre*, XXVIII (Fall), 303–22.

Erdinast-Vulcan, Daphna (1999). *The Strange Short Fiction of Joseph Conrad: Writing, Culture, and Subjectivity*. Oxford: Oxford University Press.

Ermarth, Elizabeth Deeds (1992). *Postmodernism and the Crisis of Representational Time*. Princeton: Princeton University Press.

Esonwanne, Uzoma (1996). Bolekaja criticism. In Payne, Michael (ed.), *A Dictionary of Cultural and Critical Theory*. Oxford: Blackwell, 72.

Even-Zohar, Itamar (1990). *Polysystem Studies*. Special issue of *Poetics Today*, 11(1).

Fee, Margery (1995). Who can write as other? (extracted from 'Why C. K. Stead didn't like Keri Hulme's *the bone people*: who can write as other?' *Australian and New Zealand Studies in Canada*, 1, 1989). In Ashcroft, Griffiths and Tiffin: 1995, 242–5.

Feldman, Carol Fleisher, Bruner, Jerome, Renderer, Bobbie and Spitzer, Sally (1990). Narrative comprehension. In Britton, Bruce K. and Pellegrini, Anthony D. (eds), *Narrative Thought and Narrative Language*. Hillsdale, NJ/Hove and London: Lawrence Erlbaum Associates.

Felperin, Howard (1992). *The Uses of the Canon: Elizabethan Literature and Contemporary Theory* (repr. with corrections of 1990 edn). Oxford: Clarendon Press.

Ferenczi, Sandor (1909). Introjection and transference. *First Contributions to Psychoanalysis*. London: Hogarth Press, 35–93.

Fetterley, Judith (1978). *The Resisting Reader: A Feminist Approach to American Fiction*. Bloomington: Indiana University Press.

Fiedler, Leslie (1966). *Love and Death in the American Novel* (rev. edn; first published 1960). New York: Stein & Day.

Fish, Stanley E. (1972). *Self-consuming Artifacts: The Experience of Seventeenth-century Literature*. Berkeley: University of California Press.

Fish, Stanley (1980). *Is There a Text in this Class? The Authority of Interpretive Communities*. Cambridge, MA and London: Harvard University Press.

Fludernik, Monika (1993). *The Fictions of Languages and the Languages of Fiction: The Linguistic Representation of Speech and Consciousness*. London: Routledge.

Fludernik, Monika (1996). *Towards a 'Natural' Narratology*. London: Routledge.

Forgacs, David (1986). Marxist literary theories (first published 1982). In Jefferson, Ann and Robey, David (eds), *Modern Literary Theory: A Comparative Introduction* (2nd expanded edn). London: Batsford, 166–203.

Forgacs, David (1995). The politics of modernism. In Joannou, Maroula and Margolies, David (eds), *Heart of the Heartless World: Essays in Cultural Resistance in Memory of Margot Heinemann*. London: Pluto Press, 8–18.

Forster, E. M. (1927). *Aspects of the Novel*. London: Arnold.

Foucault, Michel (1972). *The Archaeology of Knowledge*. Sheridan Smith, A. M. (trans.). London: Tavistock.

Foucault, Michel (1979). *Discipline and Punish: The Birth of the Prison*. Sheridan, Alan (trans.) (first published in French, 1975). Harmondsworth: Penguin.

Foucault, Michel (1980a). *Power/Knowledge*. Brighton: Harvester.

Foucault, Michel (1980b). What is an author? (first published in English, 1977, in Bouchard, Donald F. [ed.], *Language, Counter-memory, Practice: Selected Essays and Interviews*. New York: Cornell University Press). In Harari, J. V.: 1980, 141–60.

Foucault, Michel (1981). The order of discourse. Originally Foucault's inaugural lecture, delivered at the Collège de France, 2 December 1970. McLeod, Ian (trans.). In Young, Robert: 1981, 48–78.

Fowler, Roger (1990). *The Lost Girl*: discourse and focalization. In Brown, Keith (ed.), *Rethinking Lawrence*. Milton Keynes: Open University Press, 53–66.

Fox, Ralph (1979). *The Novel and the People* (first published 1937). London: Lawrence & Wishart.

Fox-Genovese, Elizabeth (1989), Literary criticism and the politics of the New Historicism. In Veeser:1989, 213–24.

Freud, Sigmund (1955). The uncanny. In Strachey, James and Freud, Anna (eds), *The Standard Edition of the Complete Psychological Works of Sigmund Freud*, XVII. London: Hogarth Press, 219–52.

Freud, Sigmund (1963). Female sexuality (first published 1931; repr. in Rieff, Philip [ed.], *Sigmund Freud: Sexuality and the Psychology of Love*. New York: Macmillan, 194–211).

Freud, Sigmund (1976). *The Interpretation of Dreams*. Strachey, James (ed., assisted by Alan Tyson), Strachey, James (trans.). The Pelican Freud Library, 4. Harmondsworth: Penguin.

Freud, Sigmund, and Breuer, Joseph (1974). *Studies on Hysteria*. Strachey, James and Alex (eds, assisted by Angela Richards), Strachey, James and Alex (trans.). The Pelican Freud Library, 3. Harmondsworth: Penguin.

Frow, John (1986). *Marxism and Literary History*. Oxford: Blackwell.

Frow, John (1997). *Time and Commodity Culture: Essays in Cultural Theory and Postmodernity*. Oxford: Clarendon Press.

Furbank, P. N. (1970). *Reflections on the Word 'Image'*. London: Secker & Warburg.

Fuss, Diana (1991). *Inside/Out: Lesbian Theories, Gay Theories*. New York and London: Routledge.

Gadamer, Hans-Georg (1989). *Truth and Method* (2nd, rev. edn). Trans. rev. by Weinsheimer, Joel and Marshall, Donald G. London: Sheed & Ward.

Gagnon, Madeleine (1980). Body I. An excerpt from 'Corps I' (first published in French, 1977). In Marks, Elaine and Courtivron, Isabelle de (eds), Courtivron, Isabelle de (trans.), *New French Feminisms: An Anthology*. Amherst: University of Massachusetts Press.

Galton, Ray and Simpson, Alan (1987). *The Best of Hancock: Classics from the BBC Television Series* (first published 1986). Harmondsworth: Penguin.

Garvin, Paul (ed. and trans.) (1964). *A Prague School Reader on Esthetics, Literary Structure, and Style*. Washington, DC: Georgetown University Press.

Gaunt, Philip (1996). Birmingham revisited: cultural studies in a post-Soviet world. *Journal of Popular Culture*, 30(1), 91–102.

Geertz, Clifford (1973). *The Interpretation of Cultures*. New York: Basic Books.

Genette, Gérard (1979). *L'Introduction à l'architexte*. Paris: Seuil. (English trans. by Lewin, Jane E. [1992]: *The Architext: An Introduction*. Berkeley: University of California Press.)

Genette, Gérard (1980). *Narrative Discourse*. Lewin, Jane E. (trans.). Oxford: Blackwell.

Genette, Gérard (1982). *Figures of Literary Discourse*. Sheridan, Alan (trans.). Oxford: Blackwell.

Genette, Gérard (1994). *L'Œuvre de l'art: immanence et transcendance*. Paris: Seuil.

Genette, Gérard (1997). *Paratexts: Thresholds of Interpretation* (*Literature, Culture, Theory*, 20; first published in French, 1987). Lewin, Jane E. (trans.). Cambridge: Cambridge University Press.

Gibson, Andrew (1996). *Towards a Postmodern Theory of Narrative*. Edinburgh: Edinburgh University Press.

Gilbert, Sandra M. and Gubar, Susan (1979). *The Madwoman in the Attic: The Woman Writer and the Nineteenth-Century Literary Imagination.* New Haven: Yale University Press.

Gilbert, Sandra M. and Gubar, Susan (1988). *No Man's Land: The Place of the Woman Writer in the Twentieth Century. Volume 1: The War of the Words.* New Haven: Yale University Press.

Gĩtĩtĩ, Gĩtahi (1994). African theory and criticism. In Groden, Michael and Kreiswirth, Martin (eds), *The Johns Hopkins Guide to Literary Theory and Criticism.* Baltimore: Johns Hopkins University Press, 4–8.

Goffman, Erving (1974). *Frame Analysis: An Essay on the Organization of Experience.* Cambridge, MA: Harvard University Press.

GogWilt, Christopher (1995). *The Invention of the West: Joseph Conrad and the Double-Mapping of Europe and Empire.* Stanford: Stanford University Press.

Goldmann, Lucien (1969). *The Human Sciences and Philosophy.* White, Hayden V. and Anchor, Robert (trans.). London: Cape.

Goodman, Nelson (1968). *The Languages of Art: An Approach to the Theory of Symbols.* Indianapolis: Bobbs-Merrill.

Graff, Gerald (1979). *Literature against Itself: Literary Ideas in Modern Society.* Chicago and London: University of Chicago Press.

Graff, Gerald (1989). Co-optation. In Veeser: 1989, 168–81.

Gramsci, Antonio (1971). *Selections from the Prison Notebooks of Antonio Gramsci.* Hoare, Quintin and Nowell Smith, Geoffrey (eds and trans.). London: Lawrence & Wishart.

Grant, Catherine (1994/5). Queer theorrhea (and what it might mean for feminists). *Trouble and Strife*, 29/30 (repr. in Jackson and Scott: 1996, 166–71).

Green, Michael (1976). Cultural studies at Birmingham University. In Craig, David and Heinemann, Margot (eds), *Experiments in English Teaching: New Work in Higher and Further Education.* London: Arnold, 140–51.

Greenblatt, Stephen J. (1988). *Shakespearian Negotiations.* Oxford: Clarendon Press.

Greenblatt, Stephen J. (1990). *Learning to Curse: Essays in Early Modern Culture.* London: Routledge.

Gregor, Ian (1970). Criticism as an individual activity: the approach through reading. In Bradbury, Malcolm and Palmer, David (eds), *Contemporary Criticism*, Stratford-upon-Avon Studies, 12. London: Arnold, 195–214.

Gregory, R. L. (1970). *The Intelligent Eye.* London: Weidenfeld & Nicolson.

Guattari, Félix (1998). Schizoanalysis (first published in French, 1986). Zayani, Mohamed (trans.). *The Yale Journal of Criticism*, 11(2), (Fall), 433–9.

Gugelberger, Georg M. (1994). Postcolonial cultural studies. In Groden, Michael and Kreiswirth, Martin (eds), *The Johns Hopkins Guide to Literary Theory and Criticism.* Baltimore: Johns Hopkins University Press, 581–5.

Gumperz, John (1982a). *Discourse Strategies.* Cambridge: Cambridge University Press.

Gumperz, John (1982b). *Language and Social Identity.* Cambridge: Cambridge University Press.

Hall, Stuart (1990). Cultural identity and diaspora. In Rutherford, Jonathan (ed.), *Identity: Community, Culture, Difference.* London: Lawrence & Wishart, 222–37.

Hall, Stuart and Whannel, Paddy (1964). *The Popular Arts.* London: Hutchinson.

Hallberg, Robert von (1985). *Canons*. Chicago: University of Chicago Press.

Hampton, Christopher (1990). *The Ideology of the Text*. Milton Keynes: Open University Press.

Harari, Josué V. (ed.) (1980). *Textual Strategies: Perspectives in Post-structuralist Criticism*. London: Methuen.

Haraway, Donna (1985). A manifesto for cyborgs: science, technology, and socialist feminism in the 1980s. *Socialist Review*, 80 (March/April). In Mary Eagleton: 1996, 399–403.

Haraway, Donna (1991). *Simians, Cyborgs, and Women: The Reinvention of Nature*. London: Free Association Books.

Harding, Sandra (ed.) (1987). *Feminism and Methodology: Social Science Issues*. Milton Keynes: Open University Press.

Harland, Richard (1987). *Superstructuralism: The Philosophy of Structuralism and Post-structuralism*. London: Methuen.

Hartman, Geoffrey (1970). *Beyond Formalism*. New Haven: Yale University Press.

Hartsock, Nancy C. M. (1987). The feminist standpoint: developing the ground for a specifically feminist historical materialism. In Harding: 1987, 157–80.

Harvey, David (1989). *The Condition of Postmodernity*. Oxford: Blackwell.

Hassan, Ihab (1985). The culture of postmodernism. *Theory, Culture and Society*, 2(3), 119–31.

Havránek, Bohuslav (1964). The functional differentiation of the standard language (first published in Czech, 1932). In Garvin: 1964, 3–16.

Hawthorn, Jeremy (1987). *Unlocking the Text: Fundamental Issues in Literary Theory*. London: Arnold.

Hawthorn, Jeremy (1996). *Cunning Passages: New Historicism, Cultural Materialism and Marxism in the Contemporary Literary Debate*. London: Arnold.

Hazlitt, William (n.d.). *Table Talk or Original Essays*. London: Everyman Library/J. M. Dent.

Henderson, Stephen (1973). *Understanding the New Black Poetry: Black Speech and Black Music as Poetic References*. New York: William Morrow.

Henricksen, Bruce (1992). *Nomadic Voices: Conrad and the Subject of Narrative*. Urbana and Chicago: University of Illinois Press.

Higgins, John (1999). *Raymond Williams: Literature, Marxism and Cultural Materialism*. London: Routledge.

Hinsie, L. E. and Campbell, R. J. (1960). *Psychiatric Dictionary*. Oxford and New York: Oxford University Press.

Hirsch, E. D. (1967). *Validity in Interpretation*. New Haven and London: Yale University Press.

Hirsch, E. D. (1976). *The Aims of Interpretation*. Chicago: University of Chicago Press.

Hoggart, Richard (1957). *The Uses of Literacy. Aspects of Working-class Life, with Special Reference to Publications and Entertainments*. London: Chatto & Windus.

Hoggart, Richard (1970). Contemporary cultural studies: an approach to the study of literature and society. In Bradbury, Malcolm and Palmer, David (eds), *Contemporary Criticism*, Stratford-upon-Avon Studies, 12. London: Arnold, 154–70.

Holderness, Graham (1982). *D. H. Lawrence: History, Ideology and Fiction*. Dublin and London: Gill and Macmillan.

Holderness, Graham (1991). Production, reproduction, performance: Marxism, history, theatre. In Barker, Francis, Hulme, Peter and Iversen, Margaret (eds), *Uses of History: Marxism, Postmodernism and the Renaissance*. Manchester: Manchester University Press, 153–78.

Holderness, Graham (1992). *Shakespeare Recycled: The Making of Historical Drama*. Hemel Hempstead: Harvester Wheatsheaf.

Holland, Norman N. (1975). *5 Readers Reading*. New Haven: Yale University Press.

hooks, bell (1992). *Black Looks: Race and Representation*. London: Turnaround.

Hume, Kathryn (1984). *Fantasy and Mimesis: Responses to Reality in Western Literature*. London: Methuen.

Humm, Maggie (1989). *The Dictionary of Feminist Theory*. London: Harvester Wheatsheaf.

Hunt, Alan (1977). Theory and politics in the identification of the working class. In Hunt, Alan (ed.), *Class and Class Structure*. London: Lawrence & Wishart, 81–111.

Hutcheon, Linda (1980). *Narcissistic Narrative: the Metafictional Paradox*. Waterloo, Ontario: Wilfred Laurier University Press (repr. 1984 by Methuen).

Huyssen, Andreas (1988). *After the Great Divide: Modernism, Mass Culture and Postmodernism*. London: Macmillan.

Hyam, Ronald (1990). *Empire and Sexuality: The British Experience*. Manchester: Manchester University Press.

Ingarden, Roman (1973). *The Literary Work of Art: An Investigation on the Borders of Ontology, Logic, and Theory of Literature* (first published in German, 1931). Grabowicz, George G. (trans.). Evanston: Northwestern University Press.

Irigaray, Luce (1985). *This Sex Which is Not One*. Porter, Katherine with Burke, Carolyn (trans.). New York: Cornell University Press.

Iser, Wolfgang (1974). *The Implied Reader: Patterns of Communication in Prose Fiction from Bunyan to Beckett*. Baltimore and London: Johns Hopkins University Press.

Jackson, Stevi (1978). The social construction of female sexuality. *Women's Research and Resources Centre* (repr. in Jackson and Scott: 1996, 62–73).

Jackson, Stevi and Scott, Sue (eds) (1996). *Feminism and Sexuality: A Reader*. Edinburgh: Edinburgh University Press.

Jacob, Carol (1978). *The Dissimulating Harmony: The Image of Interpretation in Nietzsche, Rilke, Artaud and Benjamin*. Baltimore: Johns Hopkins University Press.

Jahn, Manfred, Molitor, Inge and Nünning, Ansgar (1993). *COGNAC: A Concise Glossary of Narratology from Cologne*. Cologne: Englisches Seminar.

Jahn, Manfred (1997). Frames, preferences, and the reading of third-person narratives: towards a cognitive narratology. *Poetics Today*, 18, 441–68.

Jakobson, Roman (1960). Closing statement: linguistics and poetics. In Sebeok, Thomas A. (ed.), *Style in Language*. Cambridge, MA: The Technology Press/MIT; New York: John Wiley.

Jakobson, Roman (1971a). On realism in art (first published in Czech, 1921). In Matejka, Ladislav and Pomorska, Krystyna (eds), Magassy, Karol (trans.), *Readings in Russian Poetics: Formalist and Structuralist Views*. Cambridge, MA: MIT Press, 38–46.

Jakobson, Roman (1971b). The dominant (delivered as a lecture in 1935). In Matejka, Ladislav and Pomorska, Krystyna (eds), Eagle, H. (trans.), *Readings in Russian Poetics: Formalist and Structuralist Views*. Cambridge, MA: MIT Press, 82–7.

Jakobson, Roman and Halle, Morris (1971). *Fundamentals of Language* (2nd rev. edn). The Hague: Mouton.

James, Henry (1948). *The Lesson of the Master and Other Stories by Henry James*. (Place of publication not given): John Lehmann.

Jameson, Fredric (1981). *The Political Unconscious: Narrative as a Socially Symbolic Act*. London: Methuen.

Jameson, Fredric (1991). *Postmodernism, or, The Cultural Logic of Late Capitalism*. Durham, NC: Duke University Press.

Jardine, Alice A. (1985). *Gynesis: Configurations of Woman and Modernity*. New York: Cornell University Press.

Jauss, Hans Robert (1974). Literary history as a challenge to literary theory. In Cohen, Ralph (ed.), *New Directions in Literary History*. London: Routledge, 11–41.

Jay, Martin (1973). *The Dialectical Imagination: A History of the Frankfurt School and the Institute of Social Research 1923–50*. Boston: Little, Brown.

Jay, Martin (1993). *Downcast Eyes: The Denigration of Vision in Twentieth-Century French Thought*. Berkeley: University of California Press.

Jencks, Charles (1993). Letter printed in *The Times Literary Supplement*, 12 March, 15.

Jeyifo, Biodun (1996). The nature of things: arrested decolonization and critical theory (first published in 1990 in *Research in African Literatures*, 21, 33–47). Repr. in Mongia: 1996, 158–71.

Johnson, Pauline (1984). *Marxist Aesthetics: The Foundations Within Everyday Life for an Enlightened Consciousness*. London: Routledge.

Jones, Leroi (subsequently known as Baraka, Amiri) (1971). The changing same. R and B and new Black music. In Gayle, Addison, Jr, *The Black Aesthetic*. Garden City, NY: Doubleday, 112–25.

Kafka, Franz (1957). *The Castle*. Muir, Willa and Muir, Edwin (trans.) (first published in German, 1926). Harmondsworth: Penguin.

Kaplan, E. Ann (1990). *Psychoanalysis and Cinema*. New York and London: Routledge.

Kaplan, E. Ann (1997). *Looking for the Other: Feminism, Film, and the Imperial Gaze*. London: Routledge.

Keitel, Evelyne (1992). Reading as/like a woman. In Wright: 1992, 371–4.

Kenner, Hugh (1978). *Joyce's Voices*. Berkeley: University of California Press.

Kermode, Frank (1989). *An Appetite for Poetry: Essays in Literary Interpretation*. London: Collins.

Kesteloot, Lilyan (ed.) (1968). *Anthologie Négro-africaine*, Collection Marabout Université. Verviers: Gérard.

Kettle, Arnold (1988). *Literature and Liberation: Selected Essays*. Martin, Graham and Nandy, Dipak (eds). Manchester: Manchester University Press.

Klein, Melanie (1988). A contribution to the psychogenesis of manic-depressive states (first published 1945). In Klein, Melanie, *Love, Guilt and Reparation and Other Works 1921–1945*. London: Virago (first published 1975, London: Hogarth Press).

Knapp, Steven and Michaels, Walter Benn (1985). Against theory. In Mitchell, W. J. T. (ed.), *Against Theory: Literary Studies and the New Pragmatism*. Chicago and London: University of Chicago Press.

Knights, L. C. (1937). *Drama and Society in the Age of Jonson*. London: Chatto & Windus.

Konstatinov, F. V. *et al.* (1974). *The Fundamentals of Marxist-Leninist Philosophy*. Daglish, Robert (trans.). Moscow: Progress Publishers.

Korte, Barbara (1997). *Body Language in Literature*. Ens, Erica (trans.) (first published in German, 1993). Toronto: University of Toronto Press.

Kress, Gunther and Hodge, Robert (1979). *Language as Ideology*. London: Routledge.

Kristeva, Julia (1969). *Séméiotiké: recherches pour une sémanalyse*. Paris: Seuil.

Kristeva, Julia (1979). Le vréel. In Kristeva, Julia and Ribette, Jean-Michel (eds), *Folle vérité: vérité et vraisemblance du texte psychotique*. Paris: Seuil, 11–35.

Kristeva, Julia (1980). *Desire in Language: A Semiotic Approach to Literature and Art*. Roudiez, Leon S. (ed.), Gora, Thomas, Jardine, Alice and Roudiez, Leon S. (trans). Oxford: Blackwell.

Kristeva, Julia (1982). *Powers of Horror: An Essay on Abjection*. Roudiez, Leon S. (trans.) (first published in French, 1980). New York: Columbia University Press.

Kristeva, Julia (1984). *Revolution in Poetic Language* (first published in French, 1974). Waller, M. (trans.). New York: Columbia University Press.

Kuhn, Thomas S. (1970). *The Structure of Scientific Revolutions* (2nd edn). Chicago and London: University of Chicago Press.

Lacan, Jacques (1970). Of structure as an inmixing of an otherness prerequisite to any subject whatsoever. In Macksey, Richard and Donato, Eugenio (eds), *The Languages of Criticism and the Sciences of Man*. Baltimore and London: Johns Hopkins University Press, 186–95.

Lacan, Jacques (1976). Seminar on 'The Purloined Letter'. *Yale French Studies*, 48, 38–72.

Lacan, Jacques (1977). *Écrits. A Selection*. Sheridan, Alan (trans.). London: Tavistock.

Lacan, Jacques (1979). *The Four Fundamental Concepts of Psychoanalysis*. Miller, Jacques-Alain (ed.), Sheridan, Alan (trans.) (first published in French, 1973, and in English translation, 1977). Harmondsworth: Penguin.

LaCapra, Dominick (1983). *Rethinking Intellectual History: Texts, Contexts, Language*. Ithaca and London: Cornell University Press.

Lanser, Susan Sniader (1981). *The Narrative Act: Point of View in Prose Fiction*. Princeton: Princeton University Press.

Larrain, Jorge (1986). *A Reconstruction of Historical Materialism*. London: Allen & Unwin.

Lawrence, D. H. (1961). *Selected Literary Criticism*. Beal, Anthony (ed.). London: Mercury Books.

Leach, Edmund (1976). *Culture and Communication: The Logic by which Symbols are Connected*. Cambridge: Cambridge University Press.

Leavis, F. R. (1962a). *The Common Pursuit* (first published 1952). Harmondsworth: Peregrine.

Leavis, F. R. (1962b). *The Great Tradition* (first published 1948). Harmondsworth: Peregrine.

Leavis, F. R. (1964). *Revaluation: Tradition and Development in English Poetry* (first published 1936). Harmondsworth: Peregrine.

Leavis, F. R. and Thompson, Denys (1933). *Culture and Environment: The Training of Critical Awareness*. London: Chatto & Windus.

Leavis, Q. D. (1932). *Fiction and the Reading Public*. London: Chatto & Windus.

Leech, Geoffrey (1983). *Principles of Pragmatics*. Harlow: Longman.

Leech, Geoffrey N. and Short, Michael H. (1981). *Style in Fiction: A Linguistic Introduction to English Fictional Prose*. Harlow: Longman.

Lefevere, André (1983). Interface: some thoughts on the historiography of African literature written in English. In Riemenschneider, Dieter (ed.), *The History and Historiography of Commonwealth Literature*. Tübingen: Gunter Narr Verlag.

Lehman, David (1990). Derridadaism. *The Times Literary Supplement*, 18 May.

Lentricchia, Frank and McLaughlin, Thomas (eds) (1990). *Critical Terms for Literary Study*. Chicago and London: University of Chicago Press.

Lessing, Doris (1973). *The Golden Notebook* (new edition; first published 1962). Frogmore: Panther.

Levin, David Michael (1988). *The Opening of Vision: Nihilism and the Postmodern Situation*. New York and London: Routledge.

Levinson, Marjorie (1988). *Keats's Life of Allegory: The Origins of a Style*. Oxford: Blackwell.

Levinson, Stephen C. (1983). *Pragmatics*. Cambridge: Cambridge University Press.

Lévi-Strauss, Claude (1972). *The Savage Mind*. London: Weidenfeld & Nicolson.

Lodge, David (1977). *The Modes of Modern Writing: Metaphor, Metonymy, and the Typology of Modern Literature*. London: Arnold.

Lodge, David (ed.) (1988). *Modern Criticism and Theory*. London: Longman.

Lotman, Yuri (1976). *Analysis of the Poetic Text*. Johnson, D. Barton (ed. and trans.). Ann Arbor: Ardis.

Lovell, Terry (1980). *Pictures of Reality: Aesthetics, Politics and Pleasure*. London: British Film Institute.

Lucas, D. W. (1968). Appendix to Aristotle, *Poetics*. Oxford: Clarendon Press.

Lucas, Ian (1998). *Outrage! An Oral History*. London: Cassell.

Lugowski, Clemens (1990). *Form, Individuality and the Novel: An Analysis of Narrative Structure in Early German Prose* (first published in German, 1932). Halliday, John Dixon (trans.). Cambridge: Polity Press.

Lukács, Georg (1969). *The Historical Novel* (first published in German, 1937). Mitchell, Hannah and Mitchell, Stanley (trans). (Trans. first published 1962.) Harmondsworth: Peregrine.

Lüthi, Max (1984). *The Fairytale as Art Form and Portrait of Man* (first published in German, 1975). Erickson, Jon (trans.). Bloomington: Indiana University Press.

Lyotard, Jean-François (1984). *The Postmodern Condition: A Report on Knowledge* (first published in French, 1979). Bennington, Geoff and Massumi, Brian (trans.). Minneapolis: University of Minnesota Press.

Lyotard, Jean-François (1985). *Just Gaming*. Godzich, Wlad (trans.). Minneapolis: University of Minnesota Press.

McDowell, Deborah E. (1987). 'The changing same': generational connections and Black women novelists. *New Literary History*, 18(2), 281–302.

McGann, Jerome J. (1983). *A Critique of Modern Textual Criticism*. Chicago and London: University of Chicago Press.

McGann, Jerome J. (ed.) (1985a). *Historical Studies and Literary Criticism*. Madison: University of Wisconsin Press.

McGann, Jerome J. (1985b). *The Beauty of Inflections: Literary Investigations in Historical Method and Theory*. Oxford: Clarendon Press.

McGann, Jerome J. (1991). *The Textual Condition*. Princeton: Princeton University Press.

McHale, Brian (1987). *Postmodernist Fiction*. London: Methuen.

Macherey, Pierre (1978). *A Theory of Literary Production* (first published in French, 1966). Wall, Geoffrey (trans.). London: Routledge.

Machin, Richard and Norris, Christopher (eds) (1987). *Post-structuralist Readings of English Poetry*. Cambridge: Cambridge University Press.

MacKinnon, Catharine A. (1982). Feminism, Marxism, method, and the state: an agenda for theory. In Keohane, Nannerl O., Rosaldo, Michelle Z., and Gelpi, Barbara C. (eds), *Feminist Theory: A Critique of Ideology*. Brighton: Harvester, 1–30.

Macksey, Richard (1997). Foreword to Genette, Gérard, *Paratexts: Thresholds of Interpretation*. In Genette: 1997, xi–xxii.

Maclean, Ian (1986). Reading and interpretation. In Jefferson, Ann and Robey, David (eds), *Modern Literary Theory: A Comparative Introduction* (2nd edn). London: Batsford, 122–44.

McLuhan, Marshall (1964). *Understanding Media: The Extensions of Man*. London: Routledge.

McNeil, Helen (1991). She trembled at his touch. *Quarto* (May).

McQuail, Denis, Blumler, Jay G. and Brown, J. R. (1972). The television audience: a revised perspective. In McQuail, Denis (ed.), *Sociology of Mass Communications*. Harmondsworth: Penguin, 135–65.

McRobbie, Angela (1982). The politics of feminist research: between talk, text and action. *Feminist Review*, 12 (October), 46–57.

Makaryk, Irena R. (ed.) (1993). *Encyclopedia of Contemporary Literary Theory*. Toronto: University of Toronto Press.

Manocchio, Tony and Petitt, William (1975). *Families under Stress: A Psychological Interpretation*. London: Routledge.

Marx, Karl (1970a). *Capital. A Critique of Political Economy*. Volume 1: *The Process of Production* (first published in German, 1867). London: Lawrence & Wishart.

Marx, Karl (1970b). *Economic and Philosophical Manuscripts of 1844*. Struik, Dirk J. (ed.), Milligan, Martin (trans.). London: Lawrence & Wishart.

Marx, Karl (1971). *A Contribution to the Critique of Political Economy*. Ryazanskaya, S. W. (trans.). London: Lawrence & Wishart.

Marx, Karl and Engels, Frederick (1962). *Selected Works* (2 vols). London: Lawrence & Wishart.

Marx, Karl and Engels, Frederick (1970). *The German Ideology*. Part 1, with selections from Parts 2 and 3. Arthur, C. J. (ed.). London: Lawrence & Wishart.

Mast, Gerald, Cohen, Marshall and Braudy, Leo (eds) (1992). *Film Theory and Criticism: Introductory Readings* (4th edn). Oxford and New York: Oxford University Press.

Bibliography

Masterman, Len (ed.) (1984). *Television Mythologies: Stars, Shows and Signs*. London: Comedia.

Maturana, Humberto and Varela, Francisco (1980). *Autopoiesis and Cognition: The Realization of the Living*. Dordrecht: D. Reidel.

Medvedev, P. N./Bakhtin M. M. (1978). *The Formal Method in Literary Scholarship* (first published in Russian, 1928). Wehrle, Albert J. (trans.). Baltimore and London: Johns Hopkins University Press.

Megill, Allan (1989). What does the term 'postmodernism' mean? *Annals of Scholarship*, 6 (1989), 129–51.

Menton, Seymour (1983). *Magic Realism Discovered, 1918–1981*. Philadelphia: The Art Alliance Press.

Merleau-Ponty, Maurice (1962). *Phenomenology of Perception*. Smith, Colin (trans.). London: Routledge.

Mews, Siegfried (1989). The professor's novel: David Lodge's small world. *Modern Language Notes*, 104(3), 713–26.

Millard, Elaine (1989). French feminisms. In Mills, Sara, Pearce, Lynne, Spaull, Sue and Millard, Elaine, *Feminist Readings/Feminists Reading*. Hemel Hempstead: Harvester, 153–85.

Miller, J. Hillis (1982). *Fiction and Repetition: Seven English Novels*. Oxford: Blackwell.

Miller, J. Hillis (1991). *Theory Then and Now*. Hemel Hempstead: Harvester Wheatsheaf.

Miller, Nancy K. (1980). *The Heroine's Text: Readings in the French and English Novel, 1722–1782*. New York: Columbia University Press.

Millett, Kate (1970). *Sexual Politics*. Garden City, NY: Doubleday.

Minsky, Marvin (1979). A framework for representing knowledge. In Metzing, Dieter, *Frame Conceptions and Text Understanding*. Berlin: de Gruyter, 1–25.

Mistacco, Vicki (1980). The theory and practice of reading *nouveaux romans*: Robbe-Grillet's *Topologie d'une cité fantôme*. In Suleiman, Susan R. and Crosman, Inge (eds), *The Reader in the Text*. Princeton: Princeton University Press, 371–400.

Mitchell, Juliet (1974). *Psychoanalysis and Feminism*. London: Allen Lane.

Mitchell, W. J. T. (ed.) (1981). *On Narrative*. Chicago: Chicago University Press.

Mohanty, Satya P. (1997). *Literary Theory and the Claims of History: Postmodernism, Objectivity, Multicultural Politics*. Ithaca and London: Cornell University Press.

Moi, Toril (ed.) (1986a). *The Kristeva Reader*. Oxford: Blackwell.

Moi, Toril (1986b). Feminist literary criticism. In Jefferson, Ann and Robey, David (eds), *Modern Literary Theory: A Comparative Introduction* (2nd edn). London: Batsford, 204–21.

Mongia, Padmini (ed.) (1996). *Contemporary Postcolonial Theory: A Reader*. London: Arnold.

Montrose, Louis (1989). Professing the Renaissance. The poetics and politics of culture. In Veeser: 1989, 15–36.

Moody, Nickianne (1998). Mills and Boon's *Temptations*: sex and the single couple in the 1990s. In Pearce and Wisker: 1998, 141–56.

Mukařovský, Jan (1964). Standard language and poetic language, *and* The esthetics of language (both articles first published in Czech, 1932). In Garvin: 1964, 17–30 and 31–69.

Mulhern, Francis (ed.) (1992). *Contemporary Marxist Literary Criticism.* Harlow: Longman.

Mulvey, Laura (1989). *Visual and Other Pleasures.* London, Macmillan.

Mulvey, Laura (1996). *Fetishism and Curiosity.* London: BFI Publishing.

Nadelson, Regina (1987). Eating out with Atwood. Interview with Margaret Atwood. *Guardian,* 18 May.

Nead, Lynda (1988). *Myths of Sexuality: Representations of Women in Victorian Britain.* Oxford: Blackwell.

Newman, Judie (1995). *The Ballistic Bard: Postcolonial Fictions.* London: Arnold.

Newman, Robert D. (1993). Exiling history: hysterical transgression in historical narrative. In Cox, Jeffrey N. and Reynolds, Larry J. (eds), *New Historical Literary Study.* Princeton: Princeton University Press.

Norrman, Ralf (1982). *The Insecure World of Henry James's Fiction: Intensity and Ambiguity.* London: Macmillan.

Norrman, Ralf (1985). *Samuel Butler and the Meaning of Chiasmus.* London: Macmillan.

Nostbakken, Faith (1993). Cultural materialism. In Makaryk: 1993, 21–4.

Nuttall, A. D. (1983). *A New Mimesis: Shakespeare and the Representation of Reality.* London: Methuen.

Olsen, Stein Haugom (1978). *The Structure of Literary Understanding.* Cambridge: Cambridge University Press.

Olsen, Stein Haugom (1987). *The End of Literary Theory.* Cambridge: Cambridge University Press.

Onega, Susana and Landa, José Ángel García (eds) (1996). *Narratology.* Harlow: Longman.

Ong, Walter J. (1982). *Orality and Literacy: The Technologizing of the Word.* London: Methuen.

Oswell, David (1998). True love in queer times: romance, suburbia and masculinity. In Pearce and Wisker: 1998, 157–73.

O'Toole, L. M. and Shukman, Ann (1977). A contextual glossary of formalist terminology. *Russian Poetics in Translation,* 4, 13–48.

Palmer, Paulina (1987). From 'coded mannequin' to bird woman: Angela Carter's magic flight. In Roe, Sue (ed.), *Women Reading Women's Writing.* Brighton: Harvester, 179–205.

Palmer, Richard E. (1969). *Hermeneutics: Interpretation Theory in Schleiermacher, Dilthey, Heidegger, and Gadamer.* Evanston: Northwestern University Press.

Parry, Benita (1994). Resistance theory/theorizing resistance, or two cheers for nativism. In Barker, Francis *et al.* (eds), *Colonial Discourse/Postcolonial Theory.* Manchester: Manchester University Press (repr. in Mongia: 1996, 84–109).

Partridge, Eric (1984). *A Dictionary of Slang and Unconventional English* (8th edn). Beale, Paul (ed.). London: Routledge.

Pascal, Roy (1977). *The Dual Voice: Free Indirect Speech and its Functioning in the Nineteenth-century European Novel.* Manchester: Manchester University Press.

Pavel, Thomas G. (1986). *Fictional Worlds*. Cambridge, MA: Harvard University Press.

Pearce, Lynne (1994). *Reading Dialogics*. London: Arnold.

Pearce, Lynne (1997). *Feminism and the Politics of Reading*. London: Arnold.

Pearce, Lynne and Wisker, Gina (1998). *Fatal Attractions: Rescripting Romance in Contemporary Literature and Film*. London: Pluto Press.

Penley, Constance (1994). Feminism, psychoanalysis, and the study of popular culture. In Bryson, Holly, and Moxey: 1994, 302–24.

Perry, Menakhem (1979). Literary dynamics: how the order of a text creates its meanings. *Poetics Today*, 1–2, 35–64; 311–61.

Pettersson, Anders (1990). *A Theory of Literary Discourse*. Lund: Lund University Press.

Picard, Raymond (1969). *New Criticism or New Fraud?* (first published in French, 1965). Towne, Frank (trans.). Seattle: Washington State University Press.

Plekhanov, G. V. (1974). *Art and Social Life* (repr. of 1957 edn; first published in Russian, 1912). Fineberg, A. (trans.). Moscow: Progress Publishers.

Plimpton, George (ed.) (1989). *Women Writers at Work: The 'Paris Review' Interviews*. Harmondsworth: Penguin.

Poggioli, Renato (1971). *The Theory of the Avant-Garde*. Fitzgerald, Gerald (trans.). New York: Harper & Row.

Pratt, Annis (1982). *Archetypal Patterns in Women's Fiction*. Brighton: Harvester.

Pratt, Mary Louise (1977). *Toward a Speech Act Theory of Literary Discourse*. Bloomington: Indiana University Press.

Pratt, Mary Louise (1992). *Imperial Eyes: Travel Writing and Transculturation*. London: Routledge.

Prince, Gerald (1988a). *A Dictionary of Narratology*. Aldershot: Scolar Press.

Prince, Gerald (1988b). The disnarrated. *Style*, 22(1), 1–8.

Propp, Vladimir (1968). *Morphology of the Folktale* (first published in Russian, 1928). Wagner, Louis A. (ed.), Scott, Laurence (trans.). Austin: University of Texas Press.

Pynchon, Thomas (1973). *Gravity's Rainbow*. New York: Viking.

Radway, Janice A. (1991). *Reading the Romance: Women, Patriarchy, and Popular Literature* (first published 1984). With a new introduction by the author. Chapel Hill and London: University of North Carolina Press.

Ragland-Sullivan, Ellie (1992a). Death drive (Lacan). In Wright: 1992, 57–9.

Ragland-Sullivan, Ellie (1992b). The Imaginary. In Wright: 1992, 173–6.

Rayan, Krishna (1987). *Text and Sub-text: Suggestion in Literature*. London: Arnold.

Register, Cheri (1975). American feminist literary criticism: a bibliographical introduction. In Donovan, Josephine (ed.), *Feminist Literary Criticism: Explorations in Theory*. Lexington: University Press of Kentucky.

Reid, Ian (1992). *Narrative Exchanges*. London: Routledge.

Rich, Adrienne (1976). The kingdom of the fathers. *Partisan Review*, 43(1), 17–37.

Richards, I. A. (1924). *Principles of Literary Criticism*. London: Routledge & Kegan Paul.

Richards, I. A. (1964). *Practical Criticism: A Study of Literary Judgment* (first published 1929). London: Routledge.

Rickword, Edgell (1978). *Literature in Society: Essays and Opinions (II), 1931–1978*. Manchester: Carcanet.

Riffaterre, Michael (1978). *Semiotics of Poetry*. London: Methuen.

Riffaterre, Michael (1981). Interpretation and descriptive poetry: a reading of Words-worth's 'Yew Trees'. In Young: 1981, 103–32.

Rimmon-Kenan, Shlomith (1983). *Narrative Fiction: Contemporary Poetics*. London: Methuen.

Roberts, Andrew Michael (1993). Introduction to *Conrad and Gender* edition of *The Conradian*, 17(2) (Spring), v–xi.

Rock, Irvin (1983). *The Logic of Perception*. Cambridge, MA: MIT Press.

Rodway, Allan (1970). Generic criticism: the approach through type, mode and kind. In Bradbury, Malcolm and Palmer, David (eds), *Contemporary Criticism*, Stratford-upon-Avon Studies, 12. London: Arnold, 82–105.

Rorty, Richard (1982). *Consequences of Pragmatism: Essays 1972–1980*. Brighton: Harvester.

Rosenblatt, Louise M. (1978). *The Reader, The Text, The Poem: The Transactional Theory of the Literary Work*. Carbondale and Edwardsville: Southern Illinois University Press.

Rowe, John Carlos (1998). *The Other Henry James*. Durham, NC: Duke University Press.

Royle, Nicholas (1991). *Telepathy and Literature: Essays on the Reading Mind*. Oxford: Blackwell.

Ruthven, K. K. (1984). *Feminist Literary Studies: An Introduction*. Cambridge: Cambridge University Press.

Ryan, Kiernan (ed.) (1996). *New Historicism and Cultural Materialism: A Reader*. London: Arnold.

Ryle, Gilbert (1971). The thinking of thoughts. *Collected Papers*, II, *Collected Essays 1929–68*. London: Hutchinson, 480–96.

Said, Edward (1979). *Orientalism* (first published 1978). New York: Vintage Books.

Said, Edward (1984). *The World, The Text, and The Critic*. London: Faber.

Said, E. (1993). *Culture and Imperialism*. London: Chatto & Windus.

Salusinszky, Imre (1987). *Criticism in Society*. London: Methuen.

Salutin, Rick (1984). *Marginal Notes: Challenges to the Mainstream*. Toronto: Lester and Orpen Dennys.

Sangari, Kumkum (1987). The politics of the possible. *Cultural Critique*, 7 (repr. in abridged form in Ashcroft, Griffiths and Tiffin: 1995, 143–7).

Sartre, Jean-Paul (1969). *Being and Nothingness: An Essay on Phenomenological Ontology* (first published in French, 1943; first published in English, 1958). Barnes, Hazel E. (trans.). Warnock, Mary (Introduction). London: Methuen.

Sartre, Jean-Paul (1973). *Existential Psychoanalysis*. Barnes, Hazel E. (trans.). Chicago: Henry Regnery.

Saussure, Ferdinand de (1974). *Course in General Linguistics*. Bally, Charles and Sechehaye, Albert (eds), Buskin, Wade (trans.) (rev. edn). London: Peter Owen.

Schank, Roger C. and Abelson, Robert P. (1977). *Scripts, Plans, Goals and Understanding: An Inquiry into Human Knowledge*. The Artificial Intelligence Series. Hillsdale, NJ: Lawrence Erlbaum Associates.

Scholes, Robert (1982). *Semiotics and Interpretation*. New Haven: Yale University Press.

Scholes, Robert (1985). *Textual Power: Theory and the Teaching of English*. New Haven: Yale University Press.

Scholes, Robert and Kellogg, Robert (1966). *The Nature of Narrative*. London: Oxford University Press.

Scott, William T. (1990). *The Possibility of Communication*. Berlin: Mouton de Gruyter.

Searle, John R. (1969). *Speech Acts: An Essay in the Philosophy of Language*. Cambridge: Cambridge University Press.

Searle, John R. (1976). A classification of illocutionary acts. *Language in Society*, 5, 1–23 (first presented as a lecture, 1971).

Sedgwick, Eve Kosofsky (1992). *Epistemology of the Closet*. New York and London: Harvester Wheatsheaf.

Sedgwick, Eve Kosofsky (1993). *Between Men: English Literature and Male Homosocial Desire* (repr. with a new preface by the author; first published 1985). New York: Columbia University Press.

Segal, Lynne (1987). *Is the Future Female? Troubled Thoughts on Contemporary Feminism*. London: Virago.

Sell, Roger (ed.) (1991). *Literary Pragmatics*. London: Routledge (contains Sell's own essay, 'The politeness of literary texts', 208–24).

Seung, T. K. (1982). *Semiotics and Thematics in Hermeneutics*. New York: Columbia University Press.

Shannon, Claude Elwood (1949). *The Mathematical Theory of Communication*. Urbana: University of Illinois Press.

Sharpe, Jenny (1989). Figures of colonial resistance. *Modern Fiction Studies*, 35(1) (repr. in abridged form in Ashcroft, Griffiths and Tiffin: 1995, 99–103).

Sharpe, R. A. (1984). The private reader and the listening public. In Hawthorn, Jeremy (ed.), *Criticism and Critical Theory*. London: Arnold, 15–28.

Shea, Victor (1993). New historicism. In Makaryk: 1993, 124–30.

Shklovsky, Victor (1965). Art as technique (first published in Russian, 1917). In Lemon, Lee T. and Reis, Marion J. (eds and trans.), *Russian Formalist Criticism: Four Essays*. Lincoln: University of Nebraska Press.

Showalter, Elaine (1982). *A Literature of Their Own*. London: Virago.

Showalter, Elaine (1986). Feminist criticism in the wilderness (first published 1981 in *Critical Inquiry*, 8, 179–205). In Showalter, Elaine (ed.), *The New Feminist Criticism: Essays on Women, Literature and Theory*. London: Virago, 243–70.

Showalter, Elaine (1987). Critical cross-dressing: male feminists and the woman of the year. In Jardine, Alice, and Smith, Paul (eds), *Men in Feminism*. London and New York: Methuen.

Silverman, Kaja (1994). Fassbinder and Lacan: a reconsideration of gaze, look, and image. In Bryson, Holly and Moxey: 1994, 272–301.

Simpson, David (1982). *Fetishism and Imagination: Dickens, Melville, Conrad*. Baltimore and London: Johns Hopkins University Press.

Sinfield, Alan (1992). *Faultlines: Cultural Materialism and the Politics of Dissident Reading*. Oxford: Clarendon Press.

Šklovskij, Viktor (1971). The mystery novel: Dickens's *Little Dorrit* (first published in Russian, 1925). Carter, Guy (trans.). In Matejka, Ladislav and Pomorska, Krystyna (eds), *Readings in Russian Poetics: Formalist and Structuralist Views*. Cambridge, MA: MIT Press, 220–26.

Smith, Barbara Herrnstein (1968). *Poetic Closure: A Study of How Poems End*. Chicago: University of Chicago Press.

Smith, Barbara Herrnstein (1978). *On the Margins of Discourse: The Relation of Literature to Language*. Chicago: University of Chicago Press.

Smith, Dorothy E. (1987). Women's perspective as a radical critique of sociology. In Harding: 1987, 84–96.

Smith, Paul Julian (1992). Phallogocentrism. In Wright: 1992, 316–18.

Solomon, Robert C. (1980). *History and Human Nature: A Philosophical Review of European Philosophy and Culture, 1750–1850*. Brighton: Harvester.

Sontag, Susan (1964). Notes on 'camp'. *Partisan Review* 31(4), 515–30.

Soyinka, Wole (1975). Neo-Tarzanism: the poetics of pseudo-tradition. *Transition*, 48.

Soyinka, Wole (1984). The critic and society: Barthes, leftocracy and other mythologies. In Gates, Henry Louis Jr (ed.), *Black Literature and Literary Theory*. London: Methuen, 27–57.

Spivak, Gayatri Chakravorty (1984–5). Criticism, feminism and the institution. Interview with Elizabeth Gross. *Thesis Eleven*, 10–11, 175–87.

Spivak, Gayatri Chakravorty (1988). Can the subaltern speak? In Nelson, Cary and Grossberg, Lawrence (eds), *Marxism and the Interpretation of Culture*. Houndmills: Macmillan, 271–313.

Spivak, Gayatri Chakravorty (1991). Identity and alterity: an interview. *Arena*, 97, 65–76.

Spoto, Donald (1983). *The Dark Side of Genius: The Life of Alfred Hitchcock*. Boston: Little, Brown & Co.

Stam, Robert (1989). *Subversive Pleasures: Bakhtin, Cultural Criticism and Film*. Baltimore: Johns Hopkins University Press.

Stierle, Karlheinz (1980). The reading of fictional texts. In Suleiman, Susan R. and Crosman, Inge (eds), Crosman, Inge and Zachrau, Thekla (trans.), *The Reader in the Text*. Princeton: Princeton University Press, 83–105.

Stubbs, Michael (1983). *Discourse Analysis: The Sociolinguistic Analysis of Natural Language*. Oxford: Blackwell.

Thomas, Brook (1991). *The New Historicism and Other Old-Fashioned Topics*. Princeton: Princeton University Press.

Thornham, Sue (1997). *Passionate Detachments: An Introduction to Feminist Film Theory*. London: Arnold.

Tiffin, Helen (1987). Post-colonial literatures and counter-discourse. *Kunapipi*, 9(3) (repr. in abridged form in Ashcroft, Griffiths and Tiffin: 1995, 95–8).

Tillyard, E. M. W. (1944). *Shakespeare's History Plays*. London: Chatto & Windus.

Timpanaro, Sebastiano (1975). *On Materialism*. London: New Left Books.

Todd, Janet (ed.) (1982). *Women Writers Talking*. New York: Holmes & Meier.

Todorov, Tzvetan (1969). *Grammaire du Décaméron*. The Hague: Mouton.

Todorov, Tzvetan (1975). *The Fantastic: A Structural Approach to a Literary Genre*. Ithaca, NY: Cornell University Press.

Todorov, Tzvetan (1981). *Introduction to Poetics*. Howard, Richard (trans.). Brighton: Harvester.

Todorov, Tzvetan (1984). *Mikhail Bakhtin: The Dialogical Principle*. Minneapolis: University of Minnesota Press.

Tomas, David (1989). The technophilic body. On technicity in William Gibson's cyborg culture. *New Formations*, 8, 113–29.

Tomashevsky, Boris (1965). Thematics (first published in Russian, 1925). In Lemon, Lee T. and Reis, Marion J. (eds and trans.), *Russian Formalist Criticism: Four Essays*. Lincoln, NE: University of Nebraska Press.

Toolan, Michael J. (1988). *Narrative: A Critical Linguistic Introduction*. London: Routledge.

Trilling, Lionel (1966). *Beyond Culture*. London: Secker & Warburg.

Truffaut, François, with the collaboration of Scott, Helen G. (1986). *Hitchcock* (rev. edn; first published 1968). London: Paladin.

Tyler, Carole-Anne (1991). Boys will be girls: the politics of gay drag. In Fuss: 1991, 32–70.

Tynjanov, J. (1971). Rhythm as the constructive factor of verse (first published in Russian, 1924). In Matejka, Ladislav and Pomorska, Krystyna (eds), Suino, M. E. (trans.), *Readings in Russian Poetics: Formalist and Structuralist Views*. Cambridge, MA: MIT Press, 126–35.

Tynyanov, Yu. *et al.* (1977). Formalist theory. O'Toole, L. M. and Shukman, Ann (trans.). In *Russian Poetics in Translation*, 4.

Urry, John (1990). *The Tourist Gaze: Leisure and Travel in Contemporary Societies*. London: Sage.

Veeser, H. Aram (ed.) (1989). *The New Historicism*. New York and London: Routledge.

Vodička, Felix (1964). The history of the echo of literary works (first published in Czech, 1942). In Garvin: 1964, 71–81.

Vološinov, V. N. (1976). *Freudianism: A Marxist Critique*. Titunik, I. R. and Bruss, Neal H. (eds), Titunik, I. R. (trans.). New York: Academic Press.

Vološinov, V. N. (1986). *Marxism and the Philosophy of Language*. Matejka, Ladislav and Titunik, I. R. (trans.) (first published in English, 1973). Cambridge, MA: Harvard University Press.

Vygotsky, L. S. (1986). *Thought and Language*. Kozulin, Alex (rev. and ed. version of the previous trans. by Hanfmann, Eugenia and Vakar, Gertrude, 1962). (First published in Russian, 1934.) Cambridge, MA: MIT Press.

Wain, John (ed.) (1961). *Interpretations: Essays on Twelve English Poems* (first published 1955). London: Routledge.

Walder, Dennis (ed.) (1990). *Literature in the Modern World: Critical Essays and Documents*. Oxford: Oxford University Press.

Wales, Katie (1989). *A Dictionary of Stylistics*. Harlow: Longman.

Watt, Ian (1980). *Conrad in the Nineteenth Century*. London: Chatto & Windus.

Watts, Cedric (1984). *The Deceptive Text: An Introduction to Covert Plots*. Brighton: Harvester.

Watzlawick, Paul, Beavin, Janet Helmick and Jackson, Don D. (1968). *Pragmatics of Human Communication: A Study of Interactional Patterns, Pathologies, and Paradoxes*. London: Faber.

Webster, Roger (1990). *Studying Literary Theory*. London: Arnold.

Weinberg, George (1972). *Society and the Healthy Homosexual*. New York: St Martin's Press.

Weis, Elisabeth (1982). *The Silent Scream: Alfred Hitchcock's Sound Track*. Rutherford/Madison/Teaneck: Farleigh Dickinson University Press.

Weisgerber, Jean (1988). *Le Réalisme magique: roman, peinture, cinéma*. Lausanne: Editions l'Age d'homme.

Wentworth, Harold and Flexner, Stuart Berg (1975). *Dictionary of American Slang*. 2nd supplemented edn. New York: Thomas Y. Crowell.

West, Alick (1937). *Crisis and Criticism*. London: Lawrence & Wishart.

Weston, Jessie L. (1993). *From Ritual to Romance* (first published 1920). Princeton: Princeton University Press.

Wheale, Nigel (ed.) (1995a). *The Postmodern Arts: An Introductory Reader*. London and New York: Routledge.

Wheale, Nigel (1995b). Postmodernism: from elite to mass culture? In Wheale: 1995a, 33–56.

Wheale, Nigel (1995c). Recognizing a 'human-Thing': cyborgs, robots and replicants in Philip K. Dick's *Do Androids Dream of Electric Sheep?* and Ridley Scott's *Blade Runner*. In Wheale: 1995a, 101–14.

White, Hayden (1981). The value of narrativity in the representation of reality. In Mitchell, W. J. T.: 1981, 1–23. (Articles repr. from *Critical Inquiry* Autumn 1980 and Summer 1981.)

Wilden, Anthony (1968). *Language of the Self*. Baltimore: Johns Hopkins University Press.

Wilden, Anthony (1972). *System and Structure: Essays in Communication and Exchange*. London: Tavistock.

Wiener, Norbert (1949). *Cybernetics: Or Control and Communication in the Animal and the Machine*. Cambridge, MA: The Technology Press.

Willett, John (ed. and trans.) (1964). *Brecht on Theatre: The Development of an Aesthetic*. London: Eyre Methuen.

Williams, Gordon (1997). *A Dictionary of Shakespeare's Sexual Language*. London: Athlone.

Williams, Raymond (1954). *Drama in Performance*. London: Frederick Muller.

Williams, Raymond (1958). *Culture and Society 1780–1950*. London: Chatto & Windus.

Williams, Raymond (1976). *Keywords*. Glasgow: Fontana.

Williams, Raymond (1977). *Marxism and Literature*. Oxford: Oxford University Press.

Williams, Raymond (1979). *Politics and Letters: Interviews with New Left Review*. London: New Left Books.

Williams, Raymond (1980). *Problems in Materialism and Culture: Selected Essays*. London: Verso.

Williams, Raymond (1989). *What I Came to Say*. London: Hutchinson Radius.

Wimsatt, W. K. (1970). *The Verbal Icon: Studies in the Meaning of Poetry* (first published 1954). London: Methuen.

Wimsatt, W. K. and Beardsley, Monroe (1946). The intentional fallacy. In Wimsatt: 1970, 3–18.

Wimsatt, W. K. and Beardsley, Monroe (1949). The affective fallacy. In Wimsatt: 1970, 21–39.

Wings, Mary (1988). *She Came in a Flash*. London: The Women's Press.

Woolf, Virginia (1928). *Orlando*. London: Hogarth Press.

Woolf, Virginia (1929). *A Room of One's Own*. London: Hogarth Press.

Woolf, Virginia (1966a). Professions for women. *Collected Essays*, 2. London: Hogarth Press, 284–9.

Woolf, Virginia (1966b). Women and fiction. *Collected Essays*, 2. London: Hogarth Press, 141–8.

Woolf, Virginia (1967). De Quincey's autobiography. *Collected Essays*, 4. London: Hogarth Press, 1–7.

Woolf, Virginia (1977). *Three Guineas* (first published 1938). Harmondsworth: Penguin.

Wright, Elizabeth (ed.) (1992). *Feminism and Psychoanalysis: A Critical Dictionary*. Oxford: Blackwell.

Wright, Iain (1984). History, hermeneutics, deconstruction. In Hawthorn, Jeremy (ed.), *Criticism and Critical Theory*. London: Arnold, 83–96.

Yanarella, Ernest J. and Sigelman, Lee (eds) (1988). *Political Mythology and Popular Fiction*. Westport, CT: Greenwood.

Young, Robert (ed.) (1981). *Untying the Text: A Post-structuralist Reader*. London: Routledge.

Young, Robert J. C. (1995). *Colonial Desire: Hybridity in Theory, Culture and Race*. London: Routledge.

Zabus, Chantal (1991). Relexification. In *The African Palimpsest: Indigenization of Language in the West African Europhone Novel*, Cross Cultures, 4. Amsterdam: Rodopi.

Žižek, Slavoj (1990). Rossellini: woman as symptom of man. *October*, 54.

Žižek, Slavoj (1991). *Looking Awry: An Introduction to Jacques Lacan Through Popular Culture*. Cambridge, MA: MIT Press.

Žižek, Slavoj (1992). *Everything You Always Wanted to Know About Lacan (But Were Afraid to Ask Hitchcock)*. London: Verso.